Empathy

Empathy

Philosophical and Psychological Perspectives

EDITED BY
Amy Coplan and Peter Goldie

OXFORD

UNIVERSITY PRESS

Great Clarendon Street, Oxford OX2 6DP
United Kingdom

Oxford University Press is a department of the University of Oxford.
It furthers the University's objective of excellence in research, scholarship,
and education by publishing worldwide.
Oxford is a registered trade mark of Oxford University Press in the UK
and in certain other countries

© the several contributors 2011

British Library Cataloguing in Publication Data
Data available

Library of Congress Cataloging in Publication Data
Data available

ISBN 978-0-19-953995-6

Contents

Part I. Empathy and Mind

Part II. Empathy and Aesthetics

List of Figures/Images

Notes on Contributors

HEATHER D. BATTALY is Professor of Philosophy, California State University-Fullerton.

NOËL CARROLL is Distinguished Professor of Philosophy, City University of New York.

AMY COPLAN is Associate Professor of Philosophy, California State University-Fullerton.

GREGORY CURRIE is Professor of Philosophy, University of Nottingham.

STEPHEN DAVIES is Professor of Philosophy, University of Auckland.

JEAN DECETY is Irving B. Harris Professor of Psychology and Psychiatry, University of Chicago.

SUSAN L. FEAGIN is Visiting Research Professor of Philosophy, Temple University.

PETER GOLDIE is Samuel Hall Professor of Philosophy, University of Manchester.

ALVIN I. GOLDMAN is Board of Governors Professor of Philosophy and Cognitive Science, Rutgers University.

MARTIN L. HOFFMAN is Emeritus Professor of Clinical and Developmental Psychology, New York University.

MARCO IACOBONI is Professor of Psychiatry and Biobehavioral Sciences, David Geffen School of Medicine, University of California-Los Angeles.

E. ANN KAPLAN is Distinguished Professor of English and Comparative Literary and Cultural Studies, Stony Brook University.

GRAHAM MCFEE is Professor of Philosophy, University of Brighton and California State University-Fullerton.

DOMINIC MCIVER LOPES is Distinguished University Scholar and Professor in Philosophy, University of British Columbia.

DEREK MATRAVERS is Professor of Philosophy, The Open University.

ANDREW N. MELTZOFF is Professor and Job and Gertrud Tamaki Endowed Chair in Psychology, University of Washington.

ADAM MORTON is Canada Research Chair, University of Alberta.

JESSE J. PRINZ is Distinguished Professor of Philosophy, City University of New York.

MURRAY SMITH is Professor of Film Studies, University of Kent.

Introduction

Amy Coplan and Peter Goldie

This collection, which draws together eighteen chapters on empathy, follows in a long tradition of work on empathy in philosophy and psychology. For empathy has, since at least the seminal work of David Hume and Adam Smith, been seen as centrally important in at least two respects. First, it has been seen as important in relation to our capacity to gain a grasp of the content of other people's minds, and to predict and explain what they will think, feel, and do. And secondly, it has been seen as important in relation to our capacity to respond to others ethically—enabling us not only to gain a grasp of the other's suffering, but also to respond in an ethically appropriate way. Both of these aspects have been to the fore in recent discussions, and Hume and Smith are often appealed to in these discussions. First, empathy has been prominent in relation to what is now called simulation as one of the ways in which we engage with other minds, often put forward as an alternative to the idea that we deploy some kind of theory about other minds in order to understand them.[1] And secondly, empathy has been prominent in the revival of moral sentimentalism, and in the idea that it is central to an ethics of caring, often put forward as an alternative to a more 'dispassionate' ethics.[2] A third respect in which empathy has been seen as important—one which owes less to the work of Hume and Smith—is in relation to our engagement with works of art. We will turn to this in detail later in this introduction.

In the first part of this introduction, we trace the history of the concept of empathy, highlighting its role in several areas of philosophy and psychology, including the Scottish sentimentalist tradition, early twentieth-century aesthetics, phenomenology

---

[1] For early discussions of the debate between simulation theory and 'theory theory', see Gopnik and Wellman (1994), and the essays in Davies and Stone (1995a, 1995b). More recent discussions can be found in Perner & Kühberger (2005), Hutto (2005), Fisher (2006), Biggs (2007), Hurley (2008), Gordon (2009), and Schulz (2009). For critiques formulations and defenses of simulation theory, see Goldman (2006a), Currie (2004), Goldman & Sripada (2005), and Currie & Ravenscroft (2002: 49–70). For critiques of simulation theory, see Nichols & Stich (2003: 131–42) and Saxe (2009). Bertram Malle (2004, 2005) provides excellent discussions of mindreading within the context of social cognition that go beyond this debate.

[2] See, for example, Slote (2003, 2004, 2007, 2010) and Held (2006a, 2006b).

and hermeneutics, clinical psychology (including psychoanalysis), developmental and social psychology, care ethics, and contemporary cognitive neuroscience. Although we do not attempt to be comprehensive in our account of empathy's development, we specify many of the ways in which the concept has been considered significant since its inception. This provides some background and a broader context for the essays in this collection, which address a range of current questions and controversies in the study of empathy. In the second part of the introduction, we review key arguments from each of the contributed essays and explain the organization of the collection into three sections—Empathy and Mind, Empathy and Aesthetics, and Empathy and Morality. These three sections provide a framework that helps to make salient the connections among the essays as well as significant implications of the various issues they discuss.

We will begin the discussion in this Introduction with David Hume and Adam Smith's accounts of what they called 'sympathy', and it will immediately become clear that these two philosophers, like so many that have succeeded them, have understood sympathy in more than one way, and have used sympathy for more than one purpose: in particular for understanding other minds, and as the basis of ethical action. It will be important, here and throughout this volume, to be clear on precisely what empathy and sympathy mean.

David Hume and Adam Smith

In *A Treatise of Human Nature* (1739) David Hume (1711–1776) invoked the concept of sympathy to explain a variety of psychological phenomena, including the transmission of emotion from one person to another (317, 319, 363, 592), the formation of moral responses (499, 500) and desires (577–91), and aesthetic responses (576–77).[3] Since Hume used the concept in so many ways, it is difficult to say with any certainty how he defined it or whether his view remained consistent from the *Treatise* to the *Enquiry*.[4] If we restrict ourselves, however, to Hume's primary discussion of sympathy in Book II of the *Treatise*, it is clear that he understood it as a principle of communication that is fundamental to human nature:

No quality of human nature is more remarkable, both in itself and in its consequences, than that propensity we have to sympathize with others, and to receive by communication their inclinations and sentiments, however different from, or even contrary to our own. (317)

Hume characterized sympathy as a natural and automatic process. When we encounter another person experiencing an emotion or passion, we initially know this through its effects, that is, 'those external signs in the countenance and conversation, which convey an idea of it' (317). The operation of sympathy then converts this idea into an impression, which then becomes the very passion itself (317).

---

[3] See Bricke (1996) and Vitz (2004).
[4] See Vitz (2004), Debes (2007a, 2007b), and Mercer (1972) for a discussion of this issue.

Although there are numerous interpretations of Hume's account of sympathy, what is important for our purposes in this introduction is that Hume seems to have been describing a psychological mechanism that enables the fast and instantaneous spread of emotion.[5] And thus it seems that the process he referred to as sympathy is the same or at least very similar to what we will call low-level empathy or mirroring.

In *The Theory of Moral of Moral Sentiments* (1759), Adam Smith (1723–1790) took up Hume's concept of sympathy, revised it, and made it the linchpin of his moral theory.[6] Like Hume, Smith appealed to sympathy to explain how we come to experience others' emotions, but for Smith this involved imaginative perspective-taking:

By the imagination we place ourselves in his situation, we conceive ourselves enduring all the same torments, we enter as it were into his body, and become in some measure the same person with him, and thence form some idea of his sensations, and even feel something, which, though weaker in degree, is not altogether unlike them. (9)

Smith's discussions of sympathy, like Hume's, varied, seeking to get the concept to do multiple duty. Sometimes he describes an observer imagining what *she herself* would feel in the target individual's situation, and sometimes he describes an observer attempting to *imagine being the target in the target's situation*.[7] Regardless of whether sympathy for Smith is self- or other-oriented, it is usually described as a high-level process involving an imaginative component.[8] In this respect, Smith's concept differed from Hume's.[9] Whereas Hume's notion of sympathy is akin to what we call low-level empathy or mirroring, Smith's primary use of the term refers to what we call high-level empathy, essentially involving imagination.[10]

Smith sometimes argues that in order to sympathize with a target individual, one must have knowledge of the context in which the target individual's emotion has arisen.[11] Hume, like Smith, considered sympathy to be easier and more likely with family and friends and with those to whom one was in closer proximity, but he did not discuss the need for an observer to have background knowledge of a target's situation.

---

[5] Morrow (1923); Bricke (1996); and Vitz (2004).

[6] Morrow (1923); Lamb (1974); and Griswold (1999, 2006).

[7] For this distinction, see Goldie (this volume).

[8] Fontaine (1997); and Mercer (1972).

[9] For more on Smith's notion of sympathy and its role in his account of moral judgment and in his moral theory more generally, see Macfie (1959), Morrow (1923), Fontaine (1997), Mercer (1972), and Griswold (1999, 2006).

[10] Smith occasionally appeals to examples of what arguably seem to be low-level empathy, where the immediacy of the response would suggest that the conscious use of imaginative perspective-shifting is not required. For example, in one passage he discussed how we recoil our own limb at the sight of a stroke aimed at another person's leg, and how the mob at the circus 'writhe and twist and balance' their bodies as they look at the dancer on the slack rope. However, Smith insists that conscious imaginative perspective-shifting is necessary for all cases of sympathy: 'it is by the imagination only that we can form any conception of what are his sensations' (Smith 2002: 11).

[11] Fontaine (1997).

Theodor Lipps

The term *Einfühlung* (from which the English word empathy originated in a way which we will discuss shortly) was developed in works in aesthetics and psychology in the late nineteenth and early twentieth century.[12] It was first used as a technical term in aesthetics by Robert Vischer (1873).[13] Not long after this, Theodor Lipps (1851–1914) used the concept of *Einfühlung* to explain both how people experience aesthetic objects and how they come to know others' mental states (1903b). While he was almost certainly influenced by discussions in aesthetics, Lipps may also have been influenced by Hume's notion of sympathy, which he would have known well since he was the translator of the standard German translation of Hume's *A Treatise of Human Nature* and directed multiple dissertations on Hume's philosophy (Schuhmann and Smith (1987)). For Lipps, *Einfühlung*—which literally means 'feeling into'—referred to a process of inner imitation or inner resonance that is based on a natural instinct and causes us to imitate the movements and expressions we perceive in physical and social objects. We experience the other's feelings as our own because we project our own feelings onto the other. In a similar way, we experience the properties of aesthetic objects as our own because, according to Lipps, aesthetic objects elicit the same responses in us that are elicited by expressions and movements of the body, and we project these inner subjective qualities onto them.[14]

Though often criticized, Lipps's account of *Einfühlung* was enormously influential in psychology and philosophy, where it was much debated. Freud claimed to have been heavily influenced by Lipps, and philosophers in the phenomenological tradition embraced the notion of *Einfühlung* as an alternative to the 'inference from analogy' account of mental state ascription, which held that we ascribe mental states to others through a process of analogy with our own mental states.[15]

Using a transliteration of the Greek word *empatheia* to translate *Einfühlung*, Edward Titchener introduced the English term empathy in 1909 in his *Elementary Psychology of Thought Processes*. Titchener's definition of empathy changed over time, but when he first introduced it, he seemed to have in mind the same sort of process that Lipps described:

---

[12] It's worth noting that at this time, aesthetics and psychology were much more intimately connected than they were for the majority of the twentieth century. Psychologists took aesthetic questions very seriously and aestheticians often extended their treatments of questions regarding engagement with art to questions about human psychology more generally. See Currie (this collection) for a discussion of the relationship between aesthetics and psychology during this time.

[13] Vischer developed his notion of empathy in his dissertation, *On the Optical Sense of Form: A Contribution to Aesthetics* (1873). See Mallgrave & Ikonomou (1994) for a discussion of this work.

[14] For a more in depth discussion of Lipps's view, see Stueber (2006, 2008), Currie (this collection), Wispé (1986, 1987, 1991), Sawicki (1997), and Montag, Gallinat, & Heinz (2008).

[15] Zahavi (2001) and Stueber (2006, 2008).

Not only do I see gravity and modesty and pride and courtesy and stateliness, but I feel or act them in the mind's muscle. That is, I suppose, a simple case of empathy, if we may coin that term as a rendering of *Einfühlung* (21).

By the time that Titchener began discussing empathy, *Einfühlung* was already a prominent concept in psychology, aesthetics, and philosophy of social science, where, arguably, it was regarded as the primary method of the human sciences.[16]

Phenomenology and Hermeneutics

By the beginning of the twentieth century, due in large part to the influence of Lipps's account, the concept of empathy or *Einfühlung* was often associated with the concept of *Verstehen* (understanding), especially in the phenomenological and hermeneutic traditions.[17]

The phenomenologists Edmund Husserl (1859–1938), Edith Stein (1891–1942), and Max Scheler (1874–1928) all discussed empathy at length. Husserl and Stein were both highly critical of Lipps's account of empathy, but rather than dismiss it altogether, they revised it, developing their own accounts and making it central to their respective philosophical projects in general and to the problem of intersubjectivity in particular.

In broad terms, the problem of intersubjectivity, which is sometimes referred to as the problem of other minds, concerns whether or not and how we can know others' mental states. The standard response to the problem when Husserl and Stein were writing was the 'argument from analogy', according to which I infer the existence of other minds by inferring that the other is the same in this respect as I am. I thus reason analogically.[18]

Husserl and Stein both reject this solution and offer an alternative by appealing to empathy. For them, empathy is a unique mode of consciousness through which we *directly* experience others' thoughts, emotions, and desires; it enables us to experience others as 'minded' (Husserl (1989); Stein (1989)).[19] Stein argues that empathy is how we experience foreign consciousness, describing it as 'the basis of intersubjective experience' and as 'the condition of possible knowledge of the existing outer world' (Stein (1989): 60). Emphasizing the intersubjective and relational dimensions of empathy Stein argued that empathy enables us to understand others but also to understand ourselves as others experience us. Thus, through empathy I come to discern the other's

---

[16] Stueber (2000, 2006, 2008); Kögler & Stueber (2000).

[17] Several of Lipps's students began a discussion group in Munich called '*Akademische Verein für Psychologie*', which played an important role in the early phenomenological movement. Some of these students went on to collaborate with Husserl and to publish works of phenomenology. See Schuhmann and Smith (1987) and Spiegelberg and Schuhmann (1994) for more on the influence of Lipps on phenomenology, the work of his students, and students' relationship to Husserl.

[18] See Zahavi (2001) on the problem of intersubjectivity and its treatment within phenomenology.

[19] See Zahavi (2001), Miles (2003), Makkreel (1996, 2000), Throop (2008), and Stueber (2006, 2008) for more on Husserl and Stein and their analyses of empathy.

mental states while at the same time gaining self-knowledge by coming to know how the other experiences me. This self-knowledge is vital for our development.[20]

Husserl and Stein regard their notion of empathy as departing radically from the notion described by Lipps. They interpret Lipps's notion of empathy as involving a type of fusion or 'oneness', which they consider deeply problematic. On their view, there is no loss of self during the process of empathy. As Rudolf Makkreel explains, the 'Ein' in 'Einfühlung' meant 'into', not 'one' and thus Einfühlung is best understood as a process of 'feeling into', not a process of 'feeling one with'. He argues that this is why Stein makes the point that Einfühlung shouldn't be confused with Einsfühlung.[21]

Husserl wrote a great deal about empathy, which he related to Verstehen (understanding). Makkreel explains that, in Ideas II, Husserl used the concept in two different senses. The first was a psychological or naturalistic sense, which Makkreel describes as a process that falls somewhere between a straightforward presentation (Gegenwärtigung) of one's own self and an imaginative representation (Vorstellung) of a possible self (1996: 201).[22] Husserl's second sense of empathy refers to a more spiritual or cognitive process. He develops this sense of empathy after shifting his analysis from the naturalistic attitude to what he calls the personalistic attitude. Through this second type of empathy, we come to understand the spiritual meaning of what motivates the other (Makkreel (1996): 202).[23] Although this goes beyond empathy in the first sense, which reveals only the other's psychological states, the type of understanding yielded by the second sense of empathy is limited to those features or experiences of the other that are typically human.[24] According to Makkreel, empathy for Husserl and Stein is an active

---

[20] See Verducci (2000), Stueber (2006, 2008), Miles (2003), Throop (2008), Wispé (1987, 1991), and Zahavi (2001).

[21] Makkreel (1996, 2000). Karsten Stueber (2006) claims that Stein's interpretation of Lipps is uncharitable. He acknowledges that Lipps describes empathy as resulting in identification with the object but insists that this does not mean there must be a total loss of self.

[22] Makkreel explains: 'Husserl describes empathy as a process of presentification (Vergegenwärtigung) whereby I apprehend another body as belonging to another subject. The other's body is given to me in its originary presence (Urpräsenz), but the inner nature of its psychic life can only be appresented (Appräsenz) ... The other is recognized as its own originary source, but apprehended in a non-originary way' (1996: 200).

[23] The notion of 'spiritual' here has a particular meaning for Husserl, which has to do with the difference between mere signs that indicate or point to something, and expressions, which are signs that mean something. Makkreel writes that, 'Empathy initially used the body as a mere sign or indication of subjective mental states whose existence can never be confirmed. The spiritual sense of empathy, by contrast, regards the body of the other as expressing human meaning. Here the body is not apprehended as an object in itself but as a medium for the articulation of typical human meaning' (Makkreel (1996): 202).

[24] Makkreel (1996: 200–3). Makreel reports that Husserl writes about empathy elsewhere as well, expanding and questioning some of his discussion in Ideas II. In the 3 volumes Phänomenologie der Intersubjektivität (XII, XIV, XX), Husserl claims that we can sometimes empathize with those who surpass us in some way but only by imagining variations on our own experience: 'What I can re-understand (nachverstehen), to what extent I can empathize, is determined by the ideal variations of the archetypal human being: I, who am this human being, achieve normal empathy as the perception of the other; in so doing the other body that resembles mine is supplemented with the same supplementary meaning content (Sinnesbestand) that belongs to my body under corresponding circumstance and with the possible variations which belong to mine. My body as given to inwardly directed or solipsistic experience is thus the archetypal apperception and provides the necessary norm. Everything else is a variation of this norm.' (XIV: 126) Translated and quoted by Makkreel (1996: 209).

process, which is why it can contribute to understanding (1996, 2000).[25] As David Woodruff Smith puts it, 'In Husserl's analysis, empathy is the source of meaning whereby I experience a being as another 'I', another subject, another 'living body' acting by will, and so on' (Smith 2007: 65).

Max Scheler (1874–1928), who applied Husserl's phenomenology to issues in ethics, culture, and religion, focused less on empathy than on sympathy, a process that he claimed was extremely important and yet poorly understood.[26] In *The Nature of Sympathy*, Scheler criticizes sentimentalist theories that make sympathy the basis of morality and draws several distinctions between processes that are often confused with one another, including empathy, sympathy, and emotional contagion (1970/1979).[27]

Around roughly the same time that theorists were exploring and popularizing empathy within phenomenology, it began to be linked to central projects and concepts within hermeneutics. Philosophers in the hermeneutic tradition (e.g. Friedrich Schleiermacher (1768–1834), Wilhelm Dilthey (1833–1911), Robin George Collingwood (1889–1943), and Hans Georg Gadamer (1900–2002)) focused on issues of interpretation and sought to determine the appropriate methods and criteria for historical knowledge and research in the human and social sciences. These thinkers held that knowledge exists in relation to a larger background and strongly disagreed with the view of the logical positivists that all knowledge can be understood in terms of semantic reduction and logical atoms.

Theorists in the hermeneutic tradition ended up distinguishing the human sciences from the natural sciences and articulating distinctive methods and goals for each. The natural sciences take physical events as a subject matter and scientific explanation as a goal and thus researchers in the natural sciences must adopt an external perspective in order to produce explanations of events based on external causes and effects. By subsuming discrete bits of information under general laws, researchers in the natural sciences are able to specify causal relations and correlations through ahistorical explanations.

In contrast, the human sciences take human actions and the phenomena of the social world as a subject matter and *Verstehen* or understanding—rather than *Erklären* or explanation—as a goal. Work in the human and social sciences attempts to determine the *meaning of human actions*, not the *explanation of events* and for this reason it requires an interpretive process that analyzes how the meaning of particular actions and expressions is tied to the context, history, and culture in which those actions and expressions occur. And yet while theorists must understand this larger background in order to complete the interpretive process, the background itself cannot be understood independently of the specific actions and expressions that comprise it, and thus there is an inherent

---

[25] For more on Husserl's and Stein's respective treatments of empathy, see Smith (2007), Moran (2004; 2000; especially 175–6), and Sawicki (1997).

[26] Zahavi (2001).

[27] See Goldie (2000), Zahavi (2001), and Throop (2008).

circularity in all understanding and interpretation in the human sciences. Referred to as the 'hermeneutic circle', this circularity leads to a relationship of continued reciprocity between the part (i.e. the particular action or event) and the whole (i.e. the contextual, historical, and cultural background) such that anything we come to understand about the part—some particular action—changes the meaning of the whole—the background knowledge against which the part is understood.[28] This change in our understanding of the whole then leads to a change in our understanding of the part since the meaning of the part is inextricably bound up with that of the whole. In short, every interpretation relies on another interpretation, making the project of interpretation dynamic and ongoing.

It is because of their specific aims and methodological commitments that many of those working in the tradition of hermeneutics came to regard empathy as an essential epistemological tool. The human sciences were thought by many to rely on a process identical or similar to empathy in order to reconstruct meaning from other agents' points of view.[29] The most common way that empathy was linked to hermeneutics was through association with the concept of *Verstehen* (understanding), which was developed at length by the German philosopher and historian Willhelm Dilthey.

Dilthey was a pivotal figure in hermeneutics and in the development of methods and goals appropriate to the human sciences. In his early work, he characterized the fundamental method of the human sciences as a psychological process of interpretation that involved the reenactment of a subject's state of mind.[30] This early work was crucial for making empathy an important concept in hermeneutics, as many assumed and continue to assume today that Dilthey was using the concept of *Verstehen* to refer to a type of empathy. Although this reading of Dilthey is understandable, his actual view of empathy is more complicated than many have realized. Interestingly, the complications regarding his view have to do with the same sort of conceptual confusion surrounding empathy today. Not helping matters are the facts that Dilthey shifted his thinking on the nature of understanding in his later work, and that translators have occasionally translated words other than *Einfühlung* as empathy.[31]

A problem with equating empathy with *Verstehen* is that Dilthey rarely used the term and never explicated its meaning.[32] Makkreel argues that it is likely that

---

[28] Kögler & Stueber (2000); Stueber (2000, 2006); Makkreel (1992, 1996, 2000); Grondin (1994).

[29] For an in depth discussion of how the human sciences were conceived in hermeneutics and how they differ from the natural sciences, see Makkreel (2000), Kögler & Stueber (2000), and Stueber (2006). For a discussion of the hermeneutic tradition more generally, see Grondin (1994).

[30] In his later work, Dilthey no longer views introspective awareness as sufficient for understanding. He concludes that psychological interpretation or reenacting a subject's state of mind cannot serve as the basis for the human sciences. On his revised view, all awareness—of both self and others—is based on the interpretation of one's actions, politics, expressions, and so on. If one wishes to understand oneself, for example, one cannot simply introspect but must go through one's old letters, papers, diaries, etc. For more on Dilthey's later view and its relation to his early view, see Makkreel (1992).

[31] Makkreel (1992: 252–3, note 5).

[32] Makkreel (1992, 1996).

Dilthey avoided the term because he associated it with Lipps's definition, which he would have found too restrictive (Makkreel (2000)). Like Husserl and Stein, Dilthey may have interpreted Lipps as claiming that empathy is a pre-reflective state that results in fusion with the object of empathy and a complete loss of self. Such a process could not qualify as understanding for Dilthey since it would be too direct and intuitive to be considered reliable.[33]

Karsten Stueber sees the situation differently. He claims that the reason for Dilthey's infrequent use of empathy is that the term was not well established outside of aesthetics when Dilthey was writing his early work. By the time the term became popularized, Dilthey had changed his mind about the conditions for understanding. Since he no longer viewed introspective awareness as sufficient for understanding and dismissed his earlier view as too psychological, he would have had little reason to invoke the concept of empathy since he did not consider such a process to be crucial for studying the human sciences.[34]

Thinkers within the hermeneutic tradition ultimately dismissed empathy as a process capable of little other than occasionally helping us to understand those very similar to us. It was viewed as something that had nothing to contribute to the process of interpreting subjects culturally different from us, and even those thinkers who continued to employ the concept of *Verstehen* dissociated it from empathy.[35]

Stueber contends that the criticism of empathy within this tradition has been too extreme. While it may be reasonable to deny that empathy can be the primary method of the human sciences, most philosophers of social science have taken a much stronger position and denied empathy any role at all in the interpretation of others' actions and mental states. This attitude, according to Stueber, stems from theorists' association of empathy with a Cartesian conception of mind, which is now considered highly suspect in all philosophical traditions.[36]

Stueber has recently developed a defense of empathy that takes account of the concept's history in hermeneutics and the philosophy of social science and draws on recent empirical research in cognitive science and debates in philosophy of mind. He argues that re-enactive empathy, the imaginative reenactment of another's thought processes, is indispensible for predicting, explaining, and understanding others, for it is only through re-enactive empathy that we can see others' thoughts as reasons.[37]

---

[33] Makkreel (1996: 206).

[34] Stueber (2006: 223, note 17).

[35] Stueber (2006: 16–19).

[36] Stueber explains that this Cartesian conception of the mind is the view, 'according to which we are primarily acquainted with our own mental states from a first person perspective and according to which we define our mental concepts privately in reference to those inner experiences' (2006: 16).

[37] Stueber (2006). There is much more to Stueber's account, including a useful discussion and contribution to the philosophical debate between simulation theory and theory theory, which we will summarize below and which gets discussed throughout the essays in this collection.

Clinical Psychology

From the time that the concept of empathy was first introduced in clinical psychology and psychoanalysis, it was controversial, and it continues to be so today (Bohart & Greenberg (1997b); Clark (2007)). It has most often been associated with client-centered, psychodynamic, and experiential approaches to therapy, but it has received attention in almost all areas of clinical psychology, including psychoanalysis.[38]

Freud said very little about empathy but he greatly admired Theodor Lipps and claimed to have been highly influenced by Lipps's work, as we noted above (Pigman (1995); Bornstein (1984); Clark (2007); Montag, Gallinat, & Heinz (2008)). This may explain why Freud's brief mention of empathy suggests that it is important; in *Group Psychology and the Analysis of the Ego*, he wrote that empathy is 'that which plays the largest part in our understanding of what is inherently foreign to our ego in other people' (1922/1949: 66). While this statement indicates that Freud took empathy seriously, it played a minimal part, if any, in his model of the therapeutic relationship, which maintains that rational insight is what leads to change and that the analyst must occupy a detached perspective during analysis (Clark (2007); Rachman (1988)).[39]

In contrast to Freud, psychologist Carl Rogers (1902–1987), one of the founders of humanistic psychology, made empathy the centerpiece of the client-centered psychotherapeutic method he developed, which became highly popular and had a significant influence on the practice of clinical psychology.[40] Rogers argued that, to be successful, therapy must provide a supportive environment and allow for a deep understanding of the client's experience. Thus Rogers held that a successful therapist must employ empathy as both an epistemological tool that provides access to the client's private, subjective experience and in order to foster the type of environment necessary for the client to be receptive to the therapist's suggestions. Rogers wrote that when we empathize, we are:

---

[38] Clark (2007) provides an overview of thirteen different psychotherapeutic models that emphasize empathy. Additional helpful discussions of empathy's role in clinical psychology and psychoanalysis can be found in Gladstein (1984) Gladstein & Brennan (1987), Basch (1983), Lichtenberg (1981), Schwaber (1981), Hamilton (1981), and Bohart & Greenberg (1997b).

[39] In an article on Sandor Ferenczi's development of an empathic method for use in psychoanalysis (1988), Arnold Rachman reports that Freud had concerns about Ferenczi's 'empathic method' due to its potential to seem overly subjective and mystical, which Freud worried would make psychoanalysis seem less intellectually credible. In addition, many theorists argue that a psychoanalytic method employing empathy is fundamentally at odds with the therapeutic stance endorsed by Freud (Rachman (1988); Clark (2007)). See Pigman (1995) for more on the role of empathy in Freud's thought. Verducci (2000) and Clark (2007: 89–120) both speculate on why Freud chose not to explore further the concept of empathy.

[40] Rogers's method is typically referred to as 'client-centered' or 'person-centered' therapy, though it is sometimes called 'Rogerian psychotherapy' or simply 'humanistic psychology'. Although there are some areas of overlap between Rogers's view and psychoanalysis, particularly in the work of Heinz Kohut, which will be discussed below, client-centered therapy differs from psychoanalysis in a number of important respects. Kahn & Rachman (2000) explain that Rogers's theory and method are more American. For example, the focus during client-centered therapy is on the here and now rather than on the client's development, and the standard duration of therapy is typically relatively brief. In addition, client-centered therapy typically concentrates on the client's current conscious experience. Psychoanalytic psychodynamic approaches often focus on both conscious and unconscious experience (Bohart & Greenberg (1997)).

entering the private world of the other and becoming thoroughly at home in it. It involves being sensitive . . . to the changing felt meanings, which flow in this person . . . It means temporarily living in his/her life, moving about in it delicately without making judgments, sensing meanings of which he/she is scarcely aware . . . To be with another in this way means that for the time being you lay aside the views and values you hold for yourself in order to enter another world without prejudice (1975: 4).

Like Edith Stein, Rogers considered empathy to be a relational process. To empathize with the client, the therapist therefore has to communicate what she, the therapist, feels, periodically checking with the client through questions and restatement to ensure that her empathic understanding is accurate.[41]

Rogers believed that therapy could not succeed in the absence of empathy, but he also considered empathy difficult to achieve. He warned that the therapist must preserve the boundaries between herself and the client, lest she risk over-identifying with the client, which distorts understanding and interferes with the therapeutic process. In spite of these worries, Rogers insisted that empathy is critical for psycho-therapy; it is one of three conditions he considered necessary for psychotherapeutic change.[42]

As Rogers progressed in his career, further developing and refining his new model of psychotherapy, he became increasingly convinced of empathy's importance, not only for providing the therapist with invaluable information but also for enabling clients to explore and articulate their own experiences and to see themselves as the agents of that experience (Bohart & Greenberg (1997): 6). Toward the end of his life, Rogers was asked what he considered to be his most important contribution to the lives of others. After pausing for a few moments, he answered that it was his observations and work on empathy.[43] This is perhaps unsurprising given that Rogers's work established the place and importance of empathy within counseling and psychotherapy. His work initiated shifts in therapeutic methodologies and prompted numerous empirical studies. But Rogers was not the only theorist committed to organizing the therapeutic experience around empathy.

In the psychoanalytic tradition, Heinz Kohut (1913–1981) came to the conclusion that empathy was of paramount importance to the therapeutic relationship, a conclu-sion that led him to reformulate and revise many of the theoretical and therapeutic principles of traditional psychoanalysis and to create 'self psychology'. Self psychology is an influential theoretical school and psychodynamic framework that evolved from psychoanalysis in the 1960s and 1970s and remains popular today. Though it is an offshoot of psychoanalysis, self psychology departs from classical analytic theory in multiple ways. One of the most significant is the priority it places on empathy, which it viewed as the most important feature of the psychotherapeutic relationship and values

---

[41] Rogers (1959). See also Clark (2007) and Bohart & Greenberg (1997).
[42] Kahn & Rachman (2000); Clark (2007).
[43] Clark (2007: xi).

above insight and interpretation. Self psychology further differs from classical Freudian psychoanalysis in that it is not a drive theory and does not emphasize innate instincts, the ego, the Oedipal conflict, or intra-psychic conflict more generally. Instead, the focus is on subjective experience, the self, and the variables involved in its development.[44] The needs to experience a cohesive or integrated sense of self and self-esteem are thought to be the primary sources of human motivation, and relationships with other people are seen as fundamental to growth, development, and the maintenance of self-esteem. It is primarily through external relationships and social interactions that one has what self psychologists refer to as 'self-object' experiences, that is, experiences of others related to the function of defining, developing, and shoring up one's sense of self (Kohut (1984)). Self psychologists pinpoint the origin of psychopathologies, including several different types of narcissistic and anxiety disorders, in unmet or disrupted developmental needs, which lead to a lack of a continuity in one's experience of self or the inability to maintain a cohesive sense of self.

Empathy is central to self psychology in at least two important respects. During early development, one must experience empathic mirroring from one's parents in order to develop a secure sense of self and healthy self-esteem. These experiences of empathic mirroring constitute positive self-object experiences. As we discuss above, self psychologists also consider empathy to be an essential tool in the therapeutic process. It is a form of what Kohut calls 'experience near observation' and is viewed as necessary for psychoanalytic change. There are currently several different self psychological frameworks, including traditional self psychology, intersubjectivity theory, relational analysis, and motivational analysis. In spite of some important differences among these approaches, all agree about the importance of empathy.

Kohut was a major figure in psychoanalysis. He served as president of the American Psychoanalytic Association and was famous in the early part of his career for his orthodoxy regarding the practice of psychoanalysis. For these reasons, his insistence on the importance of empathy was highly controversial.[45] Kohut's clinical experience had convinced him that the detached perspective employed in Freudian psychoanalysis was ineffective and that an alternative approach was required. He therefore proposed a new psychoanalytic method that made empathy a 'necessary and defining ingredient of

---

[44] Ornstein and Ornstein (1995); Baker & Baker (1987); Sommers-Flanagan & Sommers-Flanagan (2004); Lemma (2003); Bornstein (2003).

[45] Although Kohut was the first psychoanalyst to assign empathy such a central place in the therapeutic model, and he is the theorist most often associated with introducing empathy into the practice of psychoanalysis, there were a few earlier analytic thinkers who discussed empathy and similar processes, though it is unclear whether or not Kohut was familiar with their views (Clark (2007): 89–120). For example, Arnold Rachman claims that Sandor Ferenczi paved the way for Kohut by creating a model of analysis based on mutuality, empathy, and openness. Ferenczi rejected Freud's characterization of the psychoanalytic cure in terms of intellectual interpretation and cognitive insight, arguing that much of the work of psychoanalysis concerns the emotions and the relationship between the analyst and analysand (Rachman (1988); Clark (2007): 93–8). Other psychoanalytic thinkers who considered empathy or similar processes to be important include Thedor Reik (1948), Sullivan (1953) and Sullivan & Perry (1954), Otto Fenichel (1953), Robert Fliess (1942), and Frieda Fromm-Reichmann (1959). For relevant discussion, see Clark (2007): 99–104.

the analyst's attitude as a therapist and a researcher' (1977: 304). In *The Restoration of the Self*, he writes that from 1959 on, his conceptual theoretical outlook was defined by his reliance on the 'empathic-introspective stance' (1977: xiii). A principal feature of this stance was the view that 'the essence of psychoanalysis lies in the scientific observer's protracted empathic immersion into the observed, for the purpose of data gathering and explanation' (1977: 302). This marked a radical departure from classical psycho-analysis, according to which the appropriate perspective for the analyst is one that is cool, removed, and objective with the focus on curing through insight (Clark (2007); Rachman (1988); Bohart & Greenberg (1997)). Kohut contended that the analyst (or therapist) should attempt to empathize with the analysand (the client). He defined empathy as, 'the capacity to think and feel oneself into the inner life of another person', and wrote that, 'it is the lifelong ability to experience what another person experiences, though, usually, and appropriately, to an attenuated degree' (1984: 82).

According to Kohut, empathy contributes to the psychoanalytic process in several important ways. First, it functions as an epistemological tool and a method of observa-tion by providing 'access to the inner life of men' (Kohut (1971): 300). Through empathy, the analyst gains critical information about the analysand's experience—information that would otherwise be inaccessible. A second way in which empathy contributes to psychoanalysis is as a 'fundamental mode of relatedness' (1975) that makes analysands more receptive to analysts' interpretations and provides them with a model for how to relate to themselves (Bohart & Greenberg (1997)). Thus, for Kohut, empathy is both the *primary* method appropriate for the perception of complex psychological configurations (Kohut (1971): 300) and is also beneficial on its own, independent of its ability to provide insight into analysands' experience. In 1985, Kohut writes that that the 'mere presence of empathy [used properly] possesses a beneficial, in a broad sense, effect—both in the clinical setting and in human life, in general' (1985).

Due to its endorsement by Rogers and Kohut, the concept of empathy attracted a great deal of attention during the second half of the twentieth century, not only in clinical psychology but also in experimental and social psychology, where researchers began to develop methods of measuring and testing empathy. At the same time, controversy continued to surround claims that empathy is essential to the therapeutic process (Basch (1983); Bohart & Greenberg (1997)). Within psychoanalysis, for exam-ple, many theorists continued to insist, following Freud, that the only genuine basis for psychological change is the type of insight generated by intellectual investigation.[46] They denied that empathy could provide this type of insight due to its putatively 'unscientific' character (Brenner (1968); Shapiro (1974); Shevrin (1978); Buie (1981)). Many theorists also worried about dangers associated with the therapist's adoption of the empathic stance, including the risk of over-identification with the client, which

---

[46] See, e.g. Hartmann (1964) and Shapiro (1984).

leads to an unhealthy enmeshment that impedes the therapeutic process. There was the additional risk that the therapist, rather than empathizing, would project her own concerns and experiences onto the client.

These concerns have persisted, even though evidence has emerged suggesting that empathy is indeed beneficial to the therapeutic process. After performing a meta-level analysis, reviewing numerous studies on the effectiveness of various therapies, Robyn Dawes (1994) concluded that, while the training and approach of a therapist have no significant influence on the success of therapy, therapists who are experienced by their clients as empathic are more effective.[47]

Developmental and Social Psychology

Beginning around the 1960s, empathy became a major research topic in empirical psychology. Discussions of empathy's role in psychotherapy sparked the interest of researchers in social and developmental psychology, and several distinctive research programs were established that investigated multiple aspects of empathy using a variety of methodological approaches. Some of the most influential focused on (1) constructing objective scales to study empathy,[48] (2) the development of empathy and related processes in the individual,[49] (3) empathy's role in pro-social and altruistic behavior,[50] (4) empathic accuracy,[51] and (5) gender differences in empathic responding.[52,53]

---

[47] Though significant, Dawes's conclusion is somewhat problematic since he did not operationalize the term empathy, and thus it is difficult to know what sort of processes are actually responsible for the 'successful' result he identified. For a more recent overview of the empirical research on the role and effectiveness of empathy, which points to mixed findings, see Bohart and Greenberg (1997). For a more recent meta-analysis, see Greenberg et al. (2001).

[48] See, e.g. Hogan (1969), Carkhuff (1969), Truax & Carkhuff (1967), Barrett-Lennard (1962, 1978), Campbell, Kagan, & Krathwohl (1971), Mehrabian & Epstein (1972), Stotland et al. (1978), Bryant (1982), Chlopan et al. (1985), and Davis (1983). For overviews and analyses of various empathy measures, see Gladstein (1983), Kurtz & Grummon (1972), Greenberg et al. (2001), Davis (1996), Duan & Hill (1996), Wispé (1986, 1987), Eisenberg & Fabes (1990), Eisenberg & Strayer (1987), and Eisenberg (2000).

[49] Feshbach and Roe (1968); Feshbach (1975); Eisenberg (1983, 2000, 2009a, 2009b); Hoffman (1970, 1979, 1982, 2000); Zahn-Waxler & Radke-Yarrow (1990); Moore (1990); Ungerer et al. (1990); Sagi & Hoffman (1976); Zahn-Waxler, Robinson, & Emde (1992); Nichols (2004).

[50] Hoffman (1982, 1987, 2000); Eisenberg (1983, 1987, 2000); Batson, Fultz, & Schoenrade (1987); Eisenberg & Fabes (1990); Batson (1991, 2009b); Batson & Shaw (1991); Batson et al. (1995); Batson et al. (1997); Archer (1991); Davis (1996); De Waal (2008); Nichols (2004); Van Lange (2008); Roberts & Strayer (1996); Lamm, Batson, & Decety (2007); Cialdini et al. (1997).

[51] See, e.g. essays in Ickes (1997), and Ickes (2003), Hodges & Wegner (1997), Zaki, Bolger, & Ochsner (2008, 2009), Zaki, Weber, Bolger, & Ochsner (2009), Eisenberg, Murphy, & Shepard (1997), Hancock & Ickes (1996), and Mast & Ickes (2007).

[52] Hoffman (1977); Eisenberg & Lennon (1983); Eisenberg & Fabes (1998); Eisenberg, Fabes, & Spinrad 2006; Klein & Hodges (2001); Han, Fan, & Mao (2008); Ickes, Gesn, & Graham (2000); Graham & Ickes (1997); Lennon & Eisenberg (1987); Cheng, Lee, et al. (2008).

[53] We are not attempting to provide a comprehensive history in this introduction, and this list of topics within social and developmental psychology is by no means exhaustive. For useful overviews of empathy that address areas of research in philosophy and psychology that we have not discussed, see Stueber (2006, 2008), Wispé (1986, 1987, 1991), Eisenberg & Strayer (1987), Eisenberg (2000, 2009a, 2009b), Miles (2003), Verducci (2000), Gladstein (1984), Gladstein & Brennan (1987), Sawicki (1997), Davis (1996), and Clark

Little consensus has emerged in the psychological literature about what counts as empathy, as we discuss further below in relation to the chapters in this volume, but most accounts list some type of shared emotion as an essential component. Martin Hoffman, for example, defines empathy as 'an affective response more appropriate to another's situation than one's own' (2000: 4). Nancy Eisenberg and Janet Strayer offer a more specific definition but retain the same basic idea, characterizing empathy as 'an affective response that stems from the apprehension or comprehension of another's emotional state or condition, and that is identical or very similar to what the other person is feeling or would be expected to feel' (1987: 5). An exception to the rule of defining empathy in terms of shared emotion occurs in the literature on empathic accuracy where it is more often conceptualized as an inferential process through which a subject comes to know another person's mental states (Ickes 1997).[54]

Some of the most influential and controversial work on empathy has focused on its role in moral development, social competence, and ethical life more generally.[55] Psychologists have explored this by examining the relationship between empathy and pro-social responding, which refers to 'intentional voluntary behavior that benefits another' (Eisenberg & Miller (1987): 293). Many researchers have concluded that empathy often mediates pro-social behavior, both in specific situations and at the dispositional level. In other words, both 'state empathy' and 'trait empathy' appear to promote pro-social behavior.[56]

It may seem unsurprising that empathy has been linked to pro-social behavior, but establishing this link has been no small task, for conceptual and methodological problems have plagued the research from the outset.[57] Researchers have employed several distinctive methods to measure empathy, and there has been little uniformity in the use of the key concepts.[58] As a result, what appear to be the same phenomena have been labeled 'empathic' in some experiments and 'sympathetic' in others, and different

---

(2007). It should be noted that there are rich bodies of literature on a vast array of topics related to empathy that we do not attempt to cover, including the role of empathy in medicine (Halpern (2001, 2007, 2009); More and Milligan (1994); Hojat (2007); Williams & Stickley (2010)); the role of empathy in education (Verducci (1998, 2000a, 2000b)); empathy and mental illness (essays in Farrow & Woodruff (2007)); empathy and acting (Goldstein (2009); Blair (2008b)); and empathy and fairness (essays in Bock & Goode (2006)); Singer (2007); Singer et al. (2004)).

[54] William Ickes, for example, writes that empathic inference is 'a form of complex psychological inference in which observation, memory, knowledge, and reasoning are combined to yield insights into the thoughts and feelings of others' (1997: 2).

[55] See, e.g. Hoffman (1970, 1981, 1982, 1983, 1987, 2000); essays in Zahn-Waxler, Cummings, & Ianotti (1986); Zahn-Waxler & Radke-Yarrow (1990); Eisenberg (1983, 1986, 1995, 2000, 2007); Eisenberg, Murphy, & Shephard (1997); Eisenberg & Fabes (1990); Eisenberg & Miller (1987); Eisenberg & Strayer (1987).

[56] See, e.g. Aronfreed (1970), Hoffman (1982, 1987, 2000), Batson & Coke (1981), Batson (1987), Eisenberg & Strayer (1987), Eisenberg & Miller (1987), Staub (1978). For a review of this research, see Batson, Fultz, & Schoenrade (1987), Eisenberg & Miller (1987), Eisenberg (2000), and Batson (1991).

[57] Discussions of these problems can be found in Eisenberg (1986: 30–57), Underwood & Moore (1982), and Wispé (1986).

[58] Davis (1996); Eisenberg (1986); Eisenberg & Lennon (1983); Clark (1980); Wispé (1986).

researchers have used the same term to refer to processes and behaviors that differ. This lack of uniformity in terminological usage and measurement has made it difficult to interpret and synthesize the empirical findings. Nevertheless, there is still support for the claim that sympathy and sometimes empathy correlate with pro-social behavior (e.g. Eisenberg (2000); Underwood and Moore (1982); Hoffman (2001)).

Social psychologist C. Daniel Batson, who has been at the center of the debates on the moral significance of empathy since the early 1980s, takes a strong view regarding the moral significance of empathy with his 'empathy-altruism hypothesis'. Developed on the basis of dozens of empirical studies, the hypothesis states that, in many cases, empathy evokes altruistic behavior, that is, behavior motivated by the ultimate goal of increasing another person's welfare (1991: 6). Note that empathy is understood by Batson here as 'empathic concern (other-oriented emotion felt for someone in need—sympathy, compassion, tenderness, and the like)', so it could be argued that the concept has substantial ethical content.[59]

Altruistic behavior is a specific type of pro-social behavior. While all pro-social behavior benefits another, not all of it is performed *for the sake of* benefiting the other. In egoistically motivated pro-social behavior, a subject helps a needy or distressed other in order to increase the subject's own welfare, not the distressed other's. This is almost always the case with behavior generated by personal distress. Personal distress occurs when subjects respond to others' distress by becoming distressed themselves. When this occurs, the target individual's distress causes emotional over-arousal (or aversive arousal) in the subject, which leads the subject to focus on his own distress. The subject may still help the distressed other but when he does, it will be for the sake of alleviating his own distress, not the other's.[60] In order to learn more about the helping behavior associated with empathy, Batson and his colleagues conducted a series of experiments designed to determine the underlying motivation of empathic subjects who perform pro-social behavior. These experiments varied in how easy it was for subjects to escape exposure to some needy and distressed other without having to help. Batson and his colleagues reasoned that escape—by enabling the subjects to avoid the distressing stimulus—offers subjects a viable way to decrease their own distress without having to decrease the needy other's distress. The studies therefore make it possible to determine whether subjects' motivations are altruistic or egoistic. In situations that involve exposure to a distressed and needy other where escape is relatively easy and helping is moderately costly, individuals' actions reveal their motivations. Those who choose to escape rather than to stay and help are judged to be egoistically motivated.

---

[59] See, for example, Batson's discussion in http://onthehuman.org/2009/10/empathic-concern-and-altruism-in-humans/.

[60] See, e.g. Hoffman (1984b, 2000), Davis (1980, 1983), Batson & Coke (1981), Eisenberg & Miller (1987), Batson, Fultz, & Schoenrade (1987), Eisenberg, Schaller, et al. (1988), Eisenberg, Fabes, Miller, et al. (1989), Eisenberg & Fabes (1990), Batson (1991), Okun, Shepard, & Eisenberg (2000), Eisenberg (2002), Eisenberg, Valiente, & Champion (2004), Eisenberg et al. (2006), Eisenberg & Eggum (2009), Singer & Lamm (2009), and Decety & Lamm (2009).

In contrast, those who choose to help rather than escape, even though helping is moderately costly and escape relatively easy, are judged to be altruistically motivated. After performing these experiments, Batson and his colleagues found that subjects who experience empathy in response to others' suffering are more likely to stay and help. Subjects who experience personal distress, however, are significantly less likely to stay and help.[61] Batson and many others have interpreted these findings as support for the empathy-altruism hypothesis.

Although highly significant in multiple disciplines, Batson's work has not been uncontroversial. Several researchers have disagreed with Batson's interpretation of the data yielded by his experiments, denying that altruistic empathy is the best way to explain subjects' pro-social behavior (Sober & Wilson (1998): 264–71; Cialdini et al. (1997); Nichols (2004); Stueber (2006); and Doris & Stich (2009)). Another problem with Batson's findings, which we alluded to above, is that in his discussion of the empathy-altruism hypothesis he uses the term 'empathy' more broadly, with more ethical content, than many other researchers. This makes it difficult to know whether or not he has shown that empathy leads to altruism or that some sort of combination of empathy and sympathy or perhaps even sympathy alone leads to altruism, which would be a weaker finding.

While Batson has concentrated in his research on the empathy-altruism hypothesis, developmental psychologist Martin Hoffman, who has been a key empathy researcher since the 1970s, has focused on empathy's development from infancy onwards and its role in and relationship to moral development. Hoffman highlights the role of empathy in moral emotion, motivation, and behavior. More specifically, he claims that empathic distress is a multiply determined pro-social moral motive. Because he offers the clearest and most detailed account of empathy's development, Hoffman's research has been highly influential, both in psychology and philosophy, as well as in other related disciplines.

Hoffman proposes five distinct modes of empathic arousal and five stages of empathic distress. Of the five modes of empathic arousal, three are pre-verbal, automatic, and essentially involuntary: motor mimicry and afferent feedback, classical conditioning, and direct association of cues from the target individual's experience to one's own past experience. These three pre-verbal modes are crucial for arousing empathy in childhood, especially in face-to-face situations. The remaining two modes of empathic arousal—mediated association and role-taking—are higher-order cognitive processes and contribute to the scope of one's empathic ability, allowing empathy with people who are not present (Hoffman (2000)).

Hoffman argues that the five stages of empathic distress result from the synthesis of empathic affect and a cognitive sense of others as distinct. These five stages are (1) the

---

[61] Batson (1991: 109–74) reviews 25 different studies examining the relationship between empathy and helping behavior. See also Batson and Shaw (1991), Batson, Sager, et al. (1997), Batson (1997), and Batson & Powell (2003).

reactive newborn cry, (2) egocentric empathic distress, (3) quasi-egocentric empathic distress, (4) veridical empathic distress, and (5) empathy for another's experience, beyond the immediate situation (see Hoffman (2000): 63–92). According to Hoffman's account, different cognitive processes are involved in the different kinds of empathy. At stages three, four, and five, empathic distress is transformed, in part, to a feeling of sympathetic distress, so empathy at this point again has substantial ethical content.

Another important topic of study within the social and developmental literature is empathic accuracy. Work on empathic accuracy relates closely to work in philosophy on the problem of other minds and how we come to understand and predict others' mental states. Social psychologist William Ickes, a major figure in this area, locates the study of empathic accuracy within the tradition of psychological research on interpersonal perception. Ickes defines empathic accuracy as, 'the measure of one's ability to accurately infer the specific content of other people's thought and feeling' (Ickes (1997): 3).[62]

Psychologists have taken several approaches to the study of empathic accuracy. A few have focused on the low-level physiological dimensions of how we come to grasp the valence and intensity of others' affective states. Robert Levenson & Anna Ruef (1997), for instance, argue that understanding others' emotions relies on physiological synchrony between the perceiver and the target.[63] Some researchers have examined the development of empathic accuracy. Nancy Eisenberg and her collaborators, for example, argue that empathic accuracy develops over time and relies on both social and cognitive factors (1997). Ickes (2003) has looked at differences in individuals' empathic accuracy and developed strategies for improving it.

Although the majority of the work on empathic accuracy highlights its importance, Ickes & Simpson (1997) and Ickes (2003) point out that empathy has negative dimensions and must be managed in certain contexts. In close relationships, for example, it is not always beneficial to empathize with one's loved ones since doing so can lead to disturbing knowledge. In addition, empathy is not always welcome. In many cases, individuals don't want others to empathize with them; they experience others' attempts to empathize with them as intrusive.[64]

Care Ethics

Within both psychology and philosophy, another area of research in which empathy has been important is the ethics of care. Care ethics was developed in the 1980s as a challenge to traditional principle-based ethical theories (Gilligan (1982); Noddings

---

[62] See, also, Ickes (1993), Ickes, Stinson, Bissonnette, & Garcia (1990), and Ickes (2003). It is not entirely clear in what sense Ickes is using the term 'infer', and in particular whether the inference is something of which the empathizer is aware.

[63] See, also, Hodges & Wegner (1997).

[64] See Throop (2008).

(1984); Ruddick (1989); and Held (2006a, 2006b)). Care theorists in philosophy and psychology rejected models of ethical life that emphasize impartiality and abstract rules and that characterize the ethical agent first and foremost as an autonomous, self-sufficient individual who uses reason and suppresses emotion in order to be just and fair. Proponents of care ethics argue that moral thought and action require both reason and emotion, as well as attention to the needs of particular others. In addition, they conceptualize the individual as relational and as epistemologically and morally interdependent (Held (2006a, 2006b); Slote (2007)). There are multiple versions of care ethics but almost all of them include the view that care and the practices of caring are vital to moral/ethical life.[65]

Many care theorists identify empathy as an important element in ethical life. Along with sympathy and emotional sensitivity and responsiveness, empathy is one of the emotional processes that, together with reason, creates a unique moral outlook. It is a valuable—or even essential—tool for developing our understanding of others and enabling us to determine what the best thing to do is in real world situations. Nel Noddings understands care as an activity that closely relates to empathy since caring means attending to the specific needs of particular others and attempting to understand situations from the other's point of view. To care for another requires 'feeling with' the other. Noddings says that it is possible to refer to this 'feeling with' as empathy, but only if we reject the standard notion of empathy as projecting oneself into the other so as to completely understand him, which she considers to be 'a peculiarly rational, western, masculine way of looking at "feeling with"' (1984: 30). For Noddings, empathic caring is about receptivity, not projection. We receive and share the other's feeling and, as a result, are prepared to care where we previously were not. Our 'feeling with' the other begins not with an attempt to interpret the other or solve some sort of problem, though we may learn to do this; it begins with simply attending to and sharing the other's feeling.

Philosopher Michael Slote has recently proposed an ethics of care that draws on research in social and developmental psychology, especially on the empathy-altruism hypothesis and Hoffman's developmental account. Slote's theory revives moral sentimentalism and makes empathy its core feature by using it to ground both a meta-ethical account of moral language and a normative account of moral obligation. He does this by explaining approval and disapproval in terms of empathy and then using these explanations to develop his account of moral language.

Slote's primary use of empathy is to refer to a process of contagion through which feelings can spread among individuals. He distinguishes his notion of empathy from the notion of sympathy, yet he characterizes empathy as necessarily including a feeling of 'warmth'. Regarding normative ethics, Slote argues that we will determine whether an action is morally right or wrong based on whether it expresses or exhibits the absence

---

[65] Blum (1994) provides a useful account of care ethics that specifies its virtues as well as some limitations.

of a fully developed empathic caring. Thus Slote treats empathic caring as 'critical for morality across a wide range of individual and political issues' (Slote (2007): 8). Caring motivation, for him, is based in and sustained by empathy (Slote (2007), 2010).

Slote's treatment of empathy strongly emphasizes its positive qualities, but care theorists such as Virginia Held (2001, 2006a, 2006b) are careful to point out that empathy is not an unqualified good and warn that it can be excessive and that this can lead to significant problems. Thus, for Held, empathy on its own is not enough for care ethics. To be beneficial, empathy must be conditioned appropriately and constrained by certain principles, which results from moral scrutiny and evaluations (2006a).

Recent Work in Neuroscience

During the past two decades, some of the most important contributions to the study of empathy have come from the field of neuroscience, where researchers have considered issues ranging from the nature of empathy and its role in various domains of experience to the importance of 'mirror neurons'. This research uses the tools of neuroscience to examine many of the same issues that have interested philosophers and psychologists and provides an important new source of empirical data, the significance of which is only just beginning to be understood.

One way neuroscientists have addressed questions about the nature of empathy is through attempts to determine what sorts of neurophysiological processes are involved in empathy and how they implement empathic processes.[66] This research reveals how empathy differs from related processes like personal distress. Personal distress has a number of characteristics in common with empathy and yet some have argued that it is a distinctive process. As we discussed above, when we experience personal distress while observing another in a distressing emotional state, we become so aversively aroused by the other's emotion that we end up becoming concerned primarily with our own distress and with alleviating it. And yet, in cases of empathy, observing another in a distressing emotional state causes us to become distressed by the other's emotion but not to such a degree that we end up focused on our own experience rather than the other's. As a result of this difference, empathy is more likely to result in altruistic behavior than personal distress, which may lead to pro-social behavior but which is thought to be motivated by an observer's desire to alleviate her own distress.[67]

---

[66] See, e.g. essays in this collection by Decety and Meltzoff, Iacoboni, and Goldman, and Decety & Lamm (2009), Decety & Jackson (2006), Decety & Grèzes (2006), Iacoboni (2008, 2009a), Jackson, Meltzoff, & Decety (2006), Lamm, Batson, & Decety (2007), Decety & Meyer (2008), Singer (2006), Singer, Critchley, & Preuschoff (2009), Singer et al. (2004, 2006), Vignemont & Singer (2006), and Singer & Lamm (2009).

[67] Theorists who consider personal distress to be a type of empathy include Stephanie Preston and Frans de Waal (Preston & de Waal (2002), de Waal (2009)). Preston and de Waal argue for a broad integrative model of empathy. For more on personal distress, see Coplan (this volume), and discussions in Eisenberg and Eggum (2009), Decety & Lamm (2009), Eisenberg (2000), Hoffman (1991, 2000), Batson (1991, 2009b), Toi & Batson (1982), Batson, Fultz, & Schoenrade (1987), and Eisenberg et al. (1989).

Neuroscientific research has helped to support the view that the difference between empathy and personal distress is more than one of degree. Jean Decety and Claus Lamm (2009), for example, argue that a clear distinction between these two processes can be found at the neurological level; different neural substrates underlie these two phenomena. A related line of research takes a neuroscientific approach to questions about the various roles empathy plays in human experience and in social cognition in particular. This research has been the basis of significant developments and changes in our theoretical understanding of how humans develop, interact, and flourish and of the centrality of empathy in imitation, cooperation, and deception.[68] In the area of child development, for example, the standard account of infants' early development and capacity for social connection has been completely overturned. Once thought to be asocial and egocentric, infants are now believed to be social, possessing a capacity for imitation, intersubjective communication, and social connection from the time of birth.[69]

Some additional areas of research in which neuroscientific work on empathy has figured prominently include the study of psychopathy,[70]—which has important implications for our understanding of normal development and moral psychology—the study of autism spectrum disorders,[71] and the study of different forms of pro-social behavior.[72]

Research on mirror neurons has driven much, though not all, of the neuroscientific work on empathy, revolutionizing the way we understand human interaction. In the early 1990s in Parma, Italy, Giacomo Rizzolatti and his group first discovered a special class of neurons in the macaque brain, in the ventral pre-motor area (F5). These came to be called mirror neurons. What makes these neurons special is that they are activated both when an individual performs a particular type of action (e.g. grasping an object) and when an individual observes another performing that type of action. Thus, in some cases, we *mirror* others at a neurological level. Hence the name 'mirror neurons'.

The first mirror neurons discovered were pre-motor visuo-motor neurons so the early data and many of the discussions concern motor actions (Ferrari & Gallese (2007)). Later, however, different types of mirror neurons were discovered. Audio-visual

---

[68] See essays in this collection by Iacoboni, Decety and Meltzoff, and Goldman, and Goldman (2006a), Iacoboni (2008), de Waal (2009), essays in Decety & Ickes (2009), essays in Pineda (2009a), Rizzolatti & Sinigaglia (2008), essays in Keysers & Fadiga (2009), essays in Bråten (2007), and essays in Stamenov & Gallese (2002).

[69] See the essay in this collection by Decety and Meltzoff, and Bråten (2007), Bråten & Trevarthen (2007), and Stern (2004: 241–2). It's worth noting that certain philosophers and psychologists were challenging the standard view of infants as narcissistic prior to the recent neuroscientific findings, including Meltzoff & Gopnik (1993), Cynthia Willett (1995), and Paul Harris (2000).

[70] See Blair & Blair (2009), Blair, Mitchell, & Blair (2005), Blair (1995, 2006, 2008b), Blair et al. (1997), and Decety & Moriguchi (2007).

[71] See Pfeifer & Dapretto (2009), Pfeifer, et al. (2008), Dapretto et al.(2005), Iacoboni & Dapretto (2006), Baron Cohen (1997, 2003), and Decety & Moriguchi (2007).

[72] See Batson (2009b), Eisenberg and Eggum (2009), Iacoboni (2008), Preston & de Waal (2002), and de Waal (2009).

mirror neurons, for example, are another class of F5 neurons that can be activated both by the performance of some action (e.g. breaking open a peanut) and by the sound produced by that action (Kohler et al. (2002)).[73] Multiple studies employing different experimental methodologies and techniques have demonstrated the existence of a mirroring system in humans. Part of this system involves mechanisms that make it possible for us to share the affective experience of others. As Tania Singer and Claus Lamm explain, 'consistent evidence shows that sharing the emotions of others is associated with activation in neural structures that are also active during the first-hand experience of that emotion' (2009).[74]

It would be difficult to overstate the importance of the discovery of mirror neurons, not only for the study of what we call low-level empathy but for our understanding of mental life more generally. Neuroscientist V.S. Ramachandran claims that 'mirror neurons will do for psychology what DNA did for biology: they will provide a unifying framework and help explain a host of mental abilities that have hitherto remained mysterious and inaccessible to experiments' (2000). Mirror neurons and mirror systems explain how it is that we can experience another's emotion almost instantaneously, without conscious deliberation or the use of imagination. They provide strong empirical support for simulation theory and may be the mechanism or one of the mechanisms for simulation or at least some types of simulation.[75] In his 2008 book *Mirroring People: The Science of Empathy and How We Connect with Others*, neuroscientist Marco Iacoboni says that mirror neurons are the foundation of empathy and possibly of morality and that they solve the problem of other minds.

Ethology

Another area of research on empathy that overlaps with the research in neuroscience is ethology, the study of animal behavior and social organization from a biological perspective. In his 2009 book *The Age of Empathy: Nature's Lessons for a Kinder Society*,

---

[73] See, also, the discussion in Iacoboni's essay in this collection.

[74] For more on mirroring in humans, see the essays by Iacoboni and Goldman in this collection, Iacoboni (2005, 2008, 2009a and 2009b), essays in Decety & Ickes (2009), essays in Pineda (2009a), Wicker et al. (2008), Goldman (2006a, 2008, 2009a), Goldman & Sripada (2005), Ferrari & Gallese (2007), Gallese, Keysers, & Rizzolatti (2004), and Keysers & Gazzola (2006).

[75] See Goldman's essay in this collection and Goldman (2006a: especially 113–46, 2008, 2009a), Gallese & Goldman (1998), Ferrari & Gallese (2007), and Pineda (2009a). Pineda argues that the work on mirror neurons expands the explanatory scope and empirical basis for simulation, and Ferrari and Gallese propose that simulation is a basic functional mechanism that is sub-personally instantiated by mirror neurons. As is clear in his essay in this collection and the references above, Goldman is more cautious about what we can conclude at this point about the relationship between mirror neurons and simulation. Goldman has a duplex theory of simulation that specifies two different types of simulation-based processes—low-level simulations and high-level simulations. While the low-level simulations involve direct mirroring, high-level simulations target more complex mental states and necessarily involve pretense or what Goldman calls enactment imagination. He argues that these two different levels of simulation rely on different mechanisms and operate in different ways.

ethologist and primatologist Frans de Waal states that 'empathy is the grand theme of our time', and argues that it is an ancient part of our heritage that has received far too little attention. De Waal calls for a complete overhaul of our assumptions about human nature that characterize it exclusively in terms of selfishness, competition, and aggression. It is time, he says, to correct this cardboard version of who we are that was perpetuated by the Social Darwinists and allowed to persist due to the tendency of most scientists to pay far more attention to negative emotions than positive ones, and the tendency of most philosophers to emphasize reason over emotion.

Empathy is at the center of de Waal's alternative models of human nature and social behavior in human and non-human animals. In an attempt to 'strip empathy down to its bare bones', de Waal identifies multiple levels of empathy that occur in a wide range of species that includes humans, non-human primates, monkeys, elephants, dolphins, dogs, and rodents. He traces the development of empathy and sympathy from bodily synchronization to high-level perspective-taking and 'targeted helping', describing numerous related behaviors along the way.[76]

De Waal hypothesizes that empathy works the same way in humans and non-human animals, with the only real difference being one of degree. Thus, human empathy, in some cases, possesses greater complexity than empathy in other species (2009: 132).

De Waal likens his model of empathy to a Russian doll:

The full capacity seems put together like a Russian doll. At its core is an automated process shared with a multitude of species, surrounded by outer layers that fine-tune its aim and reach. Not all species possess all layers: Only a few take another's perspective, something we are masters at. But even the most sophisticated layers of the doll remain firmly tied to its primal core. (2009: 208–9)

By explaining the evolutionary story of empathy and pointing out the pervasiveness of empathic behaviors, de Waal hopes both to provide a more accurate picture of human nature and to make it possible for us to work toward a more just society.

Overview of the Collection

Given this history of the term 'empathy', and the multiple uses to which it has been put during its short life, it is not surprising that the contributors to this volume often differ in what they mean by the term. In our view, this does not in any way present a difficulty. We believe that it would not be a good idea, even if it were possible, to attempt to regiment the term into one single meaning. Our everyday use of the term is highly varied, and often quite vague. In philosophical and psychological discussion, it is necessary to sharpen the term in a way that facilitates the particular topic and stance of

[76] See, also, the important article de Waal co-authored with Stephanie Preston, 'Empathy: its ultimate and proximate bases' that appeared in 2002 in *Behavioral and Brain Sciences* along with responses by numerous empathy researchers. It provides a review of the empathy literature and develops a broad, integrative model of empathy much like the one de Waal proposes in this more recent work.

the particular researcher and his or her readers, but it not necessary that all researchers should adopt the same meaning.

So we ask readers of this volume to be suitably aware, and not to expect us, as editors, to have forced the term 'empathy' onto a Procrustean bed. There are two corollaries to this. First, we should all take care to be clear precisely what sense of the term is being used by others when they set out their claims and arguments. Too often objections are raised to another's position which are at bottom just a protest: 'But that isn't what *I* mean by "empathy"'. Second, and obviously, we should all take care to be sure what we mean by the term when making our own claims and arguments—a certain looseness might be acceptable in everyday discourse, but not in philosophical and psychological debate.

This volume is divided into three sections, each one concerned with the relevance of empathy to larger debates in philosophy and psychology. In what follows, we will briefly set the scene for each section and then summarize the content of each chapter.

Empathy and mind

In this first section, contributors address questions of what empathy is from the perspective of psychology, neuroscience, and philosophy of mind. Some background might be helpful here to put the issues in context.

We human beings have an ability to understand, to explain, and to predict what people think, feel and do. Most of the time we exercise this ability with little or no explicit thought or reasoning on our part. This practice is sometimes called 'folk psychology', and the ability is sometimes referred to as 'mindreading', but these technical terms should not give the impression that the practice is anything other than utterly familiar to all of us from a very early age.

As we briefly discussed above, much of the debate over the last two decades has focused on what underlying cognitive or non-cognitive psychological capacities or abilities enable us to perform these tasks. One traditional view, now often called *theory theory*, has been that we take a kind of theoretical stance towards other people, very much as we take a kind of theoretical stance towards, for example, physical objects in space: one is 'folk physics', concerned with the behavior of physical objects, and the other is 'folk psychology', concerned with the behavior of people. So when we try to predict what someone will do, we deploy (perhaps tacitly) this theory, which will involve theorems such as 'if someone wants something and believes that by doing such-and-such he will be able to get it, then, all things being equal, he will do such-and-such'.[77]

The main opposition to theory theory, which was the prevailing view in analytic philosophy up to the mid 1980s, holds that our cognitive abilities in this area are quite different from our cognitive abilities in other areas. This is largely because we ourselves

---

[77] See, for example, Gopnik & Wellman (1994), Davies & Stone (1995a), Carruthers & Smith (1996), Davies & Stone (1998), Stueber (2000, 2006), and Kögler & Stueber (2000).

are minded, and this enables us to use our own minds to 'simulate' the minds of others. This view is thus often called *simulation theory*, or *simulationism*.

Although it is much debated precisely how such an account might be fleshed out in its details, simulation theory is now generally accepted to be a real alternative to theory theory.[78] We cannot go into the details of that debate here, but what has been particularly important, and what motivates many of the chapters in this section, is the role of empathy in simulation. One role for empathy, it is claimed by simulationists, is that it enables us to work out what someone else is likely to do by perspective-shifting, by imagining being in that other person's position, and thus using our imagined thoughts and feelings and decisions to determine what the other will think and feel and decide. For example, if you are asking yourself what she will do if she wants a beer and believes that there is a beer in the fridge, you do not need to deploy a theory about what people tend to do in such circumstances. Rather, you imagine what you would do in those circumstances: you imagine wanting a beer and believing that there is a beer in the fridge, and then imagine reaching a decision on the basis of having that desire and belief. You thereby conclude that that is just what she will decide to do, and what she will then in fact do. Of course your imagined decision does not result in action on your part, just because you appreciate that your thought processes are a simulation of another's thought processes: desires, beliefs, decisions, and so on are imagined, not real (they are, as it is sometimes said, 'off-line').

Empathy is now often taken to involve more than just the kind of conscious imaginative process which we have so far been considering. It is now often also taken to involve a more basic, non-conscious process of 'picking-up on' another person's thoughts and feelings. For example, we humans seem from a very early age to be able to grasp another's fear or anger from their facial expression, or to realize that someone is trying to wipe a table or to turn on a light. The exercise of these abilities seems to be so immediate and non-inferential, and so prevalent in toddlers and even very young babies, that the explanation is unlikely to involve the same kind of psychological resources as perspective-shifting—and even less likely, one might think, to involve the deployment of a theory.

In this Introduction, we will follow Alvin Goldman's lead (2006a) and call these two kinds of empathy *higher-level empathy* and *lower-level empathy*. Other terms for higher-level empathy include *re-enactive empathy* (Steuber (2006)), *reconstructive empathy* (the term which Goldman uses in his chapter in this volume), and *perspective-shifting* (Goldie this volume). Other terms for lower-level empathy include *basic empathy* (Steuber (2006)), and *mirroring* (Goldman this volume).

The arguments for the role of empathy in simulationism are partly empirical and partly a priori, although it is probably true to say that the evidence brought forward for lower-level empathy has tended to be more empirical than the evidence for higher-

---

[78] See footnote 1 for references.

level empathy. Moreover, the empirical evidence for lower-level empathy is much more robust. This is in part because lower-level or basic empathetic processes are more readily observable in, for example, toddlers and babies; and in part because these processes would seem to have more salient neural pathways—see the discussion of mirror neurons below. In contrast, a priori arguments are more at home with higher-level empathy, which is more directed towards imagining the *reasons* for someone else's mental states or action; and a priori arguments are more at home where reasons are concerned.[79] Nevertheless, there is also strong empirical evidence adduced for higher-level empathy in arguments against theory theory, including substantial work in developmental and empirical psychology, and in studies of autism.

Not surprisingly, some philosophers and psychologists have concentrated their research on one or the other of higher- or lower-level empathy. Others have concentrated on both, seeking to find reasons for unifying them in a larger theoretical framework which justifies them both being included under the single rubric of *empathy*. In her chapter, 'Understanding Empathy: Its Features and Effects', Amy Coplan gives theoretical and methodological reasons for resisting the assimilation of lower-level or basic empathy and higher-level empathy or perspective-shifting, and puts forward a conceptualization of empathy which, with one important qualification, is in line with our rough characterization of higher-level empathy which we set out above. She says, 'empathy is a complex imaginative process in which an observer simulates another person's situated psychological states [both cognitive and affective] while maintaining clear self-other differentiation' (p. 5).

Coplan goes on to consider three central elements of her definition. First, there is 'affective matching', where the imagined affective states are qualitatively the same as those of the other person, the 'target' (the term we will use for the person with whom the 'empathizer' is trying to empathize). Here Coplan makes clear the important distinction between shared affect which arises as a result of other-oriented perspective-taking, which Coplan calls *affective matching*, and shared affect which arises through other means—for example, through two persons reacting with the same emotion to the same object, or through *emotional contagion* (which we will discuss in more detail in relation to Stephen Davies' chapter in this volume). The second central element of Coplan's definition marks the important difference with our rough characterization of higher-level empathy: on her account, perspective-taking must be other-oriented rather than self-oriented. So empathy is not putting *yourself* in the other's shoes; it should not involve imagining *yourself* wanting a beer and so on. Putting yourself in the other's shoes in this way can easily result, Coplan says, in 'false consensus effects, personal distress and prediction errors based on egocentric biases' (p. 13). In contrast, other-oriented perspective-taking involves imagining being the target, having the target's thoughts and feelings, and not imagining yourself having those thoughts and

---

[79] For arguments along these lines, see especially the papers collected in Heal (2003), and Stueber (2006).

feelings. The third central element of Coplan's definition, self–other differentiation, requires that the empathizer remains conscious of the clear boundaries between the self and the other.

In 'Empathy as a Route to Knowledge', Derek Matravers begins by establishing a definition of empathy close to that of Coplan. Like Coplan, Matravers separates empathy from other, closely-related phenomena, and in particular from emotional contagion (and from other kinds of lower-level affective responses), from imagining oneself in another's shoes, and from sympathy. Empathy on this definition is a conscious imaginative project that requires a full understanding of the target's mental states in order to be able to engage with them imaginatively. Matravers then examines whether empathy, defined in this way, is a reliable route to, first, knowledge of others' mental states, and second, to knowledge of what unfamiliar mental states, in particular feelings and emotions, are like. He argues that there might be in principle some obstacles to empathy's ability to yield knowledge of the mental states of another. In particular, he questions whether two conditions which are necessary for successful empathy can, in fact, be satisfied: first, whether it is possible to provide 'inputs' to the imaginative process with the right content—right, that is, in the sense of being mental states with contents appropriate to the target; and second, whether it is possible, even with the right inputs, to reliably generate the affective states which match those of the target. Moreover, Matravers argues, there are potentially significant differences between how one imagines responding in a certain imagined situation (being faced with the prospect of death for example) and how one would actually respond if such a situation were real.

On the second topic of his chapter, the question of whether empathy can yield knowledge of what unfamiliar mental states are like, Matravers raises three requirements for the causal efficacy of an empathetic engagement with a target's experience which are, again, difficult to satisfy: the empathizer's imagined beliefs must have the right amount of 'vivacity' relative to the target's beliefs; the imagined mental states must resonate in the empathizer's mental economy in the right way relative to the target; and finally he points to the difficulty, or sometimes impossibility, for the empathizer of simulating certain triggers of the target's affect in order to give rise to that affect—simulating smells or sounds for example. Although Matravers concludes that, in the right circumstances, empathy with a target can have a cognitive advantage over mere knowledge *that* the target is in a certain mental state, nevertheless he doubts that empathy, as he defines it, 'is as common an occurrence as we might think' (p. 28).

In his chapter, 'Two Routes to Empathy: Insights from Cognitive Neuroscience', Alvin Goldman, in contrast to Coplan and Matravers, proposes a working definition of empathy which allows for two 'routes' to empathy: what he calls the 'mirroring' route and the 'reconstructive route'. These are equivalent to lower-level empathy and higher-level empathy respectively. The mirroring route is named after the discovery of mirror neurons and mirroring processes, which we briefly explained above. These are discussed in detail in the chapters by Marco Iacoboni, and by Jean Decety and

Andrew Meltzoff. Recall that, when the monkey or human observes a target's facial expression or bodily movement, the same cells are activated in the observer as in the target: thus the name *mirror* neurons and processes. This kind of mirroring has been discovered in relation to emotions, pain, touch, and action-planning. Goldman says that these mirroring episodes are 'below the threshold of consciousness' (p. 33), and accepts that terms such as 'resonance' and 'contagion' might be considered preferable.

Goldman's reconstructive route to empathy is much along the lines we have so far discussed here: reflecting on the other's situation, you imagine how you would feel if you were in his shoes. This is, Goldman says, 'a more effortful or constructive process' (p. 36) than the mirroring route; and it is less reliable. Goldman goes on to consider what the neural pathways might be for reconstructive empathy, and how they are distinct from those for mirroring; and here he registers disagreement with Iacoboni and others, who suggest that mirror neurons might be involved in both kinds of empathy.

Like Goldman, and Jean Decety and Andrew Meltzoff in their chapter, Marco Iacoboni, in 'Within Each Other: Neural Mechanisms for Empathy in the Primate Brain', addresses the question of what the neurophysiological mechanisms are that underlie empathy. He sets out a fascinating history of this inquiry, starting from the discovery of mirror neurons in the macaque brain in the late 1980s. He discusses how more recent studies have shown that macaque mirror neurons discharge not only at the sight of actions by the target, but also at the *sound* of actions—such as the sound of the breaking of a peanut. He then discusses related studies in humans, which are, for ethical reasons, restricted in their methods to measuring fMRI activation in groups of cells; he notes in particular that action sounds heard by humans give rise to activation consistent with the presence of mirror neurons, and argues that it is reasonable to hypothesize that human brains contain mirror neurons. Furthermore, he appeals to other recent studies of epileptic patients, where electrodes could be implanted on independent medical grounds, which show that mirror neurons are much more widespread in humans' brains than previously realized, beyond just mirroring of motor neurons. As we have seen, Goldman (along with many other scholars) has argued that mirror neurons cannot account for the higher-level forms of empathy—for what Goldman in his chapter calls reconstructive empathy. Against this view, Iacoboni argues that the fact that there are many different kinds of mirror neurons, and that they are also much more widely distributed in the primate brain than previously thought, suggests a very sophisticated neural system that may support complex forms of mindreading and empathizing, including higher-level empathy.

Jean Decety and Andrew Meltzoff, in 'Empathy, Imitation, and the Social Brain', bring to the fore something that is in the background in Goldman's and Iacoboni's chapters: the connection between empathy and imitation. They begin with imitation in babies, and show how their studies of neonates (only a day or so old) reveal imitation of facial expression such as tongue protrusion, explained by what they call 'active intermodal mapping'. This unifies the actions of another person, observed through perception, with the child's own actions, observed through proprioception. Imitation, functional at birth in humans, is they say, 'a marker of innate intersubjectivity in action' (p. 61). So what they call the 'Like-Me bridge' is not one that is first crossed later in life, as a developmental achievement, but is part of our human biological constitution at birth. Grounded in innate shared representations, imitation in toddlers (from 18 months old) comes to be regulated by reference to the adult's emotional reactions: a negative reaction from the adult to an observed action leads to significantly less imitation.

Bringing together these and other studies in imitation from developmental science and cognitive neuroscience, Decety and Melzoff show how imitation, including emotional sharing, plays an essential formative role in the child's developing sense of agency, self, and self-other differentiation—capacities which are involved in the emergence of empathy at age 2–4. Thus, they argue, imitation and empathy are closely linked, although they are not underpinned by identical neurological processes. They emphasize, as does Coplan, the dangers of imagining *oneself* in perspective-taking, which can result in a tendency to avoid negative emotions of one's own, and which can in turn, through egocentric bias, inhibit any tendency to mitigate the target's suffering and negative emotions. Accordingly, they say, empathy—understood as adopting the *other's* perspective—involves significant executive functions, which 'not only facilitate perspective taking, but also control attention and meta-cognitive capacities, both of which facilitate pro-social responding in reaction to another's distress' (p. 79).

Gregory Currie's 'Empathy for Objects' represents a transition point from this section, Empathy and Mind, to the next section, Empathy and Aesthetics. In this chapter, Currie argues for a more inclusive role for empathy other than with persons and their mental states. He argues that we also empathize with things. In this he recognizes a continuity of thought with what he calls the Empathists of the early twentieth century; as noted above and in this chapter by Currie, the term empathy or *Einfühlung* was first introduced in a wide sense of feeling our way into things, as what Currie calls 'a general means of knowing' (p. 83). Following Herbert Langfeld, a psychologist writing in the 1920s, he develops an idea of inner mimicry or motor imagining in our sensory engagement with objects—a process which Currie argues has an equivalent in the present-day notion of simulative processes, such as are used in our imagining the rotation of objects. Maintaining the connection with the Empathists, Currie goes on to claim that these kinds of simulative processes are involved in our engagement with the aesthetic properties of artworks such as pictures and sculptures as well as in our recognition of the emotions of other people in low-level, basic empathy. More than that, he speculates that bodily simulations are a pervasive feature of our relations to the external world, including ordinary everyday non-sentient things such as trees and telephones, sculptures and buildings. This kind of empathy, Currie says, is not merely a curious by-product of the evolution of social-empathic capacities; it is part of a sane grip on the world.

In his chapter, Currie discusses an issue in the philosophy of mind which we consider to be of the greatest importance. An intuitive temptation is to say that our simulative response to another's emotion is through perception: we *see* or *hear* the other's grief or terror. (And equivalently in the aesthetic case: we *see* the aesthetic emotional properties of the picture.) In other words, simulations of this low-level basic kind are perceptions. Currie resists this temptation. Instead, he says (with the aesthetic case in mind), 'These [simulative] processes provide information which is accessed by the visual system, and which contributes to a visual experience in which various properties of the work, or of that which is represented in it, are made manifest' (p. 90). However, he continues, 'these things are given to me in visual experience itself, as that experience is enriched by its connections with simulative processes; they are not given to me by a combination of vision and a set of distinct, simulation-based perceptual systems' (ibid.).

What we think is the important issue here—one which has not yet been fully addressed in the philosophical literature on empathy—is whether basic, low-level empathy with other people, of the kind which is non-conscious in the way discussed by Goldman for example, can *at the personal level* be thought of as a kind of perception. If, as Currie says, 'things are given to me in visual experience itself', then the fact that the deliverances of the visual system are 'enriched' by simulative connections should not force one to deny that. It might be, then, that the discovery of the marvelous complexities of the operations in the human brain, and in particular of simulative processes involving mirror neurons, should not mislead us to reject our intuitions about what to say about the *person* and the person's *mind*: we *see* in the face of the other his grief, his joy, his fear; we *see* that he intends to wipe the table, to pick up the glass, to open the suitcase, to bite the apple.

Empathy and aesthetics

As Gregory Currie's chapter foreshadowed and the first part of this introduction indicated, there is a strong historical link between the concepts of aesthetics and empathy, one which is to be found in the *Verstehen* tradition and in the work of those who Currie calls the Empathists of the early twentieth century. In many respects, this link ought not to be surprising given the role that we have already seen to be occupied by empathy in mindreading. For artworks are, like actions, the product of, and expressive of, people's feelings and intentions. Moreover, empathy can also be involved in our engagement with the characters that are portrayed in representational works of art—for example, in film, literature, and pictures. Not only are these characters the intentional products of the artist; they also have a life of their own, so to speak, which is in many respects just like ours, and which is there to be understood, and, perhaps, empathized with.

The varied, and often vague, everyday use of the term 'empathy' which we have already mentioned in relation to mindreading, is also to be found in aesthetics. In literature and film for example, readers and audiences often say that they empathize with a character, but when pressed as to exactly what this involves, they will often be unclear precisely what is going on, and precisely what sense of the term they are using.

In this section of the volume, our contributors consider the role of empathy in relation to various art forms: to film, to pictures, to music, and to literature. These discussions throw light on the different kinds of empathy that are involved, so issues of definition are as important here as they were in relation to empathy and the mind. They also reveal just how diverse are the roles of the different kinds of empathy in our engagement with the arts. And finally, a number of the discussions suggest that it would be mistaken to assume that empathy, whether higher- or lower-level, is the only method by which we engage with artworks; in this respect at least it is arguably in line with our engagement with other people in life beyond aesthetics.

Murray Smith, in 'Empathy, Expansionism, and the Extended Mind', considers the role of empathy in representational works of art, and in film in particular. His definition of empathy is as a variety of what we have called higher-level empathy: what Smith calls 'other-focused personal imagining'. It is personal imagining as it is a kind of imagining of what an experience is like from a point of view; and it is other-focused as the imagined point of view is that of another, the target, rather than the imagined point of view of oneself in the target's circumstances. Affective mimicry and emotional contagion—varieties of what we have called lower-level empathy—act, Smith says, 'as prompts to, and props within, fully-fledged imaginative projects' (p. 101), but, as he makes clear, these lower-level, non-conscious processes are excluded from his definition of empathy: empathy, for him, is a 'higher-level type of volitional imagining' (p. 104).

Smith goes on to consider the relationship between empathy thus understood and the concept of the *extended mind*—the idea that many features of human mentality can only be understood by relating the 'naked' power of the mind to the tools of technology, language, and culture. One role for empathy here, Smith suggests, lies in the *coupling* of the empathizers mind with the targets mind—as, for exmple, when we respond fearfully to the alarmed glance of another. In the other direction, so to speak, empathy can itself be enhanced as a capacity by the extended mind, and in particular by public representations and narratives such as films. Films and film-making can thus be seen, he says, as 'cognitive prostheses', aiding the development of these kinds of imaginative capacities both in their scope and in their intensity.[80]

---

[80] We cannot resist here the temptation to mention Freud's prescient description of these and other kinds of prostheses in his 'Civilization and its Discontents': 'With every tool man is perfecting his own organs, whether motor or sensory, or is removing the limits to their functioning': he mentions motor cars, telephones, telescopes, cameras, etc. He then continues: 'Man has, as it were, become a kind of prosthetic God. When he puts on all his auxiliary organs he is truly magnificent; but those organs have not grown on to him and they still give him much trouble at times. Nevertheless, he is entitled to console himself with the thought that development will not come to an end precisely with the year 1930 A.D. Future ages will bring with them new and probably unimaginably great advances in this field of civilization and will increase man's likeness to God still more. But in the interests of our investigations, we will not forget that present-day man does not feel happy in his Godlike character.' (Penguin Freud Library, volume 12, page 280).

There are important connections between Smith's discussion and the chapter from Dominic McIver Lopes, 'An Empathic Eye', which is concerned with our engagement with pictures. Both Smith and Lopes recognize the value of artworks in the development of empathy. Pictures that evoke empathy are valuable, Lopes says, in part because they can make us better at seeing empathetically. However, it is important to appreciate here that Lopes is working with what is, in one respect, a broader definition of empathy than is Smith (indeed it is broader than most of the definitions in this volume): Lopes takes empathy to include sympathy or concern for another person's suffering, a concern that might be grounded in empathetic imagining of how it is for the other to suffer.[81] He also includes the kinds of emotional sharing and emotional contagion that are involved in lower-level empathy.

Lopes acknowledges that seeing pictures can enhance empathy simply by being able to 'evoke experiences as of the scenes they represent' (p. 119), but what he is seeking here is a distinctively *different* way in which pictures contribute to our empathetic skills, and yet still in a way that 'carries over to life beyond pictures' (p. 119). Solving these two requirements at once—what he calls the *difference problem* and the *carryover problem*—is the task that Lopes sets himself. He solves the difference problem by appealing to the idea that our seeing-in pictures can evoke empathetic responses that our perception of the world beyond pictures does not: for example, we can respond sadly to a brown scene in a picture, or we can recognize the despair in the shipwrecked people portrayed in Géricault's *Raft of The Medusa* because the sea and the ship express malignant indifference to their fate, and despair is appropriate where something more powerful expresses malignant indifference. Like the ship and the sea, generally scenes in pictures can express emotion, just so long as one accepts, as Lopes does, that something can be expressive of emotion without any emotion being felt. To solve the carryover problem, Lopes turns to the phenomenon of social referencing: the child sees fear in the mother's face as she looks at an object that both child and mother can see, and as a result the child responds also with fear. Similarly, if we see fear in an experienced sailor's face as he looks at the oily-flat sea, we realize that fear of the sea is appropriate even though the sea, unlike the sea in the picture, is not expressive of a threat of the oncoming typhoon. Thus both the difference problem and the carryover problems are solved, and Lopes has shown us that pictures are prostheses for empathy just as Smith has for film.

Music too can give rise to emotions: sad music can make listeners feel sad, and happy music can make them happy. Stephen Davies, in 'Infectious Music: Music-Listener Emotional Contagion', provides an account of this which is in clear contrast to the familiar cognitive account of the emotions, according to which an emotion consists of, or depends on, a belief that the object of the emotion in some way warrants that emotion. For example, your belief that your best friend is sad warrants your feeling sad for her. So on a cognitivist account of our emotional responses to music, the music

---

[81] Recall from the discussion of the psychologist C.D. Batson above that he has a similarly wide definition; see the discussion of Jesse Prinz's chapter below.

would have to be, in fact, sad. And yet, as Davies says, 'those who are saddened by sad music are not sad *about* or *for* the music' (p. 136). In contrast to the cognitive account, Davies argues that our response to music is one of emotional contagion. He points out that emotional contagion is a very common phenomenon: we become cheerful in response to the cheerful décor of the pub or in response to the cheerful laughter of the group at the table in the corner. Note here that in this Introduction we have characterized emotional contagion as a kind of *empathy*, but the emotional contagion that is at issue in the case of the cheerful décor is one where the cause of the emotion is not another person's emotion. So the cheerful décor of the pub is the better analogy with cheerful music than is the cheerful laughter of the people in the pub. In his account, accordingly, Davies provides a definition of emotional contagion which is indifferent to the cause of the emotional state.

Davies distinguishes between two kinds of music-based emotional contagion: those occasions where we respond to 'elevator music' without being aware of the music (although of course we hear it); and those occasions where the music is the object of our attention, even though (in contrast to the cognitivist view) our emotional response is not about the music. Davies goes on to address and respond to alternative accounts of our emotional responses to music, and in particular the account of Jenefer Robinson, who also holds that our response to music can be explained by emotional contagion, but who differs from Davies in certain important respects.

The next three chapters in this section are all concerned with our empathetic engagement with literature and with literary characters. In her chapter, 'Empathizing as Simulating', Susan Feagin sets out a simulationist account of what it is to empathize with characters in literary works of art. Feagin's account of what simulation consists in is quite strict in the following respect (it is stricter than that of, for example, Goldman): for a process to simulate another process, it is necessary for it to be 'structurally similar, in relevant respects, to the process simulated' (p. 149). So it is not enough for simulation of another's mental state that one's own state ends up the same as that of the target: the process itself has to match that of the target too. Thus simulation is a process, and simulating a mental process of the person with whom one empathizes is a necessary condition of empathizing with them.

Feagin then goes on to consider simulation as a necessary condition for appreciation of, and empathy with, literary characters. Here she particularly focuses on the importance of literary devices, such as style and the use of punctuation, or the way in which the story is narrated, in enabling us to empathize with literary characters, including in particular empathizing with the phenomenology of those characters' desires and desire-like states. In this sense at least, simulation with literary characters is easier than simulation with real life people, 'since literature is written for those who would appreciate it—something not to be assumed of the 'narratives' that people create as we live our lives' (p. 161). As Feagin argues, the importance of literary devices in our engagement with literature tends to be neglected by those accounts that involve our simulation of a hypothetical reader of fact (see for example Currie (1997)).[82]

Noël Carroll, in 'On Some Affective Relationships between Audiences and the Characters in Popular Fiction', considers the various ways in which we can be engaged emotionally with the emotional states of fictional characters—especially the protagonists in popular fictions. He chooses to avoid using the term 'empathy', preferring to work with a wide notion of emotional engagement, involving 'cases where the emotional states of audience members converge, are congruent with, or otherwise resonate appropriately with what we are given to imagine are the emotions of fictional characters' (p. 163). This has some similarity to the notion of empathy that Lopes works with in his chapter, for Carroll, like Lopes, includes in the notion of 'appropriately resonating' with a fictional character what is effectively sympathizing with that character. But Carroll's aim is not to put forward any kind of definition, or to regiment our theorizing in any particular direction. On the contrary, his aim is to set out the variety of ways in which we can and do respond to the fates of fictional characters. These include: identification, including what we have called higher-level empathy; coincident emotional states; vectorially converging emotive states; sympathy, involving care and concern for another; solidarity; and mirror reflexes, of the kind we have been discussing above under lower-level empathy. Carroll concludes that 'there is no single affective relationship that describes the one and only connection between readers, listeners, and/or viewers on the one hand, and fictional characters, on the other hand' (p. 180). If this is correct, then we again have reason to question accounts of our emotional engagement with literature that are exclusively based on simulation, or in putting ourselves in the shoes of someone—whether of the protagonist, or of the hypothetical reader of fact, or of the implied author.

Graham McFee's 'Empathy: Interpersonal vs. Artistic?', a chapter strongly influenced by the work of Ludwig Wittgenstein, puts empathy in aesthetics and empathy in interpersonal relations side by side as 'objects of comparison'. With interpersonal empathy understood, roughly, as taking on in imagination the perspective and experiences of another, McFee asks what is 'carried over' to our empathizing with a character in literature. Successful interpersonal empathy involves, McFee says, a matching of one's psychological states with those of the target; success here can come in degrees— the match can be more or less precise. At this point he questions the role of empirical research in determining quite what 'success' might be in an individual interpersonal case—and further, whether empirical research has any grip at all when it is concerned with our empathetic engagement with characters in literature. McFee then considers the difficulties facing a modern male in empathizing with a Victorian woman, or with a South American gangsterista, many of whose values he does not share. Emphasizing the special importance of 'understanding' in the literary case, in the end McFee

---

[82] James Wood's discussion of free indirect style in his *How Fiction Works* (2008) is very illuminating in this regard.

expresses doubt about whether 'we can import "insight" from empathy in the inter-personal case to the empathetic reading of literature' (p. 208).

Empathy and morality

In morality, and elsewhere as we have seen, we make a very straightforward distinction between, for example, feeling the suffering of another person, and feeling *for* that person's suffering, and this distinction is one that is often (if not always—see for example Lopes above) made in terms of calling the first empathy and the second sympathy. However, the waters are considerably muddied by David Hume, who, as we previously mentioned, used the term 'sympathy' for (more or less) empathy, and 'benevolence' for (more or less) sympathy, and also by the fact that, as we have seen, many psychologists and philosophers define empathy in a way that includes pro-social motivation. In this section, however, we will restrict the term 'empathy' to a kind of 'matching' of another's psychological states, where that matching does not arise through emotional sharing (see Coplan's chapter for discussion).[83]

On this definition of empathy, it would seem that empathy is not sufficient for morality. For one could feel another's suffering and yet, like the empathetic torturer, use that sensitivity to further increase the suffering of the other person rather than to mitigate it. What is missing in this empathetic torturer is the appropriate moral motivation. Whereas sympathy, at least on most accounts, does involve the appropriate moral motivation.[84] This is not to say, of course, that, on this understanding of sympathy, the sympathetic person will necessarily act according to his feelings of sympathy: his motivation to help the other might be outweighed on a particular occasion by other considerations, such as concern for his own welfare. For example, at the airline check-in desk one might feel sympathy for one's fellow-traveler who is told that the plane is full, but still not give up one's own seat because of one's concern to get home that evening. On the strength of this example, then, it might seem that sympathy is not sufficient for morality either. But this is not a question that we will address here, except to note that there are many accounts of morality according to which neither empathy nor sympathy, nor the two together, are sufficient for morality.

Jesse Prinz's chapter asks this question: 'Is Empathy Necessary for Morality?'. Like us in this respect, Prinz avoids those definitions of empathy which include what we intuitively think of as concern for another: for example, C. D. Batson's definition of empathy as 'an other-oriented emotional response congruent with the perceived welfare of another person' (Batson, Turk et al. (1995): 300), and this seems to include empathetic concern, or concern based on empathy.[85] He also avoids those definitions

---

[83] A further issue also muddies the water. Sometimes we empathize with a target where that target does not himself feel the emotion. For example, we feel fear as the little princes innocently and unknowingly go to their place of execution. Jesse Prinz discusses this too in his chapter.

[84] See, e.g. Eisenberg & Strayer (1987), Wispé (1986, 1987, 1991), and Eisenberg (2000).

[85] For further discussion, see Slote (2007, 2010).

that involve feeling as the other *ought* to feel, for this, Prinz says, again gets us too close to sympathetic concern. The central notion of empathy that Prinz works with is of 'a kind of vicarious emotion: it's feeling what one takes another person to be feeling' (p. 213).

Prinz argues that there is little evidence for the claim that empathy, thus understood, is necessary for morality: not for moral judgment, for moral development, or for moral conduct. So far as moral judgment is concerned, he points out that many such judgments are not directly concerned with people, and here empathy has no place. Moreover, other emotions, without empathy, are sufficient for moral judgment. Turning to moral development, some recent work on psychopathology purports to show the necessity of empathy for moral competence, but Prinz challenges this account on a number of points. One such point is that it is possible that psychopaths have some third deficit which causes both a deficit in empathy and in moral competence: in particular, Prinz suggests, they lack depth in their moral emotions, which fact would also lend support to his positive claims about the source of morality in our moral sentiments—our dispositions to have moral emotions such as anger, disgust, guilt, and shame. On the role of empathy in moral motivation and moral conduct, Prinz argues instead that the source of motivation is to be found in the moral emotions; and he also claims that there is little evidence of any strong positive correlation between empathy and pro-social motivation. Finally, Prinz discusses whether moral systems that promote empathy should be encouraged, and again he expresses doubts for a variety of reasons, including empathy's fragility and biases, concluding that, 'in the moral domain, we should regard empathy with caution' (p. 229).

The authors of the next two chapters take a more positive line towards the role of empathy in particular aspects of morality. In 'Empathy, Justice, and the Law', Martin L. Hoffman argues for the importance of empathy in justice and the law—places where the traditional view is that empathy is out of place. Hoffman works with a notion of empathy and of empathetic distress which is broader than that of Prinz, in three important respects: his notion of empathy includes a pro-social sympathetic element ('feeling *for* as well as *with* the victim' (p. 235)); it involves a notion of distress towards, for example, non-psychological states such as being poor, and also towards the distress of a group; and his notion of empathy includes empathic anger, which Prinz would treat as a moral sentiment rather than as a part of empathy.

Whilst Hoffman accepts the fragility and biases involved in empathy, he argues that these can be corrected for through deliberation. He then goes on to consider the role of empathy in a number of Supreme Court decisions, including the famous *Brown v. Board of Education* and *Roe v. Wade*, and the empathetic work of individuals to help change the law which benefited distressed groups: Lyndon B. Johnson, Harriet Beecher Stowe, Ivan Turgenev, Robert Kennedy, and Yale Kamisar. In *Roe v. Wade*, concerning the right of women to have an abortion, Hoffman notes an important feature of empathy: it can give rise to conflicting empathetic concern, in this case both for the pregnant women and for what the anti-abortion lawyers called 'unborn children'. This feature alone shows that empathy can in no way be sufficient for reaching judgments in the law as there has to be some principle to decide which empathetic concern should carry the greater weight. Moreover, the degree of empathetic concern cannot be the deciding factor, for there remains the worry of empathetic biases, to which Hoffman returns towards the end of his chapter, including the potential bias from heart-rending victim-impact statements. But these observations do not imply that one should return to the traditional view of the role of empathy in the law—the view that 'the law and its underlying justice principles are, and should be, cleansed of emotion so that reason and logic can prevail' (p. 230).

E. Ann Kaplan, in 'Empathy and Trauma Culture: Imaging Catastrophe', drawing on examples such as the war in Iraq, the Holocaust, and Hurricane Katrina, considers the role of empathy in our responses to images of catastrophe and individual trauma on TV and other media. As Kaplan notes, in the West today 'we are surrounded by spectacles of individual suffering'. She sets out to show that empathy comes in various forms—she picks out three—and the kind of empathetic response that we have to trauma depends (amongst other things) on the form of the image and its context. The first form of empathy is what she calls the 'vicarious trauma response', where the pro-social motivation that empathy involves (agreeing with Hoffman here) is blocked off by the viewer's empathic overreaction to the image portrayed. The second form, 'empty empathy', arises where not only pro-social motivation is lacking but also where fleeting, transitory empathetic feelings become diminished through exposure to successive images of terrible suffering, to be replaced by a kind of bland sentimentality.

The third form of empathetic response discussed by Kaplan is 'witnessing' through images—what she calls 'ethical witnessing'. Witnessing through images necessarily involves a degree of distance, but Kaplan's concern is the potentially positive effect of being at a distance. Especially where individual suffering is focused on in the images, as was the case with many images of the Iraq war, feelings of hopelessness arise, easily leading to empty empathy. In contrast, she says, are the images from Katrina, which were less controlled by the government, and which included pictures of group suffering, often set against a background which revealed the catastrophic situation. These images 'generated more complex, varied and ethical emotional impact' (p. 270), including group empathy and, as a result, anger and shame at the injustices of the situations which were being witnessed. In this sense, then, 'witnessing leads to a broader empathic understanding of the meaning of what has been done to victims' (p. 275).

The answer to the question that Heather Battaly poses in 'Is Empathy a Virtue?' will depend, she says, on what concepts of empathy and of virtue are in play. She begins by outlining four different concepts of empathy. The first is our ordinary everyday concept of empathy, which Battaly interprets as being 'a process of caring, or sharing, or knowing, or some combination thereof' (p. 279). This is a vague concept, or to use Battaly's useful technical term here, it is 'thin', in just the sense that competent speakers of English can disagree over which combinations of these three conditions—caring, sharing, and knowing—is necessary or sufficient for application of the concept.

Empathy, being a thin concept, can be thickened in various ways, and Battaly goes on to consider three theoretically driven ways of thickening the thin everyday concept. The first such thickening is the concept of empathy as 'sharing by multiple means', where what is shared is not only affective states but mental states in general, and multiple means incorporates both higher- and lower-level empathy. Although caring could arise as a causal outcome of sharing, neither caring for the other's suffering nor knowing the other's suffering is part of the concept itself. The second thickening is empathy as sharing and knowing the other's mental states, which again does not require caring. And finally, there is empathy as knowing.

Battaly shows that these three recent theoretically developed concepts of empathy in philosophy and psychology imply that empathy is neither a moral nor an intellectual virtue, nor is it sufficient for virtue, which is, according to Battaly's Aristotelian account, a disposition of character that aims at the good. In contrast, according to the pre-theoretical everyday concept as interpreted by Battaly, empathy is a virtue. She concludes that the fact that the theoretical concepts of empathy conflict with our ordinary concept over whether empathy is a virtue does not by itself constitute sufficient grounds for rejecting them.

The last two chapters are concerned with higher-level empathy or perspective-shifting, and the difficulties that can arise in shifting our perspective in the right way onto the thoughts and feelings of another person. Peter Goldie, in 'Anti-Empathy', puts to one side in-his-shoes perspective-shifting, which involves imagining yourself in the other's circumstances, and focuses specifically on what he calls empathetic perspective-shifting, which involves imagining being the other in the other's circumstances. These are often treated as equivalent, and they will deliver up the same outcome in what Goldie calls 'base cases'. Base cases are of this kind: where the empathizer has the same psychological dispositions (including character and personality) as the target; where there are no non-rational influences on the target's thinking; where the target is not confused about his state of mind; and where the target is not psychologically conflicted in his deliberations.

When we turn to empathetic perspective-shifting beyond the base case, difficulties arise. This is not because of limitations in our imaginative powers, but for deeper, conceptual reasons. Drawing on the work of Richard Moran, Goldie argues that the deliberative, practical stance that we take in practical reason, when part of a full-blooded notion of agency, is radically first-personal. When we attempt empathetic perspective-shifting beyond the base case, it is impossible to take on in imagination the appropriately full-blooded notion of first-personal agency that is involved in deliberation, whereas in the base case all that is necessary is that the empathizer and the target share rational agency in a thin sense. To attempt to empathize with the target in this way is to attempt to usurp the target's full-blooded essentially first-personal agency, replacing it with one's own.

Adam Morton, in 'Empathy for the Devil', considers how morality can be a barrier to empathy. In particular, our sense of decency limits our capacity to empathize with those who perform atrocious acts; they become alien to us, and we are unable to imagine how we—or anyone—could possibly do such things. In such cases, Morton says, 'We can describe the motives, and we can often even imagine some of what it might have been like to do the acts, but there are deep obstacles to the kind of sympathetic identification required for empathy' (p. 321). Morton argues that we can find ways around these barriers to empathizing with evil actions, for (unlike Goldie in his chapter) Morton sees the barriers as related to the limits of our imaginative powers. He illustrates this by analogy with something outside empathy: how one can use certain techniques to overcome attitudes of one's own through, for example, re-conceptualizing the object of one's disgust, or through using a physiologically aroused state to overcome one's timidity. In respect of empathy, one technique for overcoming the barriers is to imagine doing a venial act rather than an evil one, or perhaps to remember something venial that one had done in the past, and the emotions that had led to that action; for there are psychological continuities between these more innocuous actions and the horrifying ones which one finds puzzling or repulsive. Morton here emphasizes that empathetic understanding, as contrasted with 'pseudo-empathy' requires 'a grasp of how, rather than why, a person could do what they did' (p. 329); we need to represent 'the person's actual psychology rather than a convenient metaphorical description' (p. 329). In conclusion, he leaves us with a nice dilemma. On the one hand, we want empathy with evil-doers to be as easy as possible, exploiting the psychological continuities that Morton discusses. And on the other hand, we want to 'keep a distance between us and those we despise' (p. 330).

Conclusion

What the individual chapters in this volume reveal is just how important it is, in a wide range of fields of enquiry, to bring to bear an understanding of the role of empathy in its various guises. There remains much more work to be done, but we hope that this volume will make a helpful and lasting contribution to the continuing debate, in philosophy, in psychology, and elsewhere.

We would like to express our thanks to the individual contributors for their efforts, and to Peter Momtchiloff and his colleagues at Oxford University Press for their support throughout the production process. The idea for this volume first emerged at a conference on empathy at California State University-Fullerton on June 22–23, 2006, at which a number of the chapters in this volume were first presented, and we would like to thank California State University (including Thomas Klammer, the College of Humanities and Social Sciences, the Department of Philosophy, the Office of Academic Affairs, the Department of Psychology, the Honors Program, the Department of Radio, TV & Film, and the Women's Studies Program), the American Society for Aesthetics, the British Society of Aesthetics, and Shirley Coplan for their support in making that conference possible.

PART 1

Empathy and Mind

1

Understanding Empathy:

Its Features and Effects

Amy Coplan

The concept of empathy has received an enormous amount of attention in the past few decades, appearing in the popular press,[1] political campaigns,[2] and in the study of a wide range of topics, including autism spectrum disorders,[3] psychopathy,[4] political ideologies,[5] medical care,[6] ethics and moral development,[7] justice and the court,[8] gender differences,[9] engagement with art and the media,[10] therapeutic methods in

[1] See, e.g. articles in the *New York Times* (Blakeslee, 2006), *Time* (Nash, 2007), *Scientific American* (Giacomo, Fogassi, and Gallese (2006)), and *Scientific American Mind* (Dobbs (2006)).

[2] Since he began campaigning for President, Barack Obama has invoked the concept of empathy in dozens of speeches on multiple topics. While speaking to Planned Parenthood on July 17, 2007, he famously remarked that he would use empathy as a criterion for his selection of Supreme Court Justices: 'in the overwhelming number of Supreme Court decisions, that's enough. Good intellect. You read the statute. You look at the case law, and most of the time the law is pretty clear—95% of the time . . . But it's those 5% of the cases that really count. And in those 5% of the cases what you got to look at it is: What is in the justice's heart? What's their broader vision of what America should be? You know, Justice Roberts said he saw himself just as an umpire. But the issues that come before the court are not sport. They're life and death. And we need somebody who's got the heart to recogni– the empathy to recognize what it's like to be a young, teenaged mom; the empathy to understand what it's like to be poor or African-American or gay or disabled or old. And that's the criteria by which I'm going to be selecting my judges' (quotation reported by Livingston and Murray, 2009 on *msnbc.com*).

[3] Baron-Cohen (2003, 2009); Dapretto et al. (2005); Iacoboni & Dapretto (2006); Gallese (2006); Clark, Winkielman, & McIntosh (2008); Blair (2008a).

[4] Richell, Mitchell, et al. (2003); Blair, Mitchell, & Blair (2005); King, Blair et al. (2006); Decety & Moriguchi (2007); Blair (2006, 2008a); Shirtcliff et al. (2009).

[5] Lakoff (2002, 2004); Iacoboni (2008).

[6] Halpern (2001, 2007, 2009); Stepien & Baernstein (2006); Pedersen (2010).

[7] Hoffman (2000 and this collection); Eisenberg and Fabes, et al. (1994); Eisenberg, Fabes, & Spinrad (2006); Batson, Fultz, & Schoenrade (1987); Batson (1991); Batson, Lishner, et al. (2003); Slote (2007); Einolf (2008).

[8] Hoffman (1987, 2000, and this collection).

[9] Baron-Cohen (2003); Schulte-Rüther et al. (2008); Klein & Hodges (2001); Strauss (2004); Graham & Ickes (1997); Ickes, Gesn, & Graham (2000).

[10] Feagin (1996); Walton (1990, 1997, 1999); Smith (1995); Currie & Ravenscroft (2002); Currie (2004); Coplan (2004, 2006, 2009); Kaplan (2005 and this collection); Carroll (2008 and this collection).

clinical psychology,[11] mirror neurons,[12] and theory of mind.[13] Given its central role in so many discussions and debates, it's safe to conclude that whatever empathy is, it's important.

So what is it? Depending on whom you ask, empathy can be understood as one or more of several loosely related processes or mental states.[14] Some of the most popular include the following:

(A) Feeling what someone else feels
(B) Caring about someone else
(C) Being emotionally affected by someone else's emotions and experiences, though not necessarily experiencing the same emotions
(D) Imagining oneself in another's situation
(E) Imagining being another in that other's situation
(F) Making inferences about another's mental states
(G) Some combination of the processes described in (A)–(F)

The number of competing conceptualizations circulating the literature has created a serious problem with the study of empathy by making it difficult to keep track of which process or mental state the term is being used to refer to in any given discussion. Keeping track is important because the different conceptualizations refer to distinct psychological processes that vary, sometimes widely, in their function, phenomenology, mechanisms, and effects. Further confusing things is the fact that researchers approach the examination of empathy with differing, often incommensurable approaches, from a priori theorizing to the examination and analysis of patterns of neural activation through functional magnetic resonance imaging (fMRI).

Rather than dismissing the concept of empathy altogether, a number of researchers have responded to the conceptual confusion by beginning their discussions of empathy with an acknowledgment of the varied uses of the term and then stipulating a particular definition for their discussion. This seems like a reasonable temporary solution, particularly for those interested in the role a particular process plays in a given experience or debate rather than in characterizing and analyzing the concept of empathy.

An alternative, rather ecumenical solution has been to include the multitude of diverse processes that get labeled empathy under a single broad disjunctive concept.

---

[11] Kohut (1977, 1984); Rogers (1957, 1961); Kahn & Rachman (2000); Orange (1995); Geist (2009); Clark (2007); Gladstein & Brennan (1987); and Bohart & Greenberg (1997).

[12] Iacoboni (2008, 2009a); Keysers (2009); Gallese & Goldman (1998); Goldman (2006a and this collection); essays in Pineda (2009a).

[13] Goldman (1995a, 1995b, 1995c, 2006a); Goldman & Sripada (2005); Gordon (1986, 1995, 2009); Hurley (2008); Stueber (2006, 2008).

[14] For an overview of the history of the concept, see the introduction to this collection; Stueber (2006, 2008); Gladstein (1984); Gladstein & Brennan (1987); Wispé (1986, 1987, 1991); and Eisenberg & Strayer (1987). Useful surveys of research on empathy within particular disciplines and sub-disciplines can be found in Clark (2007), Verducci (2005), Sawicki (1997), Basch (1983), Bohart & Greenberg (1997), Throop (2008), Eisenberg (2000), and Coplan (2009).

Stephanie Preston and Frans de Waal claim that the empirical data on the various processes is consistent across studies on a variety of species and propose a 'unified story' across disciplines, situations, and species.[15] Though they acknowledge differences among some of the processes, they claim that the distinctions have been 'overemphasized to the point of distraction'[16] and insist that the different views of empathy can be cohered into a unified whole if a broad view of the Perception–Action Model is taken.[17] They therefore define empathy very broadly as 'any process where the attended perception of the object generates a state in the subject that is more applicable to the object's state or situation than to the subject's own prior state or situation.'[18]

Preston and de Waal's account and others like it take us in the wrong direction. Far from being 'emphasized to the point of distraction,' the differences among processes (A)-(E) enumerated above haven't been emphasized enough, particularly those that exist between some of the higher-level processes. We need more specificity, not more generality. New developments in cognitive neuroscience and philosophy of mind on mirror neurons, mirror systems, shared representations, simulation, and emotion are revealing more about the differences among the processes labeled empathy and why they are significant. We should strive to be as precise as possible.

With this in mind, my goal in this paper is to propose a narrow conceptualization of empathy informed by recent psychological and neuroscientific research. Although I am in favor of restricting the use of the term empathy to the high-level process I'll describe, my concern is less with terminology than with clarifying the essential features of the process. In other words, it is less important that we call this process empathy than that we stop conflating it with several related processes for it is the conflation that has led to so much ambiguity and confusion, making it difficult to analyze and evaluate empathy researchers' work and threatening to hamper both philosophical and empirical efforts to study the significance of all of these processes. Under my proposed conceptualization, empathy is a complex imaginative process in which an observer simulates another person's situated psychological states while maintaining clear self-other differentiation. To say that empathy is 'complex' is to say that it is simultaneously a cognitive and affective process. To say that empathy is 'imaginative' is to say that it involves the

---

[15] Preston & de Waal (2002).

[16] Ibid. 2.

[17] Ibid. 4–5.

[18] Ibid, 4. Preston and de Waal's definition is based on Martin Hoffman's (2000). In his 2009 book *The Age of Empathy*, which is briefly discussed in the introduction to this collection, de Waal elaborates on the work he did with Preston and continues to argue for a broad conceptualization of empathy. He proposes what he calls the 'Russian Doll Model' of empathy, according to which empathy comes in many different varieties, some primitive and others highly sophisticated. De Waal objects to restricting the term empathy to high-level processes because, in his view, doing so denies how much empathy is a part of who we are. I disagree. We can be more precise in our conceptualizations without dismissing or devaluing low-level mirroring processes or ignoring the critical role they play in our lives. Preston and de Waal are right to emphasize their importance. However, they have their own unique characteristics and effects on our lives. As I will go on to argue, including them under the rubric of empathy does not elevate them; it simply confuses things.

representation of a target's states that are activated by, but not directly accessible through, the observer's perception.[19] And to say that empathy is a 'simulation' is to say that the observer replicates or reconstructs the target's experiences, while maintaining a clear sense of self–other differentiation.

Although my proposed conceptualization departs in some important respects from other recent conceptualizations offered by philosophers and social scientists, I hope to show that, in spite of this, it is conceptually cleaner, captures several of the key intuitive characteristics of the ordinary use of the term and, most importantly, that it dovetails with recent psychological and neuroscientific research. I take the view that philosophical theories should be constrained by empirical research whenever possible, and that while we as philosophers should never accept the conclusions of empirical scientists uncritically, to ignore them is to render our work less relevant, less credible, and, ultimately, less meaningful.

In the sections below, I describe what I take to be the three essential features of empathy: affective matching, other-oriented perspective-taking, and self–other differentiation. All of these features are necessary for empathy, but none is sufficient on its own. An observer affectively matches a target only if the observer's affective states are the same in kind as the target's, though they may vary in degree. In other-oriented perspective-taking, an observer imagines a target's situation, experiences, and characteristics as though he were the target. And an observer maintains self–other differentiation only if he continuously represents himself as distinct from the target, thereby avoiding confusion about their respective situations, experiences, and characteristics. Together these features make up empathy, a unique kind of understanding through which we can experience what it is like to be another person.

1.1 Affective Matching

Affect is a broad category encompassing multiple mental states, all typically thought to involve feelings and some degree of physiological arousal. Emotion and mood are paradigm cases of affect. Affective states are not necessarily directed at specific objects nor do they necessarily involve cognitive evaluations or appraisals. Although most researchers agree that empathy has an affective component, just how to characterize that component is a matter of some controversy. Under my proposal, affective matching occurs only if an observer's affective states are qualitatively identical to a target's, though they may vary in degree. The observer must therefore experience the same type of emotion (or affect) as the target. This is a stricter condition than is

---

[19] I am using imagination here to refer to a process through which one recreates or enacts some mental state. Some philosophers refer to this as recreative imagination. Alvin Goldman uses the term 'enactment' imagination, which he distinguishes from what he calls 'suppositional' imagination (2006a). As Goldman explains, when one imagines feeling X, it is not enough for one to *suppose* that one feels X; one must try to enact the feeling of X (2006a: 47–9). In other words, one must do more than entertain the idea or possibility of feeling X. One must recreate an experience of X.

proposed by researchers who argue that affective congruence—that is, mere qualitative similarity or identical valence—is a sufficient condition for the affective component of empathy.[20] Others have proposed even more relaxed conditions for the affective component of empathy, including reactive affects—that is, affects that, while resulting from an observer's perception of a target, fail to match even the valence of the target's affects.[21] For example, if the target experiences fear, and the observer experiences pity as a result, these researchers might count it as a successful case of empathy. Another example sometimes given is so-called 'empathic anger,' which results when a subject observes a target being mistreated and becomes angry in response even though the target himself is not experiencing anger.

Congruent and reactive emotions do not qualify as empathetic in my account because they are not sufficiently accurate representations of a target's situated psychological states. To say that congruent and reactive emotions are not 'sufficiently accurate' is to say that they misrepresent the type of emotion experienced by the target. Although a certain amount of disagreement exists about the types of emotions that humans experience, there is nevertheless a growing consensus among scientists that at least some emotional types do exist cross-culturally, typically identified as 'basic' emotions. These usually include fear, anger, sadness, joy, and disgust. Whatever the list of emotional types turns out to be, countenancing emotional types at all entails that representations of those types can be either accurate or inaccurate, where the criterion for representational accuracy is type-identity. Under the assumption that empathy involves the representation of a target's emotions, type-identity as the criterion for representational accuracy provides a rationale for the exclusion of congruent and reactive emotions from the category of empathetic experiences, since congruent and reactive emotions are not type-identical.[22]

To summarize, in order to qualify as the type of affective matching essential to empathy, an observer must experience affective states that are qualitatively the same as those of the target. As I will explain, this matching must come about in a particular way, namely through other-oriented perspective-taking. This means it cannot merely be the result of coincidence or of two people reacting identically to the same stimulus.[23] It also cannot be caused by emotional contagion.

---

[20] Hoffman (2000); Preston & de Waal (2002).

[21] See, e.g. Davis (1996).

[22] It must be pointed out that, in some cases, reactive or congruent emotions may not be representing or misrepresenting a target's emotions. Being triggered by the target's emotions doesn't entail that they are representing or misrepresenting at all. Moreover, depending on what is meant by 'representation,' a case could be made that reactive emotions sometimes serve as accurate representations of a target's emotion. For example, if a target individual experiences sorrow, an observer's pity may represent (in the sense of stand for or symbolize) that sorrow. As is implied by my discussion, I am using the term 'represent' in this context in a stricter sense such that accurately representing a target's emotions requires replicating those emotions. My thanks to an anonymous reader from Oxford University Press for making this point to me.

[23] For discussion of various cases of shared affect, see Goldie (1999, 2000), Goldman (2006a), Carroll (2008), and Feagin (this collection).

Psychologists Elaine Hatfield, John Cacioppo, and Richard Rapson define emotional contagion as 'the tendency to automatically mimic and synchronize expressions, vocalizations, postures, and movements with those of another person, and, consequently, to converge emotionally.'[24] In other words, emotion is transmitted from one person to another; it is as though one individual 'catches' the emotion of another. Max Scheler describes this process as 'emotional infection,' and Lauren Wispé writes that 'emotional contagion involves an involuntary spread of feelings without any conscious awareness of where the feelings began in the first place.'[25] In most cases of emotional contagion, the transfer of emotion is 'relatively automatic, unintentional, uncontrollable, and largely inaccessible to conversant awareness.'[26]

Stephen Davies refines the standard notion of emotional contagion by emphasizing that the emotion experienced by someone as a result of emotional contagion does not take the emotion of the target individual as its object: 'emotional contagion involves the arousal in B by A of an affect that corresponds to an affect felt and displayed by A . . . and B's affect does not take A's state, expressive character, or any other thing as its emotional object.'[27] This is true even in cases of attentional contagion, which Davies distinguishes from non-attentional contagion. In both the attentional and non-attentional cases, the transmission of emotion occurs via unconscious processes and is involuntary, but in the non-attentional case, the subject's attention is not on the source of the emotion. In the attentional case, the subject's attention is focused on the source of his emotion; nevertheless, he is unaware that contagion is occurring.[28]

The main processes involved in contagion are motor mimicry and the activation and feedback it generates.[29] Initiated by direct sensory perception, these processes do not involve the imagination, nor are they based on any cognitive evaluation or complex appraisal. Thus emotional contagion is a bottom-up process that operates much like a form of perception. We encounter another person, automatically react to the other's expressions of emotion through involuntary imitation, and end up experiencing the same emotion ourselves.

Due to its structure, contagion is probably more likely to yield affective matching than most attempts at empathy,[30] which may explain why it is so often conflated with or mistaken for empathy. Broad conceptualizations of empathy usually label emotional contagion as a sub-type since it involves an observer experiencing the same affective states as a target and is caused by the observer's perception of the target. Whatever labels one chooses, and in spite of these similarities, the process of emotional contagion

---

[24] Hatfield, Cacioppo, & Rapson (1992: 153–4).
[25] Wispé (1987: 76–7).
[26] Hatfield, Cacioppo, & Rapson (1994: 5).
[27] See Davies's essay in this collection.
[28] Ibid.
[29] For an overview of the empirical work on emotional contagion, see Hatfield, Cacioppo, & Rapson (1994).
[30] See Goldman (2006a) and his essay in this collection on the reliability of low-level processes.

differs substantially from the process that generates affective matching through other-oriented perspective-taking. Emotional contagion may be related to this process and may sometimes precipitate it, but when we 'catch' the emotions of the other through emotional contagion, the emotions are not experienced imaginatively or in relation to another; we experience them as our own. This is a crucial point that is too often minimized or ignored. Even though it originates in another person outside of the self, the emotion resulting from emotional contagion is not vicarious and, as such, is not 'off line.' This means that emotional contagion will not in and of itself involve any inhibition of behavior. If I contract fear from another individual through emotional contagion, I will act on the basis of that fear, as long as nothing else causes me to monitor and modulate my experience.

1.2 Self-Oriented Perspective-Taking

One of the key differences between emotional contagion and empathy is that contagion is a direct, automatic, unmediated process. Empathy is never fully unmediated since it requires perspective-taking. Roughly, perspective-taking is an imaginative process through which one constructs another person's subjective experience by simulating the experience of being in the other's situation. Although many researchers discuss only a single form of perspective-taking, which can be more or less successful, there are at least two appreciably different forms. One is self-oriented and one is other-oriented. In self-oriented perspective-taking, a person represents herself in another person's situation. Thus if I engage in self-oriented perspective-taking with you, I imagine what it's like *for me* to be in *your* situation. Peter Goldie refers to this as 'in his shoes perspective shifting,' which he distinguishes from what I'm calling empathy and he calls 'empathetic perspective shifting.'

Many conceptualize empathy in terms of perspective-taking yet fail to distinguish between the self- and other-oriented varieties. We are told to treat others as *we* would like to be treated and that we are empathetic when we try to imagine how *we* would feel if in the other's situation. Although self-oriented perspective-taking can lead to quasi-empathic experiences, this happens only in cases where there is a great deal of overlap between self and other or where the situation is the type that would lead to a fairly universal response. For example, if Dick is being chased by a lion and Jane decides to imagine that she is being chased by a lion, Jane is likely to end up with the same or very similar experiences. However, as Peter Goldie has argued, many, if not most, situations are more complex than this, and one individual's response to a set of circumstances is rarely a reliable indicator of what another's will be.[31]

---

[31] Goldie argues that in most cases, in order to adopt another's perspective, one must bring a characterization of the target individual to bear on her imaginative process, a characterization encompassing facts about the target's character, emotions, moods, dispositional tendencies, and life experiences (1999, 2000, and this collection).

In other-oriented perspective-taking, a person represents the other's situation from the other person's point of view and thus attempts to simulate the target's individual's experiences as though she were the target individual. Thus I imagine that I am you in your situation, which is to say I attempt to simulate your experiences from your point of view. Making this distinction may strike some as splitting hairs, but other-oriented perspective-taking is a different type of process than self-oriented perspective-taking, and the difference is not purely conceptual.[32] Empirical studies have shown that other-oriented perspective-taking requires greater mental flexibility and emotional regulation and often has different effects than self-oriented perspective-taking.[33] In addition, recent developments in cognitive neuroscience indicate that the neural implementation of other-oriented perspective-taking differs from that of self-oriented perspective-taking.[34]

Our default mode of mentalizing (i.e. attempting to understand and predict others' mental states) is self-oriented perspective-taking.[35] Thus, in anticipating another's psychological states or behavior, we typically imagine *ourselves* in the other's circumstances. Our engagement with the other, in this case, focuses on the other's external situation, yet we are the ones in the situation.

I propose that we conceptualize empathy so as to exclude processes that involve self-oriented perspective-taking, unless it is combined with other-oriented perspective-taking.[36] There are a number of reasons for this, not least of which is that self-oriented perspective-taking is associated with a number of psychological phenomena that are precisely the kinds of phenomena that should be distinguished from genuine empathy, including errors in prediction, misattributions, and personal distress.[37]

Our natural tendency is to assume greater similarity between self and other than typically exists, especially when we attempt to imagine how the other is feeling or what she is thinking; we are naturally subject to egocentric bias. For example, people often reason and behave as though others have the same knowledge that they themselves

---

[32] In his essay in this collection, Peter Goldie highlights the differences between self- and other-oriented perspective-taking at the conceptual level, and ultimately concludes that empathy conceived of in terms of other-oriented perspective-taking is conceptually problematic. Although I do not share his conclusion regarding the impossibility of other-oriented perspective-taking, his discussion of the differences between these two modes of perspective-taking both here and elsewhere (2000) shows why and how we must distinguish between them.

[33] Batson, Sager, et al. (1997); Batson, Lishner, et al. (2003); Decety & Sommerville (2003); Decety (2006b).

[34] Ruby & Decety (2001, 2004); Jackson, Brunet, et al. (2006).

[35] Keysar, Linn, & Barr (2003); Royzman, Cassidy, & Baron (2003); Jackson, Meltzoff, & Decety (2006b); Goldman (2006a).

[36] I suspect that in some cases, we go back and forth between self- and other-oriented perspective-taking. The trick is not to get stuck for long in the self-oriented phase, lest we fall into focusing solely on ourselves and our own experiences.

[37] For a useful discussion of the empirical literature on egocentric bias and prediction error and a theoretical explanation in relation to re-enactive empathy and high level simulation (or mindreading), see Goldman (2006a).

have even when they know that a given other is very different.[38] The assumption of similarity leads people to conclude that others will feel the same way that they feel, think the same way that they think, and want the same things that they want. Psychologists refer to such conclusions as false consensus effects and explain that they commonly lead to prediction errors regarding others' mental states and behavior. Sara Hodges and Daniel Wegner argue that this occurs due to a failure to suppress one's self-perspective.[39] In anticipating and imagining what another's experience will be in a given situation, many of us are unable to move beyond own perspective and so rely on our own imagined experiences to formulate conclusions about the other. We have difficulty not allowing our own beliefs, values, and occurrent states to influence our simulation, which is why we regularly fail to understand others or to understand them in a fine-grained way.[40]

Consider the following simple example. Generally speaking, we can say that most people are either introverted or extroverted. Introverts thrive on solitude and find it rejuvenating. Extroverts, on the other hand, dislike being alone for more than a short period of time. For them, solitude generates boredom, loneliness, and sometimes anxiety.

Suppose that I'm an introvert and my sister Bettie is an extrovert. If Bettie tells me that she's been spending lots of time alone lately and I attempt to imagine what this has been like *for her* by imagining what it would be like *for me*, I'll imagine feeling relaxed and calm. But Bettie won't have been feeling these things. She will have been anxious, upset, and longing for company.

Suppose as we're talking, it becomes clear to me (perhaps through bottom-up processes such as emotional contagion, which I then reflect upon) that Bettie is unhappy and on edge. As I was imagining how I would feel in Bettie's situation, I felt great, so now I'm confused. Normally Bettie is around people all the time. She works as a clinical professor four days a week, practices as a physician's assistant one day a week, and lives with a husband, three kids, three Labradors, and a cat. My simulation, combined with my reflections upon on it, makes me unable to figure out why she isn't thrilled to have the down time. I start to get worried that maybe something is wrong and wonder why she won't tell me. All that is wrong is that she dislikes being alone. Since this is not something I dislike, my self-oriented perspective-taking leads me to first mispredict and then misunderstand her experience. Although this example is simplistic, increasing its complexity to make it more realistic will only further prove that differences between Bettie's and my respective personality characteristics and preferences have important effects on the ways we each respond to various situations.

Rationally and theoretically, most of us understand that most people are very different from us, and yet we make these mistakes all the time. We don't just fail to

---

[38] Keysar, Lin, & Barr (2003).
[39] Hodges & Wegner (1997).
[40] Dunning, Griffin, Milojkovic, & Ross (1990). See also, Goldman (2006a).

understand others' subjective experiences; we often assume that we do understand them, which leads to a new set of problems. I contend that self-oriented perspective-taking leads to a type of pseudo-empathy since people often mistakenly believe that it provides them with access to the other's point of view when it does not. Most of us have had the experience of disclosing something to a friend, having her respond, 'I know just how you're feeling,' and then realizing within moments that she does not. It's not that she hasn't been perspective-taking; she has. But the perspective has been *her own*; only the circumstances are *ours*. Thus our friend's perspective-taking has focused on her, not on us. While this can be useful for many reasons, it does not yield empathy. One of the benefits of drawing attention to the distinction between self-oriented and other-oriented perspective-taking is that perhaps some of us will begin to stop assuming that we 'get' the other's experience, when we do not. Regardless of whether or not one accepts the conceptualization of empathy I'm proposing, it is critical to appreciate the differences between these two types of perspective-taking.

Another important distinguishing feature of self-oriented perspective-taking is its relationship to personal distress. Personal distress—also sometimes referred to as emotional distress or contagious distress—occurs when one observes another person in distress and reacts by becoming distressed himself. In cases of empathetic distress, the observer's experience of negatively valenced affective arousal is vicarious; that is, it is represented *as a simulation*. Therefore, in spite of feeling distressed, the empathizer's focus stays on the other. In cases of personal distress, however, the observer's focus is on his own distress and how to alleviate it. Psychologists characterize this response as a type of over-arousal since the observer's distress becomes overwhelming and aversive.[41] Individuals who experience personal distress typically engage in self-directed behaviors designed to alleviate their own discomfort. For example, an individual experiencing personal distress will often try to escape from the situation that triggered his distress regardless of what this will mean for the target individual whose distress initially caused the observer's distress. In some contexts, a person experiencing personal distress will display pro-social behavior but generally only when there is no alternative method of eliminating his discomfort.[42]

Conceptually, it makes sense that self-oriented perspective-taking is more likely to lead to personal distress. Imagining what it would be like *for me* to be in the awful situation you're experiencing makes it harder for me to modulate my emotions. I lose track of the fact that the experiences are actually yours and not mine and end up feeling so upset that I become completely focused on my own pain and what I can do to alleviate it. My emotional responses to imagined scenarios involving me *as me* lead to greater emotional arousal in general. These effects are decreased in other-oriented

---

[41]   Eisenberg & Strayer (1987); Eisenberg (2000); Hoffman (2000); Batson, Fultz, & Schoenrade (1987).
[42]   Batson, Early, & Salvarini (1997); Batson, Duncan, et al. (1981); Batson (1991); Batson, Sager, et al. (1997); Batson, Fultz, & Schoenrade (1987); Decety & Lamm (2009).

perspective-taking, because I suppress my self-perspective, which makes it possible for me to accurately represent the distressing emotions *as the other's*.

To summarize, personal distress, false consensus effects, and general misunderstandings of the other are all associated with self-oriented perspective-taking. When we imagine ourselves in another person's situation, it frequently results in inaccurate predictions and failed simulations of the other's thoughts, feelings, and desires. It also makes us more likely to become emotionally over-aroused and, consequently, focused solely on our own experiences. To be clear, I do not wish to suggest that self-oriented perspective-taking is a bad thing or that it never improves our understanding of someone, neither of which is true. Experiencing the other as a version of ourselves in many situations is a good thing, and it's usually far better than experiencing the other in purely instrumental terms. Very often it's motivated by a concern for the other and a desire to understand his experiences, both of which tend to be good things. It may also be the path by which we learn to engage in other oriented perspective-taking. Nevertheless, it is a significantly different mode of intersubjective engagement than one centered on other-oriented perspective-taking. We must recognize this and alter both our descriptive and normative theories accordingly.

1.3 Other-Oriented Perspective-Taking

Other-oriented perspective-taking is, as the name suggests, oriented toward the other. It therefore avoids false consensus effects, personal distress, and prediction errors based on egocentric biases. We stay focused within our simulation on the other's experiences and characteristics rather than reverting to imagining based on our own experiences and characteristics. In other-oriented perspective-taking, when I successfully adopt the target's perspective, I imagine being the target undergoing the target's experiences rather than imagining being myself undergoing the target's experiences.

To stay focused on the other and move us beyond our own experiences, perspective-taking requires mental flexibility and relies on regulatory mechanisms to modulate our level of affective arousal and suppress our own perspective.[43] It also often requires at least some knowledge of the target, though how much depends on the context.[44] Fulfilling these conditions is not easy, particularly when the other is someone very different from ourselves, since the more unlike a target we are, the more difficult it is to reconstruct her subjective experiences. As a result, empathy is subject to biases based on one's familiarity and identification with a target individual; we are more likely to empathize with those we know well and whom we judge to be like ourselves in some important respect. Not surprisingly, we're also more likely to succeed in our attempts

---

[43] Decety & Sommerville (2003); Decety & Jackson (2004); Decety & Hodges (2006); Goldman (2006a); Lamm, Meltzoff, & Decety (2009); and Decety & Meltzoff (this collection).

[44] Goldie (1999, 2000, and this collection).

to adopt their perspectives.[45] In order to represent the situation and experiences of those we know less well and with whom we fail to identify, we must work harder, and even then, we will often be unable to simulate their situated psychological states.[46]

The effort and regulation involved in other-oriented perspective-taking suggests that empathy is a motivated and controlled process, which is neither automatic nor involuntary and demands that the observer attend to relevant differences between self and other.[47] This makes it a top-down process, that is, one that must be initiated by the agent and generated from within, though it is likely that bottom-up processes such as emotional contagion may interact with this process, providing influential feedback that alters it in important ways.[48]

The differences between perspective-taking oriented toward the self and that oriented toward the other have received too little attention in philosophical discussions of empathy and of intersubjective engagement more generally;[49] however, recent developments in cognitive neuroscience and philosophy of mind are drawing attention to the existence and significance of these differences.[50] Jean Decety and his collaborators have conducted several experiments using fMRI to examine the brain activity associated with various perspective-taking tasks and have found that the neurological underpinning of other-oriented perspective-taking differs from that of self-oriented perspective-taking.[51] In one such study, Decety and Jessica Sommerville found specific activation of the frontopolar cortex, which is chiefly involved with inhibitory and regulating processes, when subjects were asked to adopt the subjective perspective of another individual when contrasted with taking a self-perspective in the same tasks.[52] Related experiments revealed that when subjects were asked to adopt another person's

---

[45] Hoffman (2000); Eisenberg (2000); Batson, Duncan et al. (1981).

[46] Decety & Jackson (2004); Lamm, Meltzoff, & Decety (2008).

[47] Goldie (1999, 2000, and this collection); Goldman (2006a, and this collection); Batson, Lishner, et. al (2003); Decety & Lamm (2009); Decety & Metlzoff (this collection); Hodges & Wegner (1997).

[48] Questions remain about the exact relationship between bottom-up processes such as emotional contagion and mirroring and top-down processes such as other-oriented perspective-taking. There is evidence to suggest a correlation between empathy scores and mirror activity (Pfeifer, Iacoboni, et al., (2008); Gazzola et al., (2006)). Other evidence, however, suggests that those highly susceptible to emotional contagion are less capable of empathy. It seems likely that bottom-up processes may help to activate an empathy response and may provide important experiential information about a target's affective state, generating a feedback loop, but at this point it is not entirely clear how these processes interact. In addition, recent research on mirroring and the mirror system has led some to conclude that mirror neurons are more complex and more widely distributed than was initially believed and that some mirror responses involve high-level processes (Iacoboni 2008, and this collection). Needless to say, the story regarding mirroring is far from complete.

[49] Discussions of intersubjectivity within Continental philosophy are typically more careful about the differences between self and others, but the concept of empathy does not figure as prominently in such discussions.

[50] Decety (2007); Decety & Chaminade (2003); Decety & Grèzes (2006); Decety & Hodges (2006); Decety & Jackson (2006); Decety & Sommerville (2003); Iacoboni (2008); Goldie (1999, 2000, and this collection); Goldman (2006a, and this collection); Hoffman (2000).

[51] Decety & Hodges (2006); Decety & Grèzes (2006); Decety & Jackson (2006); Ruby & Decety (2001, 2004).

[52] Decety & Sommerville (2003).

perspective to evaluate the other's beliefs or imagine the other's feelings as compared to their own perspective, the right inferior parietal cortex was involved.[53]

It is believed that the inhibitory and regulatory mechanisms that subserve other-oriented perspective-taking enable us to suppress our self-perspective and thus quarantine our own preferences, values, and beliefs.[54] They are also associated with the modulation of affective arousal, which provides an explanation for why other-oriented perspective-taking is much less likely to cause aversive arousal and personal distress than self-oriented perspective-taking.[55]

As scientists continue to investigate the neurophysiological substrates of various modes of intersubjective engagement and the neural implementation of shared representations, imitation, and mirroring behaviors, we will be able to increase further our understanding of how empathy and related processes work at the sub-personal level, which will improve our concepts and theorizing about these processes at the personal level. Although we have much to learn, the empirical evidence already makes it clear that the differences between various forms of perspective-taking are measurable and important.

1.4 Self–Other Differentiation

So far I have discussed affective matching and other-oriented perspective-taking—two of the three primary features of empathy under my proposed conceptualization. Affective matching and other-oriented perspective-taking are not sufficient for empathy. It also requires clear self–other differentiation, which is usually present in other-oriented perspective-taking but not always. Clear self–other differentiation is essential for empathy.

It is possible to experience affective matching and succeed in other-oriented perspective-taking and still not be empathizing. This happens when there is insufficient self–other differentiation due to a breakdown of the boundaries between the self and others. One can successfully represent a target's situation and experiences and have the same affects as the target while failing to preserve a separate sense of self. Unlike in the case of self-oriented perspective-taking, where one projects one's own thoughts, feelings, and desires onto the other, in this case the observer introjects the other's desires, feelings, and thoughts, substituting them for his own. The observer recognizes that the other is a different person and successfully adopts the other's perspective but ends up experiencing the other's perspective as his own. These sorts of cases are rarely discussed outside of clinical psychology but are not uncommon and point to the importance of self–other differentiation, not only to prevent ourselves from losing

---

[53] Ruby & Decety (2001, 2004); Jackson, Meltzoff, & Decety (2005, 2006); Lamm, Batson, et al. (2007); Decety & Meltzoff (this collection).

[54] Decety & Hodges (2006); Decety & Jackson (2006); Goldman (2006a, and this collection).

[55] Batson (1991); Batson, Fultz, & Schoenrade (1987); Batson, Lishner, et al. (2003).

sight of the other as an other, but also to prevent us from losing our awareness of our own selves as separate agents.

When we lack this awareness, we lack clear self–other differentiation, which in this case results in a kind of fusion or enmeshment. As Michael Stocker and Elizabeth Hegeman explain, when individuals are enmeshed, 'boundaries between them are too porous or nonexistent, each is too caught up in the life of the other, too involved and overly concerned with that person.'[56]

In cases of psychological engagement with clear self–other differentiation, one keeps separate one's awareness of oneself and one's own experiences from one's representations of the other and the other's experiences—in both directions. One thus remains aware of the fact that the other is a separate person and that the other has his own unique thoughts, feelings, desires, and characteristics. This enables deep engagement with the other while preventing one from losing sight of where the self ends and the other begins *and* where the other ends and the self begins. Without clear self–other differentiation, we are almost certain to fail in our attempts to empathize. We either lose our sense of self and become enmeshed or, more often, we let our imaginative process become contaminated by our self-perspective and thus end up engaged in a simulation that fails to replicate the experience of the other. Self–other differentiation allows for the optimal level of distance from the other for successful empathy. We are neither fused nor detached. We relate to the other as an other but share in the other's experience in a way that bridges but does not eliminate the gap between our experiences.[57]

Martin Hoffman argues that all mature empathizers possess clear self–other differentiation, which means that they have, 'a cognitive sense of themselves as separate physical entities with independent internal states, personal identities, and lives beyond the situation and can distinguish what happens to others from what happens to themselves.'[58] Hoffman makes self–other differentiation a defining element of the highest stage of empathic arousal in his broad model of empathy. Although he conceptualizes empathy more broadly than I do, he argues that self–other differentiation makes a critical difference to the quality of engagement and that the highest and most sophisticated level of empathy differs from the others in its effects because it involves clear self–other differentiation.

---

[56] Stocker & Hegeman (1996: 116).

[57] Peter Goldie (2000, 2002a) argues that it is possible to engage the other as an other, attending to her status as a subject from a third-person perspective without doing so impersonally, which provides an alternative to empathy based on other-oriented perspective-taking, or what he labels 'perspective-shifting.' In his essay in this collection, Goldie argues that empathy understood as perspective shifting 'is conceptually unable to operate with the appropriately *full-blooded notion of first-personal agency* that is involved in deliberation.' While I acknowledge that empathy is difficult in many cases, I consider the obstacles to it to be contingent and believe that there is something valuable in attempting to empathize in this way, even if the attempt falls short.

[58] Hoffman (2000: 63).

I maintain that clear self–other differentiation is crucial for successful empathy and that understanding its role in empathy is the key to understanding how empathy differs from related psychological processes that should be distinguished from it. Sharing another's affect in the absence of self–other differentiation provides minimal connection to or understanding of the other or his experience. Taking up one's perspective without clear self–other differentiation can result in enmeshment or in self-oriented perspective-taking, which prevents one from successfully representing the other's experience and leads to personal distress, false consensus effects, and prediction errors.

For those wishing to maintain a broad conceptualization of empathy, clear self–other differentiation provides a way to distinguish among the various processes that get labeled empathy. Emphasizing its role may be the first step toward a systematic taxonomy that can be used to organize and operationalize different accounts of empathy that use different labels to refer to the processes enumerated in the opening section of this essay.

1.5 Empathy as Experiential Understanding

Now that I have explained my conceptualization of empathy and what I take to be its three necessary features, I would like to move on to briefly consider its importance as a form of experiential understanding. Only empathy that combines affective matching, other-oriented perspective-taking, and self–other differentiation provides experiential understanding. It is for this reason that I propose restricting the term empathy to the process I've described in my essay.

What does it mean to say that empathy is a form of experiential understanding? To say that it is a 'form of understanding' is to say that it provides an observer with knowledge of another person's thoughts, feelings, and behavior—knowledge that may (though need not) subsequently figure into the explanations, predictions, and even the actions of the observer. To say that empathy is 'experiential' is to say (1) that it is itself an experience for the observer; (2) that it is a representation of, among other things, the experience of a target; and (3) that it involves representations that are not representations of causes and effects. This last sense in which empathy is 'experiential' differentiates it from most scientific explanations. Whether a scientific explanation is mechanistic, functional, dynamical, teleological, or genetic, it is very often, implicitly or explicitly, a representation of causes and effects. Empathy, in contrast, is a representation of experiences. While those experiences may very well be causes or effects, they are not, in the empathetic process, represented as such.[59]

[59] Alvin Goldman's book *Simulating Minds* (2006a) argues that re-enactive empathy plays a fundamental role in how we understand others' mental states. Karsten Stueber's book *Rediscovering Empathy* (2006) explores how the concept of empathy as an epistemological tool has been viewed in a series of historical debates (most notably those within the philosophy of social science and hermeneutics) and argues that if we are to understand other minds, we cannot do without it. Moreover Goldman and Stueber are only two among many thinkers who have participated in several longstanding debates within philosophy and psychology about the extent to

Another way of approaching the same idea is to point out that, while all scientific theories involve representations from a third-person point of view, empathy involves representations from a first-person point of view. Through empathy, we represent the other's experience by replicating that experience. Rather than attempt to apprehend the other's experience from an objective perspective, we attempt to share the other's perspective. It is tempting to conclude from this that, while the scientific study of empathy is no less third-person than the study of any other scientific topic, empathy itself has no place within the methods of science, even broadly construed. I would like recommend that we resist this conclusion, and regard empathy as one source of data among many. Admittedly, it may not be a very reliable source. But it may provide what no third-person form of scientific understanding can: understanding of another person from the 'inside.' As Gilbert Ryle explained, the longstanding view in Western thought has been that, 'the mind is its own place and in his inner life each of us lives the life of a ghostly Robinson Crusoe.'[60] I submit that, by providing us with an experiential understanding of other people, however imperfect, empathy promises to rescue us from the island of such a ghostly existence.[61]

---

which empathy is or provides understanding. Some of these are discussed in the introduction to this collection. Although these debates about different modes of understanding are relevant to my point here, they are beyond the scope of this paper.

[60]   Ryle (1949).

[61]   Earlier versions of this paper were presented at the College of the Holy Cross at the conference 'Understanding Other Minds and Moral Agency,' Cal State Fullerton at 'Empathy: An International Interdisciplinary Conference,' and in my Spring 2008 seminar on film and emotion. I would like to thank the audience members and conference participants who attended these presentations and my seminar students for very helpful comments and discussion. I am also grateful for feedback I received from Heather Battaly, Bryon Cunningham, Jean Decety, Tobyn De Marco, Marco Iacoboni, Brian Leslie, Rudolf Makkreel, Bertram Malle, Maura Priest, Jonevin Sabado, Michael Stolzle, Karsten Stueber, two anonymous readers from Oxford University Press, and especially Peter Goldie and Ryan Nichols.

2

Empathy as a Route to Knowledge[1]

Derek Matravers

In this paper I will discuss the extent to which empathy can give us knowledge. As is well known there is no consensus on the definition of 'empathy' in the literature. Some philosophers take a very broad view; for example, Karsten Steuber writes: 'Mechanisms of basic empathy have to be understood as mechanisms that underlie our theoretically unmediated quasi-perceptual ability to recognize other creatures directly as minded creatures, and to recognize them implicitly as creatures that are fundamentally like us' (Stueber (2006): 20). This links the discussion of empathy with debates about basic interpersonal understanding; centrally, the debate between simulation and theory-theory. However, that is clearly some distance from the traditional understanding of the term, introduced rather opaquely by Theodor Lipps as 'satisfaction in an object, which yet, just so far as it is an object of satisfaction, is not an object but myself; or it is satisfaction in a self which yet, just so far as it is aesthetically enjoyed, is not myself but something objective' (Lipps (1903b): 253). My focus will be on a different, and more specific phenomenon much closer to that described by Peter Goldie:

Empathy is a process or procedure by which a person centrally imagines the narrative (the thoughts, feelings, and emotions) of another person. There are three necessary conditions for empathy... First, it is necessary for empathy that I be aware of the other as a centre of consciousness distinct from myself. Secondly, it is necessary for empathy that the other should be someone of whom I have a *substantial characterization*. Thirdly, it is necessary that I have a grasp of the narrative which I can imaginatively enact, with the other as narrator. (Goldie (2000): 195)

Indeed, the phenomenon I would like to discuss is even narrower than that discussed by Goldie; I am specifically interested in an imaginative endeavour that results in us having the same type of feeling or emotion as the other person—this is what I shall mean by 'empathy' in this paper. Hence, I draw a distinction between empathy and the

[1] Thanks are due to Amy Coplan and Peter Goldie for the invitation to present a paper at the Empathy conference in Fullerton in June 2006, which was the occasion for which it was written, and for their subsequent editorial suggestions. I would also like to thank Peter Goldie and Robert Hopkins for stimulation from both their published and unpublished work, and to Jane Heal and Amy Coplan for helpful criticisms and conversation.

broader phenomenon of our ability to recognize other creatures as minded creatures (and to grasp the content of their minds). There are also distinctions on the other side, as it were, and in a helpful discussion Goldie distinguishes between empathy, emotional contagion, imagining oneself in someone else's shoes, and sympathy.

In short, we imagine the experiences of another person from the point of view of that person and our feeling the emotions that they are feeling are either part of, or a result of, this act of imagination. I will fill out this conception by looking briefly at a familiar case from the literature due to Ian Ravenscroft:

Many years ago I witnessed a rock climber struggling on an overhang, his strength rapidly ebbing. He was quite unable to reverse the difficult climbing he had already performed, and the good hand holds above the overhand were just beyond his reach. The rope was positioned in such a way that it offered him no protection, and it was obvious that a fall would be fatal. As exhaustion overcame him, he desperately sought a way out of his predicament, inspecting every crook and cranny of the rock in an unsuccessful attempt to relieve the terrible strain on his arms and fingers. Looking on, I vividly experienced what it was like to be him, and not only because, as a climber, I had been in similar situations myself: any non-climber looking on could also experience what it was like to be that poor soul. (Ravenscroft (1998): 171)

How central a case of empathy this is depends on the extent of the identification. Issues that would make it not central are that the focus of the empathy is not some particular person of whom Ravenscroft has a 'substantial characterization'; the climber is simply some person in a particular bad situation. Thus no issues about what that person in particular would feel in that situation feed into the empathetic experience. Second, there is only marginally a narrative that could be imaginatively enacted. The climber's situation is relatively un-nuanced and unchanging. Indeed, there are other ways of describing Ravenscroft's reaction which would not count as empathy. First, it might be that what Ravenscroft is feeling is horror at the perilous situation of a fellow being. It may be that the climber is also feeling horror at their situation, but having the same type of feeling is not sufficient for empathy. Second, the situation might be analogous to watching someone cut themselves; one winces and clutches one's own finger. Such a case differs from empathy in two ways. First, the experience you are having is not qualitatively similar to the experience they are having: they are feeling pain and you are not.[2] Exactly how imagined states and actual states are related in cases such as these will be considered below. Second, like Ravenscroft's case, it lacks the complexity that characterizes empathy: there is no need for a characterization, and only marginally a narrative. The third description of Ravenscroft's situation that is not empathy would be as an instance of an 'anxiety defence': the situation might be so overwhelmingly awful that Ravenscroft's psyche generates its own feelings of horror to block having to

---

[2] This bald claim is disputed in the literature: see Jackson, Rainville, & Decety (2006); Jackson, Brunet, Meltzoff, & Decety (2006); and Decety & Jackson (2006). The nature of the dispute (if dispute there is) is not clear to me, as I cannot *learn* I am in pain by reading an article. I am grateful to Amy Coplan for pointing this literature out to me.

think about it. An additional reason to be sceptical is that it is often remarked by people who have been in perilous situations that, at the time, they were possessed of a massive calm; they are totally focussed on what they need to do to get out alive. If we assume that is the case, then the observer might generate the wrong feeling altogether, as they lack just that property (being in extreme danger) which is the cause of the climber's unexpected mental state. Rather, Ravenscroft's situation would be a case of sympathy. I shall discuss the limits of the imagination as the method by which the observer replicates the circumstances of the object of their observation below.

Here is a case that is closer to the phenomenon I would like to explore. This is an excerpt from a letter by Charlotte Bronte, in which she is describing receiving a proposal of marriage from her Father's curate, a Mr Nicholls.

As usual—Mr N sat with Papa till between eight and nine o'clock. I then heard him open the parlour door as if going. I expected the clash of the front door—He stopped in the passage: he tapped: like lightning it flashed on me what was coming. He entered—he stood before me. What his words were—you can guess his manner—you can hardly realize—nor can I forget it— Shaking from head to foot, looking deadly pale, speaking low, vehemently yet with difficulty— he made me for the first time feel what it costs a man to declare affection where he doubts response. The spectacle of one ordinarily so statue-like—thus trembling, stirred, and overcome gave me a kind of strange shock. He spoke of suffering he had borne for months—of sufferings he could endure no longer—and craved leave for some hope. (Barker 2006: 377)

It is interesting that Bronte claims that she becomes familiar with an emotion she could not know from the first person perspective: 'what it cost a man to declare affection where she doubts response'. This can only be because she somehow has access to what Mr Nicholls is feeling. It is also the case that the reader is able to empathize with Mr Nicholls. That is, as we read this, we can pause and wonder what it must have been like for Mr Nicholls in that situation. We have a reasonable characterization of Mr Nicholls from other of Bronte's letters, and there is a strong narrative here. In centrally imagining the narrative from Mr Nicholls' perspective we may be able to empathize with him. What I want to examine in this paper is what we might learn from this. This falls under two headings. First, there is the issue of whether empathy could be a route to knowledge of something about Mr Nicholls in that situation, and, if so, whether empathy is the only way of gaining that knowledge. Second, there is the issue about whether through such a case we might learn something about feelings or emotions themselves.

It will help in discussing this if we have some model of the mechanism underlying empathy. One possibility is that the relevant cognitive states of Mr Nicholls are replicated 'off-line' in the mind of the reader, and they are fed into the relevant feeling-generating part of the mind (I shall refer to these as 'the inputs' into the system). If our mental structures are broadly similar to those of Mr Nicholls, and if Mr Nicholls' feelings are being generated by his real cognitive states, then the 'off line' cognitive states could generate some simulacra of Mr Nicholls' feelings—enough like Mr

Nicholls' feelings to give us knowledge of what they are like (Nichols, Stich, et al. (1996)). This might not be the only option. Another is that, in centrally imagining Mr Nicholls' situation, we imagine the mental state he is in: not only his cognitive states, but his affective states as well.

If all this second option claims is that we can imagine *that* Mr Nicholls is pouring out his heart to his beloved, and imagine *that* he is feeling anxious, then it clearly is an alternative although it falls short of empathy. If the second option is that we can imagine being in the affective state that Mr Nicholls is in without our actually being in that state, it is less clear-cut that this is a distinct option. This depends upon whether an emotion-like mental state generated off-line is an emotion as opposed to some counterpart analogous state. Some mental states have imaginative counterparts: beliefs correspond to 'make-beliefs' (imagining that something is that case), desires correspond to 'make-desires' (imagining one desires something to be the case).[3] Would the emotion-like mental state generated by off-line cognitive states really be an emotion or some imaginative analogue of an emotion? Greg Currie and Ian Ravenscroft argue that the states generated in imagined scenarios are genuine emotions; as they put it, 'imagination is transparent to emotion' (Currie & Ravenscroft (2002): 189–91). Peter Goldie has argued that this overstates the case: that it is possible to imagine being fearful, without actually being fearful. He quotes from Richard Wollheim: 'I shall use the familiar phenomenon of the erotic daydream... Let us suppose that I centrally imagine myself [that is, I imagine myself from the inside] engaged in some sexual activity with a strange figure, or a close friend. As I do so, I centrally imagine myself becoming excited, so I become excited' (Wollheim (1984): 81–2; quoted in Goldie (2005): 131). Wollheim seems to be describing a possible scenario, in which case it is possible to imagine being excited without actually being excited. If Goldie and Wollheim are right, then we will not be able to learn about others' affective states from such scenarios. This is because we will need a prior grasp of such states in order to be able to imagine them. Indeed, holding to our definition, this will not be a case of empathy as our experience is not 'qualitatively similar' to their experience. Whether or not Goldie and Wollheim are right, neither denies that that we can (and usually do) experience emotions as part of imagined states. We need not be purist about this: our two options may well both run together and borrow from each other.

2.1 Will Empathy Give Us the Right Contents?

There are two questions about the inputs: first, can the reader generate inputs with the right content, and second, what difference does it make that the reader imagines having them, while Mr Nicholls actually has them? There are also two questions about the

---

[3] For arguments in favour of 'make-desires' see Currie (2006). For arguments against see Meskin & Weinberg (2006).

feeling-generating part of the mind: is that of the reader sufficiently similar to that of Mr Nicholls, and, more broadly, is the mind able to generate feelings of which it has had no prior acquaintance?

Whether the reader can generate inputs with the right content depends on the accuracy and extent of his or her grasp of the characterization of Mr Nicholls, and the narrative in which he figures. There is an ideal here: that one has off-line versions of all Mr Nicholl's relevant propositional attitudes, all weighted correctly. The extent to which one falls short of this ideal is the extent to which one falls short of empathizing with Mr Nicholls, and instead empathizes with someone like Mr Nicholls in something like Mr Nicholls' situation. I would not want to argue for the impossibility of empathy with a particular person through setting an impossibly high benchmark. There are salient beliefs of Mr Nicholls (that I need to propose to this person; that, in doing so, I risk never seeing her again; that, whatever happens, my life is going to change completely) that are both fairly obvious and also doing most of the work. These, combined with our characterization of Mr Nicholls is enough, I suggest, to take us through this stage of empathizing with Mr Nicholls.

However, getting the content right (or nearly right) is only half the story. There is also the issue that the same contents might generate different non-cognitive mental states. One problem is the reliability of the assumption that, given similar inputs, the reader's and Mr Nicholl's minds will generate similar outputs. The grounds that the assumption is reliable in simulating contentful states do not carry across to affective states (which is why Jane Heal restricts simulation to the former states (Heal (1996/2003a): 77–8)). We are good at thinking counterfactually about different possible states of affairs, but not so good at taking on other value systems, or in making ourselves sensitive to those things which would trigger our affective states. This problem is masked if we consider only examples in which the links are obvious: being in danger and feeling fear, suffering a loss and feeling sad. However, even in such cases the assumption of reliability is insecure; one's affective attitudes to the world are greatly influenced by, amongst many other things, the idiosyncrasies of upbringing. Mr Nicholls might be more shy than the reader, more averse to confrontation, more afraid of loss. The situation in which he finds himself might trigger intrusive and disturbing thoughts from childhood, buried and yet still affecting memories and so on.

The friend of empathy might argue that this possibility is compatible with empathy being a reliable route to knowledge. Provided that empathy is generally reliable, and that on this occasion the reader has in fact simulated Mr Nicholls mental states and, on the grounds of this, formed beliefs about what Mr. Nicholls felt, then the reader knows what Mr. Nicholls felt. Knowledge requires only that the reader knows Mr. Nicholls' states, not that he knows that he knows them. Even if we agree in general with externalist accounts of knowledge there is a problem in this case. The doubts concerning the extent to which people react in similar ways may well be significant enough to throw into doubt the claim that empathy is generally reliable. If this is so, then the empathizer needs some way of working out whether it is reliable in the particular case. The problem is that it is only in fairly exceptional circumstances that our grasp of the 'substantial characterization' is so good that we can know that this is how the other will react in the circumstance. On other occasions (such as that of the reader and Mr. Nicholls) there will be no way of grasping, within the situation, the hidden particularities of the other's dispositions to react. On these occasions the empathizer will not know whether he or she has grasped the others' mental states.

There is a second issue: namely, the differences between something actually happening and something being a simulation. There are three different relations between a person feeling an emotion and the situation: that of the agent in the situation, that of a person face to face with the agent in the situation, and that of a person accessing the agent's situation indirectly (by verbal description, picture, or film). The people in the latter two relations have to centrally imagine what it is like to be in the first relation. The friend of empathy might claim that all we need to do is to be accurate in the content of our off-line representations, and they will generate what the agent's representations will generate. However, accuracy in the content of the off-line representations and accuracy in the characterization of the agent are still not sufficient for the accuracy of the identification with the agent in that situation. There may be causally relevant properties of the first relation of which no trace can be found in the other two relations (or there may be a trace in the second relation but not the third, or in some types of indirect representations and not others, or between different indirect representations within a type). There is no reason to think the empathizer will know whether the relation in which he or she stands to the situation differs from that in which the agent stands to the situation in lacking one or more of these non-representational yet causally efficacious properties. As we saw with the climber, the witness need not be aware that there are properties of the relation of being faced with the prospect of death that do not show up in the relation of witnessing being faced with the prospect of death.

There seem, then, to be at least these two difficulties in empathy as a route to knowledge: that there may be properties of the agent's make-up, or properties that are part of the face to face relation, to which the empathizer has no access. In addition, there are further issues that stand in the way of gaining knowledge of Mr Nicholl's situation through empathy. Recall that, on the mechanism that we are considering, empathy could provide knowledge of what emotions that are caused by cognitive states are like. As our beliefs cause our emotions, it is possible that running the system off-line will enable off-line beliefs to cause emotions. Putting aside my two sceptical doubts, if the patterns of causation are preserved when we move from online to off-line, this would suggest that whatever emotions can be generated by a belief, could also be generated by an off-line belief.

2.2 Can Empathy Give Us Knowledge of Feelings We Have Not Previously Experienced?

To help locate our problem against the broad geography of the area, let us consider for comparison the case of Mary, Frank Jackson's scientist who knows all the physical information there is to obtain about what goes on when we see colours, but who has only ever experienced the world as black, white, and shades of grey (the 'knowledge argument'). Jackson's claim was that Mary would lack something: namely, knowledge of what red was like (Jackson (1982/1990)). Mary could centrally imagine the experience of someone looking at a fire engine (the characterization and the narrative would not be relevant) but, if we were originally impressed that there is an epistemological gap between what Mary knows and her knowing what red is like, we will not think this is the way to bridge it. There are analogies in cases in which the feeling requires a cause that cannot be simulated, or in which, not having had the feeling before, the simulator is not able to judge whether what they are experiencing is a genuine instance of such. Instances of the former would include what one would feel like after having drunk a pint of whisky, instances of the latter might include (if the romantics are to be believed) being in love (Heal (1996/2003a): 75). It is difficult to see any role for empathy in gaining knowledge in the former case; I shall say more about the latter below.

David Lewis has argued (in a defence of physicalism against the knowledge argument) that what Mary would acquire when she first saw a red object would not be knowledge of what red is like, but a set of abilities: the ability to remember and imagine instances of the experience, and recognize the experience for what it is when it comes again (Lewis (1988): 515). The example Lewis gave is the taste of Vegemite (which is not graspable through simulation—what would be the input?). The suggestion being made is that rather than experience giving us the other three abilities, one of the other abilities (imagination) can give us experience and thus also the abilities to remember and recognize the feeling when it occurred again. The package is the same; it is simply that the 'teacher' is changed. It may seem intuitively implausible that we could cause an experience we have not had previously using off-line beliefs. We can mitigate this worry by reflecting on the nature of emotional experience. Its structure is more complicated than raw phenomenological experience, and elements of one type of emotion can enter into another. Elementarily, there are emotions which have a painful hedonic tone, and emotions which have a pleasant hedonic tone. Hence, for an emotionally mature person there are no altogether novel feelings: what novelty there is is either that one has an emotion and it has a particular, or unexpected, phenomenology, or the distinctiveness is given by the distinctiveness of the object and, through that, to the phenomenology. Even if one is surprised by Charlotte Bronte's description of Mr Nicholls, one has probably in the course of life experienced feelings of love, dread, and impending doom. Hence, one will have some grasp of what Mr Nicholls' was going through, even if one has not experienced that feeling, with that type of object, in its full particularity.

It is an interesting issue as to whether an off-line cognitive state has sufficient causal power to generate emotions. There will be a number of differences between an off-line cognitive state and a belief, which will affect their causal efficacy. First, there is the issue of what it takes to make a belief (whether on- or off-line) sufficient to cause an emotion. To do so such a state needs to be in some way salient to us. I suspect there are a range of cases here. A thought might take us by surprise; it might just enter our consciousness and produce an unexpected reaction. This might be because of its content, although it might not be because of obvious features of its content; the smallest and most unexpected thing is sometimes very affecting. Otherwise, it might be because of our current attitude; we might be feeling emotionally vulnerable, or under the influence of drugs or alcohol. The usual case, however, will be where we need to use our imaginations to give the off-line content some Humean vivacity. We need to do more than entertain thoughts; we need to vividly imagine them. Second, there are some states of affairs which, if they obtain, are pressing on us. They require our attention, and perhaps our action. If I have a problem there will be actual links between my beliefs that I have a problem and others of my beliefs, patterns of thought, motivations, and actions. It is not clear to me how this stands to imagining I have a problem. Two differences suggest themselves. First, I can imagine I have the problem without that act of imagination securing all those links. Indeed, this may be part of the difference between imagining being in danger and believing one is in danger. The combination of mental states in the latter case has different effects: in particular, the link with motivation clears the mind of fear to replace it with the mental clarity necessary for accurate planning. The second takes us back to vivacity. It might be that some actual problems have a vivacity that is out of reach of imaginative effort. The third issue that affects causal sufficiency will be the possibility of non-cognitive elements of a situation that, along with beliefs, are necessary to affect the emotions. For example, there might be a direct causal connection between the sight, sound, or even smell of Charlotte Bronte that are affecting Mr. Nicholls that are not capturable in an off-line cognitive state.

Putting aside the two sceptical doubts I argued for above, I am exploring the idea that if the patterns of causation are preserved when we move from online to off-line, whatever emotions can be generated by a belief could also be generated by an off-line belief. One way into this is to look at how we might use off-line beliefs not to find something out about a particular person (in our case, Mr. Nicholls) but rather simply to find out what certain experiences are like. One might think that this has little to do with empathy; if the point is to generate an emotion in ourselves, there seems little point in centrally imagining the state of affairs as it appears to someone else. One might as well imagine the state of affairs from one's own point of view. There is some truth in this, but it does not seem to me the straightforward matter this argument would suggest. The above considerations suggest that sometimes, somebody who is unable to imagine what something is like from their own perspective will be able to imagine what it is like from another's perspective. I shall take the three considerations I mentioned in turn.

The first was that, in order to cause emotions, off-line beliefs would need to be salient. These are not necessary connections, but—given the link between salience and immediacy—it is plausible that empathy might be a more efficient generator of emotions than first-personal imagining. Witnessing someone's life falling apart, or being told (by that person) the circumstances of their life falling apart, might have a vivacity that simply imagining that one's own life is falling apart (when one believes it is not) lacks. This is not necessarily empathetic: witnessing their being in trouble might only provoke sympathy. However, it might provoke empathy, and, if it does, the painful immediacy of the encounter might provoke an experience of that kind of traumatic feelings that is more powerful than could be obtained by imagining from, so to speak, a standing start. There is also information in the case of empathy that is lacking in the first-person case. How does one judge whether or not one's attempt at empathy has been successful? Presumably, not being surprised by, or being able to predict, fine shades of behaviour of the agent is good evidence that one has managed to identify with them. However, as this is an unfolding narrative, the behaviour of the agent will not only be a check on the extent to which the attempt as empathy has been a success, but will also aid the process of empathy. For example, one can see how the person takes bad news: they put their head in their hands, they contract into themselves. This could influence the empathizer in two ways. First, they might adopt the bodily attitudes of the object of their empathy (whether deliberately or not) to facilitate identification with them. Second, knowing the effect that the beliefs are having on the agent gives the empathizer some kind of script. This raises the question as to whether the mechanisms being run off-line are affected by beliefs about how the causation is working in the mind of the agent. To the extent that they can be affected, this information will be relevant. It is less clear that the second and third (namely, that beliefs resonate in our economy of mental states forming links in a way that off-line beliefs need not and the presence of non-simulatable triggers of affect) are reachable from the perspective of the observer. To the extent that they are not, we have an explanation of why, although the imagining from the first person is often not as epistemologically effective as empathizing, empathizing is not epistemologically as effective as being the agent in the situation oneself.

The claims made above on behalf of empathy rely on a situation in which an emotion is generated by centrally imagining a state of affairs from the perspective of another when one is face to face with that other. This is different from the situation in which we, so to speak, empathize in cold blood. In the definition given at the beginning of this paper, Goldie talks of 'having a grasp of the narrative which I can substantially enact'. On the one hand, this could describe the project of choosing to enact a narrative from another's point of view, and then carrying out that project. One settles down with one's pipe to imagine what it was like for Stoddart or Conolly in those last dreadful days in Bokhara.[4] On the other hand, it could describe an involuntary experience: one just finds oneself reliving the experiences of another. This might happen when one is face to face with another who is experiencing some strong emotions, or describing some situation with strong emotion. In these situations, the representations are likely to be vivid, and consequently—if empathy happens at all—are likely to generate emotion. If this line of thought is correct, then it seems as if empathy can be a route to the experience of emotions not previously felt, and thus a route to knowledge of what those emotions are like.

I have expressed some doubt as to whether we are correct to classify these involuntary reactions as empathy as opposed to sympathy. We are overwhelmed with *some* emotion as we relive the experiences that we are witnessing, or are being related to us. However, our behaviour is not deliberate and thus we have formed no intention about what we are doing. We are simply aware of a situation and being overwhelmed with some feeling. It is difficult to tell, from the inside, whether this is the feeling the agent is having or did have felt as a result of centrally imagining the situation from the agent's point of view, or whether it is a naturally sympathetic reaction to the agent's plight. This doubt, along with the oddity of the project of settling down in a cool hour to centrally imagine situations from the point of view of others, makes me wonder whether empathy, in the narrow sense in which I have defined it, is as common an occurrence as we might think.

2.3 What Can Empathy Teach Us?

Let us grant, then, that the reader is able—provided they have off-line beliefs of the right content, and they are making sufficient imaginative effort—to experience something of what Mr Nicholls experienced. I shall consider one further problem. What is the off-line analogue of Mr Nicholls' love for Charlotte Bronte? Mr Nicholls' has (let us assume) an intense feeling, narrowly focussed on Charlotte Bronte, that is involuntary and not under his control. Thus the reader will not be able to will themselves into this attitude to Bronte. One can imagine being in love with someone—perhaps to find out what other people see in them (experiencing her in a certain light, you hear her laugh as charming instead of just irritating). However, that does not usually involve any affective pull. An alternative would be for the make-believe to take a more complicated form. In centrally imagining the world from Mr. Nicholls' point of view, one needs to centrally imagine being in love with that woman in the chair. One could simply replace that object in Mr Nicholls' scenario with the person (if any) who plays that role in one's own life. Another possibility is that the object of love, in the make-believe scenario, is the object of one's own affections who somehow has all of Charlotte Bronte's properties.

---

[4] For an account of their end, see Hopkirk (1990).

Allowing that through some such means the reader can conjure up Mr Nicholls' attitude to Charlotte Bronte, they can relive something of the dread he must have felt even if they have not felt that dread themselves. Let us put to one side the case in which the knowledge the reader gains is knowledge of what dread is like: let us suppose the more familiar case that the reader is acquainted with feelings of that type. The question that remains for me to consider is whether this reader is epistemologically better off having empathized with Mr Nicholls than he or she would have been had they simply believed that Mr Nicholls was feeling some mixture of emotions, dominated by dread. The obvious candidate is that while the non-empathetic reader only knows certain facts about Mr Nicholls, the empathetic reader knows what it is like to be Mr Nicholls. I shall close with some brief remarks about this distinction.

The distinction is often invoked as a defence of the cognitive powers of representations (in particular, of literature). It is often held that the cognitive value of literature is not in its power to convey propositions, but rather in it enabling its readers to experience what it is like to be a participant in the scenarios being described. There are three different relevant mental states in question here: (1) the experience of being Mr Nicholls, (2) the experience of empathizing with Mr Nicholls, and (3) having true beliefs about what it is like to be Mr Nicholls. I am going to grant that if one has (1), one would be in an epistemologically superior position than if one has only (3). However, I have been arguing that we have reason to think that (2) will always fall short of (1) in some ways. Hence, the question is whether being in (2) places one in an epistemologically superior position to someone who is only in (3).

The danger would be if what it was that made (1) superior to (3) was absent from (2). That is, is it the unsimulateable parts of Mr Nicholls' experience (that is, what (1) has but (2) lacks) that make (1) superior to (3)? If so, then (2) and (3) will be on a par. What, then, will (2) be like? It will share some of the mental states of (1): it will contain elements of dread, anxiety, and impending doom. These will also be directed towards the appropriate object: Charlotte Bronte. Provided the reader has an adequate grasp of the narrative, and a substantial characterization of Mr Nicholls, we can suppose that those feelings are reasonably particular: they are Mr Nicholls' feelings of dread, anxiety, and impending doom (although recall the reader is not in a position to judge that what he or she is feeling is accurate: they are not able to know whether there might be properties of Mr Nicholls, or of the situation, that they are not replicating). The reader may not, however, be able to replicate the way in which Mr Nicholls' love for Charlotte Bronte resonates throughout his mental economy, nor certain affects that the presence of Bronte has. Is someone who is in this state (that is, (2)) epistemologically better off than someone who is in (3)? This depends on two issues: the first is whether it just is epistemologically better to feel an emotion that someone is having, rather than just believing they are having that emotion, and second, whether feeling the emotion will make one's knowledge of the subsequent mental states the person will go through more reliable.

If it is true that whatever state (2) is, someone in (3) can know that Mr Nicholls is in that state (that is, that the description of the state can be as particular as it needs to be), then it is not clear that feeling the emotion someone feels is epistemologically better than knowing that they are feeling that emotion. It does seem that, for any state, there is a proposition that will describe that state. Even if the particularity of an emotion exceeds the capacities of a brief statement in English, that does not mean that it is beyond the capacities of a longer statement, or perhaps a statement in another language (Budd (1995): 146).[5] One might nonetheless think that (2) would teach the reader *what Mr Nicholls' experience was like*. However, we are assuming that the reader is familiar with the types of emotion Mr Nicholls is undergoing, so that would not be something he or she could learn. The second issue seems to me more promising for a defence of the epistemological status of empathy. As the causal capacities of a mental state depend on more than its propositional contents, (2) will be a better replicator of the causal role of (1) than will (3). Believing that Mr Nicholls feels anxious might leave the reader in the dark about what he feels inclined to do, whilst feeling his anxiety (or something like his anxiety) might provoke the intense off-line desire to bolt out of the room, or some complex combination of desires that would include that desire vying with the desire to grab Charlotte Bronte. If this is true, then someone in (2) will be in a better position to judge Mr Nicholls' position than someone only in (3). In this respect, then, empathy (if it is possible) has an advantage over its purely cognitive rival.

---

[5] Jane Heal presents powerful reasons for doubting this claim Heal (1997/2003a).

3

Two Routes to Empathy:
Insights from Cognitive Neuroscience

Alvin I. Goldman

3.1 Definitional Overview

The concept of empathy has a considerable history in both philosophy and psychology, and may currently be enjoying an apex of attention in both. It is certainly receiving close attention in cognitive neuroscience, which brings fresh discoveries and perspectives to the subject. The term 'empathy', however, does not mean the same thing in every mouth. Nor does there seem to be a single, unified phenomenon that uniquely deserves the label. Instead, numerous empathy notions or phenomena prance about in the same corral, and part of the present task is to tease some of these notions apart. More importantly, there are fascinating new findings that should be reported, analyzed, and mutually integrated, whether one's interest in empathy is primarily driven by pure science, philosophy of mind, moral philosophy, or aesthetic theory.

As a first step in distinguishing multiple senses, grades, or varieties of empathy, consider a definition offered by Vignemont & Singer (2006):

There is empathy if: (i) one is in an affective state; (ii) this state is isomorphic to another person's affective state; (iii) this state is elicited by the observation or imagination of another person's affective state; (iv) one knows that the other person is the source of one's own affective state. (2006: 435)

Questions can be asked about this definition that might motivate alternative definitions. For example, clause (i) restricts empathic states to affective or emotional states, but this is too narrow for some purposes. Cognitive neuroscientists talk of empathy for touch (Keysers et al. (2004)) and empathy for pain (Singer et al. (2004); Jackson et al. (2004); Morrison et al. (2004)), but neither touch nor pain is usually considered an emotion (although pain has an affective dimension as well as a sensory one). Concerning clause (ii), it should be asked exactly what is meant by 'isomorphic'. If it means a state of one person that matches a state of the target, then that requirement is more restrictive than definitions offered by others. Hoffman (2000), for example, defines empathy as 'an affective response more appropriate to another's situation than one's own'. This doesn't imply that the receiver's affective state matches (or is isomorphic to) that of the target.

Clause (iii) might be questioned on a rather different ground. It seems right to restrict empathic states to ones acquired by observation or imagination of the target individual. But shouldn't the elicitation process be constrained even further? For example, David Hume writes:

'Tis indeed evident, that when we sympathize with the passions and sentiments of others, these movements appear at first in *our* mind as mere ideas, and are conceiv'd to belong to another person, as we conceive any other matter of fact... No passion of another discovers itself immediately to the mind. We are only sensible to its causes or effects. From *these* we infer the passion: and consequently *these* give rise to our sympathy. (1739–1740 (1978): 319, 576)

Hume (using the term 'sympathy' rather than 'empathy') apparently endorses a three-stage hypothesis: one observes another person's movements, one infers from those movements a certain passion in the person, and the inferred belief causes a matching passion in oneself. If this is right, the process satisfies the Vignemont-Singer definition because the affect is elicited—albeit indirectly—by observation. But many people conceptualize empathy as a spontaneous, non-inferential process. If they wish to define empathy in that fashion, the previous definition would have to be amended to exclude inferential steps.

Another dimension of empathy important to many theorists is 'care' or 'concern' for the target. This dimension is omitted in the Vignemont-Singer definition. Social psychologists are traditionally interested in empathy as the basis of altruistic behavior, and many would want to highlight that component of empathy. Other investigators are interested in empathy as a key to mindreading, and might even use the term 'empathy' to describe (what they take to be) the most common form of mindreading. In other words, they use the term 'empathize' as roughly equivalent to 'simulate' (in an intersubjective fashion). I myself am a partisan of this position (Goldman 2006a), but this will play only a secondary role in the present paper. The proffered definition is neutral on the question of mindreading, and that's fine for present purposes.

It is easy to conflate different features of empathy, so readers can sometimes be mystified as to how, exactly, a given writer uses the term. For example, in Baron-Cohen's (2003) account of autism, or Asperger's syndrome, the linchpin of the account is a deficiency in 'empathizing'. But in reading Baron-Cohen it is often difficult to tell which of three possible senses of 'empathizing' he primarily has in mind: (A) using simulation when engaging in mentalizing, (B) being curious about others' mental states, or (C) feeling concern about other people's feelings. Correspondingly, a deficiency in empathizing might consist in a sparse use of simulation, a dearth of curiosity about others' mental states, or a low-level of concern about other people's feelings.

These preliminary comments should alert the reader to the fact that different writers and researchers exhibit different approaches to empathy. In addition, however, research findings can contribute to an understanding of how empathy is produced. Is there exactly one route to empathy, that is, one cognitive system—or one *type* of cognitive system—that produces empathy, or is there more than one? How exactly does this system, or these systems, work? What different consequences might ensue as upshots of different modes of empathizing? These are the primary questions to which this paper is addressed.

3.2 The Mirroring Route to Empathy

In an earlier era, one might have been skeptical about the isomorphism, or matching, condition we provisionally accepted in the definition of empathy. Do empathizers really undergo states that match those of their targets? Are the feeling states of receivers exactly the same as those of their targets? Since the discovery of mirror neurons and mirroring processes, however, there is much less room for skepticism. There is little doubt about the existence of processes through which patterns of neural activation in one individual lead, via their observed manifestations (e.g. behavior or facial expressions), to matching patterns of activation in another individual. If the corresponding patterns of activation are not perfect duplicates, at least they resemble their corresponding states in the target in terms of the kinds or types of mental or brain activity involved. Some might balk at calling the resonant states 'mental' states, because the mirroring episodes commonly occur below the threshold of consciousness even when the episodes being mirrored are fully conscious. If the term 'mental' is used broadly, however, they are processes of 'mental mimicry.'

Mirror neurons and mirroring processes were first discovered in monkeys, and subsequently in humans, in connection with preparation for motor action (Rizzolatti et al. (1996); Gallese et al. (1996)). When a monkey plans a certain type of goal-related hand action, e.g. tearing, holding, or grasping, neural cells in its premotor cortex dedicated to the chosen type of action are activated. Surprisingly, when a monkey merely observes another monkey or human perform a similar hand action, the same cells coded for that type of action are also selectively activated. Thus for certain neurons there is a sort of neural mirroring; one thing that occurs in the actor's brain is (more or less) replicated in the brain of the observer. These kinds of cells were therefore dubbed 'mirror neurons.' There are many details concerning the precise activation properties of mirror neurons in an observer versus an actor (Rizzolatti et al. (2001)). But the basic finding is that there is robust, selective activation of the same cells in both execution and observation modes.

Using different techniques, an action-related mirror system has been found in humans, centered on the inferior parietal lobule and the premotor cortex, including Brodmann area 44 (see Rizzolatti & Sinigaglia (2008)). Cochin et al. (1998) showed that the same μ rhythm that is blocked or desynchronized when a human performs a leg or finger movement is also blocked when he merely observes a similar movement by another person. Similar results were obtained from research studies using magnetoencephalography (MEG) and transcranial magnetic stimulation (TMS). Fadiga et al. (1995) recorded the motor evoked potentials (MEPs) induced by magnetic stimulation of the left motor cortex in various muscles of the contralateral (right) hands and arms of subjects who were watching the experimenter either grasp objects with his hand or make movements unrelated to any object. In both cases a selective increase in MEPs was found in the recorded muscles. Thus, mirroring properties were detected both for the observation of goal-related actions, as in monkeys, and also for non-object-related arm movements, which is not found in monkeys.

A study by Buccino et al. (2001) showed that mirroring for action isn't restricted to actions of the hand or arm. Subjects were shown action stimuli of the following sorts: biting an apple, grasping a cup, kicking a ball, and non-object-related actions involving the mouth, hand, or foot. The results showed that observing both object-related and non-object-related actions led to the somatotopic activation of the premotor cortex, with the mouth represented laterally and the foot medially.

Which mental states are activated in the case of motor mirroring? As I have said, it is presumably plans or intentions to do specific actions. Matching motor plans are activated in the observer, but they don't normally lead to imitation. Their outputs are usually inhibited downstream. There is mental mimicry, one might say, but not behavioral mimicry.

Mimicry of action-planning states doesn't naturally invite the label of empathy. But many other mental states that partake of mirroring more naturally invite talk of empathy. Some writers might prefer other labels. One might speak of 'resonance,' for example, or 'contagion.' But I think that 'empathy' is a reasonable choice. It must be stressed, however, that in many mirroring activities the receiving end of the mirroring relationship may not be conscious. The receiver may not be aware, or not fully aware, of the mental event she is undergoing that happens to be congruent with an event in the sender. This may raise issues concerning condition (iv) of the definition discussed earlier. I think it is fair to require a receiver to have some sort of intentional attitude directed toward the target by which the resonating state is linked to him. Otherwise, it doesn't seem like a case of empathy. I suspect that condition (iv) is too strong an intentional condition of this kind, but I don't have a wholly suitable replacement for it.

Even if a suitable replacement for condition (iv) is found, 'empathy' might not be a tempting term for mental mimicry of action-planning. Let us therefore examine other categories, starting with the sensation of touch. Keysers et al. (2004) found that when a person watches another person being touched, the same brain areas are activated as those in the person being touched. More specifically, they found that touching a subject's own legs activated the primary and secondary somatosensory cortex of the subject. Large extents of the secondary somatosensory cortex also responded to the sight of someone else's legs being touched. Films used with control subjects in which the same legs were approached by an object, but never touched, produced much smaller activations. This phenomenon is naturally described as empathy for touch.

Another mirroring domain involves the sensation of pain. Pain is a complex sensory and emotional mental state associated with actual or potential body damage. Sensory components of pain evaluate the locus, duration, and intensity of a pain stimulus, and affective components evaluate the unpleasantness of the noxious stimulus. These are mapped in different nodes of the so-called 'pain matrix.' Sensorimotor cortices process sensory features of pain and display somatotopical organization (mapping locations of the stimuli in brain tissue). Affective and motivational components of pain are coded in the affective node of the pain matrix, which includes anterior cingulate cortex (ACC) and anterior insula (AI). The subjective feeling of unpleasantness is strictly associated with neural activity in these structures.

In 2004 mirroring for pain was established in three articles: Singer et al. (2004), Jackson et al. (2004), and Morrison et al. (2004). In each of these studies empathy for pain elicited neural activity mainly in the affective division of the pain matrix, suggesting that only emotional components of pain are shared between self and other. However, using transcranial magnetic stimulation, Avenanti et al. (2005, 2006) found that the direct observation of painful stimulations on a model elicits inhibitory responses in the observer's corticospinal motor system similar to responses found in subjects who actually experience painful stimulations. When participants watched a video showing a sharp needle being pushed into someone's hand, there was a reduction in corticospinal excitability in related muscles. No change in excitability occurred when they saw a Q-tip pressing the hand or a needle being pushed into a tomato. These 'mirror' responses were specific to the body part that the subjects observed being stimulated and correlated with the intensity of the pain ascribed to the model, thus hinting at the sensorimotor side of empathy for pain.

The best example of mirroring in the sphere of emotions features the emotion of disgust, and the clearest evidence comes from an fMRI study by Wicker et al. (2003). Participants were scanned while passively inhaling disgusting or pleasant odorants through a mask and, separately, while observing movies of individuals who smelled the contents of a glass (disgusting, pleasant, or neutral) and spontaneously manifested appropriate facial expressions. The core finding was that the left anterior insula— previously known to be implicated in disgust experience—and the right anterior cingulate cortex were preferentially activated both during the inhaling of disgusting odorants (compared with pleasant and neutral odors) and during the observation of disgust facial expressions (compared with pleasure-expressive and neutral faces). This shows that observing a disgust-expressive face produces mental mimicry, or empathy, in an observer of the model. To use another expression very common in the literature, part of the observer's brain *simulates* the activity of a corresponding part of the model's brain.

In addition to the fMRI demonstration of matching experiences in observers and models in the gustatory cortex, researchers have used another measure of empathy to test whether observers experienced empathy. Jabbi et al. (2007) examined whether the IFO (anterior insula and adjacent frontal operculum) was associated with observers' self-reported empathy, measured by the Interpersonal Reactivity Index (IRI). They found that participant observers' empathy scores were predictive of their gustatory IFO activation while witnessing both the pleased and the disgusted facial expressions of others.

As is evident from the foregoing, a variety of systems in the human brain have mirror properties. They do not all use the same neural network or hardware. In particular, the mirror systems associated with sensations and emotions do not use the same neural hardware as the motor mirror system, nor as one another. Nonetheless, I shall treat them all as similar for present purposes, similar in having significant mirror properties. Ascending to an appropriate level of abstraction, we can consider them all to instantiate a single *type* of route to empathy, namely, a mirroring route. This does not imply that they all employ the very same cytoarchitectural pathway.[1]

3.3 A Reconstructive Route to Empathy

Granted that mirroring constitutes *one* (type of) route to empathy, is it the only type? This section presents two reasons to suspect otherwise. Mirroring seems to be, at least in one respect, automatic. The nature and content of mirroring events seem to be 'pre-packaged'; they are not constructed on the fly. The disgust system, for example, is ready to respond to appropriate facial stimuli in a disgust-production mode. It doesn't have to manufacture a novel response to simulate the corresponding disgust experience in a model. Similarly, the action repertoire susceptible of motor mirroring is presumably pretty well fixed early in life. Although there is no consensus about the origins of mirror neurons, one promising hypothesis posits the work of the associative mechanism of 'Hebbian learning' (Heyes (2005); Keysers & Perrett (2004); Keysers & Gazzola (2006)). According to this hypothesis, mirror properties of visuomotor neurons are shaped in infancy, as a result of synchronous firing, and their subsequent activation should not require substantial online construction. In contrast with this automaticity of mirror-based empathy, a large chunk of empathy seems to involve a more effortful or constructive process. When empathizing with another, you often reflect on that person's situation, construct in imagination how things are (were, or will be) playing out for him, and imagine how you would feel if you were in his shoes. This process of perspective taking is the stuff of which most conscious empathizing, at any rate, is made. It doesn't have the effortless, automatic quality of mirroring (if mirroring is describable as having any 'quality' at all, i.e. any phenomenological 'feel'). This suggests that there is, indeed, a different kind of empathy in addition to mirroring. In fact, this other kind of empathy is more detectable in daily life than the mirroring kind, since

---

[1] However, it is also not implied that the various routes to empathy are non-overlapping. On the contrary, certain neural centers seem to be involved in the mirroring routes for several different sensations and/or emotions. Anterior insula appears to play a particularly important role in the processing of several such mental states (Singer et al., 2009).

mirroring is largely inaccessible to introspective awareness. Such a distinction between two types of empathy is embraced by Stueber (2006), who calls them 'basic' and 're-enactive' empathy respectively.

One must be careful in presenting the foregoing argument because some findings indicate that mirroring is not automatic in all respects. Singer et al. ((2006) and Vignemont & Singer (2006)) found that empathic responses to pain are modulated by learned preferences, and hence not purely automatic. In the Singer et al. experiment, participants played a Prisoner's Dilemma game in which confederates of the experimenters played either fairly or unfairly. Participants then underwent functional imaging while observing the confederates receive pain stimuli. The mirroring responses of the male participants were of special interest. Their level of pain mirroring was significantly reduced when observing painful stimuli being applied to individuals who had played unfairly. Thus, their level of pain activation was not automatic in the sense of being purely stimulus driven. Rather, it was modulated by internal preferences acquired from information about the targets. A similar result was obtained by Lamm et al. (2007), who found that subjects have a weaker empathetic response in pain-related areas when they know that the pain inflicted on another is useful as a cure.

However, the fact that mirroring can be modulated does not imply that it is a constructive activity comparable to creating an imagined scenario or adopting another person's perspective. Modulation of pain responses is inhibitory activity, something much less complex than the construction of an imagined scenario. It is the constructional aspect of many instances of empathizing I mean to highlight here. Mirroring is subject to modulation, but this doesn't make it a constructive or effortful activity, like some form of empathizing appears to be. In view of these features of the second type of empathizing, I shall call it *reconstructive* empathy (cf. Vignemont (2008)).

Another argument for this second route to empathy proceeds as follows. Assume that this kind of empathizing involves adopting the perspective of the empathic target. It is widely thought that such perspective-taking (arguably a form of simulation) is a crucial part of mindreading, or 'theory of mind' (ToM). We can then argue from functional neuroimaging data about theory of mind that this kind of empathizing is probably not the same as mirroring, because the brain regions subserving ToM have minimal overlap with either motoric mirror areas or areas involved in the mirroring of sensations or emotions. Of course, we have previously argued that mirroring is not subserved by a unique set of brain regions. In principle, then, areas involved in ToM might be mirror areas. This is possible in principle, but there is no evidence to support it. Thus, if empathizing is involved in these other types of mindreading—for example, attribution of beliefs and thoughts—it is likely to be a different type of empathizing process than mirroring.

Which brain regions are implicated in the mindreading of beliefs and other propositional attitudes? According to a number of researchers, they include the medial prefrontal cortex (MPFC), the temporo-parietal junction (right and left), and the temporal poles. Some authors contend that one area in particular, the right temporo-parietal junction (RTPJ), is specifically involved in tasks concerning belief attribution (Saxe & Kanwisher (2003); Saxe & Powell (2006); Saxe (2006)). Assuming that these brain regions are indeed involved in mindreading, what reason is there to suspect a connection between them and empathizing? What is the connection, after all, between mindreading and empathizing—especially 'reconstructive' empathizing?

According to the simulation approach to mindreading, especially as developed in my *Simulating Minds* (Goldman (2006a), there is a very tight connection. In what I call 'high-level' simulation (Goldman (2006a): ch. 7), mindreading another person's mental state involves an attempt to replicate or re-experience the target's state via a constructive process. Exploiting prior information about the target, the mindreader uses 'enactment imagination' to reproduce in his own mind what might have transpired, or may be transpiring, in the target. This coincides with the reconstructive type of empathizing proposed here. The only difference is that mindreading involves an additional final step in which one or more of the constructed mental states are categorized (commonly, in terms of both mental type and propositional content) and assigned to the target. This final stage—especially the categorization element—may be absent in empathizing.

3.4 A Possible Neural System Subserving Reconstructive Empathizing

Is there a neural system that subserves a process of reconstructive empathizing? Let us reconnoiter the subject by starting at what seems like a great distance: episodic memory. Episodic memory allows individuals to project themselves backwards in time and recollect aspects of their previous experience (Tulving, 1983; Addis et al., 2007). A growing number of investigators, however, have begun to approach episodic memory in a broader context, one that emphasizes people's ability both to re-experience episodes from the past and also imagine or 'pre-experience' episodes that may occur in the future (Atance & O'Neill (2005); D'Argembeau & Van der Linden (2004); Gilbert (2006); Klein & Loftus (2002); Schacter & Addis (2007); Schacter, Addis, & Buckner (2007); Buckner & Carroll (2007)). Evidence for a linkage between representations of past events and future events initially comes from studies of patients with episodic memory deficits. Tulving's (1985) patient K.C. suffered from total loss of episodic memory due to damage to the medial temporal and frontal lobes. K.C. was also unable to imagine specific events in his personal future, despite no loss in general imagery abilities. A second amnesic patient, D.B., also exhibited deficits in both retrieving past events and imagining future events (Klein & Loftus (2002)). D.B.'s deficit in imagining the future was also specific to his personal future; he could still imagine possible future events in the public domain (e.g. political events and issues). In general, projecting one's thoughts backward or forward in time is referred to as 'mental time travel.'

Hassabis et al. (2007) examined the ability of five amnesic patients with bilateral hippocampal damage to imagine novel experiences (see the summary by Schacter et al. (2007)). The imaginary constructions by four of the five patients were greatly reduced in richness and content compared with those of control subjects. Since this study did not specifically require patients to construct scenes pertaining to future events, they seem to suffer from a more general deficit to construct novel scenes. Recent neuroimaging studies provide insight into whether common brain systems are used while remembering the past and imagining the future. In a PET study by Okuda et al. (2003) participants talked freely about either the near or distant past or future. The scans showed evidence of shared activity during descriptions of past and future events in a set of regions that included the prefrontal cortex and parts of the medial temporal lobe—namely the hippocampus and the parahippocampal gyrus.

Drawing on these and related studies, Buckner and Carroll ((2007); see also Schacter et al. (2007); Schacter et al. (2008); Schacter & Addis (2009)) have proposed a core brain system that subserves as many as four forms of self-projection. These include remembering the past, thinking about the future (prospection), conceiving the viewpoint of others (theory of mind), and navigation. What these mental activities all share is a shift of perspective from the immediate environment to an alternative situation. All four forms rely on autobiographical information and are constructed as a 'perception' of an alternative perspective. (This brain system also goes under the label of 'the default network.')

The hypothesized core brain system involves frontal lobe systems traditionally associated with planning and medial temporal-parietal lobe systems associated with memory. How does theory of mind (ToM) fit into this picture neuroanatomically? Buckner and Carroll suggest that Saxe & Kanwisher's (2003) findings on the role of right TPJ in ToM provide further evidence that the core system extends to ToM. In the Saxe & Kanwisher (2003) study, individuals answered questions about stories that required participants to conceive a reality that was different from the current state of the world. In one condition the conceived state was a belief; in the other, it was an image held by an inanimate object (e.g. a camera). Conceiving of the beliefs of another person strongly activated the network shared by prospection and remembering, whereas the control condition did not. Buckner and Carroll also cite Gallagher & Frith's (2003) proposal that the frontopolar cortex contributes to ToM. In particular, the paracingulate cortex, the anterior-most portion of the frontal midline, is recruited in executive components of simulating others' perspectives. Thus, the Buckner-Carroll suggestion is that the core brain system is used by many diverse types of task that require mental simulation of alternative perspectives, and this includes thinking about the perspectives of other people.

Shanton (unpublished) follows up the hypothesis of Schacter, Addis, Buckner, and Carroll by identifying an assortment of experimentally confirmed parallels between episodic memory and ToM. She begins by explaining how each can be understood as a form of 'enactment imagination,' in the sense of Goldman ((2006a): chs. 2 and 7).

Enactment imagination is a species of imagination in which one tries to match a mental state or sequence of mental states in another by recreating or pre-creating this state or states in oneself. Shanton (unpublished; Shanton & Goldman 2010) argues that if the same type of simulation strategy is used for both episodic memory and mindreading tasks, there should be parallels in terms of various cognitive parameters. She reviews evidence of several such parallels, including (1) their developmental timeline and (2) their susceptibility to egocentric biases.

Consider first the fact that episodic memory and mindreading share a developmental timeline. According to Tulving (2001), episodic memory retrieval emerges around the age of 4 years. This is confirmed by Perner & Ruffman (1995), who had children between 3 and 6 years of age complete both free recall and cued recall memory tasks. These tasks tap different types of memory abilities. In cued recall tasks, semantic information is quite rich, whereas in free recall tasks, where no explicit retrieval cues are given, such information is relatively poor. Free recall tasks cannot be successfully answered without episodic memory. Perner and Ruffman found that only 4–6-year-old children, not 3-year-olds, could succeed on free recall tasks, supporting the hypothesis that episodic memory retrieval emerges around age 4. This corresponds to the traditional timeline for success in advanced mindreading tasks, such as (verbal) false-belief tasks.

Next consider the susceptibility of both high-level mindreading and episodic memory retrieval to egocentric biases. One example of egocentric bias is the 'curse of knowledge' (Camerer et al. (1989)). This is the tendency to proceed as if other people know what you do, even when you have information to the contrary. In the Camerer et al. study, well-informed people were required to predict corporate earnings forecasts that would be made by other, less-informed people. The better-informed people stood to gain if they disregarded their own knowledge when making predictions about the less-informed people, who they *knew* lacked the same knowledge. Nonetheless, they failed to disregard their own knowledge completely, letting it 'seep' into their predictions. Simulationists would say that the predictors, while attempting to imagine themselves in the shoes of the predictees, allowed their own knowledge to 'penetrate' their imaginative construction. In other words, their own genuine mental states were not excluded, or quarantined, from the construction, despite the fact that good (i.e. accurate) simulation requires such quarantining. Quarantine failure is extremely common in (high-level) mindreading. For example, Van Boven & Loewenstein (2003) asked participants to predict states like hunger and thirst in a group of hypothetical hikers lost in the woods with neither food nor water. Their predictions were solicited either before or after they vigorously exercised at a gymnasium. In the case of post-exercise participants, the combined feelings of thirst and warmth were positively associated with their predictions of the hikers' feelings. Here too there is apparent failure to quarantine one's own concurrent states while mindreading hypothetical targets.

Quarantine failure is found in episodic memory. A vivid illustration is from Levine's (1997) study of subjects' memories for their own past emotion states. During the 1992 presidential race, Levine first asked a group of Ross Perot supporters about their emotions immediately after Perot withdrew from the race in July, and later asked them again in November, after they had switched their allegiances to other candidates. Although in July they described themselves as very sad, angry, and hopeless, by November they remembered experiencing much lower levels of emotion (in July). Apparently their November memories were being influenced by their current attitudes toward Perot. Their episodic memories were constructions that were partly influenced, or colored, by the way they felt at the time of memory 'retrieval'.

Shanton argues that the best explanation of these similarities is that the two processes implement the same cognitive strategy, and she argues (based on additional evidence) that this strategy is enactment imagination. This is a different form of simulation than mirroring.

How does enactment imagination differ from mirroring? In the case of mirroring processes, the default upshot is the successful production of a match between the sender state and the receiver state. Disgust in a sender is reproduced, with reasonable accuracy, by disgust in the observer. In the case of enactment imagination, by contrast, the prospects for successful correspondence are much more tenuous. They heavily depend on the vicissitudes of prior information, construction and/or elaboration. In the case of mindreading, the vicissitudes of prior information are particularly important. If one doesn't have accurate and relevantly complete information about the prior mental states of the target, attempts to put oneself in that person's mental shoes in order to extrapolate some further mental state have relatively shaky prospects for success.

In my view, it isn't entirely clear that the same core brain system described by Buckner, Carroll, Schacter, and colleagues includes ToM, or mentalizing. For example, in describing their core system, Buckner and Carroll say that it extends to lateral parietal regions located within the inferior parietal lobule 'near' the temporo-parietal junction. But being *near* TPJ may not be sufficient to identify this area as a locus of mentalizing activity. However, my brief for a simulation system that leads to both mindreading and empathizing via *reconstruction* rather than mirroring does not depend essentially on neuroanatomical evidence. If the specific core brain system hypothesized by Buckner, Carroll, and Schacter does not extend to mindreading and empathizing, this would still be compatible with there being a constructive, or reconstructive, species of empathizing. If the core brain system does subserve mindreading and empathizing, that is just gravy.

3.5 Output Profiles of the Two Routes to Empathy

The topic of the last three sections has not been states of empathy *per se* but different *routes* to empathy. Routes to empathy are species of mental activity that (often) lead to empathic states, where empathic states are defined as indicated in section 3.1 (with possible modifications considered there). The next natural question to ask is how successful or unsuccessful are the two different routes in generating empathic states, that is, states that exemplify substantial isomorphism to those of their targets. How do they fare in comparative terms? Are there characteristic differences in the empathic outputs of the two different routes?

The question of comparative success or accuracy can be decomposed into several sub-questions. First, one can ask about the *reliability* of a route or method. Of the states produced by a given method, how many are genuinely isomorphic to those of the target?[2] Second, one can ask about the *fecundity* of a route or method. For each application of a method, how many isomorphic states (on average) are produced in the empathizer? It should not be assumed that each application generates precisely one output state. Either of the two methods may generate more states (per use) than the other, and such greater fecundity may be important because it is associated with greater intersubjective understanding.

Restricting ourselves initially to the reliability question, the issue resolves into further sub-questions, because each state has more than one dimension and we can ask with respect to each dimension whether a given method produces output states that resemble the target on that dimension. Vignemont (2010) distinguishes four main dimensions of emotional states: (1) the *type* of state, (2) the *focus* (object) of a state, (3) the *functional role* of a state, and (4) the *phenomenology* of a state. A given route or method of empathizing might be more reliable than another route with respect to some of these dimensions but less reliable with respect to others.

For reasons previously sketched, it seems likely that the mirroring method of empathizing is more reliable than the reconstructive method when it comes to the *type* of emotional state. Mirroring, by its very nature, is a highly reliable method of state generation, one that preserves at least the sameness of mental-state type (e.g. pain, disgust, fear). There is no comparable guarantee (or near-guarantee) in the case of the reconstructive method. Outputs of a constructive or reconstructive method depend heavily on the pretend inputs that the empathizer uses, and the accuracy of these inputs can vary widely depending on the quality of her background information. In short, in terms of reliability with respect to *type*, the mirroring route seems superior to the reconstructive route.

What about the focus dimension of the state: what the emotion or other state is *about*? As Vignemont argues, the mirroring method does not seem to be so helpful in this regard, whereas the reconstructive method is (or might be). Vignemont's example is seeing a smiling stranger on a train. Seeing the smile prompts a happy state in the observer by the mirroring route. But the object of the stranger's happiness remains

---

[2] The term 'reliability' is not used here in exactly the same sense in which it is used in epistemology, because we are not discussing the formation of true or false beliefs. Instead, we are discussing how much, or to what degree, one mental state is isomorphic to (resembles) another. Degrees of reliability are to be computed in terms of proportions of isomorphic versus non-isomorphic features (or something along these lines).

undisclosed by mirroring. Mirroring reproduces in the observer only happiness, not happiness *about X* or *about Y*. On the other hand, argues Vignemont, reconstructive empathizing can be helpful with respect to focus. By adopting the target's perspective, an empathizer can figure out what the object's emotion is about, or directed at, at least when appropriate information is available. Thus, reconstructive empathizing seems to be superior to mirroring in this regard.

Vignemont includes an *intensity* dimension for output states, which she subsumes under phenomenology. Although I agree that an intensity dimension is relevant here, it is not clear that it should be confined to the sphere of phenomenology. As previously indicated, mirroring states often fail to reach the threshold of consciousness, so they may have no phenomenology at all. Does this mean that they have zero intensity? This would be an unsatisfactory inference because unconscious states certainly have important functional properties, including tendencies to influence behavior. On the other hand, what alternative measure of intensity should be selected? Should some measure of neural activity be used? Which one? In any case, once a measure of intensity is chosen, the question is whether the mirroring method or the reconstructive method is more reliable, that is, which tends to produce mirrored states with greater isomorphism? It isn't obvious (to me) what the answer is; this question invites more research.

Vignemont regards the reconstructive method as superior to the mirroring method, but since she doesn't herself draw the reliability/fecundity distinction, it is an open question whether the intended superiority is supposed to hold for both reliability and fecundity, or for fecundity only. She writes:

Low-level [mirroring] empathy does not meet the condition of isomorphism [because it is limited to the *type* of emotion, and does not go beyond that]. Emotional sharing may be more exhaustive in high-level empathy. (2008)

To support this idea she considers a case of a woman learning that a friend is pregnant. Since the empathizer knows how much the friend wanted a child, she puts herself in the friend's shoes and realizes how happy she must be. She feels happy with her. The inputs in such a case of reconstructive empathizing are more complex than the inputs to mirroring empathizing, and this allows one to fill out the target's mental states more fully, or in greater detail. Continuing with the pregnancy example, the empathizer pretends that she is pregnant and that she wants a child, which leads her to feel happy. Her emotional state is *about* the pregnancy; it has the same focus as the friend's emotional state. The mirroring method, says Vignemont, 'isolates' a mirrored emotion from the rest of the target's mental life. It does not provide a fine-grained sharing of states based on a common network of associated mental states. Reconstructive empathizing does provide this.

Suppose Vignemont means to say that the reconstructive method is superior in both reliability and fecundity. I would be prepared to concede the fecundity part, because the reconstructive method is obviously capable of generating more and more detailed isomorphic states than mirroring. But is it more reliable? I am skeptical. Vignemont ignores two types of error to which only the reconstructive method is liable. The first type of error is an error of omission: omitting relevant inputs because of ignorance. If an (attempted) empathizer in the pregnancy case is unaware that her friend is pregnant or is unaware that she wants a child, application of the reconstructive method is unlikely to produce *correct* details involving the target emotion. The second type of error is an error of commission. As reviewed above, there is substantial evidence that when people try to simulate the mental states of others, they often fail to 'quarantine' their own genuine states, allowing such states to seep into the simulation process when they don't properly belong there (because the target isn't in them). This results in 'egocentric biases' in the simulation process. Both types of errors can substantially reduce the reliability of the reconstructive method, so I cannot concur with Vignemont's rosy appraisal of it. An assessment of the comparative reliability of the two methods needs more work. Nonetheless, it is good to have this problem placed squarely on the table; it deserves attention.

I have argued that there are two distinct routes to empathy, the mirroring route and the reconstructive route. It is possible, however, that the reconstructive route also involves mirror neurons. This is suggested by Iacoboni and colleagues (Iacoboni, this volume; Uddin et al. (2007)). Iacoboni (this volume) reports the recent discovery of mirror neurons in several new areas, including the amygdala, hippocampus, parahippocampal gyrus, and entorhinal cortex. He suggests that these mirror neurons may underpin what I earlier called 'high-level' mindreading and empathy (Goldman, 2006a), which correspond to what is here called reconstructive empathy.[3] Thus it is possible that even reconstructive empathy is mediated by neurons with mirror properties. Note, however, that this would not necessarily undercut the distinction between mirroring and reconstructive processes. As standardly conceived, mirror processes are automatic processes generated by observation. In addition, neurons with mirror properties might also participate in such an effortful process as imagination (see Uddin et al. (2007), box 3), a key component of reconstructive empathy. These ideas require further investigation.

---

[3] Notice that some of the areas containing mirror neurons mentioned by Iacoboni are the same as midline areas mentioned by Okuda et al. (2003) in their study of constructive imagination, specifically, the hippocampus and the parahippocampal gyrus.

4

Within Each Other:
Neural Mechanisms for Empathy in the Primate Brain

Marco Iacoboni

4.1 Introduction

Empathy is commonly defined as the ability to understand and share the feelings of another. It is obviously a very complex ability. What are the neurophysiological mechanisms that underlie empathy? For years, nobody dared to investigate this issue. The main reasons were two. First, the study of the brain mechanisms associated with emotion and emotional understanding is relatively recent. Until approximately 20 years ago, the study of the neural systems associated with higher functions was focused exclusively on 'cold' cognitive processes. The dominant metaphor was 'the mind as a computer.' The study of emotions—especially complex social emotions— clearly did not fit in the prevalent paradigm. Second, even after emotions became a popular topic in cognitive neuroscience, mostly thanks to the influential work of Antonio Damasio, the neural mechanisms of empathy remained largely unexplored. This was likely due to the perceived complexity of empathy. Indeed, the complexity of a phenomenon is generally considered an obstacle for the study of its neural correlates, especially in single cell recordings. While neurophysiologists are able to study brain activity at its most exquisite spatial and temporal resolution, that is, the spiking activity of single cells, they also tend to study this activity in relation with relatively simple phenomena, such as the perception of individual sensory stimuli or the planning and execution of relatively simple actions. For this reason, neurophysiological data on empathy were virtually nonexistent until a few years ago. In recent years, however, a new wave of studies has investigated the links between empathic behavior and brain activity. The recent studies have been inspired by the discovery of mirror neurons in the macaque brain. These cells, which I describe in detail in the next section of the chapter, have *physiological properties* that are ideal to facilitate empathy. Indeed, the properties of mirror neurons seem to map extremely well onto emotional contagion, a phenomenon studied for decades by psychologists (Hatfield et al. (1994)). Most scholars would probably agree that mirror neurons are likely critical neural elements for the relatively simple forms of empathic resonance that are observed in emotional contagion. However, most scholars would also argue that mirror neurons cannot account for more cognitively complex forms of empathy. In this chapter, I will argue instead that there are many different kinds of mirror neurons, and that they are also much more widely distributed in the primate brain than previously thought. The rich variety of mirroring responses and their diffuse anatomical localization suggest that neural mirroring may be a fundamental building block of empathy, even in its more complex forms.

In the next three sections of this chapter, I will review the single cell recordings on mirror neurons in macaques, the brain imaging data in humans that suggest links between activity in the human mirror neuron system and empathic behavior, and finally a set of unique data on single cell recordings in the human brain that demonstrate mirroring response in individual human neurons. In the final section of the chapter, I will discuss the theoretical implications of these empirical findings.

4.2 Mirror Neurons in the Macaque Brain

The first peer-reviewed scientific report on mirror neurons was published in 1992 (di Pellegrino et al. (1992)). This very short paper was followed four years later by a much more detailed report in which the term *mirror neurons* was used for the first time (Gallese et al. (1996)). The cells described in these two papers were recorded from the anterior sector of the ventral premotor cortex of *Macaca Nemestrina*. The anterior sector of the ventral premotor cortex in macaques is called area F5, and contains neurons with quite interesting motor properties (Rizzolatti et al. (1988)). The F5 motor neurons fire in relation with specific goal-oriented actions, rather than with individual movements. For instance, several F5 neurons fire during grasping actions, others during holding actions, and others during tearing actions. Interestingly, the same neuron may fire for a grasping action with the left hand *and* for a grasping action with the right hand. This firing pattern demonstrates that the firing of the cell does not occur in relation with the contraction of a specific set of muscles. Indeed, the same neuron will not fire for a different kind of action, say, scratching the head, which also involves the contraction of finger muscles used during grasping. Motor neurons in F5 show specificity of responses in relation with the *type* of grasp. Some cells discharge only during *precision grip* (opposition of thumb and index to grasp very small objects), others only during *finger prehension* (all fingers grasp a relatively small object), and others only during *whole hand prehension* (the whole hand grasps a big object). Taken together, these properties suggest that F5 motor neurons form a vocabulary of goal-oriented actions (Rizzolatti et al. (1988)), that is, as the vocabulary is the body of words of a language, the actions coded by F5 neurons seem to represent the body of actions that can achieve specific goals.

Approximately 20 to 25% of F5 motor neurons have also amazing *visual* properties. These cells fire also when the monkey is completely still and is just watching somebody else making a goal-oriented action. It is as if the monkey is watching her own actions reflected by a mirror. This is why these cells are called mirror neurons. Mirror neurons are defined exclusively on the basis of their physiological properties. They are cells that are specialized for actions, and that discharge in association with motor and perceptual aspects of actions. There are two main categories of mirror neurons: *strictly congruent* mirror neurons and *broadly congruent* mirror neurons. Strictly congruent mirror neurons discharge for the same action both when the monkey is performing it and when the monkey is simply observing it performed by somebody else. Broadly congruent mirror neurons, in contrast, fire not only for the same action, but also for different actions that achieve the same goal both when the monkey is performing the action and when the monkey is simply observing it performed by somebody else (Gallese et al. (1996)). The properties of mirror neurons suggest that these cells map the actions of others onto the motor repertoires of the observer, thereby providing an internal simulation of the actions of other individuals in the observer.

Further studies demonstrated that mirror neurons discharge also when the observed action is partially occluded (Umiltà et al.(2001)) and when the monkey does not see the action at all, but simply listens to sounds typically associated with the action (for instance, the sound of breaking a peanut) (Kohler et al. (2002)). These data suggest that mirror neurons are multimodal cells that can provide a fairly abstract representation of the actions of other individuals. How abstract? A recent experiment has addressed this question (Fogassi et al. (2005)). The single cell recordings of this recent study were performed in area PF/PFG, an area in the anterior sector of the inferior parietal cortex. This sector of the inferior parietal cortex is anatomically connected with area F5 in the ventral premotor cortex (Rizzolatti & Luppino (2001)). Parietal motor neurons in PF/PFG were recorded when the monkeys were performing grasping actions associated with different outcomes, eating or placing. In some trials the monkey was allowed to grasp food and eat it, while in others the monkey was rewarded with food only after the animal had successfully completed the trial by grasping the food and placing it in a container. While of parietal motor neurons fired equivalently for grasping to eat and for grasping to place, the remaining demonstrated differential discharges during the grasping action associated with different outcomes. Approximately ¾ of these cells discharged more vigorously for grasping to eat, while ¼ discharged more vigorously for grasping to place. Note that the neuronal discharges were measured during grasping, that is, *before* the monkey would eat or place the food in the container.

After this necessary testing of the motor properties of the parietal cells, the experimenters tested the mirror properties of the same pool of cells. In some trials, the monkey simply watched an experimenter grasping a piece of food and eating it. In some other trials, the monkey watched the experimenter grasping the food and placing it in a container. The visual cue that signaled the outcome of the grasping action was the presence of the container. If the container was present, the experimenter placed the food in it. If the container was not present, the experimenter ate the food. A subset of motor parietal neurons displayed mirror properties, that is, they discharged when the monkey simply observed the experimenter's grasping action. The discharge of these parietal mirror neurons during grasping observation mirrored the discharge previously measured during grasping execution. Cells that discharged equivalently for executed grasping actions associated with different outcomes, also discharged equivalently when the monkey simply observed grasping actions associated with different outcomes. For these mirror parietal cells, a grasp is a grasp, regardless of the outcome associated with it. Cells that discharged more when the monkey grasped to eat, also discharged more when the monkey watched the experimenter grasping to eat (the outcome was cued by the absence of the container). Also, cells that discharged more when the monkey grasped to place, also discharged more when the monkey watched the experimenter grasping to place (here the outcome was cued by the presence of the container). The preferential discharge for the same grasping action associated with different outcomes suggest that these mirror neurons do not simply code the action, but also the intention associated with it. In less mentalistic terms one could say that these cells predict the outcome of the observed grasping action, the action or actions that follow the grasp. This is evidence for a rather abstract and sophisticated coding of the observed grasp. The grasp is coded by these cells as embedded in a chain of concatenated and coordinated actions.

Mirror neurons do not simply code hand and hand-to-mouth actions. Both the ventral premotor and the inferior parietal cortex contain mirror neurons that code for mouth actions only. Two main types of actions are mirrored by these cells: ingestive and communicative actions. A recent depth electrode study demonstrated the mirroring properties of single cells in ventral premotor cortex for biting and sucking, and for lip-smacking, a communicative facial gesture with positive social valence (Ferrari et al. (2003)). The evidence that communicative facial gestures can be mirrored at the level of individual premotor neurons is theoretically important. It suggests that the evolutionary antecedents of empathy are based on relatively simple mechanisms of contagion and motor resonance.

4.3 Neural Systems with Mirroring Properties in the Human Brain

The single unit recordings in macaques described in the previous section have inspired a series of studies on humans. A common aspect of all these studies is that they cannot measure brain activity at the exquisite resolution of a single cell, as in the depth electrode studies in macaques. The neuroscience methods applied to the study of the human brain typically provide measures of *ensemble* neural activity, the activity of a large number of brain cells working together. Obviously, none of these techniques can definitely prove that the ensemble neural activity with mirroring properties truly represents the activity in concert of many mirror neurons. In principle, a neuronal ensemble may be activated during both action execution and action observation even though its individual cells do not. Let me give you an example. Suppose I am measuring activity from an ensemble of ten neurons (keep in mind that the techniques that will be discussed in this section of the chapter actually measure ensemble activity of *millions* of neurons). Four of these neurons fire during execution of a grasping action but not during observation of the same grasping action performed by somebody else. They seem classical motor neurons. Four other neurons do not fire during grasping executions but do fire during grasping observation. They are visual neurons. The remaining two neurons do not fire during both conditions. It is unclear what their properties are. In this hypothetical scenario, a neuroscience method that measures ensemble neural activity would likely show some level of activation during both action observation and action execution, even though the neuronal ensemble does not contain any mirror neuron.

In spite of these interpretational limitations, it is reasonable to hypothesize that human brain areas contain mirror neurons if at least two conditions are met: first, the brain areas demonstrate ensemble activity compatible with mirror neuron activity; second, the anatomical location of the human brain areas is consistent with the anatomical location of mirror neurons recorded in the monkey brain. This second condition, however, has generated a lot of confusion among scholars. Indeed, many scholars now conflate anatomy and physiology in their definition of mirror neurons or mirror neuron areas. This is a mistake that should be avoided. As pointed out earlier, the definition of mirror neurons in monkeys is based only on their physiological properties. While such cells have been recorded—at least so far—only in areas F5 and PF/PFG, a cell with identical physiological responses in primary motor cortex or SMA would also be called mirror neuron. In other words, the anatomical location of the recorded cell is absolutely irrelevant to the physiological characteristics of the cell. Brain imaging studies conservatively used also the anatomical location of the activation only because the brain imaging signal is, as discussed above, inherently ambiguous.

Given that mirror neurons fire during both execution and observation of the similar actions, it makes sense to hypothesize that these cells may be important neural elements for imitative abilities. Imitation is pervasive in human behavior, and it is thought to play a major role in skill learning, transmission of local cultures, and in a variety of social and cognitive domains (Hurley & Chater (2005)). The first brain imaging study that linked imitation to human brain areas presumably containing mirror neurons (Iacoboni et al. (1999)) used the pattern of firing rate changes observed in the single unit studies in monkeys to predict the pattern of brain activity measured with functional magnetic resonance imaging (fMRI). This technique measures brain activity indirectly, by looking at the level of blood oxygenation in the brain. In the healthy brain, blood oxygenation and neural activity are fairly well correlated, making it possible to monitor brain activity with techniques that respond to changes in blood oxygenation rather than neuronal firing.

The firing rate changes of mirror neurons during action observation is approximately half the firing rate changes during action execution, according to the monkey studies

(Gallese et al. (1996)). This predicts that human brain areas with mirror neurons should have increases in fMRI activity during action observation that are also approximately half the increases measured during action execution. Furthermore, given that during imitation subjects both observe and execute the imitated action, it was predicted that imitation should yield—in mirror neuron areas—fMRI signal increases that are approximately the sum of the signal increases measured during action observation and action execution. Using this relatively simple model, an fMRI study on imitation of finger movements revealed two human brain areas with a pattern of activity consistent with mirror neuron activity. The two areas were located in the posterior part of the inferior frontal cortex and in the anterior part of the inferior parietal cortex (Iacoboni et al. (1999)). These anatomical locations are consistent with the single unit recordings in monkeys demonstrating that area F5 in the inferior frontal cortex and area PF/PFG in the inferior parietal cortex contain mirror neurons (Gallese et al. (1996); (Fogassi et al. (2005)). Thus, the posterior part of the inferior frontal cortex and the anterior part of the inferior parietal cortex meet the two necessary conditions to be considered human brain areas that presumably have mirror neurons: activity profile compatible with mirror neuron activity and anatomical location consistent with the anatomical location of mirror neurons in monkeys.

Recently, a series of fMRI studies have applied the adaptation paradigm to the investigation of the human mirror neuron system. The results obtained from these studies are sometimes consistent (Chong et al. (2008); Hamilton & Grafton (2008)) and sometimes inconsistent (Dinstein et al. (2007)) with the more classical 'subtraction' studies discussed above (in which some experimental conditions are contrasted with other experimental conditions). These mixed results are not surprising, because the neural correlates of adaptation paradigms are unclear (Tolias et al. (2005); Wilke et al. (2006)) and because there is no evidence that mirror neurons adapt at all. Indeed, adaptation is not a ubiquitous property of all cortical neurons and until adaptation has been unequivocally demonstrated in mirror neurons, fMRI adaptation studies of the mirror neuron system in humans have a questionable rationale.

Other fMRI studies using the classical 'subtraction' method have linked more directly the activity of human mirror neuron areas with empathy. The first study that investigated this issue (Carr et al. (2003)) was inspired by social psychology research that demonstrated that being imitated increases liking and that more empathic individuals tend to imitate other people more than less empathic individuals (Chartrand & Bargh (1999)). These behavioral data suggested functional links between the human mirror neuron system and neural systems more traditionally associated with emotional processing. The fMRI study tested the hypothesis that empathy requires the simulation (or inner imitation) of the facial emotional expressions of other people. Mirror neurons would provide such simulation process. Their connections with the limbic system via the insula would allow mirror neurons to send signals to limbic areas, such that the observer can feel what others are feeling. This model makes two predictions: first, there should be activation of mirror neuron areas, insula, and amygdala during both observation and imitation of facial emotional expressions; second, in this network of areas the activity during imitation should be higher than during observation, as the previous study on imitation of finger movements had shown. Importantly, the higher activity during imitation should not be restricted to mirror neuron areas only. Indeed, if empathy requires the simulation of others' actions and functional links between mirror neurons and limbic areas, one would expect that the higher activity during imitation in mirror neuron areas would also spread to the insula and limbic areas. The empirical data confirmed both predictions (Carr et al. (2003)).

While this study was compelling in describing a large scale neural network supporting empathy via a simulative process implemented by mirror neurons, it did not provide any evidence linking the activity in this neural network and individual differences in empathy. Three recent fMRI studies have addressed this question. In one study, subjects listened to action sounds. As we have seen in the previous section of this chapter, action sounds trigger a discharge in mirror neurons. This predicts that human brain areas with mirror neurons should also become activated while listening to action sounds. Indeed, the study demonstrated that action sounds increased the activity of inferior frontal cortex (Gazzola et al. (2006)). This area has both activity profile and anatomical localization compatible with mirror neuron activity. Importantly, there was higher activity in subjects with high empathy scores.

Another fMRI study measured brain activity while subjects observed grasping actions (Kaplan & Iacoboni (2006)). As expected, grasping observation activated the inferior frontal cortex, where presumably human mirror neurons are located. The inferior frontal activity was correlated with empathy scores. The main difference between this study and the previous one is that while this study found a correlation between scores at scales measuring *emotional* empathy (scales that measure concern for the emotions of others and the emotional responses one experiences when watching someone else experiencing strong emotions) and activity in the mirror neuron system, the previous study found that subjects with high scores at scales measuring *cognitive* empathy (scales that measure the ability to imagine another person's perspective and the tendency to imagine oneself in the place of fictional characters in books or movies) had higher mirror neuron activity. Perhaps this difference is due to the different kind of stimuli used in the two studies. Action simulation while listening to action sounds may be mediated more by cognitive mechanisms, whereas action simulation during action observation may be based more on emotional resonance.

A more recent study has investigated the relationships between activity in mirror neuron areas and empathy in children (Pfeifer et al. (2008)). The children were asked to imitate and to simply observe facial emotional expressions displaying basic emotions. As in the previous study on adults (Carr et al. (2003)), mirror neuron areas, the insula, and the amygdala activated for both observation and imitation of facial emotional expressions, with higher activity during imitation. Correlation analyses were performed between brain activity and two types of scores: empathy scores and interpersonal competence scores. Emotional empathy scores correlated with activity in mirror neuron areas during *observation* of facial emotional expressions, in line with the study on grasping observation (Kaplan & Iacoboni (2006)). Interestingly, mirror neuron activity during *imitation* of facial emotional expressions correlated with interpersonal competence scores. Indeed, overtly mirroring the emotions of others plays an important role in social interactions. It is through this mirroring that we communicate to other people that we understand what they are feeling. The fact that activity in mirror neuron areas maps well onto interpersonal competence during emotion imitation suggests that the mirror neuron system is a fairly nuanced bio-marker of sociality.

Further evidence in support of this hypothesis comes from imaging studies of autism. A recent fMRI study of observation and imitation of facial emotional expressions has revealed not only reduced activity in mirror neuron areas in children with Autism Spectrum Disorder compared to typically developing children, but also a correlation of the severity of the disorder with mirror neuron activity (Dapretto et al. (2005)). The more severe the disorder, the more reduced the activity in mirror neuron areas.

All these studies provide compelling evidence in support of the hypothesis that the mirror neuron system is a critical neural system for empathy. However, none of these studies provided evidence of the existence of mirror neurons in humans. Obviously, it would be very puzzling if humans had no mirror neurons. However, there are many evolutionary steps between macaques and humans. It is reasonable to assume that mirror neurons have evolved too. Thus, depth electrode recordings in the human brain would be very valuable not only to provide empirical evidence for the existence of mirror neurons in humans, but also because it would allow us to compare the properties of mirror neurons in macaques and humans. The next section of the chapter describes preliminary observations on individual human neurons with mirroring properties.

4.4 Mirror Neurons in the Human Brain

In some neurological patients, epilepsy cannot be controlled efficiently by anti-epileptic drugs. In these cases, neurosurgery is necessary. It is imperative to localize the epileptogenic brain tissue with precision, and in some patients it is necessary to implant depth electrodes, stop the administration of anti-epileptic drugs, and wait until the patient seizes to find exactly where is the brain locus of epileptogenic activity. This procedure typically takes few days up to two weeks. During this time, the patient has implanted electrodes in the depth of the brain, which makes it possible to measure brain activity. Typically, these electrodes can only record EEG signal, the slow waves of electrical brain activity that represent neuronal firing of many brain cells working together. However, the group of the neurosurgeon Itzhak Fried at UCLA has modified the electrodes typically used in these patients, such that it is possible to measure activity from individual neurons (Fried et al. (1999)).

Obviously, the brain location of the implanted electrodes is exclusively determined by medical considerations and electrodes are quickly de-planted when the patients seizes. Furthermore, the modification of the electrodes that allows individual neuron recordings is located only at the tip of the electrode. These electrodes are relatively large electrodes. The way they are typically implanted determines that the tip of the electrode is always located in medial brain structures, that is, in brain areas quite different from the human brain areas that are widely presumed to contain mirror neurons. In spite of all these limitations, it makes sense to investigate mirror properties in these patients. As already discussed, there are many evolutionary steps from macaques to humans. It is reasonable to assume that the mirror neuron system evolved too, from the macaque brain to the human brain. This evolution may have taken two forms: on the one hand, an anatomical expansion of the system, such that other brain areas may contain mirror neurons (we should also keep in mind that it is possible that other brain areas in the macaque brain actually contain mirror neurons—neurophysiologists have not mapped out the properties of all neurons in the macaque brain); on the other hand, the physiological properties of the cells may have been at least in part modified by the evolutionary process.

Indeed, after recording neural activity from a total of more than 1,000 neurons in more than twenty patients, we now have evidence for the existence of mirror neurons in multiple areas of the frontal and temporal lobe of the human brain. A preliminary description of these data has been published in abstract form (Mukamel et al. (2007)). The patients were tested under a variety of experimental conditions: grasping execution (the patients grasped a mug either with precision grip or with whole hand prehension, following computer generated instructions), grasping observation (the patients watched videoclips of grasping actions, including both precision grips and whole hand prehension), execution of facial emotional expressions (smiling and frowning), observation of facial emotional expressions, and some control experimental conditions. In the frontal lobe, we found mirror neurons in all four medial frontal areas we recorded from: supplementary motor area (SMA) proper, pre-SMA, dorsal anterior cingulate cortex (ACC) and ventral ACC. The monkey homologues of these areas are anatomically connected with area F5, either directly, as is the case for area F6 (which is the homologue of pre-SMA), or indirectly, through F6 (Rizzolatti & Luppino (2001)). Thus, in principle this could be a system of mirror neurons that exerts some form of 'control' over mirror neurons located in the inferior frontal cortex (the human homologue of area F5).

Why do mirror neurons need such a control mechanisms? Given their physiological properties, the answer to this question seems obvious. If mirror neurons—which are neurons with motor properties located in premotor cortex, a brain region important for planning an action—fire uncontrollably during action observation, we may find ourselves imitating each other all the time. This is less than ideal. Indeed, even though imitation is quite pervasive in human behavior, we do not imitate all the time. It is necessary to have a neural mechanism of control to inhibit unwanted imitation. The neurons in these medial frontal areas seem to be doing exactly that. In contrast to the recordings performed in macaques, in which the large majority of neurons show increase in firing rate, we found that only one-third of mirror neurons show firing rate increase in the human medial frontal cortex. Another third of these cells demonstrates decrease of firing rate, whereas the remaining third exhibited properties never before observed in the macaque brain. These cells—which I called super mirror neurons (Iacoboni (2008))—have opposite firing rate changes for action execution and action observation. The majority of super mirror neurons increase their firing rate during action execution and decrease their firing rate during action observation, while a minority shows the opposite pattern. This pattern of firing rate change suggests that the overall neuronal population activity of these medial frontal mirror neurons shows a majority of excitatory responses during action execution and a majority of inhibitory responses during action observation. Why? While increase and decrease in firing rate do not automatically translate in excitation and inhibition (it depends on the kind of neuron firing up or down), in the cortex 85% of the units are excitatory and only 15% inhibitory (Braitenberg & Schuz (1991)). Furthermore, single unit recordings tend to measure action potentials from relatively large units, that is, pyramidal cells that are typically excitatory units. Thus, it is likely that the firing rate changes recorded in our study represent a relatively simple mechanism used by the mirror neural system in the medial frontal cortex to control unwanted imitation.

We found relatively similar proportions of excitatory, inhibitory, and super mirror neurons in all medial frontal areas we recorded from. This suggests that this system is quite widespread in the medial frontal cortex. This makes sense if this system has the important role of inhibiting unwanted imitation. One does not want to confine such an important neural system in a restricted brain area. A focal lesion might determine the loss of this important function. In keeping with this idea, the rare neurological patients with uncontrolled imitative behavior have very large lesions in the frontal lobe (Lhermitte et al. (1986)); De Renzi et al. (1996)).

The role of super mirror neurons may be relevant not only to the control of unwanted imitation. The role of these complex mirroring responses may be relevant to the differentiation between self and other. While mirroring seems a clever solution that evolution has devised to facilitate learning and social interactions, mirroring also generates the problem of differentiating between actions of the self and of other people. The opposing pattern of excitation and inhibition for actions of self and others seems an elegantly simple neuronal mechanism that helps keeping this differentiation. Indeed, the medial frontal areas we recorded from have been often associated with self-processing and the self–other distinction in the imaging literature (Gusnard et al. (2001)) (Uddin et al. (2007)).

We also recorded from the amygdala, hippocampus, parahippocampal gyrus, and entorhinal cortex. Amazingly, we found mirror neurons in these areas too. The majority of the temporal lobe mirror cells were found in the hippocampal formation (hippocampus, parahippocampal gyrus, and entorhinal cortex), which is connected with the frontal lobe through the uncinate fasciculus and other cortico-cortico projections (Blatt et al. (2003)); Kondo et al. (2005); Lavenex et al. (2002); Mohedano-Moriano et al. (2007)). Mirror neurons have been originally interpreted as neurons with motor properties (coding goal-oriented actions) that also have specific sensory properties, that is, they respond to the sight of somebody else's action. The main idea being that these cells help understanding the actions of others by mapping them onto the observer's motor repertoire. However, medial temporal lobe neurons are typically associated with higher-order visual properties and memory properties, but not with motor properties. Thus, the existence of medial temporal neurons with mirror properties requires a revision of the original notion of mirror neurons. The mirror neurons we recorded in medial temporal lobe are likely higher-order visual neurons that also discharge during goal-oriented actions (in this particular case, either grasping a mug or communicating an internal state with a facial expression). Thus, their functional role seems to be the mapping of our own actions onto our perception of the actions of others. Given the widespread presence of mimicry during social interactions, the mapping of our own actions onto our perception of others' actions may represent some form of 'neural expectation,' (Arbib & Rizzolatti (1997)) for instance the anticipation of seeing somebody else smiling in response to our own smile. Another possible interpretation of these medial temporal mirror neurons is that in order to have a *perceptual* (or maybe even conceptual) experience of our own actions, we need to invoke the neural activity typically associated with the perception of the actions of other people. This 'broader,' 'non-motor,' notion of mirror neurons also fits well with the only human neuron displaying mirroring properties that has been recorded in previous studies. This neuron in the anterior cingulate cortex seemed to be mirroring pain, rather than actions (Hutchison et al. (1999)).

4.5 Pervasive Mirroring

The empirical findings reported in the studies on mirror neurons in macaques have inspired a large literature on the theoretical implications of these cells. Obviously, mirror neurons have been invoked in support of theories of mindreading and empathy that put simulation processes at center stage (Gordon (1986); Gallese & Goldman (1998); Gordon (2005); Goldman & Sripada (2005); Goldman (2006a)). The human data demonstrating a correlation between activity in mirror neuron areas and the tendency to empathize with others have certainly reinforced this hypothesis. A classical objection to this view is that mirror neurons have properties that seem 'too simple' to account for complex forms of mindreading and empathy, since these cells seem really 'monkey see, monkey do' cells. This objection seems to ignore that two-thirds of mirror neurons in macaques are 'broadly congruent,' that is, they code for actions that achieve the same goal, but are not necessarily identical. Furthermore, the new data in humans show that mirror neurons have more complex and more flexible properties than previously thought. Mirror neurons in humans (and maybe in monkeys too) are also anatomically much more widespread than previously thought. All these combined physiological and anatomical features suggest a very sophisticated neural system that may support complex forms of mindreading and empathizing. Thus, while it has been proposed that mirror neurons and mirroring may be critical for low-level forms of mindreading and empathy, but not for high level forms (Goldman (2006a)), the new data make it entirely plausible that high-level mindreading may also be based on neural mirroring.

Another theoretically important implication of the new findings on mirror neurons in humans is that for the first time we have convincing evidence that mirroring is not a property *exclusive of motor neurons*. Because mirror neurons were discovered in the motor systems, they have been widely interpreted as reflecting the mapping of the actions of others onto the motor repertoire of the self. This interpretation, combined with the dominant tendency to put the self at the center of pretty much everything (at least in the Western world) (Kagitcibasi (1996); Triandis (1995)), led to conceptualize mirroring as a way of connecting with other people by simulating that they are 'another self' (Gallese (2006)), that is, by assimilating the other to the self. However, if neural mirroring occurs in higher-order visual areas (typically activated when we see or remember *other people* involved in their own activities, for instance when they are smiling) while we perform actions we cannot see (for instance when we smile), we must conclude that mirroring is not only simulating others as self. What is this form of mirroring supported by higher-order perceptual areas as the medial temporal cortex? In order to better understand the nature of these temporal mirror neurons we compared the timing of the activation in frontal and temporal mirror neurons. We found that frontal and temporal mirror neurons activate at the same time. This simultaneous co-activation between distant units suggests some form of Hebbian learning (Iacoboni (2009a)). Indeed, the pervasiveness of imitation and other factors (for instance, the pervasive presence of mirrors) may facilitate the coupling of activation in motor cells in the frontal cortex and in visual cells in the medial temporal cortex. When I smile, you smile back to me. The repeated co-occurrence of these two events may shape mirroring properties in both frontal (motor) and temporal (perceptual) units, such that even when I smile all by myself for whatever reason, I evoke the sight of your smile through the firing of neurons in my medial temporal cortex. When the self acts, the self also perceives the other. Self and other become two sides of the same coin. As the two sides of a coin are worthless pieces of metal when separated, self and other also make little sense when separated. Maybe this is why empathy *feels* so powerful. As Montagne wrote: 'Everyone feels its impact, but some are knocked over by it. On me it makes such an intense impression, my practice is rather to avoid it than to resist it...the sight of another's anguish gives me real pain, and my body has often taken over the sensations of some person I am with. A persistent cougher tickles my lungs and my throat.'

If self and other become deeply united in empathy and mindreading, one would predict that people that do not empathize and do not read others' minds, also refuse or resist to read their own mind. Anthropological studies seem to confirm this prediction. A number of Pacific societies behave as if it is impossible to know what goes on in another person's mind. This is called the 'doctrine of the opacity of other minds.' This attitude is amazingly extended to the self too. Indeed, when natives are asked to provide motivations for their own actions, they tend to resist any kind of intentional reading of what they have just done (Duranti).

We empathize effortlessly and automatically with each other because evolution has selected neural systems that blend self and other's actions, intentions, and emotions. The more we learn about neural mechanisms of mirroring, the more we realize that the distinction between self and other may be almost fictitious in many cases. We have created the self–other distinction in our explicit discourse, along with many other constructs that divide us. Our neurobiology, in contrast, puts us 'within each other.' This is a major revision of the long held tradition according to which our biology would lead us only to self preservation but we are able to rise above our biological make up to become 'social.' It is our biology that makes us social and empathic, even though only at implicit, non-propositional level, while our ideas often divide us and sometimes lead us to commit atrocities. Hopefully, the awareness of our neurobiological mechanisms for empathy that is finally reaching the explicit level of understanding ourselves will also change the deliberate, reflective discourse in our society (Iacoboni (2008); (Iacoboni (2007)).[1]

[1] For generous support I wish to thank the Brain Mapping Medical Research Organization, Brain Mapping Support Foundation, Pierson-Lovelace Foundation, The Ahmanson Foundation, William M. and Linda R. Dietel Philanthropic Fund at the Northern Piedmont Community Foundation, Tamkin Foundation, Jennifer Jones-Simon Foundation, Capital Group Companies Charitable Foundation, Robson Family, and Northstar Fund.

5

Empathy, Imitation, and the Social Brain

Jean Decety and Andrew N. Meltzoff

5.1 Introduction

Imitation and empathy have long been studied by developmental and social psychologists. These topics now are hotbeds of interdisciplinary activity and are being influenced by discoveries in cognitive neuroscience, which has begun to delineate the neural circuits that underpin these phenomena. The goal of this chapter is to bring together findings from developmental science and cognitive neuroscience on imitation and empathy.

We place imitation within this larger framework, and it is also proposed to be grounded in shared motor representations between self and other (Meltzoff & Decety (2003)) as well as regulated by executive functions (Decety (2006a)). Moreover, imitation has been theorized to scaffold the child's developing sense of agency, self, and self–other differentiation, which are also phenomenal characteristics involved in empathy. Thus, imitation and empathy are closely linked, but they are not underpinned by the identical neurological process. They are instead partially distinct, though inter-related. Studying the development and neural bases of these two abilities will enhance our understanding of both.

5.2 Infant Imitation and Foundations of Social Understanding and Empathy

Human infants are the most imitative creatures in the world. Although scattered imitation has been documented in other species, *Homo sapiens* imitate a larger range of behaviors than any other species, and they do so spontaneously, without any special training. Within the developmental literature, a good deal has been discovered about the origins and early development of the human capacity to imitate. A selective review of this work is provided below with the goal of assembling research that is relevant to the modern discoveries about the neural mechanisms underpinning imitation and empathy.

5.2.1 Innate imitation

Meltzoff and Moore (1977) discovered that 12- to 21-day-old infants imitated tongue protrusion, mouth opening, lip protrusion, and hand movements. Infants responded differentially to two types of lip movements (mouth opening vs lip protrusion) and two types of protrusion actions (lip protrusion vs tongue protrusion). Other research demonstrated that infants differentiated two different types of tongue movements from one another, namely tongue protrusion that is thrust off-midline (slanted towards the corner of the mouth) versus the more typical tongue protrusion-withdrawal that occurs at midline (Meltzoff & Moore (1994)). Thus the neonatal imitative response is quite specific; it is not a global or a general arousal reaction.

There is also evidence that this early matching cannot be reduced to automatic resonance and is more interesting than may first appear. In one study a pacifier was put in infants' mouths as they watched the display so that they could only observe the adult demonstration but not duplicate the gestures. After the infant observed the display, the adult assumed a passive face pose and only then removed the pacifier. After the pacifier was removed, the infants imitated the earlier displays (Meltzoff & Moore (1977)). Other research documents imitation after the memory delay of 24-hours. Six-week-old infants came in on one day, observed the gestures, and went home. They then returned the next day and observed the person who showed the gestures the day before now sitting motionless with a passive face. Infants successfully imitated based on their memory of the person's now absent motor acts (Meltzoff & Moore (1994)). If the adult had shown mouth opening the day before, the infants initiated that gesture; if the adult had shown tongue protrusion, infants responded with that gesture.

Research also reveals that the response is not rigidly fixed in the form of a 'fixed-action pattern.' Infants correct their imitative attempts so that they more and more closely converge on the model demonstrated. For example, if the adult shows a novel gesture such as tongue-protrusion-to-the-side-of-the-mouth, infants will begin with ordinary tongue protrusions. They use the proprioceptive feedback from their own actions as the basis for guiding their response to the target (Meltzoff & Moore (1997)).

The participants in the previous studies were 2- to 6-weeks old. At first glance this seems young enough to justify philosophical claims about an 'innate behavior.' But perhaps neonates had been conditioned to imitate during the first weeks of life. Perhaps imitation is dependent upon prior mother–infant interaction. To resolve the point, Meltzoff and Moore (1983) tested forty newborns in a hospital setting. The average age of the sample was 32 hours old. The youngest infant was only 42 minutes old. The results showed that the newborns differentially imitated both of the gestures shown to them, mouth opening and tongue protrusion. Nativist claims are, of course, common-place in the philosophical literature, but few tests have been conducted on newborns. You can't get much younger than 42 minutes old. *Homo sapiens* have an innate capacity to imitate. The question now becomes: What psychological and neurological mechanisms underpin this capacity?

5.2.2 The AIM mechanism for early imitation

Meltzoff and Moore proposed that facial imitation is based on 'active intermodal mapping'—the AIM account (Figure 5.1). On this view infants can, at some primitive level, recognize an equivalence between the acts they see others do and the acts they do themselves. This is not a complex mechanism that requires cognitive machinations by the infant. Rather, there appears to be a very primitive and foundational 'body scheme' that allows the infant to unify the seen acts of others and their own felt acts into one common framework. The infant's own facial gestures are invisible to them, but they are monitored by proprioception. Conversely, the adult's acts are not felt by proprioception, but they can be seen. Infants can link observation and execution through what AIM terms a common 'supramodal' coding of human acts. This is why they can correct their imitative movements. And it is why they can imitate from memory: Infants store a representation of the adult's act and it is the target against which they compare their own acts. A detailed description of the metric infants use for establishing the common 'supramodal' framework between self and other is provided elsewhere (Meltzoff & Moore (1997)). The theoretical connections between infant motor imitation and human empathic reactions warrants close attention (see subsequent sections); the discovery of early motor imitation suggests a psychological and philosophical foundation for empathy prior to human language and complex adult thought.

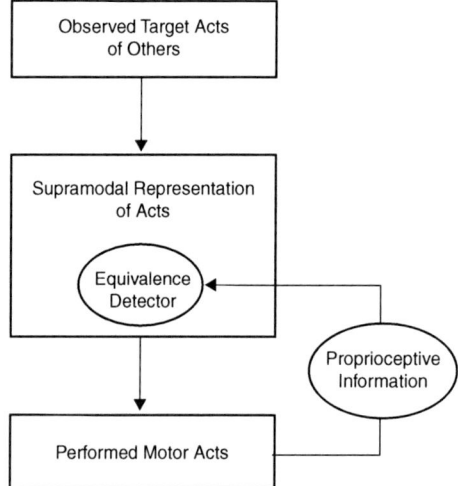

Figure 5.1 The AIM model of imitation. A supramodal representation unites the perception and production of acts within a common act space. The neural underpinnings of this supramodal representation are currently being explored (see subsequent sections of this chapter).

Source: Meltzoff & Moore (1997), with permission.

Meltzoff and Moore's hypothesis of a supramodal framework for actions emerged from developmental studies and fits well with proposals from cognitive science about action coding (the 'common coding' thesis of Prinz (1997, 2002)) and neuroscience discoveries about the mirror neuron system and shared neural circuits (see subsequent discussion in this chapter). The unique contribution from developmental science is that newborn imitation demonstrates that self–other connectedness is functional *at birth* in the human case. Imitation is a marker of innate intersubjectivity in action. At the same time, it must be underscored that newborn humans are different from both monkeys (who exhibit mirror neurons but little imitation), and from human adults. More analytic work is needed to determine whether the current convergences between the AIM hypothesis (on the psychological level), mirror neurons, and shared representations (on the neuroscience level), and other aspects of social understanding (at the philosophical level) are merely surface similarities or more substantive.

5.2.3 The 'Like Me' developmental framework

According to classical developmental theory (Piaget (1954, 1962)), newborn humans are 'solipsistic' and cannot apprehend any equivalences between self and other. The puzzle has always been to describe a developmental theory that could get an infant from such solipsistic beginnings to the empathetic, mindreading adults we see around us.

Instead of Piaget's infant solipsism theory, and based on the modern empirical work in developmental science, Meltzoff (2007a, 2007b) proposed a 'Like-Me' developmental framework for describing the infant's initial state and the early phases of intersubjectivity. The 'Like-Me' developmental framework holds that early imitation and the mechanisms that underlie it allow infants to see the behaviors of others as commensurate with their own and that this action coding in turn provides the groundwork for other developments in empathy and the grasp of other minds. The 'Like-Me' developmental framework has three steps which occur during the infancy period, prior to language (Figure 5.2). It describes the infant's innate state (step 1) and also provides an engine for change in interpersonal understanding (steps 2 and 3). The older child and adult are not locked into the same understanding of others as the newborn.

Step 1: Action representation. The first step in Meltzoff's developmental-psychological model is based on the innate equipment infants bring to interpersonal encounters. Newborn imitation provides evidence that the perception and production of acts are tightly bound in human beings. Meltzoff & Moore (1997) proposed that imitation is mediated by a 'supramodal' action representation that enables commensurate coding of acts seen and acts done (for neuroscience underpinnings, see subsequent sections of this chapter). This does not mean that the infant yet has a full blown sense of self, which surely undergoes developmental change. Rather, it suggests that there is an innate capacity to connect actions produced by the self and observed in others. This fundamental interpersonal connection is not a learned 'association,' nor acquired by looking

Action representation
Intrinsic connection between the perception and
production of acts as embodied by infant imitation

First person experience
Infants experience the regular relationship between their
own acts and underlying mental states

Understanding other minds
Others who act 'like me' have internal states 'like me'

Figure 5.2 'Like Me' developmental framework: First steps for getting empathy and perspective-taking off the ground.

Source: Meltzoff (2007b), with permission.

in the mirror. Based on the supramodal representation of action, the acts of self and other can be recognized to be equivalent from birth onwards, and this rich innate groundwork supports further development of the intersubjectivity based on infants' own particular action experience and interaction with other social agents (see Meltzoff (2007a) and below).

Step 2: First-person experience. The second step provides an engine for developmental change. Through everyday experience infants map the relation between their own bodily states and mental experiences. For example, there is an intimate relation between striving to achieve a goal and a concomitant facial expression and effortful bodily acts. Infants experience their own unfulfilled desires and the simultaneous facial/ postural behavior that accompany such states. These first-person experiences contribute to a detailed bidirectional map linking internal states and behavior. It is crucial for philosophical theories to realize that all of this can happen prior to language.

Step 3: Understanding other intentional agents 'like me'. The third step involves attribution (Meltzoff & Brooks (2008)). When infants see others acting similarly to how they have acted in the past, they ascribe the internal state that regularly goes with that behavior. There is new empirical evidence that this occurs pre-verbally, without complex reasoning (Meltzoff & Brooks (2008)).Infants' first-person experiences could not be used in this way if they did not perceive an equivalence between their own acts and those of others (step 1). Nor would it get very far if there was no systematic link between their own internal states and bodily acts (step 2). Humans, including pre-verbal infants, imbue the acts of others with felt meaning not solely (or at first) through a formal process of step-by-step reasoning, but because the other is processed as 'like me,' as manifest by early facial imitation. This is underwritten by the way infants represent action—the supramodal action code—and self experience.

Through pre-verbal interaction with other intentional agents who are viewed as 'like me,' infants develop a richer grasp of intersubjectivity and empathy for others (Meltzoff & Brooks (2008)).

Of course, philosophers have long discussed whether an analogy between self and other plays a role in our treatment of others as intentional agents. Empathy, perspective-taking, and several varieties of putting yourself in someone else's shoes emotionally seem to depend on this. A problem for philosophers has traditionally been that this self–other connection was thought to be a late achievement and perhaps dependent on language, and therefore thought not to play a formative role during the pre-verbal period of human development. Few philosophers, prior to the discovery of newborn imitation, took infant behavior as input into theories of human empathy. The modern findings from developmental science show that infants already register the equivalence between acts of self and other. It is not a derived, complex, or cognitively advanced analysis of the world. It is an innate relation to others, and must be taken seriously in our psychological and philosophical accounts of the origins of empathy.

Newborn imitation indicates that, at some level of processing no matter how primitive, infants can map actions of other people onto actions of their own body. Because human acts are seen in others and performed by the self, the infant can grasp that interpersonal connection: You can act 'like me' and I can act 'like you'—Meltzoff's (2007a) 'Like Me' bridge. This self–other equivalence provides a privileged access to people not afforded by things. It provides a groundwork for sharing and communication that goes beyond the perceived movements per se. As we will see in subsequent sections of this chapter, this basic self–other connection, empirically demonstrated in pre-verbal humans, has implications for how we conceptualize the roots of human empathy.

5.2.4 Top-down control and regulation of imitation

Imitation is also connected to empathy in deeper ways as well. Adults do not blindly and automatically imitate everything they see. If they did, it would cause chaos in normal social interaction. Instead, adults regulate their behavior and choose when to copy others. Developmental scientists have recently investigated some of the factors that regulate imitation by children. The results are intriguing, because they reveal the origins of the inhibitory control of behavior that will become important in more mature imitation and empathy for others in adults (see discussion below). In this section we review recent work on the regulation of imitation based on: (a) the perceived goals of the model, (b) the emotional consequences of the act, and (c) the prior motor experience of the child.

Goals and Intentions. In the mature adult social cognition, other people not only motorically act 'like me,' they also are understood to have other mental states, including beliefs, emotions, and intentions. When do pre-verbal infants begin to ascribe intentionality to human movement patterns? The behavioral re-enactment procedure was designed to provide a non-verbal technique for exploring intention reading in pre-verbal creatures (Meltzoff (1995)). The procedure capitalizes on children's natural tendency to re-enact or imitate, but uses it in a more abstract way to investigate whether infants can read below the literal surface behavior to the goals or intentions of the actor.

The experimental procedure involves showing infants an unsuccessful act. For example, the adult accidentally under- or overshoots his target, or he tries to pull apart a dumb-bell-shaped toy but his hand slips off the ends and he is unsuccessful. Thus the goal-state is not achieved. To an adult, it is easy to read the actor's intentions although he never fulfills them. The experimental question is whether children read through the literal body movements to the underlying goal or intention of the act. The measure of how they interpreted the event is what they choose to re-enact, in particular whether they choose to ignore what the adult literally did and instead produce the intended act despite the fact that it was never present to the senses. In a sense, the correct answer is to not copy the literal movement, but the intended act that remains unfulfilled and invisible.

Meltzoff (1995) showed 18-month-old infants an unsuccessful act, a failed effort. The study compared infants' tendency to perform the target act in several situations: (a) after they saw the full-target act demonstrated, (b) after they saw the unsuccessful attempt to perform the act, and (c) after it was neither shown nor attempted. The results showed that 18-month-olds can infer the unseen goals implied by unsuccessful attempts. Infants who saw the unsuccessful attempt and infants who saw the full-target act both produced target acts at a significantly higher rate than controls. Evidently, toddlers can understand our goals even if we fail to fulfill them.

In the adult framework, people act intentionally but inanimate things do not. To begin to examine this question of the ascription of intentionality, Meltzoff (1995) also tested how 18-month-olds responded to a mechanical device that mimicked the same movements as the actor in the unsuccessful-attempt condition. An inanimate device was constructed that had poles for arms and mechanical pincers for hands. It did not look human but it could move very similarly to a human. For the test, the pincers 'grasped' the dumb-bell at the two ends just as the human hands did. One mechanical arm was then moved outwards, just as in the human case, and its pincer slipped off the end of the dumb-bell just as the human hand did. The movement patterns of machine and man were closely matched from a purely spatio-temporal description of movements in space.

The experimental results showed that infants did not attribute a goal or intention to the movements of the inanimate device. Although they were not frightened by the device and looked at it as long as at the human display, they did not see the sequence of actions as implying a goal. Infants were no more (or less) likely to pull apart the toy after seeing the unsuccessful attempt of the inanimate device than in baseline conditions when they saw nothing. Another study pursued this point. In this study the inanimate device succeeded. The inanimate device held the dumb-bell from the two ends and successfully pulled it apart. When infants were given the dumb-bell, they too pulled it apart.

It thus appears that infants can pick up certain information from the inanimate device (they pull it apart after seeing the device do so), but they cannot pick up other information (concerning unsuccessful attempts).

By 18 months of age children have already adopted a fundamental aspect of a mature common-sense psychology—persons are understood within a framework involving goals and intentions. Just as importantly, the work shows that children did not slavishly imitate the unsuccessful motion by letting their fingers slip from the object, but instead completed the intended goal. Even though they had never seen the completed act, the children inferred the goal of the act from his try-and-try again behavior. This and other related work strongly suggests that infants can interpret what the adult is trying to do. They re-enact the goal of the act, not what was literally done.

Emotions and Attention. Recent work shows that 18-month-old infants regulate their imitation based on another person's *emotional reaction* to the act (Repacholi & Meltzoff (2007); Repacholi, Meltzoff, & Olsen (2008)). An adult model performed a series of novel acts on objects and an adult bystander either became angry at these 'forbidden acts' or remained pleasantly interested in what the model was doing. After this emotional reaction, the emoter adopted a neutral face. The infant watched this interaction between the two adults, and the question was whether infants regulated their subsequent imitation based on the emoter's reaction. A second factor that was manipulated was whether the emoter was *looking at* the toddler when the infant was given a chance to imitate. The experimental manipulations included: (a) the emoter left the room, (b) the emoter was present but had her back turned so she could not watch the infant's response, (c) the emoter was facing the infant but had her eyes closed, and (d) the emoter watched the infant's response.

The empirical results showed that if the adult had not exhibited anger at the action, the infants imitated at high levels regardless of whether or not the emoter could see them. But if the emoter had previously become angry at seeing the act, then the infants were significantly less likely to imitate the act but only when the previously angry emoter was watching them. The infants' imitated if the previously angry adult left the room, or had her back turned, or had her eyes closed, and presumably could not monitor the infant's behavior.

These effects cannot be explained simply by emotional contagion. Infants are subject to contagion, but the interesting point is that even during the pre-verbal period, their intersubjectivity is based on more than this. The infants in this study had the chance to 'catch' the adult's emotion equally well in all groups. Instead the toddlers' were regulating their imitation based on the conjunction of two factors: (a) whether the bystander had a negative reaction to the act *and* (b) whether the bystander was watching what the infant did. Evidently, infants regulate their imitative response based on the emotional reactions that others have to the target act and whether the emoter can monitor their imitative reactions or not. Infants realize that they can be a target of other people's perception and will not imitate an action when the emoter is watching them produce those actions. Imitation is thus not automatic and inflexible by

18 months of age. Instead, infants can self-regulate and actively choose when to imitate—the emotions and attention of others play a role.

Prior Motor Experience and Perceived Efficacy of the Model. Other recent studies have taken the self-regulation aspect of imitation a step further and show that young children are highly selective in choosing who, what, and when to imitate. In one series of studies 36-month-old children were tested to see if they were more open to imitating another person's technique if the child had a prior motor experience himself showing that the task was difficult to solve (Williamson, Meltzoff, & Markman (2008)). Children were randomly assigned to two independent groups. One group had an "easy experience" and the other a "difficult experience" in achieving an outcome, such as opening a drawer to retrieve an object. For the "easy" group the drawer easily slid open when the child tried to do so; for the "difficult" group the drawer was surreptitiously held shut by a resistance device. Then the model demonstrated a distinctive technique for opening the drawer. The same distinctive technique was demonstrated to both groups. The results showed that children were significantly more likely to imitate after having difficulty with the task. In a related study, children watched a model who demonstrated a particular technique, but for half the children the technique led to success and the other it led to the model's failure. The results showed that children took the model's causal efficacy into account and selectively chose to imitate the actions only when they led to success and not failure.

Across these studies, it is theoretically significant that preschoolers are actively balancing two streams of information—their own actions and the actions that they see another person perform. Future research will focus on the commensurability of these two streams and how children can learn and combine information from self and other. Taken together, this research suggests that infants and young children are not automatic, rigid imitators, but rather choose who, what, and when to imitate.

So far we have shown both the close coupling between perception and action that underlies imitation and also the fact that young children can regulate their imitation and behavior. As we will see, these two factors also play an important role in neuroscientific views of empathy (for further discussion relating imitation, the problem of other minds, and social learning, see Meltzoff, Kuhl, Movellan, & Sejnowski (2009)).

5.3 Linking to Empathy: A Neuroscience View

Like imitation, empathy is a complex term with various definitions in the literature. Broadly construed, empathy has been defined as an affective response stemming from the understanding of another's emotional state or condition similar to what the other person is feeling or would be expected to feel in the given situation, without confusion between self and other (Decety & Meyer (2008); Eisenberg, Shea, Carlo, & Knight (1991)). In line with this conception, empathy is an interaction between two individuals, with one experiencing and sharing the feeling of the other.

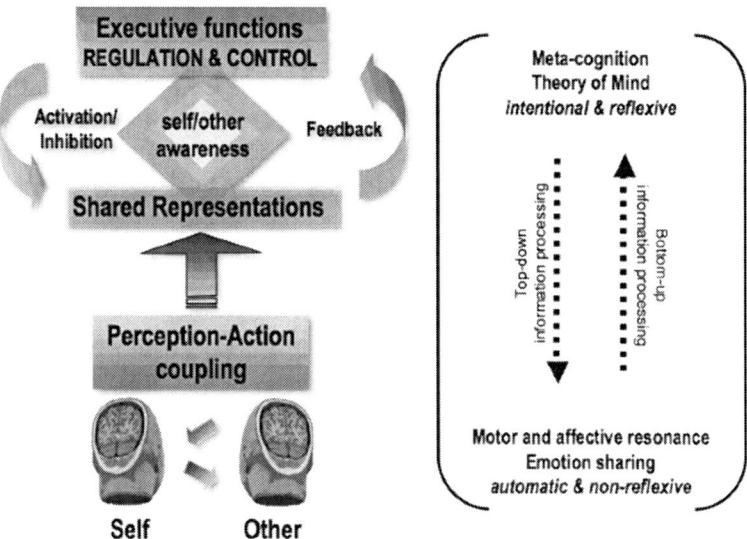

Figure 5.3 Schematic representation of the mechanisms underpinning the experience of empathy. Two dimensions interact: (1) bottom-up (i.e. matching between perception and action), and (2) top-down (i.e. regulation and control) information processing. The bottom-up processing level, which is rapidly activated (unless inhibited) by perceptual input, accounts for emotion sharing and the implicit recognition that others are like us. This aspect functions soon after birth (see also Figure 5.2). The top-down level, which overlaps with the notion of executive control is implemented in the prefrontal cortex, and develops gradually during early childhood. Executive control regulates both cognition and emotion, notably through selective attention and self-regulation. This meta-level is continuously updated by bottom-up information, and in return controls the lower level by providing top-down input. Thus, top-down regulation, through executive functions, modulates low levels and adds flexibility, allowing the individual to be less dependent on external cues. The meta-cognitive feedback plays a crucial role in taking into account one's own mental states in order to react (or not) to the affective states of others. Self–other awareness is an important aspect of this model. The computational mechanism of self–other distinction is crucial for the higher-level cognitive processing involved in social cognition such as empathy and theory of mind. Both empathy and theory of mind involves an ability to simultaneously distinguish between different possible perspectives on the same situation.

Source: Decety (2006b); Decety & Lamm (2006); Decety & Meyer (2008); with permission.

In the following sections we discuss the affective and cognitive components of empathy, reviewing first the automatic proclivity to share emotions with others, and the cognitive process of perspective-taking and executive control, which allow individuals to be aware of their intentions and feelings and keep separate self and other perspectives. We examine empathy within an overarching conceptual framework. This framework considers that empathy involves parallel and distributed processing in a number of dissociable computational mechanisms (see Figure 5.3). Shared neural circuits, self-awareness, mental flexibility, and emotion regulation constitute the basic macro-components of empathy, which are mediated by specific neural systems, including aspects of the prefrontal cortex, the anterior insula, and fronto-parietal networks. This model assumes that dysfunction in any of these macro-components may lead to an alteration of empathic behavior, and produce selective social disorders depending on which aspect is disrupted.

It should be noted that the experience of empathy does not necessarily entail imitation. Imitation can be viewed as a stepping stone in the *development* of empathy and not a sole cause or explanation. It is interesting that full-blown empathic experience does not mature until 2–4 years of age, a time in which executive functions develop rapidly. However, the initial building block of empathy is emotion sharing, which can be observed earlier in infancy. Moreover, emotion sharing itself is closely related to the perceptual-action mapping manifest in early motor imitation. More complex imitation, which involves intentional and conscious behavior matching as well as the regulation of imitation based on top-down inhibitory control, is theoretically tied to developing a sense of agency. Agency plays a role in empathy, as it facilitates knowing whose actions and emotions belongs to whom and keeps individuals from over-identifying with the observed target which would otherwise lead to empathic distress. Thus imitation and empathy are intimately intertwined. If emotion sharing fails to take place, disorders are implicated, specifically individuals with autism spectrum disorder (ASD) and psychopaths (which clearly are very different populations with different etiologies).

5.4 Emotion Sharing

5.4.1 *The automaticity of emotion sharing*

A basic building block of empathy is emotion sharing, and this process is facilitated by motor mimicry, i.e. a form of unconscious mirroring of the other person's behavior. Bodily expressions help humans and other animals communicate various types of information to members of their species.

Emotional expression not only informs an individual of another's subjective (and physiological) experience, but also serves as a sort of social glue maintaining emotional reciprocity among dyads and groups. Emotional contagion, defined as the tendency to rapidly mimic and synchronize facial expressions, vocalizations, postures, and movements with those of another person and, consequently converge emotionally with the other (Hatfield (2009); Hatfield, Cacioppo, & Rapson (1993)) is a social phenomenon of shared emotional expression that often occurs at a basic level outside of conscious awareness.

5.4.2 *Infant emotion sharing*

In classic developmental work, Meltzoff and Moore (1977, 1997) showed that infants less than one hour old mimic human actions. The findings suggest that infants enter the world with an innate sociability, grounded in action-perception coupling. Such imitative behaviors led Trevarthen (1979) to propose that infants are endowed with an innate 'primary subjectivity.' That is, infants have access to others' emotional states via perceiving the other person's actions and facial gestures. Indeed subsequent research showed that young infants can match emotion expressions of others (e.g. Field, Woodson, Greenberg, & Cohen (1982)) and engage with other people and with the actions and feelings expressed through other people's bodies (e.g. Hobson (2002)). These imitative and reciprocal bodily exchanges are critical for many facets of social functioning. For example, they facilitate attachment by regulating one's own emotions and providing information about the other's emotional state. These reciprocal gestural interactions also constitute a primary source of interpersonal engagement with others, what has been termed primary intersubjectivity (e.g. Gallagher & Meltzoff (1996)).

5.4.3 Perception-action coupling mechanism

The intrinsic mapping between self and other that was first discovered in the developmental literature is also supported by considerable empirical literature in cognitive psychology. For example, common coding theories claim that somewhere in the chain of operation that leads from perception to action, the system generates certain derivatives of stimulation and certain antecedents of action that are commensurate in the sense that they share the same system of representational dimensions (e.g. Prinz (2002, 2005)). The core assumption of the common coding theory is that actions are coded in terms of the perceivable effects (i.e. the distal perceptual events) they should generate. Performing a movement leaves behind a bidirectional association between the motor pattern it was generated by and the sensory effects that it produces. Such an association can then be used backwards to retrieve a movement by anticipating its effects (Hommel, Müsseler, Aschersleben, & Prinz (2001)).

Perception/action codes are also accessible during action observation, and perception activates action representations to the degree that the perceived and the represented actions are similar, as we saw in the case of infant imitation. Such a mechanism has also been proposed to account for emotion sharing and its contribution to the experience of empathy (Preston & de Waal (2002)). In the context of emotion processing, it is posited that perception of emotion activates in the observer the neural mechanisms that are responsible for the generation of similar emotion. It should be noted that a similar mechanism was previously proposed to account for emotion contagion. Indeed, Hatfield, Cacioppo & Rapson (1994) argued that people catch the emotions of others as a result of afferent feedback generated by elementary motor mimicry of others' expressive behavior, which produces a simultaneous matching emotional experience (see also, Meltzoff & Moore (1995)).

The motor imitation involved in emotion contagion is supported by research using measures of facial electromyography (EMG). In one study, participants were exposed very briefly (56 ms) to pictures of happy or angry facial expressions while EMG was recoded from their facial muscles (Sonnby-Borgstrom, Jonson, & Svenson (2003)).

Results demonstrate facial mimicry despite the fact that the participants were unaware of the stimuli. Furthermore, this effect was stronger for the participants who scored higher on self-reports of empathy.

Another study by Niedenthal, Brauer, Halberstadt, & Innes-Ker (2001) indicates that facial mimicry plays an imperative role in the processing of emotional expression. Participants watched one facial expression morph into another, and were asked to detect when the expression changed. Some participants were free to mimic the expressions, whereas others were prevented from imitating by holding a pencil laterally between their lips and teeth. Participants that were free to mimic detected the changes in emotional expression earlier and more efficiently for any facial expression than did participants who were prevented from imitating the expressions.

In neuroscience, some related evidence for perception/action coupling comes from electrophysiological recordings in monkeys. Neurons with sensorimotor properties, known as mirror neurons, were identified in the ventral premotor and posterior parietal cortices. These mirror neurons fire both during goal-directed actions and observation of the same actions performed by another individual. Most mirror neurons show a clear congruence between the visual actions they respond to and the motor response they code (Rizzolatti, Fogassi, & Gallese (2001)). These neurons are part of a circuit that reciprocally connect the posterior superior temporal gyrus (in which neurons respond to the sight of actions made by others), the posterior parietal cortex, and the ventral premotor cortex.

A mirror neuron system also seems to exist in humans. Numerous functional neuroimaging experiments indicate that the neural circuits involved in action representation (in the posterior parietal and premotor cortices) overlap with those activated when actions are observed (see Jackson & Decety (2004) for a review). In addition, a number of neuroimaging studies have also shown that a similar neural network is reliably activated during imagining of one's own action, imagining another's action, and imitating actions performed by a model (Decety & Grèzes (2006)). Notably, an fMRI study found similar areas engaged when individuals observe or imitate emotional facial expressions. Within this network, there was greater activity during imitation, compared with observation of emotions, in premotor areas including the inferior frontal cortex, as well as in the superior temporal cortex, insula, and amygdala (Carr, Iacoboni, Dubeau, Mazziotta, & Lenzi (2003)). Such shared circuits reflect an automatic transformation of other people's behavior (actions or emotions) into the neural representation of one's own behavior, and provides a functional bridge between first- and third-person perspectives, culminating in empathic experience (Decety & Sommerville (2003); Meltzoff (2007a)).

Recently, a growing number of functional neuroimaging studies have demonstrated striking similarities in the neural circuits involved in the processing of both the first-hand experience of pain and the second-hand experience of observing other individuals in pain (see Jackson, Rainville, & Decety (2006) for a review). For instance, Decety, Michalska and Akitsuki (2008) scanned typically developing children (range

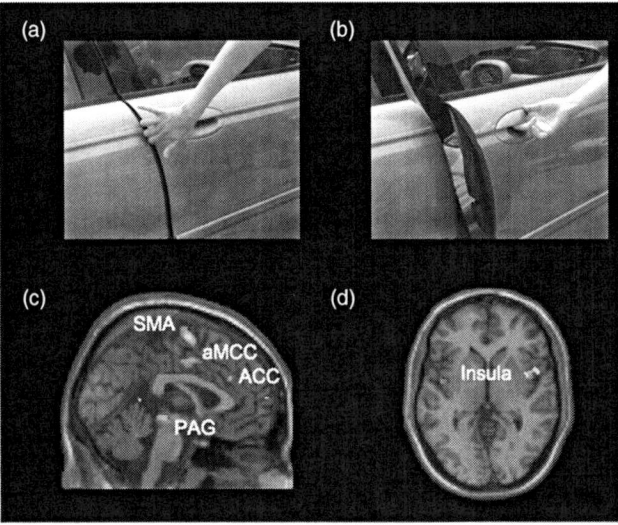

Figure 5.4 When children attend to other people accidentally in pain (A) versus no pain (B), the neuro-hemodynamic signal increases in neural regions that belong to the pain matrix, including the anterior midcingulate cortex (aMCC), anterior cingulate cortex (ACC) supplementary motor area (SMA), periaqueductal gray (PAG) (C) and middle insula (D). The somatosensory cortex was also bilaterally activated, result not shown.

Source: Adapted from Decety, Michalska, & Akitsuki (2008), with permission.

7–12 years) while presented with short animated visual stimuli depicting painful and non-painful bodily situations. The perception of other people in pain in children was associated with increased hemodynamic activity in the neural circuits involved in the processing of first-hand experience of pain, including the insula, somatosensory cortex, anterior midcingulate cortex, periaqueductal gray, and supplementary motor area (see Figure 5.4). This basic somatic sensorimotor resonance plays a critical role in the primitive building block of empathy and moral reasoning that relies on the sharing of other's distress.

5.4.4 Evidence that social deficits can be tied to poor perception-action coupling

An effective means to measure the role of perception-action coupling in emotion sharing is via EMG recording of the activation of specific facial muscles in response to viewing other people's facial expressions. Facial mimicry has been defined narrowly as the congruent facial reactions to the emotional facial displays of others, and is thus an expressive component (Hess & Blairy (2001)). Emotion contagion is an affective state that matches the other's emotional display. Thus, facial mimicry can be conceived of as a physical manifestation of emotion contagion, and it occurs at an automatic level in response to viewing others' emotions (Bush, Barr, McHugo, & Lanzetta (1989)).

Individuals with ASD are often reported to lack automatic mimicry of facial expressions. A recent study measured adolescent and adult ASD individuals and controls' automatic and voluntary mimicry of emotional facial expressions via electromyography (EMG) recordings of the cheek and brow muscle regions while participants viewed still photographs of happy, angry, and neutral facial expressions (McIntosh, Reichmann-Decker, Winkelman, & Wilbarger (2006)). The cheek and brow muscles of individuals with ASD failed to activate in response to the videos, indicating that they did not automatically mimic the facial expressions, while the muscles of the normally developing controls showed activation. In attempt to examine a potential link between neural dysfunction and developmental delay of social cognitive skills, one fMRI study found a lack of activation in the inferior frontal gyrus (a key part of the mirror neuron system) in children with ASD as compared to controls during the observation and imitation of basic facial emotion expression (Dapretto et al. (2006)). Difficulties in mimicking other people's emotional expression may prevent individuals with ASD from the afferent feedback that informs them of what others are feeling (Rogers (1999)).

The shared neural representations account in neuroscience, coupled with Meltzoff's (2007a) 'Like-Me' developmental theory, both converge in suggesting that problems with one's perceptual-motor coding or body-schema system may undermine capacities for understanding others. Consequently, it is possible that developmental problems involving sensory-motor processes may have an effect on the capabilities that are crucial for 'primary intersubjectivity,' or the ability to react contingently to others' emotional expressions (Meltzof (2007a); Trevarthen & Aitken (2001)) and therefore the child's ability to resonate emotionally with others. It thus seems plausible that the defects in social and sensory-motor problems in individuals ASD may in part reflect a disturbed motor representation matching system at the neuronal level. This speculation not only helps account for problems in primary intersubjectivity, but also the other sensory-motor symptoms of autism: oversensitivity to stimuli, repetitious and odd movements, and possibly, echolalia.

5.5 Self–Other Awareness and Agency: Mediating Whose Emotions Belong to Whom

The fact that the observation of an emotion elicits the activation of analogous motor representation in the observer, raises the question why there is not complete overlap between internally generated and externally engendered motor representations. It has been speculated that practice with intentional imitation may help infants explore who performs a given action and who is observing, and accordingly, who is the entertainer of a given subjective state and who is an observer (Meltzoff & Moore (1995)). In this way, childhood imitation may bring to conscious awareness what has been termed a sense of 'agency.' Research in the neuroscience and developmental science use the term agency to describe the ability to recognize oneself as the agent of an action, thought, or desire, which is crucial for attributing a behavior to its proper agent (Decety & Chaminade (2003)). Children who are intentionally imitated notice that their actions are being replicated by the other. Through this process, children grasp a sense that the 'other' is an intentional, goal-directed agent like the self, but whose actions are dissociable from one's own, though easily replicated (Meltzoff (2007a)).

This agentive capacity is critical for empathy: in a complete empathic experience, affective sharing must be modulated and monitored by the sense of whose feelings belong to whom (Decety & Jackson (2004)). Further, self-awareness generally and agency in particular are crucial aspects in promoting a selfless regard for the other rather than a selfish desire to escape aversive arousal (Batson, Sager, Garst, Kang, Rubchinsky, & Dawson (1997)).

In sum, the studies reviewed indicate that in addition to perception-action coupling and emotional responsivity being basic building blocks in infancy, a sense of self, agency, and self-other distinctions emerge early in the preverbal period (see also Rochat & Striano (2000)). If infants or adults were restricted only to perceiving others as 'like me,' and nothing more (and we have argued that infants and young children do more than this, see Meltzoff & Moore (1995)), this could potentially be detrimental for the altruistic function of empathy—self–other merging causes personal distress, not pro-social helping behavior (e.g. Decety & Lamm (2009); Lamm, Batson, & Decety (2007)). A sense of agency, however, helps children discriminate self-produced actions from other-produced actions. Importantly, the development of agency in children is bolstered by the emergence of intentional imitation.

5.5.1 Cognitive neuroscience of self–other awareness and agency

One role that cognitive neuroscience can contribute to the study of the self and other is to help conceptually define the distinct dimensions, aspects, and characteristics of the self and other to help address the potential separability or relatedness of each compo-nent part of self-processing. It has been proposed that non-overlapping parts of the neural circuit mediating shared representations (i.e. the areas that are activated for self-processing and not for other-processing) generate a specific signal for each form of representation (Jeannerod (1999)). This set of signals involved in the comparison between self-generated actions and actions observed from others ultimately allow the attribution of agency. It has also been suggested that the dynamics of neural activation with the shared cortical network is an important aspect in distinguishing one's own actions from the actions of others (Decety & Jackson (2004); Decety & Grèzes (2006); Jackson, Meltzoff, & Decety (2006)). Furthermore, the fact that the onset of the hemodynamic signal is earlier for the self than for others in a variety of tests (e.g. Jackson, Brunet, Meltzoff, & Decety (2006)) can be considered as a neural signature of the privileged and readily accessible self-perspective.

Accumulating evidence from neuroimaging studies in both healthy individuals and psychiatric populations, as well as lesion studies in neurological patients, indicates that the right inferior parietal cortex, at the junction with the posterior temporal cortex (also called the temporoparietal junction TPJ), plays a critical role in the distinction between self-produced actions and actions generated by others (e.g. Decety, Chaminade, Grèzes, & Meltzoff (2002); Jackson & Decety (2004)). The TPJ is a hetero-modal association cortex, which integrates input from the lateral and posterior thalamus, as well as visual, auditory, somesthetic, and limbic areas. It has reciprocal connections to the prefrontal cortex and to the temporal lobes. Because of these anatomical characteristics, this region is a key neural locus for self-processing that is involved in multi-sensory body-related information processing, as well as in the processing of phenomenological and cognitive aspects of the self (Blanke & Arzy (2005)). Its lesion can produce a variety of disorders associated with body knowledge and self-awareness such as anosognosia, asomatognosia, or somatoparaphrenia. For instance, Blanke, Ortigue, Landis, & Seeck (2002) demonstrated that out-of-body experiences (i.e. the experience of dissociation of self from body) can be induced by electrical stimulation of the right TPJ.

In addition, a number of functional imaging studies point out the involvement of the right inferior parietal lobule in the process of agency. Attribution of action to another agent has been associated with specific increased activity in the right inferior parietal lobe. In one fMRI study, Farrer & Frith (2002) instructed participants to use a joystick to drive a circle along a T-shaped path. They were told that the circle would be driven either by themselves or by the experimenter. In the former case, subjects were requested to drive the circle, to be aware that they drove the circle, and thus to mentally attribute the action seen on the screen to themselves. In the latter case, they were also requested to perform the task, but they were aware that the experimenter drove the action seen on the screen. The results showed that being aware of causing an action was associated with activation in the anterior insula, whereas being aware of not causing the action and attributing it to another person was associated with activation in the right inferior parietal cortex.

Interestingly, individuals experiencing incorrect agency judgments feel that some outside force is creating their own actions. One neuroimaging study found hyperactivity in the right inferior parietal lobule when patients with schizophrenia experienced alien control during a movement selection task (Spence et al. (1997)). Delusions of control may arise because of a disconnection between frontal brain regions, where actions are initiated, and parietal regions where the current and predicted states of limbs are represented.

Another study used a device that allowed modifying the participant's degree of control of the movements of a virtual hand presented on a screen (Farrer et al. (2003)). Experimental conditions varied to the degree of distortion of the visual feedback provided to the participants about their own movements. Results demonstrated a graded hemodynamic activity of the right inferior parietal lobule that parallels the degree of mismatch between the executed movements and the visual reafference. Strikingly, such a pattern of neural response was not detected in schizophrenic individuals who were scanned under the same procedure (Farrer et al. (2004)). Instead, an aberrant relationship between the subject's degree of control of the movements and the hemodymamic activity was found in the right inferior parietal cortex and no modulation in the insular cortex.

The right inferior parietal cortex is also found to be activated when participants mentally simulated actions from someone else's perspective but not from their own (Ruby & Decety (2001)). Similarly, this region was specifically involved when participants imagined how another person would feel in everyday life situations that elicit social emotions (Ruby & Decety (2004)) or painful experiences (e.g. Jackson et al. (2006); Lamm, Batson, & Decety (2007)) but not when they imagined these situations for themselves. Such findings point to the similarity of the neural mechanisms that account for the correct attribution of actions, emotions, pain, and thoughts to their respective agents when one mentally simulates actions for oneself or for another individual.

Some researchers have suggested that right TPJ selectively subserves the attribution of beliefs to other people (e.g. Saxe & Kanwisher (2003)). However, the fact that the TPJ is necessary for the perception of intentionality does not mean that this region is specific to that function (Stone & Gerrans (2006)). Recently, Decety, & Lamm (2007) conducted a meta-analysis of 70 functional neuroimaging studies that reported right TPJ activation in various cognitive tasks, including theory of mind, empathy, perception of agency, and attention-reorienting. Based on the results of this meta-analysis, and the overlap in activation, the authors proposed that the contribution of the right TPJ to social cognition—as seen in theory of mind or empathy tasks—relies on a low-level computational mechanism involved in attention reorientation and generating, testing, and correcting internal predictions about external sensory events (Decety & Lamm (2007)). This mechanism is necessary for the perception of agency, and precedes meta-cognitive abilities such as reading intentions and theory of mind. Based on evidence from electrophysiological recordings in monkeys as well as psychophysics and functional neuroimaging studies in humans, Corbetta and Shulman (2002) proposed that the right TPJ plays a critical function to direct attention to behaviorally relevant sensory stimuli. Additional support for the function of the TPJ was recently provided by an fMRI study that demonstrated that theory of mind and attention-reorienting tasks are associated with similar activation sites in the TPJ (Mitchell (2008)).

5.6 Empathy Demands Top-Down Regulation of First-Person Perspective

Given the sharedness of the representations of one's own emotional states and others, as well as similarities in brain circuits during first- and third-person perspective-taking, it would seem difficult not to experience emotional distress while viewing another's distressed state—and personal distress does not contribute to the empathic process

(Batson et al. (2003); Decey & Lamm (2009)). Indeed, distress in the self would hinder one's inclination to soothe.

Adopting another's perspective, which is a higher-order cognitive task that relies on executive functions, is integral to human empathy and is linked to the development of moral reasoning (Kohlberg (1976)), altruism (Batson (1991)), and a decreased likelihood of interpersonal aggression (Eisenberg, Spinrad, & Sadovsky (2006)).

Perspective-taking is truly a daunting human feat, and is more difficult than one may assume. Regulating personal self-knowledge poses particular difficulty for both human children and adults. A cognitive neuroscience study demonstrated the primacy of the self-perspective. Jackson, Meltzoff, & Decety (2006) asked participants to adopt either a first-person perspective or third-person perspective while imitating observed actions. Structures related to motor representations recruited greater activation, including the somatosensory cortex, during the first-person perspective compared to the third-person perspective, thus implying the immediacy of the first-person experience over that of the third-person perspective.

5.6.1 Perspective-taking induces empathic concern

Of special interest are findings from social psychology that document the distinction between imagining the other and imagining oneself (Batson, Early, & Salvarini (1997)). These studies show that the former may evoke empathic concern (defined as an other-oriented response congruent with the perceived distress of the person in need), while the latter induces both empathic concern and personal distress (i.e. a self-oriented aversive emotional response such as anxiety or discomfort). This observation may help explain why empathy, or sharing someone else's emotion, need not yield pro-social behavior. If perceiving another person in an emotionally or physically painful circumstance elicits personal distress, then the observer may not fully attend to the other's experience and as a result lack sympathetic behaviors.

The role of perspective-taking in generating empathic concern was originally documented in a study conducted by Stotland (1969). In his experiment, participants viewed an individual whose hand was strapped in a machine that participants were told generated painful heat. One group of subjects were instructed to watch the target person carefully, another group of participants were instructed to imagine the way the target felt, and the third group was instructed to imagine themselves in the target's situation. Physiological (palm sweating and vasoconstriction) and verbal assessments of empathy demonstrated that the deliberate acts of imagination yielded a greater response than passive viewing. Empathy seems to be sensitive to perspective-taking, as demonstrated by a series of studies demonstrating the effectiveness of perspective-taking instructions in inducing empathy (Batson et al. (1997)) and that empathy-inducing conditions do not compromise the distinction between the self and other (Batson, et al. (1997), but see Cialdini, Brown, Lewis, Luce, & Neuberg (1997) for a different account of empathy and self-other merging).

A recent functional MRI study by Lamm, Batson, & Decety (2007) investigated the distinction between empathic concern and personal distress combining a number of behavioral measures and event-related fMRI. Participants were asked to watch a series of video-clips featuring patients undergoing painful medical treatment either with the instruction to put themselves explicitly in the shoes of the patient ('imagine self'), or, in another condition, to focus their attention on the feelings and reactions of the patient ('imagine other'). Behavioral measures confirmed previous social psychology findings that projecting oneself into an aversive situation leads to higher personal distress and lower empathic concern—while focusing on the emotional and behavioral reactions of another's plight is accompanied by higher empathic concern and lower personal distress. Neuroimaging data were consistent with such findings. The self-perspective evoked stronger hemodynamic responses in brain regions involved in coding the motivational-affective dimensions of pain, including bilateral insular cortices and anterior medial cingulate cortex. In addition, the self-perspective led to stronger activation in the amygdala, a limbic structure that plays a critical role in fear-related behaviors, such as the evaluation of actual or potential threats. Interestingly, the amygdala receives nociceptive information from the spino-parabrachial pain system and the insula, and its activity appears closely tied to the context and level of aversiveness of the perceived stimuli. Imagining oneself to be in a painful and poten-tially dangerous situation thus triggers a stronger fearful and/or aversive response than imagining someone else to be in the same situation. Regarding the insular activation, it is worth noting that it was located in the mid-dorsal section of this area. This part of the insula plays a role in coding the sensory-motor aspects of painful stimulation, and it has strong connections with the basal ganglia, in which activity was also higher when adopting the self-perspective. Taken together, activity in this aspect of the insula possibly reflects the simulation of the sensory aspects of the painful experience. Such a simulation might both lead to the mobilization of motor areas (including the SMA) in order to prepare defensive or withdrawal behaviors, and to interoceptive monitoring associated with autonomic changes evoked by this simulation process.

Previous research on the neural underpinnings of empathy has been limited to affective situations experienced in a similar way by an observer and a target individual. In daily life, however, we also interact with people whose affective states can be very different from our own. In a recent functional MRI study by Lamm, Meltzoff, & Decety (2010), participants were asked to evaluate the feelings of neurological patients who had emotional reactions that were very different from the self. These patients reacted with no pain when receiving a needle injection but with pain to a soft touch by a Q-tip. Empathic understanding for these patients increased activation in areas involved in self–other distinction and cognitive control (right TPJ, dorso-medial prefrontal cortex and right ventral premotor cortex). Furthermore, neural connectivity between the latter and areas implicated in affective coding was enhanced when participants observed surgical procedures that would be painful for themselves, but were not painful for the patients. This suggests that in order to correctly infer the affective state of someone who is not like us, we have to overcome our own emotional response tendencies. These results demonstrate that fronto-cortical attention networks are crucially involved in this process, corroborating that empathy is a flexible phenomenon, which draws upon both automatic and controlled cognitive mechanisms.

5.6.2 Disorders of empathy and deficits in perspective-taking

Children with empathy deficits likewise show deficits in executive function. A series of studies found that when an experimenter feigns distress in a room where children were playing, children with ASD looked to the experimenter much less than typically developing and mentally retarded children (e.g. Corona, Dissanayake, Arbelle, Wellington, & Sigman (1998)). However, when Blair (1999) replicated such studies, but controlled for executive function demands of attention, children with ASD performed like other children: when experimenters' feigned distress was unambiguous and took place under conditions of low distractibility, children with ASD showed autonomic responses similar to controls. In studies measuring facial mimicry, when given ample time, individuals with ASD do show affective compensatory tactics to accomplish emotion reading and in emotion recognition tasks, and show activation in brain areas related to intentional attentional provision and categorization instead of automatic processing (Hall, Szechtman, & Nahmias (2003)). These data indicate that alongside bottom-up information processing deficits (e.g. mimicry), top-down executive control are also impaired in individuals with autism. The deficit in cognitive flexibility may contribute to apathetic behaviors characteristic of autism.

Violent offenders, and children with aggressive behavior problems, experience deficits in empathy, though the result of the lack of empathy manifests in behavior differently than that seen in ASD or developmental coordination disorder. The former responds aggressively to others' distress (Arsenio & Lemerise (2001)), while the latter simply lack pro-social behavior. The distinction can be understood as the difference between apathy and hostility, both of which are categorized as non-empathetic in the traditional sense, though one being 'passive,' and the other 'active.' Individuals with ASD seem to have a deficit in either an interest or capacity to resonate emotionally with others or engage in intersubjective transactions. In contrast, children with developmental aggression disorders react aggressively to the observation of others' distress.

Poor empathic ability in conduct disorder correlates with decreased noradrenergic (NA) function (Raine (1996)). In fact, a low resting heart rate (a partly heritable trait reflecting fearlessness and stimulation-seeking) at 3 years of age predicted aggressive behavior at 11 years of age (Raine, Venables, Mednick, & Sarnoff (1997)). Children with clinical levels of behavior problems, often a precursor to the development of conduct disorder, show increased disregard for others, for example anger, avoidance, and/or amusement by another's distress, a negatively toned response pattern that differs significantly from typical children's responses. It is likely that decreased NA function, which is associated with aggressive behavior, contributes to these anti-social reactions.

Of particular interest are the aggressive and non-empathetic reactions of what have colloquially been termed 'bullies.' This sub-population also falls within the category of anti-social, but their reactions seem to be specific to aggressive responses to peers in distress. Dautenhahn & Woods (2003) proposed a model to account for the empathy deficits observed in bullies. They suggest that bullies as well as psychopaths are not aggressive due to poor emotion-processing or perspective-taking, but instead have heightened goal-directed behavior, often with an aggressive, anti-social goal to inflict personal distress in the other. This model is particularly intriguing as it questions previously held beliefs that males with conduct disorders experience weak self-regulation (Gill & Calkins (2003)). This novel model has particular implications for the role of perspective-taking in empathy. Personal motivation (i.e. the desire to induce distress in the other, versus the desire to offer pro-social help) plays a crucial role—because the bully or psychopath may have the means for an empathic experience, however the goal to elicit distress.

In an initial functional MRI study, eight adolescents with aggressive conduct disorder (CD) and eight matched controls with no CD symptoms were scanned while watching animated visual stimuli depicting other people experiencing pain or not experiencing pain (Decety, Michalska, Akitsuki, & Lahey (2009)). Furthermore, these situations involved either an individual whose pain was caused by accident or an individual whose pain was inflicted on purpose by another person. The aggressive youth activated the neural circuits underpinning pain processing to the same extent, and in some cases, even more so than the control participants without conduct disorder. Aggressive adolescents showed a specific and very strong activation of the amygdala and ventral striatum (an area that responds to feeling rewarded) when watching pain inflicted on others, which suggested that they enjoyed watching pain. When watching situations in which pain was intentionally inflicted, control youths exhibited signal increase in the medial prefrontal cortex, lateral orbitofrontal cortex, and right temporo-parietal junction (regions processing intentions and involved in moral reasoning), whereas youths with CD only exhibited activation in the insula and precentral gyrus. Furthermore, connectivity analyses demonstrated that youths with CD exhibited less amygdala/prefrontal coupling when watching pain inflicted by another than did control youth.

Executive functions not only facilitate perspective-taking, but also control attention and meta-cognitive capacities, both of which facilitate pro-social responding in reaction to another's distress. Children first demonstrate responses to the distress of others with other-focused behaviors like concern, attention to the distress of the other, cognitive exploration of the event and pro-social interventions around the second year of life. At this age children manifest a multifaceted self-concept, self-conscious emotions, as well as reparative behaviors after they cause distress in the other (Zahn-Waxler, Radke-Yarrow, Wagner, & Chapman (1992)). A longitudinal study of young children's development of concern for others' distress showed that pro-social behaviors, such as hugs and pats, emerge around the beginning of the second year of life, increasing in intensity throughout this year and sometimes provide self-comfort. However, by the end of the second year, pro-social behaviors appear to be more appropriate to the victims needs, are not necessarily self-serving, and children's emotions appear to be better regulated (Radke-Yarrow & Zahn-Waxler (1984)).

The ability to regulate emotions may be subject to individual differences, and may interact with the degree to which individuals experience emotions. Eisenberg and her colleagues (1994) proposed a model suggesting an interaction between the intensity at which emotions are experienced and the extent to which individuals can regulate their emotions. In line with her model, multi-method analysis of empathy-related responses including self-reported, facial, and heart rate responses suggest that increased emotional intensity and decreased regulation predict personal distress. Emotion contagion corresponds with moderate emotionality when regulation is controlled, and perspective-taking corresponds with high regulation and high emotionality only when perspective-taking is controlled. These interactions are first seen in a primitive form in infancy, and findings from infant development demonstrate that 4-month-olds low in self-regulation are prone to personal distress at 12-months of age (Ungerer et al. (1990)). In childhood, individuals with increased levels of emotional intensity (based on self-report, teacher-parent report, and autonomic measurements) and weak regulation are prone to personal distress in response to another's predicament, as they become overwhelmed due to their vicariously induced negative emotions.

In summary, the maturation of executive functions allow for the shared representations between self and other to be mediated and pro-social behaviors follow suit. On the other hand, if executive functioning is not intact, self and other perspectives may not be regulated, and individuals may over-identify or under-identify with an observed target. In the case of childhood aggression and conduct disorder, it is likely that either over- or under-regulation contributes to empathy deficits, though other factors such as NA function, or the environmental context and past experiences also contribute to reactionary behaviors.

5.7   Conclusion

We have shown that empathy is a complex and interesting human capacity that has both developmental origins and neural correlates. We argued that imitation and empathy are linked. It seems likely that basic motor imitation and complex imitation of intentional acts support empathy development and social understanding in general. The supramodal representation of human action that underlies infant motor imitation (Meltzoff & Moore (1997)) helps explain how perception and action can be so closely coupled and provides a basis for the interpersonal bridge that exists between self and other from the early pre-verbal stages of psychological development. This review also addressed the equivalent deficits in imitation and empathy in certain developmental disorders, particularly ASD, anxiety-depression, and conduct disorders. At an applications level, imitation may serve as an excellent remediation technique for enhancing empathy in these populations.

In our view, empathy cannot be entirely conceived within an experimental or neuroscientific vacuum. Personality, temperaments, and cultural norms of emotional display also contribute to the degree to which empathy may be experienced in the observer (e.g. Posner & Rothbart (2000)) and also modulated or even inhibited. In development, girls are more prone to comprehend emotional display rules than boys, particularly in cultures in which feminine roles demand more management and control of emotion display. Likewise, children from cultures that promote reciprocal relations and cooperation tend to be better at perspective-taking tasks than children living in individualistic cultures (Eisenberg, Bridget, & Shepard (1997)). Social psychologists emphasize the role of situational context as opposed to personality in the experience of empathy (or the absence of it), although most recognize a complex interaction between situation and personality as the best predictor of social behavior (Fiske (2004)). While situational context is important, creating ecologically valid situations in a laboratory setting poses a challenge (Decety & Batson (2007)). Thus, designing ecologically valid experiments for interpersonal exchanges involving empathy remains a challenging process, especially with children.

A current trend in cognitive neuroscience is to study the interaction between affect and cognition. Empathy and imitation exemplify this complex process: Motor imitation is foundational to emotion sharing, which is the building block of empathy which in turn affects the projected mental state content during perspective-taking (with feedback/forward loops). Moreover, affective and social cognitive developmental neuroscience offers promising insights into both our understanding of typical and psychopathological social behavior.[1]

[1] We gratefully acknowledge support by grants from NSF (BCS 0718480 and SBE-0354453) and NIH (HD-22514). The views expressed in this chapter are the authors' and do not necessarily represent those of NSF or NIH.

6

Empathy for Objects[1]

Gregory Currie

We think of empathy as an intimate, feeling-based understanding of another's inner life. We do not think of it as a way of understanding inanimate objects. Yet a century ago, talk of empathy for objects would have seemed very natural; it was the theme of a group of thinkers whose writings helped to found the notion of empathy itself. They were particularly interested in empathy as a means of attending to the aesthetic properties of things. That earlier programme will be my starting point, and I'll call the participants in it the Empathists. I will move on quickly to see what light can be shed on their idea of empathy for objects by current research in the sciences of mind. I identify a class of processes which, I claim, underlie empathy for objects as well as personal empathy; these processes are often called simulative in a special sense that I will try to explain. I then have two questions to which I seek answers of at least a preliminary sort. What sort of access to worldly things, including artworks, are we given by these simulative processes; is it, in particular, a perceptual form of access? Second, what role if any does conscious awareness of these processes play in our aesthetic encounters with things?

6.1 *Einfühlung*

The work of the Empathists has now largely disappeared from view, and the contemporary research which supports some of its claims owes little to it.[2] In some respects it

[1] Versions of this paper were read to the Claremont Philosophy Colloquium at Pitzer College, and at conferences and colloquia at the Universities of Barcelona, Durham, Geneva, Illinois Urbana-Champaign, Nottingham, and Otago. Aaron Meskin, Jerome Singer, and Kathleen Stock commented on the paper at Durham and I am grateful for their criticisms and suggestions. Thanks also to Noël Carroll, Paul Harris, Henry Kripps, Patrizia Lombardo, Michele Miozzo, Margaret Moore, Kevin Mulligan, Jenefer Robinson, and Kendall Walton. Comments from Rae Langton brought about some late changes to Section 2, while Matthew Kennedy and Murray Smith were especially helpful in formulating the claims of Section 3. Discussions with Michael Mack helped me to find my way through some of the history.
[2] Kevin Mulligan brought to my attention Melchior Palágyi, an intriguing figure whose work, contemporary with that of the Empathists but not so far as I know related to it, is suggestive of the direction empirical work has subsequently taken. William Boyce Gibson wrote an appreciative, two-part account of Palágyi's work, the second part of which describes his theory of the imagination (1928).

represents a Golden Age in the philosophy of art. Aesthetics, now displaced from the centre of intellectual life in the sciences and humanities, was then a core theme for thinkers of every kind, and especially for those who walked the scarcely differentiated territories of philosophy and psychology. For forty or so years across the nineteenth and twentieth centuries there was a flowering of research into the arts, and the appearance of multi-volume psychological treatises on the perception of visual form was then an everyday occurrence. At the centre of this endeavor, crossing disciplines, traditions and continents, was the programme I'm concerned with here: the examination of the empathic basis of human aesthetic responses. It was never focused exclusively on art, and it was very variably pursued, both in methods and in doctrines. It's then most visible advocate, Theodor Lipps, is now merely a name in historical footnotes.[3] Perhaps Lipps deserves the seclusion he currently enjoys; his theory of empathy was both obscure and unsatisfactory, as we shall see. But the movement in which he was a leading figure gave us the term 'empathy', and, given the healthy survival of that concept, it is surprising that its historical roots have so far disappeared.

The term 'empathy' began life as a translation of the German *Einfühlung*, the word used by Lipps.[4] The verb *einfühlen* had been used by Herder to mean 'to understand sympathetically' (literally 'feel into') the situation of an historical agent.[5] That agent-based conception of empathy is the one that has survived. But *einfühlen* was, for the Romantics, a general means of knowing. Novalis said that one who understands nature is one 'who almost without effort recognizes the nature of all things and . . . in an intimate and manifold relationship mixes himself with all of nature by means of his feelings . . . who so to speak feels himself into them' (1802/1960: 105). The view survives in the more sober, academic philosophy of Lotze, for whom a capacity to 'feel ourselves into things'—including inanimate objects—is the basis of our understanding of and connectedness to the world. It is thus that we enter into the 'narrow round of existence of a mussel-fish', and, through a sense of bodily contortion and effort, into the 'slender proportions' of a tree, or a building (1856). No form is so unyielding', Lotze said, 'that our imagination cannot project its life into it' (ibid, p. 584.).

Fifty years later, these ideas were applied by Lipps and the Empathists to the aesthetics of visual form. Their views shifted over time in ways that are sometimes hard to associate with compelling arguments; understanding the complexities of this evolution of thought requires a historically nuanced paper that I am unable to provide. But my aim is to take up some of the philosophical issues arising from the Empathists' programme, and for this a fine-grained historical account is not helpful. Instead

---

[3] The otherwise extremely comprehensive *Encyclopedia of Aesthetics* (edited by Michael Kelly in four volumes, Oxford University Press, 1998) carries no account of his ideas. It does not mention Lee or Langfeld; Vischer and Groos are noted in passing.

[4] See Tichener (1909): 21. *Einfühlung* was first given currency in the Dissertation of Robert Vischer (1873).

[5] See Herder (1778): especially 7–8.

I identify three tendencies in Empathist thinking, the third of which points us in the direction of some contemporary research.

Lipps held that we know another only by bringing about some sort of union, by means of projection, with that other; his concept of empathy correspondingly involved an act of personal projection wherein we feel the dynamic properties of the object—an architectural column, say—as our own.[6] While an aesthetic encounter with an object is a case of experiencing aesthetic qualities within ourselves, this self is an objectified self, a self which is 'ideal' but also 'real'. There are naturalizing tendencies in Lipps' thought—he claimed that symmetry in the body is found to be beautiful because of its relation to the body's capacity indifferently to turn left and right. But Lipps rejected attempts to ground the empathic relationship in awareness of our own bodies (1903a: 105–6).

The sharpest contrast to this within the Empathists' project is found in a view held at one time by Vernon Lee: our aesthetic sense of an object is provided by episodes of sympathetic resonance within our own bodies, which we can, with effort, attend to and analyze as part of the project of aesthetic inquiry.[7] Lee had a somewhat mechanical approach to this, and there are passages which have been held up to ridicule: in viewing a jar, she tells us, I feel the pressure of my feet on the ground when I see the base, a feeling of lift as I view the body, and downward pressure on my head as I view the rim at the top.[8]

Lipps' view leaves much unclear—the union of self with the work/other, the status of the self as both objective and subjective, both real and ideal. Lee, on the other hand, threatens to reduce aesthetic appreciation to callisthenic exercises. But a third tendency is evident in such writers such as Karl Groos and Herbert Langfeld, who talked of 'inner mimicry' and of 'motor imagining'.[9] Langfeld, a Harvard psychologist speaking against the background of Jamesian sensory-motor theory, made an important point here: 'when we notice the smooth curves of a marble torso, we can probably, if we observe carefully, get a fleeting image of our hands moving in imagination around the figure' (1920: 109). Such an image of movement he calls a *motor memory*: a pattern of nerve activation like that which would produce the actual movement remembered. To do their work, these images, he says, do not need to be conscious—an important point to which we shall return.

---

[6] Max Scheler noted that Lipps' theory leaves it unclear how an act of empathic projection can amount to anything more that re-acquaintance with your own self (1970: 242).

[7] 'Vernon Lee' was the pen name of Violet Paget, whose early book on eighteenth-century Italy was much admired. She was also the author of some effective ghost stories.

[8] Lee & Anstruther-Thompson (1897: 554, 681). For critical comment see Mitchell (1907). Berenson (to be mentioned further on) claimed that Lee and Anstruther-Thompson had plagiarized his ideas for their essay. Lee's view is modified in her (1913). She strongly denied Berenson's claim. On the relation of empathy with art objects and its relation to bodily activity see Etlin (1998), especially pp. 6–7. But I have not understood Etlin's contrast between 'patterns of sentience' and 'projection of an actual bodily condition'.

[9] See e.g. Groos (1892). Groos was the author of important work on animal and human play. Lee denied that empathy could be understood in terms of inner mimicry (1913: 67).

6.2 Empathy and Bodily Simulation

Seeing empathy this way avoids the idea that it requires a Lippsian act of personal projection into the object; it also avoids Lee's idea of a motor response to an object which is literally body-involving. Rather, the object of attention generates a range of motor images. Langfeld described these in terms of activation of nerve systems that would otherwise produce the very movements in question. If we speak instead of neural systems we have something suggestive to a modern reader of *simulative* processes, the evidence for which is now very strong within psychology and the neurosciences.

The term simulation is currently used in distinct ways by different groups of researchers and I must be clear about how I am using it here. In philosophy, and in some areas of developmental psychology, the term names a theory about how it is we come to understand people's reasons, the idea being that we imagine ourselves in their position and then reproduce the reasoning which lead to their own decision or conclusion. This is an hypothesis at the personal level, an hypothesis about how the agent herself comes to understand another's reasons.[10] But here I am using 'simulation' to name a related but different theory. It is a theory about ways in which certain aspects of human performance are implemented in systems that operate within the person, are not directly under personal control, and the workings of which may be inaccessible to consciousness, though they may give rise to conscious experiences. It is a sub-personal hypothesis.[11] The flagship example here—and one central to our discussion—involves the production of simulated movements. When we ask people to make judgments about the handedness of a visual display, they seem to answer by 'mentally rotating' their own hands into the orientation of the display, taking about as long to do it as they would take actually to move their hands. Their imaginative performance is, it seems, constrained by the same biomechanical factors that constrain actual bodily movement. The neural basis of this is not fully understood but on one view these imagined movements (which may or may not be conscious) are constituted by the activation of an inner model we all possess of our own bodies: a model which has evolved so as to obey the constraints that govern bodily movement, because it evolved as an aid in the planning and control of those movements (Clark and Grush (1999)). There is evidence that this model shares neural resources with systems which activate real movements; people who are impaired in movement are often comparably impaired in their capacity to simulate movement.[12]

---

[10] See the essays in Part I of Heal (2003a).

[11] On personal and sub-personal simulation processes see Currie & Ravenscroft (2002): Part II, and Goldman (2006a): ch. 6.

[12] For a summary of relevant work, see Currie & Ravenscroft (2002): ch. 4. In thinking about the biological basis of interpersonal empathy, much is currently being made of mirror neurons, which are activated both when the subject performs an action, and when she observes someone else perform an action of that type; it has been suggested that these activations underlie processes of simulation of another's action. For one view of the relations between mirror neurons and mechanisms of empathy, see Marco Iacoboni's contribution to this volume. A clarifying account of the role of mirror neurons in empathic understanding of

Empathic understanding of emotion in other agents is also driven by a comparable sort of simulation. While disgust evolved, presumably, as an encouragement to us to avoid the noxious, its mechanisms are implicated in the recognition of disgust in others; the sight of someone with a disgusted facial expression activates brain areas used in the generation of our own feelings of disgust (Wicker et. al. (2003). And people who have damage to one of these areas—the insula—and which prevents them from feeling disgust, are impaired in their recognition of disgust in others (Calder et. al. (2000); Adolphs et. al. (2003)).[13] Some simulative processes are recruited to both personal empathy and empathy for objects. The secondary somatosensory cortex, once thought only to respond to physical touch, is strongly activated by the sight of other people being touched. Seeing inanimate objects collide generates the same activity (Keysers et al. 2004).

While simulative processes underlie empathy for objects and for persons, a variety of other tasks involve simulation, including, apparently, language processing. The motor homunculus is a region of the brain that controls voluntary movements of various body parts, so called because its shape is a distorted but recognizable model of the body within which adjacent areas control adjacent parts of the body. When people read action-related words, the motor homunculus is activated in appropriate ways, moving its feet at the sound of the word 'feet' (Hauk et. al. (2004)). Even words rather indirectly related to action have this effect: simulated hand movements can be generated merely by naming tools intended for hand-use (Martin et. al. (1996)). Work by Pulvermüller et. al. (2005) suggests that this is not an incidental connection; stimulation to the relevant motor areas speeds lexical processing.[14]

All these simulative processes are ones which may be activated by artworks, and by other kinds of objects, in ways that conform to, and sometimes extend, the claims of the Empathists. There is the sense of having your body disposed in a way which resembles (perhaps minimally) the geometry of the object viewed and its dynamical relations to other things, as one imagines standing upright supporting a heavy load, in response to the sight of a load-bearing column. Or one might imagine swaying in the wind like a tree. To this we should add those cases of simulation provoked by representational art, as when we response to artistically represented people rather than to real ones. We may, as we see the bodily dispositions of the people depicted in Rubens' *Descent from the Cross*, undergo bodily simulations which mirror aspects of

emotions, and in other aspects of mentalistic understanding, is given in Goldman (2009a), responding to a skeptically inclined paper by Pierre Jacob (2008).

[13] Adolphs et. al., whose patient B showed a remarkable inability to detect even the most obvious signs of disgust in others (describing an episode of vomiting as 'delicious food was being enjoyed'), say that 'our unpublished observations with Patient B suggest that he appears unable to feel disgust'. See also Goldman (2006a): section 6.1.

[14] The picture here is a complex one. It is reported that motor activation is significant when words are heard in isolation, less significant but still present when heard in a literal context, and not present when words are heard in a non-literal context (Raposo et. al. (2009)). I am grateful to Anezka Kuzmicova for discussion of this issue.

those dispositions. And if we need to simulate emotions ourselves in order to detect emotions in others, the same will apply to recognizing the emotions of people whose faces and/or bodies are depicted in painting and sculpture. You might have a sense of engaging with the represented object, perhaps through reaching and grasping, or passing your hands over the surface—recall Langfeld's observations about the torso.

It is also plausible that motor imagery is involved in our sense of artworks as artifacts (Langfeld (1920): 121–2). Viewers sometimes report empathic reproduction of the actions which produced the object or shaped its properties: especially so with paintings by Jackson Pollock (Freedberg & Gallese (2007)). But we do not always respond in ways which correspond closely or at all to the ways in which the object really was made, or even could be made. We may imagine squeezing the stone of a Henry Moore sculpture into its finished shape, an activity which does not correspond at all to how the object was made but which might, nonetheless, constitute the basis of an appropriate aesthetic response.[15] The same applies to the simulation of pressure induced by the sight of a load-bearing column: the column feels no pressure, but my simulation of pressure contributes to an appropriate aesthetic response to the structure, and informs my appreciation of the way the column joins the entablature.

How helpful is the notion of simulation if we want to assess the explanatory power of the Empathists' project? I think it has the capacity to help a good deal. Without it, the Empathists' programme is easily written off as focused on a gerrymandered class of operations, only some of which we would count as genuinely empathic: there is the (by our lights) recognizably empathic process of imagining one's self in the position of the maker of the object, doing various things to shape or construct it. But note two things. First, this is empathy with the maker, and not with the object. Secondly, as indicated above, some of this might consist in a wildly unrealistic yet aesthetically productive enterprise—imagining squeezing a piece of metal or stone into its current shape. Thus far we have a natural grouping of activities: the class of motor simulations which have as their target a person's activity, whether that activity is correctly or incorrectly understood, or even conceived within an imaginative project which makes no claim to verisimilitude—empathy in a broad sense, we might call it.[16] Then a further broadening that also uses the idea of empathy-as-imaginative-exploration allows us to count as empathic the response we have, or might have, to a load-bearing column, with this time a simulation of pressure or constriction rather than action. This is the best sense one can make, I think, of the idea of empathy *for* objects themselves.

---

[15] These are by no means exclusive hypotheses about how we respond to artworks; we might respond in all or any of these ways, depending on the sort of object that confronts us.

[16] Sometimes, as Kendall Walton points out, our empathic response to the making of the object combines with our recognition of representational features to give us psychological insight into the character represented in the work. Nervous-seeming brushwork can, through its simulative resonance, cause us to feel nervous and hence to attribute properties to the mind of the sitter that would not otherwise be available (1999).

But it is hard to see the simulation of movement around the torso as in Langfeld's example as a case of empathy at all—not with the object, the maker, or anything else.

Refocusing our concern from empathy to simulation will, I claim, produce a more unified and coherent project. There are a range of (bodily) simulation-based activities which are directed towards works of art or aesthetic objects more generally and which may contribute to aesthetic engagement with those objects.[17] Some of these relations are empathic in a sense we would recognize, while others are perhaps legitimate extensions of that notion; yet others really fall outside the scope of that concept altogether, and are simply cases of imagining doing various things. But they are all cases of bodily simulation.

There are two important questions to be answered about the relation between bodily simulation and engagement with art objects: one about intentionality, and one about consciousness. Addressing them helps us understand how simulative states put us in contact with works of art.

6.3 Experience of the Work

Take the case of visual art—painting and drawing. These are works in visual media because seeing them is required if we are to make the right sort of contact with them. Vision focuses us on the work—the right object. But, the argument goes, simulation of bodily movement or exertion of pressure focuses our attention on ourselves, distracting us from the work.[18]

Lipps was aware of this problem, and this is one reason he avoided a specification of bodily processes in giving his account of empathy. Langfeld, also worried by the difficulty, insisted that we only attend aesthetically to the object when we are unaware of these bodily processes; to become aware of them is to be distracted from the work.[19] But we should not follow Langfeld here; an aesthetically legitimate exploration of the work often requires our having certain conscious states; sometimes, as we shall see, it depends on our being able to reflect on their qualities and their connections. Tragedies give rise to pity and terror (or, if not precisely to these things, then to phenomenological states of some sort), while ghost stories cause fear, sometimes of a very salient kind. And we don't think of these as merely incidental effects of the tragedy or the ghost story. Works which did not move us in these ways would not be good works of their kinds.[20]

---

[17] I am grateful to Henry Kripps, Rae Langton, and Kathleen Stock for pressing me on this point.

[18] The contrast between attention to the work and attention to one's self is a theme of Wittgenstein's lectures on aesthetics in 1938; see his (1966).

[19] Langfeld (1920: 117). Palágyi held that motor imaginings could be unconscious (1924: 142). Lee offers the implausible hypothesis that, while our sense that a seen mountain is rising comes about because we raise our eyes to it, the fact that we are engrossed in the mountain makes us attribute rising (a general notion, distilled from our manifold experiences and imaginings of rising) to the mountain and not to ourselves.

[20] Going somewhat further, Sherri Irvin has recently argued that 'one's qualitative experience can itself be the object of legitimate aesthetic attention' (2008: 25).

Not that every qualitative state caused by a work counts as a way of making aesthetic contact with the work. Pity and fear (of some kinds) count as respectable responses, because they help us achieve the right kind of relation to the work; they focus us on its pitiable and fearful aspects. If *Hamlet* gave you toothache, this would not enrich your understanding of the play.[21] A worry we might have about the relation between works of art and our own states of motor simulation is that this relation is not sufficiently intentional; that there is no real sense in which the motor simulations are directed towards the work.

One response to this claims that the simulation of movement itself constitutes a form of perception of certain properties in the picture; thus the motor simulations provoked by a viewing of *Descent from the Cross* would be ways of perceiving such things as the sense of effort and muscular tension felt by the mourners as they lower the body of Christ.[22] Generalizing, we could say that mechanisms which simulate state or process S, and which are activated by another person's being in S, or being depicted as being in S, constitute states of perceiving the other's state of being in S.

I reject this view. Simulation mechanisms are too precariously related to the state of the other to count as ways of perceiving the other's state. Take the case of emotion perception. According to the story already outlined, recognizing your expression as one of disgust involves the activation of my own disgust response. But is it true that the activation, in these circumstances, of my disgust response itself constitutes a perception of your disgust? We all agree, I take it, that on many, perhaps most, occasions, the activation of my disgust response does not constitute perception of anyone's disgust; rather it is simply what happens when I am disgusted by something. At best, activation of my disgust response counts as perception of your disgust in special circumstances and only in conjunction with uncontroversially perceptual access to you by other means (I need to *see* your facial expression). So the operation of the purported 'organ of emotion perception', namely our suite of emotion-responses, is only very irregularly correlated with the presence of emotions in others, and depends for its effective operation on other senses. Neither of these things are true of sight, hearing, etc, which are very highly correlated with the things in the external world they are apt to detect, and do not operate via the operation of other senses. Further, it ought to be possible, for any mode of perception, to make a distinction between the veridical and the non-veridical case: between, say, seeing things as they are and merely being presented with certain visual appearances. Take the visual perception of faces, and grant that we normally see a person's disgust rather than merely seeing signs of disgust

---

[21] One of the concerns about the recent installation by Carsten Höller at London's Tate Modern (October 2006–April 2007) is that the experience of going down the slide is one that does not help to give us a significantly better understanding of the slide itself; the slide is more like a brute cause of the experience. There ought to be a stronger degree of intentional relatedness between the experience and the slide itself for it to count as an art object.

[22] Barbara Mondero argues that 'one proprioceives what is at the end of the mirroring system's causal path' (2006: 238). See also the discussion of 'the transparency of bodily experience' in Dokic (2003).

from which we infer the mental state. Still, an actor may fool us, in which case what we see are mere signs of disgust. But how are we to retain this distinction for the case of emotion-simulation as (purported) perception of another's emotion? In the case where our emotion-simulation is triggered by the sight of the actor, what mere appearances does the simulation expose us to? There do not seem to be any ready candidates for these appearances, other than the visual appearances. But the availability of the visual appearances makes out the case for a distinction between veridical and non-veridical *visual* perception; they can't be double counted and support a further distinction between veridical and non-veridical emotion-simulation-perception.[23]

But we need not say that simulations are perceptions in order to avoid the difficulty that troubled the Empathists. The objection was that simulative processes are not related in the right ways to objects of our aesthetic attention for those processes to count as genuinely aesthetic responses to them. And we may say that these simulative processes do have the right kinds of relations—though they are not directly perceptual relations—to objects of aesthetic attention. These processes provide information which is accessed by the visual system, and which contributes to a visual experience in which various properties of the work, or of that which is represented in it, are made manifest. When I look at Rubens' *Descent from the Cross* with the right kind of attention I am made directly, non-inferentially aware of the heaviness of Christ's represented body, and of the sense of strain represented in the bodies of the mourners as they lower the body. And these things are given to me in visual experience itself, as that experience is enriched by its connections with simulative processes; they are not given to me by a combination of vision and a set of distinct, simulation-based perceptual systems.[24] I may, in addition, have experiences constituted by the coming to consciousness of motoric simulations of bodily strain, but I think we do well to distinguish these from perceptual states. The properties I perceive in the picture are the properties I see there.

This account makes bodily simulations part of our canonical responses to pictures, but it does not make pictures multi-sensory objects, accessible through more than one sense modality; they are not available to vision *and* to a supposed motor simulative perceptual sense. What is made accessible in a picture by way of bodily simulation is seen in the picture.

This is a hypothesis about causal connections between certain mental systems: not something on which a philosopher can safely pronounce from the armchair. Is there some independent evidence to which we can appeal for support? There is. In experiments on biologically realistic motion, the movement of a light-point tracing a closed path, in this case an ellipse, looked uniform to subjects in the experiment as long at the

---

[23] I am indebted here to Millar (2000). I have put the point in a way that will, I hope, be acceptable to a disjunctivist about perception.

[24] Sometimes a similar view is taken about the role of emotions in allowing us to perceive, say, danger. According to Peter Goldie, my feeling fear as the toboggan rushes towards my child enables me to see the toboggan as 'being frightening' (2004b: 253). He does not suggest, and nor would it be plausible to suggest, that the emotions give us perceptual but non-visual access to the frighteningness of the toboggan.

motion corresponded to the motion that would be produced by a human hand tracing the ellipse. Presumably subjects were relying on a motor simulation of the motion as they would draw it, using sub-personal systems which mimic the operations, and respect the biomechanical constraints, of the hand and arm; when the motion matched that inner simulation, it looked uniform.[25] Similarly, it is probable that the marks we see on a page of handwriting look like letters and words (though their shapes do not correspond at all closely to the canonical forms of those letters) because of inputs to the visual system from the subjects' own motor representations of the movements that would be made in order to produce those marks, these motor representations providing a clue to the letter that is intended to be written.[26] Both these results strongly suggest that how things look is partly a function of inner motor processes, which must in that case have some causal connection to the visual system. Consider, finally, patient NK in a study, mentioned earlier, on the relation between impaired disgust response and impaired recognition of disgust in others (Calder et. al 2000). NK's recognition of faces is normal, as is his recognition of most emotions, but he is poor at distinguishing visual displays of disgusted faces from ones displaying anger. His own emotional reactions are in the normal range, except again for disgust. (His conceptual understanding of disgust is intact.) A plausible hypothesis is that his impaired disgust response compromises his ability to simulate disgust on seeing a disgusted face; as a consequence, a face that looks disgusted to others is much less likely to look so to him.

It is possible to draw a more general conclusion about the relation between vision and bodily simulations. Dan Zahavi (2008) rejects accounts of empathy in terms of simulation, and favours a perceptual account of the kind developed by Scheler: we perceive the emotion of the other, without experiencing that emotion ourselves. I see no reason to be dogmatic and insist that all our understanding of the emotions of others is simulation-based. But it should be clear by now that there is no inconsistency in holding that empathy is simulation based, *and* that we perceive—indeed, see—the emotions of others. For on the model just now proposed, simulative activity feeds directly into visual perception. Zahavi might grant this point and still insist that our perception of emotion is, as a matter of fact, not simulation-based, relying for support here on the phenomenology of emotion recognition. He asks, rhetorically, 'how plausible is it after all to claim that I need to become furious myself, if I am to recognize the fury in the face of my assailant?' But a simulationist need not claim this, assuming instead that conscious experience of one's self as undergoing an emotion is very variably associated with the activation of the mechanisms that underlie that emotion, and may depend on the strength of the activation. Simulation may do its causal work

---

[25] Viviani & Stucchi (1992). The actual variations in motion which are capable of seeming uniform are very large indeed; when the same motion is shown as movement along a straight line, subjects immediately recognize the highly variable speed and refuse to believe that this is the same variation as was present in the movement along the closed curve.

[26] See Knoblich, G. et al. (2002) As Paolo Viviani puts it, 'motor competence makes it possible to extract from a static trace information relating to production' (Viviani (2002)).

without reaching the threshold of consciousness, or may produce a very dim conscious experience that easily goes unnoticed. That is how it is with other kinds of simulations, for example simulated hand movements (see text to note 12 above). Consider again the perception of another being touched: this seems to produce a simulative effect, but not, in normal subjects, a conscious experience of touch. In odd circumstances, however, the simulation does produce a highly salient conscious experience. Blakemore et al. (2005) report the case of a subject who has experiences as of being touched when she sees someone else being touched. They say, 'In most people, this system would be active below a certain threshold, resulting in no conscious perception of tactile stimulation'. The visual experience we have when we see an emotion-laden face is certainly a conscious one, and may count, by dint of its connections with bodily simulation, as a perception of the emotion; but the simulation itself may be non-conscious, or so close to threshold as to go unnoticed without special effort.

There is another question we can ask about conscious awareness of motor simulations. Supposing, as seems to be the case, that we *are* sometimes conscious of motor and other bodily simulations, is there anything in our aesthetic encounter with a work of art to be gained by encouraging consciousness of these simulations? We have seen that the Empathists were divided on this, some thinking there is merit in training ourselves to be more aware of these generally rather recessive states than we normally are, while others suggest that we need to suppress consciousness of them.

I have said that these processes do not constitute a special form of perception; that effectively denies me access to one line of reasoning about this, which is the following. Suppose we are persuaded by the doctrine of the transparency of experience: that 'introspection of one's perceptual experience reveals only the mind–independent objects, qualities and relations that one learns about through perception'.[27] Then we will say that, when we try to focus on aspects of our own experience, we always end up focusing on some aspect of the world experienced: the colours and shapes and distances of things in the case of visual experience. If we thought of motor simulations as perceptual states, we could say that attending to them really amounts to attending to aspects of the world to which those simulations are related. This is not a move that is available to me. Anyway, transparency is implausible as a doctrine applied to bodily simulative states—another reason, perhaps, for denying that such states belong to the class of perceptions proper. Focusing on a simulative state presents itself as a case of focusing on something that is going on in me. In this respect, bodily simulations seem to be more like emotions than they are like perceptual states, though there are those who argue that emotions are, after all, perceptual states.[28] Focusing on an emotional state is not accounted for, without remainder, as focusing on the state of the world of which the emotion informs us, though I grant that it is partly this. There is, in addition,

---

[27]   Martin (1996): 378.
[28]   See Damasio (1999): ch. 2; Prinz (2004): 202. In Currie & Ravenscroft (2002): ch. 9, we argue that emotions are *like* perceptual states in significant ways, and I continue to hold this view.

such a thing as focusing on how you feel about that state of the world. Of course with vision we can sense a discrepancy between how things look and how they are, between the colours they seem to have and the colours they have. But in doing this, and focusing on how the colours seem, we are, once again, focusing on how things in the external world seem to be.[29] When we note that we feel afraid of something we have good reason to think is not dangerous, we are doing more than simply noticing that the thing in question seems more dangerous than it in fact is; we are noting in ourselves responses of fear which we take, in the light of other evidence, to be excessive.

The emotions are relevant here not merely as a case analogous to but better understood than the case of motor simulation. Emotions, as I have indicated, are themselves subject to simulative reproduction; we simulate the emotions of others when we encounter signs of their sadness or joy. And we do this also, as I have again indicated, when we see people represented in works of art. And here, focusing on our own conscious states of (simulated) emotion may contribute to a proper engagement with the work. As Kendall Walton suggests, there are situations in which we need to respond to a work of art by experiencing depicted characters as feeling *thusly*—where 'thusly' demonstratively picks out a way of feeling instantiated in my own case.[30] This argument applies with equal force to the case of motor simulations: part of an aesthetically aware response to *Descent from the Cross* is a vivid sense of the bodily strain experienced by the mourners as they lower the dead Christ. And my capacity to think, of one of the figures, 'He feels thusly', where 'thusly' picks out a feeling of bodily contortion and strain which I am currently simulating, gives my thought about the figures a specificity and a vividness that they would not have if I had to rely on using a descriptive concept such as 'feels some unspecific tension in his arms and shoulders'.[31]

There are other ways in which consciousness of motoric simulations might play a role in engagement with art. Consider again the case of emotional responses. The emotions we feel in response to narrative art are not merely a series of unstructured affective eruptions, but episodes which take shape in response to and in anticipation of the events of the unfolding drama, and we may sense a harmony or appropriateness in the relation between the course of the emotion and the course of the narrative; the same thing happens with music.[32] There might be a similar temporally extended relation between, say, a developing motoric imagining of strain and effort and my

---

[29] Perhaps there are occasions on which experience makes us aware of properties of the experience itself. Tim Crane argues that we are sometimes aware of aspects of our visual experience: when I take my glasses off things look blurry but it need not seem as if the objects themselves are blurry (Crane 2006: 130). This is always the case, I claim, with (felt) emotions and with (felt) bodily simulations.

[30] Walton (1999). Walton acknowledges a debt to Jane Heal's work on indexical predication (see essays in Part III of her (2003)).

[31] These considerations narrow the gap between the experience of sculpture and that of painting, which one tradition insists are entirely distinct, with painting being 'made for the eye' and sculpture for the tactile imagination (for a statement of this view, see Herder (2002)).

[32] The episodic, and in some cases 'narrative,' shape of emotions is emphasized by de Sousa (1990) and by Robinson (2005).

viewing of *Descent from the Cross*, with its variously represented postures. Attention to the phenomenology of bodily simulation might find pleasing and appropriate congruences of this kind, deepening, perhaps, my understanding of the work.

Still, a note of caution is required. It does seem to me that these motoric imaginings are somewhat unstable, difficult to control, and with the potential to distract us from the work; to that extent I agree with Langfeld. I don't think we know much about the circumstances in which, or the ways in which, consciousness of these states will deepen our experience of the work rather than detracting from it. I claim only that we should not think of them as *necessarily* a distraction.

6.4 An Aesthetics Based on Empathy?

Despite these reservations I grant that bodily imaginings, above and below the threshold of consciousness, accompany, and sometimes inform, our engagement with art objects and other aesthetic things. But while we undergo a motoric response to many artworks, mentally simulating the contortions of shape, the straining of our limbs, or the imagined activity of the maker, the same goes for our responses to things that are not artworks, and which may not have any very striking aesthetic properties, or which, whatever their aesthetic merits, we happen to have no aesthetic interest in. We need not be looking at a chair with aesthetic attention in order to activate a motor simulation of sitting on it. We might say that empathic responses are of special relevance to understanding our relations to the aesthetic, because these responses become particularly salient when we are in the presence of aesthetic things. But it is hard to see why this should be. If we do regularly have these responses, would they not be very salient in, for example, situations of sexual arousal, or danger, or other forms of heightened stimulation, not all of which count as aesthetic all of the time? Nor can empathy provide us with a standard of aesthetic excellence, as Berenson is close to suggesting when he says that Giotto's greatness in comparison with Cimabue was to have satisfied 'the first condition of painting as an art . . . to stimulate our tactile imagination'.[33] We should not construe the claim of the importance of bodily imagining in terms of 'the more the better'; representation is important in art, even though a painting is not better simply because it represents more. Bodily simulation is a subtle and complex process that contributes to pleasures and interests at many points along its many dimensions, and generally in conjunction with other qualities; these conjunctions create harmony, tension, or dissonance, in ways that may be good or bad, and which defy the formulation of rules. There is little to say in general terms about the relation between

---

[33] Berenson (1909). Berenson said that Giotto's work amounts to a kind of tactile caricature, stimulating the tactile imagination more than a comparable real object would. He valorized not merely sensory imagining in the modality of touch but also movement and muscular effort; see his discussion of Pollaiuolo's *Battle of the Nudes* ((1909): 98–9). Lipps was well aware that empathy was a concept with too general applicability to found the notion of the aesthetic.

these motoric processes and the aesthetic beyond noting, unhelpfully, that these processes play an aesthetic role when they play a role in the generation of a response which is an aesthetic one.

But motoric responses of this kind are not *irrelevant* to art and the aesthetic, any more than sight is. And if aestheticians had somehow forgotten or never noticed that colour, and the perception of colour, are relevant to painting, it would be an urgent obligation to point out their relevance. That is what I am doing with respect to motoric responses. And in addition to that, I have offered some hypotheses about the ways in which these motoric responses connect us with objects, artworks or not, to which we want to attend in an aesthetic way.

PART II

Empathy and Aesthetics

7

Empathy, Expansionism, and the Extended Mind

Murray Smith

Fever Pitch is about being a fan. I have read books written by people who obviously love *football*, but that's a different thing entirely; and I have read books written, for want of a better word, by hooligans, but at least 95 per cent of the millions who watch games every year have never hit anyone in their lives. So this is for the rest of us, and for anyone who has wondered what it might be like to be this way.

Nick Hornby, *Fever Pitch*[1]

I think people go to the movies to live other lives . . . [y]ou want to get out of your own life and kind of become someone else for a while, even if you wouldn't want to stay in that life. There's a kind of vicariousness that's a part of all art, I think. So if you're going to be Nikolai, who lives a life that is fraught with danger, I want you to experience his life as it really is.

David Cronenberg, on *Eastern Promises*[2]

Commenting recently on the landmark Pink Floyd album *The Dark Side of the Moon*, bassist and principal songwriter Roger Waters characterized the album as 'the beginning of empathy'.[3] Waters wasn't advancing the novel hypothesis that the process or the concept of empathy sprang into being in 1974, when the album was released, but rather emphasizing a shift in the mood and lyrical content of the group's work, away from the delirious, if solipsistic, psychedelia of their earlier work—the mind turned in upon itself in the exploration of 'inner space'—and towards the outer world, especially the social world of other minds. Also recently, but in a very different context, neuroscientist Marco Iacoboni has employed fMRI scanning technology in order to ascertain the motives underlying political allegiances and voting behaviour. Identifying particular regions of the brain as responsible for the processing of empathy, Iacoboni

---

[1] Hornby (1996): 11–12.
[2] Thielman (2007). Nikolai is the protagonist of Cronenberg's film *Eastern Promises* (2007).
[3] Waters makes this remark in *Classic Albums: Dark Side of the Moon*, Isis Productions (2003).

claims to have gathered evidence showing that the sense of empathic connection with favoured political candidates is eroded by negative political adverts.[4] And more generally, Iacoboni argues that we are 'wired for empathy'.[5] Waters and Iacoboni could both very well be spouting nonsense. But the fact that they both make reference to the concept of empathy, in the very different contexts of biographical art criticism and what I suppose we should call 'neuro-social scientific' research, shows that the concept of empathy is alive and, possibly though not necessarily, well.

Regrettably I won't be lingering on *The Dark Side of the Moon* in this paper. Instead, my goals here are twofold; first, to place empathy in the novel context of the theory of the 'extended mind'; and second, to address some objections to the notion of empathy, and its place within our experience of representational art in general and film in particular, objections which become particularly salient when empathy is set in this context. So let's begin at the beginning: what sort of thing do I take empathy to be?

Empathy is a kind of imagining; in particular it is a type of *personal* or *central* imagining. Such imagining takes the form of imagining perceiving or more generally experiencing events, in contrast to *impersonal* or *acentral* imagining, where we imagine that certain events have taken or are taking place, but without imagining that we perceive or experience them. In centrally imagining a situation, we mentally *simulate* experiencing it.[6] Consider the following as an example of central or personal imagining. I find myself gazing out of the window, down onto the relatively quiet, semi-rural, residential street on which we live. My eldest son is playing behind me, building a castle from wooden blocks, flying model planes in close to the towers, and bombing the hapless figures populating the structure. A car shoots by, its noise and sudden appearance startling me—it must be going at least 60 miles an hour, I think to myself—and this tips me into a brief, but quite disturbing, train of thought—of imagination—for a few seconds. What if, one day, we are outside on the street when one of these reckless drivers thunders by? What if we'd been outside just now, when that car sped by, and one of the children—lost in one of their own imaginative games—had veered into the road at the wrong moment? A queasy feeling passes through me; my breathing becomes irregular for a couple of seconds. We've all had this sort of experience—indeed, I suspect that, for some people, these alarming micro-fictions of catastrophe are quite common, part of the texture of their lives. In spite of the palpable emotional consequences of such personal imaginings, though, when we find ourselves thinking such thoughts—when, as we say, our imaginations run away with themselves—it is not as if

---

[4] Iacoboni (2008): 239–58.

[5] Iacoboni (2008): 268.

[6] The contrast between central and acentral imagining is from Wollheim (1984): 74; that between personal and impersonal imagining is from Currie 1995: ch. 6. Although subtle differences may arise from the larger conceptual schemes in which the contrasts are situated, for present purposes, they may be treated as identical. I also follow Wollheim, Currie, and many others in treating imagination as a form mental simulation. For a recent account, see Goldman (2006a). For more detail on the connections between Wollheim and Currie on empathy, see my (1997): 412–30.

we lose sight of where we actually are, of what actually is the case, of the fact that the imagining is just that: a vivid mental projection of a possible state of affairs. Our imaginations run away with themselves, but they do not hijack the mind as a whole.

In this case, I am imagining a variation on my own state of affairs. I am imagining an alternative version of myself; many aspects of the scenario are carried over directly from the way the world actually is. Let us call such imagining *self-focussed personal imagining.* Empathic imagining takes a slightly different form. In imagining how some other, *specified agent* sees the world, and in imagining how they think and feel, I empathize with them.[7] Let us call this type of imagining *other-focussed personal imagining.* Such imagining allows us not merely to recognize or understand, but to grasp directly—an idea I'll return to—the emotional frames of mind of others. And the purpose of such imagining, like the function of emotions more generally, is to lend our ascriptions of the mental states of others more 'bite'—that is, to assess them in terms of their urgency, salience, and relevance. In this way empathy functions just as emotions do in general, affectively mapping out the world in terms of its potential harms and benefits.

Empathy, however, does not take place or arise in isolation from other mental processes. In particular, empathy is systematically connected with certain other, lower-level, 'pre-reflective' responses, in particular motor and affective *mimicry*, and emotional *contagion*.[8] Consider, as an example, affective mimicry through facial expression. When we witness legible instances of the facial expressions associated with certain basic kinds of affective state—the so-called 'basic' emotions—we are apt to simulate the feeling associated with the expression, via the mechanism of facial feedback.[9] Emotional contagion is closely related, but where in affective mimicry we have some awareness that the source of the mimicked emotion lies in another person with whom we engage, in contagion we lack any such awareness of the source of the 'caught' emotion. Affective mimicry and emotional contagion can, I've suggested in earlier work, act as prompts to, and props within, fully-fledged imaginative projects. I do not say these mechanisms always work in this way; the precise effect of the expressive faces in films, for example, is very much a matter of exactly how they are deployed—framed, lit, contextualized—by filmmakers. *United 93* (Paul Greengrass (2006)), for example, gives ample screen space to the facial expressions of the hijackers—mostly expressions of anger and fear. And I think we do feel their fear by mimicry and contagion. But the film doesn't nurture a deeper imaginative engagement with the hijackers; no attempt is made to contextualize their immediate affective states in terms of their life stories. On the other hand, the film provides relatively extensive

---

[7] Note the importance of the causal history of the state here: a *parallel* state of mind—as when two people are both shocked by the same event—is not, on this definition, an empathic state of mind.

[8] For an illuminating discussion of this distinction, and a very thorough review of the pertinence of empathy for film, see Vaage (2008).

[9] For a fuller account of this process, see my (1995): 98–102. On the tie between recognizing and experiencing basic emotions, see Goldman (2006a): ch. 6.

context for many of the passengers on the plane, in this way fostering a fuller, more 'plenitudinous' imaginative engagement with them.

In passing we may note how the still emerging body of research on 'mirror neurons' relates to the account of empathy I've sketched. Mirror neurons are neurons which fire both when a subject executes and observes an action. They were first discovered, in the early 1990s, in macaque monkeys, but subsequent research has revealed that humans possess an even more active and extensive mirror neuron system.[10] The discovery of the mirror system provides further evidence in support of motor and affective mimicry, as well as specifying some of the neural mechanisms underpinning them. More recent research has shown that our understanding of at least some emotional states in others, including our old friends fear and disgust, is also mediated by a neural mirroring system. Such understanding constitutes a 'direct experiential' knowledge of these emotions, achieved by the 'direct mapping' of visual information concerning the emotions of others—in the form of expressions, gestures, and posture—'onto the same viscero-motor neural structures that determine the experience of that emotion in the observer'.[11] The mirror system does not constitute a complete neural foundation for imaginative simulation as it has been defined and debated by philosophers, but it does suggest how simulation of higher-order states can work from the platform of motor and affective mimicry. Mimicry of basic actions and emotions may *scaffold* the imagination, including the empathic imagination, of more elaborate, finely-specified states of mind.[12]

Strangers on a Train (Alfred Hitchcock (1951)) provides us with an example of the way in which vivid depictions of actions and facial expressions can scaffold more elaborate empathic imaginings. In one celebrated sequence, the film crosscuts between the desperate efforts of Bruno (Robert Walker) to retrieve a cigarette lighter that has fallen into a drain, with the no less determined attempt by Guy (Farley Granger) to win a tennis match. In both lines of action, Hitchcock presents us with highly legible close-ups of facial expressions (of concentration, exertion, anxiety, and pain) and motor actions (stretching, grasping, running, swinging) apt to trigger motor and affective mimicry of these very gestures and affective states. (Bruno's grasping for the lighter is particularly resonant in this context, since most of the early mirror neuron experiments involved subjects witnessing objects being picked up.) These mimickings may initiate, support, and enrich our broader imaginative efforts, also prompted by the film, to understand what it is like to be each of these characters—that is, to be in these situations possessing their distinctive character traits, histories, and goals. Thus we might centrally

---

[10] Gallese, Keysers, & Rizzolatti (2004): 397; Iacoboni (2008): 111; Iacoboni (this volume).

[11] Gallese et al. (2004): 397 and box 3 (p. 401). Those neural structures being (predominantly) the amygdala in the case of fear, and the insula in the case of disgust. See Gallese et al. (2004): box 1 (p. 399).

[12] Gallese et al. (2004): box 3 (p. 401). Giacomo Rizzolatti treats affective mirroring as 'a necessary condition for' fully-fledged imaginative empathy, while stressing that on its own such mirroring does not amount to empathy. Rizzolatti's perspective on mirror neurons is laid out in full in G. Rizzolatti & C. Sinigaglia (2008). The quoted phrase appears on page 190.

imagine Guy's immediate urgency as he attempts to finish off the tennis match, but also his anger towards Bruno and the excruciating injustice of his situation (in which he has every reason to resent his wife, but, appearances notwithstanding, has neither killed her nor connived with Bruno to kill her). The mirror system allows us to feel Guy's exertions on the tennis court, palpably connecting us with him, and thereby grounds and consolidates our imaginative appreciation of the larger complex of thoughts and feelings undergone by him.[13] My hypothesis, then, is twofold: *Strangers on a Train* not only shows us how a film might strive to elicit 'motor resonance'[14] and affective mimicry, but also suggests how such mimicry might go on to scaffold fully-fledged empathic imagining.

One might wonder, given the distinct types of mental process gathered under the umbrella of empathy in the discussion so far, whether the definition of the concept on offer here is really coherent. That worry might be fuelled further by considering the tangled history of the term. Introduced originally as a specialist term in psychology and art history in German, on the one hand 'empathy' has spread into ordinary English usage, and on the other hand the term has been revived—as this book testifies—as a term of art in psychology and philosophy of mind. The history of the term is further complicated by its relationship with the English 'sympathy'. In contemporary debate, empathy is typically contrasted with sympathy, where the latter is defined as a 'pro' attitude undergirding positive but *acentral* emotional responses to others—a kind of 'feeling for' others, rather than the 'feeling with' characteristic of empathy.[15] But David Hume and Adam Smith used 'sympathy' to refer to a phenomenon that we would label empathy. So long as our aim is to track and define a *phenomenon*, however, rather than give an account of the use of a *term* in ordinary or any other kind of language, the complex history of the term(s) used to refer to the phenomenon we are interested in need not derail the project. In this spirit, then, we can condense the description of empathy given in the discussion so far in the following way:

Person A empathizes with target person B if and only if A personally (or centrally) imagines perceiving, cognizing, or feeling, partially or globally, the perceiving, cognizing, and feeling of B, where such imagining involves conscious, qualitative awareness of the state imagined. A may engage in such empathy on the basis of information gleaned from perceiving B, or information inferred or otherwise derived indirectly. Various 'sub-imaginative' forms of direct responsiveness to the mental states of others, such as contagion and mimicry, may initiate and/or bolster empathy (and perhaps typically do bolster empathy); these phenomena form a family with

---

[13] The example does raise a further and somewhat unusual complication: given that the sequence (and the film as a whole) alternates our attention between two characters with opposing goals, how do we 'manage' conflicting mimickings and imaginings? Can we run, in parallel, two conflicting empathic scenarios, or does the larger context of our sympathy for Guy entail that the sequence will likely only prompt empathic imagining for him, while our response to Bruno will be 'contained' at the level of lower-level motor and affective mimicry?

[14] Iacoboni (this volume).

[15] For a fuller discussion of sympathy (and its converse, antipathy), see Smith (1995): 187ff.

empathy insofar as all are characterized by A 'feeling with' B, such that if A feels anxious, B 'takes on' this anxiety (by contagion, mimicry, or volitional simulation). But contagion and mimicry alone do not constitute fully-fledged empathy, which on this account requires the higher-level type of volitional imagining described above.

It might also be objected that the effort to render through literature or film 'what it is like' to be some other kind of person in a particular situation might involve only an 'imaginative grasp' of the situation, rather than the form of intersubjective relationship specified by empathy. There are several problems, however, with this counter-proposal. On its own, it is simply underspecified—if having an 'imaginative grasp' of a situation does not amount to simulating the states that one seeks to 'grasp', and in that sense empathizing with the person experiencing those states, we need to know what it *does* amount to. The alternative construals of 'having an imaginative grasp' that I can see are as follows:

- We recognize or understand what it would be like to be a certain kind of person in a certain situation in a purely cognitive sense—that the grief of a parent losing a child has a particular quality, for example, characterized by the ironic survival of the child by the parent. We can identify the state in terms of its relationship to various practices, norms, and other situations and states of mind. In this sense we come to understand or grasp it, but without at any point simulating it (or empathizing with the subject by simulating it).
- Our imaginative grasp of the situation takes on an emotional character, but remains an 'acentral' one, a sympathetic (in the contemporary sense) rather than empathetic response. Coming to know the character or person who experiences the grief of the loss of their child, we feel *for* them, but not *with* them. Of course, such feeling for a person necessitates the kind of intellectual or cognitive understanding of situations and states specified in our first option above—we can't feel pity for a grieving individual unless we understand in this sense the nature of grief. So in this second option, we go beyond cognitive understanding to respond emotionally, but not in the form of empathy. Our emotional response is asymmetrical with the character's—since they are responding to one situation but we are responding to their response to that situation. Empathy plays no role here, either as a prerequisite for understanding or for having a sympathetic emotional response, nor as an overall outcome of the process of engaging with the person or character.[16]
- A third possibility: having an 'imaginative grasp' of a situation might amount to 'in his shoes' imagining.[17] This form of imagining is closely related to but distinct from empathy as defined here. In such cases I might imagine how *I* would react in

---

[16] Noël Carroll has pursued this line of argument for many years. See, for example, Carroll (1990) and (2001b): 306–16. See also Goldie (this volume).

[17] Goldie (2000): ch. 7.

the situation of another—if I were in his shoes, *but possessed of my own rather than his traits, states, and history*. As I have implied through my initial example of personal imagining—the example of imagining the road accident—such imagining forms the ground of possibility for empathy. In being able to detach myself from *my* current actual state and situation and project myself imaginatively into an alternative situation, I open up the possibility of imagining how some other person might experience this situation. (Or, to put it differently, my imagining of the alternative situation might extend to include the dispositions and characters of the agents involved, in addition to its 'non-personal' elements—the setting, goals and roles at stake.) Thinking of the movement from self to imagined other in incremental terms demystifies the idea of empathy—there is no magical transplanting of one person into another, but rather the gradual and cumulative substitution of elements appropriate for myself with those appropriate for another. I have no particular anxiety around crowds, but this character does, so imagining being trapped in a surging crowd at a football stadium comes out differently if I am engaging in 'empathic' or 'in his shoes' imagining respectively. Certainly this is a process that admits of degrees, but to the extent that our imagining involves some degree of modelling on another person, empathic imagining is involved. In our experience of fictions, these two forms of personal imagining run together, either in parallel or commingled.[18]

The problem with the first two options is that they fail to take seriously the qualitative, 'what it is like' dimension of statements like Hornby's (on his football memoir *Fever Pitch*), and Cronenberg's (on his film *Eastern Promises*), quoted at the head of this essay. I think it is implausible simply to deny that many authors and filmmakers regard empathic response, along the lines described here, as among the responses they seek from readers and viewers; remarks of this type by artists are legion.[19] Perhaps such artists are simply wrong about the nature of the psychological transactions that their fictions initiate, in which case 'empathy' might be explained *away* by a kind of 'error theory'. Certainly there is often hyperbole in such statements, as in the case of Cronenberg's comments on *Eastern Promises*. But we have yet to see a really convincing version of such an error theory of empathy.[20] The third option is more plausible insofar as it addresses the qualitative dimension of empathy, but such 'in his shoes' imagining,

---

[18] Cf. Smith (1995): 80; Goldman (2006a): ch. 7. In the electronic abstract for this chapter (Oxford Scholarship Online), Goldman notes that 'an important stage of simulation for mindreading requires reflection on one's own current states'.

[19] Dan Flory notes the use of the line 'entertainment that challenges your own ability to experience the emotions of others' in the trailer for *No Way Out* (Joseph Mankiewicz (1950)), a formulation that once again points to the idea of empathy. Flory (2008): 31–2.

[20] Noël Carroll (in conversation) suggested this way of characterizing the case against empathy. Carroll and I have both pursued an 'error theory' of the notion of 'identification', arguing that all or most of the implications of the concept are conceptually confused or empirically unfounded (see my (1995), and the references to Carroll in note 16). In effect, Carroll carries over his error theory of identification to empathy, while I take the latter concept to be defensible and to pick out a real phenomenon.

I contend, is intimately bound up with empathy, both conceptually and in the actual practice and experience of engaging with fictions. 'In his shoes' imagining is not an alternative to the account I propose, but an oversimplified version of it. The third option does, however, underline an important point. Our experience of engaging with characters in fictions and other narratives cannot be understood on the basis of empathy alone. There may be particular types of narrative in which empathy plays no significant role. But every type of response assayed in the discussion so far—purely cognitive understanding, 'acentral' sympathetic responses, contagion, mimicry, 'in his shoes' imagining, and, yes, empathy—plays a role in an account of the psychology of fictional response as a whole. And empathy is usually conjoined with other responses (a point to which I return in the final section of this essay). The issue at stake in this essay is to understand the nature and place of empathy in particular, within this array of types of response, more adequately.

7.1 Expansionism and the Extended Mind

So much for an initial characterization of empathy; what about the *extended mind*? Proponents of the theory of the extended mind hold that the human mind is distinctive in part because of the manner and extent to which it exploits features of the environment to enhance its cognitive capacities, including, for example, memory, mathematical calculation, pattern recognition, and other forms of problem solving. Andy Clark and David Chalmers characterize the extended mind hypothesis as a form of '*active externalism*, based on the active role of the environment in driving cognitive processes'.[21] The use of pen and paper to perform long multiplication, physical rearranging of letter tiles in games like Scrabble, and slide rules are all offered as quotidian instances of the cognitive exploitation of 'environmental supports'. Another example for them is language, which 'appears to be a central means by which cognitive processes are extended into the world. Think of a group of people brainstorming around a table, or a philosopher who thinks best by writing, developing her ideas as she goes'.[22] What is key in such cases is that some part of the world is reliably *coupled* with the mind to form an integrated cognitive system; it is in this sense that the mind is extended into the world, structuring and co-opting part of it in order to augment its capabilities. Clark and Chalmers begin their essay with the image of a person working at a computer screen, their attempts to solve a spatial problem aided by the externalization of the problem on the screen before them. Equally we might think of a skilled musician playing their instrument, in terms of the intimate 'coupling' between person and instrument, and the enhancement of the musical cognition that this enables.[23]

---

[21] Clark & Chalmers (1998): 7.
[22] Ibid. 11–12.
[23] One of Jimi Hendrix's bass players, Billy Cox, commented on Hendrix: 'Some people thought he was crazy because they couldn't understand why a man would constantly be playing a guitar all the time. But basically what he was doing was making this instrument an extension of his body' (Wheeler (2004): 137).

A closely-related proposal, due to Stephen Kosslyn, puts the emphasis on the extension of the individual mind by *social* means, that is, through other individuals and groups. Kosslyn argues that 'Evolution has allowed our brains to be configured during development so that we are 'plug compatible' with other humans, so that others can help us extend ourselves'.[24] We will see shortly just how apt Kosslyn's description here of what he terms 'social prosthetic systems' is as a context for understanding empathy.

The extended mind thesis is a radical one that by no means commands the assent of all or even most philosophers of mind. But it comes in different strengths, and the version explicated here is considerably stronger than is necessary for my purposes (which, as will become clear, include the idea that empathy and narrative cognition may be enhanced by virtue of external elements). Frederick Adams and Kenneth Aizawa mark a distinction between the extended mind thesis, and what they regard as the more modest 'extended cognitive system hypothesis'.[25] One of Clark and Chalmers' thought experiments concerns a character called Otto, who is afflicted with Alzheimer's disease.[26] Otto relies on a notebook to record crucial new information about the world, just as Leonard—who endures anterograde amnesia—relies on polaroids and verbal tattoos in Christopher Nolan's *Memento* (2000). Otto's language skills are intact, and the notebook is always with him and poised for access. Now, according to Clark and Chalmers' extended mind thesis, the notebook is quite literally a part of Otto's mind. On Adams and Aizawa's weaker thesis, the notebook is certainly part of a system established *by* Otto's mind to assist his memory, but the notebook itself lies outside his mind. Otto's mind remains in the driving seat of an extended cognitive system; the elements outside the mind, though part of the system, do not have the same status as those elements bound by the mind in the traditional sense. And note that, though not all mental states are conscious, it doesn't look plausible to treat consciousness as arising from every element of the extended cognitive system—from the pens and paper beyond the skull as well as from the neurons beneath it. The physical seat of the conscious mind, as well as our phenomenal sense of its location, both appear to be located immediately 'north of the neck.'[27]

---

[24] Kosslyn (2007): 547.

[25] Adams & Aizawa (2008): 11; see also x and 106–32.

[26] Clark & Chalmers (1998): 12–13.

[27] The phrase—not the argument—is from Fodor (1999): 68. Two other models might deliver what is necessary to recognize the distinctive way in which the human mind expands its capacities by exploiting external resources, without demanding drastic metaphysical revisionism. The first is the familiar concept of *technology*. Film-making is a technology, obviously enough, but on this argument narrative and fiction are also (overlapping) technologies, one of whose functions is to exercise and enhance our empathic capacity. Patrick Maynard, who defines technologies as 'extenders or *amplifiers of our powers* to do things', has advanced a comprehensive account of photography as a technology expanding our powers of visualization and imagination (Maynard (1997a): 75). Maynard is also at pains to stress that 'filtering' or 'suppression' of our capacities goes hand in hand with such amplification. The second model is afforded by the notion of *niche construction*, a concept of much more recent vintage, which highlights the relevance for evolution of the way in which organisms in general, and humans particularly emphatically, are not only *adapted* to their environments, but actively *adapt* them to their needs. '[I]t is readily apparent that contemporary humans are born into a massively

So what is the relevance of all of this for the notion of empathy? There are, I think, two ways in which empathy might play a role within a theory of extended mentality. We might regard empathy as a mechanism of the *coupling* between the mind and that part of the world through which it extends itself (in which case it takes its place alongside other such mechanisms, like the visual perception which enables Otto to couple his notebook with his mind). When we empathize with another person, we extend our mind to incorporate part of his or her mind. (Iacoboni, by way of Husserl, also uses the term 'coupling' to describe the work of mirror neurons in forging empathic connections between individuals.[28]) In doing so, we exploit some part of the environment around us—in this case, another human being—and thereby learn something about the environment. Imagine that I am standing, face to face, in a conversational exchange with Amy; her eye is caught by something behind me, and an alarmed expression appears on her face. I not only immediately recognize the class of expression she exhibits, but *feel* the emotion and its force, via the mechanism of mimicry.[29] Even before I turn to discover the object of her glance, I have thus learnt something about her, and about the wider environment in which we both find ourselves—something significant and untoward has taken place and Amy is concerned about it. Much, of course, remains to be filled in; but empathy, triggered here by affective mimicry, has played a crucial initiating role, acting like a sentry alerting me to the presence of something likely to be relevant to me. I have learned something, and I have learned it in part by co-opting the perceptual and emotive capacities of another agent. (Of course, Amy's emotion and my mimicking of it are numerically distinct; she possesses and experiences her alarm, and I possess and experience my mimicking of her alarm. But my perceptual 'reach' has been extended by virtue of my uptake and mimicking of her alarm.)[30]

Alternatively, empathy might be seen as one of those capacities—alongside memory—which is *enhanced by* the extended mind; that is, it might be seen as an end as well as a means in extended mentality. And if empathy is enhanced in this way,

---

constructed world, with an ecological inheritance that includes a legacy of houses, cities, cars, farms, nations, e-commerce, and global warming. Niche construction and ecological inheritance are thus likely to have been particularly consequential in human evolution' (Odling-Smee, Laland, & Feldman (2003): 241). Storytelling in general and fiction in particular are part of the niche that humans have constructed for themselves over evolutionary time.

[28] Iacoboni (2008): 265. Iacoboni also states that 'The mirror neuron system seems to project internally ... other people onto our own brains' (260), and in his paper in this volume, he writes: 'We empathize effortlessly and automatically with each other because evolution has selected neural systems that blend self and other's actions, intentions, and emotions... Our neurobiology ... puts us "within each other"' (57).

[29] See again the references in note 9.

[30] Cf. Dominic Lopes' discussion of social referencing in 'The Empathic Eye' (this volume). Of course, it remains true in this example that, in theory, a non-empathic process of inference—of the sort associated with 'theory of mind'—would be sufficient to arrive at the conclusion that Amy is alarmed by some change in the environment. Here I simply assume that mimicry, or some such process, is in fact the characteristic way in which we make such inferences, in order to focus on how such a process would cohere with the theory of the extended mind.

the domain of representation, and especially the practice of narration, constitutes the 'environmental support' created by the mind to drive its amplified performance. Public narration—exemplified above all by the narrative arts—is the anvil on which such extension is forged. We can think, for example, of the devices of film-making as *cognitive prostheses*, in much the same way that we think of other devices, like the telescope or microscope, as perceptual prostheses—devices which reinforce our native perceptual capacities.

How, then, do the various forms of representation and narration augment empathy? They do so as part of a more general reinforcement of the imagination. We all possess an innate capacity to imagine things. We use our imaginations routinely and pervasively in the course of planning our lives, an activity which requires us to imagine and assess different paths of action that we might take in the immediate and more distant future. But now contemplate the difference between the kind and scale of imagining instantiated by, say, *War and Peace*, or *Hamlet*, or *Heimat* (Edgar Reitz (1984)), or *The Sopranos* (David Chase (1997–2008)), and the kind of imagining we can cope with unaided. 'The intrigues of people in conflict', writes Steven Pinker,

can multiply out in so many ways that no one could possibly play out the consequences of all the courses of action in the mind's eye. Fictional narratives supply us with a mental catalogue of the fatal conundrums we might face someday and the outcome of strategies we could deploy in them. What are the options if I were to suspect that my uncle killed my father, took his position, and married my mother? If my hapless older brother got no respect in the family, are there circumstances that might lead him to betray me?[31]

So it is that we extend our imaginative capacity—and thus our capacity to ponder and perhaps even solve moral and social problems—by, to take another example of public narration, arraying a set on a stage and adding some props. As Kendall Walton has argued, our first acts of mimesis are those embodied by childhood games of make-believe;[32] these games also constitute the beginnings, in the development of the individual, of the *extended imagination*.

Patrick Hogan and Lisa Zunshine have both objected to Pinker's argument, partly on the grounds that his argument makes narrative as such essentially didactic.[33] Several things can be said in response to this. First, the argument here is only that this is one

---

[31] Pinker (1999): 543. Pinker speaks here of a 'mental catalogue', but tellingly he follows his list of questions posed by well-known fictions by saying: 'The answers are to be found in any bookstore or video shop', indicating how the 'mental' extends out into, and is supported by, the physical environment. Note also that Pinker likens this to *case-based reasoning* in research on artificial intelligence. One might also connect the role of gossip and fiction in building up such a catalogue of 'cases' with a particularist view of moral psychology and reasoning: the making of moral judgements is so complex that it cannot be based (at least not solely) on the application of abstract moral principles, but must work via analogy with, or through, the database of cases. The complex domain of moral deliberation and action is a central part of the broader complexity of human interaction and conflict described by Pinker.

[32] Walton (1990).

[33] 'Instructive' is the word Zunshine uses (Zunshine (2006): 178). See also Hogan (2003): 211–12.

significant function of narrative. Second, Pinker's proposal may be more plausible if it is not put merely in terms of possible actions, but in terms of feelings and states of being which may lead to actions—what would it be or feel like to be such a person in such a situation? Take a literary example—the figure of Bonnie Clutter in Truman Capote's *In Cold Blood*, who suffers from a form of chronic depression. In one scene, Mrs Clutter is discovered weeping in her room by a visiting family friend, Wilma Kidwell. As Mrs Kidwell comforts her, Mrs Clutter speaks:

'Wilma,' she said, 'I've been listening to you, Wilma. All of you. Laughing. Having a good time. I'm missing out on everything. The best years, the children—everything. A little while, and even Kenyon [her son] will be grown up—a man. And how will he remember me? As a kind of ghost, Wilma.'[34]

Most of us, most of the time, don't think beyond stereotypes, generic ideas, and familiar imagery of experiences like 'depression'. Capote's precise delineation of Mrs Clutter's mindset, as manifest in her agonized outburst, allows us to go beyond such schematic ideas. Once we can appreciate the specificity of Mrs Clutter's situation and her feelings, the idea that we might then contemplate the possible paths of action leading from her situation—what *we* might do, and what *she* might do, in her shoes— does not seem so far-fetched. Theorists of emotion, after all, regard 'action readiness' as a typical element of an emotion (though Mrs Clutter may be a limit case, her depression precisely denying her the sense that there is anything she can do to help herself).[35] Finally, it might be that the classics invoked by Pinker are poor examples— either for the good reason that their complexity obscures this basic narrative function, or for the bad reason that we just can't stand the idea that *Hamlet* is, after all, in one respect at least, not that different to one of Aesop's fables. If we substitute, say, *United 93*, is it really such a stretch to say that the film helps us imagine what being on that flight was like for its passengers (or even, to a lesser degree, its hijackers)—and that this includes imagining deliberating over the options they had: compliance with the hijackers, resistance through subterfuge, or outright counter-attack?

The domain of artistic representation, then, provides us with the most striking and complex examples of extended imagining. But we shouldn't allow these objects to overshadow their more humdrum cousins. Gossip, everyday 'thought experiments' ('what are you going to do *if* you're made redundant?'), doodling, and sketching[36] are all ways of playing out our thoughts with the aid of external supports, in the form of both purely physical props and (as in the case of empathy) other human agents with whom we converse and exchange ideas. Such activities are tools that we use in the course of practical, social, and ethical problem-solving each and every day, and they

---

[34] Truman Capote, *In Cold Blood*, 28.
[35] See, for example, Oatley & Jenkins (1996): 96, 105–6.
[36] Patrick Maynard describes drawing as 'a way of thinking for most of us [as pre-adolescent children], for working out, observing, imagining, stating; and, for most, the fossil that remains is a doodle on a telephone pad' (1997b): 231.

form the seedbed and training ground for the artistic imagination (just as much as does 'pure' imagination—that is, imagination conceived as a mental activity in 'narrow,' purely internal terms).

Thinking of the narrative arts in this way brings my proposal into contact with another recent argument, advanced by Dominic Lopes, concerning the basis on which we study the perception and cognition of artworks in relation to perception and cognition in non-aesthetic, 'everyday' contexts. Lopes notes that most empirical research on 'artistic cognition' seeks to show how the appreciation of various sorts of artwork depends on the deployment of ordinary perceptual and cognitive capacities. Lopes distinguishes such an approach from a related but more sophisticated position that he designates *expansionism*, through a pair of proposals:

First, I propose that our engagement with most works of art, either as creators or as consumers, depends on the exercise of the very cognitive capacities we use to navigate our environment and to deal with others of our species. Second, I propose that in our engagement with works of art, these cognitive capacities are frequently extended in quite new directions, operating in ways not seen outside artistic contexts.[37]

If Lopes' first thesis is correct, we should expect that, in one sense or another, empathizing with human agents will play an important a role in our engagement with fictions.[38] If Lopes' second thesis is correct, we might expect to find empathy 'flexing its muscles fully' in the context of narrative art, that is, functioning in 'new ways, perhaps in ways never evident' in extra-artistic perception'.[39]

In what ways might empathy, then, be stretched and refined through its engagement by the narrative arts? In *scope* and *intensity*. Our ability to empathize is extended across a wide range of types of person, and sustained and intensified by virtue of the artificial, 'designed' environment of fictional experience. We are all limited, to a greater or lesser extent, in the opportunities we have to engage with situations, persons, and cultures different to a greater or lesser extent from our own. For those who want to take it up, fiction—and, once again, public narration more generally—affords a limitless horizon of opportunities for such engagement; and if empathy (along with its relatives) is as basic to human social life as the argument so far suggests, empathy will be one form of such engagement. The possibility of understanding 'from the inside'—that is, empathically imagining—human agents in social situations more or less radically different from our own emerges. We may come not only to see, but to feel, how an agent in a given situation comes to feel that there are only a particular set of 'live options'—viable choices—open to them, a much narrower range than we might believe them to possess

---

[37] Lopes (2003): 645–6. The first and second proposals here correspond, respectively, with the problems of 'carryover' and 'difference' discussed in Lopes, 'The Empathic Eye' (this volume). Lopes also speaks of pictures as 'perceptual prostheses' in that essay. See also his (1996).

[38] For a similar argument, making the link between the everyday functioning of emotion and its operation in relation to fictional entities, see Robinson (2005): 130.

[39] Lopes (2003): 645.

if we assess their situation from the outside—that is, in narrowly rational terms and without an attempt to model or simulate their state of mind.

Public forms of narration help us to sustain imaginative projects of this sort, allowing us to work through the details, and the possible dramatic patterns or 'arcs' of development, of such unfamiliar scenarios with a clarity and precision impossible without them. Consider once again the analogy with music: just as instrumentation and notation enable composers to create, and listeners to appreciate, musical form on an exponentially higher scale of elaboration than is possible without these material supports, so the novelist and the filmmaker, through the technologies of their trade, are able to sustain ambitious imaginative projects, thereby affording readers and viewers of their narrative works an opportunity to do likewise.

Along with this process of sustained elaboration comes the possibility of *intensifying* our empathic responses. This might well sound highly counterintuitive, since we are, generally speaking, accustomed to thinking of the responses we have to imagined scenarios, even those embodied and supported by material representations, as pale versions of the equivalent responses we would feel in real circumstances.[40] I can be moved by the untimely death of a sympathetic and central character, but not to the extent that I will be moved by the untimely death of an actual friend. My claim is that the crafted environment of narrative artifacts enables the authors of such objects to shape, and thus to distil and concentrate, our responses to a high degree. As Carl Plantinga has demonstrated, mainstream narrative films commonly feature one or more 'scenes of empathy', in which a critical moment in the drama is capped and highlighted by prolonged and vivid depiction of a major character in the throes of emotion.[41] Such scenes, for Plantinga, are designed to elicit an empathic response, and maximize the possibility and intensity of such a response by their sustained and detailed representation of facial and vocal expressions of affect. These expressions, as we have seen, are apt to trigger mimicry and contagion in the viewer, which may then scaffold imaginative empathy. Thus, in terms of both narrative set-up and stylistic presentation, the maker of a narrative representation has the opportunity to 'engineer' an object precisely designed to elicit empathy; not for nothing do we speak of 'tear-*jerkers*'. Just as the culinary arts enable us to refine, and intensify, the flavours available in unprocessed, natural foods, so the makers of fiction may refine and intensify certain kinds of natural emotional response. It is in this sense, and only in this sense, that I propose our empathic responses to fiction may be more intense than those to real circumstances.

---

[40] This is an assumption carried over in Gregory Currie's simulation theory of fiction; or at least, something like this is suggested by him in his (2003), where he states: 'Imaginative counterparts of beliefs and desires will have these capacities to mimic beliefs and desires [and the role of beliefs and desires in generating affective states] only in certain circumstances and even then only approximately' (294).

[41] Plantinga (1999).

7.2 Empathy Stays in the Picture

Unfortunately for me, the drift of my argument is in the opposite direction of that recently taken by at least some of those who would seem to be my natural allies. Responding to a number of arguments sceptical that imaginative simulation has any important role to play in our comprehension and appreciation of fictions, Gregory Currie concedes that 'understanding real people and understanding fictional, and especially literary characters are very different activities'.[42] However, a number of points can be made in defence of the claim that empathy (along with its relatives) plays a significant role in our apprehension of fictions and other narratives. The first of these points concerns the distinction between the *quantitative* and the *qualitative* dimensions of the claim for the significance of empathy. Sceptics tend to assume that any claim for the centrality of empathy to the process of apprehending narrative must make it quantitatively dominant, or at least among the dominant modes by which we engage with the story; it must be something, so the assumption goes, that we are doing most or much of the time when we watch a movie or read a novel. But one may ascribe qualitative significance to empathy even if it occupies, quantitatively speaking, a rather small proportion of the time we devote to engaging with the fiction. Consider again Plantinga's argument, according to which mainstream films periodically elicit an empathic response from the viewer. These moments of empathy are clearly significant, because they occur at the climactic moments in the drama of the film, even though they might occupy no more than, say, 5% of the duration of the film (and quite probably a good deal less than that).

Similarly, it is important to keep apart the *instrumental* and *intrinsic* value that we might attach to empathy. Although Currie acknowledges that there are some fictions which seem to call out for empathy with characters as an end in its own right, simulating characters' states of mind performs only an instrumental value in his scheme as a whole. Currie labels such simulation *secondary* imagining because it performs this instrumental role in relation to *primary* imagining—the business, that is, of imagining what is true-in-the-fiction.[43] But one might argue that empathy has intrinsic value in general in our experience of narrative; that empathy, so valued, is central to the institutions of narrative and fiction, and not merely of interest in the case of some exceptional narratives. In life, empathy is typically functional, a means to an end, insofar as the capacity itself most likely evolved as a result of its utility in helping us to navigate the physical and social worlds (consider again the example of my encounter with the alarmed Amy, above). In narrative art, by contrast, empathy often becomes an end as well as a means. As both Hornby and Cronenberg indicate, to know what it is like to be a certain kind of person in a certain kind of situation is something that we

---

[42] Currie (2003): 295.
[43] Currie (1995): 152–5.

value for its own sake, and a primary motivation for both the creation and consumption of fiction.

The distinction between instrumental and intrinsic value points to a tension in the literature on empathy concerning the *conditions* which are likely to elicit empathy in the context of narrative consumption, and the *purpose* of such empathy when it does arise. On the one hand we find the argument that empathy is most likely to arise when we have some, but very limited, knowledge of an agent in a situation, empathy serving in such a context to probe and reveal more of what is or might be going on inside the agent. Call this the *mindreading* function of empathy in relation to representational art. On the other hand, we find the argument that empathy is most likely to arise—or in the case of radically unfamiliar cultural settings, can only arise—when we are furnished with extensive and detailed knowledge regarding the agent and their situation. (Perhaps this is the lesson of Florian Henckel von Donnersmarck's *Das Leben der Anderen* (*The Lives of Others*) (2007): only when the Stasi agent engages in sustained surveillance of the personal life of the radical playwright he is assigned to spy on is he capable of empathically understanding *what it is like* for the dramatist.) Here empathy does not serve to uncover possible new information, but to put the information that we do possess under a new description, so to speak, allowing us to feel it 'from the inside'. Call this the *mindfeeling* function of empathy. In the first case, empathy operates at or near the base of the narrative understanding; in the second, empathy arises at the apex of such understanding.

We can explore these two very different possibilities through the following three sequences from Julio Médem's *Los amantes del círculo polar* (*Lovers of the Arctic Circle*) (1998). The opening credit sequence of the film reveals a small plane grounded in a blizzard landscape. The image fades to black, and the new image which fades in is superficially similar, but difficult to recognize as such—a black and white photograph of the plane in a newspaper which is moving up and down. The newspaper flies into air, and then we see alternating shots of a woman (played by Najwa Nimri) running, from behind, up some stairs and into an apartment, with frontal shots of a man (Fele Martínez), apparently pursuing her. Inside the apartment, the man and woman embrace, but the woman possesses a strange, glassy stare, suggesting neither relief nor passion, even though her eyes well up with tears. Careful attention reveals other enigmatic features: the man's face can be seen in the woman's eyes in certain shots, a reflection which is hard to make sense of spatially. During these opening moments of the film, we're largely at a loss as to what is going on. Disdaining the sort of dense, redundant, and direct exposition characteristic of many narrative openings, the narration here is highly elliptical. According to the mindreading hypothesis, empathic imagining might come into play quite naturally, as a means of fathoming what might be going on. Urged along by automatic, instinctive, low-level mimicry and contagion, I might imaginatively simulate being a woman, running, being pursued by a man, but then embracing the pursuer: what beliefs, emotions, and states of affair might account for such actions?[44] In initiating such imagining, we draw on what information we can perceive and infer, and our imagining may be assisted by mimicry and contagion; indeed, as I have suggested, these processes may have nudged us towards empathic imagining in the first place.

By contrast, some way into the film we witness a scene in which Otto—the male protagonist and the male character we see in the opening sequence, and no relation to Clark and Chalmers' Otto!—grieves over his mother's death. Otto is shown in medium close-up, peering through a small window into the furnace room where his mother's body is about to be cremated. His father, stepmother, and stepsister Ana—also his lover—stand behind him. As the coffin bursts into flames, Otto's hostility towards his father (Nancho Novo)—who he blames for his mother's death—recedes, the two of them falling into a grief-stricken embrace, the pain of loss clearly expressed in their facial, vocal, and bodily movements. As my commentary indicates, by this point we have a very good handle on all the major characters and their interrelationships. According to the mindfeeling hypothesis, this richly developed context, along with the cues prompting mimicry and contagion present in the scene, solicits an empathic response. (The scene also represents an example of Plantinga's 'scene of empathy', albeit a relatively attenuated one, perhaps in line with its art film status.)

Lastly, in the final scene of the film, several shots from the opening sequence are repeated, but here they are extended, supplemented by other shots elaborating the situation, and placed at the fulcrum of a fully developed narrative. We now understand that the woman, Ana, has just been hit by a car, moments before she would have been reunited with Otto. The car collides with Ana as she crosses the road to the apartment, her attention fixed on the newspaper report of the crashed plane, in which she fears Otto may have perished. As she is thrown to the ground, the newspaper flies into the air; and in the cruelest of ironies, Otto arrives at the scene only seconds later. The embrace that we witness in the opening sequence is a fantasy of what would have happened had the accident not intervened; the glassy stare is the look of a dying person; the welling tears the sole sign of sentience; the reflection of Otto in Anna's eyes is created as he kneels by her stricken body. As with the scene of grieving, the mindfeeling hypothesis suggests that it is precisely the density of information available to us by this point that is likely to precipitate fully empathic imagining.

The friend of empathy has still another card to play. We mustn't confuse, the advocate insists, *occurrent* and *retrospective* empathy: that is, empathizing in the course of reading a novel or watching a movie, and empathizing after the fact, as we reflect on the experience of the novel or the film. Pretty much the entire recent debate on simulation and fiction has been geared to our occurrent experience of artworks, for obvious, and good, reasons. Our engagement with artworks is, or rather is assumed to be, at its most intense as we engage with them; the proof of the pudding lies in the

---

[44] Currie stresses the inferential role of imaginative simulation in (2003): 294.

perception of an artwork. Surely, though, we have to allow that artworks assume their significance within a wider frame of reference than that of our direct engagement with the artwork, even if it all necessarily begins within that timeframe. We come to realize things about artworks as we reflect on them after the fact—the significance of a line of dialogue suddenly comes to us; the connection between an early and a later scene drops into place. And while movies and stage plays are traditionally consumed in one continuous block, the narrative of a novel or a television drama is much more likely to be consumed in dispersed fashion, over days, weeks, or months, so occurrent engagement with the narrative alternates with retrospective and indeed *anticipatory* engagement with it. Rereading or reviewing a narrative adds another layer to this picture. My suggestion is that, if nothing else, empathy may be an important feature of our retrospective and anticipatory engagement with a narrative, rising up in the spaces between our occurrent engagement with it.

Finally, and by way of conclusion, the role(s) I am according to empathy in our experience of narrative works is sometimes deemed implausible, I suspect, because of some lingering, problematic, Cartesian assumptions concerning the operations of the mind. Those assumptions concern the *consciousness*, *singularity*, and *seriality* of the contents of the mind. To say that I might, as a part of my imaginative engagement with the final scene in *Lovers of the Arctic Circle*, empathize with Otto's grief, is not to say that that imagined grief necessarily dominates my consciousness at any point.[45] Nor is it to say that imagining Otto's grief 'from the inside' is the only activity undertaken by my mind at a given point in the course of viewing the scene. We know that the brain processes in parallel; there are limits to its processing capacities, but it is constantly in the business of processing many items simultaneously, in different ways.[46] So in arguing that I might empathize with Otto as he discovers Ana dying in the road, we should not cash that out in terms of Otto's grief bestriding my theatre of consciousness, loudly declaiming itself to the exclusion of all other mental operations; rather, we need to think in terms of 'a complex mosaic of simulations' taking place alongside other mental activities.[47] After all, we wouldn't think it odd to claim that at the same moment I am watching—and thus visually processing—the shot of the newspaper flying into the air in the final scene of *Lovers*, that I am also remembering that I have seen this image before, recalling in which part of the film it appeared, and working out how it fits into the causal, narrative sequence of the film as a whole. If we can countenance the mind doing all these sorts of things simultaneously, why wouldn't we countenance empathic

---

[45] Indeed, counterintuitive thought it may be, it is conceivable that empathic imagining's lower-level cousins, emotional contagion and affective mimicry, may occur without breaking through to consciousness at all. Given that we know that 'blindsight' exists, can we confidently close the door on the possibility of 'blind'—non-conscious—emotion?

[46] See, for example, Clark (2001): 40–1; and Daniel Dennett's conception of the mind as a 'locus of multiple, quasiindependent [sic] processing streams' (Clark (2001): 178), or 'multiple drafts' (Dennett (1991): ch. 5).

[47] Currie (2003): 297.

imagining as one, possibly subordinate, mental activity among many taking place? Just as, in the case of my self-focussed personal imagining, I never lose sight of the fact that I am actually in the living room and my son is safely playing behind me, even as I experience the queasy sensation of fear at the thought of an accident, so in the case of this fictional imagining, I never lose sight of the overall dramatic situation and the emotions of the various other characters, nor of the fact that I am watching a fiction, even as I empathize with Otto.[48]

[48] Thanks to audiences at the 2006 Fullerton 'Empathy' conference, the 2006 Society for Cognitive Studies of the Moving Image conference in Potsdam, and especially Amy Coplan, Peter Goldie, Margrethe Vaage, Patrick Vondereau, Dan Flory, Noël Carroll, Greg Currie, Susan Feagin, and Derek Matravers for helpful comments. Thanks also to Amy and Peter for the original invitation to the very generously hosted Fullerton conference. The tea bags have been strained, the soap long since dissolved, but I still use the Moleskin notebook.

8

An Empathic Eye

Dominic McIver Lopes

What you see can shape how you feel, and the route from seeing to feeling sometimes involves empathy—as you might empathize with a woman you see grieving the death of her child. But empathy also comes from what you see in pictures: many paintings, drawings, prints, and photographs evoke empathy and are designed to do so. Going further, it seems that episodes of empathy triggered by pictures can help build up a person's capacity for empathic response. Indeed, they do so by fortifying the link between seeing and empathy in a distinctive way. To establish this thesis, we will need a broad conception of empathic response (broader than the one used elsewhere in this volume) and also the right conception of what we see in pictures.

8.1 Empathy and Seeing in Pictures

The thesis that pictures contribute in a distinctive way to empathic skill is far from trivial. On the contrary, the more obvious it is that pictures contribute at all to empathic skill, the harder it is to see how they might do so in a distinctively pictorial manner.

Some journalistic photographs are paradigms of pictures that engage empathy. An example is Eddie Adams's famous 1968 photograph of General Nguyen Ngoc Loan executing a manacled Viet Cong prisoner. It is no mystery how the photograph achieves this effect. It depicts the scene so as to enable us to experience it much as if we were there, on the spot, seeing it with our own eyes, without help from a photograph. Were we there to see the execution face-to-face, presumably we would empathize with the prisoner, all else being equal; and that is why the photograph evokes an empathic response. True, the experience of seeing a scene in the photograph is not just like an experience of seeing the scene face-to-face. The two experiences obviously differ in many respects. Nevertheless, these respects are not ones in virtue of which the photograph evokes empathy. It evokes empathy by delivering an experience that matches a face-to-face experience of the scene itself.

The same goes for non-photographic images. Goya's painting *The Third of May* also depicts an execution and evokes a strong empathic response. True, the experience of the execution in the Goya differs more from a face-to-face experience of the execution than does an experience of the execution in the Adams. The Adams seems more lifelike than the Goya. Even so, the Goya evokes an experience that is like a face-to-face experience of an execution, and the respects in which these experiences are similar are the respects in virtue of which the painting evokes an empathic response.

A little terminology drives the point home. Pictures evoke experiences as of the scenes they represent. Call these experiences 'seeing-in'. To see a man in a photograph is to have an experience, sustained by the photograph, as of a man (this is not exactly the same as what Wollheim (1987) calls 'seeing-in'). All figurative pictures sustain seeing-in in this sense. The claim is that the features of seeing-in that are responsible for evoking empathy are features with respect to which seeing-in resembles face-to-face seeing. Empathic response picks up on the very same features, whether they figure in seeing-in or face-to-face seeing.

If this is right, then it is straightforward to explain why pictures contribute to empathic skill. Exercising a skill generally improves the skill. Pictures contribute to empathic skill because evoking episodes of empathy contributes to empathic skill and they evoke episodes of empathy that are relevantly similar to extra-pictorial episodes of empathy. By way of analogy, indoor climbing walls contribute to climbing ability because climbing mountains contributes to climbing ability and indoor climbing walls afford climbs that are relevantly similar to climbs up mountains.

However, this explanation of how pictures contribute to empathic skill subverts the thesis that pictures contribute distinctively to empathic skill. The reason why pictures contribute to empathic skill at all is that they sustain empathy-affording experiences that are similar to extra-pictorial empathy-affording experiences. Pictures make the same kind of contribution to empathic skill as do episodes of empathy evoked by face-to-face seeing. So if pictures contribute to empathic skill at all, then their contribution is not distinctive.

An obvious reply denies the claim that pictures evoke empathic responses only by approximating experiences in which we empathize with people we see face-to-face. Some of the features of seeing-in that are responsible for evoking empathy are features with respect to which it fails to resemble face-to-face seeing. The problem is first to pinpoint certain features of seeing-in with respect to which seeing-in does not resemble face-to-face seeing, where the features in question are responsible for evoking episodes of empathy. Call this the 'difference problem'. Solving this problem is only the first step, however. The second step is to show that these distinctively pictorial episodes of empathy contribute to an empathic skill that is also exercised outside pictures. It would not do only to show that pictures build up abilities to empathize with people seen in pictures. What matters is that pictures contribute to a skill that carries over to life beyond pictures. Call this the 'carryover problem'. Only having addressed these two problems are we in a position to proclaim the thesis that pictures contribute in a distinctive manner to empathic ability.

Taken individually, the difference and carryover problems pose no big challenge. The trick is to solve both problems together.

Perhaps one difference between seeing a man in a picture and seeing a man face-to-face is that the former does not imply seeing a man (contra Walton (1984) and Lopes (1996): 174–93.). When you look at the Adams or the Goya, you do not see a man being shot. You see only a picture, and the picture shows the look of the scene without showing the scene itself. This is why, no matter how close seeing-in and seeing face-to-face come to each other phenomenologically, the fact remains that seeing-in is not face-to-face seeing.

From one angle, this solution to the difference problem is just what we need. After all, you might reject the above explanation of why we respond empathically to the Adams photograph. According to that explanation, we respond empathically because the photograph delivers an experience like the experience of seeing the execution face-to-face and we would empathize with the prisoner were we there to see the execution face-to-face (all else being equal). You might object that most people seeing the execution face-to-face would not respond with empathy. Empathic response would be blocked by the reality of the situation, which would trigger shock, fear, or some other response incompatible with empathy. The photograph evokes empathy only by bracketing the 'reality of the situation'.

From another angle, though, this solution to the difference problem exacerbates the carryover problem. After all, this difference between seeing-in and seeing face-to-face presumably makes a difference to empathic response. It makes a difference to visually-mediated empathic response whether or not the empathizer sees the object of his or her response. But why should any response absent the empathizee carry over to cases where the empathizee is present? It is hard to answer without putting pressure on the solution to the difference problem. Thus one answer is that when we see the Adams, we imagine seeing a man being executed, where imagining seeing the man is enough like seeing a man to solve the carryover problem. Now the problem is obvious: seeing and imagining seeing both trigger empathy because they are similar in relevant respects, so the absence of the empathizee in imagining seeing is a difference that does not make a difference to empathic response.

Here is another example of how tricky it is to solve both problems at once. Not everybody agrees that the experience of seeing a scene in a picture resembles in salient respects seeing the scene face-to-face. According to Robert Hopkins (1998), pictures elicit experiences of resemblances between features of scenes and features of the pictures themselves. Normally, looking at a picture of a man involves an experience of a resemblance between a picture and a man. But looking at a man in the flesh is normally nothing like this: it is not normally an experience of his resemblance to a picture.

If Hopkins is right, the difference problem does not even get off the ground, but the carryover problem is quite pressing. Experiences of picture-object resemblances might build an ability to detect such resemblances, and they might also strengthen any skill that implicates this resemblance-detecting ability, but why should the resemblance-detecting ability strengthen empathic skill? Why should the ability to see resemblances between pictures and people boost any capacity to respond empathetically to the sight of people? Again, it would be hasty to conclude that Hopkins is wrong about our experience of pictures. The lesson is simply that quick work with the difference problem often sharpens the carryover problem.

These examples bring out what we need in a solution to the difference problem: it must specify a difference that explains how pictures contribute distinctively to an empathic skill that carries over to extra-pictorial situations.

8.2 The Empathy Complex

Solving the difference and carryover problems requires a working account of empathy. A definition would suffice, even if it falls short of telling us everything we want to know about empathy, its biological origins, its neural implementation, its development in childhood, and its contributions to moral capacity and human thriving. Unfortunately, agreeing on a definition is hard enough. Experts characterize what they call 'empathy' in several incompatible ways, and perhaps the definitions glom onto distinct phenomena, none of which has sole claim to the title of 'empathy'. The situation calls for a little circumspection—for keeping in mind a variety of empathic or empathy-related phenomena (Eisenberg & Strayer (1987): 3–8; Goldie (1999); Preston & de Waal (2002)).

One reason for the variety of empathic phenomena is that nobody feels empathy. Although it always involves an emotion (let emotions include moods and feelings), empathy is not an emotion which belongs on a list with anger, pity, joy, optimism, and the like. Quite possibly every emotion can be involved in empathic response (although it is most often associated with negative emotions). Thus an account of empathy should try to bring out how emotions are involved in different empathic phenomena. The ambiguity of 'involving' perfectly suits the variety of empathic phenomena, each of which involves emotions in a different way.

If empathic phenomena bear nothing to each other but loose family resemblances, then the best account of empathy might be a description of each member of the family. However, we can do better than a gallery of descriptions, for the empirical and philosophical literature hints at some structure underlying the varieties of empathic response, which seem to spring from variance with respect to a small number of decently defined parameters. Seeing empathic phenomena as variants within these parameters represents them as related but distinct.

First some terminology. Vijay feels miserable because he has failed an important exam, and Abby responds empathically. Call Abby the 'subject' of the empathic response and Vijay its 'object'. Note that the object of Abby's empathic response will normally differ from the intentional object of the emotion involved in her response. The object of Abby's empathic response is Vijay, but Abby's empathy involves in some way the feeling of misery, and the object of that emotion is not Vijay but rather the failed exam. Unless otherwise qualified, let 'subject' and 'object' refer to the subject and object of the empathic response, not an associated emotion.

The emotion parameter represents how some emotion of the object is involved in the subject's empathic response. This parameter has several settings. Abby might feel just what Vijay feels. Sometimes she feels an emotion that is not identical to what he feels but is appropriately related to it. In one case, she shares Vijay's misery and in the other, she responds with an emotion other than misery—pity, perhaps. A third option is less direct: Abby brings to consciousness an experience of misery—an experience that conveys what it is like to be miserable (Green (2008)). This falls short of actually feeling miserable. Finally, Abby might just attribute misery to Vijay without feeling misery or bringing to mind its phenomenology.

The positioning parameter concerns the attitude the subject bears either to the object's situation or to the object's assessment of her situation. Suppose that Vijay believes that, having failed the exam, he has no career prospects, and so he wishes to start over. Abby might also believe that Vijay has no career prospects. Alternatively, she might go no further than attributing to Vijay this belief, without having the same belief. Finally, Abby may respond empathically to Vijay without taking any account of his situation or his assessment of his situation. She may know he is miserable and might even share his misery without knowing what he is miserable about.

The concern parameter has to do with how the subject's desires or well-being line up with with those of the object. Abby can desire that, for her sake, Vijay get what he wants (a shot at a new career); or she can desire the same thing for his sake. The latter is sometimes taken to be a necessary condition for sympathetic response (e.g. Darwall (1998)). For better or worse, sympathy is not mandatory. Abby can desire merely for her own sake that Vijay get what he wants or what is good for him. She also has the option to stand utterly indifferent to his desires and well-being. Empathic response is consistent with indifference.

Some propose that one or more of these three parameters has a setting for imaginings (e.g. Goldman (1995a)). Abby imagines that Vijay's career is in ruins and imagines desiring a new start for him. She imagines that he feels miserable. She imagines desiring, for his sake, that he gets what he wants. These imaginings are acentral: they are about Vijay but they are not from his point of view. Central imaginings can also position the subject. Abby can imagine being in Vijay's situation: she can imagine feeling miserable, anticipating a failed career, wanting a fresh start.

The beauty of this framework is that different empathic responses are modeled by setting the parameters differently. However, not all empathic responses are modeled this way, for different empathic responses can share the same parameter settings. The reason is that we get different empathic responses when there are different causal and rational relationships among the very same parameter settings.

To illustrate, here is a partial inventory of empathic responses (see Goldie (1999) for more). In emotional contagion, the object's emotion causes a like emotion in the subject. The subject feels what the object feels independently of how the concern and positioning parameters are set. In what James Harold calls 'identification', the subject feels just what the object feels as a result of sharing the object's beliefs and desires about his situation (Harold (2000): 344). Some authors define empathy proper as occurring just in case the subject feels what the object feels as a result of imagining what he believes and wants (Darwall (1998): 267–70; Gaut (1999): 206; Coplan (2004): 144). A weaker definition requires the subject to bring to awareness an experience of what it is like to feel what the object feels (Green (2008)). Susan Feagin defines empathy as the subject's wanting for the object what the object wants for himself, where the subject's wanting this results from her beliefs about what the object believes and wants (Feagin (1988)). In a variant of this, Harold defines empathy as the subject's wanting for the object what the object wants for himself, where the subject's wanting this results from her imagining what the object believes and wants (Harold (2000): 345). Completing this quick inventory takes us to what some call 'understanding' (e.g. Goldie (1999): 399–401; Harold (2000): 345) and others call 'empathy' (e.g. Goldman (1995a)). In these cases, the subject identifies but does not feel what the object feels, which identification is rationally grounded in beliefs about what the object believes and wants.

Some empathic phenomena are composites of more elementary empathic responses. A case in point is Stephen Darwall's 'proto-sympathetic empathy' ((1998): 271–2). For Darwall, this type of empathy involves as a kind of 'double vision'. On one hand, the subject centrally imagines being in the object's position and thereby imagines feeling as the object does. By imagining being in Vijay's situation, Abby imagines feeling his misery. The intentional object of her imagined feeling of misery is the failed exam. On the other hand, Abby also feels a pity which arises from imagining feeling as Vijay feels. This emotion has Vijay and what he feels as its intentional object. Darwall takes sympathy to require a particular form of concern, and a natural foundation for this concern is the double vision found in proto-sympathetic empathy. Abby is led to desire Vijay's well-being by imagining being in his situation and at the same time having a feeling of pity that represents him as feeling miserable in that situation.

In sum, different empathic phenomena emerge from different settings of the emotion, positioning, and concern parameters, together with different causal or rational relationships between these settings. This proposal can be put to several uses. One might argue that some empathic phenomena are central or paradigmatic. One might sort 'genuine' empathic phenomena from 'merely related' phenomena. Perhaps these are worthy tasks, but all we need for present purposes is to see what kinds of factors play into empathy, where empathy is understood broadly.

8.3 Empathic Skill

The claim that pictures contribute distinctively to empathic skill calls for more than an account of empathy; it also calls for an account of empathic skill. Define empathic skill as consisting in having whatever cognitive wherewithal is implicated in empathic response. Not everybody has the same degree of empathic skill; improvements can come with exercise.

Is the skill a virtue? Heather Battaly argues in this volume that there is more to a virtue of empathy than empathic skill. Any virtue has a motivational component, such that one cannot have a given virtue and regularly act in a way that flouts the end of the virtue. If curiosity is a virtue whose end is getting the truth, then there is more to curiosity than being able to look things up in books, ask questions, doubt dogmas, conduct experiments, observe the details of life, and engage in the other activities which lead to getting the truth. Having the virtue implies engaging in such activities as these without disregard for getting the truth. For example, someone who successfully engages in these truth-conducive activities 'just for fun' does not have the virtue. On this view, not everybody with empathic skill is a virtuous empathizer: some have the skill and yet lack the virtue because they lack the right motivation. If Battaly is right, the claim that pictures hone empathic skill is not identical to the claim that they contribute to a virtue of empathy. However, the former entails the latter because the skill is part of the virtue, so we can skip over the question of what effects pictures have on the motivations of their viewers.

The parameters for variance among empathic responses point to some of the components of empathic skill. The emotion and positioning parameters are key. A person cannot have much empathic skill unless she can have or represent emotions—in particular, the emotions of the object of her empathic response. She must also be able to have beliefs or imaginings about the object's situation or the object's own perspective on his situation. That is just a start, for another component of empathic response is the linkage between settings of the emotion and positioning parameters. For example, one kind of empathy consists in feeling what the object feels as a consequence of centrally imagining being in his situation. A person capable of such a response must have capacities for central imagining and feeling, and she must be wired up so that the one feeds into the other.

Not everyone can boast full empathic competence if this means being equipped for every type of empathic response. Some people are ready for some kinds of responses and not others (Kennett (2002)). Moreover, one should expect to find people with deficits covering different sets of empathic responses. An interesting empirical issue concerns deficit patterns: probably capacities for some species of empathic response imply capacities for others. Empathic skill is made up of components.

The component model of empathic skill has an important developmental consequence. Grant that empathic skill develops, like other skills, through exercise. This assumption does not by itself imply that one can only improve the ability for a given type of empathic response by exercising that very response. Take the case of Abby's sharing Vijay's emotion as a result of centrally imagining being in his situation. Underlying Abby's response are two abilities, to share emotions and to centrally imagine being in another person's situation. Each ability may be gained independently, and one might hone each ability by having many other kinds of empathic responses.

The point is crucial to appreciating how pictures contribute to empathic skill, for one conception of what the contribution requires sets the bar too low and another sets it too high. Empathic skill depends on many quite general cognitive systems such as affect, perception, belief, and general-purpose reasoning. Looking at pictures almost certainly contributes to the development and refinement of many of these. Thus it is almost trivial that pictures contribute to empathic skill. The bar is set too low. Setting the bar too high is the claim that pictures contribute to the development of a given type of empathic response only by evoking responses of that very type. Very few pictures invite their spectators to feel just what a depicted figure feels through centrally imagining being in the depicted figure's situation. Not even the Adams and the Goya require this. The same goes for other empathic responses—many types of empathic response are engaged by very few if any pictures.

The component model of empathic response sets the bar just right. Although empathy comes in several varieties, and pictures may not engage them all, the component model says that pictures exercise components of one type of empathic response by evoking a different type of empathic response if it shares some of the same components. So if pictures do not evoke the full range of empathic responses, then perhaps they engage empathic responses that share components in common with responses that they do not engage. The component model allows for pictures that help refine one type of empathic response by engaging another, different type of empathic response.

8.4 The Expressive Power of Pictures

Pictures contribute distinctively to empathic skill only if they engage empathic responses. The above characterization of the empathy complex and the components of different empathic responses provides a framework to use in seeing how they engage empathic responses. Pictures fill the positioning parameter by representing people and their circumstances. They fill the emotion parameter by expressing emotions. In expressing emotions, they sometimes parallel ordinary perceptual experience, but they also have special expressive powers, which are the key to solving the difference problem.

Begin with the positioning parameter. A face-to-face experience of a scene normally feeds the content of an attitude towards the scene. Seeing someone smoking a cigarette beside a barrel of gasoline, you come to believe that it is dangerous to stand nearby. In just the same way, what you see in a picture normally feeds an attitude towards the depicted scene. A photograph shows a firefighter facing a wall of fire. In depicting the fire, it depicts something dangerous to the represented figure. You may reasonably take the depicted figure to believe that she is in danger, you might centrally imagine facing the wall of flames, and in the right circumstances you might even believe that you are in danger too.

Empathic response also involves an emotion in one of a range of ways represented by different settings of the emotion parameter. Since danger triggers and warrants fear, your response to the photograph is likely to involve the firefighter's fear. You might, for example, attribute fear to her, centrally imagine her fear, bring to mind an awareness of what it is like to feel fear, or even share her fear. Perhaps the depicted scene brings in fear all by itself: the fireball's presence is normally sufficient reason to attribute to the firefighter a belief that she is in danger and hence to attribute to her a feeling of fear. There are further options of course. Centrally imagining facing the fire may lead to centrally imagining feeling her fear, and you feel fear if you take yourself to be facing the fire too. That said, emotions are far more often involved in empathic response through the depicted figure—in particular through the figure's expressing what he or she feels.

Pictures represent people expressing what they feel. In narrative painting, expression is typically harnessed to convey the story. Since emotions motivate action, depicting what agents feel is a way of depicting what they are motivated to do, and hence clarifies what they are depicted as doing. The expression of anger on a figure's face distinguishes her landing a blow from her shielding herself. In portraiture, expression is typically used to convey more subtle complexes of emotions that indicate the character of the sitter. Think of what the look of weariness inflected with bemusement tells us about the old man in Rembrandt's self-portrait of 1669. In expressionism, pictures typically depict what amount to pure expressive types. For example, Käthe Kollwitz's many drawings and prints of widows almost systematically explore grief and expressions of grief.

Empathy can switch objects, and pictures of multiple figures can invite or allow empathic responses to one figure after another. The prisoner about to be executed in Adams's photograph is the strongest attractor of empathic response, but it is also possible to empathize with the wincing soldier who is observing the scene (and even with the executioner). The situation observed by the wincing soldier is the situation we observe; and the photograph clues us into his feeling about that situation by showing the expression on his face. While the executioner's face is mostly hidden from sight, his situation is clear. We might attribute to him feelings of indifference. We might imagine feeling his indifference in that situation and come to pity him, if we can bring ourselves to feel concern for his good.

By representing situations and bringing in emotions in these ways, pictures contribute to empathic skill. Exercising a skill generally improves the skill. Pictures evoke episodes of empathy that are relevantly similar to extra-pictorial episodes of empathy: they exercise the same skill as gets exercised in extra-pictorial episodes of empathy. So they contribute to empathic skill. As this reasoning makes clear, though, the contribution is not distinctively pictorial. Carryover is ensured, but the difference problem is pressing.

The point is not to put down pictures' non-distinctive contributions to empathic skill. These contributions are no doubt valuable and important. As the characterization of the empathy complex makes clear, empathic response depends on the good working of sundry recognition and classification abilities. Looking at pictures that represent scenes might fine-tune the ability to recognize the relevant scenes, and looking at pictures that represent expressive figures might fine-tune the ability to recognize facial expressions. For all that, the question remains how pictures contribute in a distinctive manner to empathic response.

In a recent paper, Mitchell Green (2008) has offered a novel account of pictorial expressiveness, which ties to empathy, and which suggests how pictures contribute distinctively to empathic skill. Green begins with a relatively restrictive definition of empathy. Empathic response consists in being aware of what it is like to feel what the object feels. This falls short of actually feeling what the object feels, though it goes beyond merely attributing a feeling to the object, for it requires having an experience with an affective phenomenology. In normal circumstances, the required awareness draws from memory. Abby's memory of what it is like to feel miserable figures in her response to Vijay. Green's idea is that pictures can also supply the needed awareness.

The key for Green is the assumption that pictures of expressive figures can do more than show how emotions look: they can show how emotions feel. In general, expressions of an emotion either show how the emotion looks or how it feels. A painting shows how sadness looks when it depicts the face of a person who looks sad. That is straightforward. What about showing how an emotion feels? Green's example is the closing sequence of *Bonnie and Clyde*:

The two protagonists are finally caught in a trap and the Feds open fire on them with an absurd amount of artillery. The entire scene occurs in slow motion, giving us a sense of time stopping while we take in the carnage. In doing so, that scene not only shows us what the demise of Bonnie and Clyde might have looked like; it also shows us what a sense of crisis feels like. (Green (2008): 109)

The use of slow motion in the movie makes you aware of what a sense of crisis feels like, and thus puts you in a position to empathize with the outlaws. It positions you to be aware of what it is like to feel what they feel.

As we shall see, this account contains a useful insight; but it has two drawbacks. The first is a limitation of Green's account of the mechanism by which pictures show how emotions feel. People consistently associate experiences in a sense modality with experiences in other sense modalities. For example, piccolos are judged to be bright and the oboe is judged to be dim; vanilla is said to smell smooth and musk to smell rough. The congruence even obtains for the sounds of words: yellow is ping and orange is pong; triangles are ping and ovals are pong. Green adds that yellow is happy and brown is sad, and this is why yellow shows how happiness feels and brown shows how sadness feels. More generally, this is how visible properties show how emotions feel. However, congruence effects are limited in scope. People agree that yellow is happy and brown is sad, but they do not agree on the color of embarrassment or optimism, so no colors show how embarrassment or optimism feel. If pictures engage empathic responses by showing how emotions feel and if showing how emotions feel relies on congruence effects, then pictures can engage only a limited range of empathic responses.

The second problem connects to the difference and carryover problems. Pictures contribute to empathic skill by sustaining experiences of seeing-in that evoke empathic responses in their viewers. They contribute distinctively to empathic skill only when some of the response-evoking features of seeing-in are not features of face-to-face seeing. The difference problem is to identify these features of seeing-in, and Green's account adroitly solves this problem. Many features of your seeing a sad person face-to-face factor into your empathic response—perhaps you take note of his situation (the broken toy) or his facial expression (tears). But it would be unusual, to say the least, were these factors to include the world's looking brown. Nevertheless, your seeing in a picture a scene with a brown cast shows you how sadness feels and thereby grounds your empathic response. Characterizing pictures as triggering empathic responses by exploiting congruence effects to show how emotions feel solves the difference problem.

The trick is also to solve the carryover problem. The question is whether empathic responses to pictures that show how emotions feel boost empathic skill in a way that carries over to extra-pictorial empathic skill. Responding empathically because you see a brown scene in a picture may well contribute to your ability to respond empathically to scenes in pictures. Not only do you get better at responding empathically to the sadness of other brown pictures, but perhaps you also get better at responding empathically to the happiness of yellow pictures. However, it is less plausible that these benefits carry over as improvements in abilities to respond to emotions that are not color-keyed.

The source of the difficulty is a relatively narrow conception of empathy as being aware of what it is like to feel what the object feels. Starting with this conception means that pictures trigger empathy only if experiences of seeing-in are vehicles for this awareness. Positing that pictures deliver phenomenologically distinctive experiences solves the difference problem but risks any traction we might have on the carryover problem.

Yet Green's account contains a useful insight. One might think that pictures engage empathic responses by expressing emotions only when they depict figures as expressing the emotions. Green demonstrates that this is not the case. Yellow shows how happiness feels, though happy people do not look yellow, and *Bonnie and Clyde* does not express a sense of crisis by depicting the expressive gestures of the outlaws themselves—people never express a sense of crisis by moving very slowly. So some pictures do not express emotions by depicting figures expressing the emotions. Perhaps pictures can engage empathic response by expressing an emotion that is not expressed by any depicted figures.

At this stage, a survey of the expressive powers of pictures should come in handy (Lopes (2005): 50–7). The survey goes beyond

figure expression: an expression that is wholly attributable to some depicted person.

For example, in Goya's *Third of May*, the terror expressed by the white-shirted captive is wholly attributable to that depicted figure, and the hint of bemusement in Rembrandt's 1669 self-portrait is wholly attributable to the sitter. But there is more to expression in pictures than figure expression. Some expressive pictures depict no figures. Landscapes of a certain period often express a sad nostalgia; Saenredam's empty church interiors express a religious purity of heart; mountain scenes often express awe. These are instances of

scene expression: an expression that is attributable to a depicted scene and that is not wholly attributable to any depicted persons.

This definition leaves it open that some of what a picture expresses is attributable both to the scene and to the figures depicted. The dancers in Matisse's *Danse* express joy through their dancing, and so too does the scene in which they dance. With that in mind, return to the closing sequence of *Bonnie and Clyde*. The slow motion is expressive, but although the outlaws feel a sense of crisis, they do not express what they feel by slowing the apparent passage of time.

Empathic responses triggered by pictures involve getting at what the object feels via what the picture depicts (e.g. danger) or expresses (e.g. a look of fear). What a figure expresses indicates what the figure feels—attributing fear to Goya's captive makes sense of his expression of fear. In addition, what the depicted scene expresses can also indicate what the figure feels. Here are two kinds of cases.

Some depicted scenes express emotions that are attributable to depicted figures. The claim is not that the scene expresses the emotion of the figure. It is not as if the picture depicts the figure's emotion as reaching out to modify the figure's world in the same way as it modifies the figure's face and body. Rather, the scene expresses an emotion that lines up with what the figure feels. The scene in *Danse* expresses joy, and joy is attributable to the dancers, but the scene is not an expression of the dancers' joy. In *Bonnie and Clyde*, the scene expresses a sense of crisis and this feeling is attributable to the outlaws even though they do not express their feeling by slowing down the pace of time. Call this

reflective scene expression: an expression E of a token emotion F, where E is attributable to a depicted scene and not wholly attributable to any depicted person S, where token emotion F* is attributable to S, and where F and F* are tokens of the same emotion type.

In reflective scene expression, the scene's expressing an emotion is a reason to attribute the same emotion to a depicted figure. The depicted figure's feeling that emotion makes sense of the scene's expressing what it does.

Not all scene expression is reflective, however. Consider Théodore Géricault's *Raft of the Medusa*. The Medusa, a French vessel, had broken up in the seas off the west coast of Africa. Its survivors, clinging to debris, beset by sharks, cannibalized each other to keep alive. The living figures in Géricault's painting express despair and desperation. The sea is relentless and dangerous, but it expresses a malignant indifference as well; and the tiny ship almost out of sight on the horizon expresses blind indifference. Attributing despair to the shipwrecks makes sense both of what they express and also of what the sea and the distance ship express. Their expressing indifference is reason to think that the shipwrecks feel despair. That this is so does not depend, however, on the scene's reflecting what the figures express. Call this phenomenon

reactive scene expression: an expression E that is attributable to a depicted scene and not wholly attributable to any depicted persons S, but where emotion F is attributable to S because S's feeling F is warranted as a response to E.

The model for reactive scene expression is reactive emotions in ordinary interpersonal communication. Attila's glowering at Benedict is a reason to attribute fear to Benedict because feeling fear is warranted as a response to glowering looks. In reactive scene expression, figures are represented as reacting emotionally to what scenes express.

Empathizing always involves getting at what another person feels, so as to share the emotion (or imagine sharing it), react to it (or imagine reacting to it), bring it to mind what it feels like, or merely attribute it. Pictures guide their viewers in several ways to the emotion that is involved in empathic response. They depict the scene as one to which the emotion is the expected response and they depict figures as expressing the emotion. Getting at the emotion in these ways is much like what we do when we respond empathically to real people. However, pictures also guide us to the emotion by reflective and reactive scene expression. This has no parallel in non-pictorial experience, which does not represent bits of inanimate nature as expressing emotions. Herein lies the special expressive power of pictures.

Is the idea of scene expression coherent? One might object that an expression is an expression of an emotion, and an emotion is a mental state of a sentient creature, but since seas and ships are not sentient creatures, they have no emotions, and thus can express nothing. Of course, seas and ships can be represented as sentient—as are the dancing broomsticks of Walt Disney and the scowling trees of Hieronymous Bosch. However, the sea and the ship in the Medusa are not represented as sentient, so they cannot be represented as expressing any emotions. One response to this objection attributes what depicted scenes express to a sentient creature who is not depicted—a 'persona,' for example (along the lines of Robinson (1994); Levinson (1996)). An alternative reply is that expression does not require emotion (Lopes (2005): 69–78). True, Green's account of expression in art is inconsistent with this reply, but that is no reason against the reply so long as we are considering the viability of the proposal that scene expression can play a role in distinctively pictorial empathic responses.

The component model of empathic response implies that pictures may exercise components of one type of empathic response by evoking a different type of empathic response which shares some of the same components. According to Green, some pictures make visible what certain emotions are like, but few types of empathic response involve an awareness of what an emotion is like. Another component of empathic response is engaged by pictures that represent scenes as intentional objects of emotions or that represent figures and scenes as expressing emotions. Moreover, some of these pictures engage empathy in distinctively pictorial ways—in ways not seen in ordinary perception. That takes care of the difference problem. What about the carryover problem?

8.5 Pictorial Referencing

Empathic responses are distinctively pictorial when pictures elicit empathy by means of scene expression: and as long as these responses contribute to empathic skill, then pictures contribute distinctively to empathic skill. The difference problem is solved. Yet the carryover problem looks as hopeless as ever. Suppose empathizing with the shipwrecks in the *Raft of the Medusa* involves seeing their despair as warranted by the ship's expressing indifference. How does this help us to empathize with people we see face-to-face unless we see bits of the inanimate world as expressing emotions? One might answer that we do in fact see bits of the inanimate world as expressing emotions —perhaps, indeed, as a result of familiarity with pictorial scene expression. However, this solution to the carryover problem unravels the solution to the difference problem. We must seek another kind of solution. Materials come from the phenomenon of social referencing.

Social referencing is a key strategy for dealing with a complex world where signals about what is harmful and beneficial, pleasant and painful are not always clear (see Feinman et al. (1992) for a review). Children confront a relatively high proportion of unfamiliar situations, and social referencing is crucial to their coping. In social referencing, one person uses another person's affective response to a situation in order to assess the situation, guide his behavior, and perhaps determine his own affective response. Children develop a capacity for this within their first year and it is fully in place by eighteen months. When put in an unfamiliar and ambiguous situation, they will try to keep within sight of their mother's face, they will engage in visual 'check back' behaviors, and they will inhibit play when she is preoccupied. When they do detect a significant expression on their mother's face, their behavior is profoundly modified. Clearly, social referencing involves reading facial expressions. It also means identifying the environmental situation that is the object of the emotion expressed, since the mother's look must be identified as expressing fear at the toy monster.

In general, social referencing comes in handy when it is not clear to an agent how she should respond to a situation in her environment. She checks with an expert, whose facial expression tells her what response is warranted. If the expert expresses fear, she learns that the situation is dangerous. She can then generalize, honing her ability to detect danger and react appropriately.

As in social referencing, where one person uses another person's expression to cue an assessment of a shared situation, spectators can use what pictures express to cue assessments of a depicted scene. Of course, referencing may not be needed to assess the depicted scene. The wall of flames is evidently dangerous, and so is the sea in the *Raft of the Medusa*. However, assessments of situations can depend on quite subtle and sophisticated discrimination abilities, and they can have fine-grained contents. These features of depicted scenes can be cued by the expressions worn by depicted figures; and this amounts to a pictorial version of social referencing.

That is not all. What a scene expresses also cues the viewer into what emotional response the scene warrants, and thus indirectly implies an assessment of the scene. Keep in mind that social referencing is not mimicry; it is an advance on mimicry. The child checks the mother's face in order to find out about the world—to find out how to view the world in light of her mother's responding as she does. Likewise, scene expression can function to mark the features of a situation that warrant a response either reflecting or reacting to what is expressed. By marking features of a scene, the picture enables us to see the features as ones that warrant a certain response. Scene expression tags an assessment of the scene, just as does a mother's look of concern.

Any sailor knows that the sea is dangerous, and the sea in the Géricault is certainly depicted as rough. However, the sea's expression of malignant indifference brings home how dangerous it is and so how desperate is the plight of the shipwrecks. What the sea expresses makes sense of what the shipwrecks feel and express. At the same time, by showing what response is warranted, the sea's expression picks out features of the situation as warranting that response. It helps the viewer appraise the situation.

A kind of dramatic irony arises when an assessment implied by reactive scene expression conflicts with the assessment actually expressed by depicted figures. The scene expresses an emotion in response to which one is warranted in feeling E, but the depicted figures do not express E. They do not assess the situation in the same way as we are led to when we take in what the scene expresses. We know something that they do not. The skull in a memento mori painting expresses grief at a wasted life, but all this is wasted on the depicted figure who dances footloose upon the earth. Pictures that trade on this kind of dramatic irony display not only how to assess a situation but also illustrate how a situation can be assessed differently, as befitting different emotional responses. They put viewers in a position to judge what response is appropriate and hence to second or dissent from the emotion a figure is depicted as expressing. The lesson of social referencing is that expressions of emotion are doubly informative. A person's emotional expression tells us how they feel and it also tells us something about their situation. Indeed, the expression tells us about their situation by telling us how they feel. So we can learn to read situations by reading expressions reacting to those situations. Likewise, expressive scenes in pictures mark features of the scenes for the purpose of appraising them. We can learn about the scenes and how to react to them from the messages about them carried by scene expression.

A solution to the carryover problem lies within reach. We respond empathically with some figures we see in pictures. Sometimes this response involves our seeing a scene as expressive, though the expression is not attributable to the figure. Since we do not normally see bits of the inanimate world as expressing anything, this is a distinctively pictorial response. Moreover, scene expression can play a referencing role, marking features of situations as warranting responses. The cognitive pay-off is that we learn to recognize situations as warranting certain responses even when the expressive element is removed. That is carryover. The carryover and difference problems are solved together.

In sum, pictures contribute to empathic skill. This is not because they directly engage every type of empathic response, nor is it merely because they engage some component of some empathic response. Rather, pictures engage a type of empathic response that has benefits for general empathic skill. They place their viewers in a position to attribute an emotion, to assess a scene, and to see the former as appropriate to the latter. In so far as they accomplish this through scene expression, they contribute to empathic skill in a distinctive manner.

Pictures are perceptual prostheses: they expand the power of perception (Lopes (1996)). Since perception leads to emotional responses and also to empathy in its various guises, it should be no surprise that pictures also expand empathic skill. What engages the heart tends to be absorbing, and so pictures like Adams's photograph, the *Third of May*, and the *Raft of the Medusa* address us as empathic creatures. Pictures are valuable in so far as we would be worse off as empathic creatures without them. You might now ask if this forms part of their aesthetic or artistic value, but that is a question for another occasion.[1]

[1] My thanks to audiences at Scripps College, the University of British Columbia, and the University of Fribourg for helpful suggestions—and especially to Amy Coplan, Fabian Dorsch, Peter Goldie, and two anonymous referees.

9

Infectious Music:

Music–Listener Emotional Contagion

Stephen Davies

I have long been interested in the expression of emotion in music and in the response this calls forth from the listener. One such response is a mirroring or echoing one; sad music tends to make (some) listeners feel sad and happy music to make them happy. This mirroring reaction is brought about by what I have called emotional contagion. We tend to resonate with the emotional tenor of the music, much as we catch the emotional ambience emanating from other people.[1]

Reflecting on the musical case not only enhances understanding of the listener's response, it provides a novel objection to the cognitive theory of the emotions favored by many philosophers and invites critical consideration of the models for human-to-human emotional contagion proposed by psychologists. As I try to show, the most common accounts of emotional contagion should be developed and refined in light of analysis of emotional contagion in the musical case, which recommends, for example, that we distinguish attention from non-attentional modes of emotional transmission and, in general, avoid defining the phenomenon reductively in terms of the routes and mechanisms of communication.

In the 1960s and 70s, philosophers (Kenny (1963); Solomon (1976); Lyons (1980)) developed what became known as the cognitive account of the emotions. Emotions are object-directed states characterized in terms of the beliefs under which their intentional objects are subsumed. For example, if I am afraid for myself I am afraid *of* or *about* something—a rise in the mortgage rate, say—and I *believe* that a rise in the mortgage rate will injure me or otherwise affect me adversely. A rise in the interest rate is the *intentional object* (or *emotional object*) of my fear, and the belief that the intentional object of my response will injure me or otherwise affect me adversely, a description sometimes known as the *formal object* of fear, is what characterizes the response as fearful.

---

[1] I reject the arousal theory, according to which 'the music is sad' is true if and only if the music arouses sadness in the listener. (For detailed discussion, see Davies (1994a): ch. 4.) In other words, I regard the music's expressive quality as distinct from the response. For further comment, see footnote 9.

Similarly, for my emotion to be one of envy I must believe that another possesses something that I desire and do not have, and so on.

Though proponents of the theory occasionally suggest that the nature of the belief is sufficient to determine what emotion is involved, the more circumspect view is that the relevant belief is necessary and that no other condition is also sufficient. In other words, other conditions might be necessary for an emotion's being one of fear, but among the conditions that are jointly sufficient for an emotion's being fear is the condition that the relevant beliefs, ones about dangers posed by the emotion's object, are present.[2] It is the centrality that this theory accords to the role of belief that led to its being called a cognitive account of the emotions.

A number of fairly obvious putative counterexamples can be ranged against the cognitive theory of the emotions. Phobias either involve beliefs not appropriate to the emotion's object or are impervious to beliefs that should block the response. Reflexive affective responses of the kind sometimes called quick and dirty or fast and frugal by psychologists also seem to operate independently of, and be unaffected by, the responder's belief systems. As Darwin ((1998): 43–4) famously observed, he flinched in fear of a striking snake even as he knew it was separated from him by an unbreakable glass barrier. Meanwhile, emotional reactions to fictions recognized as such, as when I feel sad at Mimi's death in *La Bohème*, or to counterfactually entertained scenarios, as when I feel sad as a result of imagining a world without birds, also do not involve beliefs that should be crucial: that Mimi exists or existed and therefore suffered the fate depicted, or that the earth will be bereft of birds. As well as these cases, all of which question the claimed tie between the emotion's kind and the content of the beliefs of the person who experiences it, there are others denying that emotions necessarily take emotional objects. Apparently there are objectless moods and feelings, as when one is gloomy but not about anything in particular or where one experiences an undirected sense of dread or foreboding.

There are a number of replies the cognitivist can offer. Emotional reactions that are based on irrational or otherwise mistaken beliefs are inappropriate to the way the real world is but are not otherwise unintelligible. And reactions that do not engage the responder's beliefs perhaps should not be put together with full-blooded emotions. In this view, reflexive reactions either are not emotions at all or they form a minor, peripheral class within the wider group in which cognitively founded, object-directed emotions are central and paradigmatic.[3] As for moods and anxieties that appear to be objectless, it could be argued that they take relatively general objects rather than specific ones (Goldie (2000): 143)—one is depressed about the condition of the

---

[2] For instance, certain behavioral dispositions might also be necessary for some if not all emotions.

[3] If emotions serve adaptive functions, as is widely claimed ((Plutchik) 1980; Lazarus (1991); Le Doux (1996)), and if we share many emotions with less cognitively sophisticated species, as seems hard to deny, the cognitive theory does look to be parochial and narrow. On the other hand, Griffiths' conclusion (1997), that 'conceptual analysis' provides no coherent account of cognitively sophisticated emotions and that they are beyond the pale because psychologists' methodologies cannot deal with them, seems equally biased.

world at large, though not at a particular part of it (Solomon (1976): 172–3)—or that their objects are unconscious (Lyons (1980)).[4] Or again, perhaps the claims of objectless moods and dreads to unequivocal standing as emotions should be doubted.

Meanwhile, our responsiveness to what we know to be fictional characters and situations has attracted a spread of theories. There is the option of denial. Kendall Walton (1990, 1997) stands by cognitivism. He holds that *fictional emotions*—by which he means not that the states are merely imagined but that they occur in the context of games of make-belief prescribed for the consumption and appreciation of fictional works—are not kosher, despite their emotion-like phenomenological and physiologi-cal profile. An implausible alternative is Coleridge's suggestion that one suspends—or in contemporary jargon, puts off-line—one's awareness of the fictionality of the events shown or described. There is the proposal that the response is non-rational, either because beliefs in the existence of their objects are absent or, for other reasons, because one does not believe one's responses can affect or engage with the object of the response. Colin Radford (1975), who endorses this proposal, apparently thinks irratio-nal reactions can be tolerated by the cognitivist as exceptions that prove the rule. Alex Neill (1993) argues that cognitivism does not require the belief that the fictional target of one's emotional response exists in the actual world. According to Neill, one can pity a fictional character provided one believes that the character exists in a pitiable situation in the world of the fiction. Another attractive suggestion (offered in Carroll (1990), Feagin (1996), Lamarque (1996)) recommends modifying the cognitive theory to allow that the relevant cognitive role can be played sometimes by make-belief, not only by belief. The emotional evocativeness of fictions entertained as such then no longer calls the cognitive theory into doubt.

In Davies (1980) (also in 1983, 1994a, 2001), I drew attention to a different kind of counterexample to the cognitive theory. People respond emotionally to music. Some of these reactions fit the model proposed by the cognitivist. I might be happy that the work is entertaining or irritated by the performance's dreary tempo. Others, however, do not. It is widely accepted that even purely instrumental music can express or present the appearance of emotions such as happiness and sadness. It is also generally acknowl-edged that happy music sometimes makes people feel happy and sad music sometimes make them feel sad. Music can give rise to an affective reaction that mirrors or echoes its own expressive character. But, and here is the point, those who are saddened by sad music are not sad *about* or *for* the music. The music is the perceptual object and cause of the sad reaction. Indeed, the music is the attentional focus of the response, which tracks the expressiveness as it unfolds in the music's progress.[5] However, the music is not the

---

[4] For discussion, see Lamb (1987).

[5] The disposition to echo the music's expressiveness might be overridden, though, in light of a broader view of its expressive character. I might not be cheered by the occasional happy moments because I recognize them in the work's overall pattern as best thought of as smiling through tears, not as expressions of unalloyed joy.

emotional object of the listener's response—the response is *to* the music without being *about* it—because moved listeners do not believe of the music that it satisfies the formal object of sadness.[6] In other words, they do not believe it suffers or is otherwise unfortunate or regrettable. They might regard the slow movement of Mahler's Fifth Symphony, say, as expressing a profound sadness, and on that account, as a magnificent human achievement that should be celebrated, not mourned, yet hearing it inclines them to share in its sadness.

I claim that responses of this kind are familiar more generally. We often catch the emotional ambience of our environment or of those around us. I referred to the phenomenon, including the musical case, as involving emotional contagion, transmission, infection, or osmosis.

It may be useful to distinguish two types of emotional contagion in which music could take part. Music is played as background sound in stores and elevators where it serves to calm those who encounter it.[7] To produce its effect it must be heard. (I assume the feelings of deaf people are not influenced by ambient music.) Typically, though, it is not listened to. It is the perceptual object of the response, but the person calmed by it may be oblivious of this fact and may remain unaware throughout of the musical wallpaper. The sense of well-being experienced as a result of this barely aware or subconscious perception is not appreciated as a response to its cause and is not directed to the background music. In other words, the music generates an objectless mood that reflects its own, calm expressive character.

The second kind of music-based emotional contagion is the one I described earlier. The music is the object of attention and is inevitably recognized as the source (or one of the sources) of the response it calls forth. The listener responds *to* the music, though the response is not *about* the music. The response is experienced as occasioned by and linked to the music, not as some undirected mood (Davies (1994a)).[8]

To say the response is attentional is, of course, not to maintain that the person subject to emotional contagion attends to or is even aware of the causal mechanisms responsible for the transmission of affect. Typically she is not. She attends to the source of contagion, the music's expressive character, without following the process by which this affect becomes one she shares. In many cases, however, the attention she pays to

---

[6] Philosophers interested in analyzing the emotions sometimes discuss the musical case without noticing how peculiar it is in this respect; see Wilson (1972): 82–5 for an example.

[7] For discussion of the use of music in marketing, see Milliman (1982) and (1986), Bruner (1990), and North & Hargreaves (1997). Shatin (1970) discusses the use of music to control and change the listener's mood; see also Bunt & Pavlicevic (2001) and the practical guide to music selections associated with desired emotional responses edited by Capurso et al. (1952).

[8] Maddell (2002) objects to accounts of music's expressiveness like mine (Davies (1980, (1994a)) and Kivy's (1989) that they leave the listener's response only loosely tied to the music. He cites Radford (1991), and the objection does seem relevant to Radford's view, in which music is a cause of objectless moods that are about 'everything and nothing'. The objection does not have much force against the position I defend, however, which stresses the attentional dependence of the response on the music's expressive development.

expressions of the source emotion plays a crucial role in opening her up to the relevant triggers of emotional communication.

Film music may turn out sometimes to involve the one kind of contagion, at others the other, or to involve the one kind more often with one group of viewers than with the rest. Many movie-goers are not aware of the film's accompanying music as they hear it, while others are aware of but not focused on the music, yet both kinds of viewers are liable to be emotionally primed by the music they hear. At other times, the music draws attention to itself and clearly establishes an emotional tone for (or tension against) the movie action that is to follow. If there is emotional contagion in either case, it is non-attentional in the first and attentional in the second. As well, some members of the audience may be inclined to listen more often and more carefully to the movie's music, in which case if they are infected by the music they are likely to be conscious more often of its working on their emotions.

What characterizes emotional contagion? Intuitively, the hallmarks are these: one emotional state, appearance, or condition is transmitted to a person (or creature) who comes to feel the same way; the display of the first emotional state plays a causal role in the process of transmission and the first emotional state must be perceived, either attentionally or non-attentionally, by the emotion's recipient; the first emotional state is not the emotional object of the response, however, because the responder does not hold about the first emotional state beliefs that make it an appropriate intentional object for the response in question.

Emotional contagion should be distinguished from some conditions that are out-wardly similar in that *A* and *B* experience the same emotion. The following do not fit the characterization of emotional contagion that was just offered: we both feel the same emotion because our emotions have a common intentional object about which we both hold the same emotion-relevant beliefs. (We both react with fear to the nearby charging lion, or we both laugh at the same joke.) I react to your emotion by feeling the same, because I believe the basis of your reaction will also provide me with a reason to react similarly. (Seeing you flee in terror, I do the same without waiting to discover what you are terrified of, or I begin to share your humor at a joke you are about to tell.) Your emotion is the emotional object of my response and our emotions are the same. (You are angry that we are delayed, and I am angry that you are angry because you promised you would keep your cool.) I try to work out what you are feeling by imaginatively simulating your situation, or I use knowledge of your character and circumstances, and thereby empathically share your state. And finally, our recognizing that we share some reaction modifies that reaction, for instance, by augmenting it—people laugh thirty times more often when they are with strangers who also display their amusement than when they are alone (Provine (1996))—or by coloring it—as when we feel a sense of community, or alternatively become self-conscious and embarrassed, to react as the other does.

Emotional contagion does not always occur when two people share the same emotion, or even when this sharing is caused by one person's emotional state impinging on the other. What is crucial, as I have noted, is that the mirroring response does not take the initial emotional state, appearance, or condition as its emotional object and does not involve the kinds of beliefs about that state, appearance, or condition that are distinctive to emotions of the kind elicited. Nor does one adopt the response in the process of trying to understand what affective state another is undergoing. Even if it arises via contagion, however, that other people are similarly affected may trigger the effects of sharing, such as an amplification of the response.

Not all philosophers of music agree that the mirroring response to music's expressiveness involves contagion. Kivy, who is a dedicated cognitivist, at first (1987, 1989) denied that anyone (apart from the pathological) is ever saddened by sad music.[9] This view dismisses the testimony of many music lovers as well as the experimental results of psychologists' studies.[10] Later (1993, 1994), Kivy ameliorates his position, accepting that music weakly tends to move some listeners. Radford (1989, 1991) allows that music can produce a generalized, objectless reaction, but seems to take as his model the case of non-attentional emotional infection, and thereby mischaracterizes the important musical case. Jerrold Levinson (1996, 2006; see also Robinson (2005)) argues that music is expressive because we experience it imaginatively as a narrative about an indefinite persona we hear as inhabiting it. He suggests that sometimes our responses are to the fate of this persona. Or finally, instead of proposing a rival account, one can file it in the 'too hard' basket: 'And only music, with its capacity not only to go beyond words but to exist only beyond words, can provide an explanation of why we respond the way we do to it. We are confusing the issue further by attempting to package this emotive understanding in terms of language, or in terms of objects and beliefs. Perhaps this is where both music as well as emotion should, as Wittgenstein suggests, be passed over in silence' (Worth 2000: 106).

I find all these alternatives unconvincing and have argued against most of them elsewhere (Davies 1994a, 1994b, 1997, 2006). I will not recapitulate those discussions. Instead, I consider criticisms of my position recently proposed by Robinson. She thinks that music is a source of emotional contagion, but she regards my story about this as flawed. She writes: 'Davies's account cannot be quite right for two reasons. For one thing, emotional contagion normally occurs automatically without our being aware of what's happening: the expression is acquired automatically by some form of motor

---

[9]   Kivy (1987, 1989) conflates the arousal account of music's expressiveness—music expresses an emotion *E* if and only if it arouses (or tends to arouse) *E* in a suitably qualified listener—with the claim that music sometimes arouses echoing responses in the listener. He writes as if he can demonstrate that music never arouses a mirroring response if he can show that the arousal theory is false. These views should be kept apart, however. There is no inconsistency in maintaining (as I do) both that music's expressiveness does not depend on its arousing any emotion (and hence that the arousal theory is false) and also that music regularly does arouse the emotion it expresses.

[10]   Carol Krumhansl (1997) sets out specifically to test Kivy's position and concludes he is wrong to claim that listeners do not experience the emotions they recognize in music. For a review of the literature and empirical evidence of contagion from music to listener, see Gabrielsson (2002). For Kivy's critique of Krumhansl's experiment, see Kivy (2006).

mimicry. *Recognition* of the expression is not necessary as Davies stipulates, and may even prevent or moderate the effect of contagion' (2005: 385; here, as in subsequent quotations, italics are as in the original).

This first objection insists that emotional contagion normally does not depend on one's recognizing the expressive character of that to which one responds. By this, I take it that Robinson holds the emotional contagion is commonly non-attentional, so the attentional response I characterize cannot be 'quite right'. But this has to be wrong. Robinson cites with approval the work of psychologists Elaine Hatfield, John T. Cacioppo, and Richard L. Rapson and indicates them as her primary source on emotional contagion. Apparently, Robinson overlooks this: 'People should be more likely to catch others' emotions if their attention is riveted on the others than if they are oblivious to others' emotions' (Hatfield et al. 1994: 148). Hatfield et al. (1994: 148–52) provide compelling evidence for the truth of this hypothesis. And common sense and experience suggest that one is more likely to catch another's mood by recognizing his emotions and signals of affect than by being unaware of them. Film-makers know this and focus spectators' attention on characters' expressive facial features in order to elicit emotional contagion or empathy (Plantinga (1999); Coplan (2006)).

In fact, Robinson regularly cites psychologists' experiments in which the subjects were asked to listen to—that is, attend to and recognize—the music's expressive character. The experimenters measured the subjects' physiological or behavioral responses or obtained self-reports afterwards. One of Robinson's favorite cases is an experiment by Krumhansl (1997) of exactly this kind: the physiology of half the subjects was monitored as they attended closely to the music, while the other half recorded their emotional responses as they listened. Robinson (2005: 395) also mentions Dale Bartlett's review (1996) of 130 studies showing how listening to music produces physiological effects in listeners. As she should be aware, the vast majority of the studies listed by Bartlett are recognitional. In only a tiny minority is the music played as background while the subject focuses on something else, such as a puzzle task, for instance. Robinson offers these recognitional experiments as evidence of a kind of emotional contagion she labels the 'jazzercise effect'. So, she cannot consistently maintain against my view that emotional contagion in the musical case is normally non-attentional.

It is true, as I noted earlier, that the listener subject to emotional contagion is usually oblivious to the way the affect is transmitted. Nevertheless, her recognition of and attention to the music's expressiveness primes her to catch the music's mood. Her focus on the music's expressive character encourages and invigorates the transmission of affect, as is indicated by experimental evidence both for emotional transfer from person to person and from music to person. So, there is nothing amiss in my suggestion that music is involved in attentional emotional contagion. Indeed, one would expect this to be usually more powerful and reliable than non-attentional contagion from musical sources.

Robinson's second objection is as follows:

On Davies's account music is *like* an expression of emotion—just as is the configuration of the basset hound's face—but it isn't one really. We are programmed to respond with sadness to an expression of sadness in another human being. The fact that we are probably programmed to respond to other human faces (on the grounds that sad *human* expression usually indicate sad humans) probably has no implications for our responses to doggy faces. (After all, if living with a basset hound were like living with a depressed person, would normal folk choose a basset hound as their life's companion?) And by parity of reasoning we are probably not programmed to respond to musical sounds by virtue of the fact that they are *like* expressions of emotion in some way. (2005: 388).[11]

It seems to me that these are empirical claims and that the evidence favors my view rather than counting against it. To take a non-musical case, I surmise that when we are cheered by a warm and jolly décor, this is most easily explained as involving contagion. Presumably the original source of the cheerfulness of yellow and the gloominess of grey is the weather, and it is not difficult to understand why we might be programmed to react positively to sunny weather and to be depressed by rain and fog. (Such responses are neither inevitable nor uncontrollable, however. Any number of local factors might block what is initially a weak tendency to respond via contagion.) Though the interior décor of a house is never likely to be mistaken for the local weather, nevertheless, it inherits the positive and negative values of the weather and we respond via contagion to this.

As this case testifies, our valuations and responses to our natural environments, as well as to our human cohorts, can become generalized and applied over a range of contexts. Synaesthetic generalizations are common in the musical case, in particular. We conceive of music in terms of human, spatial, and other categories. Timbres are warm, metallic, dark, and brittle, rhythms are jagged or square, notes are high or low. Melody and music in general contain movement, conflict, statements, questions, dialogue, wit, and humor. The progress of music makes sense much as human behavior does: we do not regard it as mechanically determined, yet we expect to be able to understand each event in terms of what went before. We anticipate that the music will present a coherent pattern much as we anticipate that a person will act in character, though both can also be bafflingly unpredictable on occasion. Above all, we hear in music humanly created emotional expression. The *image* of human expressiveness is often as evocative as the real thing. There are good biological reasons for this fact. Our first reaction as social creatures that rely on our mindreading abilities is to respond to the outward show as a window on the human soul. That is how (and why) we react to expressiveness in music: it is no less a human form of expression, though it is a far more sophisticated one, than weeping is.

---

[11] Robinson is correct that I regard music as expressive by virtue of its presenting appearances of emotion. I do allow that real emotions of the composer can be expressed in his or her work, but I also hold this to be a sophisticated act of expression achieved via the composer's appropriation of the expressive character of the music he or she writes (see Davies (1986), (1994a)).

Few deny that music often powerfully calls from them an emotional echo of its own expressiveness. I think we respond directly to that expressiveness—and not that we respond to a persona we imagine to inhabit the music, for example—so I do not find it at all implausible to regard that response as suggesting we find music evocative of contagious responses. Because there is money to be made, marketers and the psychologists they employ have taken the trouble to establish that music can affect us subliminally through contagion. Why think it would not do so more directly when we focus on its expressive power?

Why do people choose basset hounds as pets? No doubt there can be many reasons, but I guess that many a basset pup has elicited a sympathetic 'oooh, poor baby' from its owner-to-be. Why do basset hounds not drive their owners to suicide via contagion? We can soon become inured to the surface mood of our environment. When we know that basset hounds are as fun loving as other breeds through living with them on a daily basis, the subliminal tendency we have to be affected negatively by the humanly sad-looking character of their faces is easily held in abeyance. If your partner had the misfortune to suffer a stroke that left him or her with a permanently down-turned mouth, you would probably learn not to let this outward appearance of sadness affect you. So it is, I assume, for the owners of basset hounds.[12]

As we have seen, Robinson's second objection to my account of music's contagious powers fares no better than the misconceived first. How well does her own theory of musical expressive transmission by infection stand up? I find it confusing. What she offers as the primary example of musical contagion either looks like something else or supports a view like mine, as I now demonstrate.

Robinson's jazzercise effect, which illustrates her model of emotional contagion, works like this: music arouses physiological changes; the subject aware of these changes looks for and latches on to cues in the environment and responds emotionally to them. Robinson's model here is a notorious experiment performed by Stanley Schachter and Jerome Singer (1962).[13] The experimenters used a drug to induce arousal in their subjects. These subjects, who were unaware of how or why their bodies were stimulated, matched their emotions to a stooge who behaved angrily with his situation in some cases and who cheerfully horsed around in others.

---

[12] Peter Kivy, in a commentary on a draft of this chapter, has described this concession as 'utterly devastating' for my view, because we have resided with sad music our entire lives and therefore should never respond to it via contagion. I do not agree. My claim is that there is a disposition toward contagious responses that is realized in some cases. One way it can be dulled or deadened is by over-exposure to a given piece. As for the ubiquity of sad music, it is important to recall that we react to the expressive detail of particular works (Davies (1999)), so it is not surprising if our emotions are gripped when we return to those works, despite having been exposed to other, similarly expressive pieces in the meantime.

[13] I call the experiment notorious because the methodology is suspect, the results have proved difficult or impossible to replicate, and the interpretation of the outcome is contested. For a review of psychologists' criticisms, see Carlson & Hatfield (1992). Philosophers have often discussed the experiment; for recent critical comments, see Griffiths (1997) and Prinz (2004).

My proposal is that at least sometimes music plays a role similar to that which the epinephrine played in Schachter's famous experiment. It *arouses* listeners and puts them in a bodily mood or state. But, as in the experiment, listeners have no good explanation for their state of arousal. Why, after all, should music make me feel anxious or fearful? . . . So what they do is what the subjects in the Schachter experiment did: they look around for an appropriate label for their vaguely felt affective state, and they *label* their state of arousal depending on the context they bring to the experience. (Robinson (2005): 401)

Here is the process Robinson describes: the music causes me to feel tense, say. Perhaps matters end there; I feel an objectless irritability. Alternatively, I find myself thinking of tomorrow's dental appointment and thereby come to identify my reaction as one of apprehension. Or again, perhaps I pick up on the affective tone of those around me, so that I come to share their all-too-apparent irritation.

Now, the first two cases—unfocussed irritability and apprehension at tomorrow's dental appointment—are not ones of emotional contagion. I experience an objectless mood in the first and an object-directed response of the ordinary, cognitively founded kind in the second. And if the third example—I pick up on the irritation of others—is one of contagion, the communication of affect is not to me from the music, but to me from people in my environment. In all these cases, the music is relevant because it heightens my physiological condition and in that way disposes me more than might otherwise be the case to adopt an affective stance, so that I come to experience a mood or to resonate emotionally with some aspect of my environment. But the music is always remote from the response. It plays a role in making me receptive to emotional experience, but this role might have been played instead by three cups of espresso or a shot of adrenaline. Certainly, the response is not made *to* the music.

I do not deny that people sometimes react affectively in the way just described or that music sometimes initiates the process by which this occurs. I agree, that is, that music can affect the listener's physiological state in ways of which she is not directly aware, and that this can lead her to interrogate her wider environment for cues as to the character of her affective state. For the examples previously described, however, I deny that the response involves catching the music's expressive character. If contagion occurs, it does not directly involve the music. So, when developed this way, Robinson's would not be an account of *musical* contagion.

How could the music play a more prominent role? Schachter's experiment has been taken as an instance of emotional contagion (as in Hatfield et al. (1994): 111–13) because the subjects tended to catch the confederate's emotion. If the music not only initiated the change in the listener but also participated in her reaction, much as the confederate did in the experiment, the result would involve musical contagion, the transmission of affect from the music to the listener. Moreover, the suggestion is plausible. It would not be surprising if the listener latched on to the music, to which she is attending already, and in particular, to the emotional character she recognizes in the sounds it presents. Her attention to the music then closes a causal circle: the music affects her physiology, which makes her attend more closely to what it expresses and disposes her to account for her own reaction in similar terms. This description is consistent with a very familiar case—we are physiologically affected by events in our neighborhood, which makes them perceptually and cognitively salient, which leads to our taking them as the intentional objects of our emotion—except that, for music, where we are aware that its sadness, say, is not an appropriate object for our sympathy, it is the echoing response, not sympathy, that is elicited.

Is this how Robinson's account should be understood? As I say, this story is one of emotional contagion via music and is plausible.[14] Nevertheless, it cannot be the interpretation Robinson wants for her view, because it describes the emotional contagion produced by music as normally of the attentional kind. Moreover, this story matches my own theory of the echoing response, which Robinson would rather reject.

Despite Robinson's doubts, I remain convinced that the idea of attentional emotional contagion provides the most convincing characterization of the emotional reaction of the listener who attends closely to an instrumental work and, as a result, finds herself inclined to be moved to mirror the music's overall expressive character.

I now turn from philosophers to psychologists. Many psychologists are not interested in the intentionality and cognitive subtlety of emotions. They prefer to focus on physiological changes (e.g. in the autonomic nervous system, body chemistry, neurological activity, or sub-muscular movements) or on behavioral displays (e.g. facial expressions) that can be accurately measured without relying on self-reports. Much work has been done to show that there are basic affects—fear, anger, happiness, sadness, surprise, and disgust—that have universally recognizable facial displays and that are modular in the sense that they are triggered and operate independently of conscious reflection (Ekman (1972, 1980, 1992)).[15] These are called 'affect programs', though it is not uncommon for psychologists to proceed as if this technical term designates all that is covered by the word 'emotion' in its ordinary, day-to-day use.

As well, psychologists and others have long been interested in empathy, sympathy, mob psychology, social conformity, and emotional communication, but emotional contagion was not usually distinguished from other versions of these modes of emotional engagement.[16] It was in the 1990s that the topic of emotional contagion attracted the attention of psychologists in its own right. A key work, mentioned earlier,

---

[14] I am not convinced, however, that physiological change *always* precedes perceptual inspection and cognitive evaluation, as this account implies.

[15] Note that non-cognitive reactions of these kinds were discussed above as possible counterexamples to the cognitive theory of the emotions.

[16] Wheeler (1966) was among the first psychologists to attempt to distinguish contagion from other types of social and emotional influence. An appropriate subtlety is apparent in some recent empirical studies of empathy, for instance, which portray empathy as more sophisticated than, and as involving a different degree of self- and other-awareness from, emotional contagion—see Decety & Jackson (2004) and Decety & Hodges (2006). For a philosophical account of some of the relevant distinctions, see Goldie (2000): ch. 7, and for discussion of the difference when the response is occasioned by films, see Coplan (2004).

is by Hatfield et al. (1994).[17] Their definition of primitive emotional contagion occurs in this passage: 'The focus in this text is on rudimentary or *primitive* emotional contagion—that which is relatively automatic, unintentional, uncontrollable, and largely inaccessible to conversant awareness. This is defined as the tendency to automatically mimic and synchronize facial expressions, vocalizations, postures, and movements with those of another person and, consequently, to converge emotionally' (1994: 5). They emphasize mimicry and feedback in explaining emotional contagion.

Proposition 1. In conversation, people tend automatically and continuously to mimic and synchronize their movement with the facial expressions, voices, postures, movements, and instrumental behaviors of others.

Proposition 2. Subjective emotional experiences are affected, moment to moment, by the activation and/or feedback from such mimicry.

Proposition 3. Given Propositions 1 and 2, people tend to 'catch' others' emotions, moment to moment (1994: 10–11).

The idea, then, is that, when dealing face-to-face with another, I tend to mimic his behavior and facial expressions without being aware of doing so; I 'read' my feelings off from my facial expressions and behaviors; so, I come to feel the way my interlocutor does.

Hatfield et al. defend the premises of this argument. Some psychologists regard facial feedback as singularly important in this process, while others see other factors sometimes as equally relevant. When they review the psychological literature, Hatfield et al. find strong experimental evidence in favor of the facial feedback hypothesis (1994: 53–63). Evidence for vocal and postural feedback is positive, but the tie is not so close as that with facial expression (1994: 63–76).[18] They conclude: 'subjective emotional experience is affected by feedback from facial, vocal, and postural muscular movements, as well as by feedback from instrumental emotional activity. We also expect subjective emotional experience to be influenced by feedback from the facial, vocal, and postural movements that are mimicked' (1994: 52–3).

Teresa Brennan identifies a quite different mechanism of transmission as crucial: 'If contagion exists (and the study of crowds says it does), how is it effected? Images and mimesis explain some of it . . . but olfactory and auditory entrainment offer more comprehensive explanations . . . Research on chemical communication and entrainment suggests answers centered on the analysis of pheromones, substances that are not

---

[17] Even their treatment sometimes lacks care. The cover of their book shows a wonderful picture from the 1937 All-Ireland Road Bowls Championship. The bowler and scores of onlookers are shown attempting to use body English to control the course of the (out-of-shot) bowl's movement. The authors identify this as 'an example of postural mimicry' when clearly it is no such thing. Everyone's eyes are fixed on the bowl, not the bowler, and each, independently of the rest, is attempting to guide its course. There is behavioral coincidence with, not mimicry of, the bowler.

[18] Later in the book, however, they allow: 'people vary greatly in the extent to which they rely on facial, vocal, and postural feedback in determining what they feel' (1994: 159). For a review of work on facial feedback in mood contagion, see Adelman & Zajonc (1989).

released into the blood but are emitted externally' (2004: 68–9). Pheromones play a role not only in sexual behavior but also in communication, she argues.[19]

Now, if there is emotional contagion between music and humans, or between house décors and humans, it cannot be facial mimicry that underpins it because music and house décors do not present a human physiognomy, and it cannot be the detection of pheromones that cause it because music and house décors do not emit pheromones. Rather than abandoning talk of emotional contagion for such cases, where it seems perfectly apt, it is the psychologists' accounts that should be questioned. It is my impression that psychologists are sometimes inclined to define experiential processes or phenomena reductively, in terms of the causal mechanisms by which they are frequently brought about.[20] And because they naturally focus on the human-to-human case, the relevant causes are identified with neurological, physiological, or behavioral patterns that are distinctively human (or animal).

There is a lesson philosophers have learned from functionalist theories of the mind. A given state or process might be realized in different ways by different systems. That process or state should be identified in terms of its functional role in the system's operation or ecology rather than in terms of factors that are contingently dependent on the form in which the system exists or on the materials of which it is built. This lesson is appropriate to the case in hand. Emotional contagion should be characterized in terms of what is distinctive to the affective relation, not solely in terms of its underlying etiology (or etiologies). Here is the relevant account: *emotional contagion involves the arousal in B by A of an affect that corresponds either to an affect felt and displayed by A or, where A is non-sentient, as for the case of music and house décors, to the expressive character experienced by B as displayed in A's appearance, and while B's arousal must derive from A's displaying the relevant affect, so that A's affect is the perceptual object of B's reaction, A's affect is not the emotional object of B's response, because B does not believe (or imagine) of A's affect what is required to make it an appropriate emotional object of the response B experiences.* We can be agnostic about the mechanism of transmission. Between humans, there are many possibilities, from subtle facial mimicry to the detection of emitted pheromones. Between music and humans, or home décors and humans, different causal routes might produce the relevant outcome.

---

[19] The experiments cited by Brennan concern the regulation of human ovulation and show how exposure both to men's and women's perspiration affect the cycle. As well, there is interesting work she does not cite indicating that females detect male MHC (major histocompatibility complex) alleles (and vice versa). A male with MHC alleles differing from a given female's alleles thereby signals his capacity to father children with stronger immune systems. Women prefer such men at the peak of monthly fertility, but otherwise take as partners men with MHC alleles nearer their own. For discussion, see Milinski (2003) and Thornhill & Gangestad (2003).

[20] Hatfield et al. (2004) take care to identify their topic as *primitive* emotional contagion and they allow that attentional, cognitively more complex forms of contagion are possible. Nothing in their account commits them to analyze non-primitive emotional transmission in terms of the causal mechanisms they highlight for primitive emotional contagion.

What are these causal routes in the musical case? That would be for scientists to discover, but it is possible to offer some speculative suggestions. I favor the view that music is expressive because we experience it as presenting the kind of carriage, gait, or demeanor that can be symptomatic of states such as happiness, sadness, anger, sassy sexuality, and so on.[21] If contagion operates through mimicry, we might then expect the listener to adopt bodily postures and attitudes (or posturally relevant muscular proprioceptions) like those apparent in the music's progress.[22] This would be more likely, I guess, than facial mimicry, since music is not experienced as presenting a facial aspect. Vocal mimicry, in the form of subtle tensing or flexing of vocal muscles, would also be a predictable response to vocal music or to acts of subvocal singing along with instrumental music.[23] And to return to features highlighted by Robinson and others, where the flux of music is felt as an articulated pattern of tensing and relaxing, this is likely to be imaged and mimed within the body, perhaps in ways that are neither subpostural nor subvocal. Finally, there is the possibility that music works on the brain, not only by eliciting physical-cum-physiological changes that nudge the subject as she becomes aware of them toward affective appraisals and responses, but also more immediately, by directly stimulating cortical regions linked with emotional recognitions and responses. Many and diverse routes of emotional transmission might be involved, perhaps simultaneously.

That music sometimes leads the attentive listener to share the emotions she hears it as expressing calls into question the cognitive theory of the emotions, because the listener does not believe of the music's expressiveness what would make it an apt emotional object of the response and she does not pick up on some other aspect of the environment as the response's emotional object. This phenomenon is best understood as involving emotional infection or osmosis. Emotional infection requires perception of the music's character but may be non-attentional or attentional. The mirroring response of the music-focused listener is of this second variety. She is very likely to identify the music's expressiveness as the cause of her response because her reaction tracks her following of the music and recognition of its expressive character, but she is unlikely to be aware of details of the causal mechanisms that forge the connection. The evocative power of purely instrumental music to call forth such a reaction does not depend on the listener's taking the music as expressing someone's felt emotion. As social beings, we are primed to detect and react to mere appearances or presentations of emotions (provided we judge that cheating is not an issue). Psychologists' attempts to

---

[21] For empirical work on the human capacity to identify a person's emotion by observing only the abstract form of human motion (that is, motion as displayed only as light points on an otherwise invisible body), see Grammer et al. (2003).

[22] For relevant empirical data, see Janata & Grafton (2003).

[23] For relevant empirical data, see Koelsch et al. (2006). Juslin & Laukka (2003) and Juslin & Västfjäll (2008), who postulate that the response to music can be explained as involving emotional contagion, make the comparison not with facial mimicry but with the communication of affect through vocal cues. See also Neumann & Strack (2000).

characterize the nature of emotional contagion do not readily accommodate the musical case, however. This is because they are inclined to describe the phenomenon primarily in terms of the causal mechanisms of transmission from human to human. An account of emotional contagion referring to what distinguishes it from other emotional states and relations is preferable to one attempting to reduce it to an underlying causal process or route of communication. Meanwhile, empirical study of the many possible paths and mechanisms of transmission is far from complete, and the musical case presents intriguing prospects and challenges for work in the area.

10

Empathizing as Simulating

Susan L. Feagin

The main objective of this paper is to explain a simulation account of what it is to empathize with characters in literary works of art. I ascribe to the view that simulating a mental process of the characters with whom one empathizes is a necessary condition of empathizing with them, and that for one process to simulate another it is necessary for it to be structurally similar, in relevant respects, to the process simulated. Further, I propose that it is in virtue of the similarity of the structure of the process that simulating provides an understanding of a character, part of what it is like to be that character, in a literary work of art.

I take such an understanding to be one aspect of appreciating the literary arts, including both narrative fiction and non-fiction. Much of the recent interest in emotional and other affective responses to literature has been generated by the paradox of fiction, in which the primary philosophical problem is to explain how emotional responses to what readers know to be untrue are both possible and rational (Radford (1975); Weston (1975)). Differences of belief and the reasonableness of belief with respect to the truth or falsehood of what one is reading may of course be relevant to one's affective responses and to the appreciation of literature. Yet, the philosophical debate has moved beyond the paradox itself, and for good reason. One reason is that the account of emotions as involving beliefs has been seriously undermined.[1] Another reason is that, even if a subset of emotions, 'emotions proper' or 'emotions' narrowly defined, are taken to require beliefs, appropriate responses to literature include other affectively-laden mental states and processes, such as moods and feelings, which are not typically thought to involve beliefs, and their appropriateness needs to be explained as well. Third, in appreciating fiction, one typically has many reasonable beliefs about how a fictional work relates to the world that may well be implicated in the generation of one's emotional responses. Finally, in part because of this third reason, the distinction between fiction and non-fiction is itself significantly problematic, and is not

---

[1] Though there were some defenders early on of the view that emotions do not require certain types of beliefs (e.g. Greenspan (1988)), it has become more common (Robinson (2005); Prinz (2004)).

tracked by the distinction between whether what a work 'says' or presupposes should be believed. An appreciation of the significance of these last two facts is, I suspect, at least partly responsible for moving the discussion within philosophy of art from debates about the *rationality* of one's responses to literature to debates about their *morality*, or, put another way, from imagination and emotion made possible by the suspension of disbelief to imagination and emotion made possible by the suspension of one's values.

In suggesting that simulating is a necessary rather than a sufficient condition for empathizing, I allow that other conditions may be required. For example, in ordinary usage, the word 'empathy' refers only to responses to other people's pain or discomfort, and not to their pleasures: one empathizes in times of loss, not with triumph or success.[2] Simulating, in contrast, does not discriminate between pains and pleasures, and has the potential advantage of explaining vicarious pleasures as well as empathic pains.

Another necessary condition for empathizing that has commonly been suggested is that one must first identify an individual with whom one empathizes, variously referred to as one's 'target' or 'protagonist' (even if one does not initiate the process with the intention of empathizing with that individual). In reading literature, however, one may realize after the fact that the mental process one has gone through is one that it is reasonable to attribute to a character, rather than identify a character in advance with whom one will empathize. The point could be put this way: the *understanding* of the character, the 'empathic content' itself, exists in virtue of the structural similarities between the simulator's mental process and that of the protagonist, but understanding *the character* requires the identification of a protagonist whose mental processes one simulates, something that may take place after the fact.

I begin with a brief explanation of what I take simulating a mental process to be and contrast it with the idea that the process is to be described in functional terms, that is, in terms of relationships between 'inputs' and 'outputs'. In Section 10.2, I rehearse briefly some problems with accounts that describe the process both in functional terms and as initiated by a state or set of states, the input, in the form of 'simulated beliefs' and 'simulated desires'. Finally, in Section 10.3, I explore the crucial role that desires and desire-like phenomena may have in establishing the structure of a mental process, components that have been largely neglected or rejected, but that are nevertheless significant when accounting for the affective quality of the experience when empathizing with a character.

10. 1 Simulating Mental Processes: Structural Similarities

I propose that a necessary condition for empathizing with a character in a literary work is that one simulates the relevant mental process of that character, and for one process to

---

[2] Some hold that the possibility of empathizing is not restricted to someone else's pain, e.g. Peter Goldie holds that one can empathize with Mother Theresa's serenity (Goldie (2000)). Gregory Currie is unusual in holding that, with empathy, 'the shared mental states need not involve feeling' at all ((2004): 108).

simulate another it is necessary for it to be structurally similar, in relevant respects, to the process simulated. I also propose that it is the structural properties of a process that account for, at least to some extent, the affective or phenomenological 'feel' of the experience, and hence for the types and degrees of understanding one may have of a character with respect to the mental process being simulated.

Two processes may be initiated in the same way and yield the same results, but have different structures. For example, suppose that John and Joan are both excellent spellers, and that if you ask either one of them how to spell the word 'believe', they will both invariably provide the right answer, even though they both have some trouble with that tricky part involving the ordering of the 'i' and the 'e'. On the one hand, let us suppose that John, in order to deal with that tricky part, conjures a visual image of an inscription of 'believe' spelled correctly, which enables him to reply correctly. Let us suppose that Joan, on the other hand, runs through the well-known rule, '"I" before "e", except after "c"' in order to make sure she orders the vowels correctly. The two processes are *structurally different* in that one involves a visual image, deploying memories of how the word looks when it is written correctly, and the other the application of a rule that has previously been memorized.

Yet, John's and Joan's mental processes are also *structurally similar* in that they both employ a 'double-checking' mechanism for spelling a word. In this respect, the processes that John and Joan go through contrast with what Sheila does when asked how to spell 'believe': she just rattles it off from memory without having to double-check anything. The more abstract similarities, as in the application of a double-checking mechanism, might yield an understanding of a person (what is going on in that person) who takes longer to answer than another person, who is able simply to spell the word without having to double-check the sequence of vowels. John and Joan may each be able to empathize with the other in this respect. Yet, empathizing only at this higher level of abstraction will not necessarily enable one to understand someone who double-checks in a particular way, e.g. against a visual image. Joan may be imaginatively clueless with respect to how a visual image can be recruited to serve as a double-checking mechanism. Another type of abstract structural difference may exist between processes that involve deliberate effort in the application of a double-checking mechanism and those where one double-checks automatically, by force of habit.[3]

It may be that, ultimately, what I describe as the structure of a process is in fact a type of *functional* relation between what initiates the process and the state the process leaves one in as a result. I do not have any objection in principle to this characterization, but it is not always as clear as it might be what the functionalist account of a particular mental phenomenon might be, and hence whether it would be the same as what I describe as a structure. First, functionalism is typically offered as an account of mental *states* rather

---

[3] My account differs in this respect from Alvin Goldman's distinction between two types of simulation that are both, on his view, involved in mindreading, since his distinction depends on one of them not being deliberate or even conscious.

than of mental processes. Processes involve, minimally, a *change* of state. Second, the structure of a mental process is not to be equated simply with a particular sequence of mental states. Consider the process of reasoning to a conclusion: to reason to a conclusion is not merely to have a particular sequence of thoughts, but to believe one of those thoughts, what we call the conclusion, at least to some extent on the basis of or because it follows from the content of other thoughts, what we call the premises. To have a sequence of thoughts is not, per se, to reach the last thought, the conclusion, on the basis of the others. I may have no trouble thinking a particular sequence of thoughts, but have no sense of how or why one could come to believe the last thought I think of on the basis of the others.

In *Simulating Minds*, Alvin Goldman also insists that simulations are processes and that they are simulations of processes (2006a: 36–8). However, when he begins his discussion of how simulations might be used 'to answer a [third person] mindreading question', he takes such a question to ask what mental *state* another person is in rather than what mental process(es) are going on (2006a: 39). He writes, 'People often use mental simulations or attempted mental simulations to answer questions about other people's mental *states*' (2006a: 39; emphasis added). Such a notion of simulation requires that the output, the state the simulation leaves one in, be the same as the other person's mental state. The fact that the simulation (allegedly) leaves one in the same mental state is what Goldman sees as important about it. In contrast, I urge that it is the structural similarity of the processes that is necessary for a simulation, and that is what figures in the activity of empathizing with someone, whether or not the processes are initiated by or terminate in the same mental states.

On Goldman's view, one attributes one of one's own states, which occurs 'in simulation mode, to be sure', to the other person (2006a: 40). He calls 'the act of assigning a state of one's own to someone else *projection*', and explains that, on his view, simulation, which he then identifies as simulation-for-mindreading, is basically a 'simulation-plus-projection' view (2006a: 40; original emphasis).[4] Further, he takes someone's 'simply assum[ing] that certain things she believes are also believed by the target' to be the limiting case of simulation-plus-projection, which he calls 'simulation' for short. That is, he ends up admitting as cases of simulation mental processes (simple projections) in which no simulation occurs at all. This may indeed, in some sense, enhance the explanatory power of his version of a simulation theory, but extending it to cover cases of simple projection misses the opportunity to show the *distinctive* way a simulation captures the character of a mental *process*.

Finally, two processes may be structurally the same even if what initiates each of the two processes and the states in which they leave one are different. For illustration,

---

[4] It should be noted that the emphasis on the fact that for a simulation one must assign a state *of one's own* to another person does help to contrast the simulation theory with the so-called theory-theory of how we go about attributing mental states to others, but it also obscures the nature of simulation in the process in that it doesn't distinguish the different ways in which one may come to be in that state.

I again offer a spelling example, this time with the request to spell the word 'neighbor'. Sheila, remember, has no problem with 'believe'; she can rattle it off on demand. But she cannot do so with 'neighbor', and has therefore adopted the practice of visualizing an inscription of the word in order to make sure she has the vowel sequence correct. The mental process Sheila goes through is structurally similar in this respect to that of the double-checkers of 'believe', even though the input, the question, is different and the output, the answer, is also different. Sheila may thus understand, to this extent, the double-checkers of 'believe' because she does the same sort of thing with 'neighbor'. Even with different inputs and outputs, processes may be similar or different with respect to different levels of abstraction, and the levels of abstraction may account for significantly different *types* and *degrees* of understanding.

10.2 How Simulations Begin

In much of the literature on mental simulation, simulations are said to be initiated by a simulated or pretend mental state. Alvin Goldman, for example, describes simulation as a heuristic for discovering another person's mental states, and says that 'pretend initial states', such as 'simulated desires and beliefs,' are fed into a 'decision-making system and allow it to generate the same choice it would produce given genuine beliefs and desires' (1995c: 718).[5] The initial state is described as a *simulated* belief or desire because of its functional role—in terms of the output generated—something the simulator presumably does not know it will produce at the initial stage of the process. The initial state is a simulation in part because of what happens later, not because of some inherent quality or characteristic of the state itself or of the process.

Gregory Currie endorses a similar view, holding that the initial stage of a simulation involves simulated beliefs, as opposed to real beliefs, which are described as such because they play a functional role that is similar to but not identical with that of real beliefs in one's cognitive economy. He writes that 'human beings have the capacity to generate and manipulate simulative *states* such as simulated beliefs and desires' (2004: 177; emphasis added), although he also states clearly that 'simulation' always refers to a mental *activity* (2004: 179). The claim that simulations are always mental activities is reconcilable with his reference to simulated beliefs and simulated desires if having a belief (or desire) is also a mental activity, perhaps at a deeper psychological level. And it is possible that a mental process could initiate another mental process, but the onto-logical implications of how a process could serve as a cause is in need of further attention. Currie makes similar claims about empathy, that it is, like simulation, 'a functional notion: it is the concept of a *state* that plays a characteristic role in a larger pattern of thought, feeling, and behaviour' (2004: 183; emphasis added). So described,

---

[5] Goldman (2006a) criticizes this sort of view and claims instead that enactment imagination should be considered to be a certain kind of process, something closer to the view I defend here, but he still develops the view in terms of simulated *states*.

empathy does not appear to be a process but a mental state, where the state counts as a particular type of simulated state because of the cognitive, affective, and behavioral functional roles that it plays, i.e. what outputs it produces. He of course grants that one may not know whether it will play that role 'at the time the [initial] state is experienced' (2004: 183).

It is appealing to identify the initial states of a simulation process as themselves simulations because they help to bring about results that are both similar to and crucially different from what actual beliefs and desires would (allegedly) produce. For example, both an actual belief and a simulated belief may lead to one's making a given decision, but, whereas the actual belief would likely lead to one's taking action on the basis of that decision, the simulated belief, given that it is *simulated*, would not. Simulated beliefs are sometimes described as functioning 'off-line', in so far as they do not, and are not supposed to, lead to overt action. Thus, both similarities and differences between so-called simulated beliefs (and desires) and actual beliefs (and desires) are effectively highlighted.

As this all too brief rehearsal of views reveals, referring to the initial states of a simulation as 'simulated' or 'pretend' states tends to undermine the idea that what is simulated is a process. Further, the view that the initial states are simulations of other states because of their functional role, i.e. because of what outputs or behavior they do or do not produce, has a more important vulnerability: it is unclear how one 'knows' which pretend states to recruit in order to initiate a simulation.[6] If one is 'trying out' a mental state to see if it may plausibly be attributed to another person, an explanation is still needed for how one comes up with the hypothesis that the other person might be in that state to begin with. The account seems to presuppose that one already has the information that the simulating is supposed to provide. This is a common criticism of empathy as simulation, one to which the account of simulation as structural similarity is not vulnerable since it does not require that a simulation be initiated by the same mental state, or type of mental state, as the process simulated.

But the structural account is vulnerable in another equally important way: one should be able to explain how one is able to generate a process having the requisite structure from the initial state (whatever that state is). This concern is especially important in light of the distinction between simulating how someone else is responding in a given situation and imagining how *I* would respond in that situation—sometimes referred to as 'in his shoes' imagining—that is, imagining how I would behave or respond were I in the situation that the person is in. The extent to which the former departs from the latter is exactly the extent to which engaging in the relevant imagining is challenging, according to some, or simply impossible, according to others.

---

[6] Shaun Nichols and Stephen Stich make a similar point in arguing against simulation-based explanations of desire attributions of the sort Robert Gordon and Gregory Currie employ (Nichols and Stich (2003): 138–40).

Currie carries the view that the inputs, the initial states of simulator and target, must be the same one step further, a step that seems designed to address these two concerns (how one knows what the particular initial state should be, and how one is able to engage in a psychological process of the right structural type). On his view, the relevant type of imagining 'is a matter of having substitute versions of the states [the other person] possesses' (Currie (1997): 67). He refers to these as imagined beliefs and imagined desires ('beliefs^i' and 'desires^i'). There are two ways, he explains, that 'the empathizer's i-states [are] like real beliefs and desires' (1997: 67). First, they have the same content (and it is notable that in both cases their content is said to be propositional). Second, they play a similar though not identical causal role as the genuine beliefs and desires would. Currie then adds a third requirement, that 'readers of fiction simulate the state of a hypothetical reader of fact . . . As a reader of fiction, I simulate someone who is reading a factual account of' whatever the work is about (1997: 68). Thus, according to Currie, simulation is transitive: one simulates what is going on in someone, a hypothetical-reader-of-fact, who simulates what's going on in the character; and by this route, the actual-reader-of-fiction simulates what is going on in the character.

Though Currie may have backed away somewhat from the hypothetical-reader-of-fact account, Goldman takes his view as a model for how to address the relevant issues in philosophy of art, pointing out that the hypothetical-reader-of-fact account is a bit 'baroque', but ultimately not taking this fact to be a sufficient reason to reject it. Goldman sagely notes that 'optimal aesthetic appreciation' will hardly accrue 'from adopting this simple perspective on the narrative to the exclusion of any other' and so instead takes it as a '*baseline* for all further responses to the work' (2006a: 287; original emphasis). Nevertheless, the hypothetical-reader-of fact account does not serve as an adequate baseline, and for a variety of reasons. First, it is far too often not at all clear how to imagine being a hypothetical reader of fact, and, second, it fails to identify what is distinctive about the role of empathizing in literary appreciation. There is a third problem as well: What explains how one is to respond when reading non-fiction literature? It may seem natural to take empathizing with real people as primary and empathizing with fictional characters as derivative from how it is done with real people, though I shall not pursue the distinction between a hypothetical 'real person' from a fictional character; Goldie (2003: 55–9) has a sensitive treatment of its implications. But the responses of readers of fact are far from being unproblematic. Certainly not everyone reading for facts would respond in relevantly similar ways. Equally important, from the standpoint of a philosophy of art, is that such a perspective leaves out the literary aspects of a work, whether fiction or non-fiction. It is hence not a view that will help us better understand simulation as a necessary condition for the appreciation of fiction or non-fiction as literature.[7]

---

[7] Goldie also criticizes the alleged derivative character of responses to fictional characters by drawing attention to similarities between fictional characters and non-factual but real persons (2003: 55–9).

Goldman and Currie occasionally use films as examples, where it is at least arguably more plausible to hold that one imagines a hypothetical-*observer*-of-fact as 'seeing an unfolding scenario from the camera's perspective' (Goldman (2006a): 287), than it is to hold that a hypothetical-*reader*-of-fact reads a description of actual events from, say, a narrator's or the author's perspective. Goldman includes some mental activities that are 'largely automatic and unconscious' as an 'important class of cases' falling within the rubric of simulation. His featured case of such an activity is a type of visually-based perceptual achievement, 'Face-based emotion recognition' or FaBER, since the case for FaBER as involved in the attribution of emotions to other people is 'very substantial' (2006a: 113). Nevertheless, even with films, such things as the cutting and alterations in color and focus—aspects of film that are *different* from what a person might see, even in a point-of-view shot—that provide a film with some of its affective power and hence that are to some degree responsible for initiating or providing the input for a viewer's empathizing with a character. Not only is it hard to know what a hypothetical-observer-of-fact would make of such visual experiences, since they are not the normal ways one sees things, but it is also difficult to account for the significance of such *artistic* devices for a hypothetical-observer-of-fact.

Similarly, there is a question of how an actual reader, in simulating a hypothetical-reader-of-fact, would recruit a sensitivity to *literary* features of a work—such as prose style, imagery, alliteration, and length of sentences—while reading for so-called facts.[8] By way of illustration, I offer an example involving punctuation, in this case, the lowly comma. Jack Kerouac's original typescript of *On the Road* is a 120-foot long, continuous role of pieces of paper that he taped together before inserting one end into the typewriter. He wrote the first-person narrative in a mere three weeks, and numerous passages in the original draft exude a feverish impatience. This quality is due in part to Kerouac's minimalist attitude towards punctuation. Luc Sante, in his review of the reprint (in book form) of the original scroll, employs a musical metaphor to describe a rather lengthy, unpunctuated passage, where, as he puts it, there is a 'frantic rush of 16th-notes that . . . [is] finally . . . punctuated half-way down the page by a thunderous "Yes!"' (2007: 13). It is easy to empathize with the narrator-character when reading such passages: it's a great ride; one relishes getting carried along in the rush. By contrast, in the previously published version, Sante points out that the 'rush' is stifled by 'six unnecessary commas' inserted by Kerouac's editor, commas that 'groom and house-break the character as well as his jazz' (2007: 13). Appreciators of the original typescript of the novel should be, *will* be, affectively sensitive to the presence or absence of commas in a way that facilitates empathizing, though it is not at all clear how or why a hypothetical-reader-of fact might respond to Kerouac's 'punctuational' anomalies. One might say that a hypothetical-reader-of-fact would respond to punctuation in so far as the facts one reads for include an understanding of the narrator's psychological

---

[8] See also Goldie (2003) on this point, 61–2.

state or dispositions. But, if so, what it is to respond as a hypothetical-reader-of fact is being explicated in terms of one's sensitivities to what one is reading as literature, rather than the other way around.

10.3 The Importance of Desires and Desire-Like Phenomena

I have been arguing that one should not think of simulated or pretend beliefs as input for a mental process that is in turn taken to be a simulation of some other process. And though I do not argue for it directly here, I also hold that one should not take emotions (or feelings) to be the output of a process that simulates some other process. Nevertheless, it is very tempting to describe feelings and emotions as psychological states, and as the outputs, products, or results of a process. This third (and last) section is designed to point to a different way of conceiving the phenomenological character of empathizing, one that is accounted for by the structure of the process itself.

For purposes of illustration, I begin with a stripped down version of the classic belief-desire account of emotion that takes each type of emotion to consist of a particular constellation of beliefs and desires. Fear, for example, involves the belief that one is in danger and the desire to avoid harm; indignation, the belief that something is unjust and the desire that such an injustice not occur; envy, the belief that someone else has possessions that one desires for oneself; resentment towards a person, the belief that one has been offended by that person and the desire that the offender suffer for it; and so on. The unpleasant aspect of the phenomenology of such emotional experiences as these is due to, roughly put, the *conflicts* that exist among each emotion's constituent beliefs and desires. The unpleasant feeling of fear, for example, would be explained by the conflict between what one believes to be the case (that one is, will be, or will likely be in danger) and what one desires to be the case (to avoid serious personal harm). The same type of explanation is available for the feeling quality of pleasurable emotions. The pleasures of eager anticipation are explained by the *collusion* between what one believes to be the case—that one will shortly achieve the object of one's desire—and the existence of that desire. I use 'conflict' and 'collusion' to cover a range of fit and misfit among beliefs and desires, not merely the narrower relations of inconsistency and consistency, which apply, strictly speaking, only in relation to propositional contents.

Some desires take the form of propositional attitudes: desires *that* something be the case, or that it not be the case. But there are also desires *to do*: stronger or weaker *urges*, or dispositions to act, or to refrain from acting in various ways. I take habits to be on the same continuum; they have a kind of automaticity that one becomes aware of, in an unpleasant way, when one tries to break them, or merely to act contrary to them. Some people, for example, have a hard time sitting still; they have an urge—sometimes we call it a 'need'—to stand up and move around. Urges can have cascading effects. One may be annoyed that all the seats at the ends of the rows in the lecture hall are taken so that one will not be able, without producing a disturbance, to get up and move before the lecture is over. One may be angry with the speaker for talking even longer than her allotted time, embarrassed by being so fidgety in one's seat and hence a distraction to others. Such urges or desires play a role in generating patterns of thought and related dispositional conditions. The need to stay put may even involve palpable physical discomfort.[9] One may resist calling all of these kinds of things (urges, dispositions, habits, and so on) 'desires'—I have taken to referring inclusively to desires and desire-like phenomena—but it can hardly be gainsaid that they need to be taken into account when understanding affective responses to anything, including literature.

The example of the frustrated audience member raises a problem for accounts of emotion that subvert the ordinary roles for desires and desire-like phenomena, such as that defended by Jenefer Robinson in *Deeper than Reason: Emotion and its Role in Literature, Music, and Art*. On Robinson's account, separate belief and desire components of emotions are merged and morphed into initial 'affective appraisals' or 'evaluative assessments'. Having an emotion is a process triggered by a quick-and-dirty affective assessment of a state of affairs, followed rapidly by some combination of physiological changes (heart rate, galvanic skin responses, etc.) and involuntary behavior (e.g. movements of facial muscles), and then by cognitive monitoring and assessments of the earlier stages of this process and the suitability of the responses to the situation or environment in which they arose. The feeling component of the emotion, the affective arousal, is thus (allegedly) accounted for at the very first stage of the process in the form of the affective appraisal, which has a broadly positive or negative valence. Following Le Doux, Robinson is partial to the view that many of the assessments arise from a few basic, innate emotion systems, though she emphasizes that triggers for the assessments can be altered and supplemented throughout the course of one's life (2005: 48).

The problem is that emotions and feelings do not arise exclusively to new events or changes in one's environment; sometimes they arise because the relevant aspects of the situation have *not* changed. It does not seem right to say in such cases that what initiates the emotion process is a quick-and-dirty preconscious affective appraisal of the situation, whether innate or acquired. Rather, a desire in the form of a disposition *to act* may become stronger with time, with an attendant increase in frustration, and perhaps also anger. In other cases, it could be curiosity or a desire for stimulation that is frustrated, manifesting itself as boredom. And in still other cases, the desire may simply evaporate.

In light of this, one possible move is to expand the pool of survival mechanisms to include those that predicate reproductive and survival value not merely on the 'quick-and-dirty', but also on the 'slow-but-has-its-limits', a basic emotion system with an inherent unwillingness to remain physically stationary or mentally inert for very long. However this plays out, it seems to me that the effort to discover basic conative sources

---

[9] Goldman (2006a), to my mind, makes too sharp a break between mental processes and physical behavior, but this concern will have to be addressed elsewhere.

of actions and affects (much more so their evolutionary 'just-so' stories) points us in the wrong direction for understanding empathizing with characters in literature and our affective responses to literature in general. Appreciating literature as art draws on mental capacities and abilities that lie at the more sophisticated end of the mental spectrum, in particular, our abilities to engage in abstract processes of imagination involving (1) the accumulation and application of complicated bundles of information, (2) shifting focuses of attention, and (3) capacities for affective flexibility. This may hardly sound like news, but it is at odds with the commitment to seeking some type of foundation or grounding of responses rather than to more general mental powers and flexibilities.

Consider the first of these elements, the accumulation and application of complicated bundles of information. Richard Wollheim writes of a 'cognitive stock' or 'repertoire' of information that is used in our various imaginings (1984). Peter Goldie makes a similar appeal, while also advocating that the process (of understanding) is essentially narrative in form, something that empathizing with actual people and empathizing with characters in literature share. Goldie proposes that I have a 'substantial characterization' of that other person and 'that I have a grasp of the narrative which I can imaginatively enact, with the other as narrator' as two necessary conditions for empathy.[10] Virtually all commentators on the subject mention how difficult it is to select out the relevant bits of information that enable one to simulate people's mental processes and hence to empathize with them.

Well, not so fast: it can be difficult, but the difficulties can also be overestimated. I described one example of how literary devices help out, that is, in the way punctuation is used. But the narratives themselves, the telling of the story or tale, can facilitate our engaging in the mental processes having the requisite structure because they control how relevant bits of cognitive stock are acquired and brought to mind. Some features of a narrative, the telling of a story or a tale, are especially relevant to empathizing with characters. First, the central cases of narratives are those that tell of the activities of human beings.[11] Second, there is something distinctive about human beings and our activities that accounts for the fact that the central cases of narratives involve us, and this is our ability to act as agents. That is, a story does not simply recount a series of actions and events, but it represents them as connected in significant ways. Consider, in particular, Michael Bratman's idea that temporal cross-references in the form of plans and policies are central to human agency. On Bratman's view, human agents are necessarily temporally extended beings (at least) in the following sense: we make plans for the future and adopt policies to carry out those plans. Plans and policies display temporal cross-reference when the primary roles of these states and attitudes,

---

[10] (2000: 195). He also proposes 'that I be aware of the other as a centre of consciousness distinct from myself' (195) as a necessary condition, but I do not address this condition here.

[11] Perhaps John Deigh (2004) would disagree, since he sees it as incumbent on any theory of emotion to explain how we (allegedly) can share emotions with non-human animals.

according to Bratman, 'include the support of coordination by way of the connections and continuities which . . . help constitute the identity of the agent over time' (2000: 45–6). Reflection, to which some have given a more crucial role in the analysis of agency, constitutes, on this view, one relevant type of temporal cross-reference, at least when we do not merely monitor our states and attitudes, but use what we learn about ourselves to organize and coordinate future actions primarily by issuing in plans and policies. These include what we should allow ourselves to do, what we should be on guard against, what we should suppress, and so on, which are then implicated in other intentions and actions.[12]

Plans and policies fall into the category of desire-like phenomena. They cannot exist in a vacuum and need not have an affective dimension in themselves in order to figure in mental processes that have affective dimensions. They may conflict or collude with, for example, our dispositions and urges, on the one hand, and beliefs and thoughts, on the other, and therein make a difference in how we feel. The conflicts and collusions among these various phenomena are partly responsible for the structure of a mental process and hence account for (at least some of) its affective quality.

The first sentence of Harriet Doerr's *Stones for Ibarra*, reveals how a talented author can convey crucial information involving temporal cross-reference, explicitly and implicitly, which readers can internalize very rapidly. 'Here they are, two North Americans, a man and a woman just over and just under forty, come to spend their lives in Mexico and already lost as they travel cross-country over the central plateau' (1984: 1). One might first note a slightly disoriented feeling created by the use of the term 'North Americans' to refer to the couple. Its operation is accommodated by what Goldman describes as simple projection. But the chances are higher that readers will (correctly) assume such things as that the man and woman are a married couple and that they are driving across the plateau in a car, both of which are rife with temporal cross-references. We learn that they are in early middle age and have made a momentous decision about how to spend the rest of their lives. This decision will have been filled out with a variety of plans, and their current action, 'travel[ing] cross-country over the central plateau' of Mexico, is an action undertaken as part of a plan. It is a richly-textured but inauspicious beginning to the rest of their lives, and indeed no more than this is needed to empathize with their discomfort in being lost.

When engaged in the project of attributing mental properties to real people one encounters in real life, making inferences on the basis of established psychological generalizations and particular bits of information about the individuals in question may be generally more reliable than attempts to simulate their mental processes. But

---

[12] There is considerable debate over whether mental states, such as decisions, beliefs, and intentions, *cause* mental events or overt behavior, and functionalist theories generally take inputs to be causes and outputs to be effects. There is not space to argue the point here, though I have intentionally avoided such talk with respect to plans and policies, representing them not as *causing* mental events or overt behavior, but as directing and focusing our minds and actions.

different sets of considerations come into play when reading literature as an art. It is obvious but worth repeating that appreciators of literature are human agents whose reading processes—including empathizing with characters—are more or less informed by relevant plans and policies with respect to reading literature. We recognize that authors are selective in what they present to us, controlling how much access we have to the relevant 'back story', what assumptions we will make, and what questions will arise. What would impel the Evertons to make this momentous decision? Will things eventually work out? Empathizing may facilitate raising questions such as these, questions that are appropriately raised as part of one's effort to understand the narrative, structured, in part, by the complex web of plans and policies operative for the characters involved.

In sum, I have here proposed an account of empathizing with a character as simulating the mental activity of that character, where simulating involves engaging in a mental process that is structurally, rather than functionally, similar to the process simulated. Structural similarities between processes may be manifested in the phenomenological character of one's experience, which is due to, broadly stated, simulating the conflicts and collusions among beliefs or belief-like phenomena and desires or desire-like phenomena. Simulating mental activity is likely to be easier with respect to characters in narrative literature than with actual people since literature is written for those who would appreciate it—something not to be assumed of the 'narratives' that people create as we live our lives. Good literature will often provide, through style and substance, opportunities for empathizing with characters, activities that, in turn, may enhance appreciation. As when reading *On the Road*, sensitivity to such a simple thing as a few commas can affect one's inclination to empathize. I have not attempted to provide principles here for when empathizing contributes to appreciation and when it does not. My task has rather been to explain empathizing as simulating a mental process or activity in a way that clarifies its differences from other current accounts and its distinctive strengths, including how it helps to account for the phenomenological character of experience when reading narrative works of literature as works of art.

11

On Some Affective Relations between Audiences and the Characters in Popular Fictions

Noël Carroll

11.1 Introduction

The focus of this paper concerns aesthetics in the sense that Alexander Baumgarten introduced that concept. It is about sensations, especially about a certain class of feelings in relation to works of art, notably narrative fictions. The feelings in question involve the emotive responses of audiences to fictional characters. Specifically, I will explore a range of cases where, for the most part, the emotive and other affective responses of readers, viewers, and listeners tend to converge, to be congruent, or otherwise to resonate appropriately with what the fiction presents as the emotional states of characters, particularly those characters whom we label the protagonists.

Although I think that my observations are relevant to the understanding of narrative art in general, for methodological reasons, I will pay especially close attention to the ways in which the characters in *popular* fictions engage our emotional responses. For, in those cases, typically, the emotions are, by design, extremely pronounced and clear cut. This is due to the fact that standardly it is part of the job description of the popular fictioneer to make his productions immediately accessible. Thus, popular fictions may afford perspicuously insight into the affective structures that also operate in so-called high art, where the emotive address may be more complex, ambiguous, and/or recessive, and, therefore, harder to pith.

As some readers have probably already noticed, rather than labeling my topic with a single term like 'empathy,' I have chosen instead to describe it—to say that I am interested in cases where the emotional states of audience members converge, are congruent with, or otherwise resonate appropriately with what we are given to imagine are the emotions of fictional characters. I have resorted to these circumlocutions and avoided the word 'empathy' because I have been unable to find much consensus in either ordinary language or the relevant technical literatures about how we are to understand *empathy*.[1]

As occurs with people's usage of other emotion-vocabularies, speakers and writers, including experts, employ the relevant terminology in diverse, often conflicting, incommensurate, and/or mutually canceling ways. For example, even what are called emotions can vary appreciably. Some count reflexes and phobias to be emotions, while other categorize moods as emotions—for example, what some psychologists call 'mood-induction' procedures might be more accurately be called 'emotion-induction' procedures, since what they elicit are short-lived, episodic states rather than more enduring ones.

This kind of terminological disagreement is very evident with respect to talk of empathy. Although most of us think of it as taking another person as its object, the term was apparently coined by Titchener who was inspired by the concept of 'feeling our way into' as that was used in aesthetics to describe our affective response to objects with pronounced expressive properties, such as the impression of muscularity imparted by bulging architectural columns.[2] As well, some draw a distinction between empathy and sympathy, when they come to define their concepts; yet we find that highly respected researchers may map the terrain in very different ways. Often in his excellent book, *Empathy and Moral Development*, Martin Hoffman characterizes empathy as others define sympathy, insofar as on his account empathy appears to involve a pro-social disposition of beneficence toward its object.[3] Others restrict empathy to the experience of cognate affective states with no necessary smidgen of concern on the part of the empath. To complicate matters, Lauren Wispé, in contrast, appears to define 'sympathy' in the way that the former theorists define 'empathy,' namely as a condition where the spectator merely undergoes the same emotive state as the victim—which state, for Wispé, must be exclusively some negative experience, like pain and or distress; thus, whereas some theorists think that sympathizers can share happiness with others, Wispé thinks that only negative affect can be the medium of sympathy.[4]

For some, the object of empathy is a person; for others, a situation. Sometimes empathy only seems to pertain to simply *understanding* another person's viewpoint which, of course, is possible without feeling anything. According to other authorities, feelings are requisite, although which feelings vary. So, some regard empathy as essentially cognitive, some treat it as essentially affective, and, in addition, others think it is a mixture of cognitive and affective elements.[5]

---

[1] My suspicions are corroborated in Eisenberg & Strayer (1987).
[2] See Wispé (1987):. 20–3. Throughout this essay, I have benefited from Wispé's useful historical overview.
[3] Hoffman (2000). See for example, p. 30.
[4] Wispé (1991).
[5] Hoffman (2000): 29.

Of those who maintain the relationship involves affect, some require that the empath suffer the identical emotion-types as does the empathee; others slacken the requirement of a perfect match and ask no more than that the emotions or feelings of the emoter be suitable to the emotive state of the object of empathy; for example, Simon Baron-Cohen says empathy involves understanding the situation of another and responding with the appropriate emotion.[6] This may involve no more than feeling some negative affect in response to another's distress, or something positive when the other feels pleasure.[7]

With all this diversity of usage, the temptation to legislate is strong. This is what I think Paul Griffiths does in his book *What Emotions Really Are*.[8] He elects one candidate for the title of *emotion,* and tells us little about what we are to make of the rest of the phenomena that have often been slotted under that rubric. Having shown that certain variants of the cognitive theory of the emotions are not comprehensive, Griffiths offers an alternative account of the emotions: that emotions are really affect programs. But this decision unfortunately tells us virtually nothing about how to theorize the kinds of mental states—like academic envy—that the ostracized cognitive theories handled so neatly.

On my view, such terminological vagaries should not serve as invitations to regiment matters à la Griffiths. They are rather signs that it is very likely that there are more kinds of phenomena lurking in this domain than heretofore recognized. Our nomenclature gets confusing, because we don't have enough labels to go around. So, different folks keep redeploying the same linguistic repertoire to mark whatever it is that interests them. Successive generations of psychologists, for example, keep employing earlier concepts in behalf of new research programs.

The discourse gets tangled up like a reel of fishing tackle in the hands of an amateur like me because there are so many different things to be interested in this sphere of inquiry and so few markers in ordinary language, or even the available technical languages. Given this, on my view, it may be less profitable to quibble over labels, and more useful at this point to initiate an exploration of the range of the phenomena in this arena—that is, to start, at least, to develop a conceptual cartography of what we might call the realm of affect. With regard to aesthetics, this involves beginning to identify some of the dominant emotive relationships between fictional characters and their audiences. Though I may no pretense to exhaustiveness in this matter, that is the purpose of this essay.

---

[6] Simon Baron-Cohen writes 'Empathizing... involves recognizing what another person may be feeling or thinking and responding to those feelings with an appropriate emotion of *one's own*' (2005: A15; emphasis added).

[7] Interestingly, Baron-Cohen's conception of empathy covers the notion of sympathy that will be developed later in this article.

[8] Griffiths (1997).

11.2 Identification

The natural place to start a discussion about the relation between readers, viewers, and listeners and the fictional characters to whom they attend is with the notion of identification. There are several reasons for this. First, when asked for an account of our emotive relation to fictional characters, especially to protagonists, referring to this alleged process is likely to be the answer most people, including a great many professionals, are apt to give. It is probably the oldest account in the western tradition where it was first introduced by Plato who feared that citizens would become possessed by the undesirable emotions, such as fear of death, portrayed by characters in the texts of poets like Homer.

Identification is also interesting for our purposes because there is one version of the notion of identification that some might be tempted to appropriate as one possible explication of empathy.

Moreover, we can use the notion of *identification* or, at least, one version of it, in order to probe critically the range of different emotive relations between audiences and fictional characters. That is, by working through various of the inadequacies of the leading notion of identification, we can begin to uncover the rich array of audience/character relationships occluded by the idea of identification.

Of course, identification, like empathy, and almost every other concept in this field of discourse, is fraught with multiple meanings—some more or less misleading, and others completely unobjectionable. In some cases, to identify with a character comes down to wishing one were like that character. It makes no claim to any sort of identity, affective or otherwise, between me and the pertinent fictional being. I wish I felt as fearless as Superman does, but, alas, I have vertigo. And I'd like to have the romantic flair of a James Bond, but I'm too afraid of rejection. But perhaps these cases shouldn't be called identification at all, but rather wishful fantasizing. Furthermore, it is not clear how much of this wishful fantasizing I can indulge while consuming a fiction without losing track of the story. And if the fiction is a movie, how will I keep up with the rapid editing, if I am off dreaming about being invulnerable and/or irresistible?

Frequently, when people say that they identify with a character, they mean no more than that they like the character or, as teenagers say, they think 'he's cool.' Or maybe it comes down to indicating that they've had a similar experience. The character has been dumped and so have they been. These usages come without the Platonic insinuation that the imagined emotional states of the characters have infected the audience. These variants of 'identification' really amount to feeling some affinity for the characters in question and might be better called 'affiliation' rather than 'identification.'

Alternatively, sometimes identification is parsed in terms of putting myself in the place of the character. This is not a matter of putting myself in the character's shoes, as they say, but of putting the character in my shoes.[9] But why suppose that this entails that the character and I are in the same emotive states? This might be better labeled *projection* rather than *identification*.[10]

What I suspect is the core concept of identification, and, for some, the core of empathy as well, involves the supposition that the audience member is in the same type-identical emotional state in which fictionally the character is.[11] This is certainly what Plato had in mind. The character in the poem fears death and then the reader likewise fears death. Likewise, this is the view of present day Platonists: the protagonist evinces aggressiveness, and then the viewers, or, at least, the adolescent male viewers, are contaminated with the selfsame species of aggressiveness too.[12]

But identity of emotion-types, even if necessary, is not enough to constitute identification in the variation that I am exploring. The fans of a certain team at a soccer match may be in the same emotive state—they all hate the opposing team. Yet we wouldn't call this identification (let alone empathy). For, with whom are they identifying? Although they may all be inflamed to the same degree with hatred for the rival team, they are not identifying with each other, since they may not even be aware of the presence of the others, so wrapped up are they in the game they are witnessing before them. Or they may be home alone, watching the game on TV, oblivious to the existence of other fans.

Nor is it plausible that they are identifying, in the relevant sense, with any of the soccer players—the players are probably too absorbed in the activity on the field to be emoting anything, and, in any event, it is unlikely that they literally *hate* their opponents. That kind of sports-hatred is for the fans, not for the professionals.

---

[9] This is sometimes called perspective-taking. There are two kinds of perspective-taking, the sort described above and the case where I attempt to embrace the perspective of the other wholesale. However, there is a real question about the extent to which the latter form of perspective-taking (a.k.a. empathy and/or identification) is conceptually possible. For, we can never be sure that there isn't a mismatch between the kind of person I am and the kind of person whose perspective I intend to take on (where the kind of person I am depends upon many variables of which I am typically unawares). For more sophisticated objections to this sort of perspective-taking, see Peter Goldie's 'Against Empathy' in this volume.

[10] Alessandro Giovannelli regards this as one form of empathy. I don't see why, since someone in this state could be totally misunderstanding the empathee as well as experiencing an utterly different emotion. Moreover, contra Giovannelli, experimental data indicate that this projective state cannot be empathy while taking the perspective of the other is empathy, if empathy means having type-identical feelings with the target. For magnetic imagining experiments, when one is one's own target, the results differ from cases when another is the target. However, if empathy involves identical feelings, all of the cases should be the same. See Giovannelli (2009). See also Jackson, Brunet, et al. (2006): 752–61.

[11] Here I am only requiring that the emotion-types be congruent. I am not stipulating that the audience member and the character must have the emotion in the same degree. I suspect that even those who believe in infectious identification will say that the emotions formed in reaction to the character may differ in intensity from those the character is imagined to suffer. Our emotions, it may be said, can be more or less intense than the characters'. Of course, this may be yet another reason to be suspicious of the notion of infectious identification, but I will not press the issue in this essay.

[12] Some have suggested to me that this is not the core concept of identification and have maintained that all that most people mean by 'identification' is that they feel in some way similar to the pertinent characters. I question this because it seems weaker than people intend when they use 'identification' and because it doesn't seem plausible to call such a weak connection 'identification.'

But if the sharing of type-identical emotional states is not sufficient for identification, what needs to be added? That the viewers be in the emotional state in question *because* that is the state they think that the characters are in. That is, putatively I identify, in this sense, with Anne Darrow when I am horrified by King Kong *because* she is—or I imagine her to be—horrified by King Kong. In short, the version of identification on the table is: someone x identifies with a fictional character y if and only if (1) x is in the same type-identical emotive state that y is in (2) *because* y is in—or, x imagines y to be in—that state. To speak metaphorically, the audience member has been infected by the ostensible emotive state of the character. Furthermore, this is, I submit, probably the dominant sense of the notion of identification nowadays.

I have no reason to believe that this phenomenon (or something like it) never occurs, especially in *real* life. There is empirical evidence that infants feel distress, when they detect distress in their caregivers. I am not sure that this is a full-blown emotive state, rather than merely an affective reflex. But for now, let that pass; I will talk about affective reflexes like this toward the end of this paper.

Similarly, recent research shows that women respond to fMRI scans of their significant others being subjected to electrical shocks with the activation—to a certain extent—of the same neural pathways in themselves that are registering pain in their spouses.[13] Again, the question arises about whether these are emotive states (it depends on how you categorize pain),[14] but it doesn't seem altogether improbable to me that some emotional states, like anger, might be transmitted in this way, especially between people involved in intimate personal relationships. Nevertheless, the question remains whether this model of identification has much to offer aestheticians when it comes to our emotive responses to fictional characters. By way of preview, let me say that there is abundant cause for skepticism here.

First, let us consider the preceding characterization of emotive identification—which, for convenience, we might call the *infection model*—as a comprehensive account of our relation to fictional characters. I do not think that I am exaggerating when I say that many subscribe to this view, especially pre-reflectively. That is, they think that this account pretty much covers most, if not all, of our emotive relations with fictional characters, or, at least, with the protagonists.

Nevertheless, even a cursory review of the data shows this is false. In the story, the candidate is pumped up by the adulation with which his acceptance speech as been greeted by the crowd; but we know that she is standing in the cross-hairs of a rocket-launcher, manned by an enemy assassin. We do not feel the thrill that the candidate

---

[13] Singer, Seymour, O'Doherty, Kaube, et al. (2004): 1157–62.

[14] Feeling the pain of the other is often adduced as evidence for identification and empathy-as-identification. But surely we cannot be feeling the *same* pain as the empathee. None save perhaps the most inveterate masochist could stay seated while experiencing the same pain that Jesus experiences as the Roman soldiers flail him in Mel Gibson's *Passion of the Christ*.

does; we feel suspense, even anxiety. Our emotional states are not type-identical. Nor should they be, since the fiction mandates that we fear for the candidate's life.

This asymmetry of affect is also common throughout comic fictions. Every time the would-be suitor is discovered in a compromising situation, we are amused while he is discomfited. When Bertie Wooster is flustered, we are merry.

Situations in which the emotional states of the characters diverge from those of the audiences abound in fictions of all sorts. One reason for this, obviously, is that generally there is a significant differential between what we know and what the characters know, and this, of course, can have a discernibly different impact on what is felt on both sides of the audience/fiction divide. In some cases, we know more than the characters; we tremble for them as they plunge ahead ignoring clear and present danger. On the other hand, Sherlock Holmes always knows more than we do, so we never share his aplomb in the face of peril.

Circumstances like these are not rare. They may even predominate statistically. But, be that as it may, there are more than enough cases like these to establish that the infection model of identification cannot be comprehensive on readily observed empirical grounds. Furthermore, there are also conceptual considerations that invite us to suspect the infection model. Quite often both the cause and the object of the audience's emotional state differ from that of the protagonist's affective condition. We are told that the character's son, Moe, died last year. That event was the cause of her grief; the object is her son. But the cause of the audience's emotional state is the character's grieving; and our object is the grieving mother.

Our emotion gestalts a wider situation than the mother's, while also including the object of the mother's state as a constitutory component. Moreover, our emotion is pity for the mother, not grief—who is Moe to us? It is his mother with whom we have become acquainted through the fiction. Indeed, Moe may never even have had his moment on the stage in the fiction under consideration. Since quite frequently, our emotional states have different causes and take different objects than the putative mental states of the protagonists, the suggestion that our emotions always, or even most often, match each other perfectly is highly unlikely. So, again, the infection model must be abandoned as a comprehensive picture of our emotive relations to fictional characters.

Indeed, there are certain cases, perhaps many, where the audience member's emotional state can only be reasonably thought to be an onlooker's state rather than one that corresponds to the object's. When we feel nail-biting suspense as the protagonist claws his way to safety, he cannot be feeling that emotion; he is probably not feeling anything. He is so caught up in and focused upon his task that his anxieties are on hold.

Nevertheless, the proponent of infectious identification may point out that, even if there are many cases where the inner states of the audience members and those of the characters diverge, there are also a significant number of cases where the emotive states at issue would appear to be type-identical. In an episode of *Law and Order: Special*

Victims Unit, say, the character recoils in contempt at the child molester's ploys; so do we. Emotive symmetry obtains.

Therefore, even if the infection model fails to be applicable across the board, perhaps the argument can be made that it has compelling authority with cases like these. However, in order to test this suggestion, we need to introduce a distinction between emotions that are held in common or coincidently versus emotions shared due to some intimate causal connection between them.

11.3 Coincident versus Connected Emotional States

Jet bombers have streaked past their fail-safe points and they are winging their way to Beijing. They are freighted with nuclear devices. Atomic warfare looms; millions will die. The protagonist, the President of the United States, is stricken with fear; so are we. Isn't this a case where infectious identification can be said to obtain?

I think that it is not. The infection model of identification requires not only that our emotions match those of the protagonists, but also that our emotions be a causal consequence of the protagonists being in precisely the selfsame mental states. Nevertheless, in a great many of the cases in which we find ourselves in the same emotive condition as the protagonist, including the preceding example, it is pretty obvious that we have gotten there by our own route, so to speak. We are not anxious because the president is anxious. We are anxious because we have been encouraged to imagine that a nuclear exchange, threatening a catastrophic number of deaths, is in the offing.

Perhaps some evidence for this is that the fiction could be told without reference to the president's anxiety and we would still feel anxiety. We would feel the same sort of anxiety because the fictional situation has been structured in a way that makes certain features that are appropriate to the state of fear salient—such as assessments of how much explosive power those jet bombers are carrying, their capacity to evade radar detection, their imperviousness to any and all anti-aircraft defenses as well as the putatively uneasy diplomatic relations between the United States and China.

Elsewhere I have called this sort of structure criterial prefocussing.[15] By that I mean that the fiction, by means of either visual depiction, enactment, and/or verbal description, organizes or filters the situations and events it presents in such a way that the features the creators select for emphasis are those that are criterially apposite to the emotional states intended to be excited by the work. In the Odessa Steps sequence of *Potemkin*, Eisenstein foregrounds the callous massacre of old people, a young boy, two mothers, and an infant—in short, those who are culturally figured as defenseless and harmless. His selection of these vignettes, instead of shots of the clouds overhead, is designed to activate the viewer's emotions of moral outrage. For, the sequence has been forcefully designed so that these factors, which are criterial to moral indignation,

---

[15] Carroll (2001a).

unavoidably command attention in a way that leads the viewer, unless he is a White Russian or a Cossack, to appraise the episode as evil and, in consequent, to feel visceral distress.

Most often, I contend, when the feelings of audiences are congruent with those of the protagonist's, it is a result of criterial prefocussing, not infectious identification. The difference is that in the case where criterial prefocussing leads to emotive uptake on the part of audience members, the correspondence between what the audience feels and what the characters are imagined to feel is coincident rather than causal. That is, the audience has been effectively led to the emotional state it is in by a pathway that can be causally independent of what, if anything, the protagonist feels. Thus, cases of congruent emotions between audience members and protagonists, though quite frequent, are typically not instances of infectious identification, but are better regarded as coincidentally congruent emotive states engineered by means of criterial prefocussing.

Indeed, it seems to me that postulating infectious identification in most cases is to take on excess theoretical baggage, since typically congruent emotional states, where they occur, can, *ceteris paribus*, be adequately and exhaustively explained by means of criterial prefocussing. That is, since infectious identification will also presumably involve something like criterial prefocussing, it is more parsimonious to explain what is going on by means of criterial prefocussing alone.

Of course, it may be pointed out that often the way in which situations are criterially prefocused in fictions tends to parallel the way the protagonist sees things. Even if the narration is omniscient and not channeled explicitly through the point of view of the protagonist, fictional narrators often depict or describe the fictional world from the perspective of leading characters. The gloominess of the portrayal of the environment echoes the apprehensiveness of the hero as he enters the realm of Lord Voldemort.

This is a fair point, but it does not, I think, revive the model of infectious identification, however. For, on the one hand, the audience need not be aware that it is the character's viewpoint that he is being invited to take on; it is the perspective of the narrative. And, furthermore, the critierial prefocussing will work in the same way whether or not it is crafted in a way that reflects the point of view of the protagonist.

Here it is interesting to consider the case where the fiction explicitly establishes that the way in which events are criterially prefocussed are congruent with the emotive states of the protagonist. A striking example of this is the use of point-of-view shots in the editing of audio-visual arrays. The character looks off-screen, her visage etched with horror; then there is a shot of a slimy creature—part reptile and part arachnid and part lawyer with a maw like a chain saw—and we are horrified too. Isn't that a case of infectious identification? Again, I think not for the simple reason that we would probably feel the same level of horror, if the sequence were shown without the shot of the character looking off-screen.[16]

---

[16] It might be interesting for psychologists to design an experiment to test this.

So, once again, hypothesizing infectious identification appears unnecessary. In the larges number of cases, I suspect that its conjecture violates the principle of theoretical parsimony.

Of course, this leaves open the question of why such point-of-view shots—and other perspective disclosing devices—are used by fictioneers. The short answer, I think, is that they are a means to prime or to prepare the audience by communicating to them in a very broad way the general kind of affect the audience should bring to the objects, persons, situations, and events they are about to encounter. I will have more to say about how this communication works later in my remarks regarding mirror reflexes.

11.4 Vectorially Converging Emotive States

I have challenged the second condition of the model of infectious identification on the grounds that, even if the audience is in an emotive state congruent with the imagined mental state of the protagonist, that is generally the result of the reader, viewer, or listener having arrived at that state by a process situated in his or her own emotive-appraisal system, independently of any necessary causal input involving the character being in the selfsame emotional state. In other words, as those jet bombers race toward Beijing, I fear for humanity because human life is, in the fiction, endangered and not because the protagonist fears for human life. The protagonist's fears need not be a causal ingredient in my fear, even though our fearful states are congruent. My fear is coincident or conjoint with the protagonist's while, at the same time, being causally independent from it. Or so I maintain is the standard case.

However, it is important not to misinterpret this example. The claim is not that we are never emotively influenced by the emotional states of characters, especially the protagonists and others to whom we bear a pro-attitude. For example, at the end of *The Gold Rush*, the Tramp accidentally meets up again with Georgia, the woman of his dreams; the two embrace, they kiss, and they fade out into the land of happily-ever-after. They are in love, and their successful match gladdens us. Scenes like this happen all of the time in popular fictions. However, our previous objections to the infection model of identification should not be taken as an attempt to deny their existence. For, cases like these should not be taken as cases of infectious identification.

True, the emotive states of the characters do cause us to be in a euphoric state. But our euphoric state is not precisely the state that the lovers are in. Their emotional state is one of infatuation. That is not our state; we are happy for the couple. I am not in love with Georgia. Were I in love with Georgia, I wouldn't be so happy; I'd be jealous of the Tramp. So I am not in the state of infectious identification. But I am in a state of roughly the same emotive valence. They are, let us say, euphoric and I am euphoric as well. Our emotive states converge vectorially—they both belong on the positively charged side of the scale of the emotions. We are not in the same emotional states, but our states are in broad categorical agreement and we are in that vectorially converging state with the state of the characters, because they are in that condition.

Contrariwise, when the monster in the concluding scenes of *Bride of Frankenstein* is reviled by his reanimated betrothed, we feel sorry for him. Our emotion does not match his. We do not feel the pain of the unrequited lover. Indeed, I doubt that any viewers, no matter how desperate, harbor any desires for the frizzy-haired, electrified corpse, played by Elsa Lanchester. But we do respond to the monster's misery with sorrow. It is in this sense that we share his misery. We are not miserable for being lovelorn but we do pity the monster.

Both misery and pity, of course, are dysphoric or negative emotions. Both sit on the distressful, discomforting, disturbing, or painful pole of emotional states. Again our emotions are broadly similar in their general valence. They converge vectorially in their negative direction. Our emotions are causally coordinated. But this does not support the notion of infectious identification, unless identification means nothing more than a somewhat similarly charged feeling. But why mobilize the notion of *identity* to describe that?

I suppose that if I were empowered to legislate linguistically in these matters, the category of vectorially converging emotional states would be my preferred candidate for 'empathy,' since it captures the idea that the audience is resonating emotionally or 'communing' with the pertinent characters, while not requiring that the audience and the protagonists be precisely in emotional synch. It is only that our emotional states are 'like' each other.

The notion of vectorially converging emotions also seems to mesh with Titchener's early conception of empathy which maintains that empathy involves feeling our way into the mental state of others. For, with vectorially converging emotions, we grasp the general valence of the internal states of others by means of the directionality of our own inner dispositions. We do not replicate the emotional state of others exactly, but instead approximate its general drift.[17] When we say our feelings are *like* those of the empathee, I suspect we intend this similarity in terms of vectorially converging emotions.

Moreover, since we empathize, in my sense, with The Tramp rather than identifying with him, we are happy for his good fortune and not jealous of him, as we would be if we identified with him emotionally and, like him, loved Georgia possessively. However, I do realize that this suggestion on my part remains stipulative, since many use 'empathy' to signal precisely matching feeling-states rather than merely vectorially converging ones.[18]

[17] Sometimes simulation theorists speak of our *resonating* in feeling with the targets of our attention. 'Resonating' seems to me a useful way of describing the relation between our emotions and fictional characters in cases of vectorially converging emotions. See Goldman (2006a): 132.

[18] Perhaps needless to say, I think that many claims made to the effect that our emotions perfectly match those of the characters turn out, upon scrutiny, to be vectorially converging emotions. In fact, my money is

11.5 Sympathy

Mention of empathy invites a discussion of sympathy, insofar as the two states are, though closely related, often differentiated. Sympathy is probably a concept that is used with as many various definitions as is empathy. For present purposes, I will describe sympathy as non-fleeting care, concern, or, more broadly, a non-passing pro-attitude toward another person under which rubric I include fictional characters and anthropomorphized beings of any sort whatsoever (such as Charlotte in her web). Sympathy involves a supportive response to its objects. It provides an impulse toward benevolent action with respect to those toward whom it is directed, though, of course, that impulse need not and often is not acted upon, frequently because it conflicts with other interests that we might have. And, needless to say, with fictional characters that impulse cannot be acted upon. Perhaps, one reason we are so free with our sympathies towards fictional characters is that, since we need not ever act on their behalf, their needs never threaten to fall afoul of our interests.[19]

Sympathy, construed as an emotional state, involves visceral feelings of distress when the interests of the objects of our pro-attitudes are imperiled and feelings of elation, closure, or satisfaction when their welfare is secured. The emotion of sympathy under discussion possesses as a component the presiding desire that things work out well for whomever it focuses upon—that their objective interests, goals, and desires be realized. In order to be the object of this pro-attitude, the person in question must be thought to be worthy of our benevolence as a result of our interests, projects, loyalties, allegiances, and/or moral commitments. When someone is appraised to be worthy of our non-passing desire that things go well with her and this is linked to positive feeling tones when gratified and negative ones when stymied, then that person is the object of the emotional state that I am calling sympathy. Likewise our response is sympathetic if we hope a character we esteem makes the right choice, as we do when, in reading *Middlemarch,* we wish that Dorothea not give into Casaubon's demands.[20] If you don't like calling this state 'sympathy,' you can call it feeling benevolently.

Initially, this account may seem indistinguishable from the one I recommended for empathy. The Tramp's fortunes, romantic and otherwise, flourish and we feel happy for him; our emotions converge vectorially. Nevertheless, sympathy does not always track how the protagonist feels. Sympathy concerns what we believe to be the genuine or objective well-being of the character. Should the protagonist go head over heels for the nefarious *femme fatale,* he may be overjoyed, but we will feel anxiety, because we surmise that his interests are endangered. So although empathy, as I've characterized

behind the claim that this is what is going on in the vast number of cases where we appear to 'commune' with protagonists.

[19] Amy Coplan points out that this a reason why we often sympathize with fictional characters more readily than with actual people. Rousseau would have concurred, but he would have added that this made theater (the topic of his concern) morally suspect.

[20] The example comes from Feagin (1996): 114–15.

it—that is, as a vectorially converging emotion—may sometimes be a part of sympathy, it need not be. Though the two states may overlap, they are nevertheless discriminable.

Moreover, I suspect that at least with regard to the characters in popular fictions, it is probably the case that sympathy generally governs empathy (in my sense). That is, we rejoice when the character rejoices over circumstances we judge to be actually beneficial to him because he is already an object of our benevolence. We do not rejoice when the villain rejoices, because the villain is not an object of our sympathy; his well-being is not something about which we could give a fig. I would not make a similar claim about the relation of sympathy and empathy in everyday life. But in popular fictions, characters come to us marked as worthy of our concern almost upon arrival.

In life outside of our fictions, our benevolent or altruistic attitudes toward others depend on factors such as kinship, group memberships of all sorts, and group interests. Of course, for both artistic and economic reasons, creators of popular fictions are aiming at larger audiences than a single extended family and often at audiences that exceed regional, ethnic, national, and religious boundaries. And even where their targets are less than global, they must be careful not to trigger the sectarian differences that always exist in virtually every large group. This obviously presents the creator of popular fictions with a problem to be solved, namely, how to enlist the care and concern—the sympathetic feelings—of mass audiences for fictional characters.

In order for us to feel sympathy for a fictional character, we must find the character worthy of our emotions. There must be some reason grounding our wishes that they fare well. But how will the maker of popular fictions motivate diverse audiences with often vastly variegated and sometimes even conflicting real-world interests to get behind the protagonists? As an empirical generalization, my conjecture is that the most frequent solution by far to this design problem is to construct protagonists and the other characters intended to warrant our concern in such a way that we perceive them to be, broadly speaking, morally good.

Morality, especially of a fairly widely shared and often nearly universal variety, gives the popular fictioneer the interest, or project, or loyalty, or touchstone of allegiance upon which audiences from similar cultures, and even sometimes dissimilar ones, can converge. The protagonists protect the lame and the halt, the helpless and the sick, the young, the old and the defenseless, while simultaneously treating them with dignity and respect. They evince a sense of fairness, justice, loyalty, honor, and are altogether pro-social, and especially pro-family, at least, where the families in question are portrayed as wholesome ones. These characters tell the truth and they keep their promises to good people, because they, themselves, are what we call good people.

By designing protagonists who are morally appealing, the producer of popular fictions purchases the criterial wherewithal necessary to engender the sympathy requisite for keeping audiences emotionally absorbed in the story. The pertinent fictional characters satisfy the criterion of being deserving of our benevolence because, in short, they are fundamentally morally deserving. They exhibit virtue, including Grecian or pagan virtues. Morality, in a very generous sense, is the project that we share with them—usually one wide enough to be recognized by Christian, Jew, Moslem, Hindu, Yankee, Korean, and Chilean alike.

Protagonists are usually good guys, since good guys are exactly what are apt to elicit pro-attitudes from the heterogeneous audiences for popular fictions whose interests and loyalties are varied and even otherwise at odds. Such characters are attractive, but it is important to emphasize that a significant amount of their attractiveness has to do with their virtue. Morality, of the fairly generic sort found in popular fictions, is something upon which people from different backgrounds are apt to agree. Who would dare to cast the first stone at Cinderella? Even the so-called anti-heroes of popular fictions are seen to be righteous, once you get beyond their gruff exteriors. In the end, for example, Sam Spade turns out to be almost Kantian in his sense of duty.

Sympathy, in my estimation, is the central emotional response that we bestow upon the protagonists in popular fictions.[21] Needless to say, in the course of a popular fiction we may undergo a gamut of emotional reactions to the relevant characters. But it is the sympathy we feel with regard to these characters that generally plays the major structuring role vis à vis whatever accompanying feelings may emerge. For, we are proud of the hero's success because his well-being is an object of our concern and we are angry at the heroine for sneaking off with the city slicker because we do not think that is in her best interests. Sympathy is the primary glue that binds us emotively to the protagonists and their fates in popular fictions.

11.6 Solidarity[22]

If sympathy is as central to our emotional response to fictional protagonists as I have maintained, then instances of the strongest version of infectious emotive identification cannot be common, since, sympathetic feelings, construed as emotions, are not ones that we share with their objects. Sympathy, by definition, is directed at others. The protagonist does not feel sympathy for himself; were he to do so—to any extent—that would probably turn the audience off. However, though crucial to our emotional bonding with protagonists, sympathy pure and simple is usually not the whole story of our emotional connections with protagonists. It is usually supplemented by another emotional state—which we may call solidarity.

Some fictions have only protagonists. The film *Just my Luck* is an example. There are two major characters—Ashley Albright and Jake Harden. Their names are clues to their most important attributes. She is always the beneficiary of deliriously good fortune. When she leaves her apartment without an umbrella, it immediately stops raining. And so on. He is just the opposite; if he bends down, his pants will split; if he picks up a five

---

[21] I think that this view would also be shared by Smith (1995).

[22] The notion of solidarity in this essay is meant to replace the more cumbersome idea of sympathy-cum-antipathy in Carroll (2007).

dollar bill, it will be smeared with canine feces. But their luck changes hands at a masquerade ball when they kiss while dancing. Now everything Ashley attempts leads to disaster, while Jake becomes a very successful record producer. The rest of the story involves Ashley tracking Jake down in order to reclaim her good fortune with another kiss. However, they fall in love and kiss their way to some kind of providential equilibrium; they will live happily and unhappily ever after in the normal proportions.

What is striking about *Just My Luck*—and I think this is true of many romantic comedies—is that there is no real villain. There are some people who present temporary obstacles to the main characters, but they are not full-fledged antagonists. They are not on the scene long enough for our antipathy toward them to take root. We are encouraged to feel care and concern for Ashley and Jake. But there are no real bad guys in the film.

Most popular fictions, however, are not like this. Most popular fictions pit the protagonists and the other nice people against some adversaries. We are not only prompted emotionally to embrace the good people as members of a generic 'Us;' their opponents belong to 'Them.'[23]

If sympathy toward the 'Us' is characteristically elicited by portraying the protagonists and the other nice people in the fiction as morally good, then the antipathy generated toward the 'Them' is generally provoked by representing Them as morally blemished. Whereas the protagonist is nice to nice people—treating good people with good manners—the villain is at least rude to inferiors and very often much worse. The antagonists pillage, cheat, rob, kill, lie, and so forth. The hero pets the old dog sleeping on the doorstep; the bad guy kicks it out of his way.

Popular fictions are most frequently *political* in Carl Schmitt's sense.[24] The fictional population is partitioned into friends and enemies—into Us and Them. Sympathy, motivated by morality, disposes us to assimilate the protagonists as belonging to Us. But the bond is usually further strengthened by introducing enemies who, in popular fictions, are customarily marked by being constructed as bad people. As I am using the term, 'solidarity' is the name of the complex emotive relation of sympathy-for-the-protagonists plus antipathy-for-the-antagonists, which state is typically incited in audiences in response to popular fictions.[25] The reader, listener, and/or viewer feels emotionally allied to the protagonist and against the antagonist. The antagonist instills anger, indignation, hatred, and sometimes even moral disgust in us.

Unlike sympathy in everyday life which we tend, all things being equal, to extend quite readily to most of those around us by default, in fictions our sympathy must be won. In popular fictions, the most efficient way of doing this is to render the relevant characters morally appealing. Our bond with these characters can then be reinforced by

---

[23] See Berreby (2009), especially chapter 9.
[24] Schmitt (1996).
[25] 'Solidarity' as a real world phenomenon, of course, also includes a sense of responsibility to other members of the Us, but, of course, this is not practicable with respect to fictional characters.

setting an array of nemeses against them whom we find repulsive, customarily because their various moral failings—from petty vices to outright viciousness—are emphatically foregrounded by means of criterial prefocussing.

I suspect that, in most cases, our sympathy for various characters is enlisted by their evident virtues. However, in some instances, characters may obtain our sympathy on the rebound, so to speak. That is, we may be so appalled by the villain that our care and concern goes out to whomever he opposes. In other words, sometimes solidarity in popular fictions may result from the 'enemy-of-my-enemy-is-my-friend' phenomenon. This, moreover, explains why it is that we sometimes find ourselves siding with characters whose morals we do not otherwise share, like Hannibal Lector. It is that we find his enemies, the people who are trying to kill him, so much more depraved than he is, bent, as they are, to feeding him to giant, slavering pigs.[26]

Solidarity involves sympathy and antipathy viscerally felt. Though our sympathetic feelings toward the protagonists are not shared by them, our hatred for the villains often is. But we do not hate the villain simply because the protagonist does. Rather, we have detected coincidentally on our own many of the same morally noxious characteristics of the antagonists that have impressed the protagonists. Thus, when it is congruent with the protagonist's hatred of the bad guy, the antipathy component of our feelings of solidarity with the hero is basically conjoint with his. We may vent our hatred of the bad guy at the same time the hero does, but primarily as a result of our own processes of moral appraisal.

11.7 Mirror Reflexes

So far I have explored several kinds of emotional relationships between audiences and characters in popular fictions. These have included circumstances: (1) where our emotions may be type-identical with those of the protagonists, but only due to our own independent appraisals of the relevant situations, (2) where our emotions vectorially converge upon the emotional states of the characters, (3) where we sympathize with the character (which, of course, can be an instance of a vectorially converging emotion), and (4) where we emote in solidarity with the protagonist (where the antipathy component may be an instance of a congruent response that we find ourselves in as result of our own appraisal of the situation). None of these cases correspond to the popular model of infectious identification which requires that the audience member be in an emotional state that is type-identical with the protagonist's precisely because the relevant character is in that state. But let me conclude by briefly examining a fifth affective relation—one which comes closer to the notion of infectious identification—and whose very existence probably lends a modicum of credibility to talk about our identification with fictional characters.

---

[26] For further discussion, see Carroll (2004).

What I have in mind can be called 'mirror reflexes.'[27] This is the sort of motor imitation that Gordon Allport had in mind when he wrote: 'the imitative assumption of the postures and facial expressions of other people plays a greater part in ordinary life than is commonly realized.'[28] When conversing with another, we often observe ourselves knitting our brows as they knit their brows. They chuckle; we chuckle. They grimace; we grimace.

Moreover, these imitative responses are not confined to facial expressions. They extend to postures as well. We tend to fall into step with our companions; when they're walking tall, so are we. They rub their chin, we do likewise.[29] This mimicry is not restricted to real life encounters; when Hamlet's muscles bunch up—on either stage or screen—we feel a tug in our own. In short, we have an involuntary tendency to replicate automatically in our own bodies the behavior, particularly the expressive behavior, of our conspecifics. Furthermore, this tendency is inborn and already evident in infancy.[30]

These imitative reflexes grant us some inkling of what others are feeling. When we configure our faces in the shape of another's—frowning when he frowns, for example—the feedback from our facial muscles stimulate our autonomic system in a way that is somewhat similar to his inner feelings, so long as he is sincere. This need not give us full access to his emotional state, but it supplies us with a valuable clue to the nature of that state by providing us with an experiential sense of the bodily-component—the feeling state—of the occurrent emotion of the other person.

This feature of the human organism has great adaptive value and is probably bred in the bone.[31] These advantages are especially pertinent for communication. When I 'catch' the negative vibes or feelings of distress of another, I immediately survey the environment to locate the source of his discomfort. His negative affect alerts me in my own musculature to the likelihood that I may soon need to mobilize some vectorially converging, negative emotion, such as fear or possibly anger.

Of course, mirror reflexes, which *may* be linked to mirror neurons,[32] are not only relevant for the purposes of gathering information about what surrounds other people.[33] By relaying to us something of what others are feeling, they help us cope with others. Detecting that one's brother is in a bad mood via mirror reflexes is helpful in

---

[27] See Wispé (1991), especially chapters 7 and 8. See also Hatfield, Cacioppo, & (1994), especially chapter 2.

[28] Allport (1924): 530.

[29] Meltzoff & Decety (2003): 494.

[30] Meltzoff & Moore (1977): 75–8; Meltzoff & Moore (1997): 179–92.

[31] Plutchik (1987).

[32] On mirror neurons, see: Rizzolatti, Fadiga, Matelli, et al. (1996): 246–52; Jellema, Baker, Perrett, & Perrett (2002); Fadiga, Fogassi, Paves, & Rizzolatti (1995): 2608–61. See also the articles by Iacoboni and Decety & Meltzoff in this volume.

[33] It should be noted that presently the mirror neurons that have been identified by researchers seem primarily dedicated to perceptual, motor, and pain mimicry rather than to emotive mimicry. This is one of the reasons for the caution in the sentence above.

deciding when to ask him for a loan. And, of course, mirror reflexes are immensely useful for coordinating group activities—for getting the troops reeved-up as they march off singing in lockstep comraderie.

The communicative potential of mirror reflexes is widely exploited in audio-visual fictions, especially the theater arts and moving images of all sorts from films to CGI. The Soviet director Sergei Eisenstein, having read Theodor Lipps on the topic, quite consciously attempted to exploit mirror reflexes in his film-making. He showed close-ups of clenched fists and horrified faces in the expectation that audiences would mimic these gestures in a way that would jump-start bodily feelings of consternation in them which, given the narrative context, would then segue into the emotional state with which Eisenstein wanted them to respond to the situation. Whether or not they realize their debt to Eisenstein, motion picture makers ever since have been following his example.

Arguably, mirror reflexes are not fully articulated emotional states, but only not-quite-specific, bodily-feeling states, such as vague intimations of distress. Since these mirror reflexes are not full scale emotional states, they do not supply evidence for *emotional* identification.[34] But mirror reflexes are undoubtedly affective states and they are contagious.[35] Furthermore, we can use the information that we gather in this way about the putative inner states of fictional characters in the formation of our own, integrated emotional reactions to them. That is, mirror reflexes may function as sub-routines in the activation of our emotional responses to characters by alerting us to the general valence—whether positive or negative—of the characters, enabling us, there-by, to mobilize the appropriate, perhaps vectorially converging, emotional reaction to them—for example, sorrow if we detect that they are in spiritual pain. Mirror reflexes, in this respect, supply us with clues to the way in which we should size-up the situation in which characters find themselves.

Perhaps it is the existence of mirror reflexes that has led people to endorse the notion of the infectious emotional identification. This is understandable, since we do share feelings somewhat similar to those that the characters evince as a result of their ostensible manifestation of the pertinent states. Yet what is shared are not full-blown emotions, but only bodily feelings, and merely roughly similar ones at that. That is,

---

[34] Some, like Iacoboni and Decety & Meltzoff in this volume, write as though mirror reflexes and related patterns of mirror neuron firings are tantamount to empathizing. But if empathy is an emotion, then this seems unlikely, since these reflexes don't involve appraisals, whereas emotions do necessarily. Moreover, if empathy involves understanding then these states can't amount to empathy, since they are pure feeling-states. Nevertheless, as I indicate above, these states may contribute to the formation of emotional states. Regarding Iacoboni, and Decety & Meltzoff, see footnote 32.

[35] I wonder whether Meltzoff and Decety would agree with me about this. In their article, they indicate that behavioral imitation and its neural substrate precede mentalizing. Does that mean that these states in children are not yet emotions, properly so-called? On the other hand, the authors speak of 'empathy.' Nevertheless, it is not clear if by 'empathy,' they are speaking of empathy as infectious identification or merely about resonances (which might be only vectorially converging sensations) or simply feeling that we are *like* others. But if the latter, these would appear to fall far short of the notion of empathy as infectious identification.

unlike emotions, mirror reflexes do not necessarily involve appraisals, though they may afford data pertinent to forming an appraisal.[36]

Nevertheless, mirror reflexes afford the creators of audio-visual fictions with a powerful repertoire of devices that are unparalleled in literary fiction and which can be deployed to keep spectators in virtually continuous affective contact with the pertinent characters. By exploiting our biological endowments, mirror reflexes enable us to feel our way into popular visual narratives with an impressive level of ease, accuracy, and assurance which we nevertheless take for granted.

11.8 Summary

There is no single affective relationship that describes the one and only connection between readers, listeners, and/or viewers, on the one hand, and fictional characters, on the other hand. There are a number relations; I do not know how many. In this essay, I have explored several: coincidentally occurring emotions which may include the antipathy element of solidarity; vectorially converging emotions, which can encompass certain episodes of sympathetic feeling and which is my preferred candidate for the title of empathy (should we wish to retain that label); as well, I have discussed mirror reflexes, affective states that, though not precisely fully articulated emotions, can nevertheless contribute to their formation. In charting these affective states, I have been skeptical about the degree to which infectious identification—and empathy construed as infectious identification—accounts for our emotional bond with fictional characters, especially protagonists. However, I grant that there are more species of affective relationships in this neighborhood of the heart than I have enumerated here, which relations I hope future research will disclose.[37]

Appendix: A Competing View

Alessandro Giovanelli would undoubtedly agree about the importance that I assign to sympathy in our commerce with fictional characters. However, since his view of sympathy is at odds with mine, his position is a rival one. For Giovanelli, a certain kind of sympathy—which he calls *paradigmatic sympathy*—requires empathy as a

---

[36] I do not think that mirror reflexes involve appraisals, since we may detect distress in a fictional character by means of mirror reflexes, but that may lead to a sympathetic appraisal, if the character is the heroine, or a triumphant appraisal, if she is the villain.

[37] I have profited from comments on the body of this paper from Amy Coplans, Murray Smith, Jesse Prinz, Peter Goldie, Margaret Moore, Susan Feagin, William Seeley, Stephen Davies, Graham McFee, Martin Hoffman, E. Anne Kaplan, and the other participants in the conference on empathy at California State University, Fullerton, 2006. I have also benefited from a discussion of the main section of this paper at the Myrifield Institute for Cognition and the Arts in July, 2008, where my commentators included David Miall, Keith Oately, Willi van Peer, Margaret Freeman, Donald Freeman, Reuven Tsur, and Ellen Dissanayake. None of these scholars are responsible for the flaws in this paper. For despite their sage advice, I did it my way.

component.[38] Empathy, in turn, is thought of by Giovanelli in terms of an empathizer vicariously experiencing the mental states and emotions of another, as if they were her own. Thus, Giovanelli thinks that some sort of identification is a part of sympathy and, therefore, denies my hypothesis that it is sympathy, construed as a state contrasting to identification, that is the primary glue that emotively attaches us to fictional characters.

Giovanelli's reason for this view is that since identification/empathy is a part of sympathy, it makes no sense to say that sympathy is a more comprehensive emotive fixative than identification/empathy, because they are, in a significant number of cases, a package deal.

It is not always easy to follow Giovanelli's discussion, since he frequently uses 'sympathy' interchangeably with 'paradigmatic sympathy'—i.e. sympathy plus identificatory empathy.[39] Thus, he will say that something is a necessary component of sympathy, where counterexamples are easy to come by. But then he will say that he is talking about paradigmatic sympathy, rather than sympathy more generally.

Giovanelli knows that sympathy in general does not require empathy. As he himself notes, a husband may sympathize with his wife who is enduring labor pains, although he lacks the equipment to experience them vicariously. Likewise a male audience member may sympathize with the sentiments expressed by the characters in *The Vagina Monologues*, but be incapable of representing those experiences to himself. Similarly, we may not be able to imagine the experiences of those stricken by exotic diseases or by unprecedented catastrophes. And, although Giovanelli does not mention this case, we may be sympathetically indignant with respect to the treatment of others—such as the prisoners at Abu Graib—because we feel their suffering to be unjust, even though we do not feel ourselves to be suffering that injustice. I don't have to vicariously experience humiliation in order to mobilize my sympathies for those who are so humiliated.

Giovanelli will concede all this, I think, but go on to say that he is not speaking of sympathy broadly, but only of paradigmatic sympathy. Yet, this raises the question of why this kind of sympathy—if there is such a thing—counts as paradigmatic and why Giovanelli thinks it should be accorded theoretical primacy. Giovanelli offers three considerations, none of which I find compelling.

The first consideration might be called 'the-best-sort-of-sympathy argument.' The idea here seems to be that paradigmatic sympathy is deeper than sympathy sans empathy. It is more sensitive. In everyday life, Giovanelli asserts, we want sympathy that comes garnished with empathy in contrast to sympathy *simpliciter*. With regard to our relation with fictional characters, we value the opportunity for this more sensitive sort of sympathy just because it engages us more deeply to the relevant characters. Moreover, this deeper sort of sympathy may act as a bulwark against the possibility of being manipulated sentimentally.

---

[38] See Giovanelli (2009) and (2008): 11–24.

[39] In fairness, it should be acknowledged that he warns us that he will do this, but it is still a little confusing at times.

None of this seems persuasive to me. Paradigmatic sympathy is said to be more *sensitive* than other types of sympathy. But surely there is an equivocation here. It may be more sensitive with respect to the feelings or sensations supposedly experienced vicariously, but that does not mean that it is a more discerning kind of sympathy. I see no reason to doubt that sympathy, without the alleged accompaniment of identificatory empathy, can also be the equal and often surpass what Giovanelli calls paradigmatic sympathy in discerning the concern we ought to bring to others. This will be the case especially where the target of our sympathies is attracted to something not in her best interests. Furthermore, I doubt Giovanelli's assertion that we want those who sympathize with us to vicariously experience what I am feeling. Although I am glad to have their sympathy, I do not want my family or my doctor to feel my pain as I lie in my hospital bed with third-degree burns.

Just because I am unconvinced that so-called paradigmatic sympathy is more sensitive in an artistically pertinent sense than sympathy, as I construe it above, I question whether we value it as the best sort of sympathy to indulge with regard to fictional characters. Nor do I see why Giovanelli thinks that paradigmatic sympathy blocks the threat of sentimentality. Indeed, I think that many, like Plato, who endorse the idea of identification, worry that taking on the experiences of characters will mislead our sympathies, often in an extremely superficial direction.

Govanelli's next set of reasons for defending his notion of paradigmatic sympathy involve the claim that this idea can handle certain problem cases between than competing theories. These problem cases are labeled respectively as *anticipatory sympathy, conditional sympathy*, and *sympathy by proxy*. Anticipatory sympathy occurs when we muster sympathy for a character before ill fortune befalls her and her lamentations commence; for example, we feel anticipatory sympathy for the character who is about to learn that the rest of her family is dead. Conditional sympathy is extended to characters who will never know about some setback to their interests, such as the dead man who never learns his will has been overturned by his feckless children. And lastly, there is sympathy by proxy; this involves sympathy for someone who is keenly attracted to some prospect that is not in his best interest, such as the eighty-year- old millionaire smitten by the nubile, young gold-digger. Nevertheless, we feel sympathy for him, which, on Giovanelli's account, should imply we are vicariously experiencing what he experiences.

As the last example underscores, these might appear to be cases where empathy is inapposite, since the vicarious feelings of empathizers will be strikingly different than what the targets are experiencing at the moment that our sympathy takes hold.

But not so, claims Giovanelli. He says that with anticipatory sympathy, we empathize with a future or possible state of the character. In the case of conditional sympathy, we empathize counterfactually with what the character *would* feel, were he apprized of the way in which his will has been disrespected. And when it comes to sympathy by proxy, we are said to empathize with what the silly old millionaire *should* be feeling.

I find these suggestions very strange, if we are to conceive as empathy as a form of identification, since, following Giovanelli's instructions, it does not appear that I am actually imagining the experiences of these characters as experiences of my own, for the simple reason that the experiences I am entertaining are radically different than the experiences these characters are thought to be having. How can we be said to have the same experiences of the characters when they themselves are not having said experiences? Perhaps we can send our imaginations in the directions that Giovanelli suggests. But we are not identifying with the characters in question by way of sharing their experiences vicariously.

Giovanelli considers his approach to these three problems in contrast to Susan Feargin's account of audience sympathies as directed toward characters, which account, like the view sketched by me above, sees the relevant sort of sympathy as grounded in our endorsement of the interests and desires of the characters, rather than in empathetic identification.[40] According to Giovanelli, his approach can explain the differences in sympathetic reactions to the characters when they are undergoing the emotions we putatively, vicariously emulate versus when they are not suffering the feelings we emote on their behalf.

But I am not sure that there is always a difference in our experience of sympathy across these cases, and, even if there is, I doubt that it is systematic, and thus, I suspect, the differences would need to be adjudicated on a case by case basis, where, in fact, the model that Feagin and I embrace would not appear to be obviously disadvantaged. Moreover, on the basis of what he has said so far, I am not certain what the differences in sympathetic response are that Giovanelli has in mind nor is it clear to me how exactly his view explains them.

In relation to the preceding point, it also needs to be emphasized that Giovanelli has failed to appreciate the methodological problem the competing theories of sympathy, based on audience alignment with the interests and desires of characters, pose for his empathy/sympathy view. For, since the interest/desire view does a nice job dealing with the cases that Giovanelli introduces, it is incumbent on him to demonstrate what explanatory pressure remains that is being relieved by the postulation of identificatory empathy. Without that, Giovanelli has failed to motivate his conjecture to the effect that empathy is a *necessary* part of (even just some sort of) sympathy. Instead, he's added a wheel to the mechanism that turns nothing, or, to put is less poetically, he's violated the methodological principle of parsimony. Until Giovanelli adduces some compelling explanatory gap in my account of sympathy that can only be closed by introducing the alleged process of identificatory empathy, a theory of sympathy, like the one I proposed earlier, has no reason to take empathy/identification on board. The burden of proof here belongs to Giovanelli.

[40] Feagin (1996).

Finally, Giovanelli believes that an account of sympathy as entailing empathy gains support from the causal connection between empathy and sympathy—namely, that empathy often leads to sympathy. Giovanelli proposes this consideration despite the fact that he realizes that the notion of empathy that he presupposes is compatible with the empathizer being hostile or indifferent to the target.

For example, it is often suggested in the literature that the Complete Sadist should be an astute empathizer—all the better to grock what torments his victim. Likewise, suppose I could engender Hitler's feelings towards Jewish people in my own heart; but that could lead me to anathematize him. Nor is there any contradiction involved in suggesting that I might empathize, in Giovanelli's sense, with the rodeo star's experience but just remain indifferent to his interests and desires because I'm just not an-at-home-on-the-range kinda' guy.

Clearly, if there is a causal connection between empathy à la Giovanelli, and sympathy, it is an empirical question, not a conceptual one. But in order to convince us empirically that there is such a connection, Giovanelli will have to show that empathy must be added to the audience member's endorsement of the character's goals, interests, and desires in order to explain our sympathy for the protagonist. Until Giovanelli can adduce some reasons why identificatory empathy has to be added to accounts of sympathy like the one I've sketched, adding empathy/identification to sympathy seems like so much excess theoretical baggage.

12

Empathy:
Interpersonal vs Artistic?

Graham McFee

12.1 Introduction

Although I have not typically thought about contact with artworks (and especially with literary works) in terms of empathy,[1] I had an experience which might seem to point in that direction. On one occasion, while suffering from heatstroke, I read at one 'sitting' a translation of De Lampedusa's novel, *The Leopard*. Confined to bed, my attention to the novel took on a peculiar focused quality, in which I 'imaginatively identified' (for want of a better expression) with a central character, throughout his trials and tribulations as recounted in the book. And my 'identification' was quite extreme: for instance, those circumstances made it seem easy to put oneself into the climatic conditions. It seems to me very plausible to see my relation to that central character in terms of *empathy*. But, of course, this case is very much more than just my being one of those 'readers [who] adopt the perspective of one or more characters in fictional narratives' (Coplan (2004): 141). Indeed, it is this stronger (than usual) sense of identification that clearly warrants the term *empathy* here.

Now, a case so peculiar shows us nothing directly about reading, about empathy, or about literature. My reading of *The Leopard* in a semi-hypnoid state cannot be our model of the usual experience of literature. Still, in that unusual case, my empathy was with the character as depicted, not with the author. And this would, I take it, be a characteristic of any such identification—although the situation might become clouded when the writing had a strong autobiographical flavor. But that would just generate the familiar problem of distinguishing the implied author (and his acts) from

[1] Thoughts raised by the 'Empathy' conference at California State University Fullerton, June, 2006 led to this paper. I am conscious that some readers might see this as 'inventing the wheel': my only reply is that most of the other offerings on this topic do not seem appropriately *round* to me. (My avoiding the term 'circular' is important!) And I would like to thank all those who by word or deed encouraged me to shape those thoughts into a chapter; especially, in alphabetical order, Heather Battaly, Amy Coplan, Terry Diffey, Peter Goldie, and Derek Matravers. And then, again, to the editors for help later on.

the author in reality (and his). Thus, in *My Family and Other Animals* (1956), Gerald Durrell writes as if his brother Lawrence lived only a small distance from the rest of the family. Although that does not in fact replicate the living arrangements of the real Durrell clan in Greece, it is the *facts* of the 'world' Gerald describes or creates in that novel. Then, there are facts relevant in my case of reading *The Leopard* beyond those described in the novel (combined perhaps with some facts of a very general kind about Sicily at the time the novel was set), facts I need to be aware of in making sense of it, but which the characters in the novel need never bring to mind. Hence there is no character (and certainly no person) whose state of mind (or some such) I would be 'matching' in being empathetic here.

In what follows, I begin by asking what relevance, if any, such a genuine case of empathetic reading of a novel has for our more general understanding of that grasp of novels achieved through reading them. That leads to a reconsideration of the place of an appeal to *empathy*. And, then, what can we learn from an empathetic reading of a fictional narrative? As such, my primary focus should be on cases relating to literary works, rather than on cases of interpersonal empathy. But, although the cases are quite different, features of the one may be brought out by placing it side-by-side with the other, noticing similarities and differences that strike us as relevant—articulating in this way '*objects of comparison*' (PI § 130[2]) to help us in thinking about aspects of our case we might otherwise have missed, perhaps because of their simplicity and familiarity. At its heart, such a comparison illuminates the sense in which an empathetic response is an *achievement* (see below).

Perhaps it is unfair to begin characterizing *empathy* in terms of this admittedly extreme case: am I begging the question against a more general account of an empathetic response to literature? There may be cases *weaker* than my example: but are they definitely empathy? Or should we prefer some other explanatory concept? The primary difficulties in replying accurately come from the problem of deciding what one would be *putting aside* if one began to speak regularly of empathetic responses in this context: what did I say before? And, if that was adequate, what could motivate me to *add* to my conceptual repertoire here? Further, do I have only one account of reading fiction? Obviously not. Moreover, does recognizing some (but not others) of the fictions as *literature* make it more or less likely that I will engage with them

---

[2] Standard abbreviations are used for the works of Wittgenstein:
  Wittgenstein, 1953—cited as 'PI' [also 2001—see below].
  Wittgenstein, 1969—cited as 'OC'.
  Wittgenstein, 1976—cited as 'LFM'.
  Wittgenstein, 1993—cited as 'PO'.
  Wittgenstein, 2005—cited as 'BT'.
  Wittgenstein & Waismann, 2003—cited as 'VoW'.
On *objects of comparison*, see Baker (2004): 48 note 15; 81–2; 128—importantly, comparing A with B is not saying that A *is* B (nor vice versa).

empathetically? Again, there seems no reason to say 'yes'. So there seems no reason to suppose that, in setting aside *empathy* as an explanatory concept, one *automatically* leaves out something typically of relevance to the reading of, say, novels. Still, there may yet be cases where *empathy* just seems the right concept.

As often in philosophy (see PI §79), if we understand the situation, we can *say* what we like: the key thing is what *contrasts* we are respecting. Then, a fairly robust view will be preferable: there should be some reason to talk of *empathy* here. Thus, for example, if the case is happily described without appeal to that idea, we have no reason to invoke it.[3] Here, an emphasis on *empathy* must pick out at least the taking up of another's psychological perspective. Indeed, while there are disputes as to whether an account of *empathy* should stress emotion,[4] this aspect—of perspective-taking—is widely acknowledged. For instance:[5]

Empathy is a process or procedure by which a person *centrally imagines the narrative* (the thoughts, feelings, and emotions) of another person. (Goldie (2000): 195)

Or:

when I empathize with another, I imaginatively experience his or her emotional states, while simultaneously imaginatively experiencing his or her cognitive states. (Coplan (2004): 144)

Or:

[the term] 'Empathy' is often used...to designate an imaginative reconstruction of another person's experience. (Nussbaum (2001): 301–2)

Notice, here, the emphasis on the *experience* of that other person; and on one's taking that experience *as one's own*, if only in imagination. These, at least, seem features which might justify our use of the term 'empathy'.

So, applied to reading literary fictions, it must amount (roughly) to a taking up of the psychological perspective of a character. But exactly what features of my empathizing with a person are supposed to carry over?

---

[3] Suppose, then, that someone urges that empathy can be used predictively: knowing you are in such-and-such a state, and wanting to know what you will do, I imagine myself in that state, and imagine what I would do. And then you do that. Well, this would clearly be insufficient to justify success in *empathy*—not least because this kind of imagination is as well explained as *sympathy* (see below). But also the mere fact of prediction here is quite compatible with my having failed to genuinely imagine (as from my own perspective) what you were feeling—getting this wrong could still result in successful prediction.

[4] See Coplan (2004) note 15.

[5] Some other accounts of empathy include: Simon Blackburn (2005: 113): 'the state of being emotionally and cognitively "in tune with" another person, particularly by feeling what their situation is like from the inside or what it is like for them'. Robert M. Gordon, in Audi (1999: 261): 'imaginative projection into another person's life, especially for vicarious capture of its emotional and motivational qualities'. Sarah Richmond, in Honderich (2005: 242): 'States of mind in which someone shares the feelings or outlook of another, sometimes prompted by imaginative exercises such as "stepping into another's shoes"'.

12.2 Getting the Metaphysics Right?

Before we can come to that topic, we must set some guidelines for our discussion: what constraints can we invoke, such that what we produce will be more plausibly thought philosophy?

For me, at least four points seem key here. First, one must say only as much as is profitable, where the danger is one clearly identified by Wittgenstein: 'to begin at the beginning. And not try to go further back' (OC §471). Second, one must be able to say something here without needing to say *everything*: if too many other, general commitments are required, we shall have to defer this topic until they are resolved. (I have in mind, especially, commitments in the philosophy of mind.) Thus, in going forward, we are implicitly conceding that this is not the case. In combination, these two ideas should make us hesitant about introducing yet more theoretical machinery. Certainly, we cannot *assume* that there is some abstract structure, underlying our appreciation of literature, which we might discover by analysis: at best, such a structure would be an abstraction *from* what real practitioners do—as when art students are required to 'make visual images', as though this was the underpinning of their more normal activities of drawing the figure, painting the still-life, and so on. So we cannot just build-in the thought that, say, all novels (or even most) *require* empathetic reading. In this way, our account here should roughly mirror the pre-theoretical or 'everyday' one. Then, third, if one thinks in terms of rescuing our understanding from the excesses of philosophical invention, or of 'bringing back' from metaphysical uses (see PI §109), the 'everyday' is just the default position, *not* some specific thesis. So we should not begin from some rich or ripe metaphysical world: at least, I will not be beginning there.

The fourth point involves recognizing the connection of *this* interest in literary art with other interests in it, and other theorizations of it. For, in so far as this is an inquiry in philosophical aesthetics, it will draw on a grasp, however tenuous, of the nature and contribution of literary works, especially novels. It helps to sketch a plausible one. Then, the rough thought might take works of literature to 'have cognitive benefits, [so] that we can learn . . . from them, that we can be improved by them' (Lamarque (2001): 456), where this might be cashed out in terms of 'an artist's way of "looking at the world"' (Iris Murdoch, quoted in Lamarque (2001): 456[6]). This is partly a matter of recognizing how one moves from, say, seeing Proust's *world* to seeing the world as Proust does—where this second, too, is only an invitation to 'try out'. Thus we might begin with the general idea of literature as *revealing*:[7] that, for example, the typical novel 'instructs us in how to view the world' (Lamarque (1996): 105). Then the empathetic

---

[6] See, for example, Murdoch (1998: 326): 'study of literature . . . is an education in how to picture and understand human situations'. Or again: 'what we learn . . . is something about the real quality of human vision, when it is envisaged, in the artist's just and compassionate vision, with a clarity which does not belong to the self-centred rush of ordinary life' (Murdoch (1998): 353).

[7] Compare Wisdom (1953: 224) for the thought that art can reveal anew the familiar from life, exemplified by discussion of some novels.

reading might offer the possibility of viewing the world from the perspective of some character or other. And we might take some novels as so structured either to permit or to require such a reading. (Of course, by our earlier point, they may be few-and-far-between.)

Clearly, this is the beginnings of an account of *some* of what is involved in reading *some* novels on *some* occasions, partly explaining the insight we feel these novels offer us. Were it not, it would be very odd to appeal to *empathy* here at all: and yet people (and critics[8]) regularly do just that, directly and indirectly, when commenting on novels. However, this might—and typically will—fall far short of my empathetic engagement with *The Leopard*, described above, even though that case would be included within the broad remit. Here, though, the instruction on how to *see* the world (as constituted by such-and-such novel: see above) includes, of course, aspects of how to *feel* in that world, and what to feel in response to it.

Still, seeing a concern with empathy in this light may already cast some shadows across it. For instance, Nick Hornby characterizes his fictionalized autobiography, *Fever Pitch* (1992: 11[9]), as 'an attempt to gain some kind of angle on my obsession', and explains that the text is 'for anyone who has wondered what it might be like to be that way' (12). The implication of such an appeal (I take it) is that I can, for example, learn *what it is like* to be a soccer fan through reading Hornby's book; and that, somehow, I do this by empathizing with the book's narrator. So I take for granted that some kind of appeal to *empathy* is indeed warranted in respect of one's understanding of *some* novels on *some* occasions—but that concession is a place-holder. For what does empathy *amount to* in that context? In particular, we cannot assume that what we know of empathy in respect of fellow humans and *their* situations (in so far as we know *anything*) simply carries over to this account of the art case. Although I have no complete argument to show that it does not, what follows presents some considerations in that direction, focusing especially on the requirement that, in empathy, my psychological states *match* yours (see below). But, given *my* account of artistic judgment (McFee (2005), and see below), we should certainly expect the two cases of empathy to differ in important ways. Also, the general problems of ascribing psychological states to art-works—especially to the physical-object kinds—point in the same direction.[10] So I will take as the default position here that the concept *empathy* will operate differently in the art case, when contrasted with the inter-personal case.[11]

---

[8] One instance: John Gardner (1978: 112) writes of 'the queer experience of falling through the print on the page into something like a dream, an imaginary world', in order to make concrete his claim that '[o]ne of the essentials of our humanness . . . is that we empathize' (112).

[9] My thanks to Murray Smith whose mention of this book at the 'Empathy' conference reminded me of it; and also for his discussion of related themes with me. [It is very important to distinguish the content of the book—about 'football' = soccer—from that of the feature film, about baseball!]

[10] For a convenient summary of such problems for cognitivist account of the emotions and their application in philosophical aesthetics, see Kivy (2002): 25–6; 110–34.

[11] That default position certainly seemed granted by presentations at the 'Empathy' conference, even those more sympathetic that I am to some role for empathy here.

12.3 What Might We Learn from Thinking About Interpersonal Empathy?

Still, it may be helpful to address the interpersonal case, since it offers uncontentious examples of *empathy* with others.[12] Here *empathy* must require more than just, say, getting a sense of what another felt from, for instance, his expression or demeanor— that is just our ordinary understanding of another person, with no need for a special name or process.

So let us begin by noting that *empathy* is regularly and rightly contrasted with *sympathy*: for example, Peter Goldie (2000: 176) writes of 'a tendency to confuse sympathy with empathy'. Thus, I am sympathetic to the famine victim, but I certainly do not try to feel what he or she feels. And we regularly regard efforts to do just that, when we find them, as unusual, if not excessive (as with Simone Weil's restricting her diet to that of her war-time compatriots, even though she could have eaten more). So in broad brush-strokes—especially as our interest here is not in this case—*roughly*, in sympathy I do not *share* your '*mental state*':[13] the implication is that, in empathy, I do share your 'mental state'. And 'definitions' characteristically offered reflect this idea: for example, that from Goldie (2000: 195, quoted above[14]). Again, this highlights why merely imagining what it would be like to experience what another is experiencing is not yet a helpful characterization of *empathy*: it does not yet make the connection to my responses being emotional or affective ones (too).

Two related points can be extracted from this fact that, in empathy, we imaginatively put ourselves in the other's position, while still recognizing our individuality.

---

[12] Of course, a fuller treatment might find revealing *objects of comparison* in one's responses to, say, biographies or autobiographies. Given that the interpersonal case *seems* at first the simplest, and that the evocative writing in novels has a stronger claim on our *emotional* responses than such cases (as well as being my chief interest), those are the examples from which I begin, and then use throughout. And, of course, my emphasis on the case of literature is of a piece with my commitment to the distinctive character of appreciation of the arts (see McFee (2005)).

[13] The idea of a 'mental state' was one which generally Wittgenstein preferred to resist: see, for instance, PI §149. See also VoW: 5 on: 'so-called mental states'. In particular, Wittgenstein had reservations about taking any form of *understanding* to be a mental state. A key feature here is temporal location: as Wittgenstein imagines being asked there: '*When* did you know how to play chess? All the time? or just when you were making a move? And the whole of chess during each move?' Then he comments ironically: 'How queer that knowing how to play chess should take such as short time, and the game so much longer!' (PI §50 note). [The remark is from BT §36 (p. 114).] See also his remark about what *time* there was a change in the price of shares on the stock market, if the Exchange opened at the new price (PO: 405; MS, 119): 'If the price of a commodity has changed between yesterday and today, when did it change? How much was it at midnight, when nobody was buying?'.

[14] Compare also Smith (1995): 87: 'In sympathizing with the protagonist I do not simulate or mimic her occurent mental state.' The implication, then, is that in empathy I do so simulate or mimic. See also Feagin (1996): 95: 'Empathy with another person requires that one "share" another's feelings, that one "feel" things as that person does or did.' (I assume the scare-quotes pick out the 'in imagination' condition.) Also consider Feagin (1996): 114: 'Empathy involves simulating the mental activity and processes of the person with whom one empathizes'. (Compare note 26.)

First, and negatively, it suggests limits to empathy; second, and positively, it offers a strategy for conceptualizing complete or perfect empathy.

Let us take them in that order. So, what constrains such a process of imaginatively entering the other's emotional world? Stephen Pinker[15] offers a slogan that might have a wide scope:

The body is the ultimate barrier to empathy. Your toothache simply does not hurt me the way it hurts you.

Pinker might seem to be arguing simply that my pain cannot be *numerically identical* with yours: but there is no *numerical* identity condition here—also we cannot easily see what a 'qualitative identity' would be like. In fact, Pinker's insight concerns the power of the connection between my psychological states and my anatomy and physiology. For key limitations will flow from my distinctive central nervous system—but also from other, similar differences between us: in particular, differences of gender, and of range of experiences. In effect, what I can *imagine* sets a kind of limit here—for empathy between us, my imagined version of your psychological state must agree with your *actual* state (to some degree) or I have failed to empathize with you. And this is what is meant here by my psychological states *matching* yours.

Thus, suppose I read in a newspaper about a South American woman who has been involved with drug-running. The article includes a striking photograph. I become fascinated with this character (perhaps the striking image is important here), and try to find out more. Perhaps, then, I go to her trial—and I try to find myself in her shoes, to *empathize* with her. We can readily highlight some blocks to, or limitations of, empathy here. For instance (a version of Pinker's point?), our difference of gender might mean that I could not readily imagine the connections of responses to anatomy and physiology. In effect, this might limit *my* (current) capacity to imaginatively entertain her position. But there are also limitations on the degree to which I can imaginatively enter her world: it is South America (I've never been); it is a world of vicious killers, and so on. In short, it is nothing like my world.

Does this suggest that I can only empathize with those like me? Certainly, some practical limitations here will be set by the scope of what, at present, I can realistically imagine, as opposed to merely guessing. For one cannot be empathetic unless (or to the degree that) one is successful in 'matching' the other's psychological states. Then here too what *I* can imagine may set boundaries to what I can make sense of, given that some of my concepts may depend on my having the anatomy and physiology I do. So Pinker's constraint also applies when we ask about *getting it right*! For, in practice, we will be similarly limited, through our imagination as at present, in the extent to which we can successfully 'match' the psychological state of someone at some remove

---

[15] From his *How The Mind Works* (1997), quoted in Brockman (2006): 146.

from us. And my emphasis here on *matching* is to avoid getting bogged down in the detail of how this might be achieved.

Then, as the second crucial point noted above, this 'constraint' could be read positively, as elaborating the key success condition. Thus, with a real woman, it seems at first sight that we know what *would be* required for empathy in the highest degree: namely, that I should imaginatively enter her world so that my emotional state is the same as hers, although of course mine is only taken on 'in imagination'. So we have a rough model for empathetic engagement with another person to the highest degree: namely, that my mental state should 'match' hers (completely), putting aside the 'in imagination' qualification.[16] Of course, we do not expect to get such 'total empathy' in any real case: it functions here as an idealization. But to talk of empathy at all is to approach that ideal, to some extent: to grant a *role* to that ideal. And, at every turn, that is to conceive of my psychological states matching the others': or that I '*centrally imagine* . . . the thoughts, feelings, and emotions of another person' (Goldie (2000): 195); that I might 'imaginatively experience his or her emotional states, while simultaneously imaginatively experiencing his or her cognitive states' (Coplan (2004): 144); or have 'an imaginative reconstruction of another person's experience' (Nussbaum (2001): 302). For all of *these* can be cashed out as such matching, since each takes empathy to involve my imaginative engagement with what the *other* is feeling. And other versions worthy of the term 'empathy' (say, in contrast to *sympathy*) must grant the same point. Then the degree to which I achieve empathy in any actual case will be the degree to which there is such matching.

In this way the metaphor of *matching* seems fundamental to any detailed account of empathy here. For genuine empathy occurs only with matching of this sort. So empathy is, in this way, *relational* in a stronger sense than, say, even sympathy. My sympathy with you (or for you) does not require that you feel anything: but at the centre of the idea of empathy is precisely a *sharing* of some psychological state or condition. So both your contribution and mine are required. And clearly it will not be sufficient for *empathy* that, say, you are afraid and so am I. Rather, in empathy, I am seeking to enter into your emotional state, if only in imagination: in this sense, success in empathy requires that my emotional state *match* yours. Of course, it seems that such matching can be *to some specific degree* or other, including totally. Further, we might expect to investigate to *which* degree. If this were right, the same should be true of empathy. So, to repeat, empathy can be *to some degree* since my emotional state may match yours *to some degree*. This thought too will be fundamental to an elaboration of the concept of empathy, reflecting how such empathy is regarded: that it can be to some degree or other. And the *matching* model offers an account of that fact. Yet nothing here says how to make out that matching; hence, it offers no guidance as to how *empathy* is to be elucidated.

---

[16] My thought here is that including the 'in imagination' requirement will make it more *difficult* to cash out this 'matching' metaphor: so putting it aside is a way to support the advocates of empathy-theory.

On such a picture, empathy *appears* like an achievement, even if only achieved to some degree. An elaboration may forestall any misunderstanding at this point. For this view is not the extreme one that only 'total empathy' counts. Rather, it is about the usefulness of the empathy model: I am urging that such a model has a degree of matching as its success condition; and that, without some such condition, it would not be attractive to us, especially in aesthetics. For the idea is precisely that I might *succeed* in imaginatively entering the other's world: hence that I 'take on' psychological states *of hers*.

So, to repeat, empathy *appears* like an achievement, on such a picture. For, in this context, my having empathy for you involves my adopting some aspects from your psychological state (such as affective tone or perspective). As we said, the success condition here can be thought a kind of 'matching'. Then what of cases where I do not in fact 'match' your mental state at all (in the relevant respect)? Is this *failed* empathy, or not empathy? However that (terminological?) debate is resolved, at the least we can grant that—despite my best efforts at empathetic engagement—things may not go well. Thus we must recognize cases where, for whatever reason, the upshot of my fellow-feeling for the person in the plight is, from my side, empathy—that is, I intend it to be empathy and I take it for empathy: I take myself to be 'matching' the emotional state of that person in the relevant way. But, in the event, I fail: my mental states do not, after all, 'match' those of the person with whom I took myself to be empathetically engaged. (Since we have empathy only when we 'match', there must clearly be cases like this—of *intended* empathy, perhaps—where empathy fails despite my best efforts.)

Of course, there are, no doubt, also failures of empathy which amount to my simply making nothing of your situation. But these are not the cases under consideration. Rather, in the cases before us, I do *something*. So, in such cases, failing to empathize is not, of course, like failing to see or failing to notice. When I fail to *see*, or fail to *notice*, the step—or the sheep—there may be nothing that I in fact *do*: I merely do not attain *those* achievements. By contrast, in the favored cases considered, the failure to empathize is, in effect, the failure of match between (to put it tendentiously) my psychological states and those of another. So we can see this as my *striving* for empathy: my projecting what I hope will be empathetic—in failure to empathize, there is simply no 'match' between my psychological state and that of the person with whom I am trying to empathize. Then this is what, earlier, I called 'intended empathy'. But, again, this is not really empathy at all.

This sense of empathy as an *achievement*—that one only has (genuine) empathy when one's emotional states *match* those of the empathized-with—is central to the standard views of empathy, as represented in those accounts quoted/cited above. If empathy is, in this sense, an *achievement*, we must be very clear when it *is* and—especially—when it is *not* achieved: we should look, as it were, to its *failure conditions*. For, if conceptual importance is to be urged for *empathy* (with some 'work' asked of it[17]), it must at least *make sense* to say that there is or is not empathy: hence that there is or is not such matching. And, as above, talk of 'matching' here will be both *to some degree* (we do not require total matching) and *in respect of . . .* whatever psychological states are at issue (rather than across the board). One question will be whether we can, in some way, make the common sense account of empathy more robust. So, below, I will consider two or three attempts to do just that, either by treating the matching as quantifiable or by modeling it as a comparison of brain states. Neither of these seems promising. But they represent efforts to give a more explicit 'cash-value' to talk of *empathy* Then we will be better placed to evaluate the more general usefulness of the concept *empathy*: in particular, its usefulness in philosophical aesthetics. And this paper is shaped by such an investigation.

Let us return to success in empathy. Then my empathizing with you, say in respect of your fear on hearing a noise in the night, leaves me with at least *something like* a feeling of the fears you experience: my psychological state matches yours. So far, this is harmless. If you grant that I have understood you, and I claim empathy (in this respect), perhaps 'accompanying' my comments with 'suitable' behavior, there seems no reason to deny that my psychological state matched yours. And perhaps our interest is exhausted by my claim to empathy and your granting of it. So, to elaborate, this is a case accepted as empathy but with no *explicit* matching of my psychological states with yours. There might be nothing more to say. (One might still wonder why I insist on the term 'empathy'.) But this is, so far, not a very helpful way to explore my empathetic engagement with you. For example, why is this *empathy* and not, say, sympathy? I am not denying that it *is*: yet why? My assertion of empathy here seems sufficient for some purposes, but scarcely if someone raises a serious objection to that claim.

If my claim were challenged, or you not around (or not inclined) to comment, there would be no strategy for elaborating such a claim; for making it more robust—in short, for *proving* it. We cannot check the matching independently; say, by comparing my psychological states with yours. And such a challenge might reasonably arise. We have already conceded that (merely) *intending* empathy is not enough. In particular, we may need more robust claims to empathy precisely when more turns on its being, or not being, genuine *empathy*—say, in contrast to *sympathy* ('Yes, you do feel for us—but you don't know what it is like for us'). And the hope to use the concept of empathy productively within philosophical aesthetics assumes of it just this kind of robustness:

---

[17] Of course, if empathy were really just a humanistic (or 'folk-psychological') notion, and if one had no particular designs on utilizing the concept of empathy in an explanatory way, one might rest content with a humanistic account here—that I am good at seeing the world through your eyes and feeling it through your 'shoes' just to the degree that I am: to the degree, perhaps, that I know you well, and hence understand what you are thinking and feeling. That is to say, having assumed that there was no 'logical bar' (Dilman (1975): 211) to knowing the thoughts and feelings of another, the account would draw on such knowledge as we find it in our everyday lives. But a concept such as this will not sustain the kinds of precise distinctions (say, from sympathy) which must be deployed by anyone pressing the distinctive claims of empathy, for instance in philosophical aesthetics.

without that, there will be no real reason to prefer the term 'empathy' to others, such as 'sympathy', when considering emotional and identificatory readings of (in our case) novels. As above, our strategy is to ask with what *empathy* is being *contrasted*. When, as with the contrast with sympathy, we recognize what empathy here is *not*, we can see how its claims might be defeated. But that does not help elucidate our understanding of *success* in empathy. Hence this loose sense of 'matching' cannot be elaborated into a theoretical structure for use in philosophical aesthetics.

But might more be made of the concept of empathy? Well, genuine empathy, as opposed to (mere) intended empathy, requires what I have called 'the matching of psychological states' that is built into even those accounts where it is not mentioned explicitly. And, thus far, the problems for matching may *seem* to concern our knowing, or being sure, of the empathy: an epistemological problem. Once we move beyond the simple case, where the claim to empathy is not contested, is there a way forward? As we will see, my response illustrates why, in fact, the original difficulty is not centrally epistemological at all.

One feature of my previous discussion might seem to offer hope to the theorist of empathy. Above, in looking towards the 'matching' central to empathy, I spoke of the match as 'to some degree'. This might seem to suggest that one's account here could be made more robust: that the 'degree' could be specified, at least in principle. For, without some such stronger version, talk of 'to some degree' may seem contentless. (We will return to that idea below.) Yet this is not my point. Instead my thought was to recognize it as 'to some degree' by specifying where, and how, it failed. For instance, we might offer an explanation of my failure to empathize with a Victorian woman as a failure to 'match'—say, I could not really see the world *as a woman* might, although managing to empathize with the Victorian character of the other (or vice versa). So saying that the match was 'to some degree' is justified by pointing out its failures: that is all there is to the thought of partial failure or success here. This sense of 'match' would be unexceptionable. Yet, equally, this sense of 'matching' could not sustain any further elaboration. In fact, at this level we do not pursue the idea of *having* matched, but only the cases of intended empathy through having *failed* to match—by elaborating where exactly this failure occurred. There is no *precision* to be had here beyond this.

This might suggest a stronger version: that one should make this 'degree' of match more explicit, thereby producing a more robust version of the 'matching' criterion. Yet there is no *quantifiable level* of failure here—it was not, say, a case of '70% success'; and could not be, because there is no finite totality of (relevant) aspects to match or not match. And the requirement here should, for me, both be within the powers of humans in a reasonable timescale and be the sorts of things we can come to by steps: *complete*-minus-two, *complete*-minus-one, and then *complete*. This is to import a certain conception of finite totalities[18] as involved in the claim to *all* or to *completeness*. Lacking

---

[18] The strictly mathematical model here is misleading; and this is part of my point. As Wittgenstein recognized, someone asked how many numerals she had learned to write down might reply, 'Aleph-null'

such a finite totality, the idea of a *complete match* makes no sense. (Rather, there is no 'complete'!) Then since, in principle, it makes no sense to talk of a 100% match, it is equally senseless to assay other numerical results. This means that a strategy of this kind, which seeks to quantify the degree of *matching*, is misconceived. Hence it seems unpromising to attempt to make more precise the degree of empathy by making the *degree* of matching more exact. But, as we have seen, the *question* of matching here is crucial: as traditional accounts agree, with no 'match', there can be no empathy, since your psychological states do not relevantly resemble mine—it is *intended* empathy only!

Yet perhaps we can explain the problem so as to suggest a way forward. For if this whole idea of 'matching' *seems* problematic, isn't that 'only because of our too slight acquaintance with what goes on in the brain and central nervous system' (PI §158)? Isn't that the 'matching' to which we should really aspire? Again, that thought, although misguided, tells us something important. For it might seem that, if the issue concerned our brain states only, mine might match with yours to such-and-such an extent—on the occasion, all of your c-fibers are firing, but only 70% of mine (and so on). That might reinstate the matching metaphor.

In fact, the difficulty is more profound. For resolving the question of *success* in empathy cannot wait until empathizer and empathizee are in some scanner (or, worse, on a post-mortem table): we should in principle be able to determine successes and failures 'at the human level', at least as reliably as we can where the psychological states of others are at issue. After all, the 'matching' here is done by humans. Given that we cannot readily explain functional equivalence here *divorced* from similarities of causal structure, this would seem to set one limit, by constraining my empathy to (at best) creatures whose physical structures resembled mine sufficiently closely. Yet it cannot really be a case of my *brain states* matching yours, unless we first import what is at issue; namely, that parallels at the level of achievement must *always*, or at least typically, depend on parallels in the causal substrate.[19] And, again, that is an assumption we must criticize.

As an extreme example, suppose some research identifies a pattern of brain activity it regards as constituting the loving response to an image of a beloved—what should we make of, say, a loved one whose brain *does not* fire when (say) he sees the picture of the beloved?[20] I imagine the person who has read a lot of cognitive science might find a doubt raised in her mind—does this person *really* love me? But it would be misguided

---

($\aleph_0$). And this answer is, in a clear sense, absolutely right. But then, first, Wittgenstein points out that we might 'say, "How wonderful—to learn Aleph-null ($\aleph_0$) numerals, and in so short a time! How clever we are!"' (LFM: 31). Then, second, he notes that now 'it is illuminating to ask, "What would it be like to learn only 100,000 numerals?"' (LFM: p. 31), rather than Aleph-null ($\aleph_0$). For that highlights the sense in which our first reply was not strictly a numerical one.

[19] Perhaps, in line with functionalist thinking, mental states should be explained ('defined') by their causal roles: 'in principle, a machine . . . , a human being, a creature with a silicon chemistry . . . could all work much the same when described at the relevant level of abstraction, and . . . [so] it is just wrong to think that the essence of our minds is our "hardware"' (Putnam (1988): xii).

[20] Compare Fisher (2004): especially 56–64.

to give weight to this sort of example,[21] as two cases clearly illustrate. First, consider building up the correlation: if, at that stage, there are cases where the relevant part of the brain does not fire as predicted, these must simply count against any such generalization. Why? Because we do not have *independent* access here to both *what X feels* and to his/her brain states; and only independent access would allow us to build up a correlation *detached* from the reports of persons. Yet, in the nature of the beast (reflecting Pinker's point), one cannot have such *independent* access. So we must determine which brain states are under consideration by first granting the accuracy of the personal reports (in their behavioral context). And that would mean recognizing the imagined scenario as a counterexample to one's thesis about which part of the brain is involved in 'beloved-recognition'.

Then, second, there is a big mistake in *priority* here, akin to giving a modern creativity test to, say, Mozart or Picasso—if the test scores show (or seem to show) that Mozart or Picasso were not creative (if they score low) . . . well, so much the worse for the test. And this too relates to the structure of building-up the correlations that 'validate' the test: since we know the 'creativity status' of Mozart and Picasso (they are!), this knowledge can become data in evaluating the test. And the same goes for our lovers: their love is the case from which the whole discussion began. Hence there is no (useful) inference to be drawn from the facts as described to the standard concern, 'He/she loves me, he/she loves me not'. (Indeed, one might as well be pulling the petals off a daisy!) Thinking otherwise just *takes for granted* what is, or should be, at issue in current theory about how brain states instantiate psychological ones.

This means, of course, that no great weight can be attached to this way of cashing out the metaphor of the matching of psychological states, and hence of the success or otherwise of empathy: it may have seemed a promising strategy, but it never can be.

The moral here may be hard to see, but it is this: there is no finite totality of powers and capacities here to which empathetic 'matching' could aspire—hence there is no 100% match, no 70% match, and so on. Rather the whole model of 'matching' is a humanistic confection, a metaphor to which no numerical weight can be given. And this despite our recognizing that our empathy is often limited, and our explaining its limitations in terms of a failure to 'match'. So my point is not that we lack a clear idea of what represents a total match, nor that there is insufficient matching in some cases, nor (again) that we do not know *if* there is 'matching'. Rather, my objection is to the whole metaphor of matching: since there is no finite totality of features to consider, any detailed idea of matching is rendered incoherent if we try to use it as the kind of success condition needed—and its incoherence is inherited by the picture of empathy it sustains.

---

[21] With Bernard Williams (1981: 18), we may think this 'one question too many'. For a discussion along my lines, see Frankfurt (2004): 36ff.

12.4 Empathy and Text-Processing: Some Empirical Considerations?

One thought might be that empirical investigations of empathy (and related phenomena) may sharpen our understanding. For instance, in her perceptive discussion, Amy Coplan (2004: 147) urges that it is 'the lack of consensus among scholars concerning the definition of empathy' that renders problematic a debate in the philosophical literature. By way of clarification, she turns to some psychological literature, commenting '[i]t is in part because of the confusion in the [philosophical?] literature regarding the meanings of these terms ['empathy', 'emotional contagion', 'identification'] that I developed my account of empathy on the basis of models in psychology' (Coplan 2004: 147). Further, she draws explicitly on some of the empirical findings of psychology. Here, I will comment briefly on some of the detail to which she appeals, as well as on her general procedure, selecting her discussion for its strengths (especially its clarity) rather than any deficiencies[22]—although my own predisposition is to find such psychology a collection of 'experimental methods and *conceptual confusion*' (PI p. 197[23])!

Coplan's paper uses 'recent relevant empirical work on text processing and narrative comprehension' (Coplan (2004): 141): that is, she deploys work on texts (and hence on *reading* more generally). So, we are already discussing empathy in the contexts of *texts*, a small plus given that our interest is ultimately in novels. What should we make of this material?

First, one difficulty is partly *methodological*: do the so-called 'data' bear on the real issues? The intention here must be to replace armchair psychology, or—as Guyer (2005: 335) augments the list—'concert-hall or gallery psychology', with *real* psychology. But then success, if granted, at best involves what passes for proof in psychology; philosophy has a different set of obligations. In particular, philosophy must avoid, as various *causal fallacies*, giving weight to what one can in fact believe, or how one came to this belief (given one's general background). Thus, it can never be philosophically revealing that, say, so-and-so *thinks* or *claims* to be unable to imagine such-and-such, if the topic is the limits of imagination. Hence it cannot be helpful to line up, via a survey, a collection of such people. For, if the issue is whether or not they can, say, *imagine* such-and-such, the constraints cannot be *of the same kind* as those these experiments invoke. The same might apply to the 'psychological' data presented here.

But let us put such points aside. Then, second, consider the issue of narrative comprehension: we are offered psychological research in which 'readers were experiencing the narrative from the spatio-temporal standpoint of the protagonist' (Coplan (2004): 141). But also, and without comment, research which concluded that adult

---

[22] My model here is Austin (1962): 1: 'I choose them for their merits and not for their deficiencies.'

[23] My use of the 50th Anniversary edition of *Philosophical Investigations* (Wittgenstein (2001)) means that the pagination for Part Two is different from that usually employed.

readers (certainly the ones of most interest for aestheticians) regularly 'take up an internal perspective (i.e. the perspective within the framework of the story)' (Coplan (2004): 142). In this second case, of course, no specific character is identified: hence, even were this the basis for an emotional reaction, no empathetic response would be possible—there is no one with whom to empathize!

Further, third, the issue of 'emotional dimensions of a point of view', explained as 'how readers process characters' emotions' (Coplan (2004): 142) and as treating 'the emotional implications of a narrative from the standpoint of one of the protagonists' (Coplan (2004): 142). Now, it is far from clear that these are equivalent. But one justification—rightly voiced by Coplan—is that the literature contains no sustained treatment of the relevant issues; that we must do our best to pull together whatever is revealing.

One question here also is broadly methodological: for the results draw on the thought that 'target sentences matching the character's emotions [in some passage] should be processed more quickly than sentences not matching it' (Coplan (2004): 143). That was the prediction; and, we are told, '[t]his was exactly what they found' (Coplan (2004): 143). But what exactly could be the test for one sentence being 'processed more quickly' than another? Is it that one understands more quickly? One set of problems here comes from the term 'processed'—what exactly is that, and how does it differ, for a sentence, from the more commonly recognized 'processes', such as reading and understanding? It seems that there is some test here, such that the psychologists could determine whether or not the relevant processing had taken place. But surely what is needed is to gauge when the sentence was appropriately *understood*: that will not be readily quantified. Further, note that both reading and understanding can be 'completed' partially or sketchily, to some degree or other, such that one might go back to read again or to understand more. Can one similarly *process* sentences to some degree or other? If so, what degree of such processing was required to count, in the experiment, as having processed? And, if not, how can such 'processing' be *informative* about reading and understanding, given that they can be partial?

A related set of problems comes from the term 'quickly'. (Compare, too, reference to another study looking at who would 'read the emotional attribution more quickly': Coplan (2004): 143.) For how would one know how quickly something *read* had been understood? Suppose I ask you to read a passage and to raise your hand when you have read it: here we have a clear sense of 'more quickly' for reading—whoever's hand goes up first was the quickest. And then we might want to test whether or not our winner had read *all* the words. But, for our experiment, is merely having *read* enough? One's level of understanding of the passage might be relevant: how fully or completely have you understood? Or, even, have you understood it at all? (Perhaps I could read a passage phonetically but very quickly, as I might read a passage in a foreign language, without understanding it—that would not do.) And might there not be very many factors relevant here? For instance, the vocabulary used (not to mention the language) might affect reading and comprehension differentially, without the difference reflecting differences in one's identification with the position described: they might simply grasp the words less well, rather than the emotions. The difficulty is that these all seem like instruments too blunt to determine the character of the responses to these stories. (And, of course, one complicates the task hugely by offering an account from a literary work—and, perhaps, complicates it again by selecting the passage from literary works where this seems especially problematic: say, James Joyce's *Ulysses*.)

Then again is the *right* gloss put on the empirical evidence, even granting its conclusions? Does it lead us automatically to consider *empathy*? Suppose instead that the empirical research (either this lot, or something similar) arrived at the unsurprising conclusion that the participants in these experiments could better understand—even if they persist in treating *better* in terms of more quickly—when they could *sympathize* with the protagonists: that is, when they could grasp the problems, issues, concerns of the protagonists. Then suppose sympathy 'involves caring about another individual— feeling for another' (Coplan (2004): 145). Of course, this cannot be how its *authors* understand this research material: but their perspective is not automatically correct. Would a reading in terms of, roughly, *sympathy* offer a plausible alternative? (This might reflect a general methodological question here: is no other explanation possible?)

Well, this 'sympathy' talk, understood this way, sounds exactly like what one needs to explain, for instance, making sense of some stories ('emotionally charged narratives' (Coplan (2004): 143) at the center of the research design discussed here. In the stories there deployed, protagonists meet a doctor to discuss the results of a brain scan. Yet, while the official topic concerns the audience's identification with the protagonists of the narratives, the actual research protocol reflects—not *understanding* as such—but the relative speed of 'processing', and hence of response. But is that necessarily empathetic? In those cases, what is needed is to understand what that person is feeling: either knowing (for the informed narratives) that the protagonist understands that 'major problems' (Coplan (2004): 143) have been ruled out, or (for the uninformed) that this was so, *even though* the protagonist did not know it, would facilitate understanding what the protagonist was feeling, perhaps. For I recognize the different degrees of distress appropriate to the different conditions of knowledge. Further, it seems entirely likely in such cases that I might then 'focus on the protagonist's feelings' (Coplan (2004): 143), rather than the 'objective situation'. But why should that suggest that I am *identifying* with those feelings? And, in particular, why should I be taking up the protagonist's perspective, so as to 'imaginatively experience, to some degree or other, what he or she experiences' (Coplan (2004): 143)? First, this is not an experience I should want for myself; nor can I think, as I might for a literary fiction, that I am caught up in it; second, if one wants to explain my concern with that protagonist, it is unnecessary for my experience to be identificatory—the appeal to a sympathetic response on my part is quite sufficient.

So it is not clear that this discussion really requires an *empathy*-reading; hence that it really exemplifies that '*empathetic* perspective taking is a standard part of the readers' engagement with narrative fictions' (Coplan (2004): 143; my emphasis).

Of course, the distinctive feature required for such a characterization as *empathy* returns us to our emphasis on the *achievement* of empathy: it would then involve stressing the involvement of 'emotions that are *qualitatively the same* as those of the target' (Coplan (2004): 144). But, as our discussion of interpersonal empathy illustrated, this feature is inherently problematic. For it returns us to the 'matching' theme. Perhaps, after all, it makes sense for my emotional state to be *qualitatively the same* as that of another person, although this too might be disputed.[24] Whatever we make of *that* case, how could one guarantee *qualitatively the same* emotions, when the 'subject' of the 'match' for my emotions is a character in a novel? For that character's emotional states are whatever the novelist puts into them—in this fashion, they are *closed* in a way mine, or any other person's, are not. Any emotional states ascribed to that character will be answerable to some passage in the novel, while no such requirement operates for *my* emotional states. In another way, the character's emotional states are *under-described* (relative to *real* states) in ways mine are not: their duration and intensity is left uncharacterized to the degree that these details are not written-up, while mine depend on how I presently feel, together with my dispositions, and such like.[25] So, while there is no finite totality of properties for *my* emotional states,[26] the dependence of the character's emotional states on the text means that *his/her* states are circumscribed by that text. Yet, in turn, that must speak against our states being (definitely) *qualitatively the same*.

Here we might, with profit, return to Nick Hornby: if we took the narrative of *Fever Pitch* to be just autobiographical, we might see the 'matching' emotional states required for empathy in terms of Hornby's own states. But, then, do we extract our understanding of these states from the book or the man? If from the book, we have made no progress over other examples; if from the man, the book now seems irrelevant.

Further (a topic for the next section), how is this empirical data even possibly relevant *for the art case* (namely, the novel), when it is drawn for the 'regular' interpersonal relations case? What debatable assumptions would we be importing if we thought it was?

12.5 And What About Literature?

So far we have considered some reasons why talk of empathy is not likely to be revealing vis-à-vis aesthetic matters: namely, that the failure conditions for *achievement* of empathy seem inherently problematic and ill-suited to dealing with fictional narratives—it certainly does not reflect our usual mode of engagement with literary

---

[24] See, for instance, Malcolm (1977): 104–32, especially 115–29.

[25] And, of course, to dispute much of *this* is just to dispute the idea of a psychological *state*.

[26] A simplified version of the argument here, applied to description quite generally, is in McFee (2000): 117–24.

works, such as stories,[27] even when we identify with central characters. The psychological literature offers neither a compelling reason to conceptualize understanding narrative fictions in terms of such empathy nor a clear picture of what emotions being *qualitatively the same* would mean here.

In the examples above, discussions of empathy sometimes use the term 'reading' and its cognates when addressing our understanding of other people. Thus Goldie (2000: 195) writes, 'I have a grasp of a narrative which I can imaginatively enact, with the other as narrator'—but this requirement is for empathy quite generally (that is, for interpersonal empathy): its references to *narratives* and *narrators* are at best figurative, or some such, picking out how the 'other' understands his life. Some cases, considered earlier, seem to reflect a kind of proto-reading: 'text processing'. Yet other cases are clearly concerned with reading in general.

Therefore, as implied above, a powerful line of objection is open to aestheticians, questioning the *relevance* of this material. For are the discussions here about *art* (that is, *literary* fiction)? Or just about (any old) narrative fiction? We know that there is a distinction here, even if few would insist on it in *my* terms.[28] And both *what* is seen and *how* it is seen can matter. Thus (on a parallel) Wollheim's baby daughter, photographed in his *Painting as an Art* (1987: 54) looking at a painted image, is not seeing *art*, although (a) she is looking at an artwork, and (b) she is seeing (and arguably recognizing) a depiction: and that fact is crucial to understanding what is going on in that case. So, is the investigation here research into (the literary versions of) *art* and *artistic judgment*? To put the case simply, should the conclusions, if accurate, apply as well to kinds of light-weight novels that are the standard fare of airport lounges[29] as to *Pride and Prejudice* and *Wuthering Heights*, and vice versa? My thought is that empathetic reading of the kind envisaged by its 'fans' is more likely in the first set of cases,[30] perhaps because I imagine the appeal of such texts resides in the identifications their readers make. Certainly, nothing here (yet) refers to the specific kind of *value* for the literary.

---

[27] As Coplan ((2004): 151 note 35) notes, some writers—she cites Susan Feagin in her excellent *Reading with Feeling: The Aesthetics of Appreciation* (Feagin (1996))—take some other process to underlie both interpersonal empathy and empathetic reading of literature. In Feagin's case, her choice (*simulation*) seems to me a further level of going back beyond the beginning. Like Searle (2002: 69), and for similar reasons, I am puzzled by this technical use of the term 'simulation'; for, as he writes of the everyday use, 'simulation should not be confused with duplication, whether the subject-matter is the mind, or anything else'.

[28] On my version (see McFee (2005)), terms such as 'beautiful' amount to something different applied to artworks than they do applied to non-art objects of aesthetic appreciation. Although the correct explanation here lies in the occasion-sensitive uses of these terms, I occasionally put the point loosely by saying that such terms are 'systematically ambiguous' (McFee (2005): 384)—this version puts bluntly what is 'one step too far' for most aestheticians.

[29] In the UK, these might well be called 'bodice-ripper' or 'bonk-buster' novels: expressions for a certain kind of quasi-romantic work of fiction (not to be mistaken for literature) perhaps familiar from the writings of Posy Simmonds (*Gemma Bovary* (2000)) and Helen Fielding (*Bridget Jones's Diary* (1997)—including Hollywood's version!).

[30] We should also remind ourselves that the category choice here is not limited to 'bodice-ripper or Booker Prize candidate'.

Now, rather than asking, 'Is, for instance, *reading such-and-such literary work* best understood as an exercise of empathy?', we should ask:

- In contrast to what? (So, how *else* might it be explained?)
- In what circumstances?

This issue, for us, would not just be about *reading* in general (which is surely rarely or never empathetic; see below) nor even *reading a literary work*. For both of these are insufficiently particular—we may need to go further: say, by contrasting the reading of *this* literary work with the reading of that one; or even considering sections within each.

But, to get a starting point, what is ordinary, non-art, *reading* like? Is *that* even possibly 'empathy-involving'? (For most cases, I'd say, 'no'.) Could reading a car manual or a typical newspaper article be understood empathetically? While I see no need to preclude either absolutely, in both cases the suggestion would at least involve a *peculiar* reading of the text—for example, I do not need empathy to agree with the newspaper article's conclusions about, say, George W. Bush's foreign policy as it applies in Iraq: I need only both to follow the article's argument (thereby seeing that it is validly formed) and to grant the truth of its premises—perhaps on the basis of other material it includes. For the article, as I imagine it, should move me by *logic*. While the conclusion may have an affective component in its content, regarding the piece as an *argument* means that this conclusion is not reached by affect alone. Even if our journalist relied instead on rhetorical force to 'arrive' at his conclusion, what moved me then was not identification: it was . . . well, rhetoric! That is to say, the *writing*, and not (for instance) the psychological states of its writer. And, of course, conclusions driven solely by affect *here* are likely to be rightly dismissible as sentimental. Further, merely *sharing* the emotion should be contrasted with empathizing. Moreover, *whatever* taking an empathetic stance would involve, it certainly does not amount to matching the affect of the author of either the article or the manual. While the article's author may *have* some affective position (I assume the manual's author does not), understanding either work is certainly not equivalent to some kind of *matching* of that sort. To see this clearly, assume that the article is in a conservative newspaper, with a stance with which its author disagrees. But he cannot get work published elsewhere. So the tone of the piece is not *his* tone.

Again, this is revealing: when we come to literary artworks too, it is only infre-quently (even when empathy is important) that the view of the real *author* herself—that person—is at issue when the discussion of empathy is introduced. And we recognized that fact much earlier. This suggests, of course, the obvious point—again, embodied in the standard definitions—that empathy centrally involves, as a key part, *affect*. Hence there will be no purchase for an empathy-based explanation of affectless objects (the car manual) and affect-irrelevant objects (the newspaper article; and also the philosophy paper)—of course, saying this is not saying anything profound.

We have suggested, though, that *empathy* (as opposed to mere *intended* empathy) requires a 'matching' of the other's psychological state—that 'no match, no empathy'. And, in so far as that psychological state has an affective dimension, that too must be matched.

But what constrains that affect; and especially its understanding by a reader? Above, I deliberately chose cases where this might be problematic: for instance, where the central character is a woman, and often a woman of a past era—to what degree *can* I, as a male of *this* era, empathize there? In another language,[31] does the airport-lounge novel *address* me as, say, a Victorian woman? Well, its doing so cannot require that I *be* (say) a Victorian woman, or it would have no audience. So what weaker condition is required? It would be odd to *deny* that I can make *anything* of such a narrative, at least in typical cases: that grants too much by way of limitations on our imaginative powers.

So could a fictional narrative address me *as a woman*? Well, the term 'woman' here has no specific content as such: it needs to be augmented in terms of the powers, capacities, and so on thereby assumed for, or attributed to, *women*. If artworks can require, for their understanding, an audience suitably knowledgeable and suitably sensitive,[32] there seems no reason to preclude some version of this requirement for understanding, even for fictional works *not* art, such as those from our airport lounge. So there could be (in principle) an implied audience for such a novel which assumed certain, say, *values*: then the novel assumes that its (appropriate) spectators *share*, or at least recognize, the values of, for instance, a Victorian woman (or a certain conception of Victorian women or Victorian femininity)—for example, I have read accounts of Edith Wharton's *The Age of Innocence* in these terms. Were they correct, my mastery of that novel (to the degree I can) might suggest that I have the requisite understanding.

We have recognized that a narrative that requires of its audience, say, understanding the values of, for instance, *Victorian women* cannot thereby require that the audience be composed of Victorian women. But does my *not* being a Victorian woman entail that I will *misperceive* the work in question? No doubt, in practice, I will: but is the requirement that I so misperceive a conceptual one, such that it follows no matter how sympathetic, sensitive, and well-prepared I am? Suppose that it does not: then the requirement here seems to be for a sympathetic recognition of the values, and such like. Then, viewed as a 'best case scenario' from the perspective of my knowledge, understanding, and sensitivity, a work which addresses me as a Victorian woman might do so *even though* I (personally) fail both aspects. Again, this situation seems both harmless and familiar to literary criticism (or art criticism more generally): namely,

---

[31]   See, for instance, Wollheim (1987): 96: 'Necessarily communication is either addressed to an identifiable audience, as when a speaker answers a question put to him by another or when an orator harangues an audience, or is undertaken in the hope an audience will materialize, as when a shipwrecked sailor raises a signal of distress.'

[32]   These are Richard Wollheim's requirements for an audience for *art*: compare, for instance: 'What is properly visible in the surface of the picture is a matter of what experiences appropriate information allows a sensitive spectator to have in front of it' (Wollheim (1993): 189).

as building-in the assumed values of an audience for this novel, or whatever—and then some discussion would follow about what happened when those assumptions were not met, either wholly or to some degree.

As I imagine such a case, the difficulties here concern my specific (and hence in principle remediable) ignorance—or some such. These difficulties are essentially practical, generated by what I do not know, or by values I do not currently share and cannot adopt 'in imagination'.

We should, of course, contrast this case with an imaginary one where—since I am *not* a Victoria woman—the work *cannot* engage with me: where the 'bar' here is somehow *conceptual* or *logical*. But it is much harder to envisage what exactly precludes *in principle* my coming to the appropriate understanding. For instance, does this particular work automatically address me and, say, a female colleague *differentially*? That is, so that the differences did not come down to ones about our relative experience, knowledge, and so on: differences like that would be remediable *in principle*. I would say 'no': for what, exactly, am I supposed *necessarily* to lack? If the issues concern values, or understanding, or even empathy, there seems no reason to regard these as *in principle* beyond a super-sympathetic me. But, if that is right, then there could be no such case of 'in principle' unintelligibility.

Of course, in reality, compared to our stylized Victorian woman, there are certain perceptions I do not share, certain values I do not have, certain narratives of art (and similar) in which I *cannot* locate the work under discussion, as our candidate Victorian woman could—and certain narratives 'second-nature' to me which are unavailable to her. Yet all (or at least, most) of this would be equally true of a contemporary female colleague: so that suggestion simply replicates in more detail our general point about the need for a suitably knowledgeable, suitably sensitive audience. And that just reinstates, with more detail given, the case sketched above. But we have no reason to expect a single uniform resolution to the difficulty which these cases indicate: hence, no neat account of the place of my knowledge, values, and such like in my making sense of fictional narratives.

Then how would the cases where we simply have a narrative text differ from confronting a work of literature? Our previous discussion offers an object of comparison. We have already asked to what extent I can enter the emotional world of a woman from South America. The case might be posed sharply by my 'identification' (or something similar) in my reading of a literary work, such as Arturo Pérez-Reverte's novel *The Queen of the South* (2002[33]), where the central character is *exactly* the kind of South American gangsterista described earlier. Perhaps what a psychologically-driven novel of this sort can offer differs from my knowledge of such a *real* person, if I could get it—here at least I know a lot of facts about that central character, Teresa Mendoza, including psychological ones.

---

[33] Put aside the issue of my reading a translation!

As already noticed, this case differs substantially from the case of interpersonal empathy, in that the psychology to which I must 'match' is one specified, to the degree that it is, by the author, along with those presuppositions about persons his practice imports.[34] Moreover, this feature points in two directions. On the one hand, Teresa Mendoza's psychological states are more circumscribed than those of a real person: all there is to know of them is from the text. Hence we can know all (but only) what the text offers us. For we can have before us all the words that comprise it. On the other hand, the text can leave certain questions unanswered (and hence unanswerable). Supposedly, no answer to L. C. Knights's question,[35] 'How many children had Lady Macbeth?', was forthcoming *from the text*: each real woman has some determinate number of children, including none; but this inference cannot be drawn for fictional characters. For if there is no information in the text, there can be no *fact of the matter* on this topic. The same is true of psychological states: each real woman was in some psychological state or other (including being anaesthetized) at a particular time. We cannot reliably say this for fictional women: again, there may be no *fact of the matter*, if (say) the novel is silent.

This gives us some leeway when we turn again to 'matching' here: we are not trying to match the (fixed?) psychological states of some person at some particular time. Instead, we will do the best we can on the basis of the author's words. But then one's reading of a novel can make concrete the emotional states of its protagonists, where there may be more than one way of unfolding those states (whether or not this is true of real persons). That, in turn, points us towards some explanatory mechanisms and away from others. So my ultimate strategy is this: to find two different occasions superficially similar. If one's relation to an artwork were (correctly) explained *differently* on two occasions—as answers to two different *questions*, as it were—this speaks against reducing that explanation to anything plausibly the same on both occasions; say, to brain states, or to the firing of groups of neurons (or whatever is the preferred neurological explanation today). Then we have a basis for not drawing on neurophysiology to explain empathy in the case of literature (or anywhere?).

Perhaps an example might work as follows. You notice my fascination with Teresa in *The Queen of the South*, my treating all the events from her perspective (facilitated by the way the novel was written): asked to explain this 'reading', I do so in terms of empathetic engagement—to the degree that I can manage—with Teresa. And I explain this, as classically, in terms of a 'matching' of our psychological states, at least to some degree. This makes sense to you, as a fan of the idea of empathetic readings of novels.

---

[34] Another case here: would my possibilities for empathy be stronger if, instead of Teresa, we considered my reading about the life of fellow Scot and fellow philosophy student Isabel Dalhousie, in (say) *The Right Attitude to Rain* (McCall Smith (2006))? For real people, the similarities between my world and hers would clearly be a relevant consideration, seeming to facilitate empathy (as noted earlier). But, for novels, the quality of the *writing* seems more important.

[35] The title of an essay in Knights (1964).

But now your brother asks me about that novel. When I describe the novel and its events to him, I adopt an *internal perspective* (see above) all right, but without characterizing the events of the novel just from Teresa's emotional perspective. Thus, with the 'blurb',[36] we agree that '[y]ou are inexorably drawn into Teresa's world', such that 'one is left wondering where Teresa is today': and, in summary, are struck by 'the author's ability . . . to plumb the recesses of a character's psyche'. But none of these moves is explained in terms of *taking* her emotional perspective, as opposed to merely understanding it. (So there need be no 'matching' in this case.)

In both of these discussions (as elsewhere), I am being scrupulously honest: your brother put the question about themes and ideas within the novel with a slightly different emphasis or tone—so that I answered, in effect, a different question. But, at base, there is only one reading of the novel (mine): I respond differently to each of you, but that does not leave me with two readings of the novel. Or, more exactly, it certainly *need* not. Hence my first, 'empathetic' reading cannot amount to certain brain states of mine at the time I offer it. For, at that time, I might have said either of these things—so the states of my brain when reading the novel sustain (at least) two 'readings' of it. Yet, one might say, there is but one brain state at issue (mine). Thus there can be no simple equation of brain state to 'reading' nor vice versa. Then, whatever we decide to say about interpersonal empathy—which will no doubt reflect our predilections in the philosophy of mind more generally—we should recognize the need to say something different here, faced with a case of artistic judgment.

Thus, one crucial factor, mentioned previously, is that this case deals with objects of literary *art*, not with (mere) fictions. That, in turn, sets limits on the resources required to make sense of the work. As Roger Scruton (2000: 21) recognizes, from the perspective of a *critical reading*:

[i]n the nature of things, the arguments of a critic are only addressed to those who have sufficient reverence for literature; for only they will see the point of detailed study and moral investigation.

As such, we must treat the work of literature differently from other fiction, granting it value of a different *kind* (see McFee (2005): 379). So, again, that makes it less likely that we can import 'insight' from empathy in the interpersonal case to the empathetic reading of literature.[37]

12.6 Conclusion

I have followed a path from my own experiences of what might seem a hyper-empathetic reading by considering whether a comparison with interpersonal empathy is likely to be revealing in respect of the empathetic reading of fictions: in particular,

---

[36] These quotations all come from the publicity materials to the 2005 Blume edition.
[37] Of course, this is not yet to explain *empathy* in this context, with Aurel Kolnai (1978: 209), as 'arbitrary subjective fantasy'!

how badly it reflects the *achievement* character of empathy. And, concluding that (at least) empathetic reading of fictions was not likely to be the norm, I have shown how some of the material from psychology that might seem to support such a reading cannot offer the promised help. Further, I have suggested that the peculiarities of the *artistic* case (here, the novel) require an account all of its own, if at all. To end, I will mention another example: perhaps it shows us something useful about a more humanistic picture of empathy in art appreciation.

At the end of the film *Cast Away* (2000), the Tom Hanks character looks wistfully after the young woman whose package he had saved during his time on the island, and finally delivered. There are no words: he has already considered the other three dusty roads away from the junction. He smiles slightly. Seen one way, we do not know what he is going to do; there is no explicit clue. Perhaps, in the minutes after the screen goes dark, he will look elsewhere, and drive off in one of the other directions. But if, throughout his tribulations, we have been identifying to some degree with the character Hanks plays, we know he will follow her. And a part of our understanding lies in our sharing both his sense of having nowhere to go and his seeing her as offering some possibilities for a life. Is our understanding of that character *empathetic*? I do not know. But it does not seem to depend on any precise 'matching' of our psychological states—at best, I understand his state, and that understanding is evocative. There is a kind of identification, but it is certainly not the kind from which I began, in respect of *The Leopard*. Perhaps this is the only moment in the film in which we feel this degree of identification. But that is a strength of that moment, and of the film. And perhaps this is the moment we should seek to understand.

PART III

Empathy and Morality

13

Is Empathy Necessary for Morality?

Jesse J. Prinz

13.1 Introduction

It is widely believed that empathy is a good thing, from a moral point of view. It is something we should cultivate because it makes us better people. Perhaps that's true. But it is also sometimes suggested that empathy is somehow *necessary* for morality. That is the hypothesis I want to interrogate and challenge. Not only is there little evidence for the claim that empathy is necessary, there is also reason to think empathy can interfere with the ends of morality. A capacity for empathy might make us better people, but placing empathy at the center of our moral lives may be ill-advised. That is not to say that morality shouldn't centrally involve emotions. I think emotions are essential for moral judgment and moral motivation (Prinz (2007)). It's just that empathetic emotions are not ideally suited for these jobs.

Before embarking on this campaign against empathy, I want to say a little more about the target of the attack. What is empathy? And what would it mean to say empathy is necessary for morality? With respect to the first question, much has been written. Theories of empathy abound. Batson et al. (1995: 1042) define empathy 'as an other-oriented emotional response congruent with the perceived welfare of another person.' This is not the definition I will be using. Batson's construct might be better characterized as 'concern,' because of its focus on another person's welfare. Indeed, in much of his research he talks about 'empathetic concern.' Notice that this construct seems to be a combination of two separable things. Being concerned for someone is worrying about their welfare, which is something one can do even if one doesn't feel what it would be like to be in their place. One can have concern for a plant, for example, and an insect, or even an artifact, like a beautiful building that has fallen into disrepair. Empathy seems to connote a kind of feeling that has to be at least possible for the object of empathy. If so, 'empathetic concern' combines two different things—a kind of feeling-for an object and a feeling-on-behalf-of an object. Much of the empirical literature, including the superb research that Batson has done, fails to isolate these components, and, as a result, some of the existing studies are confounded. They purport to show the value of empathy, but may really show the value of concern. My focus below will be on empathy, and I leave it as an open possibility that concern is highly important, if not necessary, for morality. Indeed, concern often seems to involve an element or kind of moral anger, which I will argue is very important to morality.

It is also important to distinguish empathy from sympathy. Suppose I feel outraged for someone who has been brainwashed into thinking she should follow a cult leader who is urging mass suicide. That would not necessarily qualify as empathy. As Darwall (1998: 261) points out, sympathy is a third-person emotional response, whereas empathy involves putting oneself in another person's shoes. But Darwall's definition is also somewhat problematic. He says, 'Empathy consists in feeling what one imagines he feels, or perhaps should feel (fear, say), or in some imagined copy of these feelings, whether one comes thereby to be concerned... or not.' This definition has two features, which I would like to avoid. First, the appeal to imagination seems overly intellectual. Imagination sounds like a kind of mental act that requires effort on the part of the imaginer. As Darwall recognizes, empathy in its simplest form is just emotional contagion: catching the emotion that another person feels (Hatfield et al. (1994); Hoffman (2000)). It seems inflated to call contagion an imaginative act. Also, I want to resist Darwall's application of 'empathy' to cases where one has a feeling that someone *should* feel, but does not feel. The problem is that this tends to blur the distinction between empathy and sympathy. Suppose I encounter a member of a cult who is delighted by the cult leader's nefarious plans. The cult member *should* be afraid, but is not. If I feel fear on the cult member's behalf, that is not putting myself in the cult member's shoes. As I will use the term, empathy requires a kind of emotional mimicry.

I do not wish to imply that empathy is always an automatic process, in the way that emotional contagion is. Sometimes imagination is required, and sometimes we experience emotions that we think someone *would* be experiencing, even if we have not seen direct evidence that the emotion is, in fact, being experienced. For example, one might feel empathetic hope for a marathon runner who is a few steps behind the runner in first place, or anxiety for the first-place runner, and the second-place runner catches up. We can experience these feelings even if the runners' facial expressions reveal little more than muscular contortions associated with concentration and physical exertion. A situation can reveal a feeling. The core idea, as I will use the term, is that empathy is a kind of vicarious emotion: it's feeling what one takes another person to be feeling. And the 'taking' here can be a matter of automatic contagion or the result of a complicated exercise of the imagination.

I don't think there is anything anachronistic about this notion of empathy. I think it has a long tradition in moral philosophy, even though the term 'empathy' is only 100 years old. The British moralists, including David Hume and Adam Smith, used 'sympathy' in a way that is similar to the way I want to use 'empathy.' Here is Smith (1759/2002: II.i): 'Whatever is the passion which arises from any object in the person principally concerned, an analogous emotion springs up, at the thought of his situation, in the breast of every attentive spectator.' My question, in the pages that follow, is whether empathy so-defined is necessary for morality. I should note again, in advance, that the empirical literature does not always distinguish between the constructs I have been discussing, but I do think that all the studies I discuss below can, by inference at least, shed some light on empathy as defined here.

The suggestion that empathy is necessary for morality can be interpreted in at least three different ways. One might hold the view that empathy is necessary for making moral judgment. One might think empathy is necessary for moral development. And one might think empathy is necessary for motivating moral conduct. I think each of these conjectures is false. Empathy is not necessary for any of these things. We can have moral systems without empathy. Of course, it doesn't follow directly that empathy should be eliminated from morality. One might think the modal question—Can there be morality without empathy?—and the related descriptive question—Do our moral responses depend on empathy?—are uninteresting. One might even think that the answers to these questions are obviously negative and don't need to be argued for. The interesting question, one might think, is whether empathy *should* play an integral role in morality. In the final part of this paper, I will offer a skeptical response to this question, and I will draw on the lessons of earlier parts in making this case. I will not try to prove that empathy is useless, or even that there is no aspect of morality for which empathy might not prove essential. Perhaps empathy is a moral virtue, and, thus, having empathy is necessary for being completely virtuous. My goal is rather to argue that empathy is not necessary for the capacities that make up basic moral competence: one can acquire moral values, make moral judgments, and act morally without empathy. Put this way, my thesis may look rather modest, but I think it's actually quite surprising. I think empathy looks on initial reflection like an integral part of morality. In seeing why it isn't, we will also begin to see why it shouldn't be.

13.2 Is Empathy Necessary for Moral Judgment?

Let's begin with the conjecture that empathy is necessary for making moral judgments. For simplicity, let's restrict the account of judgments that are expressed with the term 'good' and 'bad.' For example, one might judge that charity is good, or that wife-beating is bad. According to the view under consideration, these judgments depend on empathetic responses: we empathize with the positive feelings experienced by the recipients of charity and with the negative feelings of those who fall prey to domestic violence. It is these empathetic responses that allow one to see these actions as good and bad respectively. Without empathy, we could mouth the words that 'charity is good' and 'abuse is bad,' but we wouldn't speak with true understanding; we wouldn't be grasping the judgments that such sentences have the function of expressing.

A view like this can be attributed to David Hume. He writes,

We partake of [victims of injustice's] uneasiness by sympathy; and as every thing, which gives uneasiness in human actions, upon the general survey, is called Vice, and whatever produces satisfaction, in the same manner, is denominated Virtue . . . [S]ympathy with public interest is the source of the moral approbation, which attends that virtue. (Hume (1739/1978): II.ii)

As I read him, Hume's theory of moral judgment can be broken down into the following claims: a virtuous action is one that intentionally brings about pleasure and a vicious action is one that intentionally brings about pain; when we contemplate the pleasure or pain of another person, we feel empathy (what Hume calls 'sympathy'); our empathetic response to the recipients of virtuous and vicious actions arouses in us feelings of approbation and disapprobation, respectively; these feelings of approbation and disapprobation constitute our judgments that something is morally good or bad. On this interpretation, empathy is an essential precursor to moral judgment. If we had no empathy, the pain brought about by a vicious action would leave us cold, and no disapprobation would follow. Thus empathy, while not a component of moral judgment, is a precondition.

Whether or not this is an accurate reading of Hume, the account has an initial ring of plausibility. It is plausible that empathy plays an epistemological role, leading us to have negative regard for those actions that harm people and positive regard for those actions that help. If moral judgment consists in a certain kind of negative or positive regard, empathy looks like it might be fundamental to moral cognition. But close analysis severs this link.

First, consider cases where deontological considerations overrule utilitarian principles. For example, one might judge that it is bad to kill an innocent person even if his vital organs could be used to save five others who desperately need transplants. Here, arguably, we feel cumulatively more empathy for the five people in need than for the one healthy person, but our moral judgment does not track that empathetic response. Second, consider the moral judgments one might issue from behind a Rawlsian veil of ignorance; you might decide it's good to distribute resources to the needy because *you* might be needy. Here there is no empathy for the needy, but rather concern for the self. Third, while on the topic of the self, consider cases in which you yourself are the victim of a moral transgression. You judge that you've been wronged, but you don't thereby empathize with yourself, whatever that would mean. Fourth, consider cases in which there is no salient victim. One can judge that it would be wrong to evade taxes or steal from a department store, for instance, without dwelling first on the suffering of those who would be harmed. Fifth, there are victimless transgressions, such as necrophilia, consensual sibling incest, destruction of (unpopulated) places in the environment, or desecration of a grave of someone who has no surviving relative. Empathy makes no sense in these cases. As a descriptive claim it seems wrong to suppose that empathy is a precondition for moral judgment.

Moreover, there is reason to believe that other emotions are sufficient for moral judgment even when empathy is absent. Recall the Humean model on which empathy leads to disapprobation. A simpler alternative would say that disapprobation can arise directly upon consideration of various kinds of action. To see this, it's helpful to have a firmer idea of what disapprobation is. Elsewhere, I offer the following analysis (Prinz (2007): ch. 2; drawing on Rozin et al. (1999)). Disapprobation, I claim, is a sentiment, rather than an emotion. Sentiments are dispositions to have emotions. Disapprobation is a disposition to have emotions of blame towards self and others. If I have a sentiment of disapprobation towards stealing, I am disposed to have bad feelings towards myself if I steal and bad feelings towards you if you steal. The feelings depend on the kind of action under consideration. Stealing is a crime against a person, and when such actions are performed by others, they elicit anger, and when performed by the self, they elicit guilt. In contrast there are crimes against nature: such as necrophilia, incest, or bestiality. In these cases, the dominant emotional response is disgust, when the action is performed by another, and shame if we perform or even consider performing such an action ourselves. In addition, there are crimes against community, such as the violation of public trust, which tend to elicit contempt or some kind of self-loathing. On any given occasion, when I judge that something is wrong, that judgment token derives from a sentiment, and consists in the appropriate emotional response. If I judge that I was wrong to eat the last cookie, my judgment consists in a feeling of guilt about my action. That guilt is a manifestation of my disapprobation of last-cookie-eating, or, more likely, an indirect manifestation of a more generalized disapprobation of greed.

With this picture in hand, we can formulate the alternative to the empathy-based theory of moral judgment as follows. A (negative) moral judgment arises when an action elicits an emotional response in virtue of the fact that the judger has a sentiment of disapprobation towards actions of that kind. (Positive moral judgments may sometimes involve sentiments of approbation, which may dispose us to positive feelings, such as gratitude, pride in good conduct, or admiration). So the question at hand is, is empathy needed for disapprobation if this story is right? For example, do I need to empathize with anyone in order to feel guilty about taking the last cookie? It seems plausible that I do not. If I construe my action as greedy, I may immediately feel a pang of guilt. It might be objected that empathy is needed to construe an action as greedy, but I find that implausible. I can recognize an action as greedy without putting myself in someone else's shoes. It's cognitively cumbersome to think through the simulation of another person every time I classify some behavior as greedy (or thieving, or murderous, or incestuous, or nepotistic, or indecent, and so on, for everything I am apt to condemn as morally bad). Morally significant actions can be recognized without empathy, even if those actions are ones that involve harm. We need not reflect on the harm to see that the action is bad. Perhaps you are delighted that I ate the last cookie. I recognize that, empathetically, and I still feel guilty; I still think I should have offered the cookie to you.

If this is right, then empathy is not a necessary precursor to moral judgment. I emphasize this point, because it is sometimes presumed that sentimentalist theories of moral judgment should be empathy-based theories (e.g., Slote (2005)). The tradition that includes David Hume and Adam Smith has placed empathy in a central place. It might even be presumed that empathy is the fundamental affective response involved in moral judgment. That is a mistake. The emotions just mentioned have been demonstrated to play a major part in morality. One can advance a sentimentalist theory based on such emotions as anger and guilt, while giving only marginal import to empathy. Empathy may help us come to the conclusion that a particular action is wrong on a particular occasion, but it hardly seems necessary for that purpose.

13.3 Is Empathy Necessary for Moral Development?

The Humean theory of moral judgment that I've just been discussing is a synchronic theory: it's a theory of what moral judgments are like when we make them here and now. I argued that the theory is false; we often make moral judgments in the absence of empathetic responses. But this conclusion is consistent with the possibility that empathy plays a diachronic role: emotions may be necessary for the development of the capacity to make moral judgments in the first place.

The idea that empathy plays a role in moral development has been pursued by some developmental psychologists. The emergence of empathy has been extensively investigated, and some developmentalists speculate that empathy plays an essential role in developing a sense of morality (Hoffman (2000)). Conceptually, the idea has much appeal. Morality centrally regards the regulation of behavior towards others, and one can acquire a concern for others' well-being by empathizing with them. If a child were not empathetic, she could not fully appreciate how her actions affected others, and, without that, she might not come to appreciate when her actions were wrong.

It's somewhat difficult to find evidence for developmental hypotheses of this kind. Most studies of normally developing children measure relationships between empathy and morally relevant *behaviors* such as aggression and helping behaviors (Eisenberg et al. (2006b)). But the issue I want to address is whether empathy gives rise to the capacity to make moral *judgments*. If one can acquire this capacity without empathy, then empathy is not required for acquiring a moral sense. Studies do show that children engage in empathetic reasoning when making moral judgments (Eisenberg-Berg (1979)), but they do not show that empathy is essential to moral judgment. Even a high positive correlation between empathy and healthy moral judgments would not speak directly to the necessity thesis. Such correlations would not show that, without empathy, a capacity for moral judgment would not be acquired.

To assess the necessity thesis, researchers must consider pathological populations. They must identify people who lack empathy and see whether they lack moral competence as a result. Blair (1995) takes on precisely this challenge. His study investigates morality in psychopaths. Lack of empathy is a diagnostic criterion for psychopathy (Hare (1991)), and Blair shows that psychopaths also suffer from a profound deficit in moral competence. In particular, they do not draw a distinction between moral rules (e.g. don't hit people) and conventional rules (e.g. rules about what clothing to wear in school). Blair concludes that psychopaths' failure to draw this distinction indicates that they do not comprehend the essence of moral rules. When they say that something is 'morally wrong,' they don't really understand what these words mean. Blair speculates that this failure is a direct result of the empathy deficit. His developmental model goes roughly like this: normally developing children have an innate tendency to empathize with observed distress. So, if one child causes another child to cry, the offending child will catch the observed emotion and feel badly. This bad feeling serves as an inhibition signal that causes her to cease the actions that are causing the distress and to associate bad feelings with that kind of action in the future. Blair conceptualizes this as a violence inhibition mechanism, akin to what we observe in non-human animals. If two dogs are fighting, the stronger will stop aggressing when the weaker bears its throat. Blair thinks that violence inhibition is mediated by empathetic distress, and, in humans, distress becomes associated with moral rules, but not conventional rules, because conventional violations do not cause distress. Normally developing children can distinguish moral and conventional rules because the former are emotionally grounded. Absent emotional grounding, the distinction would not be drawn. Absent empathy, moral rules would never acquire emotional grounding. Thus, Blair concludes, empathy is necessary for moral development. He does not, however, assume that empathy arises whenever moral judgments are made in adulthood. Once negative emotions have been associated with an action type, one can recognize its wrongness without contemplating any one in distress.

Blair's account can be challenged in various ways. First, it is not clear that there is a violence inhibition mechanism. The status of such a mechanism is controversial in ethology and has not been established in human beings. Second, many of the most important moral rules we learn involve non-violent behaviors, such as stealing or sexual impropriety. One of the diagnostic criteria for psychopathy is 'criminal versatility,' which suggests that psychopathy does not stem from a specific deficit in violence inhibition, as Blair's model suggests. Third, there is evidence that normally developing children draw the moral/conventional distinction well before they associate empathy with morality. Smetana and Braeges (1990) show sensitivity to the distinction before the third birthday, and Eisenberg-Berg (1979) shows that empathy does not enter actively into moral reasoning until high school. Fourth, there are other explanations of why psychopaths have deficits in both empathy and moral competence: these two deficits may arise from a third cause. In particular, psychopaths suffer from a more general deficit in moral emotions. 'Shallow Affect' is one of the diagnostic criteria on psychopathy. Here's how Cleckley (1976: 364) puts it:

Vexation, spite, quick and labile flashes of quasi-affection, peevish resentment, shallow moods of self-pity, puerile attitudes of vanity, and absurd and showy poses of indignation are all within his emotional scale and are freely sounded as the circumstances of life play upon him. But mature, wholehearted anger, true or consistent indignation, honest, solid grief, sustaining pride, deep joy, and genuine despair are reactions not likely to be found within this scale.

Psychopaths are also poor at recognizing emotions, especially fear and sadness—and recognition deficits are known to be correlated with deficits in emotional experience

(Blair et al. (2002)). These affective abnormalities could explain both the low levels of empathy in psychopaths and the lack of moral competence. Empathy requires a disposition to experience emotions appropriate for another person, and a person with shallow affect and poor emotional recognition will have a diminished capacity for empathy as a result. The emotion deficit will also make an individual comparatively insensitive to common methods of moral education: they will be relatively indifferent to punishment, because they have low levels of fear, and they will be unmoved by love withdrawal, because they have low levels of sadness. They will also have a diminished capacity for emotions like guilt, which seem to have sadness as a component (Prinz (2004)), and moral anger. So psychopaths will lack emotions that facilitate moral education as well as the emotions that constitute moral judgments on the model that I outlined in the previous section. Therefore, the deficit in moral competence can be explained without appeal to the empathy deficit.

Given the availability of this alternative explanation, Blair's hypothesis that empathy is necessary for moral development is in need of further support. And given the fact the empathy enters into moral discourse fairly late in development, the alternative explanation is to be preferred. Young children are empathetic, but there is little evidence linking their empathetic responses to their capacity to make moral judgments. Let me emphasize that I don't take the foregoing arguments to refute the hypothesis that empathy is essential for moral development. It is always possible that a child without empathy would never care enough about morality to acquire sensitivity to moral rules. I have tried to suggest that Blair fails to establish such a conclusion, but I welcome other efforts to do so. My main reason for skepticism is that other emotional responses seem to be both necessary and sufficient for moral judgment, and, if I am right about that, it is hard to see why empathy would be needed to get morality off the ground. At best, empathetic responses in young children have been linked to moral behavior. But, even here, the links are quite limited, as we will now see.

13.4 Is Empathy Necessary for Moral Conduct?

So far I have been arguing that empathy is not necessary for making moral judgments, either synchronically or diachronically. Still it might be conjectured that empathy is necessary in another way: it might be necessary for moral motivation. Let's suppose someone arrives at the judgment that it would be good to give to charity. It might be possible to make such a judgment without feeling motivated to act on it. Perhaps empathy with the recipients of charity is what converts moral judgment into moral conduct. Or suppose someone comes to think it's bad to abuse his spouse. Without empathy for her, he might continue to be abusive. It seems plausible, on the face of it, that empathy is the key to converting judgment into action.

There are good reasons to resist this picture. First of all, on the account I sketched above, moral judgments have an emotional basis. Token moral judgments contain emotions such as anger, disgust, guilt, and shame. Emotions are motivating states, and each of these moral emotions has a behavioral profile. Anger promotes aggression, disgust promotes withdrawal, guilt promotes reparation, and shame promotes self-concealment. More generally, these emotions are negatively valenced, and negative emotions are things we work to avoid (Prinz (2004)). If we anticipate that an action will make us feel guilty, we will be thereby inclined to avoid that action. The guilt-prone would-be wife beater might learn to overcome his abusive rages. It follows from this that moral judgments, which contain emotions, are intrinsically motivating states. A person who judges that stealing is wrong, for example, will be motivated to resist the urge to steal, even when it would be easy and lucrative. Such a person will also be motivated to prevent others from stealing; for example, those who think stealing is wrong might report a shoplifter to the store clerk even though this intervention carries some risk and no direct reward. And this is just half the story. I have been focusing on disapprobation. There may also be a suite of positive emotions associated with moral approbation. Good behavior by others elicits admiration and gratitude, as remarked above. And the person who engages in good behavior feels pride or gratification. Anticipating these good feelings can lead to good actions. On this view, moral judgments have plenty of motivational impact in the absence of empathy.

Moreover, the emotions involved in approbation and disapprobation may have greater motivational force than the emotions associated with empathy. That empathy leads to action is actually quite weak. Let's begin by considering research on empathy in children. In an extensive meta-analysis, Underwood and Moore (1982) show that there is a positive correlation between emotion *attribution* and pro-social behavior in children, but no correlation between *empathy* and pro-social behavior. Indeed, a number of the studies show negative correlations between empathy and altruism. Critics have worried that the studies contained in this meta-analysis are flawed because they measure empathy by self-report (though measures include non-verbal self-report, such as asking children to point out a facial expression corresponding to how they feel). In lieu of self-report, Eisenberg et al. (1989) used observers' reports and found that pro-social behavior is positively correlated with 'concerned attention' in children. A child who wrinkles her brow when watching someone in need is more likely to help. But no correlation was found for 'shared emotion.' Empathy essentially involves sharing emotions, so this result suggests that empathy does not contribute to pro-social behavior in children. Attention and concern matter, but empathy does not.

The situation is a little less bleak when it comes to adults. There are modest correlations in adults between pro-social behavior and shared sadness (Eisenberg et al. (1989)). Adults who looked sad while watching a film about a woman whose children had been in a car wreck were slightly more likely to offer to help that woman with yard work when, later in the experiment, they read a letter from her requesting help. But this study does not establish that empathy, in general, relates to altruism, because it is restricted to sadness. And curiously, there is no correlation between expressions of sadness while reading the letter, and the decision to help, which is made just afterwards. So, empathetic sadness is not the immediate cause of helpfulness.

Moreover, many people who showed no shared emotions were helpful as well, so the study provides no evidence for the conclusion that empathy is necessary for moral conduct.

The Eisenberg et al. (1989) study is typical. A meta-analysis shows that empathy only weakly correlated with pro-social behavior (Neuberg, et al. (1997)). More strikingly, the correlation appears only when there is little cost. If someone has to do something as easy as crossing a street to help someone in need, they are not especially likely to, and those who are empathetic show no greater tendency to help in such circumstances than those who are not. Now it must be noted that most of the research summarized in this meta-analysis does not carefully distinguish between empathy, sympathy, and concern. One can't be sure that the studies in question are ones in which the participants actually experienced emotions akin to those of the people they were in a position to help. But I think the failure to find strong motivation associated with the various forms of fellow-feeling, provides evidence for thinking that empathy is not a great motivator. It's overwhelmingly likely that empathy is experienced by participants in many of the studies reviewed by Neuberg et al. Moreover, there are independent reasons for predicting that empathy should have limited motivational force. First, an emotion caught from another person is likely to be far weaker than an emotion that originates in oneself. Second, when we consider others in need, the emotions we are likely to catch are things such as sadness, misery, and distress. These emotions may not be great motivators. Misery might even promote social withdrawal. So there is little reason to think empathy, defined in terms of vicarious emotions, would do much to make us work on behalf of people in need.

The meager effects of empathy are greatly overshadowed by other emotions. Consider, for example, positive affect. Above, I suggested the feelings of approbation are positive and positive emotions may help to explain why people do good things. Empirical support for this hypothesis comes from the large literature on positive emotions and helping (Carlson et al. (1988)). For example, Isen & Levin (1972) induced positive affect by planting a dime in a neighborhood phone booth. They then watched to see whether the person who found the dime would help a passerby who dropped some papers. Among those who found the dime, 87.5% helped. Among those in the control condition, where there was no dime planted in the phone, only 4% helped. Other studies have not always shown such a large effect size, but they do tend to confirm that a small dose of happiness seems to promote considerable altruism. This is often true even when the altruism is costly. For example, Weyant (1978) found that people who are made to feel good by being given an easy test to solve are almost twice as likely, when compared to neutral controls, to volunteer for a charity that requires going door to door collecting donations. Happiness seems to make us work for people in need. This conclusion is embarrassing for those who think empathy is crucial for altruism because vicarious distress presumably has a negative correlation with positive happiness. It could be that vicarious distress reduces helpfulness by diminishing positive affect.

There is also evidence that the emotions associated with disapprobation are highly motivating. Consider anger. Lerner et al. (1998) showed subjects emotion-inducing film clips and then probed their attitudes towards punishment on unrelated vignettes. Subjects who watched anger-inducing films recommended harsher punishments than those in the control condition. Studies using economic games have shown that, when angry, people are even willing to pay significant costs to punish those who fail to cooperate (Fehr and Gächter, 2002). This contrasts strikingly with empathy, which does not motivate moral behavior when there are significant costs. Guilt is also a great motivator. In a study by Carlsmith and Gross (1969) subjects were asked to make some fund-raising phone calls for a charity organization after they administered shocks to an innocent person. These subjects made more than three times as many fund-raising calls as the subjects in a control condition where no shocks were administered.

These studies suggest that empathy is not a major player when it comes to moral motivation. Its contribution is negligible in children, modest in adults, and non-existent when costs are significant. Other emotions, including those associated with approbation and disapprobation appear to have much greater impact. Thus, the hypothesis that empathy is necessary for moral conduct—or even important—enjoys little support.

13.5 Should We Cultivate An Empathy-Based Morality?

At this point, we can draw an initial conclusion: empathy probably isn't necessary for morality in any of the senses that I have been considering. But that does not mean empathy plays no role in morality. Presumably it does. Presumably empathy can induce a moral judgment, factor into moral development, and facilitate moral motivation. It probably plays all these roles to some degree. I have tried to suggest that the degree may be limited. That is a descriptive claim. One might think that this claim is uninteresting from the perspective of ethical theory. The question that really matters is normative, not descriptive. Even if empathy does not play a central role in morality, perhaps it could. Should we, then, try to increase the role for empathy in morality? Should we cultivate moral systems that are based on empathy?

To address this question, I want to begin by reflecting on what an empathy-based moral system might look like. To keep this plausible, I will reflect on some actual moral systems that seem to place empathy in a position of prominence. So far, in this discussion I have talked about morality (or even 'our morality') as if it were just one thing. In reality, there are many different moralities—different systems of moral rules that have been internalized by different groups of people. These may vary in the degree to which they emphasize morality. Looking at empathetic moralities may help us address the normative question under consideration here. I will consider three examples. My goal is here not to show that empathy leads to social ills, but that it is highly compatible with such ills, and that should give us pause when reflecting on whether empathy is the key to a well functioning moral system.

Let's begin by looking at moral values in collectivist cultures. Collectivism can be defined as: 'a social pattern consisting of closely linked individuals who see themselves as parts of one or more collectives...; are primarily motivated by the norms of... those collectives [and] emphasize their connectedness to other members of those collectives' (Triandis (1995): 2). Collectivist cultures can be found in the Far East, South Asia, South America, the Middle East, and the Mediterranean. The cultures in these regions also differ from each other, but their members tend to share a similar tendency to prioritize group membership in their self-conceptions and values. Individualist cultures, like those found in the United States and Western Europe, are comprised by 'loosely linked individuals who view themselves as independent of collective [and] are primarily motivated by their own preferences, needs, rights, and the contract they have established with others' (Triandis (1995): 2). In short, collectivists tend to value group cohesion above all, and individualists value autonomy.

Collectivism, by its very nature, may place more emphasis on empathy than individualism. Consider child-rearing practices in Japan. Greenfield and Suzuki (1998) found that, in contrast to Americans, Japanese parents had more contact with their children, were more indulgent and calming, and introduced toys into play as opportunities for sharing, rather than, say, skill mastery. American parenting practices foster independence and probably decrease children's tendency to view each other empathetically, promoting interpersonal relationships that are more likely to be competitive than collaborative. If children view each other as competitors over toys, rather than sharing partners, they may be less likely to respond to each other empathetically. The emphasis on groups also shapes moral values in collectivist cultures. In many, strong emphasis is placed on respect for parents and family. The wrongdoings of the individual are seen as reflecting on the group in a way that suggests deep empathetic connections. Collectivists also differ from individualists when it comes to questions of distributive justice. Leung and Bond (1984) found that, unlike Americans, people in China prefer distributions that are equal as opposed to equitable, i.e. proportionate to individual achievement. This again may reflect a more empathetic and less adversarial orientation towards others. More direct evidence comes from a study by Tobin et al. (1989). They asked Japanese and American parents to list the most important things to teach children. 80% of Japanese respondents listed empathy as opposed to 39% of Americans. This presumably affects moral education and the resulting values. It's reasonable to speculate, then, that collectivist cultures have more empathetic moralities then individualist cultures.

Consider a second example that can be found within Western culture. One of the most salient moral divides in the West is between liberals and conservatives. These political orientations can be conceptualized as moral value systems, and the differences are quite pronounced. Lakoff (2002) tries to capture this by suggesting that liberals and conservatives both base their views about how to run a society on stereotypical ideals for how to run a household, but they draw on different stereotypes. For conservatives, the ideal is a household run by an authoritarian father, and for liberals it's a nurturing mother. This translates into the following moral frameworks. Conservatives value self-reliance and self-discipline; they emphasize the importance of punishment and reward; they strive to protect society from evil; and to uphold 'moral order.' Liberals, in contrast, want to help the helpless; protect the vulnerable; and promote fulfillment. If someone transgresses a norm, it is not construed as evil, but rather as the result of bad influences, or confusion, or perhaps even a botched attempt at self-expression. The wrongdoer should be helped or reformed. For conservatives, there is little tolerance for transgression; three strikes and you're out. Lakoff captures the liberal value system by saying that for liberals, morality is empathy. The construct of empathy is essential. Liberals try to empathize with both victims and transgressors and, instead of dividing the world into good and evil, they try to put themselves in the shoes of people on both sides of every divide. In foreign policy, conservatives see members of countries that are hostile to their homeland as enemies, where as liberals see them as freedom fighters trying to protect themselves against aggression. In domestic policy, liberals support social welfare programs to help people in need. Conservatives tend to be less empathetic, and they think the needy should pull themselves together and solve their own problems rather than be looking for handouts.

As a final example, consider gender differences in morality. Though highly controversial, there is evidence that men and women have different moral orientations that derive from the different roles they play and experiences they have in gender- stratified societies. Gilligan (1982) famously argued that women tend to have an ethics based on care, rather than rigid principles. The empirical case for Gilligan's thesis has been mixed, especially when using traditional study methods, which measure gender differences in reasoning style. Walker (1984) found support for Gilligan in only 8 out of 108 Kohlberg-styles studies. Jaffee and Hyde (2000) found more consistent support for Gilligan in their more recent meta-analysis, but the overall contribution of gender that they report is relatively small. One reason for these modest results may be that traditional tests exhibit a male gender bias, insofar as they ask people to argue for their moral decisions rather than probing the underlying feelings. When feelings are examined, differences emerge. First of all, there is strong evidence that women are more prone to empathy than men (Eisenberg and Lennon (1983)). And this seems to have significant implications for morality. Gibbs et al. (1984) found that women made twice as many appeals to empathy in moral justification (53% vs 27%). Singer et al. (2006) found evidence for this in the brain: when men watched a wrongdoer getting shocked, they showed activity in reward centers of the brains (the nucleus accumbens), whereas women showed no reward activity and significant activation in pain centers, suggesting an empathetic pain response. Correspondingly, women were less than half as likely to desire revenge. Finally, in studies of trolley dilemmas, Mikhail (2002) found women twice as likely to say it is impermissible to sacrifice one life in order to save five people in harm's way (by switching a runaway trolley onto an alternate track).

These differences are quite dramatic, and, in each case, they suggest a moral orientation that is more empathetic. Before moving on, I must add a cautionary note against essentialism. I am not suggesting that gender differences have a biological basis. There is evidence that parents socialize their female children to be more empathetic. Parents use emotion words twice as frequently when talking to their daughters (Adams et al. (1995)), and the observed differences seem to correlate better with gender roles than with biological sex (Karniol et al. (1998)). The gender differences in empathy also seem to be motivational in nature, and disappear under some testing conditions (Klein and Hodges (2001)). There are a number of social factors that might promote an empathy-based orientation in women. First, women have lower status than men in male dominant societies, and sensitivity to the emotions of others may be a good coping strategy under such circumstances. Second, because women are often subordinate to men, they may develop more concern for the underdog because they can relate. Third, because women play a disproportionate role in childcare, they may develop more nurturance skills. And finally, lack of employment opportunities may lead to higher degrees of collectivism: individualism is fuelled by competitive marketplaces. The result of these factors seems to be that women are more skilled than men at taking the perspective of others, and this informs women's moral outlook.

These examples help us see how moral systems can vary in the degree to which they emphasize empathy. They also help us see why a more empathetic approach might seem desirable. Given the sociology of academia, most readers of this chapter are probably disposed to think that collectivism, liberalism, and feminism are good things. If collectivist, liberal, and feminist approaches to morality all emphasize empathy, that's an indication that empathy might be something we should actively promote. I think that would be a hasty conclusion.

To see this, it is important to notice that collectivism, liberalism, and empathy-based feminist ethics all have dark sides. Collectivism has been used as a tool to promote dangerous kinds of group thinking and intolerance. In Japan, it is not uncommon for groups of school kids to beat up peers who are perceived as different. Bullying (or *Ijime*) is widespread and often targets those who do not fit in. More disturbingly, Pol Pot exploited collectivist thinking when he got the Khmer Rouge to kill dissenters and intellectuals. Pol Pot made explicit use of collectivist rhetoric and collectivist ideology helped legitimate his campaigns (see e.g. Valentino (1994): 135f.). Collectivist thinking has also been implicated in suicide bombers. Atran (2003) argues that suicide bombers are bonding by a 'fictive' sense of kinship, which allows them to lay down their lives for a group. Arguably, empathy plays a role in establishing the bonds that allow for such collective behaviors.

Liberalism may have a dark side too. The politics of empathy tends to treat the victims of inequality without targeting root causes. Social welfare does ease the suffering of the poor, but it does not undo the cycles of intergenerational poverty. Poverty is often inherited and social stratification remains in a place across generations. The politics of empathy is also subject to empathetic biases (on which more below); policy makers empathize more with some people than with others. Social welfare programs were introduced to help white mothers, not people of color, though now people of color are more likely to be on welfare (relative to population size) and more likely to stay on welfare intergenerationally because the existence of such programs promotes a kind of complacency that leads liberal attention away from the challenging problems associated with bias in labor markets and the social capital deficits that result from ghettoization. Ironically, the stigmatization makes the recipients of welfare less easy to empathize with and thus more likely to be blamed for economic hardships. The relevant question here is what kinds of emotional responses would help promote a campaign against the root causes of economic injustice, rather than merely offering the (very helpful) support to its victims? The answer probably isn't empathy, but rather indignation.

A similar point pertains to any brand of feminist ethics that promotes empathy as the central moral construct. The fact that women are more empathetic than men is, I suggested, a consequence of social roles that emerge under conditions of male dominance. This raises an urgent question: is the empathetic orientation in women's morality a useful tool for liberation or does it rather serve to sustain the inequality from which it springs? There are reasons to suspect that the latter might be true to some extent. Liberation, it seems, requires outrage: total intolerance to oppression and a correspondingly aggressive pursuit of change. If 'aggression' is treated as a bad (and phallocentric) word, and replaced by a moral stance that is predominantly empathetic, inaction may result. If the emotional response to gender inequality is to feel empathic sadness for those who are adversely affected, the resulting interventions may be limited because sadness tends to reduce motivation, rather than increasing it. If, in contrast, critics of inequality get angry or 'uppity' (as the anger of the oppressed is called), more radical change may be actively sought. A feminist morality bent on liberation should not be an empathy-based morality if that label is meant to describe a morality that makes empathy into the primary emotional resource. An outrage-based morality might be more effective.

The point of these remarks has not been to criticize empathy so much as bring out some limitations. When we look for moral systems that have placed greater emphasis on empathy, we can see that empathy is a double-edged sword: it can promote compliance and complacency. Of course, empathy can also promote moral concern, and that, one might think, is a good thing. But there are some more general problems with empathy that should raise doubts about its role as a central moral emotion. Many of these problems also apply to sympathy and to what Batson calls 'empathetic concern.' Indeed, some of the studies I will mention now were done with one of these other constructs in mind, though I think they apply to empathy as well. What I offer here is a laundry list of worries about empathy, some of which I have already mentioned. I invite the reader to reflect on whether these worries threaten all species of fellow-feeling.

First, as we have seen, empathy is not very motivating. So even if empathy elevates the level of concern, it doesn't do so in a way that guarantees action on behalf of those in need. Vicarious anger also constitutes a species of concern, and it may be a better motivator.

Second, empathy may lead to preferential treatment. Batson et al. (1995) presented subjects with a vignette about a woman, Sheri, awaiting medical treatment, and then asked them if they wanted to move Sheri to the top of the waitlist, above others who were more needy. In the control condition, the majority declined to move her up the list, but in a condition where they were encouraged to empathize with Sheri, they overwhelmingly elected to move her up at the expense of those in greater need.

Third, empathy may be subject to unfortunate biases including cuteness effects. Batson et al. (2005) found that college students were more likely to feel empathetic concern for children, dogs, and puppies than their own peers. Batson's notion of empathetic concern is not equivalent to empathy, as I am defining it, because it does not require feeling what the object of empathy should feel, but I think cuteness effects would also arise for empathy. For example, I'd wager that we would feel more vicarious sadness for a dying mouse than a rat, and more vicarious fear for a frog crossing the highway than a lizard. It has also been found that empathetic accuracy—which includes the ability to identify someone else's emotions, and, thus, perhaps, to mirror them—increases when the target is viewed as attractive (Ickes et al. (1990)).

Fourth, empathy can be easily manipulated. Tsoudis (2002) found that in mock trials, a jury's recommendation for sentencing could be influenced by whether or not victims and defendants expressed emotions. When sadness was expressed, empathy went up, ingratiating the jury to the one who expressed the sadness. Sad victims evoked harsher sentences, and sad defendants got lighter sentences.

Fifth, empathy can be highly selective. Think about the experience of watching a boxing match. You might feel great empathy when the boxer you are rooting for takes a blow, but great delight when he delivers an equally punishing blow to his opponent. In both cases, you are watching the same violent act, but the allocation of empathy can vary dramatically as a function of morally arbitrary concerns about who will win.

Sixth, empathy is prone to in-group biases. We have more empathy for those we see as like us, and that empathy is also more efficacious. Brown et al. (2006) found that when viewing pictures of faces, people show more empathetic responses, as measured by physiology and self-report, for members of the same ethnic group. Stürmer et al. (2005) found that empathy leads to helping only in cases when the person in need is a member of the in-group. In one of their studies, participants learn about someone who may have contracted hepatitis and their willingness to offer support, such as talking on the phone, depended on both empathy and whether the person had the same sexual orientation as the participant. This strong in-group bias doesn't show up in every study, but even if only occasional, it is something that defenders of empathy should worry about.

Seventh, empathy is subject to proximity effects. There was an outpouring of support for the Katrina hurricane victims in the United States in 2005, and passionate expressions of empathy for the victims is still frequently expressed in public discourse in the United States. The death toll was 1,836. A year later, an earthquake in Java killed 5,782 people and there was little news coverage in comparison. I would venture to guess that few Americans remember the incident. Nor was there much discussion of the Indian Ocean Tsunami a year before Katrina. People recall that event, but discuss it with less pathos than Katrina, despite the fact that the death toll was 315,000. It might be suggested that Katrina continues to command our attention because the bungled relief efforts draw attention to the nation's ongoing problems with racial prejudice, and, to that extent, the disaster remains relevant after the fact. But American prejudice can also be implicated in our failure to prevent the attempted genocide in Rwanda, in which at least 800,000 Tutsis were killed. That's more that 435 times the death toll in Katrina, but public discussion of the events is rare. The best explanation is that empathy increases for those who are nearby, culturally and geographically.

Eighth, empathy is subject to salience effects. Natural disasters and wars are salient, newsworthy events. This happens during temporally circumscribed periods in localized areas, and can be characterized in narrative terms (preconditions, the catastrophe, the aftermath). Other causes of mass death are less salient, because they are too constant and diffuse to be news items. This is the case with hunger and disease. To put some depressing numbers on the problem consider the following: malaria is estimated to kill between 1.5 and 4 million people a year; tuberculosis kills 2 million; and AIDS kills 2.8 million. Hunger is the biggest killer of all: 9 million die each year for lack of food. That means that every single day, there are 24 Katrinas. 10.5 times the number of people who died in Katrina die each day from preventable diseases, and 13.5 times as many people die from malnutrition. These deaths are not salient, so they induce little empathy.

In sum, empathy has serious shortcomings. It is not especially motivating, and it is so vulnerable to bias and selectivity that it fails to provide a broad umbrella of moral concern. A morality based on empathy would lead to preferential treatment and grotesque crimes of omission. I don't mean to imply that such problems arise for empathy alone. Perhaps moral indignation is greatest when we are personally involved. But there is an important difference on this score between indignation and empathy. Indignation can be directed towards types of conduct, whereas empathy is focused on individual persons. In cases of mass murder, empathy may be hard because victims are treated as statistics, but indignation is easy. In cases where the victims are members of an out-group (as when the U.S. bombs Iraq), empathy may not arise spontaneously, but outrage will. Indeed, I suspect that limitations on moral indignation may be most likely to arise *as a result of* empathetic interference. In cases where indignation is effected by proximity, for example, that may result from the fact that we don't empathize with victims; if we focused on the crime rather than the victims, such effects might diminish. The point might be summarized by saying that the limitations of empathy are intrinsic to it: empathy is biased towards the near and dear, whereas disapprobation is not. Therefore empathy is less well suited to serve as the central motivational component of morality.

13.6 Concluding Question: Can We Improve Empathy?

The limitations of empathy can be summarized by saying that empathy lacks motivational strength and tends to be highly selective. Defenders of empathy might argue that these limitations can be overcome. Perhaps we should try to improve empathy rather than giving it a marginal role. Perhaps an improved capacity for empathy would be worthy of exalting to a central position is morality.

An improved empathy would require two fundamental changes. First, we would need to do something to give empathy more force in promoting action: a mechanism of motivation. One possibility would be to train ourselves to combine empathy with the emotions that constitute the sentiments of approbation and disapprobation. For example, we might combine empathy with pride, so that when we help those in need we feel good about ourselves. We know that people will work to attain positive feelings, and recent research suggests that pride has motivational force above and beyond the fact that it feels good, even when there is considerable cost (Williams and Desteno (2008)). Empathy can also be combined with various forms of disapprobation. For example, when we learn about people who have been victims of injustice, we could combine empathy with indignation. We know people will incur considerable costs when they are angry. If we got angry when we empathized with those who have been harmed, we might be more likely to work on their behalf. Second, we would need to overcome the selective nature of empathy by devising a way to make us empathize with a broader range of people: a mechanism for determining moral considerability. For example, we might adopt a Kantian approach to cultivate a cosmopolitan outlook that exposed proximity biases and made distant strangers seem more worthy of moral concern. Or we might try to adopt the position of an ideal observer, in the spirit of Adam Smith, when making moral judgments. Of course, it is difficult to adopt a cosmopolitan perspective, and even more difficult to be an ideal observer. Therefore, my own recommendation would actually be to make use of less demanding alternatives to these two. If we focus our moral judgments on *types of actions* (stealing, torture, rape, etc.) and make an effort *not* to reflect on the specific victims, we may be able to achieve a kind of impartiality that does not require the epistemic availability of a truly cosmopolitan outlook or a truly ideal position of observation. I cannot flesh out the idea here, but the basic idea is that we make a concerted effort to focus moral reflection on *what* has happened not on *whom* it has happened to, because the whom question invites bias.

In principle, empathy could be improved by combining it with (dis)approbation and some procedure for achieving impartiality. But once we have these other mechanisms in place, empathy might prove superfluous. If we can learn to see distant strangers as worthy of concern, and if we become outraged when their needs are unanswered and delighted when we help them, then we will be motivated to act on their behalf. Empathy drops out of the picture. And, on my own recommendation, *any* focus on the victim of a transgression should be avoided, because of potential bias. If I am right, the most reliable method of achieving impartiality actually involves bracketing off thoughts about victims, and, thus, empathy might actually be something we want to avoid.

In response, the proponent of empathy might say that we need to empathize with distant others in order to become outraged when they are harmed. But this suggestion is false and futile. It's false, because we can directly condition each other to be outraged at the thought of iniquity, genocide, and neglect. Like other emotions, anger can be learned directly. For example, anger can be conditioned through imitation. If we express outrage at injustice, our children will feel outrage at injustice. A focus on empathy, as a means to anger, would be futile because empathy is a response directed at individuals, and many of the most urgent moral events involve large numbers of people. We cannot empathize with a group, except by considering each member. The magnitude of some catastrophes is so large that it would be impossible to empathize with all the victims. And, if we could empathize with a large number, the agony of vicarious pain would cripple us into inaction. It is important to remember that death tolls are not just statistics—they involve real people—but empathizing with multitudes of victims is neither possible nor productive. What we really need is an intellectual recognition of our common humanity, combined with a keen sense that human suffering is outrageous. If we could cultivate these two things, we would achieve greater commitment to global welfare.

I do not want to suggest that we should actively suppress empathy. Perhaps it enriches the lives of those who experience it, and perhaps it helps to foster close dyadic relations in personal life. But, in the moral domain, we should regard empathy with caution, given empathetic biases, and recognize that it cannot serve the central motivational role in driving pro-social behavior. Perhaps empathy has a place in morality, but other emotions may be much more important: emotions such as guilt and anger. When confronted with moral offenses, it's not enough to commiserate with victims. We should get uppity.[1]

---

[1] In writing this paper, I received generous, detailed, and illuminating comments from Daniel Batson, Amy Coplan, Peter Goldie, and two anonymous referees. I learned as much from those comments as I learned in doing the research for my initial draft, and it would be an understatement to say I am grateful. The paper would have been considerably stronger if I had incorporated more of their valuable insights and if I had been able to address all of their penetrating objections. Batson, whose influence is detectable throughout, convinced me that his notion of empathetic concern may be immune to many of the worries raised here.

14

Empathy, Justice, and the Law

Martin L. Hoffman

For decades legal scholars and philosophers from Kant to Rawls assumed that the law and its underlying justice principles are, and should be, cleansed of emotion, so that reason and logic can prevail. In recent years, however, legal scholars acknowledge that emotions inevitably creep in and influence not only legal judgments and decisions by jurors and judges but at times law's very substance (Maroney (2006)). This literature revolves heavily around empathy—for plaintiffs, defendants, individuals, groups. Some writers, including former Supreme Court Justice Blackmun, support empathy's role in law because it takes people's needs into account and provides a humane counterpoint to cold abstract argumentation; and, further, it can fill gaps and provide information needed to carry out the full intent and spirit of the law (Greenhouse (2005); Zipursky (1990)). But others disagree and argue with equal force that just and predictable law cannot tolerate empathy (Bandes (1996)).

My aim is to contribute to this literature by situating empathy's relation to law solidly within a broad empathy framework (Hoffman (2000)). I do this first by summarizing my empathy theory's main points: its definition, evidence for its being a pro-social moral motive, its modes of arousal, its developmental stages, and how it is shaped by causal attribution into various affects including empathic anger, guilt, and especially empathic feeling of injustice that may motivate action in certain law-relevant situations. I then illustrate with real examples two rather different ways in which empathy may contribute to law: (1) by contributing to individual personalities that interact with historical events to help prepare the country for initiating and changing laws; and (2) by contributing to how laws are made, changed, and applied in the courtroom, especially the U.S. Supreme Court. And finally, I discuss empathy's inherent biases that may limit its value in legal contexts.

14.1 Overview of Main Points of my Empathy Theory

14.1.1 Empathy defined

There are two types of empathy which may be broadly defined as cognitive empathy or awareness of another's feelings, and affective empathy or feeling what another feels.

My focus is affective empathy although the two types often occur together, as for example in the courtroom when a judge or jury member becomes aware of an absent victim's plight, imagines how the victim feels, and the resulting image triggers affective empathy.

Affective empathy (I'll just say empathy from now on for convenience) may be defined as an emotional state triggered by another's emotional state or situation, in which one feels what the other feels or may normally be expected to feel in his or her situation. Since empathy-relevant laws typically involve people in distress (e.g. victims of violence, fraud, or injustice), our primary concern here is empathic distress. There may be a match between one's feeling and the victim's feelings but contrary to some writers (Ickes (1997a)), a match is not necessary. Mature adult empathy, which I assume when discussing empathy's links to law, has a meta-cognitive dimension: one is aware of empathizing—that is, one feels distressed but knows this is a response to another's misfortune, not one's own, and has an idea of how the other feels. One also has a sense of self and others as separate beings with independent inner states (feelings, thoughts, perceptions) that are only partly reflected in outward behavior and facial expression, and with separate identities and life conditions.

14.1.2 Empathy as a motive

Empathy's importance for law is based on its presumed motivational properties. As we might expect, under certain conditions such as anger, dislike, and competition people might feel pleasure rather than pain at another's misfortune (Hareli & Weiner (2002)). The overwhelming evidence, however, is that most people, when they witness someone in distress, feel empathically distressed and motivated to help. Thus empathy has been found repeatedly to correlate positively with helping others in distress, even strangers, and negatively with aggression and manipulative behavior. More important, experiments show that empathy arousal leads observers to help victims, and further-more they are more quick to help the more intense their empathic distress and the more intense the victims' pain. Additionally, observers' empathic distress decreases more quickly and they feel better when they help than when they don't help and when despite their best efforts the victim's distress is not alleviated. For details of these experiments and correlation studies and further discussion of their relevance to em-pathy's being a pro-social motive, see Hoffman (1978, 2000, 2008) and Eisenberg & Miller (1987).

In the real world, empathy and empathy-derived emotions like guilt and feeling of injustice (described below) have been found to help motivate some of the Germans who saved Jews from Nazis (Oliner & Oliner (1988), American Civil Rights activists in the 1960's (Keniston (1968)), and Latvian pro-social activists in the early post-Soviet years (Linden (2008)). Finally, there are the five individuals described below whose empathy for suffering or disadvantaged groups motivated sustained action on their behalf that contributed to initiating and changing laws.

In sum, empathic distress thus has all the attributes of a pro-social motive.

14.1.3 Modes of empathic arousal

I have identified five modes of empathic arousal (Hoffman (1978, 2000)). I now summarize them briefly, including the first three which are often neglected in the literature. Though these three modes are pre-verbal and automatic, they are important because they are not replaced by the advanced modes but continue to operate along with them throughout adulthood and are therefore relevant to empathy's contribution to law:

(a) mimicry—the generally accepted explanation of mimicry, since Lipps (1903a), involves two steps: (1) one automatically imitates the victim's facial, vocal, and postural expression of distress, and (2) the resulting changes in one's own facial, vocal, and postural musculature trigger neural circuits to the brain and feedback from the brain that produce feelings which match the victim's feelings. The recent discovery of 'mirror neurons' in rhesus monkeys (Iacoboni (2005)) may, if they are also found to exist and function the same way in humans (Iacoboni, Molnar-Szkacs, et al. (2005), provide a more direct neural explanation of mimicry;

(b) conditioning—empathic distress becomes a conditioned response through observing others in distress at the same time that one is experiencing actual distress;

(c) direct association—makes the connection between a victim's expression of distress or cues in the victim's situation and one's own painful past experience, without requiring conditioning. For example, having had an experience of separation from one's parents for a long time may be all it takes for one to empathize with someone in the midst of a distressing separation.

Empathy aroused by these three modes is passive, involuntary, based on surface cues, and requires little cognitive processing. These modes are important however because they show that one's empathic distress can result from another's painful experience even in early childhood, before the emergence of meta-cognitive concepts and language, while also giving empathy an involuntary dimension in adulthood and through life because they continue as accompaniments of the higher-order cognitive modes, which follow:

(d) verbally mediated association—another's distress is communicated and connected to one's own painful past experience through the medium of language, which makes it possible to empathize with someone who is absent. When the victim is absent and the communication is only through language (a letter from the victim, someone else's description of the victim's plight, a newspaper article), semantic processing is necessary to mediate the connection between victim's distress and observer's empathy. This semantic processing may put distance between victim and observer.

The distancing is often reduced, however, when the decoded message leads the observer to construct visual or auditory images of the victim (sad face, blood, cries, moans), and respond empathically to the images through pre-verbal modes. When the victim is present, distancing can be reduced further by the direct activation of pre-verbal modes by the victim's facial and other expressions of distress. Alternatively, empathy may first be aroused by the relatively quick-acting preverbal modes and then fine-tuned by semantic processing of the verbal message;

(e) perspective-taking—this is not a new mode, going back at least to David Hume, who wrote that because people are constituted similarly and have similar life experiences, imagining oneself in another's place converts the other's situation into mental images that evoke the same feeling in oneself (1751/1957). Adam Smith went further and more deeply into the experience of empathy: 'By the imagination we place ourselves in the other's situation, we conceive ourselves enduring all the same torments, enter, as it were, into his body, and become in some measure the same person with him and thence form some idea of the sensations and even feel something which, though weaker in degree, is not altogether unlike them' (1759/1976:.261).

The modern research, begun in the 1950's reveals three types of perspective-taking: (a) self-focused—imagining how one would feel if the stimuli impinging on the victim were impinging on oneself. This mode, imagining oneself in the other's place can, especially when enhanced by association with similar painful events in one's own past, produce as much, at times even more pain than that felt by the victim (Hoffman (2004)); (b) other-focused—one focuses attention on the *victim's* feelings, current life condition or typical behavior in similar situations; this mode, focusing on the other's plight arouses empathic distress, though it is less intense than that resulting from self-focused perspective-taking (Batson, Early, & Salvarani (1997)). I suggest it may be less intense because focusing on the other makes associations with one's own painful past less likely than focusing on oneself. The overall effect of other-focused perspective-taking is magnified, however, when the empathic distress it arouses leads one to introspect and imagine oneself in the other's place, that is, when other-focused induces self-focused. This leads to the third type of perspective-taking: (c) combined self–other focused—one focuses on both the victim and the self, simultaneously or more likely sequentially as just described. This mode is important for empathy's contribution to law because it benefits from both the emotional intensity of self-focused and the enlarged scope and sustained attention to the victim afforded by other-focused perspective-taking. The three types of perspective-taking correspond to my above definition of empathy as including affective empathy, cognitive empathy, and the co-occurrence of the two.

To summarize, the five arousal modes can operate alone or in any combination. The pre-verbal modes allow empathic arousal in infants but continue operating and add an involuntary dimension to empathy in adults. The cognitive modes enlarge empathy's scope to include subtle types of distress (e.g. disappointment in oneself) and allow empathy with victims who are absent. Multiple modes thus enable one to respond empathically to whatever distress cues are available: facial, vocal, and postural cues are picked up mainly through mimicry; situational cues through conditioning and association; distress expressed verbally, in writing, or by someone else can arouse empathy through the cognitive modes. Multiple modes not only enable but often compel one to respond to another's distress empathically—instantly, automatically, with little or no awareness. Even the cognitive modes, often drawn out and voluntarily controlled, can kick in immediately if one attends closely to the victim. This multi-determined quality makes empathic distress a reliable response and may explain why it likely survived human evolutionary pressures (Hoffman (1981b), de Waal (2008)) and has a hereditary component (Zahn-Waxler, Robinson, & Emde (1992)).

A note about mirror neurons, which have received a lot of attention recently. It should be clear from the above discussion of multiple empathy arousal modes that although mirror neurons, if they exist and function in humans as in monkeys, may account for mimicry, an important empathy arousal mode when victims are present, they can by no means account for all of empathy as assumed by some neuroscientists and psychologists (e.g. Iacoboni, Molnar-Szakacs, et al. (2005)). Also please note the important role played by cognitive processes involved in the higher-order modes especially when victims are absent, which rules mirror neurons out, as in many cases involving the law.

14.1.4 Empathy development

Young children, before 3 or 4 years of age, can empathize but with little or no meta-cognitive awareness, through the three pre-verbal modes. This suggested to me that empathy continues to develop along with cognitive self–other concepts, in six stages (Hoffman (1978, 2000)). The first three early childhood stages (unlike the three pre-verbal modes) are superseded by later stages and thus irrelevant to mature adult empathy and its relation to law, so I'll skip them—except for one developmental transition which is relevant to mature adult empathy and thus to law.

This transition occurs in toddlerhood, at around 2 years of age. As the sense of self and others as separate beings begins to emerge, empathic distress is transformed in part into sympathetic distress. That is, the child continues to feel empathic distress, more or less matching and operating in parallel with the victim's feeling, but the child now also has a reactive feeling of sympathetic distress or compassion for the victim. From then on, through the last three empathy development stages and throughout adult life, empathic distress has a sympathetic component. This is crucial because the sympathetic component gives empathic distress a clearly pro-social dimension (see Hoffman (1978, 2007) for empirical evidence and a theoretical analysis of the processes underlying this transition). That is, one is now motivated to reduce another's distress, not only to reduce one's own empathic distress. The term empathic/sympathetic distress would be a more exact description but I'll stick with the less cumbersome 'empathic distress' for convenience. But please keep in mind the sympathetic component: empathic distress past toddlerhood and throughout adult life involves feeling *for* as well as *with* the victim. The last three stages, all important for empathy's relation to law, follow:

(a) *Veridical empathy.* By mid-childhood children have a clear sense of one's body as a physical entity that exists outside one's subjective self and can be seen by others. They are also aware that others have inner states (thoughts, feeling, desires) independent of their own, and they can recognize and empathize with another's feelings, take another's perspective, and offer help that fits the other's needs. Their empathic ability becomes more complex with the growing awareness that people can display emotions not felt and feel emotions not displayed, and with increased understanding of the causes, consequences, and correlates of different emotions, which allows them to empathize not only with simple but subtle distress feelings such as disappointment, fear of failing tests important for one's future, ambivalence, low self-esteem, desire for independence, and even fear of losing face if one accepts help.

(b) *Empathic distress over another's life condition.* By 7–10 years of age, due to the emerging conception of oneself and others as continuous persons with separate histories and identities, children become aware that others feel joy, anger, sadness, fear, low esteem not only in the situation but also in their lives beyond the situation. Consequently, they not only respond empathically to another's immediate distress but also to what they imagine is the other's chronically sad or unpleasant life. They can thus empathize with someone who is chronically ill, emotionally deprived, hopelessly poor—regardless of his immediate state. If he seems sad, knowing his life is sad may intensify one's empathic distress. If he seems happy, the contradiction may make one stop short and rather than feel empathic joy one may realize that a sad life is a more compelling index of well-being, and respond with empathic sadness, or at least a mixture of joy and sadness (Hoffman (2000); Szporn (2001)). Mature empathy is thus a response to a network of cues from another's behavior, emotional expression, immediate situation, and life condition.

(c) *Empathy for distressed groups.* When children start forming social concepts and classifying people they can comprehend the plight not only of individuals but also groups or classes of people (e.g. chronically ill, homeless, slaves, paupers, victims and survivors of natural disasters, the Holocaust, ethnic cleansing, war, terrorism, prejudice, discrimination, unfair laws). They are therefore able to empathize not only with an individual's but also with a group's distressing life condition ('empathy narrative'). The two may go together, as when empathy generalizes from an individual victim to a group, for example from the famous photograph several years ago of a burned baby in a fireman's arms to all Oklahoma City bombing victims (which I call media-enhanced empathic distress for a group.) Indeed, it may be difficult to empathize with a mass—it's too abstract—without first empathizing with an individual victim and then, realizing others are in the same boat, generalizing one's empathy to the group. At this stage one can also be empathically distressed by the destruction of inanimate objects that symbolize the life of a group—ancient artworks, churches, mosques, synagogues, temples, and other types of cultural and religious property. An example is the public's empathic response to the Taliban's blowing up the giant Buddhist statues of Bamiron, Afganistan (Hoffman (2001a)).

As with a single victim, one can empathize with a group's life condition that contradicts its behavior:

When I read accounts of slaves in America who were extremely religious and joyful in religious ceremonies, I feel sort of happy that they were doing something that gave them a sense of joy, even ecstasy, but I am reminded that they were oppressed and this is a false sense of joy or hope in the midst of a distressing, unfair life. I feel happy that they're happy despite being enslaved, but I feel bad for them too because this religious hope or joy is really a false sense of security. It was a bitter irony that they took joy from the promised salvation of this religion, given them by the slave owners whom they wanted to be liberated from. (From a student of mine's term paper.)

Empathy for a distressed group may progress to a point that Kaplan (2006, and this volume) and Laub (1995) call 'witnessing.' Kaplan's witnessing exemplar is Susan Sontag's self-described experience of shock, numbness, and 'being changed forever' by images of atrocity at age 12 when first exposed to Holocaust photos. It affected her life work, which featured mass suffering, culminating in *Regarding the Pain of Others*, her last book (Sontag (2003)). I would add (thanks to John Gibbs) Craig Kielburger, an award-winning Canadian author and Noble Peace Prize nominee (Kielburger (1998)). Like Sontag, he was 12 when he saw a life-changing newspaper photo of a Pakistani boy who had been bonded into labor at 5, escaped from the factory where he knotted carpets as a virtual slave, traveled widely speaking against child labor, and, finally, was murdered under suspicious conditions. The photo and story so empathically disturbed Kielburger that he went to the library, called various organizations to learn about child labor, traveled to Pakistan, and eventually founded and raised money for Free the Children, the world's largest network of children helping children through education. A third exemplar is Harriet Beecher Stowe, whose son's death, as noted below, was the occasion for mobilizing her empathy for slaves and turning it into the driving force behind writing *Uncle Tom's Cabin*. Other witnessing exemplars noted below include Lyndon Johnson, who pushed through America's first Civil Rights Law, and Tsar Alexander, who freed Russian serfs.

I define witnessing specifically as empathic distress that becomes so intense ('empathic over-arousal') and penetrates so deeply into one's motive system that it changes one's behavior beyond the immediate situation. One not only feels compelled to help the group in the present but becomes committed to act on their behalf beyond the situation and often over an extended period of time and at great personal cost. This level of empathic identification and behavior may constitute an advanced, seventh stage of empathy development. In any case, empathy with victim groups and witnessing can be crucial links between empathy and law, as we shall see.

14.1.5 Empathy is shaped by causal attribution

It is well established that humans spontaneously attribute causality to events (Weiner (1985)). It therefore seems reasonable to assume that most people attribute causality when witnessing someone in distress. If they blame the victim, empathic distress is reduced. Otherwise, depending on the attribution, empathic distress may be transformed in whole or part into one of the following feelings:

(a) sympathetic distress or compassion results when the cause is beyond a victim's control as in illness, accident, or loss, and when the cause is unknown. Also when the cause is beyond one's comprehension, as in the developmental transition from empathic to sympathetic distress in toddlerhood, noted above;

(b) empathy-based guilt results when one's efforts to help have not alleviated the victim's distress (Batson & Weeks (1996)), or guilt over inaction when one has not even tried to help, as this allows the victim to suffer. The anticipation of guilt over inaction motivated some of the Civil Rights activists and Germans who saved Jews, mentioned earlier;

(c) empathic anger results when someone else is the cause. If the victim is distressed (sad, disappointed, afraid) but not angry at the perpetrator one may still feel empathic anger towards the perpetrator on the victim's behalf (a prime example of a lack of match between victim's and empathic observer's feeling);

(d) empathic feeling of injustice results when a victim gets less, or is punished more than he deserves. Empathy over injustice and empathic anger, separately or combined, are especially relevant to the law and so I give them special attention.

14.2 Empathy's Contribution to Law

14.2.1 Empathic feelings of injustice and anger

Humans seem to have a natural preference for fairness, reciprocity, equity (Lerner, Ross, & Miller (2002); Peterson & Cary (2002)). There are evolutionary grounds for this preference (Trivers (1971)) and evidence of a neural basis for liking and empathizing more with a fair person in distress than an unfair person (Singer, Seymour, O'Dougherty, et al. (2006). It seems reasonable to conclude that most people believe that one should get what one deserves—based on such things as performance, effort, good deeds, and character; also that one's rights as a citizen should be respected, punishment should fit the crime, and rules should be applied fairly and impersonally. When one sees someone get paid too little for hard work, cheated out of his or her savings, denied legal rights, disadvantaged by racist laws, falsely accused of a crime, or punished excessively, the preference for fairness is violated. This violation of justice may transform one's empathic distress for the victim into an empathic feeling of injustice (or simply empathy over injustice) and motivate action to right the wrong and restore justice (Hoffman (1987, 2000)).

The underlying process may be that one first responds empathically to someone in distress, then, realizing the cause is an injustice transforms the empathic distress into an empathic feeling of injustice. Or, one's pre-existing, abstract notion of injustice interacts with the empathy aroused on encountering, hearing about, or imagining an actual victim of injustice, and transforms it into an empathic feeling of injustice. In other words either the empathic distress or awareness of justice violation may come first; what's important is they end up as a unit—empathy over injustice—which combines empathic affect and a justice concept that motivates action to make, apply, or change laws.

If a perpetrator is involved, one may feel empathic anger toward the perpetrator, whether it's an individual, group, law, or the state. John Stuart Mill (1861/1979) connected empathic anger, justice, and law as follows: 'the natural feeling of retaliation rendered by intellect and sympathy applicable to those hurts that wound us through wounding others . . . serves as the guardian of justice.' This suggests empathic feeling of injustice, reinforced when appropriate by empathic anger, may be a crucial link between individuals and laws by providing the voices needed in law-based societies to uphold justice, object to people and laws that abuse others, and be ready to punish perpetrators and change laws when necessary.

14.3 Individuals Whose Empathy Helped Change Laws

I now turn to individuals whose empathy with societies' disadvantaged led to actions on their behalf, which in turn contributed significantly to changes in laws that not only benefited the disadvantaged but also had consequences for society as a whole. The actions of some of these individuals, as mentioned earlier, exemplify 'witnessing,' where exposure to others' trauma or stressful life condition produces intense empathic distress and a commitment to helpful long-term action beyond the situation.

14.3.1 Harriet Beecher Stowe and the abolition of slavery

In her historical novel *Uncle Tom's Cabin* (1852/2009), Harriet Beecher Stowe humanized and described the living conditions of slaves in the South. She wrote the book for the express purpose of turning people against slavery, targeting especially the Fugitive Slave Law, as in this incident in the novel: An affluent politically uninvolved housewife's deeply felt empathy for slaves she personally knew who 'have been abused and oppressed all their lives' motivates her to oppose a new law against giving food, clothes, or shelter to escaping slaves. She argues with her husband, a government official who supports the law, saying 'the Bible says we should feed the hungry, clothe the naked, comfort the desolate,' adding that 'people don't run away when they're happy, but out of suffering.' She becomes intensely opposed to the 'shameful, wicked, abominable' law and vows to break it at the earliest opportunity. (This fictional character is also an example of a 'witness.')

Is there evidence for Stowe's own personal empathy? The high level of detail in depicting slaves' harsh living conditions, their personalities, and their anguish clearly shows cognitive empathy and suggests the likelihood of empathic feeling as well. More direct evidence for Stowe's empathic feeling and its motive property appears in this quote from a letter she wrote to Eliza Cabot Fallon, an abolitionist friend (Stowe (1952)):

> I have been the mother of seven children, the most loved of all lies buried near my Cincinatti residence . . . at his dying bed and grave I learned what a poor slave mother must feel when her child is torn away from her. In those immeasurable depths of sorrow it was my only prayer to God that such anguish might not be suffered in vain . . . the most cruel suffering that I felt could never be consoled for unless this crushing of my own heart might enable me to work out some great good to others . . . I allude to this here because I have often felt that much that is in that book had its roots in the awful scenes and bitter sorrow of that summer . . . It has left now no trace in my mind except a deep compassion for the sorrowful, especially for mothers who are separated from their children.

This letter is a good example of intense empathic distress motivating long-term pro-social action as well as being evidence in this particular case that empathic distress was a prime motivator of Stowe's writing *Uncle Tom's Cabin*.

Did the book accomplish her goal of abolishing slavery? First, a comment on the often cited greeting by Abraham Lincoln on meeting Stowe, 'So this is the little lady who started this big war,' which historians interpret either as serious, frivolous, or tactical. The book surely didn't start the war but the first year after it was published 300,000 copies were sold in the U.S., a million copies in England and two-and-a half million worldwide, which is important because it intensified the political pressure on the U.S. coming from Europe in favour of emancipation. It was the best-selling book in the world (after the Bible) during the nineteenth century.

The book did not abolish slavery but it probably did as much as any book could. See Hanne (1994) for a wide-ranging discussion of the book's impact on abolition and the war as well as on Lincoln's election and building support for the Republican Party. I'll just give three quotes. The first, from a *New York Times* article: 'The story of *Uncle Tom's Cabin* served admirably to quicken the national conscience until the great blot of slavery was removed from our escutcheon' (Anonymous (1896)). The second, by Frederick Douglas, the famous black anti-slavery campaigner, as cited by Hanne (1994: 77): the book was 'a flash to light a million camp fires in front of the embattled hosts of slavery.' The third: 'While no one should underestimate the great services of abolitionists like Garrison and Phillips and Parker and Sumner, who cast their fortunes into the effort to free the slave, it is truth to say that all their efforts were but a drop in the bucket compared with the stir and power that were in *Uncle Tom's Cabin*. Never in human history has a work devoted to a great cause had such an instantaneous effect' (Ward (1896)). The last is surely an exaggeration, but most historians do agree that the book did play a significant role in preparing the nation psychologically for emancipation and laws supporting it.

I suggest this is a rather pure instance of a person's empathy for a victimized group making an indirect contribution to the law—not by changing the law but by writing a book that affects the culture, changes individuals' attitudes, sways public opinion, and thus helps create the necessary cultural support for changing the law.

14.3.2 Ivan Turgenev, Tsar Alexander, and emancipation of Russian serfs

Stowe showed that a writer's empathy over the plight of societies' victims could help change laws in a democracy with a large reading public. Could this happen in an autocratic state with far fewer people who read? Apparently yes. A book written by Ivan Turgenev, one of Russia's great nineteenth century novelists, which, like *Uncle Tom's Cabin*, portrayed the serfs as human and exposed their cruel treatment in great personal detail is generally credited by historians with helping revolutionize Russia's serfdom system (Ripp (1980)). The book consisted of a series of individual stories initially published in a literary periodical between 1847 and 1851 and collected and published as a single volume, *A Sportsman's Notebook*, in 1852 (the same year as *Uncle Tom's Cabin*!).

Like Stowe, Turgenev includes occasional landowners who treated serfs fairly, and serfs who lived contented lives, but what came through to readers, whose previous knowledge of the serfs' harsh existence had been largely abstract, are incidents like these: serfs who were flogged or sent to the army for displeasing their master; and serfs who were prohibited from marrying, renamed, or sent to work in a factory for wages that were paid to their owner. In one story, landowners were said to 'treat the peasant like a doll: they turn him this way and that, they break him and throw him away.'

Turgenev's personal empathy for serfs is revealed in an argument with his mother over her cruel treatment of the family's 2000 serfs:

MOTHER: ...but they're well-fed, shod, and clothed, even paid wages...
IVAN: ...but, momma, I didn't say that they were starving or not well clothed. Just think about what it must be like for a man to live constantly in such a state of fear! Imagine a whole life of fear, and nothing but fear! Their grandmothers, their fathers and they themselves are all afraid...must their children also be doomed?
MOTHER: ...What fear...?
IVAN: ...The fear of not being safe for a day, or for a single hour of their existence; today here; tomorrow there, where you will. That is not life. (Moser (1972): 4.)

Turgenev's books' route to power was similar but also differed from Stowe's. It was similar in making the predominantly upper class and serf-holding reading public aware of the serfs' human qualities and the cruelties they suffered, and thus helping to cultivate and enhance sentiment for reform already existing in Russian society. This contributed to Tsar Alexander's emancipation manifesto, the legal basis of serfdom reform in Russia, in 1861, a year before Lincoln's Emancipation Proclamation (Freeborn (1960)).

The difference was the important role played by Tsar Alexander. When he was nineteen and still a Grand Duke he was, at the behest of his father, taken on a seven-month tour of the Empire by his tutor. During the tour he insisted, against his father's instructions, on stopping frequently to enter peasant huts and talk to the serfs. According to Hanne (1994), one of Alexander's biographers describes him as displaying 'obvious anguish' (empathic over-arousal) as he discovered the conditions of existence of many of the serfs (Almedingen (1962)), and another notes that during the tour 'the people's sorrow became Alexander's sorrow' (Schumacher, no reference given). Hanne's summary is that ten years before reading Turgenev's first story, Alexander had a series of direct encounters of his own with serfs and been deeply moved by the desperate conditions in which he saw many of them living.

Reading Turgenev's stories years after his own personal encounters apparently revived Alexander's empathy; he was deeply moved once again, by Turgenev's vivid descriptions of the serfs' plight, their personalities, and their feelings of desperation—not unlike Stowe's description of slaves' lives—which he read and discussed enthusiastically with his wife. This apparently enhanced and consolidated his empathy for the serfs, but more importantly it was also at least partly responsible for adding a significant new twist: the motivation to abolish serfdom which he resolved to do at the earliest opportunity. He succeeded to the throne in 1855 and almost immediately initiated moves to bring about emancipation, which finally came about in 1861. He accomplished emancipation against strong opposition from the landed serf-owning gentry and others who were already aware of the serf's problems but also saw them as a potential threat, by asserting his power and above all by arguing forcefully that freeing the serfs from the top was better than risking a revolution.

Besides directly influencing the Tsar, Turgenev's book's describing the serfs as individual human beings with intellectual and spiritual potentialities contributed to a general change of attitude towards them. This helped put an end to the tendency even among liberals desiring emancipation, to treat serfs with derision and contempt (Schapiro (1978)). This shift in 'public opinion' was an ally that helped strengthen the Tsar's case for emancipation. There was thus in effect an empathic one-two punch that contributed to emancipation: Turgenev's book reactivated the Tsar's travel-based empathy with serfs, and it energized the anti-serfdom sentiment in the small but influential reading public. We can also add the general awareness in Russia of the U.S. Civil War and slavery's abolition throughout Europe.

A final question: did Turgenev, like Stowe, write for the express purpose of achieving emancipation. He apparently once said yes and called the book 'a political manifesto', but he more often claimed to be detached from social and political concerns. In any case he was happy with the outcome: 'If I had any pride in these matters, my one desire for my tomb would be that they should engrave upon it what my books accomplished for emancipation of the serfs. Yes, that's all I ask.' (Goncourt (1962): 198). He also claimed that the Tsar had personally communicated his thanks for the book; and the Tsar's biographers vouch for the truth of this claim (Hanne (1994); Almedingen (1962)).

A final note. I think Tsar Alexander, even more so perhaps than Ivan Turgenev, qualifies as a 'witness.'

14.3.3 Lyndon B. Johnson and civil rights legislation

Lyndon Johnson's accomplishments, in contrast to Stowe's and Turgenev's indirect impact on law through literature, provide a relatively pure illustration of empathy's direct impact when embodied in a powerful person's motivational structure: the person can play a direct role in changing and passing laws.

In discussing Lyndon Johnson I quote freely and paraphrase the prize-winning 1200- page biography (Caro (2002)), which describes Johnson's 'deeply felt empathy for the plight of African-Americans since the emancipation of slavery and continuing through World War 2 and into the 1950s' (see also Kluger (1975)). According to Caro, Johnson

'was able to win those (Civil Rights) victories in the Senate in part because of empathy—a deep sense of identification with the poor, including the dark-skinned poor; he understood their thoughts and emotions and *felt* their thoughts and emotions as if they were his own . . . this empathy for poor dark skinned people came from personal experience with them plus his rare ability to read people so deeply, to see so truly what they were feeling that he could feel it himself —and could therefore put himself in their place. (718–19).

When he was 21 Johnson spent a year teaching Mexican children in the South Texas brush country. He visited their homes, saw the poverty, learned their fathers were paid slave wages by 'Anglo' farmers, and (in his own colorful, empathic language) 'I saw hunger in their eyes and pain in their bellies. Those little brown bodies had so little and needed so much . . . I could never forget the disappointment in their eyes and the quizzical expression on their faces . . . they seemed to be asking why didn't people like me? Why do they hate me because I am brown?' Seeing how the Anglos treated them turned part of Johnson's empathy into empathic anger. Empathy is a pro-social motive to help and it was this for Johnson: besides teach, he tried to inspire them and he helped them (e.g. worked hard to get the school board to buy play equipment, arranged games with other schools) but the circumstances of their lives, permeated with injustice, interfered.

Added to empathic anger was an empathic feeling of injustice which fueled a promise of future action on their behalf: 'I swore then and there that if I ever had a chance to help those underprivileged kids I was going to do it.' That, he said later, was where his dream began of an America 'where race, religion, language, and colour didn't count against you' (720). Clearly, he was unusually empathic with and moti-vated to help this country's underprivileged long before being in the position to help them. (It was a focused empathy to be sure; I found no evidence that he was empathic to other groups or that he was in general an empathic person).

Johnson could accomplish these goals not only because of empathy but also his skills, drive, and, above all, personal ambition to do so. As a U.S. Senator, he was driven by his empathy for the poor which operated in parallel with his personal ambition and, (like Tsar Alexander) working against overwhelming odds and relentless opposition from his Southern colleagues, using his extraordinary persuasive skills, managed to manipulate the Senate in an unprecedented manner into passing America's first major Civil Rights legislation, in 1968.

He later backtracked when his strong stand on civil rights conflicted with his personal ambition to be President. But even as President his empathy had enough staying power for him to appoint the first African-American member of the Supreme Court, Thurgood Marshall. And to win a major addition to the battery of civil-rights laws he had obtained in Congress: the Fair Housing Act which made it unlawful to refuse to sell or rent—or to refuse to negotiate, or advertise the sale or rental of any dwelling in any way that indicates any preference, limitation, or discrimination based on race, religion, or national origin, or even to pretend that a dwelling is not available for inspection, sale, or rental when in fact it was. Johnson's aim here was to get rid of what he called the 'ghettoization' of black America, similar to desegregation of the schools.

I'll skip over Johnson's big misadventure, the Vietnam War, which became a major distraction as well as a drain on the country's financial resources resulting in under-funding of his wide-ranging domestic programs. The upshot is that despite his many empathy-driven accomplishments, Johnson ended up being substantially discredited and reviled by many. Still, Lyndon Johnson's accomplishments stand as strong evidence for empathy's potential impact on law (and society) when it is allied with a person in power's egoistic motives. They also show empathy's fragility when it conflicts with rather than operates in parallel with those same motives and is opposed by overwhelming social and political forces.

Putting it all together, including the ups and downs, I would say Johnson's following through on the resolution he made as a young man qualifies him, along with Harriet Beecher Stowe and Tsar Alexander, as a 'witness.'

14.3.4 Robert Kennedy

Robert Kennedy died in 1968, the same year Lyndon Johnson pushed the Civil Rights bill through Congress. Despite Kennedy's elitist background, tough-minded approach as US Attorney General, and previous reputation for ruthless, pragmatic politics, he developed in his later years an intense, deep feeling of empathic distress and anger on behalf of oppressed and disadvantaged people, and feelings of injustice at the wasted lives and opportunities denied them—all of which contributed to his becoming a serious presidential candidate (Thomas (2000)). The causes of these changes in him were many: the lesson of the Cuban missile crisis about the importance of putting oneself 'in the other guy's place'; first-hand experience with poor blacks in the Mississippi Delta and in South Africa; the suffering he experienced after his brother's assassination that fed his growing angry compassion over human misery (sort of like Harriet Beecher Stowe's suffering over losing her son). In any event, he exposed and talked openly of the 'obscenity' of poverty in a wealthy country (empathic anger and feeling of injustice) and worked long and hard attempting to change welfare policy. His efforts led among other things to formation of a select committee on hunger and poverty. Had he lived longer, as Senator or President, he would no doubt have continued to work on these issues and might have produced new laws.

He didn't, but he may have had an impact on laws in another unpredictable and indirect way and in another country. Gordon Brown, former Prime Minister of Great Britain, has claimed Bobby Kennedy as his 'moral beacon,' precisely because of Kennedy's deep empathic feeling for and efforts on behalf of the oppressed and disadvantaged (Brown (2007)). Whether Brown was sincere or just connecting himself to Kennedy for political purposes, it implies at least that empathy has appeal and importance in the British value system. Regardless of whether empathy actually influenced British law under Brown, it does point up an interesting new way in which a person's empathy might influence politics and law: by providing a role model for a powerful leader.

14.3.5 Yale Kamisar and the right of the accused to be silent and have a lawyer

Yale Kamisar is unknown except to legal scholars in the U.S., who describe him as an enemy of injustice whose empathy was combined with an 'incredibly logical and rational approach to Constitutional law.' His passion for law took the form of a 'fiery' empathy for those he referred to as the 'little guy' especially those accused of crimes. He was concerned primarily with confessions elicited by police using varying degrees of coercion and techniques of subtle persuasion. These quotes from his writings are another illustration of what I call the language of empathy, empathic anger, and empathic feeling of injustice.

'The atmosphere and environment of incommunicado interrogation is inherently intimidating . . . the temptation to press the victim unduly, to browbeat him if he is timid or reluctant, to push him into a corner and entrap him into fatal contradictions, which is so painfully evident in many (state trials) . . . make the system so odious as to give rise to a demand for its abolition . . . In many cases police resort to physical brutality—beating, kicking, hanging, whipping, placing cigarette butts on his back—and sustained and protracted questioning incommunicado in order to extort confession or inform on a third party . . . and which put the suspect in such an emotional state as to impair his capacity for rational judgment.

Kamisar's articles on police interrogation procedures, cited by the Supreme Court judges, were a major factor in the Court's 1966 *Miranda v. Arizona* decision which linked these procedures to the Fifth Amendment's clause against self-incrimination and gave the accused the right to remain silent and to have a lawyer present during interrogation. He has also continued supporting *Miranda* when attacked by judges and congressmen who see it as an obstacle to criminal investigations (Kamisar (2000)).

Note: I mention the 'language of empathy' here and elsewhere. An author's empathy can of course be communicated directly by describing his or her feelings for victims, but it is more likely to be expressed indirectly, for example by pointing up in fine detail what's happening to victims and their physical and psychological pain and distress, as in most of the cases I cite.

14.4 Empathy in U.S. Supreme Court Decisions

The cases that are the glory of the Supreme Court are the cases where the little guy won. The cases that are its shame are those where he lost (Malcolm (2006)).

14.4.1 School desegregation

I begin briefly with Justice Harlan's lone dissent more than a century ago (1896) in the U.S. Supreme Court decision (*Plessy v. Ferguson*) which legalized the segregation of black children in America as long as the schools they attended were equal to White schools. In his dissent, Harlan pointed out that compelling black children to attend different schools in the context of the widespread race discrimination existing at the time, especially in Southern states, was degrading to them even if the educational facilities were equal. The opinion is suffused with empathic concern for the individual experience of race discrimination; it also expresses empathic anger ('loathing' to be exact) for certain forms of race discrimination and Southern lawyers' dissembling about racial motivations (Pillsbury (1999)). Harlan's dissent regarding separate-but-equal doctrine is an example of empathic feeling of injustice. It is also an appropriate lead-in to empathy's role in the Supreme Court's decision to overturn that doctrine sixty years later, especially since it prefigured the major arguments that led to the overturn.

The Supreme Court initially argued this case (*Brown v. Board of Education*), which combined cases from several Southern states with the actual *Brown* case from Kansas, in 1952, re-argued it in 1953, and finally decided to overturn segregation and impose desegregation in 1954. Empathy's role in the decision is pointed up in the *Michigan Law Review*:

Brown 1 was remarkable and remains so in large part because it is a human opinion responding to the pain inflicted on outsiders by the law . . . In it legality clashed with empathy, and empathy ultimately transformed legality . . . The justices' understanding of racism was radically illuminated; as a result the Court subsequently de-legitimized segregation in other areas (e.g., transportation) . . . The case transformed constitutional law. (Henderson (1985): 1594–5).

In other words, empathy not only contributed to changing laws but in so doing had a profound impact on society.

How did it happen? To answer this question I rely heavily on Henderson's (1985) account. Henderson begins by noting that in arguing the case before the Court,

Thurgood Marshall, the National Association for the Advancement of Colored People's (NAACP) lead attorney, did not use conventional modes of legal argumentation. Instead he used the narrative of black school children's experience (their 'empathy narrative') to show how the South's school segregation policy destroyed their self-respect, 'stamped them with a badge of inferiority,' and 'put up road blocks in their minds.' He also brought in expert testimony by social scientists, including the famous study of black children who preferred white dolls and labeled black dolls as 'bad,' to describe the nature of the humiliation and self-hatred caused by segregation. Finally, he showed that the impact of these detrimental effects is greater when segregation is legitimized by law.

The Southern state's main argument, on the separate-but-equal legal grounds then in force (since 1896 as noted above), was that it had made every effort 'to wipe out all inequalities between its white and colored schools' (equal funding, class size, etc.) and 'that ended the matter under the law.' Their response to Thurgood Marshall's empathy narratives was a form of blaming the victim: if segregation of blacks stamps them with feelings of inferiority 'that's because they choose to construe it that way;' being segregated doesn't necessarily mean one is inferior. And they argued further that psychological reactions to laws are something the state lacks the power to deal with; in other words, legality precludes empathy.

The nine Supreme Court justices initially differed in response to the empathy appeal (Henderson (1985); Kluger (1975)). Some openly empathized with the black children but were concerned about empathy's relevance to the law. Justice Jackson, fully aware of the horrible effects of race prejudice from his experience as chief prosecutor in the Nuremberg trials following World War 2, 'did not doubt that segregation was painful to Negroes' but believed that the Court should not incorporate into law 'these elusive psychological and subjective factors.' He considered them 'politically' but not legally relevant, which fit with the South's position. He finally decided, however, that segregation's being painful to Negro children and making them feel inferior was a significant enough issue that striking down segregation was 'a political decision he could go along with.'

Justice Frankfurter, known to worship the letter of the law, had been advisory counsel to the NAACP, and as a Jew a member of a group subjected to the worst forms of racism, prejudice, and torture throughout history, sympathized with the pain of another oppressed minority. He wanted very much to strike down school segregation but like Jackson, couldn't find appropriate legal grounds. He wavered for a long time, finally persuading the Court to postpone arguments for a year. He never did find a traditional legal concept that fit the case but finally voted against segregation because of what was then a new idea: 'the effects of changes in society's feelings for what is right and just was relevant to determining whether a discrimination denies the U.S. Constitution's guarantee of equal protection of the laws.' In other words, he ended up linking his concern for the black children to what society now felt was a Bill of Rights violation: victims' distress due to law-based injustice. Put differently, he linked his concern to what I call 'society's empathic feeling of injustice' and this enabled him to vote for desegregation as well as alter his view of the law more generally so that changes in societies' (in this case empathic) feelings over injustice become a relevant issue.

Some of the justices apparently had less trouble accepting the empathy narratives. Justice Black, from Alabama and briefly in his past a racist Ku Klux Klan member, knew the purpose of segregation was to discriminate against blacks in the belief that they were inferior, not to give them a separate but equal education. Justice Minton thought *Plessy v. Ferguson* was unconstitutional to begin with and segregation's only justification was belief in blacks' inferiority. Chief Justice Warren, known as always putting himself in the other's place 'to get to the essence of the case' was less worried about traditional legalisms since the injustice was clear. Justice Reed, a southerner whose ideology about race may have limited his ability to respond to the empathy narratives, was finally swayed by Warren to make the Court's decision unanimous 'for the good of the country' (Henderson (1985): 1607).

The Court's opinion was world-shaking at the time.

We conclude that in the field of public education the doctrine of separate but equal has no place . . . Segregation of white and colored children in public school has a detrimental effect on colored children. The impact is greater when it has the sanction of law, for the policy of separating the races is usually interpreted as denoting the inferiority of the Negro group. A sense of inferiority affects the motivation of the child to learn. Segregation with the sanction of law therefore has a tendency to [retard] the educational and mental development of Negro children . . . Separate educational facilities are thus *inherently* unequal. Therefore we hold that the plaintiffs and others similarly situated are deprived of the equal protection of the laws guaranteed by the (Constitution's) 14th amendment.

To summarize and highlight empathy's role, the Court's decision clearly takes the perspective of segregated children, their feelings about themselves, and is sensitive to their pain; and the justices weighed these considerations more heavily than state's rights, the existing separate-but-equal law and the South's efforts to uphold it, and the claim that white kids would be distressed by having to sit with black kids [interesting that the South felt compelled to use an empathic appeal]. It may therefore be called at least partly an empathic decision, and it seems reasonable to assume that most of the justices who voted for it were to some extent empathically motivated. The evidence for this is the fact that they voted for it, and also their behavior. Some justices openly expressed empathic feeling for segregated children's pain but before they voted needed and spent a lot of time and effort searching for legal grounds to support desegregation; some did not express their feelings but were aware of the children's pain (cognitive empathy) and voted for desegregation when they found the necessary legal grounds; others were moved, at least influenced enough to vote by Thurgood Marshall's emotionally evocative empathy narratives.

We can't be sure how much each judge's motivation was based on affective empathy, cognitive empathy, or both (historians might wish to explore this). But it doesn't seem much of a stretch to conclude that in the aggregate the judges' decision was largely based on empathy—not empathy alone but hooked to legal concepts involving unfair treatment: the Constitution's equal protection clause and the segregation law's intensifying the harm to victims. The 'court's empathy over injustice' might be an appropriate term. Said differently, empathy alone didn't make the judges support desegregation (some almost voted against it), but it did help them realize that the previously accepted separate-but-equal principle was violated (separate-but-equal may be an oxymoron). This is a good example of empathy clarifying an important legal concept for judges (Zipursky (1990)).

That's the good news. As I note later, empathy is fragile and it is not surprising that the same is true of laws that lean heavily on empathy; they too are apt to be fragile. After *Brown I* came powerful Southern resistance (Virginia's governor declared 'I shall use every legal means at my command to continue segregated schools in Virginia'), congressional criticism of the decision, executive inaction (President Eisenhower openly regretted choosing Warren as Chief Justice). The Court's one-year postponement increased the opportunity for second thoughts and the external pressure during that time may have persuaded the judges to stick to traditional, non-empathy-influenced legality, as they did the following year in '*Brown II*', which I do not discuss here except to note its partial undermining of *Brown I*.

The upshot, six decades later, is general agreement that *Brown I* inspired widespread school desegregation but did not achieve its school integration goals. It did not lack impact or consequence, however: 'A review of education litigation since then reveals the decision's influence has penetrated many different areas beyond desegregation including school finance, school choice, and single-sex education' (Heise (2005)). And, as Henderson (1985) notes, '*Brown I* remains a powerful example of Supreme Court Justices' ability to hear a different—empathic—narrative, to understand the pain created in that world by a law; and to respond to that pain . . . The pain caused by discrimination against Blacks because they were black and the privileges whiteness gives to life did reach the justices.'

Regarding empathy's long-term impact, the powerful image of children in segregated schools who preferred white dolls to black dolls still resonates as a lasting symbol of the Court's opinion, despite the research evidence presented by the South's lead attorney that black children in Northern states did the same thing. This and other challenges have failed to diminish the doll study's powerful imagery, as evidenced by a recent *Cornell Law Review* article's title, 'Betrayal of the children with dolls: The broken promise of constitutional protection for victims of race discrimination' (Rich (2005)).

14.4.2 Legalizing abortion (Roe v. Wade)

The 1973 decision to permit women access to abortion is celebrated as the Supreme Court's greatest gift to women. So I expected the opinion to be loaded with empathy for women with unwanted pregnancies. I was wrong, as were others: 'such empathic understanding was strangely lacking in the Supreme Court opinion' (Henderson (1985)). What happened?

From an empathy perspective the abortion issue is more complex than *Brown*. It is a 'multiple claimant dilemma' (Hoffman (2000)), that is, it involves two conflicting moral claimants (potential victims): the woman desperate for an abortion and the unborn fetus. Efforts were indeed made in amicus briefs and oral arguments to the Court to tell the story of the horrible effects of unwanted pregnancy on women, but just as much attention was paid to the effects on fetuses who anti-abortion lawyers humanized by calling them 'unborn children not fertilized eggs or blastocysts,' 'human beings,' the 'true silent majority that needs someone to speak for them and protect their rights.'

The Supreme Court justices did vote to allow abortion but not because of empathy for women. The narrative of unwanted pregnancy appeared near the end of the Court's 51-page opinion in a single paragraph acknowledging the physical and emotional harm, the distressful future life consequences, and the continuing stigma of unwed motherhood that might be involved. Empathy is here to be sure, at least cognitive empathy, but unlike *Brown 1,* this recognition of the impact on personal lives was not mentioned in the decision or hooked to a legal concept. Instead, the decision allowed abortion for other reasons: Justice Blackmun focused on the professional rights of doctors; Justice Stewart said abortion was a professional medical judgment; Justices Brennan, Marshall, and Douglas supported an opinion based on 'broad grounds of women's constitutional rights' rather than the stressful impact on their lives of being denied the opportunity to have an abortion. Justice Powell, who came closest to an empathic response at least by implication, was moved by arguments that the constitutional right of liberty included reproductive choices and abortion was a moral decision that shouldn't be imposed by force of law but also by horror stories from relatives of his about back-alley abortionists, to conclude that anti-abortion laws were 'atrocious' (Henderson (1985)).

Empathy for women was thus lacking in the Court's written opinion but legal experts differ on whether it was lacking among the judges personally and served as a silent motive behind their vote. The view that seems most convincing to me is that the seven judges who voted to allow abortion did empathize with the women, although some may have felt a decisional paralysis because they also empathized with unborn fetuses; and they took a less controversial way out of the moral dilemma by framing the legal issue in terms of women's broad constitutional rights and the expertise of medical professionals.

In any case, the Court's majority opinions in subsequent related cases undermined *Roe v. Wade* in bits and pieces—for example, by abolishing federal funding for abortions except when the mother's life would otherwise be endangered. The minority judges in these cases, notably Blackmun, Brennan, and Marshall wrote strongly worded dissenting opinions filled with empathic language and images mainly on behalf of poor women who would suffer economically as a result of the decision. Finally, in

Thornburg v. American College of Obstetricians (1986) a bare majority of the Court staved off an attempt to have *Roe v. Wade* overruled in the face of an amicus brief by the Reagan administration urging that it be overruled. Contributing to this decision was an amicus brief submitted by The National Abortion Rights Action League (NARAL) for the express purpose of 'placing the realities in women's lives before the Court and urging it to reaffirm Roe.' It consisted largely of letters written by women who, anonymously, told the stories of their own abortion experiences and made concrete its reality for women. Included were horror stories of abortions before *Roe v. Wade*, narratives of women having to leave jobs, quit school. The stories showed that the women who chose abortion were not immoral but had carefully considered their choice. These were not just empathy narratives but part of a NARAL brief that hooked them to legal concepts by giving them an equal protection dimension: with the right to choose abortion, women are able to enjoy, like men, the right to fully use the powers of their minds and bodies.

The majority opinion, written by Blackmun and heavily influenced by the NARAL brief, acknowledges explicitly some of the narratives of women with unwanted pregnancies lacking in *Roe v. Wade* and other previous abortion decisions. Equally important for our purposes, the Court's decision hooks empathy to legal concepts:

the Constitution embodies a promise that a certain private sphere of individual liberty will be kept largely beyond the reach of government. That promise extends to women as well as men. Few decisions are more personal and intimate, more properly private, or more basic to individual dignity and autonomy, than a woman's decision—with the guidance of her physician and within the limits specified in *Roe v. Wade*—whether to end her pregnancy. A woman's right to make that decision freely is fundamental. Any other result, in our view, would protect inadequately a central part of the sphere of liberty that our law guarantees equally to all.

It seems reasonable to conclude that empathic feelings of injustice in Supreme Court justices played an important role in preserving *Roe v. Wade* and women's abortion rights, just as they apparently did in a Supreme Court made up of different individuals two decades earlier that supported school desegregation.

14.5 The Negative Side of Empathy in the Courtroom

So far I have treated empathy's impact on law positively. I now take up its more problematic side: empathic bias and its role in victim-impact statements.

14.5.1 Empathy's limitations

Though clearly a pro-social motive, empathy is limited by its fragility, dependence on the salience and intensity of distress cues, and susceptibility to influence by one's relationship to the victim (for details, see Hoffman (1984a, 1987, 2000, 2008)). Thus it can be trumped by egoistic motives such as fear or personal ambition (Lyndon Johnson's presidential ambitions), and one may not help even if it makes one feel guilty. Second, empathic distress increases with the intensity of victims' distress, as noted earlier, which is all to the good except for the fact that it can become so painful ('empathic over-arousal') that bystanders may shift attention away from the victim to avoid their own personal distress, or leave the situation, or if they remain in the situation think of other things in order to turn off the image of the victim (Hoffman (1987)). Trauma therapists can't turn away from their patients and may experience 'vicarious trauma' which is not only painful for them but can interfere with treatment (although it may also help therapists to grasp a patient's perspective), as noted by Hoffman (2002, 2008) and Pearlman & Saakvitne (1995). Something similar may happen to lawyers who represent clients who have been traumatized (Silver, Portnoy, & Peters (2004)).

Third, though the research shows that people empathize with almost anyone in distress including strangers, they empathize more with kin, friends, and their own ethnic group. I call this in-group or familiarity bias; it may not be a problem in ethnically homogeneous societies except when there are multiple victims and one must choose whom to help. It can be a serious problem, however, in multicultural settings when inter-group rivalry fosters hostility toward out-groups that are seen as a threat to one's fellow group members, resulting in empathic anger. Fourth, people empathize more with victims who are physically present than with absent victims or potential victims, which I call here-and-now or salience bias and has been shown experimentally by Batson, Batson, Todd, et al. (1995). The two types of bias can be especially damaging in the courtroom.

14.5.2 Empathic bias in the courtroom

The influence of empathy on jurors has long been known. Courtroom training manuals in the U.S. teach law students how to select jurors and get them to empathize with their clients. Clarence Darrow, the famous defense attorney, said the main task of a trial lawyer is to 'make a jury like his client, or at least feel sympathy for him.' In a University of Chicago Law School study forty years ago, Kalven and Zeisel (1966) cite many instances where judges disagreed with juries they felt voted to acquit out of sympathy with defendants, against the weight of the evidence that clearly warranted a guilty verdict. (Of course the judges could have been biased too.) I mentioned two types of empathic bias: in-group or familiarity bias and here-and-now or salience bias. Examples of both types abound in the law literature. For a full discussion of the issues see Linder (1996) especially on race bias in white juries. Here-and-now bias, perhaps less obvious and less well known, has been shown experimentally by Batson et al., as noted. Circuit Court Judge and author Richard Posner (1999) views it as a manifestation of the 'availability heuristic' in the courtroom when judges give too much weight to vivid immediate impressions and hence pay too much attention to the feelings, interest, and humanity of the parties in the courtroom and too little to absent persons likely to be affected by the decision. You don't need much empathy to be moved by a well represented litigant pleading before you. The challenge to the empathic imagination is to be moved by thinking or reading about the consequences of the litigation for absent—often completely unknown or even unborn—others who will be affected by your decision. Posner calls being moved by consequences to absent as well as present others 'judicial empathy,' a concept that I think deserves a lot of attention.

An example of empathy's fragility, here-and-now bias, and also its potentially fickle nature, is the highly publicized 1997 trial in Boston of a British nanny (Hoffman (2000)). When the 8-month-old child in her care was shaken to death, there was widespread condemnation of the nanny and an outpouring of public sympathy for the baby's parents. After the nanny's trial and conviction, the empathic tide shifted in her favor: she became the victim and the recipient of widespread empathic distress in this country as well as in her homeland. This was due largely to her severe sentence, life in prison for second degree murder; the defense attorney had disallowed manslaughter, which everyone agreed was the appropriate charge, gambling that she would be acquitted rather than convicted of murder. Seven months later, apparently responding to the public outcry, the judge reduced the charge to manslaughter. He then surprised everyone: he not only decided against a retrial but reduced her sentence to time served and freed her to return home immediately—thus confirming the defense's go-for-broke strategy—in order to 'to bring this matter to a compassionate conclusion.'

My point does not concern guilt or innocence or the wisdom of the original sentence. It is that the compassion in the U.S. for this young woman who became the focus of attention and, aided by the media, *the victim of the moment*, largely replaced the compassion for the dead baby and his parents who were the original, true victims but no longer salient. Indeed, many people ended up 'blaming the victim,' that is, blaming the mother for expecting too much of the young woman, being too cheap to hire a professional nanny, or working instead of being home with her baby. This is a clear instance of empathy's fragility, potentially fickle nature, and vulnerability to media enhanced here-and-now bias, not only in the public but also in a state judge.

There may also be a useful lesson here: had the manslaughter charge and the act it was based on been kept in mind, that is, had empathy's connection to legality been maintained, it might have restrained empathy's tendency to go to the salient victim at the expense of the absent victim. It also illustrates my general point that for empathy to play a constructive role in law it must be hooked to a legal concept; its influence can be destructive when it pops up unannounced and unhooked.

14.5.3 Victim-impact statements and empathic bias

I noted earlier how Yale Kamisar's empathy ended up helping the criminally accused in police interrogations. Empathy also helps the accused in the courtroom when evidence is presented for their good character, unfortunate life circumstances, and other mitigating factors. Arousing empathy for the *victim*, however, can do the accused great harm. Consider this statement that was made in court by a woman whose daughter and granddaughter were murdered (Bandes (1996): 361): 'He cries for his mom. He doesn't understand why she doesn't come home. And he cries for his sister Lacie. He comes to me. He comes to me many times during the week and asks me, Grandma, do you miss my Lacie.'

The question has been raised, should jurors be allowed to hear such heartbreaking testimony? The Supreme Court has gone back and forth on this issue. In 1991 it answered yes, overruling its 1987 decision that impact statements by the victim's family were not admissible at a capital sentencing hearing. Some legal scholars weigh the pros and cons, and say on balance, yes they should be allowed, mainly to give the otherwise silenced victims a voice in the proceedings and allow them or their families to present the full reality of human suffering the defendant has produced; and also to counter the witnesses who testify to the defendant's character or pressures beyond normal experience that drove him to commit his crime. Others say no, because victim impact statements may appeal to hatred, vengeance, and bigotry and they may diminish juries' ability to process evidence that bears on defendants' innocence or guilt or might be mitigating; besides, they are unnecessary because juries naturally empathize with victims. Whichever side is right, it shows empathy's power in the courtroom. For full discussion of the issues, see Bandes (1996) and Blume (2003).

14.6 Conclusion

It should now be clear that the question does empathy play a role in law must be answered, yes it does. It can have an impact on making laws and on creating the social and emotional climate and support for changing them, as well as on the practice of implementing them in the courtroom. It goes without saying, however, that empathy is not enough. The judges' empathy in *Brown 1* may have been necessary to overturn the separate-but-equal doctrine when it did but it surely was not sufficient: the country had to be ready for it politically, economically, and socially. The judges' empathy may have advanced the process by a year or two, perhaps more, however, which is nothing to sneeze at. With *Roe v. Wade* empathy was not enough the first time around although it may have indirectly affected the Court's opinion, but it clearly seemed to tip the balance in the later decision that preserved abortion rights in the face of strong political opposition. Regarding Lyndon Johnson's empathy for the 'dark-skinned' poor, his empathy was surely not enough; the country had to be ready. But given the enormous opposition in the Senate and Johnson's unique talents at persuasion, his empathy may well have produced the country's first Civil Rights Law years, perhaps decades sooner than otherwise. Similar analyses could be made for Harriet Beecher Stowe's, Ivan Turgenev's, and Yale Kamisar's impact on U.S. law.

An obvious problem is that empathy can serve many masters and is vulnerable to bias. When and if empathy is appropriate or inappropriate is a problem legal scholars are wrestling with but have not yet solved. I suggest we begin with my argument that empathy is in general less likely to be biased when embedded in moral principles like caring and justice (Hoffman (2000)). Since law's purpose is to serve justice, empathy becomes relevant and appropriate to law when linked to legal principles, especially pro-social legal principles like citizens' Constitutional rights, as in the Supreme Court cases discussed above. Empathy is likely to be biased and inappropriate when it is a simple unreflective empathic distress for someone in the courtroom, as appears to have been the case with the judge in the Nanny trial. Whether empathy in victim-impact or defendant's-good-character statements is appropriate in criminal trials may also depend on whether it is linked to legal concepts but the issue is more complicated when both types of statements are employed in the courtroom, because they argue in opposite directions.

Empathic bias is likely the outcome of natural selection and other evolutionary pressures and must therefore be considered part of human nature. To overcome it will undoubtedly require cognitive effort and socialization, as well as educational practices designed to counteract it. For example, people might be taught to think and consider the consequences for others, including those who are not present before engaging in an action. Or, playing into familiarity bias, one might be taught to imagine that an absent potential victim is one's kin or a close friend (Hoffman (2000)). Law professors could encourage students to consider absent potential victims of judicial decisions and to imagine relatives or close friends among them. In any case, empathic bias must be kept in mind and given consideration in any legal context that might involve empathy.

15

Empathy and Trauma Culture:
Imaging Catastrophe

E. Ann Kaplan

Media scholars have begun to discuss new digital viewing contexts, such as cell phones, ipods, internet, video games, and more (see Marsha Kinder (1991) or Anne Friedberg (2006)) but few have explored processes involved in responding to images of catastrophe in a rapidly expanding visual culture. Scholars have mainly studied exhibition sites, visual techniques, ideological meanings, and how new global networks are structured. Response to an image is partly determined by the way it has been composed—editing, visual style, purpose—and partly by its context for exhibition, but scholars have assumed that cognition—meaning—is primary. My view is that response is also, especially in regard to images of catastrophe, emotional. We bring culturally shaped emotions to reception, and in turn, our emotions are aroused (we might say *constructed*) by images. For the purposes of this chapter, I will focus on empathy as an emotion central to response to images of disaster.

While psychologists often ignore issues of cultural coding in analyzing emotions, these are important for humanities scholars working at the intersection of virtual and social worlds. We need to think about where emotions come from. Sara Ahmed has argued that emotions circulate in cultures and certain emotions become attached to certain bodies (Ahmed (2004)).[1] Teresa Brennan has analyzed what she terms 'the transmission of affect,' and the phenomenon of emotional contagion crucial to public feelings (Brennan (2004)). For these scholars, emotions are not only something that we have prior to, but something that is also produced in, encounters in the social world, which has become increasingly a world of images. Journalism, advertisements, television, movies, the internet, political and religious propaganda, and other sorts of appeals

---

[1] José Esteban Muñoz (2000) goes further and suggests that there is an unofficial national affect that he calls 'whiteness' (no less powerfully entrenched than the requirement for English as a national language). 'Whiteness, he claims, 'is a cultural logic which can be understood as an affective code that positions itself as the Law' (2000: 69).

enlist the power of images to move their audiences under the radar of cognition. Emotions produced in these ways may be called 'Public Feelings.'

Empathy, as is well known, is a complex pro-social emotion, with limitations. It is by no means always a response that serves the best cause or that necessarily has positive results. And yet, humans would be totally lost without empathy. Martin Hoffman has theorized six stages (summarized in this volume) through which empathy develops in humans, with adults achieving a mature empathy that is my focus here (Hoffman (2000)). Important for my project is Hoffman's demonstration that from childhood and 'throughout adult life empathic distress has a sympathetic component.' For Hoffman, this is crucial 'because the sympathetic component turns empathic distress into a clearly pro-social motive' (Hoffman (2000): 88; see also Hoffman (1986, 2007) and his chapter in this volume). In what follows, working with film and TV-mediated empathic responses to trauma, I will explore the intricate interrelationship of three kinds of empathic response to images. At the two extremes are what I call 'empty empathy' and 'witnessing,' with 'vicarious trauma' an in between response. All three are manifestations of living in a 'trauma culture' (Kaplan (2005)). By this I mean that when representations of victims prevail in a culture, then people other than the direct victims become vulnerable to traumatization through the media—second-hand, as it were. All three types of response demonstrate the different ways in which empathy may be both created and mobilized. I will explore the different kinds of empathic arousal by an image, which depend on the context (situation within which an image is received, what the viewer brings to the image) and aesthetic form (the kind of appeal an image offers, its aesthetic quality).

In this chapter, then, I define, analyze, and critique these three possible empathic responses to images of catastrophe, depending on the form an image takes, where it is placed, and the situation of the viewer. All three responses involve empathy, but what my case studies try to show is that empathy has multiple forms—that empathy is far from a monolithic emotion. I'll discuss how the form of the image, its placement, and context, will influence the type of empathy one experiences. These three responses are (a) secondary or vicarious trauma (VT), a response in which the viewer is shocked to the extent of being emotionally over-aroused; that is, the empathic response to an image of a catastrophe may be so strong and personally painful that the individual turns away, or thinks distracting thoughts, unable to endure the feelings aroused; (b) a response I call 'empty empathy' because of the transitory, fleeting nature of the empathic emotions that viewers often experience; that is, what starts as an empathic response gets transformed into numbing by the succession of catastrophes displayed before the viewer, as in TV newscasts or reading a newspaper; and finally (c) what I call 'witnessing'—a response that may change the viewer in a positive pro-social manner, and that, more than the first two types of response, involves ethics. Witnessing is especially important in what follows because of the special relationship between empathy and 'witnessing'—a term whose common meaning I extend. That is, while much of the research on empathy focuses on processes through which an individual comes to empathize with another, 'witnessing' requires much more than empathizing with suffering of a person one sees in front of her (whether an image or a live event). It involves feeling so shocked by suffering that one is moved to act. One may feel vaguely responsible, but in any case one is motivated to see that justice is done. In witnessing we understand empathy's potential social impact, especially when it is deeply and enduringly felt. This is in contrast to empathy's fragility which emerges in some of my case studies in the phenomena of 'vicarious trauma' and 'empty empathy.'[2]

15.1 Trauma Culture and Images of Catastrophe

After 9/11, trauma moved to the center of U.S. consciousness. And the government, and more germane to my argument, the U.S. media, has seen fit to create a culture of trauma through continuing focus on terrorism—which is linked to, and was used as justification for, the invasion of Iraq. I am not denying that terrorism is a serious issue. I want rather to discuss the *emotional* work that media discourses of trauma, war, and terrorism do in the U.S. today. I have chosen to discuss newspaper images and (briefly) TV reports because these are entities we deal with daily, in the course of our everyday movements. Film is still (even with DVD and internet access) a type of activity we have to set aside time for. I have dealt with trauma and film elsewhere (Kaplan (2005)), and some of the theories I outline in dealing with reporting may apply to film. But my aim here is to theorize how empathy is involved in the impact of daily images of catastrophe, although I also look briefly at other sites such as the internet and the museum.[3]

An example of the daily barrage of images may be found in a randomly selected issue of *The New York Times*. On October 12, 2005, each turn of the page brought a new disaster for the reader to confront, from the earthquake in Pakistan, to poverty in Africa, disasters in Iraq and Guatamala, and on to Hurricane Katrina. Viewing traumatic events has become a worrying national preoccupation. While newspapers, radio, and television have *always* focused on tragic or horrific happenings, media were not as central to people's daily lives as they now are. Images of trauma bombard us daily.[4] Traumatized people speak to us of their pain and suffering. Twenty-four hour television, like CNN, with reporters all over the world, bring catastrophes to us live, with continuing coverage as they are happening. New digital technologies, especially the internet, make global communication of catastrophe instantaneous. On a day like October 12, do we escape from this series of disasters into mindless entertainment? Do we turn away from such images because they have become routine? What happens to viewers in regard to empathy as we watch reporters interview individuals about their

---

[2] Martin Hoffman has begun to theorize 'depth of empathic feeling.' See Hoffman (2008): 449–52.

[3] For the purposes of my argument, my case studies are limited to the period 2003–2005. Readers will understand the logic of this as the chapter develops.

[4] Brian Massumi (1996) asks us to 'Think of the image/expression events in which we bathe. Think interruption. Think of the fast cuts of the video clip or the too-cool TV commercials...Think of our bombardment by commercial images off the screen, at every step in our daily rounds' (234).

pain, sometimes immediately after, or even during, a catastrophe?[5] If it is true that we are surrounded by spectacles of individual suffering, what effect is this having on the millions of people consuming these images? How is empathy (and its complexities, its limitations, and varied forms) in particular central to understanding the role of images in our lives today?

There are many ways in which the realities of terrorism, war, and catastrophe could be handled by reporters. While I understand a certain serendipity in what images finally appear on our screens and newspapers, the specific form that results is important since empathic response regarding catastrophes will depend partly on images people are given.[6] Response will also vary according to what viewers bring to an image both in regard to idiosyncratic emotional make-up and to norms of a subject's culture. The generally liberal politics of contemporary Eurocentric cultures together with emotional conventions (initiated by Hollywood) tends to foster sensitivity to suffering. But, as I will show, this is less empathy proper (as may be found in non-Eurocentric cultures accustomed to caring for the community) than the degraded form that is sentimentality.[7] I am not, then, claiming that all viewers will respond in similar ways to the same images. Indeed, the experience of teaching has confirmed my sense that images are wild cards that can be interpreted in numerous ways, depending on what frameworks a viewer brings to an image as well as on historical and other contexts. Often, as Roland Barthes noted years ago, an image is anchored by some text or commentary (essential for advertisements) but when that is not the case, readings vary widely.[8] However, I do claim (with appropriate evidence) that the three kinds of response I outline occur frequently, whether in relation to images I discuss or in relation to other images.

15.1.1 The Vicarious Trauma (VT) response

Before discussing VT, it will help to have a definition of trauma as experienced by individuals. In *Trauma Culture* (Kaplan (2005)), I discuss theories of psychic trauma

[5] Or, for that matter, as we engage with television talk shows with live audiences also having people discuss horrible events, as if it is therapeutic.

[6] The daily business of putting newspaper or TV reporting together involves numerous processes and rapid decisions. Thus, I am not talking about a specific process on any given day, but rather about an often unconscious culture of reporting that individuals may not even be aware of. It is by analyzing the result that we can deduce certain things about U.S. culture. That is my aim here as I work from select images to theorizing potential response.

[7] Hollywood's sentimentality involves manipulating viewers' emotions to market films. Viewers enjoy fleeting sadness because they know all will come out right in the end. They do not have to confront the reality of trauma and suffering which cannot have a happy ending. For more on different conceptions of the subject in Eurocentric and non-Eurocentric cultures, see Teresa Brennan (2004), chs 1 and 2. 'The emotionally contained subject,' Brennan says, 'is a residual bastion of Eurocentrism . . . non-Western as well as premodern, preindustrial cultures assume that the person is *not* affectively contained' (2).

[8] Indeed, as Sontag (1977) (following Barthes) noted 'even an entirely accurate caption is only one interpretation, necessarily a limiting one, of the photograph to which it is attached.' The caption, Sontag notes, can easily be undermined 'by the plurality of meanings that every photograph carries . . . and by the aesthetic relation to their subjects which all photographs inevitably propose' (109).

developed at the end of the nineteenth century as the industrial era got underway with resulting train and factory accidents that traumatized passengers and workers. Doctors and psychiatrists of the period debated physical versus psychic trauma, but Freud and his colleague Breuer added to ongoing theories in their studies of hysteria. Freud was later personally involved in debates about shell shock in World War I (Freud, (1919/ 1948)), and war trauma continued to be debated in the wake of World War II. Much later, psychologists working with Vietnam veterans and with child abuse victims in the early 1970's gathered more data about trauma (Herman (1992/1997)), and finally first in 1984 and then (a more extended account) in 1987 the American Psychiatric Society provided a diagnostic definition.[9] From all this, literary theorists, such as Cathy Caruth (working with Psychiatry Professor, Bessel Van der Kolk), adopted a working definition of trauma as a shocking event that overwhelms the victim's cognitive mechanism (Caruth (1995)). The event bypasses the brain's meaning-making processes and is lodged in the body, dissociated from ordinary consciousness. In this view, trauma is known by its symptoms—that is through phobias, flashbacks, hallucinations, and nightmares—rather than by memory per se.[10]

Little noted in the research is that one's specific positioning vis-à-vis a traumatic event makes a difference in terms of its impact.[11] A sequence of varied relationships to the experience of trauma includes the position of bystander (one step removed) or that of a clinician listening to a patient discussing a traumatic experience.[12] Most people encounter large public traumatic events through visually and verbally mediated trauma (i.e. viewing trauma on film or other media, or reading a trauma narrative and constructing visual images from semantic data) (two steps removed), which is why (given my interest in trauma culture) I focus on so-called 'mediatized' secondary trauma in viewing images.

What data can we find about images of catastrophe producing vicarious trauma, and thus contributing to a U.S. 'trauma culture'? And to what degree does Vicarious Trauma involve empathy? Clearly, following the above definition, for the person

[9] Laura S. Brown (1995) discusses the changes being made to APA's DSM IV diagnostic manual, partly inspired by feminist clinicians like herself and Judith Herman, in regard to Post-Traumatic Stress Syndrome.

[10] This definition has been adjusted by those who claim that some traumas are accessible directly, and by others who argue that traumatic events may suffer what memory in general suffers, namely subjection to unconscious fantasies and distortions. These differing views need not trouble us here.

[11] I also argue in the book that trauma produces new subjects, that the political-ideological context within which traumatic events occur shapes their impact, and that it is hard to separate individual and collective trauma. I stress further the difficulties of generalizing about trauma and its impact, for, as Freud pointed out long ago, how one reacts to a traumatic event depends on one's individual psychic history, on memories inevitably mixed with fantasies of prior catastrophes, and on the particular cultural and political context within which a catastrophe takes place, especially how it is 'managed' by institutional forces.

[12] That is, (1) Direct experience of trauma (trauma victim); (2) Relative or close friend of trauma victim or clinical worker brought in to help the victim (close but one step removed from direct experience); (3) Direct observation by a bystander of another's trauma (also one step removed); (4) Clinician hearing a patient's trauma narrative (a complex position involving both visual and semantic channels; it involves the face-to-face encounter with the survivor or the bystander within the intimacy of the counseling session) (also one step removed); (5) Visually and verbally mediated trauma.

experiencing a traumatic catastrophe first-hand, empathy is not in the picture. But for the viewer in cultures where feeling for the suffering of others is a norm, looking at an image of catastrophe may *start* with empathy. Martin Hoffman's definition of empathy as 'the involvement of psychological processes that make a person have feelings that are more congruent with another's situation than with his own situation' is pertinent (Hoffman (2000): 30). I am suggesting that what draws the viewer initially to the image of catastrophe is some sort of empathy. However, in the case of empathic over-arousal, including VT, the original empathic impulse to help turns back on the viewer or listener because the shock is too much; it overwhelms and freezes the subject.

I offer three sets of data of varying kinds and degrees of relevance to support the claim that VT as a form of empathic over-arousal is a genuine phenomenon that needs attention. First, data collected by psychologists Hoffman and Friedman from interviews with therapists treating trauma victims allows us to understand secondary trauma symptoms, and how empathy may be involved.[13] In this data, therapists reporting their work with trauma patients start with an empathic response to the patient, but interestingly (for my purposes here) often use language that sounds as if they are creating a film in their minds of the events people narrate. One therapist said, I quote: 'I created an image in my own mind, like a movie, of what she was describing' (patient thrown from Disneyland ride), and of another case, 'As I write this, I see the picture of the man who hurt her in my mind's eye (the picture I created in my imagination as she spoke);' and a third recounted that she 'had images of her in the situations she (the patient) described. She was usually very articulate so her narrative created flashes of visual images of her traumas, along with the feelings that went with those images.' Others seem haunted by images, as when a clinician reported 'horror and images of faces, body parts, smells of blood and flesh.' One therapist notes that she 'was hyper-vigilant for three days, worried over what she might do, about suicide.' Another respondent said, 'Sometimes after hearing incidents like this, I cannot be exposed to anything else that hints of violence against people as I cannot get enough distance from the event. I think about what if such had happened to me or to my children . . . I refuse to watch TV or violent movies, as it feels too real to me' (Quoted in interview data collected by Martin Hoffman and Tatiana Friedman at New York University, and used by Hoffman in his chapter in this volume). Here, the border between TV or movie images and the 'reality' of her patient's experiences is blurred for the therapist. The comment confirms the power of visual media to trigger symptoms of vicarious trauma.

But is VT only a result of an interpersonal relationship? Does it apply to viewing images, say on TV? My second data set, a psychological study of student responses to

---

[13] The study was done by Martin L Hoffman and Tatiana Friedman at New York University. Some of the clinicians' replies to Hoffman/Friedman's questions suggest that visuality links cinema, victims' accounts, and therapists' responses to those accounts. See also research by L.A. Pearlman and P.S. Maclan on vicarious traumatization (1995).

seeing an Australian ethnographic film about circumcision, would support the claim that films can produce vicarious trauma attributed to overwhelming the spectator, leading to the 'belatedness' of response, and spectators avoiding screen images (Step 5 in sequence described in Footnote 12). Richard Lazarus et al., studying stress in the 1960s at UC Berkeley, turned to using film in laboratory experiments because film avoided both deception and 'losing the realism of the naturalistic state' usual in experimental laboratory conditions (Lazarus et al. (1962): 2). Lazarus notes that the 'delay in obtaining a disturbed response was surprising' (he is referring here to the well-known *nachträglichkeit* of trauma (8); later studies by Mardi Jan Horowitz extending Lazarus' use of the circumcision film, cited symptoms now commonly known as vicarious trauma, including again the delayed traumatic reaction to the film.[14] Horowitz noted that 'The period after the traumatic film lead to more reports of film references, and more instances of forgetting' (556).

How common are such over-arousal reactions in response to daily images on TV or in newspapers? And what difference would it make if the subjects in the case of images U.S. publics daily consume involve individuals less remote than Australian Aborigines? The case of the Vietnam War, when some shocking news images were shown, suggests that empathic over-arousal can take place from viewing pictures. Some readers will recall the impact of the image of a little girl having been napalmed running from her village (see Image 15.1). (We now know a great deal about this girl, Kim Phuc, whose book describing her experiences is widely available[15]). The form of the image with the little girl's tortured screaming face directed at the viewer, her burned arms held away from her body in extreme pain, perhaps first elicited empathic identification (what if this happened to me?) before shock set in. In this and other cases noted below, I would argue, following Hoffman, that the empathic distress such images cause has a sympathetic component. This makes the element of empathy in VT different from that in other cases to be studied below. Because the sympathetic component in images from Vietnam may have lead to anti-war protests, generally editors of daily newspapers and TV programs shy away from disturbing images partly because they worry about the politics of such over-arousal.

I'll briefly mention three less common instances of images causing a vicarious trauma reaction in which the response starts with empathy involving a sympathetic component, but becomes too arousing as the full impact of the image registers. All require more examination than I can give here. First, images of ethnic slaughter in Rwanda. These are mainly found in documentaries, although the Hollywood film, *Hotel Rwanda,* had several graphic scenes, and others appeared in select newspapers and

---

[14] It should be noted that these psychology researchers were not interested (as I am) in the pro-social impact of trauma films, in their moral or political import, or the aesthetic strategies that produce traumatic effect in the viewers.
[15] See Denis Chong's (2000) narrative about Kim Phuc in *The Girl in the Picture: The Story of Kim Phuc, the Photograph and the Vietnam War.*

Image 15.1 Vietnam 1972: Kim Phuc running after being Napalmed.
With permission of Nick Ut/Associated Press.

journals. One image of female bodies left in a field that I found on the internet was especially shocking. It showed a mother in the foreground feeding her baby at her breast while dying, and in the background other, presumably raped, women. Elsewhere, I discuss diverse reactions to clips from a Rwanda documentary shown in a class I taught. Students' responses to the images of rape and genocide showed that images can produce powerful and varied emotional reactions in viewers that remain disturbing for days.[16]

Second, images of dire poverty in Africa. My example is from Sebastiao Salgado, who is famous for his dedication to documenting the devastating impact of vast numbers of peoples displaced by neo-colonialism, especially in Africa. His photographs can be seen in exhibitions or in the many books showcasing his work. These images are powerful and disturbing, even as Salgado tries to soften the horror through artistic strategies—such as lighting and composition—showing the dignity and grace of people living on the edge of catastrophe.[17] One image comments bitterly on classic icons of

[16] In *Trauma Culture* I discuss responses to images of rape and genocide in Rwanda in a class on trauma that I taught in 2001. A Journalism student presented her research about a Rwandan documentary in which women were interviewed about the violent tragic inter-ethnic war, showing long clips of the film.
[17] The topic of making photographs of pain and suffering is getting new attention—as in a City University of New York conference on 'Picturing Atrocity: Photographs in Crisis' (December 9 2005), or studies of the Brazilian photographer, Sebastiao Salgado. Salgado's amazing (graphic, beautiful) photographs of migrants,

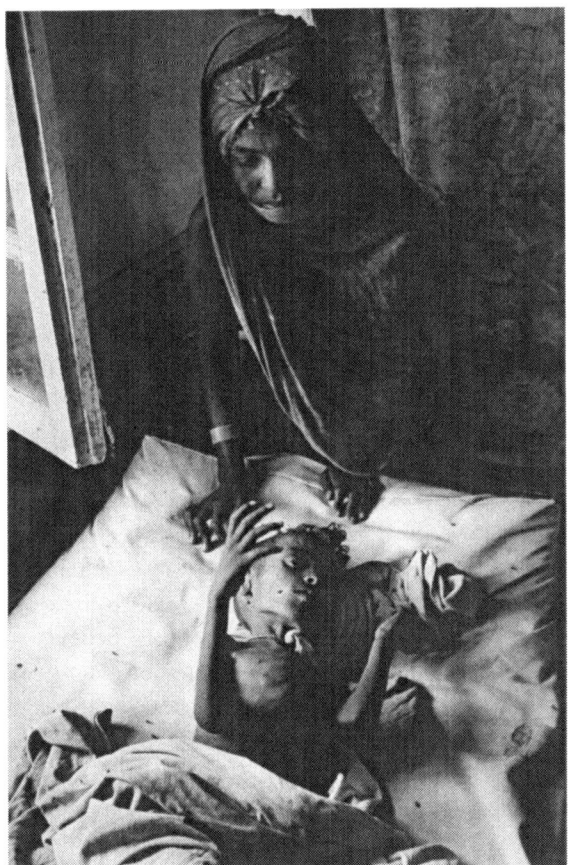

Image 15.2 A mother gazes at her starved child.

From Sebastiao Salgado's *Sahel: The End of the Road*, Africa. Courtesy of Sebastiao Salgado/Amazonas/ Contact Press Images.

Virgin and Child in showing a painfully thin mourning mother, draped like the Virgin Mary, leaning over a all but dead skeletal child. See Image 15.2.

Finally, images of lynching in the American South (gathered together by James Allen (2000) in his powerful volume *Without Sanctuary: Lynching Photographs in America*) are especially disturbing for two reasons. First, they show white people enjoying themselves as at a picnic while the lynching is taking place; and second, the images were made into postcards sent to relatives and friends. One image shows the white people, including children, looking at the camera (some even smiling) while above their heads a black man hangs from a tree. These images are too shocking to be shown in any class,

displaced peoples, and extreme global poverty have provoked a productive debate about photographing victims, their intended audience, and what aesthetics such images should offer, which I discuss briefly below.

although part of me would want to insist that Americans confront our inhumanity that is part of U.S. history.

But to what end, the over-arousal, you might ask? Doesn't the experience simply leave the viewer preoccupied with her own feelings, and unable to complete the empathic impulse of pro-social helping? May empathic over-arousal rather lead to a deadening or denial of affect, or habituation to catastrophe? Let me turn to the second type of response before attending to these questions.

15.2 Empty Empathy

Given the definition of empathy above, 'empty' empathy is empathy that does not result in pro-social behavior but is also not an empathetic/sympathetic response to a shocking image like those above. Here it is perhaps useful to extend Hoffman's empathy definition so as to take into account the difference between empathic response in the here and now of lived experience and in relation to viewing a media image. In the here and now situation, a person observes and is part of the total situation in which a catastrophe happens. This is not usually the case with images. Differences in media empathy partly depend on how far an image *is* able to convey the situation and context to a viewer. Empathy that is 'empty' is produced by images that occur in at least two ways. First, images that are received in succession. My opening discussion of the October 12 *New York Times* series of pictures of catastrophe is a good example. In this case, one's empathy for victims may be aroused by each image, but then as images come in succession, it dissipates. Each image of catastrophe cancels out or interferes with the empathic impact of the prior image. Second is the concept of fragmentation leading to empty empathy. Here the array of separate images of suffering without any context or background information provided, and focusing on the pain of strange individuals whom we see at a distance cannot elicit more than a fleeting empathy. There is then a rapid diminution of the affect. There is no socio-political context for actually putting ourselves in the situation of those suffering from catastrophe, for experiencing it deeply and enduringly. Succession and fragmentation usually involve either close-ups of suffering individuals or images of an anonymous mass of people. For example, think of the sweeping images (taken from airplanes) of refugee camps in Darfur which appear as dots in a sea of sand. When the camera closes in, it is often on an exhausted western United Nations or other representative, or an overwhelmed white nurse or doctor. While we might empathize with such individuals in their distressful work, we do not have an idea of the whole situation. The 'Others' were only indicated by the 'dots' on the aerial image. To complete the situation, we would need to be presented with the perspective of the 'Other' who remains invisible. That's why images of these kinds only elicit empty empathy.

As I noted earlier, Eurocentric cultures do encourage sympathetic feelings for suffering in others, but while this may be allied to empathy, it does not involve the complexity of, in Hoffman's words (quoted earlier) 'involvement of psychological processes that make person have feelings that are more congruent with another's situation than with his own situation.' Instead, the person reacts on a superficial level that does not get as far as truly congruent feelings, but instead she remains preoccupied with her own tears. Several humanities scholars have rightly objected to a culture of 'wounded attachments' and sentimentality (Wendy Brown (1995); Lauren Berlant (1997)). The concept of empty empathy illuminates how a certain kind of media reporting encourages sentimentality by presenting TV viewers or newspaper readers with a daily barrage of images of individual pain. Using as my case study for 'empty empathy' the 2003 coverage of the war on Iraq, I'll argue that the media coverage was either characterized by succession and fragmentation and thus aroused only 'empty' empathy, closely allied to sentimentality; or that images deliberately avoided arousing empathy in an effort to elicit emotions in another register—namely supporting U.S. troops presumably in Iraq to help people to a better life. The deliberate censoring of images of U.S. casualties and corpses was not new. Images of casualties were discouraged in World War II as well, but it is especially remarkable in the case of a war that is arguably not really a war as such. Perhaps the Iraq reporting took its cue from what authorities learned from Vietnam reporting, as I note below.[18]

A typical kind of coverage involved a reporter interviewing an individual soldier or commander about his or her experiences, but perhaps the most graphic example of reporting resorting to melodrama was the case of Jessica Lynch—a drama that included later doubts about the heroism of the capture. The Lynch story occupied hours of TV time with details of Jessica's life, interviews with her family, and retelling of her original capture by the Iraqis, her wounding, and (supposed) recapture by American forces. Lynch's photograph made the front cover of *Newsweek* (April 14, 2003), with an inside story showing images of Jessica's childhood and of her family. Subsequently, a TV movie was made about the episode.[19] In such an elaborated story, viewers may experience genuine empathy for the individual, but the melodramatic form of the story prevents the empathy from lasting and turning toward the collectivity I'll describe in a moment.

Newspaper coverage in daily images in the March 2003 *New York Times*' 'A Nation at War' section focused on individuals.[20] On Sunday March 30 2003, the focus was 'the faces and stories of the first American casualties' (A1, B7). Portraits of the 27 dead soldiers remind one of the portraits of those killed in 9/11. We do not see maimed and bloodied images, but rather neat posed official photographs, situating the soldiers

---

[18] For more on war photography and its history, see Sontag's last book, *Regarding the Pain of Others* (2003).

[19] In this kind of media reporting, spectators are asked to peek in on an individual's life in war rather than to think about the ethics of the war, human rights, and other important topics. We are encouraged to identify with specific people—to enter their personal lives.

[20] I do not claim the *New York Times* represents a national consensus, but the images I'll discuss were distributed widely across a range of newspapers and media. Many news stories and images are shared via news services, then reprinted as a group in special issues of magazines like *Time* (many newspaper images were gathered into *Time*'s 'Best Images of 2005) and' can be found in internet image files like Google's.

Image 15.3 A Marine doctor holds an Iraqi girl whose mother has been killed.
With permission of Daniel Sagoli/Reuters.

as having died in a noble national cause. And there are similar stories to those told about 9/11 victims in the accompanying article. We feel empathy for their loss and for grieving families, but the soldiers are strangers. Sentimental patriotism would seem the predominant fleeting emotion. There is nothing for us to think and feel further about.

Some images may have aroused sympathy for the dangerous plight of soldiers involved in a guerilla war. Images of men with guns on tanks or warily parading through areas where terrorists were suspected, capable of being blown up momentarily aroused fleeting empathy, as did images of soldiers hurriedly forced to put on gas masks because of supposed biological warfare. But heroic images of men on the battlefield or caring for wounded Iraqis or, as in the famous photo of a male marine holding an Iraqi child in his capacious arms, interfered with compassion for the soldiers because they were in the 'strong' helping position. His masculinity in this case was enhanced by the addition of the comforting 'softness' of cuddling the child.[21] Maleness as protecting, taking care of the small ones is a common trope in war imagery. See Image 15.3.

---

[21] I was reminded of two widely disparate images—King Kong in the recent remake of the 1930's film, and the Pieta.

Images of the Iraq War reveal much about how commercial visual media function in relation to the 'real'—that is, we can see that visual media shape how we feel about our lived worlds, how they 'hail' us as particular kinds of U.S.-identified subjects, how in this case they constructed the war for U.S. citizens through highly select images.[22] While this is not unusual (images were restricted in the case of World War II), in the case of Iraq it's hard not to see it as political given the lack of consensus about this, as also the Vietnam, war. Indeed, as briefly noted, some images from Vietnam evidently did over-arouse and encourage an anti-war sentiment the media did not intend to foster in regard to Iraq. Thus in the first year there were no images of maimed soldiers or corpses littering the landscape after a suicide or other bombings. Only belatedly and in select magazines were such realities offered in graphic stories about (still individual, but real) suffering.[23] Lacking in mainstream reporting was information about reasons for invading Iraq, and its sociocultural impact. Empty empathy prevailed.

The Abu Ghraib images, released unofficially, were shocking but not in the sense of images shown earlier as producing VT. These images, in fact, would require discussion of yet another category, namely voyeurism and sadism, which I cannot develop here. The images were shocking for what they showed about the perverse sexualities and behaviors of soldiers in extreme situations but not in the sense of empathic over-arousal. The images may have even provided some titillation for certain viewers. Susan Sontag suggested that images of the repulsive are alluring (or are seductive, if you prefer) (2003), but she did not discuss why—an area that would surely require looking at Freud and sadism.

The third preferred kind of image to be discussed, namely 'witnessing,' produces a different level of response to catastrophe. My case studies here come first from daily news reporting, and then from images of paintings in a museum.

15.3 Witnessing—and Its Ethics

As one of the few film scholars to discuss vicarious trauma in any depth, Joshua Hirsch notes that despite the mediation involved in seeing images, 'the relaying of trauma to the public through photographic imagery' can be most graphically demonstrated in Susan Sontag's description of her initial reaction to photographs of concentration camps. Sontag describes her life as divided into two parts, 'before I saw those photographs (I was twelve) and after, though it was several years before I understood fully what they were about.' She describes how 'When I looked at those photographs, something broke. Some limit had been reached, and not only that of horror; I felt

---

[22] Journalist reporting follows certain codes (or rhetorical strategies) that govern what is shown and what may be said. Briefly, in the U.S., the genre requires a focus on individual suffering and pain, on the drama of catastrophe as it affects personal lives. Personal stories sell: it's what we want to hear, rather than our feelings being evoked in a way that moves beyond the individual to the collective, in the sense of collective responsibility, not of a mere image community other scholars have discussed.

[23] See Denis Chong's narrative about Kim Phuc in Chong (2000).

irrevocably grieved, wounded, but a part of my feelings started to tighten; something went dead; something is still crying' (Sontag (1977): 19–20).

As Hirsch notes, Sontag's account provides a clear example of vicarious image-induced trauma, such as 'the sense of shock, of numbing, of being forever changed,' along with references to the 'belatedness' characteristic of traumatic reactions (Hirsch (2004): 6). But this is not only a case of VT (similar to those discussed earlier) but also an example of what I call an 'ethics of witnessing.' In line with this ethics, Sontag has been essentially transformed by the experience of seeing the holocaust photographs. Powerful feeling came first, later cognition. She continued to be interested in catastrophes and researching the question of a photograph's impact. The holocaust photographs haunted her as she grappled with questions about morality, meaning, and emotion in images, and one of the last acts of her life was electing to go to Sarajevo in the midst of the ethnic war to see how she could help. Her last book, *Regarding the Pain of Others*, returns to the question of images of horror, inspired partly by the Abu Ghraib photographs that had just appeared. The image of a Goya war etching on the cover suggests that human savagery is not new and recalls the lynching image from the American South that repeats the iconography of a hanging man and an onlooker (see Image 15.4). However, there is an important difference. In the Goya etching the soldier looks up at the hanged man, suggesting a degree of humanity, while in the lynching the white families ignore the hanged man and smile at the camera taking a photo to send to friends.

Sontag's position in her 2003 book has changed less than it may seem. While she still agrees that film and TV images change how we see the world, she adds that because we are 'not totally transformed by images of atrocity does not impugn the ethical value of *an assault by image*' (Sontag (2003): 116). 'Images,' she says, 'have been reproached for being a way of watching suffering at a distance, as if there were some other way of watching' (117). Yet that is not my critique of such images. I am rather troubled by the sentimentality of the distanced but brief and sentimental response, not just that *there is* distance. Indeed, the concept of ethical witnessing requires a degree of distance. But the distance involved in ethical self-examination and character change is a consequence of the affect experience, not a distancing that prevents emotional response. When Sontag says that 'There is nothing wrong with standing back and thinking' (118), she comes close to the ethics I have in mind. If images, as John Leonard notes in a review of *Regarding the Pain of Others*, can be 'an invitation to pay attention, to reflect, to learn, to examine the rationalization for mass suffering offered by established powers' (Leonard (2003): 10), then they are ethical. But neither Sontag nor Leonard specify which images invite us to reflect, learn—a question I turn to next.

I want to suggest that national publics need exposure to images that ask us to do a different kind of work than daily images of victims do, and that provoke a response other than those of vicarious trauma and empty empathy which, we have seen, can be limited. The trouble with images that arouse empty empathy is the passive position such pictures put the viewer in. Even the magnificent photographs of Sebastiao

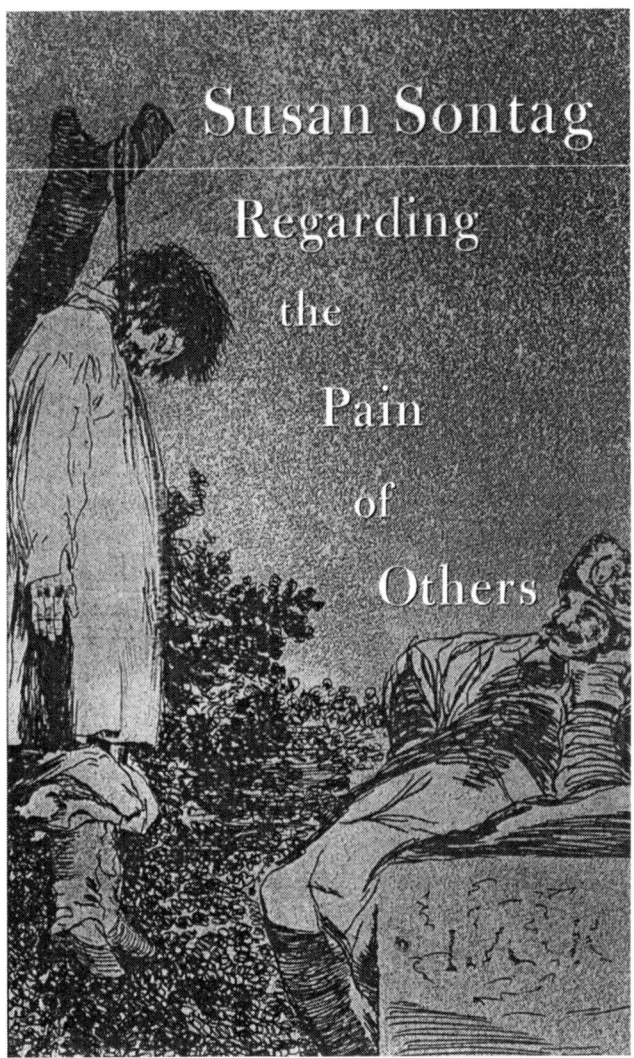

Image 15.4 Goya etching from "The Disasters of War," imaged on Susan Sontag's *Regarding the Pain of Others.*
Courtesy of Farrar, Straus, & Giroux.

Salgado reveal only the victims. While these photographs stress the subjects' dignity and perseverance against all odds, they do not move the viewer to action. They rather make one feel hopeless. Empty empathy is linked to this feeling of hopelessness, of not wanting to believe people have to suffer in these ways, to live like the photos show them living and dying. As one critic puts it, Salgado's interest in eye contact with his subjects works against his desire for social change in not showing the people angry or enraged about their situation, or showing the perpetrators.[24]

Witnessing as I conceive it involves an element of both vicarious trauma—the shock of recognition of humans' capacity for evil—and empathy proper, that is as Hoffman put it, a deep and enduring identification with what the victims in the case feel. Just observing would not be witnessing in this enhanced sense. Observing might produce VT, but again that alone would not be witnessing. Something else has to come in for witnessing to take place. The pro-social aspect of empathy sets the stage for witnessing, since taking responsibility for injustice by listening carefully to victims or actually doing something about injustice as Sontag did, is required for witnessing. I'll return to these issues after looking at case studies.

The first Katrina images gestured toward the kind of reporting that might come close to witnessing because viewers had a sense of the whole situation and could vicariously experience the impact on many, not just individuals. It is instructive to compare and contrast the media reporting from images brought to us from Iraq with images from Hurricane Katrina. While from the start, images of the war in Iraq were heavily controlled, resulting in the empty empathy and other emotions, in the case of Katrina the government was so out of the loop, so unaware or uncaring about New Orleans and the dangers certain areas faced, that the reporters were on the ground or in the air sending digital images before anyone at the White House knew or understood the implications of their unconscious carelessness about the largely African American people in areas of danger. One striking difference between the early Iraq photos focused on close-ups of soldiers and these early Katrina images is that here we see individuals as members of groups, not the focus *only* on individuals as in the early Iraq photos. The implicit government control in the case of Iraq has two consequences. First, this control limited what images reporters were allowed to print (at this stage, no images of severely wounded American soldiers, no images of coffins being flown back to the U.S., no images of badly mutilated veterans, etc.).[25] Second, government control entailed images taking the forms I discussed that generated patriotic emotions. In the case of Katrina, the early lack of control allowed for a greater variety of forms that generated more complex, varied, and ethical emotional impact involving both empathy and shock.

For example, let's look at a sequence of Katrina images that appeared together in *The New York Times*. First, an image of people crowded outside the superdome waiting to get in allowed us to see the entire situation (Image 15.5). The people here do not form an anonymous group without context as in the shots of camps in Darfur mentioned

---

[24] Nancy Scheper-Hughes (2003) wonders why Salgado doesn't show perpetrators: 'Might the next big book by Sebastiao be entitled *Capitalism*, depicting the great, clanking, grinding gears of global capitalism? . . . Might we fantasize a series of portraits . . . not of children but of the agents of capital?' (42).

[25] This very censoring confirms that images do have a powerful emotional impact or else why forbid them?

Image 15.5 Katrina 2005: Outside the Superdome. Thousands of people waited for buses to take them away.

With permission of Nicole Benginveno/*The New York Times*/Redux.

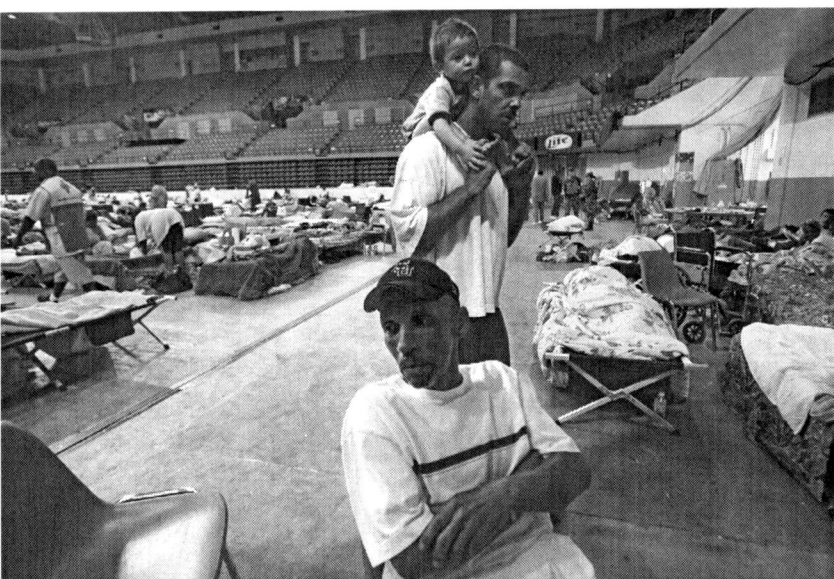

Image 15.6 Katrina 2005: Inside the Superdome. People settling into the dome.

With permission of Vincent Laforet/*The New York Times*/Redux.

Image 15.7 Katrina 2005: In the streets. After the floodwaters, silent streets tell tales.
With permission of Nicole Benginveno/ *The New York Times*/Redux.

before. We see their bodies and some faces, and can empathize with their plight as they wait for relief. Second, the camera moves inside the dome (Image 15.6). This image allows the viewer to move on from empathic emotions elicited by the dejection and hopelessness of the individual in the foreground to many others further back in the dome. Here the space in the background is shown as well as a close-up of a man in the foreground. Third, photos of the devastated environment without any people in sight suggest much about the suffering and about the general situation as opposed to one person's specific loss (Image 15.7). The doll lying abandoned suggests the haste with which a child was rushed out of the area, and the sneaker too indicates no time even to pick up a shoe. There were also devastating images of corpses floating in the water, or of simple shrines to the dead. There was no government prohibition on images of devastation or of suffering because at first Katrina was considered only a 'natural' disaster. Only later did the (perhaps unconscious) politics emerge in regard to the relationship between lack of preparation for the hurricane and the social group most vulnerable to it.

These first images did not, perhaps could not, fall into the personal story genre that was firmly kept in place for the reporting of the Iraq War. The chaos was such that at first there were no spokespersons for the victims as there were in the well-organized U.S. Military in Iraq, who colluded with government wishes about what to show and say, and what to keep hidden. The people in New Orleans were struggling simply to escape and survive, leaving it to reporters to catch what images they could of the catastrophe. As time went on, journalists resorted to the personal story but still editorials and columnists in the *New York Times* continued, especially with the investigation into FEMA (Federal Emergency Management Agency) and into the extent and timing of government knowledge, to discuss larger issues in which emerged emotions like shame about the abandonment of a largely African American population to the horrendous fatal floods.

Images of people left to drown, waiting for busses that never came, of the old people left in retirement communities to die, of those finally seeming to be safe in the superdome only to discover it was insecure and without provisions, aroused my empathy but also anger and shame that this could happen in the U.S. In registering the injustice, I was providing a witness to people's pain. The relatively free flow of images under the radar of government control allowed political knowledge to be felt in a way not possible in reporting from Iraq with their accompanying rhetoric of heroism, bravery, sacrifice.

The Katrina images permitted a certain level of witnessing to unconscious racism in the U.S. through inviting viewers to move from empathic identification with the individual to the group, the community, the context. In experiencing the affect of the images, then, we were lead from empathy with the individual to the mass (perhaps the only way that we can come to empathize with a group), and a model for what we can hope for through 'witnessing.' We had to think about how it was that a mass of people were under such needless duress. We became witnesses to the catastrophe and its injustice.

My final case studies come from paintings in a museum. Jerome Witkin's 'Entering Darkness' was inspired by an account by a Red Cross Nurse, Dorothy Wahlstrom, in Rhonda Lewin's *Witnesses to the Holocaust* (see Image 15.8). This painting at once offers the viewer identification with a protagonist, the Nurse entering Dachau as part of the liberation of camps in 1945, while at the same time, on another level, the painting renders the horror of what the Nazis did through ghastly surreal images beyond the Nurse's single consciousness. In a way, her consciousness is located as just one element of the traumatic shock of the liberators and the western world at understanding what had gone on in the camps. The painting, then, partly expresses horror through the Nurse, but the images also move beyond her purview to mythical, allegorical levels that gesture towards a common trope of revulsion at violence and human devastation of other humans.

Richard Harden's 'My Breath' and 'Falling,' another huge composite painting, is made up of two linked parts, and takes a less realist narrative position (Image 15.9). Here we see first what looks like an innocent field of poppies (although those of us who know Anselm Kiefer's work would immediately suspect something) only to find, as we continue to gaze, what looks like a corpse or skeleton scattered amongst the flowers. The side panels figure nude women, their gaze turned from the viewer, apparently sinking down in a whirling mass of ashes. The viewer is placed so as to

Image 15.8 *Entering Darkness*, by Jerome Witkin.
Courtesy of Jack Rutberg Fine Arts Los Angeles.

Image 15.9 *My Breath* and *Falling*, by Richard Harden.
Courtesy of Richard Harden.

understand this is a world gone awry: natural beauty contains horror; women, made vulnerable by nakedness and falling amid ashes, brings up Nazi camp associations although this work evidently refers to Kosovo. The uncertainty of which catastrophe is indicated adds to the generalization crucial to an ethics of witnessing, and to a certain distancing effect that is necessary for an ethical impact.

We might call response to these paintings the 'Sontag Effect,' referring back to my earlier discussion of Sontag's reaction to seeing images of Holocaust victims. Dori Laub's reflections on his work with Holocaust victims also illuminate witnessing as against the simpler experience of empathy or vicarious trauma (Laub (1995)). For Laub, what makes the Holocaust so horrifying is that, 'during its historical occurrence, *the event produced no witnesses'* (1995: 65).[26] Here Laub is not saying that there were no *observers* but as noted earlier, observing is not witnessing. Arguably the difference involves distance. Inside the camps, there was no distance, no ability to situate what was happening against some other reality. Empathic sharing entails closeness but may lead to the over-arousal of vicarious trauma, or the sentimentalism of empty empathy. Witnessing has to do with an image producing a deliberate ethical consciousness through empathic affect not related only to a specific person or character. For in bearing witness, in the sense I intend here, one not only provides a witness where no one was there to witness before, but relatedly, one may feel motivated to see that justice is done. Witnessing involves wanting to change the kind of world where injustice, of whatever kind, is common. While individual efforts, as in therapy, are immensely important (and therapists, like Laub, are often witnesses of a sort), there is also a need to mobilize the consciousness of large communities, such as the nation state, in which people elect their leaders and vote for or against policies that affect people's daily lives. The concept of empathy has to be extended from identification with a victim in the here and now to identification with groups, and from there to thinking about who is responsible for suffering. 'Witnessing' is the term I use for prompting an ethical response that will perhaps radically change the way someone views the world, or thinks about justice. Vicarious traumatization may be a component of witnessing (as we saw in the Vietnam images), but instead of only intensifying the desire to help an individual in front of one, witnessing leads to a broader empathic understanding of the meaning of what has been done to victims, of the politics of trauma being possible.[27]

Most images that we see are part of consumer culture, and hence usually participate in prevailing culture codes that promote a focus on individual pain made public. It's as if personal pain is politics, leaving no room for a concept of the collective or of our collective response-ability (see Oliver (2004)) for national or international policies. Iraq War photos imaging individual soldiers and marines on the battlefield mask the Real of what is going on. They create an illusory screen hiding the unconscious that knows but does not know the devastation and loss of life the invasion has caused. We are not invited to understand the situation and its wrongs, as was more possible in the early Katrina images. The Iraq images concealed what they could not show (and still have trouble showing, namely horrible wounds, civilian deaths, impossible missions, etc.).[28]

---

[26] Most importantly for my purposes, 'it is the encounter and the coming together between the survivor and the listener (standing in for the community) which makes possible something like a repossession of the act of witnessing. This joint responsibility is the source of the emerging truth' (69).

[27] One of the therapists in Hoffman's study treated several abused girls. She became an activist against such abuse. Her experiences with her patients thus transformed her and moved her to actively trying to help victims.

[28] On Sunday May 14, a *New York Times* article, 'Army Concerned About HBO War Film,' discussed senior military officials' worry over graphic footage of soldiers in a Baghdad Hospital being treated for wounds from roadside bombs and in combat. One HBO official noted that 'Anything showing the grim realities of war is, in a sense, antiwar.' Others however see the documentary as a tribute to the heroism of both soldiers and medical personnel (*New York Times*, Sunday May 14, 2006, p.24).

One of the main characteristics of the witnessing position is the deliberate refusal of an identification only with the specificity of individuals—a deliberate distancing from the subject to enable the interviewer to take in and respond to the traumatic *situation* (see David Becker (2003)), as in Witkin's and Harden's paintings. When a work constructs this sort of position for the spectator, it opens the text out to larger social and political meanings. Empathic identification with an individual is only the start: the narrative and structure of the paintings lead the viewer on from individuals to collectivities.

15.4 Epilogue

In this chapter, I have drawn on three genealogies—that of the history of images, of the new cultural studies research on public feelings, and psychology research on empathy—showing that images of catastrophe are the point of intersection of these genealogies or archives. Traumatic images are the site where feelings become public. Yet recent humanities research on public feelings has seldom considered the emotional impact of daily viewing of images of catastrophe.[29] This is partly because evidence is hard to obtain.[30] Witnessing is necessary for national traumas. People as collectively responsible require structures within which often silently endured traumatic experiences can be 'spoken' or imaged, and through which we can change the way we see the world, feeling (through empathic identification instead of only cognizing) injustice as something to be fought against collectively. In other words, one aim of the project is to make caring about injustice a predominant public feeling.

---

[29] In addition, in looking at the three dominant ways of responding to images of catastrophe, I have shown first how public feelings become private (e.g. how the media portrayal of the Iraq invasion as patriotism produces individual patriotic feeling); second, how private feelings become paradigms for public policy (e.g. how love for an individual's white child becomes a public policy that implicitly sanctions racism—as in Hurricane Katrina); and finally, I showed how the public sphere mobilizes individual feelings as (or instead of) political discourse (Berlant (1997)) (Iraq and Jessica Lynch). Overall, I showed how in our era of proliferation of traumatic images, private and public feelings become merged; rationality and emotion are all but impossible to separate. In this situation, it is more important than ever for scholars to study the relationship of viewers to media images, including the emotions involved in increasing ideological bias across corporate media

[30] Rather than neglect this important area of enquiry, as you have seen, I have used what data I found, including case studies drawn from my own and my students' experiences in order to begin the process of theorizing emotional response provoked by public images of catastrophes.

16

Is Empathy a Virtue?

Heather D. Battaly

Is empathy a virtue?[1] Pre-theoretically, we think that empathy involves caring about, or sharing the emotions of, or knowing another person. To see this, we need only consider paradigm cases of empathy; for example, the empathy of a close friend, or therapist. Empathic friends and therapists care about the subject, share in her emotional highs and lows, and reliably predict her thoughts, feelings, and behavior. Is empathy, so construed, a virtue? Pre-theoretically, we treat it as one. After all, we think that empathy in friends and therapists makes them better people, and that it is morally good to care, know about, and share the emotions of others. We also resoundingly agree that it is morally good for doctors, teachers, and even fellow citizens to be empathic. We regularly praise doctors and teachers for caring about their patients and students, and reproach them when they do not. We also commend the empathic citizen who stops to aid victims of an accident, and judge those who pass by to be of lesser character. Pre-theoretically, we conceive of empathy as a quality that makes us morally good—as a moral virtue, ordinarily construed.[2]

Philosophers and psychologists have tried to improve on our ordinary, pre-theoretical concept of empathy by making it more accurate and precise. I will argue that if we adopt their current 'improved' concepts of empathy, then empathy is neither a moral nor an intellectual virtue. Ironically, our ordinary, 'unimproved' concept of empathy is better-suited for arguing that empathy is a virtue; but because it is, as it stands, a vague folk concept, such arguments will not get far. In section 16.1, I provide a conceptual overview which enumerates four different concepts of empathy, the first

[1] I would like to thank Peter Goldie, Amy Coplan and her 2008 seminar students, Jason Baehr and his 2007 seminar students, and two anonymous referees for comments on an earlier draft. I am also grateful to Bruce Russell, the participants of the 2008 Russell IV workshop, and to the participants of the Fall 2007 Carlsberg Foundation UCLA epistemology workshop, especially Nikolaj Pedersen and Mikkel Gerken. Thanks also to audiences at the 2006 Empathy Conference at Cal State Fullerton and the 2007 Conference on Understanding Other Minds and Moral Agency at Holy Cross College.
[2] Our ordinary, or folk, concept of a moral virtue is silent with respect to whether virtues are, or are not, dispositions. Our folk concept of a moral virtue centers on the notion that virtues are qualities that make us morally good people.

of which captures the ordinary, pre-theoretical concept of empathy described above, and the remaining three of which emerge from the contemporary philosophical and psychological literature. In section 16.2, I introduce the main features of virtues, skills, and capacities. I argue that there are three primary differences between virtues and skills. My arguments make use of work in virtue ethics and virtue epistemology. In section 16.3, I contend that if we adopt any of the three theoretical concepts of empathy that are prevalent in the philosophical and psychological literature, then empathy is not a virtue. Specifically, empathy, so construed, is not sufficient for virtue. I do not attempt to determine whether it is necessary, nor do I deny that it might help us attain virtues. If empathy, so construed, turned out to be necessary for virtue possession, then it would have some moral value.[3] The point of section 16.3 is just that empathy, so construed, is not itself a virtue. It will be a skill only if it is a voluntary ability, rather than an involuntary capacity. Does this mean that philosophers and psychologists have led us astray—that we should reject the three theoretical concepts of empathy? Not necessarily. In Section 16.4, I argue that the fact that these theoretical concepts of empathy conflict with our ordinary concept does not by itself constitute sufficient grounds for rejecting them. Ordinary concepts do not automatically trump theoretical concepts.[4]

16.1 Concepts of Empathy: An Overview

I identify four different concepts of empathy: (1) empathy as caring, and/or sharing, and/or knowing; (2) empathy as sharing by multiple means; (3) empathy as sharing and knowing; and (4) empathy as knowing by multiple means. The first is meant to capture our ordinary, pre-theoretical concept of empathy. Concepts (2) and (3) are in wide use in the contemporary philosophical and psychological literature. Concept (4) is present in that same literature, though less dominant. My current goal is not to decide which of these is the 'real' concept of empathy, if there even is such a thing. It is only to demonstrate that when we adopt concept (2), (3), *or* (4), empathy is not a virtue.

16.1.1 Concept (1): empathy as caring, and/or sharing, and/or knowing

Empathy is a process of caring, or sharing, or knowing, or some combination thereof. This is the broadest and least precise of the four concepts. It is meant to capture the empathy of one's best friend or therapist, ordinarily construed. Best friends and therapists often *care* about the target for his own sake; their motivations are often altruistic. They often *share* the emotions (or other mental states) of the target, and they

---

[3] Granted, empathy might then be instrumentally morally valuable rather than intrinsically morally valuable.

[4] Nor do theoretical concepts automatically trump ordinary concepts. Here, I neither endorse nor reject the folk concept of empathy; nor endorse nor reject any of the theoretical concepts of empathy. See section 16.4.

typically understand, *know*, and can predict the target's emotions, beliefs, and actions. As a folk concept, we can expect (1) to be vague about exactly what is required for caring, sharing, and knowing. We can also expect it to be vague about whether each of these three components is necessary or (in combination) sufficient for empathy. In other words, this concept of empathy is combinatorially vague or thin: there is no definite answer as to which combination of conditions is necessary or sufficient for its application.[5]

A concept is combinatorially vague if and only if: (a) it has multiple conditions of application; (b) different fluent speakers appeal to different combinations of those conditions in applying the concept; and (c) there is no definite answer as to which of those combinations of conditions is necessary or sufficient for its application (Battaly (2001): 99). Our ordinary concepts of art, science, and religion are vague in this way. Take the ordinary concept of religion. When we examine paradigm cases of religion, we find that they exhibit certain features, including: prayer, belief in supernatural beings, ritualistic behavior, the identification of sacred objects, and a world view that defines the role of the individual in the world.[6] When *all* of these conditions are met, as in the case of Judaism, fluent speakers will agree that the concept of religion applies, and when *none* are met, as in the case of piano-playing, we will agree that it does not apply. But, there are cases where some but not all of the conditions are met (e.g. Communism meets the last three conditions), in which fluent speakers will be uncertain, or disagree, about whether the concept applies. Such disagreements are not caused by a lack of information—we all know which conditions are satisfied—but by the concept's combinatorial vagueness.[7] In short, there is no definite answer as to which combination of the above conditions is necessary for the application of 'religion,' or which, short of the whole, is sufficient. Those who think that the final three conditions are sufficient will claim that Communism is a religion, whereas those who require a belief in supernatural beings will deny this. Since the ordinary concept of religion does not determine which of the above conditions are necessary or sufficient for its application, both of these applications—'Communism is a religion', and 'Communism is not a religion'—are correct. To borrow a metaphor from Michael Lynch, a vague concept is like a roughly drawn sketch which can be completed in different ways (Lynch (1998): 72). No one way of completing it is any less correct than another. It is no less correct to apply the concept of religion by emphasizing belief in supernatural beings than it is to apply the concept by emphasizing ritualistic behavior. Both of these

---

[5] See H. Battaly (2008a, 2001). This notion of thin concepts is not identical to Bernard Williams' notion. This notion claims that thin concepts are combinatorially vague. Thin concepts can be purely descriptive, purely evaluative, or simultaneously descriptive and evaluative. In contrast, for Williams, thin ethical concepts, like 'right' and 'wrong' are purely evaluative, not descriptive (Williams (1985): 152).

[6] This example is William Alston's. See Alston (1964) and (1967): 218–21; Battaly (2001).

[7] Similarly, concepts like 'tall' and 'bald' admit of borderline cases. Fluent speakers might know S's exact height, and still disagree about whether S is tall. See Keefe & Smith (1996) and Williamson (1994).

ways of applying the concept are correct, even though these different emphases will yield different extensions.[8]

Just as there is more than one correct way to apply the ordinary concept of religion, there is more than one correct way to apply the ordinary concept of empathy. Fluent speakers will agree that the concept of empathy applies to best friends and therapists, like *Star Trek: The Next Generation*'s Deanna Troi, who cares about *and* knows us, *and* shares our emotions.[9] We will also agree that the concept does not apply to Ebenezer Scrooge, who meets none of these conditions. Moreover, there will be cases where some but not all of these conditions are met, in which we will be uncertain, or disagree, about whether the concept applies. Consider Dexter, the protagonist of the eponymous television series, who works for the Miami police department by day, and murders criminals by night. Arguably, Dexter neither cares about nor shares the emotions of his victims, but knows and predicts their mental states and actions. When fluent speakers disagree about whether Dexter is empathic, we do not do so because of a lack of information—we all know which conditions Dexter satisfies. Rather, we disagree because our ordinary concept of empathy is combinatorially vague. There is no definite answer as to which combination of caring, sharing, and knowing is necessary for its application, or which, short of the whole, is sufficient. Those who think that knowing is sufficient will claim that Dexter is empathic; those who think that caring or sharing is necessary will not. Since the ordinary concept of empathy does not fix which of these conditions should be used, both of these applications are correct. The ordinary concept of empathy can also be correctly applied to agents who share the affect of, but do not care about or know, the target, and to agents who care about the target, but do not know the target or share her affect.

Applications of our ordinary concept of empathy abound in contemporary popular culture, and occasionally appear in the philosophical and psychological literature. Nancy Sherman suggests that our intuitive concept of empathy is informed by Heinz Kohut's clinical concept of empathy. According to Sherman, Kohut's concept 'combines both the notion of empathy as a mode of understanding . . . and as an affective mode by which to communicate that understanding in supportive ways' (Sherman (1998): 96). She describes our intuitive concept as follows: 'to be empathetic is to be a good listener, to imaginatively engage in another's thoughts and feelings without becoming overly enmeshed in them . . . It is to understand but also to let another know, in a supportive way, how and what one understands' (Sherman (1998): 96). The

---

[8] In the literature on vagueness, it is often held that sentences of the form 'either S is P or S is not P', where P is a vague predicate, violate the law of the excluded middle. For example, because 'religion' and 'tall' are vague predicates, 'Either Communism is a religion or it is not a religion' and 'S is either tall or not tall' arguably violate the law of the excluded middle. See Keefe & Smith (1996) and Williamson (1994). I am grateful to an anonymous referee for raising this issue.

[9] The character Deanna Troi is a member of a species of 'empaths,' and therapist to the crew of the Enterprise. She meets all of the conditions associated with the ordinary concept of empathy. She shares the emotions of her crew, knows and can predict their mental states and actions, and cares about and counsels them through problems.

concept Sherman describes approximates the folk concept that I am trying to capture.[10] The same three features are represented: the empathic person cares about and supports the target, shares the target's affect, and knows that the target has particular mental states. Adam Smith's notion of sympathy, often cited as a starting point in the contemporary philosophical and psychological literature, also approximates our folk concept of empathy.[11] Smith thinks that sympathy makes us interested in 'the fortune of others, and render[s] their happiness necessary to [us], though [we] derive nothing from it' (Smith (1759/1976): 9). In short, sympathy involves caring about others. According to Smith, the source of our sympathy for others involves 'changing places' with them (Smith (1759/1976): 10). In his words, 'By the imagination we place ourselves in his situation . . . and become in some measure the same person with him, and thence form some idea of his sensations, and even feel something which, though weaker in degree, is not altogether unlike them' (Smith (1759/1976): 9). That is, sharing the target's affect and knowing his feelings is said to give rise to caring about the target.

The three theoretical concepts of empathy examined below try to improve on our ordinary concept of empathy by making it more accurate and precise. It is no accident that they try to do so by emphasizing one, or another, of the conditions associated with our ordinary concept. Because our ordinary concept of empathy is vague, it can be filled out in different ways, yielding distinct theoretical concepts. Each of the three theoretical concepts fills out our ordinary concept by highlighting a different condition or combination of conditions: sharing, sharing and knowing, or knowing, respectively. Each completes the empathy 'sketch' differently, and in so doing, carves out a distinct extension.[12]

Below, we will see that all three of these extensions exclude agents who care but neither share nor know. In contrast, the extension of our ordinary concept of empathy includes 'merely caring' agents. Hence, all three theoretical concepts are incompatible with part of our ordinary concept (they are erasing part of the original sketch). This sort of result is not unusual: theoretical concepts sometimes conflict with parts of ordinary concepts. Indeed, insofar as we assign theoretical concepts the task of correcting inaccuracies in ordinary concepts, we should expect such conflict.[13] In this vein, Saul Kripke argues that it is possible to discover, via theory, that some of the conditions associated with our ordinary concepts of natural kinds, like 'gold,' are incorrect. According to Kripke, though we ordinarily conceive of gold as a yellow metal, 'some of these marks may not really be true of gold. We might discover that we were wrong about them' (Kripke (1980): 118–19). We might discover, via theory, that

---

[10] Sherman's concept is too strong. It implies that caring, sharing, and knowing are each necessary for empathy. The folk concept that I describe does not imply this.

[11] Smith's concept may also be too strong.

[12] Their extensions partly overlap, but they are not identical.

[13] Alvin Goldman assigns theoretical concepts this role in his 'Epistemic Folkways and Scientific Epistemology', in Goldman (1992): 155–77.

gold must have the atomic number 79—a condition not included in our ordinary concept—but that it need not be yellow.

Something similar can be said of our ordinary concept of empathy: it is *possible* to discover, via theory, that we are wrong about some of the conditions associated with our folk concept of empathy. This does *not* mean that we have already made such discoveries: it does *not* mean that we have already discovered that empathy is not a virtue (though we have already discovered that gold need not be yellow.) Nor does it mean that in cases of conflict, theoretical concepts are always correct and ordinary concepts always incorrect. Though the above conflict over 'gold' favors the theoretical concept, some conflicts favor ordinary concepts. For instance, if a theoretical concept of consciousness entailed that human beings were not conscious, we would reject the theoretical concept.[14] Some will argue that we should likewise reject any theoretical concept of empathy that entails that empathy is not a virtue.[15]

Can we use our ordinary concept of empathy to argue that empathy is a virtue? If we use our folk concept as it stands, without further theoretical 'improvement', our arguments will not get far. Granted, we ordinarily think that it is morally good to care about and know others, and share their emotions. But, at best, this will only enable us to contend that empathy, ordinarily construed, is a virtue, ordinarily construed. This is not philosophically satisfying. What we want, as philosophers, are more precise concepts of empathy and virtue: we want our theoretical concepts to improve on our ordinary concepts. Only after we have developed more precise concepts of empathy and virtue, will it be worthwhile for us to ask whether empathy is a virtue. None of this entails that our current theoretical concepts of empathy are correct. As we shall see in section 16.3, if we adopt concept (2), (3), or (4), then empathy is not a virtue. One possible response to this state of affairs is to claim that since theoretical concepts (2), (3), and (4) conflict with our ordinary intuition that empathy *is* a virtue, (2), (3), and (4) are all incorrect. In which case, one might return to our ordinary concept of empathy and use it to develop new theoretical concepts, perhaps concepts that emphasize the caring condition. A new theoretical concept might enable us to argue that empathy is a virtue.[16]

16.1.2 Concept (2): empathy as sharing by multiple means

Empathy is the sharing of mental states including, but not limited to, affect. One empathizes with the target if and only if one has roughly the same mental state as the target. According to Nancy Eisenberg and Janet Strayer, 'empathizing involves the vicarious sharing of affect' (1987: 3). They define empathy as 'an emotional response that stems from another's emotional state or condition and that is congruent with the other's emotional state or situation' (1987: 5). Similarly, Martin Hoffman argues that

---

[14] Thanks to Peter Goldie for this example.
[15] I think such claims are premature. See section 16.4.
[16] Thanks to Jason Baehr for this suggestion.

empathy is a set of 'psychological processes that make a person have feelings that are more congruent with another's situation than with his own situation' (2000: 30). Empathy is 'the vicarious affective response to another person' whereby one 'feels what the other feels' (Hoffman (2000): 29–30). In his recent work, Alvin Goldman endorses a 'dual-process' account of empathy, whereby empathy includes both low- and high-level simulation (Goldman (2006a): 207). According to Goldman, the minimal condition for successful mental simulation is a match in mental states (2006a: 132).

One can empathically share affect, or other mental states, by different means. Eisenberg and Strayer acknowledge that their concept of empathy includes both emotional contagion, and perspective-taking. Contagion occurs when one involuntarily 'catches' an emotion from someone else; for instance, when one catches happiness from a roomful of laughing people. In 'catching' happiness from another, one shares the other's affect, but one need not recognize that one shares the other's affect, that one caught the affect, or that the other exists at all (Eisenberg & Strayer (1987): 6). In contrast with contagion, perspective-taking is a voluntary and effortful process, whereby the subject imagines what emotions the target would have in a particular situation. In addition to producing shared affect, successful perspective-taking is usually thought to produce epistemic output—a cognitive awareness, belief, or knowledge that the target has said affect (Eisenberg & Strayer (1987): 9).

Hoffman argues that there are five empathy-arousing modes: (1) mimicry; (2) conditioning; (3) direct association; (4) mediated association; and (5) perspective-taking (Hoffman (2000): 37–59). Briefly, (1) facial and postural mimicry of others occurs automatically in infants (and adults), and produces emotional states in them that match the emotional states of the other. One can share another's feeling of (say) distress via (2) conditioning, when one is repeatedly exposed to someone in distress while simultaneously feeling distressed oneself; or via (3) direct association, when the other is present and her situation triggers a memory that causes distress. One can share the feelings of absent others via (4) mediated association when hearing or reading about them triggers memories that produce feelings of the same type. Finally, one can share the affect of others via (5) perspective-taking. In self-focused perspective-taking, the observer imagines how she (the observer) would feel in the other's situation; whereas in other-focused perspective-taking, the observer imagines how the other would feel in that situation. Hoffman claims that mimicry, conditioning, and direct association are involuntary, and do not require epistemic awareness that one's emotion is a response to another's emotion. In contrast, mediated association and perspective-taking can be subject to voluntary control, and do produce epistemic outputs about how the target feels (Hoffman (2000): 49).

Goldman argues that there are two routes to empathy: low- and high-level simulation. The prototype of low-level simulation is mirroring, which occurs when the mirror neurons and resonance systems of an observer cause her to share the target's mental state (Goldman (2006a): 133). According to Goldman, mirroring is involuntary and automatic, and does not entail mindreading or epistemic output of any kind. It requires only that the 'receiver' undergo a matching mental event via her mirror system. The receiver need not 'know (or believe) that such a mirroring event occurs,' or 'know about her own mental event,' or 'know that it matches an event occurring in a sender. She may not think about the sender or connect her own mental event with an event in the sender' (Goldman (2006a): 133). In contrast, the prototype of high-level simulation is enactment imagination, an often effortful type of perspective-taking. The observer 'E-imagines' the affect of the target by pretending to be the target. She does this by generating inputs—pretend mental states that are supposed to match the target's actual input states—which she feeds into her own affect-generating mechanism. The observer's mechanism outputs an affective state that is supposed to match the affect of the target. Finally, the observer ascribes this affective state to the target. Goldman claims that this ascription is a belief about the target's mental state. Hence, E-imagination produces beliefs about the target's mental states, but low-level mirroring does not. In short, the views of Eisenberg and Strayer, Hoffman, and Goldman demonstrate that the notion of empathy as sharing by multiple means requires (with few exceptions[17]) *sharing* the mental state of the other, but does not require *knowing* that the other has that mental state. Contagion, mimicry, mirroring, conditioning, and direct association are ways of empathizing that do not produce epistemic output.

Their views also demonstrate that the concept of empathy as sharing by multiple means does not require caring about others. With regard to caring—altruistic motivation—Eisenberg and Strayer offer a definition of sympathy that differs from their definition of empathy: 'Sympathy is 'feeling for' someone,' and 'often involves feelings of concern' (1987: 6). They argue that empathy is not sufficient for sympathy.

Hoffman is sometimes interpreted to claim that empathy, or at least empathic distress, conceptually entails caring about others. This interpretation is incorrect. Granted, Hoffman does state that 'empathic distress is a prosocial motive' (2000: 30); and that after age two, empathic distress is 'transformed . . . into a . . . reciprocal feeling of concern for the victim, and . . . a motive to help the victim' (2000: 87), and thus includes 'a sympathetic component' (2000: 88). But, Hoffman's claims are contingent and causal, not conceptual. Hoffman is arguing that empathic distress usually causes altruistic motives; not that altruistic motives are conceptually entailed by empathic distress. Two points validate this interpretation. First, Hoffman uses empirical studies to argue that empathic distress is correlated with altruistic motivation (2000: 30–6). He treats this hypothesized correlation as one that can be confirmed or disconfirmed by empirical evidence; as a contingent claim that might be false. The studies Hoffman cites confirm the hypothesized correlation; but had those studies found it to be false, Hoffman would *not* have asserted that subjects in them lacked empathic distress, only that their empathic distress did not cause altruistic motives. Second, Hoffman identifies

---

[17] Hoffman contends that though successful empathy standardly involves a close match in the observer's and target's affect, there are some exceptions. See Hoffman (2000): 80–6, 98.

cases in which empathic distress does *not* cause altruistic motivation. For instance, in the earliest developmental stages of empathy—newborn reactive cry and egocentric empathic distress—infants lack altruistic motives. Additionally, in cases of over-arousal, the empathic distress of the observer is so painful that it causes her to ignore the target and focus solely on alleviating her own distress (Hoffman (2000: 198–205). And in cases of 'habituation' or 'compassion fatigue,' an observer's repeated exposure to a victim's distress causes the observer's empathic distress to 'diminish to the point of indifference to the victim's suffering.' (Hoffman (2000): 203) In short, Hoffman is arguing that empathic distress usually causes caring about the target, not that empathic distress conceptually entails caring about the target.

Goldman also argues that the connection between empathy and caring is causal, not conceptual. Neither mirroring nor E-imagination is conceptually sufficient for caring about the target. Mirroring and contagion do not 'constitute a form of altruistic motivation, such as concern... to help' because a 'motivation to help would require mindreading of the other, attributing to the other a state of distress' (Goldman (2006a): 291–2). For Goldman, neither mirroring nor contagion entails mindreading. E-imagination does not entail altruistic motivation because psychopaths can E-imagine without caring about the target. Following Shaun Nichols (2004: 56–60), Goldman posits a concern mechanism, which is conceptually distinct from, but causally triggered in normals by, mirroring and E-imagination (Goldman (2006a): 294). In sum, the views of Eisenberg and Strayer, Hoffman, and Goldman demonstrate that the notion of empathy as sharing by multiple means requires (with few exceptions) *sharing* the mental state of the other, but does not require *caring* about the other or *knowing* her mental states.

16.1.3 Concept (3): empathy as sharing and knowing/mindreading

Empathy is a process that produces shared mental states *and* a cognitive grasp of, belief about, or knowledge of another's mental states. Hence, one empathizes with the target only if one shares the target's mental state and cognitively assigns that mental state to the target. This notion of empathy includes high-level simulation processes, like imaginative perspective-taking. Low-level simulation processes (e.g. mirroring, mimicry, contagion) are excluded on the grounds that they do not conceptually entail mindreading.

This concept of empathy includes both of Peter Goldie's (2000) main varieties of imaginative perspective-taking—what he calls 'in-his-shoes imagining' and 'empathy'—and Amy Coplan's (2004) version of perspective-taking—what she calls 'empathy'. All three of these versions of perspective-taking involve simulating the mental states of the target and cognitively assigning those mental states to the target. Goldie argues that empathy is a process by which one 'centrally imagines the... thoughts, feelings, and emotions... of another person' (Goldie (2000): 195). To empathize with a target, one must imaginatively experience the target's mental states. For instance, one must imaginatively *feel* the target's shame—thus, sharing her affect—rather than imagine *that* the target is ashamed (Goldie (2000): 195). The agent must also have background knowledge of the target's character and current situation, and recognize that she and the target are distinct—that the target's character traits, beliefs, and desires may differ from her own. In contrast, Goldie's 'in-his-shoes' imagining (like Hoffman's self-focused perspective-taking) does not require the agent to distinguish herself from the target. Instead, it requires the agent to imagine what mental state she—the agent— would have in the target's situation. Goldie thinks that both empathy and 'in-his-shoes' imagining produce epistemic output. Successful empathy is one (but hardly the only) way of knowing what the target's mental states are. 'In-his-shoes' imagining produces beliefs about the target's mental states, but those beliefs may well be false (Goldie (2000): 202).

On Coplan's view, to empathize with a target, one must: (1) share the mental states of the target; (2) 'imaginatively experience the target's [mental states] from the target's point of view'; (3) attain (1) as a result of (2); and (4) maintain a distinction between oneself and the target (Coplan (2004): 144). According to Coplan, one cannot successfully empathize with a target unless one experiences (say) affect that is qualitatively the same as the target's affect. Nor can one successfully empathize unless one maintains self–other differentiation. To do the latter, one must avoid fusing with the target: avoid thinking that, or acting as if, the simulated emotion is one's own emotion rather than the target's. In Coplan's words, when I successfully empathize with (say) Joe, 'imaginatively experiencing what he experiences, I am still aware of the fact that those experiences are Joe's and not mine' (Coplan (2004): 144). I share Joe's affect, but I also realize that the affect is his, not my own. Coplan does not explicitly claim that successful empathizers form full-blown beliefs about the target's mental states. But, her account of self–other differentiation commits her to claiming that the empathizer is cognitively aware that the simulated mental state is the target's (rather than her own).

The views of Goldie and Coplan demonstrate that the notion of empathy as sharing and knowing requires *sharing* the mental state of the target, and *knowing* or cognitively grasping the target's mental state, but does not require *caring* about the target. Goldie and Coplan both explicitly deny that empathy conceptually entails sympathy. Goldie contends that unlike sympathy, empathy and in-his-shoes imagining do not conceptually entail the motivation to alleviate the target's distress. Rather, they are consistent with: utter indifference with respect to the target's suffering, rejoicing in the target's suffering, and the motivation to alleviate one's own suffering rather than the target's (Goldie (2000): 215). Coplan argues that though there is an empirical correlation between empathy and sympathy, the two phenomena are distinct: 'empathy . . . does not in and of itself involve . . . an impulse [to help the other]' (2004: 146).

16.1.4 Concept (4): empathy as knowing/mindreading by multiple means

Empathy is the process by which one attains a cognitive grasp of, belief about, or knowledge of another's mental states. In short, empathy is the answer to the theory of mind debate. It is whatever process or processes we use to ascribe mental states to others, even if one of those processes turns out to be the theory-theory. According to the theory-theory, we attain knowledge of the target's mental states by deducing them from the principles of folk psychology and information about the target. Whereas concept (3) requires a 'hot' process (sharing affect), concept (4) includes any process of mindreading, whether 'hot' like simulation, or 'cold' like the theory-theory. Concept (4) is not as prevalent in the literature as are concepts (2) and (3). Some readers may even find it odd to think of the theory-theory as included in the concept of empathy. Perhaps this is because the theory of mind debate has led to analyses of 'empathy' in its own right, and these analyses have been largely simulationist. Still, concept (4) is employed in the recent work of William Ickes.

In *Everyday Mind Reading*, Ickes asserts that empathic inference is mindreading—the ability to infer the mental states of others (2003: 43). He intends mindreading to include both simulation and the theory-theory, and argues that normal humans use both processes. Thus, 'Normal humans are cognitively sophisticated enough to reason deductively about other people's thoughts, but they . . . don't exert the . . . effort required to do this all the time. Instead, they typically revert to the . . . more automatic mode of mindreading . . . that depends upon the mirror system . . . and the incipient simulation of the other's acts in one's own conscious experience' (Ickes (2003): 325–6). For Ickes, empathy is mindreading, and one can mindread by multiple means, including the theory-theory. Accordingly, his notion of empathy does not require *sharing* the mental state of the target, since one can deduce the target's mental state via the 'cold' theory-theory. Nor does Ickes's concept of empathy entail *caring* about the target. Some of his studies found no correlation between Empathic Accuracy—successfully inferring the content of the target's mental states—and concern for the target (Ickes (2003): 81). Moreover, Ickes argues that Empathic Accuracy 'can be used to harm as well as to help, it can be as essential to the sadism of a . . . torturer as it is to the altruism of a . . . nurse' (2003: 293).

16.2 Virtues and Skills

Is empathy, as construed by concepts (2), (3), and (4), a virtue? In this section, I introduce the main features of virtues, skills, and capacities. I address both moral and intellectual virtues because empathy may be confused with moral virtues like benevolence and intellectual virtues like open-mindedness. We are far more likely to mistake skills for virtues than we are to mistake capacities for virtues. This is because virtues and skills are both voluntary, but capacities are not. I draw three distinctions between virtues and skills. Together, these distinctions entail that no skills are themselves virtues. Since capacities are involuntary, no capacities are themselves virtues either. Still, it is reasonable to think that there must be some capacities (and perhaps skills) that are causally necessary for virtue acquisition. If so, they would have some moral value.

16.2.1 Virtues, skills, and capacities: the basics

Virtues are character traits of agents. Agents can have a wide variety of good qualities, from a sonorous voice to excellent social skills to benevolence and open-mindedness. Virtues like benevolence and open-mindedness are a particular type of good quality: they are good qualities of character. Specifically, virtues are dispositions of appropriate action, emotion, perception, and motivation. The virtues are acquired, and difficult to acquire at that! They are not automatic, involuntary capacities; they are voluntary—we exert some control over their acquisition and operation.

16.2.1.1 Moral Virtues. Readers will likely recognize this account as Aristotelian. Aristotle argues that moral virtues, like courage and temperance, are acquired states of character that lie in a mean. In his words: 'Virtue . . . is a state of character concerned with choice, lying in a mean, the mean relative to us, this being determined by a rational principle, and by that principle by which the man of practical wisdom would determine it' (NE 1106b36–1107a2). To illustrate, the courageous person fears and yet faces the appropriate things, at the appropriate times, in the appropriate ways, because of appropriate motivations. To be courageous, one must at a minimum perform courageous acts—one must do what the courageous person would do. This is more difficult than it sounds because the virtues are not canned responses. Courageous people do not always stand and fight; they sometimes flee. Courage lies in a mean between two extremes: a vice of excess—rashness—and a vice of deficiency—cowardice. The rash person stands when he should run, while the coward runs when he should stand. Hitting the mean with respect to one's actions, and thus succeeding in performing courageous acts, does not make one a courageous person. After all, one might perform a courageous act but do so under the guidance of another (as children do) or with inappropriate emotions or motivations. To possess the virtue of courage, one must hit the mean with respect to one's emotions: one must feel fear, and confidence, when it is appropriate to do so. The coward is inappropriately afraid; the rash person, inappropriately confident. The person with Aristotelian virtue is also appropriately motivated; she performs virtuous actions for their own sakes (NE 1105a30–1105a32). She does not perform courageous actions to impress or manipulate others, or to win awards or fame, but because she (correctly) thinks they are morally good. Analogously, the benevolent person helps the appropriate people, at the appropriate times, in the appropriate ways, because of appropriate motivations. The benevolent person notices opportunities to help others, cares about others when it is appropriate to do so, helps others appropriately, and performs such acts because she (correctly) thinks they are good. In contrast, the cruel person fails to care about or help others when she should, while the servile person cares about or helps others even when she should not.

16.2.1.2 Intellectual Virtues. Readers may be unfamiliar with the contemporary use of Aristotelian virtue ethics in epistemology. Some virtue epistemologists have argued that the intellectual virtues are epistemic analogues of the Aristotelian moral virtues.[18] The intellectual virtues—like open-mindedness, intellectual courage, and intellectual autonomy—are character traits. They are acquired dispositions of intellectual action and intellectual motivation (Battaly (2007)). Like Aristotelian moral virtues, the intellectual virtues require that one perform virtuous actions, possess virtuous motivations, and hit the mean.

To illustrate, the open-minded person appropriately considers alternative ideas, and does so because she is appropriately motivated. To be open-minded one must, at minimum, perform open-minded acts—one must do what the open-minded person would do. But, open-minded people do not always act the same way—they do not always entertain every alternative. Open-mindedness lies in a mean between two vices—dogmatism and naïveté. To illustrate, suppose that Jane is an open-minded police detective who has taken on the homicide of a prostitute in London. In forming a belief about the identity of the murderer, she entertains various alternatives, each of which has a high probability of being true (the employer, or a client, did it.) She does not ignore alternatives that are likely to be true, or consider alternatives that are highly likely to be false (the Secretary-General of the United Nations did it.) She hits the mean with respect to her intellectual actions; in this case, how many and which alternatives she entertains. In contrast, the dogmatic person entertains too few alternatives, ignoring probable alternatives that undermine her chosen hypothesis; while the naïve person entertains too many, even those that are patently false (Battaly (2007): 159).

Performing open-minded acts is not sufficient for being open-minded. One must also perform those acts because one's motivations are intellectually virtuous. For a motivation to be intellectually virtuous, its end must be epistemically valuable, and one must desire it because it is epistemically valuable (and not for some ulterior reason). The motivation to attain truth for its own sake is intellectually virtuous, as is the motivation to attain understanding.[19] In contrast, the motivations to believe whatever it is easiest to believe, or whatever will make one feel good are not. In short, the open-minded person entertains alternatives appropriately because she is motivated to attain truth for its own sake. She (correctly) thinks that attaining truth is epistemically good.

One can fall short of possessing the moral and intellectual virtues, without possessing vices, by being *enkratic* or *akratic*. The virtuous person is motivated to perform virtuous acts 'for their own sakes;' that is, because she desires the good and (correctly) thinks that virtuous acts are good. She does not have competing motivations, nor does she struggle to perform virtuous acts. In contrast, the *enkratic* (continent) person has competing

---

[18] See Zagzebski (1996); Montmarquet (1993). For an overview, see Battaly (2006, 2008b).
[19] See Battaly (2007): 158; Zagzebski (1996).

motivations. She struggles, but succeeds in performing virtuous acts. The *akratic* person suffers from weakness of will. Not only does she possess competing motivations, those motivations defeat her virtuous motivations, thus preventing her from performing virtuous acts.

16.2.1.3 Skills. A skill is an acquired ability to reliably attain a particular end. To be skilled at, say, doing derivations in logic, hitting tennis serves, or speaking a language, one must be more successful than not at completing correct derivations, landing serves inside the court, and correctly forming grammatical sentences, respectively. There are three preliminary points to make about skills. First, skills require reliable success in attaining their ends. In my view, the intellectual virtues require reliability in hitting the mean in one's actions, but do not require the reliable production of true beliefs. Since nothing in my argument hangs on this, those who think that the intellectual virtues do require the reliable production of true beliefs can still endorse what I say below. Second, one who accidentally but repeatedly produces correctly formed grammatical sentences is not skilled (Aristotle NE 1105a22–1105a26). Skills are grounded in the experience of, or knowledge possessed by, the agent. Relatedly, the agent must be able to apply that experience or knowledge to new situations. Rote memorization is insufficient for skill possession. Unlike a rote memorizer, one who is skilled at doing derivations in logic can apply her experience to derivations she has never seen before. Third, skills are voluntary abilities—they are acquired, and we exert some control over their acquisition and exercise. Skills are not involuntary; if they were, it would be easy to be skilled. Rather, they are acquired and improved via effortful practice. Hence, the existence of tennis camps, music lessons, and language schools. Even those who have 'natural' proclivities for tennis, music, and the like can improve their skills via effortful practice. (It is rumored that Steffi Graf used to practice each shot one hundred times before moving on to the next.)

16.2.1.4 Capacities. There are two primary features of capacities. First, capacities are involuntary. They are either innate, or acquired in the standard course of development. We lack control over their acquisition and operation: capacities are not the sort of thing that can be improved via effortful practice. Consider vision, a paradigmatic capacity. For those of us who lack 20/20 vision, effortful practice will not help us attain it; there are no vision improvement lessons, only corrective lenses and surgery.[20] Arguably, mimicry and mirroring are involuntary in this way. There is little or nothing we can do to control their development or operation; they are activated automatically.

---

[20] In ordinary discourse, we sometimes say that the capacity to (e.g.) lift things can be improved through training. But on my view, capacities cannot be improved; they are involuntary. It is skills that can be improved. Our capacity to lift things is equivalent to what Aristotle calls a 'first potentiality' (see below). A person who could lift things, but has not yet made the effort to acquire the skill of lifting things, has a capacity or 'first potentiality' for lifting things. I am grateful to an anonymous referee for raising this point.

Likewise, it is reasonable to think that for those of us who lack properly functioning mimicry and mirroring systems, effortful practice will not help us attain them.[21] Alvin Goldman has suggested that impairments in mirroring systems might be linked to impairments in mimicry, which in turn might be linked to Autism Spectrum Disorders (Goldman (2006a): 205–6). Though mirroring and ASD fall outside my range of expertise, I take it that none of the experts would suggest that impaired mirroring systems can be substantially improved or corrected via effortful practice. By way of contrast, it is reasonable to think that perspective-taking can be substantially improved via effortful practice. For instance, practice may help one learn to successfully differentiate between oneself and others—to avoid both fusion and 'self-focused' perspective-taking. It may also help one learn to overcome familiarity biases.[22] Mimicry and mirroring are excellent candidates for capacities, perspective-taking is not.

Because capacities are involuntary, and virtues are voluntary, no capacities are virtues. Virtues are voluntary—they are acquired, and we exert some control over their acquisition and exercise. This is not to say that, once acquired, virtues cannot be spontaneously triggered—they often are. But it is to say that unlike involuntary capacities, we have some control over their acquisition and operation. Moral praise and blame presuppose such control. This is a version of the 'ought implies can' principle. If an agent could not have avoided a particular trait, capacity, or behavior, then she does not warrant moral praise or blame for it. Virtues qualify for moral praise or blame because they are acquired via effortful practice—agents might easily have failed to possess them. The benevolent agent could have been cruel instead. Granted, we do sometimes praise and blame people for their involuntary capacities, for example, when we cheer 'natural' athleticism and bemoan 'innate' intellectual deficiencies. But, this praise and blame is not moral. It should reflect the fact that these qualities are involuntary and unavoidable. In short, because capacities are involuntary, they are not themselves virtues.

But, second, we cannot possess virtues without possessing some capacities. Capacities underlie all of our voluntary dispositions and abilities, including virtues and skills. One cannot acquire the skill of speaking Japanese unless one has the capacity to acquire that skill. Nor can one acquire the virtue of benevolence without the capacity to acquire benevolence. In this sense, a capacity is what Aristotle calls a 'first potentiality.'[23] To illustrate, one who could learn to speak Japanese, but has not yet made the effort to acquire the skill of doing so, has a 'first potentiality' for speaking Japanese. One who activates that first potentiality, and acquires the skill of speaking Japanese has reached a 'second potentiality' for speaking Japanese. The first potentiality is required for the second potentiality. This example also reinforces my contention that capacity

---

[21] Though it is possible that practice of some sort might help us compensate in other ways for their absence.

[22] On overcoming familiarity biases, see Goldman (2006a): 297–8; Hoffman (2000): 213.

[23] See Aristotle (1984): 412a18–26.

possession is not sufficient for possessing virtues or skills: capacities can go 'untapped'. Surely some insurance executives possess the capacity (first potentiality) for benevolence, though they have never bothered to activate it.[24]

Because virtues and skills are both voluntary, we tend to conflate them. Prizing them apart requires some work.[25] In the remainder of this section, I argue that there are three primary distinctions between virtues and skills. Since these distinctions presuppose some degree of control, they do not apply to capacities.

16.2.2 Distinction 1: foregoing opportunities

First, skills are abilities, but virtues are habits or dispositions. According to William Alston, virtues differ from abilities because the former indicate 'what one *would* do under certain circumstances,' what one is disposed to do; whilst the latter indicate 'what one is *able* to do' (Alston (1993)). Though one could have a skill that one (knowingly or unknowingly) failed to exercise when given the opportunity, one could not have a virtue that one (knowingly or unknowingly) failed to exercise when given the opportunity. To illustrate, one could *unknowingly* forego an opportunity to cook a meal (because one failed to perceive that opportunity), but still be a skilled chef.[26] Whereas, one could not unknowingly forego an opportunity to appropriately help another (because one failed to perceive that opportunity), and still be benevolent. Part of what it is to be benevolent is to detect opportunities to appropriately help others. Those who fail to recognize such opportunities are not yet benevolent. One can also *knowingly* fail to exercise a skill but not a virtue. Thus, one could knowingly forego opportunities to do logic derivations (because one is bored), but still be perfectly skilled at doing derivations. Whereas, one could not knowingly fail to listen to the smart objections of one's colleagues on the appropriate occasions (because one is bored), and still be open-minded. The speaker who knowingly succumbs to boredom during the question-and-answer period of her talk, or 'just doesn't feel like listening' is at best *akratic*, not open-minded. Competing motivations prevent her from performing virtuous actions.

One might object that this standard is too high, making virtue unattainable for humans. After all, we are not perfect—even virtuous people occasionally have bad days. In reply, I add the following qualification: unlike skills, which indicate what one is able to do, virtues indicate what one would do *with few exceptions*. Roughly, virtues indicate what one would do, except when the most salient cause of what one does or fails to do is an event that one cannot control. When the most salient cause is not under the agent's control, all bets are off—the agent might fail to perform a virtuous act, but still be virtuous. To illustrate, one could, as a result of a scoundrel's physical force or

---

[24] Thanks to Susanna Schellenberg and Brian McLaughlin for discussions of 'first potentiality.'

[25] Especially since both Annas and Bloomfield have recently argued that virtues are a type of skill. See Annas (2003): 15–33, and Bloomfield (2000): 23–43.

[26] This is not true of skills of perception.

deceit, fail to help a friend in need, and still be benevolent. One could also, on rare occasion, accidentally make mistakes in detecting opportunities to help others, or in determining how to attain the end of benevolence (how to help a grieving friend), without forfeiting one's benevolence. After all, humans have never been flawless calculators. But, one could not (knowingly or unknowingly) fail to perform virtuous acts as a result of events that are under one's control and still be virtuous. Virtuous people only have bad days when events are out of their control. In sum, failing to perform virtuous acts, when the most salient cause is under one's control, does show that one lacks virtue. But, failing to perform skillful acts, whether or not the most salient cause is under one's control, does *not* show that one lacks skill.

Nor are the virtues *mindless* habits, as it is sometimes charged. The open-minded person is not habituated to respond to every opportunity with the same behavior. Rather, she is habituated to stand-at-the-ready in a certain way—she is habituated to look for and be alert to opportunities for open-mindedness, and once she has perceived these opportunities, to exert the appropriate effort to determine whether and to what degree she should entertain alternative ideas. Unlike an automaton with canned responses, she recognizes that each situation must be judged on its own merits—that it is neither always right to consider alternatives, nor always wrong to ignore them.

16.2.3 Distinction 2: deliberate errors

Not only can one forego opportunities to exercise a skill without forfeiting it, one can even deliberately flout the end of a skill. In *Nicomachean Ethics* VI.5, Aristotle claims that amongst the skilled, 'he who errs willingly is preferable', but amongst the practically wise, and the morally virtuous, the reverse is true (NE 1140b22–24). In other words, one can deliberately flout the end of a skill and still be skilled, but one cannot deliberately flout the end of a virtue and still be virtuous.

To illustrate, one can deliberately misspell a word simply because one is bored with perfect spelling and still be skilled in spelling. But one cannot deliberately perform cruel acts, simply because one is bored with benevolent acts, and still possess the virtue of benevolence. According to Philippa Foot, an intentional spelling error does not count against one's skill in spelling because the response, 'I did it deliberately,' rebuts accusations that one lacks the skill. The same can be said of deliberate errors in logic derivations and tennis serves. In contrast, contends Foot, 'if a man acts unjustly or uncharitably, or in a cowardly or intemperate manner "I did it deliberately" cannot . . . lead to exculpation' (Foot (1997): 169). Recall that the benevolent person is disposed to care about others appropriately, help others appropriately, and perform such acts because she thinks they are good. Benevolent people do not struggle to perform benevolent acts—they do not have competing motivations.[27]

---

[27] Even Robert C. Roberts, who thinks that some virtues are corrective, argues that benevolence is 'motivational': it requires the motivation to help others and the absence of competing motivations. See Roberts (1987): 121–36.

Now, consider Beatriz, a kindergarten teacher who appropriately helped her students until she grew bored with helping and began deliberately performing cruel acts—intentionally glowering at her students to make them cry. Beatriz does not harm her students because of an external threat, or because she judges the acts required by benevolence to conflict with the acts required by a competing virtue. She recognizes that she has the opportunity to treat her students benevolently and knows how to do so, but deliberately harms them for no other reason than to vary her standard routine. Unlike the deliberate misspeller who is skilled in spelling, Beatriz does not possess the virtue of benevolence. Beatriz is, at best, *akratic*. Her competing motivation—to alleviate her boredom—defeats her virtuous motivation, thus causing her to perform acts that are not virtuous. Knowingly performing cruel acts without mitigating reasons demonstrates that one is not disposed to care about or help others appropriately, and thus that one lacks benevolence. Beatriz' 'I did it deliberately' serves to convict rather than to exculpate her.

16.2.4 Distinction 3: aiming at the good

Virtuous people are motivated to perform virtuous acts 'for their own sakes,' because the acts are 'good in themselves,' not for ulterior reasons. In other words, to be benevolent, one must be motivated to help others because one desires the moral good and believes that helping others is morally good. Likewise, to be open-minded, one must be motivated to attain truths because one desires the epistemic good and believes that truth is epistemically good. Those who are motivated to help others or attain truths for ulterior reasons—e.g. pleasure, fame, personal gain at the expense of others—are not virtuous. Virtuous people are motivated to attain what they believe to be good, and since their beliefs about the good are correct, they are motivated to attain what is actually good. There is no such restriction on skilled people. Skilled people need not be motivated to attain what they believe to be good, and may be motivated by ulterior reasons, some of which are objectively bad. Hence, skills can ultimately aim at bad ends, but virtues cannot.

To explicate, I begin with an insight from Aristotle. Aristotle argues that the ends at which the virtuous person aims must be rational ends.[28] In contrast, the ends at which the skilled person aims need not be rational. Rational ends are the objects of Aristotelian rational desires. Unlike appetites, which aim at the pleasant (wealth, power, etc.), rational desires aim at that which appears good. Thus, (i) the ends at which the virtuous person aims must appear good to her; whereas (ii) the ends at which the skilled person aims need not appear good to him. In brief defense of (i), those who help others for some ulterior reason (e.g. personal gain), not because they value helping for its own sake, are not virtuous.

---

[28] See Aristotle, *Nicomachean Ethics*, III.2–III.4; Irwin (1980): 117–56; Wiggins (1980): 221–40.

In defense of (ii), the skilled person may be motivated to attain the ends at which he aims because he thinks they will make him wealthy, popular, or powerful, not because he thinks they are good. To illustrate, a skilled doctor will figure out how best to treat patient P by using her knowledge of medicine to determine which course of action—surgery or physical therapy—is most conducive to restoring P's health. A skilled scientist will figure out how best to test hypothesis H by using his knowledge of the methods of his field to determine which course of action—collecting new samples or running a different test on old samples—is most conducive to deciding whether H is true or false. Likewise, a skilled general will figure out how best to neutralize enemy E by using her knowledge of military strategy to determine which course of action—bombing or ground assault—is most conducive to advancing the military interests of her own country. Each practitioner performs an act that issues from skill, but the ends at which they aim (health, etc.) need not be rational ends. Our doctor can desire curing patients (and, more generally, health) simply because she wants wealth, and not because she thinks promoting health is good. Our scientist can desire the confirmation or disconfirmation of H, or even truth, simply because he wants to get his name in the trendy journals, not because he thinks that truth is epistemically good. And, our general can desire the destruction of the enemy simply because she craves political power, not because she thinks destroying the enemy is good. In each case, the skilled practitioner's motive is something other than the apparent good: wealth, fame, and power. So, skilled people need not aim at what appears good to them. Their skilled actions may be solely motivated by appetites; in theory, they may lack rational desires altogether.[29] Skilled people may even aim at ends that are clearly objectively bad (whether or not they think they are bad). For instance, our skilled general may desire the destruction of the enemy because she wants to dominate the world and enslave conquered populations, an objectively bad end if there ever was one.

16.3 Is Empathy a Virtue?

In this section, I argue that empathy, as construed by concepts (2), (3), and (4), is neither a moral nor an intellectual virtue. Empathy, so construed, will be a skill only if it is a voluntary ability rather than an automatic capacity. I begin by arguing that empathy, as construed by concept (2), is a capacity, not a virtue. Second, I argue that one can possess empathy, as construed by concepts (3) and (4), while foregoing opportunities to be empathic. Third, one also can possess empathy, as construed by (3) and (4), while deliberately flouting the ends of empathy. Finally, I argue that the empathic person, so construed, need not aim at the apparent good. Hence, empathy, as construed by concepts (3) and (4) is (if reliable) a skill, not a virtue.

---

[29] Alternatively, skilled people might be *akratic* with respect to their ulterior motives (they might believe that their ulterior motives are bad, but act on them anyway), or they might aim at what they think is bad. See Stocker (1979): 738–53.

16.3.1 Concept (2): empathy is a capacity, not a virtue

According to concept (2)—sharing by multiple means—empathy can be involuntary and automatic. Recall Eisenberg and Strayer's inclusion of contagion, Goldman's inclusion of mirroring, and Hoffman's inclusion of mimicry, conditioning, and direct association. But, insofar as empathy is involuntary and automatic, it is a capacity, not a virtue. Automatic involuntary capacities like mirroring, mimicry, etc., are not virtues because they do not warrant moral praise or blame. Hence, empathy as construed by concept (2) is insufficient for virtue.

In 16.2.1.4, I argued that virtue possession requires the possession of some capacities. It could turn out that it requires the possession of capacities like mimicry and mirroring. If so, empathy, as construed by concept (2), would be necessary for virtue possession. Mimicry and mirroring would be instrumentally morally valuable.

16.3.2 Concepts (3) and (4): foregoing opportunities

Empathy, as construed by concepts (3) and (4) is voluntary. We have some control over perspective-taking and our deployment of the principles of folk psychology, and each can be improved via effortful practice. So, is empathy, as construed by concepts (3) and (4), a virtue or a skill? In the remaining sections, I apply the three distinctions between virtues and skills (foregoing opportunities, deliberate errors, and aiming at the good) to concepts (3) and (4). Recall that, other things being equal, foregoing opportunities to appropriately entertain objections demonstrates that one does not possess the virtue of open-mindedness. Can something similar be said of empathy, as construed by concept (3)? If so, it is a virtue. If not, provided that it is reliable, it is a skill.

According to Goldie and Coplan, empathy is the voluntary process of imaginative perspective-taking, which results in sharing and knowing the target's mental states. Suppose that, other things being equal, an agent foregoes opportunities to engage in imaginative perspective-taking. Does this demonstrate that she is not a good imaginative perspective-taker—that she lacks empathy so construed? It does not.

Suppose that Katie is a seasoned therapist who is quite reliable at imaginative perspective-taking. She routinely succeeds in using her imagination to share the affect of her clients and others, and know their mental states. But, today, she is bored and complacent. When her final client of the day arrives, Katie knowingly foregoes opportunities to engage in perspective-taking. I submit that in foregoing these opportunities, she does not forfeit her imaginative ability. For *if* she *were* to exercise it, her perspective-taking would reliably produce shared affect and true beliefs. Rather, she is what we might call an 'empathic underachiever'. Katie can be censured for failing to do her job to the best of her ability, or failing to care about her clients or the truth; but she cannot be censured for failing to be a good imaginative perspective-taker. Foregoing opportunities to engage in perspective-taking does not demonstrate that one is not a good perspective-taker, and hence does not demonstrate that one lacks empathy, so construed. What it may well demonstrate is that some perspective-takers are not sufficiently motivated to care about others or about the truth. In short, it may demonstrate that perspective-takers can lack the motivations that are required for the virtues of benevolence and open-mindedness. In sum, imaginative perspective-taking is an ability, not a habit. Hence, empathy as construed by concept (3) is not a virtue. Given that it reliably produces shared affect and knowledge of others' mental states (when activated), it is a skill.

Something similar can be said of empathy as construed by concept (4)—*knowing* the target's mental states. Let's focus on the theory-theory, which, like perspective-taking, is voluntary. Using the theory-theory requires both possessing 'the theory'—having beliefs about the principles of folk psychology—and deploying 'the theory.' Can one forego opportunities to deploy one's principles of folk psychology, and still be good at deploying those principles? One can. Just as one can opt out of applying the principles of deductive logic to what one reads in the newspaper without thereby sacrificing one's logical prowess, one can opt out of activating one's knowledge of folk psychology without sacrificing one's prowess in mindreading via the theory-theory. Failing to deploy the principles of folk psychology demonstrates that one lacks sufficient concern for the truth, not that one fails to be good at mindreading via the theory-theory. Hence, mindreading via the theory-theory is not a virtue either. Given that it reliably produces knowledge of others' mental states (when activated), it is a skill.

In sum, perspective-taking and mindreading via the theory-theory are not virtues, but abilities. I have suggested that when we forego exercising these abilities it is because we are insufficiently motivated to help others or attain the truth. This claim supports, and is supported by, some empirical findings. Hoffman identifies two types of empathic bias. First, an agent is 'more likely to empathize with and help those who are members of his . . . [own] family, [or] ethnic or racial group' (Hoffman (2000): 206). Second, agents are more likely to empathize with and help people who are present. In short, we (often) forego opportunities to empathize with targets who are absent or different from us. Of course, it is sometimes wrong to forego such opportunities. I submit that if we cared appropriately about others and about the truth, if we possessed the virtues of benevolence and open-mindedness, then we would not wrongly forego such opportunities.

16.3.3 Concepts (3) and (4): deliberate errors

Can one be empathic, as construed by concept (3) or (4), and deliberately produce results or perform acts that are inconsistent with the ends of empathy? If so, empathy (so construed) is at best a skill, not a virtue. Let's begin with concept (3). The ends of imaginative perspective-taking are shared affect and an epistemic grasp of the target's mental states. Suppose that, other things being equal, the agent deliberately engages in a process that she knows will produce botched affect and false beliefs about the target's mental states. Does this demonstrate that the agent is not a good imaginative perspective-taker—that she lacks empathy so construed? It does not.

Suppose that Jackie and Joan are adult sisters. Jackie excels at imaginative perspective-taking with respect to Joan, but Joan does not excel at perspective-taking with respect to Jackie. Jackie reliably and repeatedly grasps Joan's frustration with her job, Joan's unhappiness about her marriage, and any number of Joan's emotional reactions. But, Joan does not grasp Jackie's emotional reactions. Suppose that in today's conversation with Joan, Jackie is tired of being taken for granted. As a result, Jackie deliberately engages in a sub-standard imaginative process, knowing that it will result in skewed affect and false beliefs about Joan's emotions. I submit that in so doing, Jackie does not forfeit her imaginative ability. For if she were to exercise it, instead of the sub-standard process she actually exercised, she would reliably produce shared affect and true beliefs about Joan's mental states. Jackie can be censured for not caring sufficiently about truth, (perhaps) for not caring sufficiently about her sister, and for failing to produce shared affect and a true belief on this occasion; but she cannot be censured for failing to be a good perspective-taker. Deliberately engaging in a skewed imaginative process does not demonstrate that one is not a good perspective-taker, and hence does not demonstrate that one lacks empathy, so construed. Again, what it may well demonstrate is that some perspective-takers lack the motivations necessary for virtue possession. Hence, empathy as construed by concept (3) is not a virtue. Given that it is voluntary, if it is reliable, it is a skill.

Something similar can be said of empathy as construed by concept (4). The end of the theory-theory is true beliefs about others' mental states. Can one deliberately engage in an epistemic process that one knows will produce false beliefs about others' mental states and still be good at mindreading via the theory-theory? One can. Suppose that Tony has fallen in love with Cleo; but his love is unrequited. Tony has some evidence for thinking that Cleo does not love him, but he desperately wants to believe that she does. Accordingly, he deliberately and knowingly engages in wishful thinking, which produces the false belief that Cleo loves him. This does not demonstrate that Tony is not good at mindreading via the theory-theory, and hence does not show that he lacks empathy so construed. Deliberately circumventing an epistemic process does not show that one fails to be good at using that process when one does use it. It only shows that Tony fails to have sufficient concern for the truth. Tony might be highly reliable at mindreading when using the theory-theory, and might deliberately use wishful thinking in this case because he does not want to know Cleo's feelings. So, again, empathy as construed by concept (4) is not a virtue. If reliable, it is a skill.

One of Ickes's studies supports the claim that agents can flout the ends of mindreading, but still be good mindreaders. Ickes argues that 'motivated inaccuracy' occurs when partners are 'motivated to avoid accurately inferring each other's thoughts and feelings to spare themselves and their relationship the damage that might result if more accurate inferences were made' (Ickes (2003): 227). Ickes reports that in relationship-threatening situations, partners' beliefs about each other's mental states were wildly inaccurate: only 5% of their beliefs were true (Ickes (2003): 234). I submit that in threatening situations, partners are using sub-standard processes that produce false beliefs. Sometimes this use of sub-standard processes will be deliberate. But, provided that partners reliably infer each other's mental states in non-threatening situations, they will still be good mindreaders.

16.3.4 Concepts (3) and (4): aiming at the good

Finally, must the ends at which empathizers (as construed by concepts (3) and (4)) aim appear good to them? And, must the ends at which they aim actually be good? If both answers are affirmative, then empathy (so construed) is a virtue; if not, it is, if reliable, a skill. Recall that the ends at which virtuous people aim must appear good to them; and since their beliefs about the good are correct, their ends are actually good. In contrast, the ends at which skilled people aim need not appear good to them. Skilled people may be motivated by ulterior reasons, some of which are objectively bad (whether or not they believe them to be bad).

So, beginning with concept (3), must the ends at which a good perspective-taker aims appear good to her? They need not. A good perspective-taker must aim at (and reliably attain) shared affect and true beliefs about the target's mental states, but she need not think that these ends are good. Suppose that Katie the therapist aims at shared affect and true beliefs about her clients' mental states because she wants wealth, not because she thinks that shared affect or true beliefs are morally or epistemically good. Does this demonstrate that Katie is not a good perspective-taker? It does not. Katie might be highly reliable at perspective-taking: she might be a veritable expert at sharing the affect of and attaining true beliefs about the mental states of her clients. After all, wealth can be a proficient motivator. Good perspective-takers are like skilled doctors, scientists, and generals—they may be motivated by appetites for wealth, fame, or power rather than by rational desires. Something similar can be said of concept (4). An adept user of the theory-theory must aim at (and reliably attain) true beliefs about the target's mental states, but she need not think that truth is epistemically good. She may be aiming at truth because she wants to impress others, or win bets, not because she values it for its own sake.

Must the ends at which good perspective-takers and users of the theory-theory aim actually be good? Here, moral and epistemic cases diverge. One can be empathic, as construed by concepts (3) and (4), while lacking any ends that are in fact morally good. But, one cannot be empathic, as construed by concepts (3) and (4), while lacking any ends that are in fact epistemically good. First, the moral cases. Good perspective-takers and users of the theory-theory must aim at sharing affect and attaining true beliefs, but they need not aim at helping others or any other end that is in fact morally good. Successful confidence men are not motivated to help others, but often excel at perspective-taking and mindreading via the theory-theory. Genocidal murderers, torturers, and others whose aims are clearly morally bad, can also be good perspective-takers and users of the theory-theory. As Ickes and Hoffman have suggested, it is possible to use empathy for morally bad ends.[30] Now, the epistemic cases. If one is a good perspective-taker or user of the theory-theory, then one must at minimum aim at, and reliably attain, true beliefs about the mental states of others. One cannot be empathic, as construed by concepts (3) and (4), without aiming at the truth. Since truth is an objectively good end, one cannot be empathic, so construed, without having at least one end that is in fact epistemically good. But, this is insufficient for virtue possession because empathizers may also have competing or ulterior motives that are epistemically bad; for instance, the motivations to believe whatever will make one feel good, or whatever it is easiest to believe.

Hence, we again find that empathy as construed by concepts (3) and (4) is not a virtue. The benevolent person is motivated to appropriately help others because she thinks it is good to do so. She aims at an end that is objectively morally good. In contrast, empathizers, as construed by concepts (3) and (4), need not aim at ends that are objectively morally good; and even if they do aim at some ends that are objectively morally good, they need not aim at them because they are good. The open-minded person is motivated to attain truth because she thinks it is good to do so. She aims at an end that is objectively epistemically good. In contrast, though empathizers, as construed by concepts (3) and (4), are motivated to attain truth, they need not be motivated to attain truth because it is good. Even though one of their ends is epistemically good, they may have ulterior ends that are epistemically bad. Empathy, so construed, is distinct from the virtues of benevolence and open-mindedness.

16.4 Conclusion

In conclusion, I have argued that empathy as construed by concepts (2), (3), and (4) is neither a moral nor an intellectual virtue. If it is voluntary (concepts (3) and (4)) and reliable, it is a skill. If it is involuntary (concept 2), it is a capacity. Briefly, does this demonstrate that we should reject our leading theoretical concepts of empathy? Not necessarily.

Granted, one might argue that we should reject concepts (2), (3), and (4) because they conflict with the ordinary intuition captured in concept (1)—that empathy is a virtue. This argument proceeds as follows:

I.   If any of concepts (2), (3), or (4) are correct, then empathy is not a virtue.
II. But, empathy is a virtue.
III. So, theoretical concepts (2), (3), and (4) are incorrect.[31]

---

[30] Ickes (2003): 293; Hoffman in discussion of his paper 'What We Know about Empathy and Where to Go from Here' at the 2007 Conference on Understanding Other Minds and Moral Agency, Holy Cross College.

[31] In conversation, several philosophers have raised exactly this objection, claiming that I have shown that (2), (3), and (4) must be wrong.

We do sometimes reject theoretical concepts because they conflict with our ordinary intuitions. We would reject any theoretical concept of consciousness that entailed that humans were not conscious. But, as Kripke has shown, conflicts between ordinary and theoretical concepts do not always favor the ordinary. We sometimes reject ordinary intuitions because they conflict with our theoretical concepts. We no longer think that gold must be yellow. Applying this reasoning to concepts of empathy, we can instead argue that:

I. If any of concepts (2), (3), or (4) are correct, then empathy is not a virtue.
Not III. One of (2), (3), or (4) is correct.
So, not II, empathy is not a virtue.

So, the fact that (2), (3), and (4) conflict with our ordinary concept does not by itself constitute sufficient grounds for rejecting (2), (3), and (4). Ordinary concepts do not automatically trump theoretical concepts; but nor do the latter automatically trump the former. For now, we are stuck in a stalemate in which 'one person's modus ponens is another's modus tollens.' Breaking it will require a philosophically satisfying argument either for the conclusion that empathy is a virtue or for the conclusion that one of (2), (3), or (4) is correct.

Suppose, for the moment, that we are able to develop a philosophically satisfying argument for the conclusion that one of (2), (3), or (4) is correct. Would this entail that empathy is unrelated to the virtues? Of course not. It might even turn out that capacities like mirroring, and skills like perspective-taking and the deployment of the principles of folk psychology, are necessary for possessing virtues like benevolence and open-mindedness. If so, empathy, as construed by (2), (3), or (4), would be a capacity or skill that underlies at least some of the moral and intellectual virtues.

Suppose, instead, that we pursue the alternative route: how might we develop a philosophically satisfying argument for the conclusion that empathy is a virtue? We might begin by returning to our ordinary concept of empathy (1), and using it to develop a new theoretical concept. Would this entail that we ignore mirroring, perspective-taking, and the use of the 'theory-theory'? Of course not. But given the argument of section 16.3, it would entail that we emphasize entrenched motivations, specifically, the dispositions to care about others, and about the truth, for their own sakes. It is these motivations that prevent us from foregoing opportunities, making deliberate errors, and aiming at ends for ulterior reasons (like wealth).[32]

---

[32] I am grateful to two anonymous referees for raising this issue.

17

Anti-Empathy

Peter Goldie

17.1 Introduction

To say that I am against empathy might seem at first somewhat like saying that I am against motherhood; surely empathy is so obviously a Good Thing that if someone is against it, either there must be something wrong with him, or he must be confused as to what it is.

My first task will be to restrict what I am against to a particular kind of empathy. The term 'empathy' is understood in so many different ways—not only in philosophical and psychological theorizing, but also in our everyday discourse—that making precise the kind of empathy that is my target will take a little while.[1] Very roughly speaking, what I am against is what I will call *empathetic perspective-shifting*: consciously and intentionally shifting your perspective in order to imagine *being* the other person, and thereby sharing in *his or her* thoughts, feelings, decisions, and other aspects of their psychology. I am not against what I will call *in-his-shoes perspective-shifting*: consciously and intentionally shifting your perspective in order to imagine what thoughts, feelings, decisions, and so on *you* would arrive at if you were in the other's circumstances. These two kinds of perspective-taking are both kinds of higher-level empathy, in the helpful terminology of Alvin Goldman (2006a and this volume), and they are often either confused or not sufficiently distinguished. What I want to do here is to show just how different they are, and how deep the problems are for empathetic perspective-shifting.

I have always had the intuition, which I think others share, that perspective-shifting works alright, more or less, in the simple cases, but when it gets to the more complex, more *important*, cases, it fails. (Sometimes the importance lies in the ethical domain, sometimes in the domain of personal choice, and sometimes both; often such cases are found in good literature.) I think I am now able to put my finger on why this is—on what grounds my intuition. The problem is not (as I used to think) a contingent one, concerned only with the limits to our powers of imagination.

---

[1] See Battaly this volume.

The problem is, rather, a conceptual one, concerned specifically with the empathetic variety of perspective-shifting, whether deployed for prediction, for explanation, or for understanding. Essentially, empathetic perspective-shifting is conceptually unable to operate with the appropriately *full-blooded notion of first-personal agency* that is involved in deliberation. In particular it usurps the agent's own first-personal stance towards what he is thinking; only the agent *himself* can take *his* stance towards his own thoughts, decisions, and intentions. This problem, which is not shared by in-his-shoes perspective-shifting, only manifests itself in the less simple cases—in cases other than what I will call the *base case*—and this gives the misleading impression that the problem is a contingent one, to do with limitations of our imaginative powers. But the problem exists in all cases of empathetic perspective-shifting, even though it is below the surface when deployed in base cases.[2]

So when I say I am against empathy, it is only empathetic perspective-shifting that is in my sights. But before I get into the problems that it faces, I need first to say more about what perspective-shifting is in general, and what distinguishes the empathetic variety from the in-his-shoes variety.

17.2 Perspective-Shifting

To begin with, we need to distinguish between empathy as outcome and empathy as process.[3] There are a number of definitions of empathy which differ in various ways, but which are united in seeking to define empathy as outcome. For example, Martin Hoffman's definition of empathy is of any kind of process which has a certain outcome, and in this sense, he rightly observes, it is 'multi-determined': 'The key requirement of an empathetic response according to my definition', he says, 'is *the involvement of psychological processes that make a person have feelings that are more congruent with another's situation than with his own situation*' (Hoffman (2000): 30).[4] And Adam Morton's definition (this volume) is 'One person, A, has empathy for another, B, with respect to a particular state of mind, when B experiences an emotion or attitude and A has a representation of B's state which shares its affective tone and perspective'. So on either of these definitions, empathy can take place more or less regardless of what kind of psychological process is involved.

---

[2] There is a positive part to my overall view which I do not have the space for here. There is an alternative to empathy as perspective-shifting which is wholly commonplace in our everyday lives, and yet in much of the recent debate concerning how we think about others' thoughts, feelings, and actions, and in making predictions, this alternative is neglected. As a result, it often seems as if there are only two possibilities (or some combination of these two): either empathy in some form; or theorizing about the other person, deploying a range of psychological laws. The neglected alternative is the possibility of seeing the other *as another person*, understanding and responding to him as having dispositions and attitudes perhaps deeply different from one's own, whilst not theorizing about him as one might theorize over other kinds of thing. The point of view is third-personal, but in no way impersonal. I discuss some of these issues elsewhere (2000; 2002b).

[3] See Feagin this volume.

[4] But see Hoffman this volume for a somewhat different definition.

Empathy as process is, in a sense, a refinement of empathy as outcome, in that it distinguishes between the various kinds of process by which the outcome of shared states of mind is achieved. One such process is a kind of 'resonance' which is more or less non-conscious. This is what Alvin Goldman calls 'primitive, 'low-level' mind-reading' (2006a: 113), and Karsten Steuber (2006) calls 'basic empathy'. For example, in recognizing another's face as expressing a certain emotion, 'the observer's emotional system "resonates" with that of the target, and this is the matching event on which the attribution is based' (Goldman 2006a: 132). Goldman draws on a wide range of empirical data to lend support to the existence of this kind of low-level simulation, much of it based on the fascinating recent work on mirror neurons (see also Goldman this volume and Iacoboni this volume). Now, whether or not it is right to call these processes empathy, or even simulation, is a point which I do not want to dwell on.[5] The point I do want to emphasize, though, is that it is not these low-level empathetic processes that I am concerned with here.

In contrast to these lower-level empathetic processes is what Goldman calls 'higher-level mind-reading', Steuber calls 're-enactive empathy', and I am calling 'perspective-shifting'. Goldman gives a rough characterization of this kind of process: '(a) it targets mental states of a relatively complex nature, such as propositional attitudes; (b) some components of the mindreading process are subject to voluntary control; and (c) the process has some degree of accessibility to consciousness' (2006a: 147). Importantly, this process, unlike lower-level empathy, uses a form a *pretence*, a species of imagination; Goldman calls it 'enactment imagination', or 'E-imagination'.[6] He discusses how this works where the 'target' is engaged in a piece of means-end reasoning which results in a decision to perform a certain action. The attributor, deploying enactment imagination, creates a pretend desire and a pretend means-end belief:

These states are then fed as inputs into a decision-making, or practical reasoning, mechanism . . . A decision-making mechanism normally takes genuine (nonpretend) desires and beliefs as inputs and then outputs a genuine (nonpretend) decision. In simulation exercises, the decision-making mechanism is applied to pretend desires and beliefs and outputs pretend decisions. . . . The final step of the decision-prediction routine is to use the pretend decision to form a (genuine, not merely pretend) belief about the target, namely, that the target will make that decision. With this final belief, the sequence of states constitutes a process of mental attribution. (2006: 29)

As this citation illustrates, Goldman characterizes higher-level empathy as a 'process' in the information-processing sense of that term—in a way which is congenial to the

---

[5] It is however, something I would want to dwell on in putting forward a positive alternative to empathetic perspective-shifting which is not theory-driven: on this positive account, low-level empathy would belong more naturally on the side of perception; for discussion, see Goldie (2007).

[6] In a later paper, responding to criticism from Frederique de Vignemont about the vagueness of his distinction between higher-level and lower-level empathy, Goldman (2009b: 485) defined higher-level empathy as follows: 'A high-level simulational event is an event produced by the imagination (usually in concert with one or more other subsystems)'.

empirical investigations of the cognitive sciences (using terms such as 'input', 'output', and 'mechanism'). However, I do not want the idea of perspective-shifting as a process to point only towards this information-processing sense of 'process', for there is also a more everyday sense which is not tied to any particular scientific model. Jane Heal, in a series of insightful papers, has argued that there are significant a priori considerations in favour of this kind of thinking as against theorizing: she calls it *co-cognition*, which is, roughly, someone's thinking about the same subject matter as the other person is thinking about, and I will take this to be also a kind of perspective-shifting.[7] This is Heal's account of how the 'basic strategy' for co-cognition works, and it bears a clear family resemblance to Goldman's account, albeit at the personal level and without the information-processing terminology:

The other thinks that p_1–p_n, and is wondering whether q. I would like to know what she will conclude. . . . So I ask myself 'Would the obtaining of p_1–p_n necessitate or make likely the obtaining of q?' To answer this question I must myself think about the states of affairs in question, as the other is also doing, that is, I must co-cognize with the other. If I come to the answer that a state of affairs in which p_1–p_n would necessitate or make likely that q, then I shall expect the other to arrive at the belief that q. (1998/2003a: 103)

The a priori considerations that Heal raises for co-cognition are essentially grounded in a conception of our rationality as shared with others: in wondering what conclusion the other person will reach, or what the other person will decide to do, we deploy our own rationality, on the tacit assumption that the other, like us, thinks things, feels things, and does things for reasons. Steuber echoes this, arguing that 'only through *reenactive empathy*—that is, by using our cognitive and deliberative capacities in order to re-enact or imitate in our own mind the thought processes of the other person—are we able to conceive of another person's more complex social behavior as the behavior of a rational agent who acts for a reason' (2006: 21).

This account of perspective-shifting is so far neutral between the two varieties that I want to distinguish here. Roughly and intuitively, the difference between in-his-shoes perspective-shifting and empathetic perspective-shifting lies in the content of the imaginative project: who, *in the imaginative project*, is doing the thinking. So if A is wondering what B will decide in some situation, it will be in-his-shoes perspective-taking if A imagines *himself* in that situation, imagines *himself* deliberating and deciding what to do—off-line as Goldman and others put it. In contrast it will be empathetic perspective-shifting if A imagines *being B* in that situation, deliberating and deciding what to do.

Before considering these two kinds of perspective-shifting, though, there is another kind of imagining, which I will call *imagining-how-it-is*, which must be sharply

---

[7] See the collection of paper in Heal (2003a). I do not want to engage here in the debate between Heal and Goldman as to whether the a priori, co-cognition approach, or the empirical, off-line simulation approach to the process of empathy as perspective-shifting is to be preferred. See also Heal (1994) and Goldman (2006a) for further discussion.

distinguished from perspective-shifting (of both varieties). An example will illustrate the difference. I am thinking about my wife, who is at a business meeting with someone I know to be particularly difficult. In thinking about her at that meeting, I am imagining how it is for her: I imagine how stressed she must be, and how she will be trying to keep her sense of humour in spite of having to face up to her difficult opponent. In doing this, in imagining how it is for her, I need in no way be imagining *from the inside* what it is like for her. Only the latter is a form of perspective-shifting. Of course one can imagine how it is for someone by perspective-shifting, but the important point is that this is by no means necessary. I might imagine how it is for a mouse caught in a trap but still very much alive, and realize it must be terrifying, but to do this, I don't have to take up the mouse's perspective.

The confusion between perspective-shifting and imagining-how-it-is often arises in our discussion of our engagement with literary figures: in reading *War and Peace* we say that we imagine how it is for Pierre, and then jump to the conclusion that we are *empathizing* with Pierre, imagining what it is like for Pierre from the inside. But, as with the mouse, we might just imagine how it is for him—terrifying perhaps, or delightful.

The confusion between perspective-shifting and imagining-how-it-is is sometimes compounded in the social psychology literature. For example, Daniel Batson's experiments (Batson, Early, et al. (1997) for example) often involve asking participants to adopt what Batson calls an 'imagine-other' perspective (as contrasted with an 'imagine-self' perspective and an 'objective' perspective). But the instructions to participants for the 'imagine-other' perspective are unclear on precisely the point at issue. The instructions are as follows in Batson, Early, et al. (1997) (for discussion see also Decety and Meltzoff this volume): 'While you are listening to this broadcast, try to imagine how the other person feels about what has happened and how it affects his or her life. Try not to concern yourself with attending to all the information presented. Just concentrate on trying to imagine how the person interviewed in the broadcast feels'. This by no means requires perspective-shifting; the instructions are simply ambiguous between perspective-shifting to the other person and imagining-how-it-is for the other person.

Let us now put to one side imagining-how-it-is, and return to the two varieties of perspective-shifting. An intuitive way of appreciating the difference between the two arises in perceptual imagining: whether one can imagine meeting the target of the perspective-shifting. If A is engaged in empathetic perspective-shifting with B, he is, as I have just made clear, imagining *being* B, so obviously A cannot imagine meeting B. Whereas if A puts himself in B's shoes, he can imagine meeting B.[8] But, as we will see, there is much more to the difference than this.

---

[8] My concern here, however, is not mainly with perceptual imagining in perspective-shifting; for seminal discussion, see Wollheim (1984). I discuss the difference between the two kinds of perspective-shifting in Goldie (2000: 194–205), although using slightly different terminology. My view about the difficulties of empathetic perspective-shifting have become more negative since then, for the reasons which I will discuss here.

17.3 Perspective-Shifting and Base Cases

One of the reasons why little attention is paid to the difference between the two kinds of perspective-shifting is that in simple cases—what I am calling here *base cases*—they will each produce the same result, the same 'output'. A *base case* of perspective-shifting is one in which:

(i) there are no relevant differences in the psychological dispositions of A, the person attempting to empathize, and of B, the target of the attempt; in particular, both A and B are minimally rational; (ii) there are no relevant non-rational influences on B's psychological make-up or decision-making process; (iii) there is no significant confusion in B's psychological make-up; and (iv) B is not faced with a psychological conflict, such as having to make a choice between two or more alternatives where it is not clear to B which alternative is to be preferred.

Let us consider an example of a base case involving means–end practical reasoning, along the lines discussed by Alvin Goldman in the passage I cited earlier. B wants to eat a sandwich for lunch and believes that Joe's Café is the only place in the vicinity which serves sandwiches. A is wondering what B will decide to do. In perspective-shifting, as Goldman puts it, A applies the decision-making mechanism to a pretend desire (to eat a sandwich) and to a pretend belief (that Joe's Café is the only place in the vicinity which serves sandwiches), and thus outputs a pretend decision (to go to Joe's Café). This enables A to conclude that B will decide to go to Joe's Café. A has thus achieved mental attribution to B through this process of perspective-shifting.

Another example would involve reasoning of the kind discussed by Jane Heal above. B is trying to decide which apples to buy. B believes that English apples are the best kind of apples to choose in the autumn, and she also believes that the current month is September, which, being at present in England, she believes to be the autumn. A is wondering which apples B will decide to buy. A, in co-cognizing with B, must herself 'think about the states of affairs in question', as B is doing. A concludes that this state of affairs would make it likely that English apples are the best ones to buy, and accordingly she can reasonably expect B to come to the same conclusion.

So in both examples, A is able to come up with the correct prediction through perspective-shifting. And, because these examples are base cases, A's prediction would be the same whether the perspective-shifting is of the in-his-shoes or the empathetic variety. The reason why the two kinds of perspective-shifting produce the same result in base cases is simply because all one needs to operate with is a *thin notion of rational agency*—one that is, indeed, shared between A and B. In other words, it doesn't matter what sort of people A and B are, just so long as each is a minimally rational agent, and just so long as the case is a base case in the other respects I set out above. Deliberation and choice is, on this model of practical reason, *impersonal*. Of course it is personal in the sense that it presupposes a thin notion of rationality of the kind ascribed to persons, but what matters here is that it is impersonal in the sense that it is irrelevant who—what sort of person—is doing the deliberation and the choosing. The question really is what would X decide to do, where 'X' ranges over all and only minimally rational agents, including both A and B.

Perspective-shifting involving base cases is a very familiar and everyday phenomenon, deployed in prediction, explanation, and understanding. So it is not surprising that so much of the debate about simulation, empathy, or co-cognition focuses on base case perspective-shifting. But still, there is something deeply misleading about doing this, for it gives the impression that deliberation and choice in practical reasoning is *essentially* impersonal, in the sense that impersonality is supposed to be an essential feature of practical reason, so that any minimally rational agent, any such substitution for X, can be the deliberator, whatever might be the subject-matter.[9]

Sometimes, of course, practical reasoning does allow substitution of the agent, of A for B or of B for A, as was the case in the examples of Joe's Café and of the English apples. But, as we will see, it cannot be generalized to all cases of practical reasoning, and in particular it cannot be generalized to cases outside the base case. To generalize in this way, as is so often done in the simulation debate, results in a blurring of the distinction between the two kinds of perspective-shifting, making it a matter of indifference whether A is imagining *herself* deliberating in B's place, or whether A is imagining *being* B doing the deliberating. The distinction is important not just because the outcome of the two kinds of perspective-shifting could be substantially different if any of conditions (i) to (iv) do not hold. It is important for deeper, conceptual reasons—reasons which will emerge when we consider in detail cases beyond the base case.

17.4 Perspective-Shifting Beyond the Base Case

Condition (i): Differences in psychological dispositions

Sometimes the psychological dispositions of A (the empathizer) and B (the target) differ in a way that impinges on the process of perspective-shifting. These are what I have called in earlier work differences of *characterization*. Aspects of characterization go beyond the thin notion of rational agency towards a more full-blooded notion of agency, which includes not only traits of character and of personality, but also intellectual traits and abilities, such as open-mindedness and quick-wittedness, and emotional dispositions, such as being compassionate towards the homeless, or loving one's spouse.

As I have already pointed out, in base cases, such as Joe's Café and apple-choosing, A need only be concerned to put herself in B's shoes. This is perfectly reasonably just

---

[9] I owe the term 'essentially impersonal' to Rai Gaita (1991). Gaita (1991: 104) puts the point like this: 'For a "logician" of practical reasoning, the fact that it is a particular individual who must act is irrelevant; practical reasoning, in so far as it is reasoning, is essentially impersonal. In contemporary philosophy this is most transparently at work in decision theory which depends upon the idea of a perfectly rational agent in whom practical reason works without error'.

because differences of characterization are quite irrelevant—they have no impact on the outcome of the process. A might not even be clear in her own mind as to whether what she is doing is in-his-shoes perspective-shifting (imagining herself deliberating in B's shoes) or empathetic perspective-shifting (imagining being B doing the deliberating). Our way of thinking and talking about these imaginative processes is after all notoriously imprecise.

But where the full-blooded notion of agency comes into play, A's attempt at perspective-shifting to B's psychology will have to involve taking on those aspects of B's characterization which differ from her own *whilst at the same time not being conscious of them as such*. The reason for this is that the typical role of these dispositions is passive or in the background in the sense that our conscious thoughts and feelings that feature in our deliberations are shaped by, *but are not directed towards*, these dispositions. The kind person has kind thoughts and feelings, but these thoughts and feelings are not typically *about* the disposition of which they are an expression. The person who loves his spouse seldom thinks that he is doing loving things *because* he loves her; and for the modest person, as Bernard Williams says, 'it is a notorious truth that a modest person does not act under the title of modesty' (1985: 10).

At this point I need to explain, in outline, a distinction that Richard Moran (2001) makes between two kinds of stance that one can take towards oneself: the essentially first-personal deliberative or practical stance; and the theoretical or empirical stance. When we are deliberating about what to do, it is the former that is at work, and the question 'What am I going to do?' has 'a practical and not a theoretical application' (2001: 56). 'What we're calling a theoretical question about oneself, then, is one that is answered by discovery of the fact of which one was ignorant, whereas a practical or deliberative question is answered by a decision or commitment of some sort, and it is not a response to ignorance of some antecedent fact about oneself' (2001: 58). So, in deciding what one ought to do (or think or feel), it is a feature of the deliberative or practical stance as part of full-blooded agency that one's characterization is not treated as an empirical fact about oneself; if it is, the deliberative 'ought' becomes merely a theoretical or predictive 'ought'.

This typical role of characterization in first-personal deliberation simply cannot be matched through empathetic perspective-shifting onto another. A cannot, as part of a consciously willed project, keep B's characterization in the non-conscious background in her imaginative exercise of wondering what B will decide to do in a certain situation. A will be obliged, in trying to shift to B's perspective, to treat B's characterization through the theoretical or empirical stance, as one typically does when considering the role of character in explaining or predicting other people's decisions, actions, and so on ('I expect she will help him because she is a kind person'). In effect, B's full-blooded agency, including his characterization, becomes merely another empirical fact for A to take into account in her imaginative project. And this produces a fundamentally distorted model of B's thinking.

There are no doubt *atypical* cases of first-personal deliberation where one's trait is in the foreground, and in particular where it features as a reason for forming an intention, or for adopting an attitude towards something, or for making a decision about what to do. But in these atypical cases, one is put at a psychological distance from one's own thoughts, feelings, and decisions; part of one's thinking about one's own agency has become theoretical or empirical. Just as one says of the other person that the reason why she helped him was because she is a kind person, so, in these non-typical cases, one decides that one should help him because one is a kind person. But if I say this about myself, as Moran argues,

I stand here towards my character as toward some fixed, objective, psychological datum ... But at the same time, the very act of judgment itself demonstrates that I am not in thrall to this 'character', for I can judge it from a standpoint superior in both clarity and freedom. There is a sort of deliverance of myself in the assessment of my character as 'just the way I am', for it absolves me of a kind of responsibility for it. At the same time, there is another kind of deliverance involved in feeling that my very act of naming and judgment demonstrates that I am really superior to this given character, not determined by it. (2001: 173)

The distortion of B's thinking in empathetic perceptive-shifting can then be summarized as follows: A, in foregrounding B's characterization in the process of empathetic perspective-shifting—as she will have to do where there are relevant character differences—will be foisting onto B (in A's imagination) this kind of 'double-minded' thinking, both deliberative or practical *and* theoretical or empirical. This kind of thinking is not only atypical; it is also undermining of the notion of character and of agency with which we began. Moran notes this about Jean-Paul Sartre's discussion: 'Something very much like this same structure lies behind Sartre's insistence on the inherent double-mindedness in any such estimation of oneself'. He then cites Sartre in *Being and Nothingness*: 'The man who confesses that he is evil has exchanged his disturbing "freedom from evil" for an inanimate character of evil; he *is* evil, he clings to himself, he is what he is. But by the same stroke, he escapes from that *thing*, since it is he who contemplates it' (cited in Moran (2001): 172).

In-his-shoes perspective-shifting is less ambitious, and because of this it does not face the problems which confront empathetic perspective-shifting. Of course, where there are relevant differences in characterization, in-his-shoes perspective-shifting will often come up with the wrong answer, due, as Goldman puts it, to 'input inadequacy'. But, as he rightly points out, input inadequacy does not undermine in-his-shoes perspective-shifting, for any relevant 'input' differences between A and B can be adjusted after the process of perspective-shifting is completed. As Goldman has put it, 'There can be adjustments here for factual information about interpersonal differences, but this is just a corrective to the basic tactic of simulation' (1995: 84). I am not in any way arguing against this approach here (although I do have doubts about its usefulness), any more than I am against in-his-shoes perspective-shifting in general.

However, there is an issue concerned with just how ambitious in-his-shoes perspective-shifting really is, and how ambitious it should be.[10] Assume (simplifying for the sake of example) that A is not a kind person, and is putting herself in the shoes of B, who is a kind person, in order to predict what B will do in the circumstances in which B is placed. If the circumstances are such that kind thoughts and kind actions are appropriate then it is likely that A, not being kind, will come up with the wrong prediction of what B will do ('Well, *I* wouldn't give up my seat to someone older at the start of such a long train journey, so I presume B wouldn't either'). At this point, 'adjustments for factual information about interpersonal differences'—namely in this case for B's being a kind person—will be necessary in order correctly to predict what B will do ('Well, *I* wouldn't give up my seat, but B is a kind person, so I expect he would').

This is unambitious in-his-shoes perspective-shifting. A more ambitious variety would seek to build into the imagined circumstances aspects of B's characterization. So in this case, A would imagine himself *being a kind person* in B's circumstances ('Well, if I were in B's circumstances, and if I were a kind person like B—which by the way I'm not—I would think that giving up my seat would be what a kind person like me ought to do'). At this point, this more ambitious variety of in-his-shoes perspective-shifting begins to suffer from exactly the same problems as empathetic perspective-shifting: B's thinking is being distorted in just the same way. The lesson from this for in-his-shoes perspective-shifting, I think, is that it should not be too ambitious. Some 'interpersonal differences' can no doubt be built into the circumstances without distortion ('Well, I suppose I might give my seat up, but poor B's ankle is broken and in plaster, so I wouldn't if I were in his shoes'). In contrast, it is those interpersonal differences of characterization which are involved in our full-blooded agency, operating in the background of our deliberation, that give rise to the difficulties which I have been canvassing here.

Condition (ii): Non-rational influences on thinking

The second move beyond the base case is where there are significant non-rational influences on B's thinking. One such influence can be mood. If B is feeling irritable from drinking too much coffee and A is not, A's attempt to perspective-shift to B's psychological states may well fail for this reason; for example, if A is wondering what B will decide to do if he (B) sees someone queue-barging in front of him.[11] Mood, like our character traits and emotional dispositions, typically plays a background role in our deliberations, and we seldom take a theoretical stance towards them ('Given the mood I'm in, I'll probably shout at him if he tries to queue-barge'). This is even more so with what Matthew Ratcliffe (2008) calls 'existential feelings', such as a feeling of being out of touch with the world. These feelings can colour our whole way of thinking in ways

---

[10] Thanks to Joel Smith for pressing me on this.
[11] I discuss this kind of example in Goldie (2002a).

that we are often not conscious of, and hardly ever take a theoretical stance towards (except in therapy and the like).

The kind of non-rational influence that I want to concentrate on here is the complexity of temptation, and of akrasia or weakness of will,[12] which will enable me to explore further the tension between the deliberative and the theoretical stances. Both Heal and Goldman, and most other proponents of versions of empathy as perspective-shifting, are at pains to acknowledge these kinds of complexity, and accept that they can often lead to incorrect results. Heal, for example, discusses the difficulties of imagining the effects of non-rational influences such as tiredness, emotional distur-bance, drinking whisky, depression, and akrasia.[13] This is why she insists that the proper domain for perspective-shifting (co-cognition) is where there are 'rational or intelligible linkages' between 'items with content'. With the connections between emotion and value judgement in mind, she says that 'simulation will be applicable and will cope when the links of value judgement to the other elements of the situation (e.g. strength of motivation and feeling) are all intelligibly in order, but will fail when there is akrasia or other non-intelligible or non-content-involving factors affecting the outcome' (1996/2003a: 82).

One of the important facts about our emotions is that they can induce irrationalities in ways that the agent is not aware of at the time. Emotions have a tendency to 'skew the epistemic landscape': to make what is irrational or unfounded appear to the agent as rational or well-founded.[14] This leads us to the further difficulty with empathetic perspective-shifting which arises where the other person, B, is in such a condition. Very much as with character and characterization, which I considered earlier, there is no way in which A can *consciously and intentionally* replicate B's state of irrationality *of which B is unaware*; for it is only in those cases of fully conscious irrationality that one's irrationality is to the foreground in deliberation. In other words, here too we inflict 'double-minded' thinking on B in a way that distorts B's psychology in an important way.

As I have already mentioned, Goldman, in his discussion of what he calls 'input inadequacy', considers the many examples of failures successfully to empathize through perspective-shifting (high-level simulation), and argues that their existence, and the existence of what he calls 'rampant egocentrism' count, somewhat ironically, in favour of this kind of simulation (at least when considered against its opponent, theory): roughly speaking, we should not be surprised that pretend inputs should be inaccurate on certain kinds of occasion. For example, when trying to simulate the experiences of subjects in the Milgram experiments, students get it wrong, Goldman says, because 'their E-imaginative efforts are woefully deficient' (2006a: 175). It is not enough, he rightly says, merely to *suppose* that one is a subject in the Milgram experiment; what is

---

[12] For the distinction between akrasia and weakness of will, see Holton (1999).

[13] These examples of non-rational influences are all mentioned in various places in her 1996/2003a.

[14] I discuss this phenomenon in Goldie (2008a). I owe the expression to Finn Spicer.

needed is E-imagination in order to 're-create the psychological circumstances opera-tive in a decision-making task' (2006a: 175).

Goldman discusses further circumstances where perspective-shifting fails, not be-cause of non-rational, non-intelligible linkages of the kinds just discussed, but also through general failures to 'quarantine' our own psychological states so that they do not interfere with or 'contaminate' the process (see also Goldman this volume). And of course this is going to be far from easy to do, or to know reliably when it has been done successfully, particularly given the fact that our emotions can mislead us in ways that are systematically hard to detect.

So far it might seem that most of the problems discussed are contingent limitations on the success of empathetic perspective-shifting—epistemic limits on quarantining, or on getting the right 'inputs', and limits on individuals' imaginative powers where the other is unlike oneself. Perhaps some kind of 'method-acting' transformation will be sufficient; Robert Gordon, for example, has argued that 'by transforming ourselves much as actors do', A can simulate B rather than merely simulating himself in B's situation (1995: 57). But I now want to turn to the third and fourth difficulties which seem to be little discussed in relation to perspective-shifting and the wider debate about the merits of simulation, and which will, I hope, bring out profound conceptual problems for empathetic perspective-shifting.

Condition (iii): Confusion

We are, as Charles Taylor (1985) says, 'self-interpreting animals', capable of reflecting on, and interpreting, our own psychological states. A feature of this capacity—which, as we have seen, is an aspect of the deliberative, practical stance—is that one's activity of self-interpretation can change the psychological states on which one is reflecting. Of course someone can be wrong about how he feels, but, as Stuart Hampshire says, 'his claim to knowledge still has authority just because his *thought* of his state of mind as having a certain cause, and therefore being of a certain kind, is one of the factors which determines what his state of mind actually is'.[15]

Following on from this, a number of writers have made the point that when we are uncertain or confused about how we think or feel, this is not like the uncertainty or confusion that we can have about an independent object. When I say 'I don't know what I feel about this', this does not imply that 'There is a way that I feel about this and I don't know what it is'; in other words, in this respect it is not like my saying 'I don't know what that thing in the corner of room is'.[16] When the agent deliberates about,

---

[15] 1972: 237. Moran cites Sartre's *Being and Nothingness*: 'It is often said that the act of reflection alters the fact of consciousness on which it is directed' (2001: 37).

[16] Both Moran and Hampshire discuss the fundamental difference in these respects between uncertainty about one's own psychological states and uncertainty about physical objects in the world. Moran, for example, says that 'the relation . . . is not like that of an object to the observation of it' (2001: 39); and Hampshire says that 'recognizing what one thinks, feels, or wants, is apt to be wrongly assimilated to recognizing and identifying an independent physical object, where an independent object is something

and decides on, his confusion, only the agent can avow the thought 'On reflection, I really do feel ashamed about what I did', and this is just because the avowal is also the expression *of a decision*, one which only the agent can reach about his thoughts. This self-interpreting deliberative stance is essentially first-personal: one has an authority here which others cannot usurp, because each of us is uniquely able to take the deliberative stance towards our own mind—and also because each of us uniquely has an insight into our own confusion.

Two citations, from Moran and Hampshire, help to bring out what is special about the first-personal perspective. Moran says this:

If reflective self-consciousness imposes either the assumption or the evasion of responsibilities peculiar to the first-person position, responsibilities that involve the acknowledgement of one's deliberative and not just theoretical role with respect to one's own state of mind, then we should expect that the apprehension of one's own mind will not only be a matter of special privilege and authority, but will also involve its own complexities and uncertainties that are not characteristic of the apprehension of other minds. On this view the privileges of the first-person position are internally related to its special limits and infirmities, and the awareness of one's mental life presents difficulties which are *not* shared by the corresponding third-person perspective'. (2001: 153–4)

Hampshire discusses a man who is in a state of uncertainty and confusion about how he feels about his past action, about just what his feeling of uneasiness might be, and is asking himself 'What is this feeling that I have?':

While he is unsure of the correct diagnosis himself, and while he is still putting this question to himself, at least his conscious feeling has not crystallised into one of these determinate forms. No one can truthfully attribute to him one of these determinate sentiments yet. He still has to make up his mind what he thinks, and therefore, in more specific terms, exactly what he feels, apart from just feeling unhappy. And his making up of his mind is, in many typical cases, like a kind of decision, being a conscious adoption of a specific attitude. (1972: 242)

Confusion of the mind, deliberation about our confusion, and decision about what we feel, reveal profound difficulties for empathetic perspective-shifting. First, B's confusion is not a condition that A can 'take on' in imagination; surely A cannot imagine being in a state which is indeterminate in the required way. And secondly, even if A were able to do this (although I believe it to be conceptually impossible), how could *A* make the decision to *remove* that confusion, for this *essentially* involves a decision which is *first-personal to B*, a decision which is an expression of the sort of person B is. In other words, A, in perspective-shifting to B, cannot at time T_1 have (co-cognize, empathize with) this thought of B's: 'I don't know what I feel about what I did'; nor can A at time T_2 decide on, and then avow, this thought on behalf of B 'On reflection, I really do

that can be observed by different observers from different points of view, and will change its appearance, but not its real properties, as the point of view changes' (1972: 244).

feel ashamed about what I did'. The avowal, the expression of a *decision*, is one which only *B* can make about his thoughts.

The ability to reflect on our confusion, and decide what we think or feel, has at its heart the full-blooded notion of agency in relation to our own minds. Thoughts are thought, feelings felt, decisions and choices made, *by particular agents*, and the identity of the agent in this full-blooded sense can make a difference to what is thought, felt, decided on, or chosen. It is not as though all thoughts, feelings, decisions, and choices can be 'processed' by *any* agent, impersonally, just so long as that agent is minimally rational.

Condition (iv): Conflict

The full-blooded notion of agency in relation to our thoughts comes into play even more clearly when we turn to psychological conflict which arises on those occasions— frequent enough in our lives—when we have to make a *personal decision*, choosing between competing or conflicting considerations. Personal decisions range from the tragic ethical dilemmas like the one faced by Agamemnon at Aulis, to the kind of personal decision we have to make about which of two careers is the right one for us to pursue. It is a mark of personal decisions that one is not willing to delegate the decision to someone else ('I can't decide what is the right thing to do; you decide for me'). These are decisions that one has to live with. The idea that practical reasoning is essentially impersonal mistakenly assimilates them to the base case.

I suggest that a related kind of assimilation is at work in the simulation debate, assimilating simulation of base cases such as deciding what any minimally rational agent ought to do if he or she desires a sandwich and believes that Joe's Café is the only place in the vicinity which serves sandwiches, to simulation of deciding what one ought to do if one is deciding which career to choose.

Spelling out exactly what the role is of the agent in deliberation and decision is no easy matter. Even in the more banal base case, just involving the thinner notion of rational agency, the process of decision has a certain mystery, and it is sometimes taken to be a kind of exercise of one's freedom. Those who have written on the subject have different formulations of what is involved, but the insight that all of them share is that at the heart of a full-blooded conception of agency is a conception of oneself as a temporally persisting agent who, in the words of Michael Bratman, 'begins, continues, and completes temporally extended projects' (2007a: 59), and who has the capacity to reflect on, and decide or settle on, desires, values, plans and so on. When one decides what to think or what to do, one does so (or so one hopes) in a way that is expressive of this full-blooded conception of oneself, but—just as we saw earlier with character and personality traits—one does not typically decide with this full-blooded conception of oneself as part of one's conscious deliberation, as merely another empirical fact to be taken into consideration.

Bratman, in a series of papers on agency, deliberation, and choice, has drawn out Robert Nozick's idea that, instead of 'weighing up' the options before us when we make a decision, as if the options have their weights exhibited on their sleeves, we make 'a self-subsuming decision that bestows weights to reasons on the basis of a then chosen conception of oneself and one's appropriate life' (2007b: 127, citing Nozick (1981): 300). This kind of decision, the 'bestowal' of weights, being an expression of one's conception of oneself, is radically first-personal. Especially (but not only) in the ethical case, the existence of dilemmas and difficult choices is often, rightly in my view, taken to throw light not only on the radical first-personal nature of choice, but also, as Rai Gaita (1991) and others have argued, on why the notion of a moral 'expert' is incoherent. Accordingly, this notion of agency cannot be captured with the idea that reflection and decision in the face of conflict is something that can be done on the agent's behalf, 'delegated' to some other 'agency', as one might to an expert.

The suggestion, then, is that in empathetic perspective-shifting, where A thinks B's thoughts, and then in imagination decides what is the right thing for B to think or to do, A *usurps* B's agency, replacing it with her own. To bring the point home, consider a case where B is trying to decide whether to abandon his life as an architect to become a hill-farmer. B, of course, might ask for advice from his friends, one of whom is A. Now at this point, T_1, B is undecided. As he might put it to A, he doesn't know what is for the best. Then, at T_2, B decides what to do—he makes his choice. How can A in empathetic perspective-shifting, emulate this process: conflict and indecision at T_1, and at T_2 the resolution of the conflict through the making of the decision (through the 'bestowal of weights'), without her decision being expressive of her own full-blooded agency and not B's? Even if A were to treat B's characterization as an empirical fact to be taken into consideration in the attempt to empathize, A would still be left with her own full-blooded agency, which would continue to play its covert, non-speaking part in the deliberation—a particularly virulent form of contamination.[17]

17.5 Conclusion

At this point it might be objected that I have missed the whole point of the simulationist program as contrasted with its opponent, the theoretical stance.[18] For, it is often asserted, what is precisely *right* about simulation—and perspective-shifting in particular—is that it models our thinking about the other on the way that we ourselves

[17] Steuber (2006, Chapter 6: 'The Limits of Empathy'), has a nice discussion of the arguments against empathy from the hermeneutical tradition. He refers to what Gadamer has called the 'prejudicial structure of understanding': 'Understanding another person's reasons for his actions or grasping his thoughts cannot merely be understood as re-enactment or as a form of inner imitation because the manner in which we 'think' that thought is always already—to use one of the signature phrases of hermeneutic thinkers—colored by our system of beliefs and values, which can differ considerably from that of the interpretee' (2006: 205). Although Steuber agrees that these difficulties are too much neglected in the current debate, his own conclusion is more optimistic than mine.

[18] Heal might add that my anti-empathy stance might have some bite against Goldman's information-processing approach, but not against hers, which is, she rightly insists, simulation at the *personal* level.

think; what A does is make her mind like B's, to paraphrase Heal, and part of this involves A making her agency like B's.

The truth in the objection only reaches so far as the base case, and, correlatively, only so far as in-his-shoes perspective-shifting where deliberation can be impersonal. What can be 'emulated' in base case simulation is the minimally rational stance towards the subject matter being deliberated on: when A makes her mind like B's, she adopts a rational stance which, it is assumed, is relevantly like that of B. But emulation of this rational stance—of thin rational agency—falls far short of emulation of the deliberative, practical stance that I have been putting forward here as part of a full-blooded notion of agency.[19] The thin notion of agency has no place for all those traits of character and personality, and other psychological dispositions, which come to be expressed in the kind of full-blooded agency which is implicated in deciding about one's own confused states of mind, and in deciding what to think and do in situations of conflict. There is simply no place in perspective-shifting for this full-blooded notion of agency *of the other person*, for the deliberative or practical stance of *the other person*, infused as it is with dispositions of character and personality, and with a conception of oneself as having a past and a future in the light of which decisions and choices are made—decisions and choices which one has to live with. To the extent that there is a place for this full-blooded notion of agency in A's attempt at empathetic perspective-shifting, it can only be *A*'s agency that is brought to bear in deliberation and in decisions in the face of confusion and conflict; and it is in just this respect that A usurps B's agency. And if A were to try to bring to bear *B*'s agency, it could only be achieved in the 'double-minded' way that is profoundly unrepresentative of the typical role of our agency in our practical reasoning, and more generally in our inner lives.[20]

[19] In a way, this could be seen as a vindication of Heal's thought, that simulation as co-cognition has to be restricted to rational linkages between contents.

[20] Many thanks to Amy Coplan, Derek Matravers, Joel Smith, and to participants at a workshop at Durham University on moral phenomenology for their comments on earlier versions of this chapter.

18

Empathy for the Devil

Adam Morton

18.1 An Unwelcome Conclusion

You may not like what I am going to say. I shall argue that there is a blinkering effect to decency. Being a morally sensitive person, and having internalized a code of behavior that restricts the range of actions that one takes as live options for oneself, constrains one's imagination. It becomes harder to identify imaginatively with important parts of human possibility. In particular—the part of the claim that I will argue for in this chapter—it limits one's capacity to empathize with those who perform atrocious acts. They become alien to one. This is an obstacle to understanding many important, if awful, human actions. But it also creates obstacles to understanding some very ordinary, relatively harmless, actions. It is a problem that decent people have to grapple with.

The shape of my argument will be clearer if I make clear at the outset that the empathy I am interested in applies our emotional and imaginative capacities to the task of understanding others. (The role of empathy in understanding others is a theme of Steuber (2006), which discusses a long tradition in sociology and the philosophy of the social sciences.) It is real understanding that gives one a grasp of the motivation of another. An emotion of similarity and closeness that misleads one about the actual state of another is pretend empathy, in my book. I think that real understanding is a large part of what we need empathy for, and that we try to encourage it in cases where we need it. But this means that we must select among all the possible empathetic emotions to another, to find the accurate ones. It is the difficulty of doing this that causes the phenomena I am concerned with. Or so I claim, and for this reason a large part of the paper consists in evoking the variety of attitudes that are candidates for empathy.

18.2 Why versus How

To begin, an account of the explanatory force of empathy: how taking another's point of view can result in understanding their actions better. Empathy is not a luxury in human affairs. We need it in order to negotiate our way around one another, with our diverse motives and characters. It is intrinsic to our efforts to get real explanations of why people do what they do. To elaborate on this, I will have to give my understanding of what empathy is. I think the following is reasonably close to the consensus among contemporary philosophers and psychologists. (Ravenscroft (1998), Goldie (2002a), Hutto (2002), Preston & de Waal (2002), Currie (2004).)

One person, A, has empathy for another, B, with respect to a particular state of mind, when B experiences an emotion or attitude and A has a representation of B's state which shares its affective tone and perspective.

The definition is not completely sharp, but neither is the concept of empathy. In particular it requires that the empathizer share some of the 'tone and perspective' of the person they are empathizing with. That can be taken several ways. To require that 'the same emotion' be shared would be too weak, as it would allow a representation of annoyance as empathy for rage, since both are instances of anger. But emotional identity is too strong, or we would rarely empathize with despair or agony. Talking of imagination may help here, since one can imagine more than one can experience. (One can in some sense imagine the extent of space, or the origin of the universe.) But some imagination is too distanced to support empathy.

I have required just that one 'represent' the state of the other person, but in a way that captures its affective tone and perspective. I intend this to involve the same sort of emotion felt in the same sort of way, but I am not requiring that the fit be perfect. I do have in mind, though I am not writing it into the definition, that the way one represents another's state of mind in empathizing with them enable the kind of understanding of the person that empathy should support.

An example: B is pausing on the high board and will either dive into the pool below or back out and descend. A is watching and knows two things. First he knows that B is fearful, and in fact he knows how B's knees shake and how the water seems far, far below. And, second, he knows that B's fear is shaped around being in that position on the board, looking along and down, and imagining two possible futures (each in a different way unwanted.) By representing B's state as having this affect, its particular feel of fear, and this perspective, spatially and temporally, A's grasp of B's fearful indecision is one of empathy.

As I am telling the example and using the term, A does not have to like or approve of B. A may think that B is silly and selfish, having got herself into a situation she could easily have anticipated and wasting the time of other divers lining up at the steps. That does not matter. It is still empathy. For that matter, A may be B, considering her own situation from some time later. (And a sex-change, given my use of pronouns, but we can ignore that.) Identity will not ensure that empathy succeeds: sometimes one has no fellow-feeling for one's former self.

Now suppose that B after an inner struggle gets herself to run along the board and dive, with a hesitating departure that results in an awkward entry into the water below. A has a grasp of what lay behind B's action, based in part on his empathy. So here we have an important function for empathy: it can allow us to grasp how a person managed to act on the motives that she did. But the empathy is not needed for B to know *why* B dove at that moment. In fact it is not particularly helpful in the why-explanation. For that, A needs to know B's desires—what possibilities she is aiming at in diving then—and her beliefs—what situation she takes herself to be in. And if A knows these things in sufficient detail he knows why B did what she did. But this will not allow A to know *how* B was able to do it. That is, given the scary height and the competing attraction of coming down feet-first on the ladder rather than head-first in the air, A can identify B's motives without understanding why these were the motives on which she acted.

To put it differently, knowing why a person performed an act is not the same as knowing why the person did that act rather than others for which there were also strong motives. This distinction is obscured by descriptions of human choice that assume that there is always a comparison of the all-things-considered motives for competing actions, so that a rational agent can simply choose the act with the stronger motives. (Or that the options have equally strong appeal, in which case the agent can make a trivial and arbitrary choice between them.) I shall assume, as I take to be overwhelmingly plausible, that these are unrealistic descriptions. Life is just not like that; we can rarely rank our motives in such a simple way. Usually, it takes something else to push us in one direction or the other. (Morton (1990), Richardson (1994).)

Sometimes, to go in one direction or the other we have to overcome some barrier or inhibition, based on fear, sympathy, disgust, or decency. Then empathy can be vital in allowing us to understand the barrier and how it was overcome. The barrier of decency is the one that concerns me here. Suppose that instead of hesitating on a diving board B is pausing before pulling the trigger of a gun pointed at the head of another person. Suppose that the other is her husband and after years of abuse she has finally been pushed to a point where given an opportunity to express her rage and despair, and to avoid the beating that will otherwise soon follow, she is prepared to kill. Still she hesitates. She is not a violent person; she takes killing to be forbidden; and once she loved this man. But after a few seconds of indecision that feel like hours, she shoots. She will have overcome a deeply ingrained barrier against violence, and another against acts she has been raised to abhor. (See chapter two of Morton (2004).)

We can tell the story so that her act is wrong. There are alternatives to killing that she could have seen and would have preferred if she had been able to reflect. The consequences of allowing him to live are, while nasty, not dire enough to justify killing. Then the barriers that she had to overcome in order to pull the trigger are rightly placed. They should be preventing her from acting. Still, we can empathize with her. We can represent to ourselves an emotion that is directed along the axes of her situation and that gives us some grasp, not of why she made a choice that rid her of a great menace, but of how she was able to make it.

You may wonder about the accuracy of the empathy in this case. Is the emotion we feel on her behalf similar enough to the emotion that allowed her to act, that we do in fact grasp something real about how she could do it? That is a serious question, central to this paper. Not everything that feels like empathy can do empathy's work.

18.3 Evil Acts

The example of the abused wife is special, in that while we may think, intellectually, that she should have acted differently, the tone of our condemnation is rather muted. We sympathize. We are not sure that in similar circumstances we might not have done something similar. Things are different with cases in which the act is truly repugnant, where it would damage our self-respect to believe that we could have done anything analogous. There is no shortage of horrors to choose from, but think of the rape and murder of a young child, or active and enthusiastic participation in genocide. We have no sympathy for the perpetrators here, and while we often know reasonably well why they act as they do, we have a deep and troubling puzzlement about how they could do it. A murderous pedophile, for example, may have sex with children in order to satisfy desires that may be no more continuous with other things he wants than those of adults with less harmfully satisfied sexualities, and kills simply to cover up his crimes and the immense shame that their discovery would bring. But, we imagine, were we to have his desires we would force chastity on ourselves with a rigor fuelled by horror of the alternative. We imagine these even while being distantly aware that there is something unrealistic and self-deceptive in what we are telling ourselves. Not that long ago, many people used to tell themselves similar stories beginning 'if, God forbid, I had been homosexual.' The fact is, that when we try to find anything like real empathy for people who commit real atrocities we come up against a barrier. We can describe the motives, and we can often even imagine some of what it might be like to do the acts, but there are deep obstacles to the kind of sympathetic identification required for empathy.

I am interested in the nature of this barrier. Here is a hypothesis about it. It is made of the same materials as the barriers against choosing dangerous, disgusting, or immoral actions. These barriers affect our imagination of choice as well as our actual choices, so that they inhibit us from making nasty choices vivid. (As a by product, we can find it puzzling how the barrier was overcome in imagination, as we can be puzzled how it was in fact. So a higher-order empathy is possible, addressed to a higher-order puzzlement: how was this person able to empathize with this atrocious act?) To make the similar-barrier hypothesis intelligible, perhaps even plausible consider some examples.

A-assault. A has an unpredictable violent temper. His irritation at another person can grow to a point where he seizes on a small detail of that person's behavior, or an incidental fact about them, as a pretext for an assault. A is married to B, who wishes A were not so volatile and despairs of the trouble that surrounds their life. But very often she takes A's side, and even joins in. Reacting typically, A is irked by the slow and meticulous way in which a co-worker, C, is performing a task. After half an hour's work C is near to finishing it, though A would have done a sloppier job in ten minutes.

A fidgets impatiently, trying to urge speed on C with his body language, until he gets a whiff of C's aftershave and notices his freshly shaved face and nicely manicured hands. 'You fucking pretty boys, you don't know how to do fucking anything', he shouts; 'if you wanted to take so long you should have started early at work instead of taking time to get pretty for your fag friends.' And he grabs C's shoulder to push him into quicker motion. C resists and in a moment a brawl has begun. B arrives as this is all beginning, bringing lunch for both men, and hopes that A will not make trouble with his only remaining co-worker. She can see that C is irritatingly slow and needs to be hurried, but she can also see the bad consequences of yet another explosion. So she is taken aback by the verbal and physical assault. This is her man, though, and she has a lot of practice at tracking his point of view. She can easily recreate his reaction to C's fastidious appearance, and see how A links it to his meticulous style of work. So she soon understands what is moving A, and once the emotion is available as explanation it is also available as motive. She wades into the brawl, grabs C by his tie. 'Mind your manners with my husband, you goddam fashion model': holding him so that A can get in a few good blows.

This is an imagined example, but it is easy to imagine. It shows how, at least in the way we imagine people in narration, we can find the process that can get a person past a barrier to empathy to carry them further, past the barrier to action. And this particular case also suggests a basic reason why we are reluctant to overcome a barrier to empathy. Overcoming it may carry one along further than one wants.

Imagining past a barrier does not always make the acts more available. Consider a case that is in some ways an opposite of the one I have just described.

X-taxi. X devotes a lot of his time and energy visiting criminals in prison, getting to a condition of mutual comprehension with them, and then providing support for them on their release. He is a deeply religious person, and his particular beliefs emphasize the sinfulness of all humanity, himself included. He often analyzes his motives on occasions when he has strayed from duty or kindness. When he thinks about times he has been discourteous, misleading, or devious he finds similar attitudes to those he takes to have led his criminal acquaintances to murder, rape, or assault. At any rate this is the way he understands himself and them.

X has been visiting A in prison: A of the previous example, whose assault on B produced serious injuries, so that his parole for an earlier yet more serious assault was revoked. Although A is not by far the most hardened criminal X has dealt with, he finds his motivation particularly hard to grasp intuitively. He thinks about the assault on C and an analogy from his own experience strikes him. Not long ago he was taking a taxi to an airport, not having left quite enough time and so wanting the driver to hurry. When the driver stopped at a light that was just beginning to turn orange, X found himself glancing a the driver's identification plaque, noticing that the driver's home country was Somalia, and exclaiming 'you know, some of us were raised with a concept of precise time.' Later he berated himself for his racist reaction, and the way he had seized on an irrelevant attribute of the driver to hang his irritation on. Now, thinking about A, he sees the analogy. Both of them had used the emotional force of their reaction to an incidental feature of the other person as a vehicle for overcoming an obstacle to an action that would otherwise have been off-limits. One result of this link between him and A is that he begins to compare notes with A about all the little traits of people that annoy them. His aim is to help A to contain his reactions, before they facilitate disasters. X now feels he can empathize with A. He can summon a representation that allows him to grasp how A can have done what he did.

18.4 Smith, Hume, and Imagining the Context

I am trying to account for the barriers to empathizing with an evil action. But on some accounts the issue is trivial. For example Adam Smith in his *The Theory of Moral Sentiments*, discussing 'sympathy', which is closely related to what I and other contributors to this book call empathy[1], says

> When the original passions of the person principally concerned are in perfect concord with the sympathetic emotions of the spectator, they necessarily appear to this last just and proper, and suitable to their objects; and, on the contrary, when . . . he finds that they do not coincide with what he feels, they necessarily appear to him unjust and improper, . . . To approve of the passions of another, therefore, . . . is the same thing as to observe that we entirely sympathize with them; and not to approve of them as such, is the same thing as to observe that we do not entirely sympathize with them. (Part I, Chapter 3, p. 20)

According to Smith, we sympathize with, *and approve of*, only the emotions that we feel, or which we would feel were we in the situation of the person concerned. In particular

> There are some passions of which the expressions excite no sort of sympathy, but before we are acquainted with what gave occasion to them, serve rather to disgust and provoke us against them. The furious behaviour of an angry man is more likely to exasperate us against himself than against his enemies. (Ibid., Part I, Chapter 1, p. 7)

The reason is that sympathy is derived from putting oneself imaginatively in someone's situation and then experiencing in a reduced form the resulting emotion.

> the spectator must, first of all, endeavour, as much as he can, to put himself in the situation of the other, and to bring home to himself every little circumstance of distress which can possibly occur to the sufferer. He must adopt the whole case of his companion with all its minutest incidents; and strive to render as perfect as possible, that imaginary change of situation upon which his sympathy is founded. (Ibid., Part I, Chapter 1, p. 35)

If one can do this for the feelings that motivate an action, then one will approve of it as the person acting does. If not, not.

---

[1] I think in fact that there are important differences that can be marked by distinguishing between sympathy and empathy, but that is a topic for another occasion.

This is clearly much too simple. Leaving aside the difference between sharing a motivating emotion and approving of an action, which would lead us into controversial questions in meta-ethics, sympathy or empathy cannot simply be the result of imagining oneself into all the details of the other person's situation. There are unimaginably many details in any person's situation, relevant to any one of their acts or emotions. To grasp another's situation one ignores some of these, imagines some of them in a rudimentary not-very-vivid way, and imagines a few in a vivid way that incorporates the person's perspective. Moreover the person's situation includes their desires, beliefs, and even their emotions. These too have to be ignored or imagined with varying degrees of intensity. As a result, it can happen that although in the situation in which another finds herself one would in fact feel just as she does, when one tries hard to load enough relevant details into one's imagination one comes up with a different emotion, or none at all. Or, more to the point here, it can happen that when one imagines some of the details of someone's situation one gets an emotion that is much like the one attributed to the other, but is not in fact what one would feel if one was in that full situation. The question of the accuracy or appropriateness of the resulting empathy then arises, as it does not given Smith's simplistic account.

Adam Smith's friend David Hume also described limits to what we can imagine. Hume's point is not that we cannot sympathize with wrongdoers but that we have difficulty imagining that what is wrong is right. A work of fiction, in particular, may require us to imagine humans battling dinosaurs, or time travel, or a human turning into a beetle, and we manage to imagine all of these. But a fictional presupposition that rape is a noble action, or that one may eat babies on a whim, is practically impossible to comply with. As Hume puts it

Whatever speculative errors may be found in the polite writings of any age or country, they detract but little from the value of those compositions. There needs but a certain turn of thought or imagination to make us enter into all the opinions, which then prevailed, and relish the sentiments or conclusions derived from them. But a very violent effort is requisite to change our judgment of manners, and excite sentiments of approbation or blame, love or hatred, different from those to which the mind from long custom has been familiarized. And where a man is confident of the rectitude of that moral standard, by which he judges, he is justly jealous of it, and will not pervert the sentiments of his heart for a moment, in complaisance to any writer whatsoever. (Hume (1757), paragraph 33)

There are many issues here, and recent writers have done a lot to disentangle them. (See Walton (2006, Gendler (2006).) Many of the issues have no direct connection with the themes of this chapter. There is a connection, though, with our attitude to fictional characters with awful motivation. We do identify with Macbeth or Raskolnikov, and experience something like empathy for them. If Hume is denying that, he seems clearly wrong. And the reasons why we can empathize with awful characters are closely related to the reasons that Adam Smith is overstating his case: a skilful author will direct the imagination to aspects of the fictional situation, including aspects of the fictional character's motivation, that are similar to those of the reader, so that one gets a partial imagination of the motivation of deeds that one would not consider doing oneself (at least in one's current circumstances, as discussed in a moment.) But a partial grasp of motivation is all one ever has: if there is any empathy at all it rests on partial imagination. So, to deny something Hume may not be asserting, we can empathize with the motives of repugnant characters in part because empathy can be selective in its choice of an imaginative basis, and in fiction the issue of accuracy is very problematic.

Issues about the limits of imagination connect also with an enormous and important issue that I shall not discuss. One of the deepest and most troubling issues of modern times is the realization that ordinary decent people willingly participate in atrocities. The point was first made by Hannah Arendt in Arendt (1963) and in other writings (see especially Arendt (1971)). It is a motivation for work in social psychology by Millgram and others (for a summary, see Nisbett & Ross (1991)) which shows that if placed in a suitable context just about anyone will acquiesce in acts that in other contexts they would find morally repugnant. These facts are a surprise to the people concerned, as they are to the whole culture, because we find it very hard to imagine taking part in such actions. And as a result we find it hard to empathize with people who are complicit in atrocities even when they are psychologically very similar to us. The reason for this, I think, is of a piece with what is going on with the claims by Smith and Hume: when we imagine an action we focus on a small number of relevant factors, holding others implicit. We usually keep out of focus factors concerning the general context of action, concentrating our limited imaginative resources on the thinking and motivation that a person experiences in that context. As a result, we are not used to imagining actions performed in significantly different contexts to those in which we find ourselves. So given a repugnant action performed in different circumstances our simple efforts to imagine it, or gain empathy for the agent, fail.

This is too quick. It deserves a much fuller treatment, which I am not going to give here. The important point is just the link between issues about the limits of imagination and the incredulity we feel at the suggestion that we might act atrociously.

18.5 A Choice of Empathies

Before touching on issues arising from Smith, Hume, and Arendt, we were discussing cases in which people do manage to have empathy for an evil act. I used an example of a person X who models the violent actions of another person, A, on his own failures to be courteous. There is something suspect about X's empathy. It is not particularly plausible that X is identifying anything close to the emotion that allowed A to commit his assaults. Which is not to say that he is obviously wrong, but he seems to be leaping from the assumption that if he can condemn himself and A under the same description he will have got onto A's moral-psychological wavelength.

Since I am interested in accurate empathy, empathy that can help us really understand people, it is important to me to bring out the variety of ways that X's task could be done. So in this section I show different ways of doing similar tasks. In a real case, one of them may fit the facts better than another. In an imaginary case, told in a few paragraphs, there is no telling.

X did one thing right. He tried to empathize with an atrocious act by focusing on a venial one. He made two mistakes. One was thinking that all he had to do was to present to himself an emotion with somewhat similar functioning, and then crank up the moral seriousness. The other was to think that the emotion he chose, and its function, had to serve an immoral end, even if a less seriously immoral one. These may not seem like mistakes. After all empathy for an act one would not have performed oneself will have to be based on analogy rather than identity. And if empathy is to bring morally relevant understanding one might expect empathy for an evil act to link it to motivation that is at any rate wrong. I think the first of these points is right, but not the second. To see why, consider some alternative explanations of A's actions, with empathy-producing potential.

Smoking. S is a former nicotine addict who has weaned herself off cigarettes after a long and difficult struggle. One day, after she has been nicotine-free for six months, she is talking to a friend who is in despair over her stalled career and her failed marriage. The friend has also quit smoking but says that what she would find most comforting at the moment would be just a few puffs to calm her down while she talks. It is more important to be able to talk out one's troubles than to preserve nico-purity, S argues, and so she dashes into a shop and gets a pack of cigarettes. They both puff, and the conversation is comforting, but they finish the packet, and a month later both of them are still smoking. Looking back, S sees the impulse to comfort her friend with a cigarette as prompted by the whisper of her buried addiction, and regrets it.

Propositioning. T is a shy young man who while very attentive and relaxed with old friends has difficulty making new friends. He is fascinated by a woman he meets at a party, but cannot summon the nerve to contact her later. A month after the party he sees her on a bus and watches her unobtrusively. She gets off, leaving a book behind on her seat. T goes to the seat, picks up the book, realizes that it is a library book, rushes to the front of the bus, persuades the driver to stop, gets off, and runs after her with the book. When he finally catches up with her, he is out of breath and, panting and holding on to a parking meter for support he hands her the book. She recognizes him from the party, says 'I was hoping we'd meet again', and touches him on the arm. As he slowly regains the ability to speak, he finds he is still in the adrenaline rush of his decision in the bus and his dash down the street. He deliberately uses it to make himself look and speak directly at her and suggests that in that case they have a cup of coffee right away.

Dog poop. U is very proud of her Shiba Inu. She has never owned a dog before, and this is not an easy breed, but U and the dog get on well and the dog is obedient and affectionate. And well cared for, with one exception. On their walks U does not pick up after the dog. She has a loathing of excrement, and cannot bear to touch it even through a plastic bag. This failure creates tension with her neighbors, and disapproval from other dog owners who think she is undermining the acceptability of urban dogs. One day U is sitting in the park with her dog, enjoying a picnic with her partner, when she notices a lump of the chocolate cake she was eating has fallen onto her partner's dress. She takes a paper napkin and stealthily removes the lump, depositing it into the garbage bag they have brought. Then, picking up her cake again, she realizes that the slice is intact, and what had dropped on the dress could not have been cake. But scooping it and depositing it had been easy, as long as she did not think of it as shit. From then on, when her dog defecates she imagines the lump as wayward cake, and the grass or sidewalk as a dress to be saved from a stain. With this mental trick, the task is easy.

Any of these stories might throw the right kind of light on A's assaults. That is, if one was the protagonist in one of them, or intuitively close enough to the protagonist, one could apply them as analogies to get a feel for A's motivation, for how he managed to act in ways that would come less readily to most of us. But one couldn't apply all of them: if one of them is a good fit then the others are not. The main differences between them lie along three dimensions. First there is the aspect of the kind of barrier to be overcome: in the examples resolution, timidity, and disgust. Then there is the aspect of the person's considered attitude to overcoming it. In *Smoking* S regrets having taken the forbidden puff, even though she may think that the immediate result was helpful to her friend. In *Propositioning* and *Dog poop* the protagonists are glad that they got to the other side of the obstacle. In *Propositioning* it may be a one-time-only trip: he can't run a hundred yards every time he wants to make friends. In *Dog poop* it is a permanently available device, which she will access several times a day, and eventually become unconscious of using. The third aspect is that of the nature of the emotion or motivation that facilitates the process. In *Smoking* it is sympathy, operating against the person's will in the service of a suppressed desire. In *Propositioning* it is general physiological arousal, deliberately used in the service of an acknowledged desire. In *Dog poop* it is a deliberate re-conceptualization, a controlled seeing-as, used as a device for removing an unwanted obstacle.

There are obviously more possibilities than these. Very few of them are mutually compatible, in the sense that the motives and emotions in most of them exclude those of others. None of them require that the act be wrong. The resemblance to a morally repugnant act lies in the repugnance, rather than the immorality. In each case a barrier is overcome, in a specific way, and in each case the way it happened could be very similar to that in which a barrier to atrocity is overcome. But there are many barriers to atrocity, and they operate in many different ways. A connection with an evil action that preserves moral character at the price of describing the wrong kind of barrier makes pseudo-empathy, an empathetic feeling that is not accompanied by understanding. A connection with a non-evil action that yields some insight into the nature of the barrier and the way it is overcome is a much more powerful thing. It allows an empathy that brings some insight.

Return to X's empathy for A's action. (The prison visitor and the rage-prone assailant.) In X's encounter with the taxi driver the barrier was one against incivility, and it was overcome by the force of X's fear of not getting to the airport on time. It was a once-only event and X remained his usually considerate self. It resulted in a state that X regretted getting to. There are some similarities and also important dissimilarities with A's assault on C. There too the transition was facilitated by an irrelevant triviality, and there too the outcome was something that was not part of the person's plan. On the other hand, the transition was habitual in A's case. He could use the same path to facilitate rage on just about any occasion. In this respect it is like *Dog poop*. And it led to a state that A did not regret as part of his personality, though on many particular occasions he could see it as inconvenient. In this respect it is like *Propositioning*. Moreover the motive that was satisfied once the barrier was overcome was one that was constantly in the background, exerting a pressure on the person's general response to situations. In this respect it is more like *Smoking*.

So which of these analogies, *X-taxi, Smoking, Propositioning, Dog-poop*, is the best basis for empathy for A's actions? Are any of them acceptable? Any could be, though some are more likely than others. The *X-taxi* case would be one of the less likely, I suspect, in a real case with real people. That is, if we choose at random a real human case that fits the outline description I gave of *A-assault*, and a real human case that fits the equally schematic description of *X-taxi*, then the chances are that the real human protagonist of the situation with the *A-assault* outline will have too little retrospective regret, and too much connection with a continuing motivational force, for the protagonist of the case fitting the *X-taxi* outline to find that imagining the other person through their own experience gave them an accurate empathetic grasp. One consequence is that the empathizing person (the X-role) is unlikely to find that they can anticipate the actions, thoughts, and feelings of the target person (the A-role) better as a result.

This is an intuition, a guess. I am not claiming to have shown that X's empathy is inadequate. After all, there might be a real case in which X-like empathy was spot-on for A-like motivation. The explanatory depth or adequacy of the empathy depends on the psychological facts in particular cases; it cannot be read off schematic descriptions such as those I have been giving. The use of such examples is rather to reveal the variety of connections between one person's life and another that can be the basis for empathy, and the reasons that such a connection might or might not give real understanding of the other person.

18.6 Conclusion: Worrying Continuity

One basic function of empathy is to transfer understanding from the familiar to the unfamiliar. You see that what someone is going through—what is going through someone—leading to acts that you find puzzling or repulsive, is continuous with what you yourself have gone through on some occasion, or which you can in detail imagine going through. (And sometimes it is your own puzzling or repulsive action that you can link with some less problematic earlier occasion, though we do not usually call this empathy.) I argued earlier that when this understanding is empathetic it often gives a grasp of how, rather than why, a person could do what they did.

The continuities have to be real ones, though. If 'empathy' describes simply a feeling of common motivation between people, then there can be empathy that is completely hollow in terms of the understanding of one person that it gives to another. The empathy that I am discussing is a form of understanding that is relevant to the moral assessment of another person. This does not mean judging the other, but assessing their potentialities for important interactions. In giving one person a sense of how another could do something, it gives valuable information about when to trust, what projects to share in what ways, and what appeals to make. In Goldilocks terms, some people are bad news—they too easily find themselves doing things they should not have more than considered—some people are no addition to your own efforts—their barriers to action are too rigid or too orthodox—and a few are perfect complements to your own initiatives—they consider things you would not have but should and they hesitate where you do not and should. One function of empathy is to fill out the finer structure of these assessments, often in terms that one cannot explicitly describe. (I have discussed the accuracy of imagination in Morton (2004), with particular attention to capturing the perspective of the person imagined.)

An important test of continuity comes with increased seriousness. Suppose that S, the person in the *Smoking* case, later takes part in an atrocity. Perhaps one like A's assault. Would a person who had had the attitude to her given by my description of *Smoking* think, retrospectively, that they had seen the signs in advance, and perhaps feel that they should have anticipated the atrocity? In fact it takes more than a single pair of cases to set up such a continuity, so we would need a series of *Smoking*-like incidents, leading to increasingly worrying actions. Would that set up retrospective concern? It would depend on the details of the cases, as they are imagined by the concerned person, but some series of cases are better candidates than others. But it is only when the empathy for the person concerned represents the person's actual psychology rather than a convenient metaphorical description—when it is not what I have called pseudo-empathy—that such retrospective continuity makes sense. But when we can find it we take there to be a deep similarity between the joined cases. We think that attitudes towards one can be applied, perhaps in attenuated form, to the others.

This is where the blinkering effect of decency enters. Since we need to know how people are able to do what they can—what other things they are also capable of—we need a general intuitive sense of their barrier-overcoming profiles. We need to know if they are more like the people in the *A-assault, X-taxi, Smoking, Propositioning, Dog poop*, or other similar cases. So we need to explore continuities between the barrier-hopping potentialities in a variety of cases. But when we do this we find too many. We find that many ordinary actions are continuous with many atrocious ones. As indeed they are, though the chains of continuity are long and we cannot be sure of the psychological accuracy of our intuitions to crucial cases. But we need empathy in everyday cases with everyday acceptable acts, in order to have a sense of one another as cooperators. Yet we do not want constant and telling comparisons with evil-doers. So we have a dilemma: we want to take empathy as easy, to ease everyday interaction, and we want to take it as difficult, to keep a distance between us and those we despise.

We react in two ways. We exaggerate the ease with which we can get accurate, non-pseudo, empathy in ordinary cases. We take it that any fellow-feeling that does not actually interfere with shared activity can be taken to represent real and significant psychological factors. And we minimize the ease with which we can make continuities with atrocious acts.

The result is that we do not think of ourselves as capable of empathy with the performers of atrocious acts, and we do think of ourselves as understanding acts where all we have is a warm empathetic feeling. We mis-distribute our estimates of what we can intuitively understand. If we did not do this then we would have a deeper understanding, and a more solid empathy, for some very ordinary actions. We would see them in a brighter light that brought into relief their sinister potentialities. But we would also be forced to admit puzzlement about how in many very ordinary cases someone we know well could do what they did.

Bibliography

Adams, F. & Aizawa, K. (2008) *The Bounds of Cognition*. Malden, MA: Blackwell.

Adams, S., Kueblie, J., Bayle, P.A., & Fivush, R. (1995) 'Gender Differences in Parent-Child Conversations About Past Emotions: A Longitudinal Investigation', *Sex Roles* 33: 309–23.

Addis, D.R., Wong, A.T., & Schacter, D.L. (2007) 'Remembering the Past and Imagining the Future: Common and Distinct Neural Substrates during Event Construction and Elaboration', *Neuropsychologia* 45: 1363–77.

Adelman, P.K. & Zajonc, R.B. (1989) 'Facial Efference and the Experience of Emotion', *Annual Review of Psychology* 40: 249–80.

Adolphs, R., Tranel, D., & Damasio, A.R. (2003) 'Dissociable Neural Systems for Recognizing Emotions', *Brain and Cognition* 52(1): 61–9.

Ahmed, S. (2004) *The Cultural Politics of Emotion*. London: Routledge.

Allen, J. (2000) *Without Sanctuary: Lynching Photographs in America*. San Francisco: Twin Palms Press.

Allport, G. (1924) *Social Psychology*. Boston: Houghton Mifflin.

Almedingen, Edith M. (1962) *The Emperor Alexander II: A Study*. London: Badley Head.

Alston, W.P. (1964) *Philosophy of Language*. Englewood Cliffs, NJ: Prentice Hall.

Alston, W.P. (1967) 'Vagueness'. In: *Encyclopedia of Philosophy*, P. Edwards (ed.), pp. 218–21. New York: Macmillan,.

Alston, W.P. (1993) Review of Ernest Sosa, *Knowledge in Perspective: Selected Essays in Epistemology*, *Mind* 102: 199–203.

Annas, J. (2003) 'The Structure of Virtue'. In: *Intellectual Virtue*, M. DePaul & L. Zagzebski (eds), pp. 15–33. Oxford: Oxford University Press.

Anonymous (1896) 'Mrs. Stowe Eulogized', *New York Times* (6 July), p. 8.

Arbib, M.A. & Mundhenk, T.N. (2005) 'Schizophrenia and the Mirror System: An Essay', *Neuropsychologia* 43: 268–80.

Arbib, M.A. & Rizzolatti, G. (1997) 'Neural Expectations: A Possible Evolutionary Path From Manual Skill to Language', *Communication and Cognition* 29: 393–424.

Archer, R.L. (1991) 'Dispositional Empathy and a Pluralism of Prosocial Motives', *Psychological Inquiry*, 2(2): 123–4.

Arendt, H. (1963) *Eichmann in Jerusalem: A Report on the Banality of Evil* (Revised and Enlarged Edition). London: Penguin Books.

Arendt, H. (1971) 'Thinking and Moral Considerations: A Lecture', *Social Research* 38: 417–46.

Aristotle (1984) 'On the Soul'. In: *The Complete Works of Aristotle*, J. Barnes (ed.), pp. 641–92. Princeton: Princeton University Press.

Aristotle (1992) *Nicomachean Ethics*, D. Ross (trans.). Oxford: Oxford University Press.

Aronfreed, J. (1970) 'The Socialization of Altruistic and Sympathetic Behavior: Some Theoretical and Experimental Analyses'. In: *Altruism and Helping Behavior: Social Psychological Studies of Some Antecedents and Consequences*, J. Macaulay & L. Berkowitz (eds), pp. 103–26. New York: Academic Press.

Arsenio, W.F. & Lemerise, E.A. (2001) 'Varieties of Childhood Bullying: Values, Emotion, Processes, and Social Competence', *Social Development* 10: 59–73.

Atance, C.M. & O'Neill, D.K.(2005) 'The Emergence of Episodic Future Thinking in Humans', *Learning and Motivation* 36: 126–44.

Atran, S. (2003) 'Genesis of Suicide Terrorism', *Science* 299: 1534–9.

Audi, R. (1999) *The Cambridge Dictionary of Philosophy* (second edition). Cambridge: Cambridge University Press.

Austin, J.L. (1962) *Sense and Sensibilia*. Oxford: Clarendon.

Avenanti, A., Bueti, D., Galati, G., & Aglioti, S.M. (2005), 'Transcranial Magnetic Stimulation Highlights the Sensorimotor Side of Empathy for Pain', *Nature Neuroscience* 8: 955–60.

Avenanti, A., Paluello, I.M., Bufalari, I., & Aglioti, S.M. (2006) 'Stimulus-driven Modulation of Motor-evoked Potentials During Observation of Others' Pain', *NeuroImage* 32: 316–24.

Baker, G. (2004) *Wittgenstein's Method: Neglected Aspects*. Oxford: Blackwell.

Baker, H.S. & Baker, M.N. (1987) 'Heinz Kohut's Self Psychology: An Overview', *American Journal of Psychiatry*, 144(1): 1–9.

Bandes, S.A. (1996) 'Empathy, Narrative, and Victim Impact Statements', *The University of Chicago Law Review* 63: 361–412.

Bandes, S.A. (1999) (ed.) *The Passions of Law*. New York: New York University Press.

Barker, J. (2006) (ed) *The Brontes: A Life in Letters*. London: The Folio Society.

Baron-Cohen, S. (1997) *Mindblindness: An Essay on Autism and Theory of Mind*. Cambridge, Mass.: MIT Press.

Baron-Cohen, S. (2003) *The Essential Difference: The Truth about the Male and Female Brain*. New York: Basic Books.

Baron-Cohen, S. (2005) 'The Male Condition', *The New York Times* (8 August), p. A15.

Baron-Cohen, S. (2009) 'Autism: the Empathizing—Systemizing (ES) Theory', *Annals of the New York Academy of Sciences* 1156 (The Year in Cognitive Neuroscience 2009): 68–80.

Barrett-Lennard, G.T. (1962) *Dimensions of Therapist Response as Causal Factors in Therapeutic Change*.(Psychological Monographs: General and Applied), vol. 76, n. 43.

Barrett-Lennard, G.T. (1978) 'The Relationship inventory', *JSAS Catalog of selected Documents in Psychology*, 8.

Barthes, R. (1972) *Mythologies*, A. Lavers (selection and translation). New York: Hill and Wang.

Bartlett, D.L. (1996) 'Physiological Responses to Music and Sound Stimuli'. In: *Handbook of Music Psychology* (second edition), D.A. Hodges (ed.), pp. 343–85. San Antonio, TX: Institute for Music Research Press.

Basch, M.F. (1983) 'Empathic Understanding: A Review of the Concept and Some Theoretical Considerations', *Journal of the American Psychoanalytic Association* 31(1): 101–26.

Batson, C.D. (1987) 'Prosocial Motivation: Is it Ever Truly Altruistic?' In: *Advances in Experimental Social Psychology*, L. Berkowitz (ed.), pp. 65–122. New York: Academic Press

Batson, C.D. (1991) *The Altruism Question: Toward a Social-Psychological Answer*. Hove, UK: Lawrence Erlbaum Associates.

Batson, C.D. (1997). 'Self-other merging and the empathy-altruism hypothesis: Reply to Neuberg et al. (1997)', *Journal of Personality and Social Psychology* 73(3): 517–22.

Batson, C.D. (2009a) 'Empathic Concern and Altruism in Humans', http://onthehuman.org/2009/10/empathic-concern-and-altruism-in-humans/

Batson, C.D. (2009b) 'These Things Called Empathy: Eight Related but Distinct Phenomena'. In: *The Social Neuroscience of Empathy*, J. Decety & W. Ickes (eds), pp. 3–15. Cambridge, Mass.: MIT Press.

Batson, C.D., Batson, J.G., Slingsby, J.K., Harrell, K.L., Peekna, H.M., & Todd, R.M. (1991) 'Empathic Joy and the Empathy-Altruism Hypothesis', *Journal of Personality and Social Psychology* 61(3): 413–26.

Batson, C.D., Batson, J.G., Todd, R.M., Brummett, B.H., Shaw, L.L., & Aldeguer, C.M.R. (1995) 'Empathy and the Collective Good: Caring for One of the Others in a Social Dilemma', *Journal of Personality and Social Psychology* 68(4): 619–31.

Batson, C.D. & Coke, J.S. (1981) 'Empathy: A Source of Altruistic Motivation for Helping'. In: *Altruism and Helping Behavior: Social, Personality, and Developmental Perspectives*, J.P. Rushton & R.M. Sorrentino (eds), pp. 167–87, Hillsdale, NJ: Lawrence Erlbaum Associates.

Batson, C.D., Duncan, B.D., Ackerman, P., Buckley, T., & Birch, K. (1981) 'Is Empathic Emotion a Source of Altruistic Motivation', *Journal of Personality and Social Psychology* 40(2): 290–302.

Batson, C.D., Early, S., & Salvarini, G. (1997) 'Perspective Taking: Imagining How Another Feels Versus Imagining How You Would Feel', *Personality & Social Personality Bulletin* 23: 751–8.

Batson, C.D., Fultz, J., & Schoenrade, P. A. (1987) 'Distress and Empathy: Two Qualitatively Distinct Vicarious Emotions with Different Motivational Consequences', *Journal of Personality* 55: 19–39.

Batson, C.D., Klein, T. R., Highberger, L., & Shaw, L.L. (1995) 'Immorality from Empathy-induced Altruism: When Compassion and Justice Conflict', *Journal of Personality and Social Psychology* 68: 1042–54.

Batson, C.D., Lishner, D. A., Carpenter, A., Dulin, L., Harjusola-Webb, S., Stocks, E. L., Gale, S., Hassan, O., & Sampat, B. (2003) 'As You Would Have Them Do Unto You: Does Imagining Yourself in the Other's Place Stimulate Moral Action?', *Personality and Social Psychology Bulletin* 29: 1190–201.

Batson, C.D., Lishner, D., Cook, J., & Sawyer, S. (2005) 'Similarity and Nurturance: Two Possible Sources of Empathy for Strangers', *Basic and Applied Social Psychology* 27: 15–25.

Batson, C.D., Polycarpou, M.P., Harmon-Jones, E., Imhoff, H.J., Mitchener, E.C., Bednar, L.L., Klein, T.R., & Highberger, L. (1997) 'Empathy and Attitudes: Can Feeling for a Member of a Stigmatized Group Improve Feelings Toward the Group?', *Journal of Personality and Social Psychology* 72(1): 105–18.

Batson, C.D. & Powell, A.A. (2003) 'Altruism and Prosocial Behavior'. In: *Handbook of Psychology: Personality and Social Psychology*, T. Millon & M.J. Lerner (eds), pp. 463–84). Hoboken, NJ: Wiley.

Batson, C.D., Sager, K., Garst, E., Kang, M., Rubchinsky, K., & Dawson, K. (1997) 'Is Empathy-Induced Helping Due to Self-Other Merging?' *Journal of Personality and Social Psychology* 73: 495–509.

Batson, C.D. & Shaw, L.L. (1991) 'Evidence for Altruism: Toward a Pluralism of Prosocial Motives', *Psychological Inquiry* 2(2): 107–22.

Batson, C.D., Turk, C.L., Shaw, L.L., & Klein, T.R. (1995) 'Information Function of Empathic Emotion: Learning that We Value the Other's Welfare', *Journal of Personality and Social Psychology* 68(2): 300–13.

Batson, C.D. & Weeks, J.L. (1996) 'Mood Effects of Unsuccessful Helping: Another Test of the Empathy-Altruism Hypothesis', *Personality and Social Psychology Bulletin* 22: 148–57.

Battaly, H. (2001) 'Thin Concepts to the Rescue: Thinning the Concepts of Epistemic Justification and Intellectual Virtue'. In: *Virtue Epistemology*, A. Fairweather & L. Zagzebski (eds.), pp. 98–116. Oxford: Oxford University Press.

Battaly, H. (2006) 'Teaching Intellectual Virtues', *Teaching Philosophy* 29(3): 191–222.

Battaly, H. (2007) 'Intellectual Virtue and Knowing One's Sexual Orientation'. In: *Sex and Ethics*, R. Halwani (ed.), pp. 149–61. London: Palgrave Macmillan.

Battaly, H. (2008a) 'Metaethics Meets Virtue Epistemology: Salvaging Disagreement about the Epistemically Thick', *Philosophical Papers* 37: 435–54.

Battaly, H. (2008b) 'Virtue Epistemology', *Philosophy Compass: Epistemology* 3(4): 639–63 .

BBC (2006) 'Classic Albums: Dark Side of the Moon', Broadcast.

Becker, D. (2003) 'Dealing With the Consequences of Organized Violence in Trauma Work'. In: *Berghof Handbook for Conflict Transformation*, pp. 1–21. Berlin: Berghof Research Center for Constructive Conflict Management.

Berenson, B. (1909) *Florentine Painters of the Renaissance* (third edition). New York: G. P. Putnam's Sons.

Berlant, L. (1997) *The Queen of America Goes to Washington City: Essays on Sex and Citizenship*. Durham, NC: Duke University Press.

Berreby, D. (2005) *Us and Them: Understanding Your Tribal Mind*. Boston: Little Brown.

Biggs, Stephen (2007) 'The Phenomenal Mindreader: a Case for Phenomenal Simulation', *Philosophical Psychology* 20(1): 29–42.

Blackburn, S. (2005) *Oxford Dictionary of Philosophy* (second edition). Oxford: Oxford University Press.

Blair, R.J.R. (1995) 'A Cognitive Developmental Approach to Morality: Investigating the Psychopath', *Cognition* 57: 1–29.

Blair, R.J.R. (1999) 'Psycho-Physiological Responsiveness to the Distress of Others in Children with Autism', *Personality and Individual Differences* 26: 477–85.

Blair, R.J.R. (2005) 'Responding to the Emotions of Others: Dissociating Forms of Empathy through the Study of Typical and Psychiatric Populations', *Consciousness and Cognition* 14(4): 698–718.

Blair, R.J.R. (2006) 'The Emergence of Psychopathy: Implications for the Neuropsychological Approach to Developmental Disorders', *Cognition* 101(2): 414–42.

Blair, R.J.R. (2008a) 'Fine Cuts of Empathy and the Amygdala: Dissociable Deficits in Psychopathy and Autism', *Quarterly Journal of Experimental Psychology (2006)* 61(1): 157–70.

Blair, R.J.R. (2008b) *The Actor, Image, and Action: Acting and Cognitive Neuroscience*. London and New York: Routledge.

Blair, R.J.R. & Blair, K.S. (2009) 'Empathy, Morality, and Social Convention: Evidence from the Study of Psychopathy and Other Psychiatric Disorders'. In: *The Social Neuroscience of Empathy*, J. Decety & W. Ickes (eds), pp. 139–52. Cambridge, MA: MIT Press.

Blair, R.J.R., Jones, L., Clark, F., & Smith, M. (1997) 'The Psychopathic Individual: A Lack of Responsiveness to Distress Cues?', *Psychophysiology* 34(2): 192–8.

Blair, R.J.R., Mitchell, D., & Blair, K.S. (2005) *The Psychopath: Emotion and the Brain*. Malden, MA: Blackwell.

Blair, R.J.R., Mitchell, D.G.V., Richell, R.A., Kelly, S., Leonard, A., Newman, C., & Scott, S.K. (2002) 'Turning a Deaf Ear to Fear: Impaired Recognition of Vocal Affect in Psychopathic Individuals', *Journal of Abnormal Psychology* 111: 682–6.

Blakemore, S.-J., Bristow, D., Bird, G., Frith, C., & Ward, J. (2005) 'Somatosensory Activations During the Observation of Touch and a Case of Vision–touch Synaesthesia', *Brain* 128(7): 1571–83.

Blakeslee, S. (2006) 'Cells that Read Minds', *New York Times* (10 January), pp. 131–41.

Blanke, O. & Arzy, S. (2005) 'The Out-of-body Experience: Disturbed Self-Processing at the Temporo-parietal Junction', *The Neuroscientist* 11: 16–24.

Blanke, O., Ortigue, S., Landis, T., & Seeck, M. (2002) 'Stimulating Illusory Own-body Perceptions: The Part of the Brain that can Induce Out-of-body Experiences Has Been Located', *Nature* 419: 269–70.

Blatt, G.J., Pandya, D.N., & Rosene, D.L. (2003) 'Parcellation of Cortical Afferents to Three Distinct Sectors in the Parahippocampal Gyrus of the Rhesus Monkey: An Anatomical and Neurophysiological Study', *Journal of Comparative Neurology* 466: 161–79.

Bloomfield, P. (2000) 'Virtue Epistemology and the Epistemology of Virtue', *Philosophy and Phenomenological Research* 60: 23–43.

Blum, L.A. (1994) *Moral Perception and Particularity*. Cambridge and New York: Cambridge University Press.

Blume, J.H. (2003) 'Ten Years of Payne: Victim Impact Evidence in Capital Cases', *Cornell Law Review* 88: 257–81.

Bohart, A.C. & Greenberg, L.S. (1997a). 'Empathy and Psychotherapy: An Introductory Overview'. In: *Empathy Reconsidered: New Directions in Psychotherapy*, A.C. Bohart & L.S. Greenberg (eds), pp. 3–31. Washington, D.C.: American Psychological Association.

Bohart, A.C. & Greenberg, L.S. (1997b) (eds) *Empathy Reconsidered: New Directions in Psychotherapy*. Washington, D.C.: American Psychological Association.

Bornstein, M. (1984) 'Introductory Remarks'. In: *Empathy II*, J. Lichtenberg, M. Bornstein & D. Silver (eds), pp. 107–12. Hillsdale, NJ: The Analytic Press.

Bornstein, R.F. (2003) 'Psychodynamic Models of Personality'. In: *Handbook of Psychology: Personality and Social psychology*, T. Millon & M.J. Lerner (eds), pp. 117–34. Hoboken, NJ: Wiley and Sons.

Boyce Gibson, W.R. (1928) 'The Philosophy of Melchior Palágyi. (II) The Theory of Life and Mind', *Journal of Philosophical Studies* 3: 158–72.

Braitenberg, V. & Schuz, A. (1991) *Anatomy of the Cortex: Statistics and Geometry*, V. Braitenberg (ed.). New York: Springer-Verlag.

Bråten, S. (2007) (ed.) *On Being Moved: From Mirror Neurons to Empathy*. Amsterdam: John Benjamin's Publishing Company.

Bråten, S. & Trevarthen, C. (2007) 'From Infant Intersubjectivity and Participant Movements to Simulation and Conversation in Cultural Common Sense'. In: *On Being Moved: From Mirror Neurons to Empathy*, S. Bråten (ed), pp. 21–47. Amsterdam: John Benjamin's Publishing Company.

Bratman, M. (2000) 'Reflection, Planning, and Temporally Extended Agency', *Philosophical Review* 109: 35–61.

Bratman, M. (2007a) 'Valuing and the Will'. In his *Structures of Agency: Essays*, pp. 47–67. Oxford: Oxford University Press.

Bratman, M. (2007b) 'Appendix: Nozick, Free Will, and the Problem of Agential Authority'. In his *Structures of Agency: Essays*, pp. 127–36. Oxford: Oxford University Press.

Brennan, T. (2004) *The Transmission of Affect*. Ithaca, NY: Cornell University Press.

Brenner, C. (1968) 'Archaic Features of Ego Functioning', *The International Journal of Psychoanalysis* 49(2): 426–30.

Bricke, J. (1996) *Mind and Morality: An Examination of Hume's Moral Psychology*. New York: Oxford University Press.

Brock, G. & Good, Jamie (2007) (eds) *Empathy and Fairness* (Novartis Foundation). Chichester, UK: John Wiley & Sons.

Brockman, J. (2006) (ed.) *Intelligent Thought: Science Versus the Intelligent Design Movement*. New York: Vintage Books.

Brown, G. (2007) 'Bobby: My Moral Beacon', *New Statesman* (April 30). London.

Brown, L.M., Bradley, M., & Lang, P. (2006) 'Affective Reactions to Pictures of Ingroup and Outgroup Members', *Biological Psychology* 71: 303–11.

Brown, L.S. (1995) 'Not Outside the Range: One Feminist Perspective on Psychic Trauma'. In: *Trauma: Explorations in Memory*, C. Caruth (ed.), pp. 100–12. Baltimore: The Johns Hopkins Press,.

Brown, W. (1995) 'Wounded Attachments'. In her *States of Injury: Power and Freedom in Late Modernity*, pp. 52–76. Princeton: Princeton University Press.

Brüne, M. (2005) '"Theory of Mind" in Schizophrenia: A Review of the Literature', *Schizophrenia Bulletin* 31: 21–42.

Bruner, G.C. (1990) 'Music, Mood, and Marketing', *Journal of Marketing* 54(4): 94–104.

Bryant, B.K. (1982) 'An Index of Empathy for Children and Adolescents', *Child Development* 53: 413–25.

Buccino, G., Binkofski, F., Fink, G.R., Fadiga, L., Fogassi, L., Gallese, V., Seitz, R.J., Zilles, K., Rizzolatti, G., & Freund, H.-J. (2001) 'Action Observation Activates Premotor and Parietal Areas in a Somatotopic Manner: An fMRI Study', *European Journal of Neuroscience* 13(2): 400–4.

Buckner, R.L. & Carroll, D.C. (2007) 'Self-projection and the Brain', *Trends in Cognitive Sciences* 11: 49–57.

Budd, M. (1995) *Values of Art: Pictures, Poetry, Music*. Harmondsworth, UK: Penguin.

Buie, D.H. (1981) 'Empathy: Its Nature and Limitations', *Journal of the American Psychoanalytic Association* 29(2): 281.

Bunt, L. & Pavlicevic, M. (2001) 'Music and Emotion: Perspectives from Music Therapy'. In: *Music and Emotion: Theory and Research*, P. N. Juslin & J. A. Sloboda (eds), pp. 181–201. Oxford: Oxford University Press.

Bush, L.K., Barr, C.L., McHugo, G.J., & Lanzetta, J.T. (1989) 'The Effects of Facial Control and Facial Mimicry on Subjective Reactions to Comedy Routines', *Motivation and Emotion* 13: 31–52.

Calder, A.J., Keane, J., Manes, F., Antoun, N., & Young, A.W. (2000) 'Impaired Recognition and Experience of Disgust Following Brain Injury', *Nature Neuroscience* (3): 1077–8.

Camerer, C., Loewenstein, G., & Weber, M. (1989) 'The Curse of Knowledge in Economic Settings: An Experimental Analysis', *Journal of Political Economy* 97: 1232–54.

Campbell, R.J., Kagan, N., & Krathwohl, D.R. (1971) 'The Development and Validation of a Scale to Measure Affective Sensitivity (Empathy)', *Journal of Counseling Psychology* 18(5): 407–12.

Capote, T. (2000) *In Cold Blood*. London: Penguin.

Capurso, A., Fisichelli, V.R., Gilman, L., Gutheil, E.A., Wright, J.T., & Paperte, F. (eds.) (1952) *Music and Your Emotions: A Practical Guide to Music Selections Associated with Desired Emotional Responses*. New York: Liveright.

Carkhuff, R.R. (1969) *Helping and Human Relations*, Vol. I & II. New York: Holt, Rinehart & Winston.

Carlsmith, J.M. & Gross, A.E. (1969) 'Some Effects of Guilt on Compliance', *Journal of Personality and Social Psychology* 11: 232–9.

Carlson, J.E. & Hatfield, E. (1992) *Psychology of Emotion*. Fort Worth, TX: Harcourt, Brace, Jovanovitch.

Carlson, M., Charlin, V., & Miller, N. (1988) 'Positive Mood and Helping Behavior: A Test of Six Hypotheses', *Journal of Personality and Social Psychology* 55: 211–29.

Caro, R.A. (2002) *Master of the Senate*. New York: Knopf/Random House.

Carr, L., Iacoboni, M., Dubeau, M.C., Mazziotta, J.C., & Lenzi, G.L. (2003) 'Neural Mechanisms of Empathy in Humans: A Relay from Neural Systems for Imitation to Limbic Areas', *Proceedings of the National Academy of Sciences USA* 100: 5497–502.

Carroll, N. (1990) *The Philosophy of Horror; or, Paradoxes of the Heart*. New York: Routledge.

Carroll, N. (2001a) 'Art, Narrative and Emotion'. In his *Beyond Aesthetics: Philosophical Essays*, pp. 215–34. Cambridge: Cambridge University Press.

Carroll, N. (2001b) 'Simulation, Emotions, and Morality'. In his *Beyond Aesthetics: Philosophical Essays*, pp. 306–17. Cambridge: Cambridge University Press.

Carroll, N. (2004) 'Sympathy for the Devil'. In: *The Sopranos and Philosophy*, R. Greene & P. Vernezze (eds.), pp. 128-36. LaSalle, IL: Open Court.

Carroll, N. (2007) 'On the Ties That Bind: Characters, the Emotions, and Popular Fictions'. In: *Philosophy and the Interpretation of Pop Culture*, W. Irwin & J.J. E. Gracia (eds.), pp. 89–116. Lanham: MD: Rowman & Littlefield Publishers.

Carroll, N. (2008) *The Philosophy of Motion Pictures*. Malden, MA: Blackwell.

Carruthers, P. & Smith, P.K. (1996) (eds) *Theories of Theories of Mind*. Cambridge: Cambridge University Press.

Caruth, C. (1995) (ed.) *Trauma: Explorations in Memory*. Baltimore: Johns Hopkins University Press.

Chartrand, T.L., Bargh, J.A. (1999) 'The Chameleon Effect: The Perception-behavior Link and Social Interaction', *Journal of Personality & Social Psychology* 76: 893–910.

Cheng, Y., Lee, P.L., Yang, C.Y., Lin, C.P., Hung, D., & Decety, J. (2008) 'Gender Differences in the Mu Rhythm of the Human Mirror-Neuron System', *PLoS ONE* 3(5): e2113.

Chlopan, B.E. & McCain, M.L., Carbonell. J.L., & Hagen, R.L. (1985) 'Empathy: Review of Available Measures', *Journal of Personality and Social Psychology* 48(3): 635–53.

Chong, D. (2000) *The Girl in the Picture: The Story of Kim Phuc, the Photograph and the Vietnam War*. New York: Viking.

Chong, T.T., Cunnington, R., Williams, M.A., Kanwisher, N., & Mattingley, J.B. (2008) 'fMRI Adaptation Reveals Mirror Neurons in Human Inferior Parietal Cortex', *Curr Biol*, 18(20): 1576–80.

Cialdini, R., Brown, S., Lewis, B., Luce, C., & Neuberg, S. (1997) 'Reinterpreting the Empathy-altruism Relationship: When One Into One Equals Oneness', *Journal of Personality and Social Psychology* 73: 481–94.

Clark, A. (2001) *Mindware*. Oxford: Oxford University Press.

Clark, A. & Chalmers, D. (1998) 'The Extended Mind', *Analysis* 58(1): 7–19.

Clark, A. & Grush, R. (1999) 'Towards a Cognitive Robotics', *Adaptive Behavior* 7: 5–16.

Clark, A.J. (2007) *Empathy in Counseling and Psychotherapy: Perspectives and Practices*. Mahwah, NJ: Lawrence Erlbaum.

Clark, K.B. (1980) 'Empathy: A Neglected Topic in Psychological Research', *American Psychologist* 35(2): 87–90.

Clark, T.F., Winkielman, P., & McIntosh, D.N. (2008) 'Autism and the Extraction of Emotion from Briefly Presented Facial Expressions: Stumbling at the First Step of Empathy', *Emotion* 8(6): 803–9.

Cleckley, H.M. (1976) *The Mask of Sanity: An Attempt to Reinterpret the So-called Psychopathic Personality* (fourth edition). St. Louis, MO: The C.V. Mosby Company.

Cochin, S., Bethelemy, C., Lejeune, B., Roux, S., & Martineau, I. (1998) 'Perception of Motion and EEG Activity in Human Adults'. *Electroencephalography and Clinical Neurophysiology* 107: 287–95.

Coplan, A. (2004) 'Empathic Engagement with Narrative Fictions', *Journal of Aesthetics and Art Criticism* 62/2: 141–52.

Coplan, A. (2006) 'Catching Characters' Emotions: Emotional Contagion Responses to Narrative Fiction Film', *Film Studies: An International Review* 8: 26–38.

Coplan, A. (2009) 'Empathy and Character Engagement'. In: *The Routledge Companion to Philosophy and Film*, P. Livingston & C. Plantinga (eds), pp. 97–110. London and New York: Routledge.

Corbetta, M., & Shulman, G.L. (2002) 'Control of goal-directed and stimulus-driven attention in the brain', *Nature Reviews Neuroscience* 3: 201–15.

Corona, R., Dissanayake, C., Arbelle, A., Wellington, P., & Sigman, M. (1998) 'Is Affect Aversive to Young Children with Autism? Behavioral and Cardiac Responses to Experimenter Distress', *Child Development* 69: 1494–502.

Crane, T. (2006) 'Is There a Perceptual Relation?'. In: *Perceptual Experience*, T.S. Gendler & J. Hawthorne (eds), pp. 126–46. Oxford: Oxford University Press.

Currie, G. (1995) *Image and Mind: Film, Philosophy, and Cognitive Science*. Cambridge: Cambridge University Press.

Currie, G. (1997) 'The Paradox of Caring'. In: *Emotion and the Arts*, M. Hjort & S. Laver (eds), pp. 63–77. Oxford: Oxford University Press.

Currie, G. (2003) 'The Capacities that Enable Us to Produce and Consume Art'. In: *Imagination, Philosophy and the Arts*, M. Kieran & D.M. Lopes (eds), pp. 293–304. London: Routledge.

Currie, G. (2004) *Arts and Minds*. Oxford: Oxford Univerity Press.

Currie, G. (2006) 'Anne Bronte and the Uses of Imagination'. In: *Contemporary Discussions in Aesthetics and Philosophy of Art*, M. Kieran (ed.), pp. 209–21. Oxford: Blackwell.

Currie, G. & Ravenscroft, I. (2002) *Recreative Minds*. Oxford: Oxford University Press.

Cvetkovich, A. (2003) *An Archive of Feelings: Trauma, Sexuality, and Lesbian Public Cultures*. Durham, NC: Duke University Press.

D'Argembeau, A. & Van der Linden, M. (2004) 'Phenomenal Characteristics Associated with Projecting Oneself Back into the Past and Forward into the Future: Influence of Valence and Temporal Distance', *Consciousness and Cognition* 13: 844–58.

Damasio, A. (1999) *The Feeling of What Happens*. London: Heinemann.

Dapretto, M., Davies, M.S., Pfeifer, J.H., Scott, A.A., Sigman, M., Bookheimer, S.Y., & Iacoboni, M. (2006) 'Understanding Emotions in Others: Mirror Neuron Dysfunction in Children with Autism Spectrum Disorders', *Nature Neuroscience* 9: 28–30.

Darwall, S. (1998) 'Empathy, Sympathy, Care', *Philosophical Studies* 89: 261–82.

Darwin, C. (1998) *The Expression of Emotion in Man and Animals*. London: Harper Collins.

Dautenhahn, K. & Woods, S. (2003) 'Possible Connections Between Bullying Behaviour, Empathy, and Imitation. In: *Proceedings of the Second International Symposium on Imitation in Animals and Artifacts*, K. Dautenham & C. Nehaniv (eds), pp. 68–77).

Davies, M. & Stone, T. (1995a) (eds) *Folk Psychology: The Theory of Mind Debate (Readings in Mind and Language Series, No. 3)*. Oxford: Blackwell.

Davies, M. & Stone, T. (1995b) (eds) *Mental Simulation: Evaluations and Applications*. Oxford: Blackwell.

Davies, M. & Stone, T. (1998) 'Folk Psychology and Mental Simulation', *Royal Institute of Philosophy Supplement* 43: 53–82.

Davies, S. (1980) 'The Expression of Emotion in Music', *Mind* 89: 67–86.

Davies, S. (1983) 'The Rationality of Aesthetic Responses', *British Journal of Aesthetics* 23: 38–47.

Davies, S. (1986) 'The Expression Theory Again', *Theoria* 52: 146–67.

Davies, S. (1994a) *Musical Meaning and Expression*. Ithaca, NY: Cornell University Press.

Davies, S. (1994b) 'Kivy on Auditors' Emotions', *Journal of Aesthetics and Art Criticism* 52: 235–6.

Davies, S. (1997) 'Contra the Hypothetical Persona in Music'. In: *Emotion and the Arts,*, M. Hjort & S. Laver (eds), pp. 95–109. Oxford: Oxford University Press.

Davies, S. (1999) 'Response to Robert Stecker', *British Journal of Aesthetics* 39: 282–7.

Davies, S. (2001) 'Philosophical Perspectives on Music's Expressiveness'. In: *Music and Emotion*, P.N. Juslin & J. Sloboda (eds.), pp. 23–44. Oxford: Oxford University Press.

Davies, S. (2006) 'Artistic Expression and the Hard Case of Pure Music'. In: *Contemporary Debates in Aesthetics and the Philosophy of Art*, M. Kieran (ed.), pp. 179–91. Oxford: Blackwell.

Davis, M.H. (1980) 'A Multidimensional Approach to Individual Differences in Empathy', *JSAS Catalog of Selected Documents in Psychology* 10(4): 85.

Davis, M.H. (1983) 'Measuring Individual Differences in Empathy: Evidence for a Multidimensional Approach', *Journal of Personality and Social Psychology* 44(1): 113–26.

Davis, M.H. (1996) *Empathy: A Social Psychological Approach*. Boulder, CO: Westview Press.

Dawes, R.M. (1994) *House of Cards: Psychology and Psychotherapy Built on Myth*. New York: Free Press.

Debes, R. (2007a) 'Has Anything Changed? Hume's Theory of Association and Sympathy after the Treatise', *British Journal for the History of Philosophy* 15(2): 313–38.

Debes, R. (2007b) 'Humanity, Sympathy and the Puzzle of Hume's Second Enquiry', *British Journal for the History of Philosophy* 15(1): 27–57.

Decety, J. (2006a) 'A Cognitive Neuroscience View of Imitation'. In: *Imitation and the Social Mind: Autism and Typical Development*, S. Rogers & J. Williams (eds), pp. 251–74. New York: Guilford Publication.

Decety, J. (2006b) 'Human Empathy', *Japanese Journal of Neuropsychology* 22: 11–33.

Decety, J. (2007) 'A Social Cognitive Neuroscience Model of Human Empathy'. In: *Social Neuroscience: Integrating Biological and Psychological Explanations of Social Behavior*, E Harmon-Jones & P. Winkielman (eds), pp. 246–70. New York: Guilford Publications.

Decety, J. & Batson, C.D. (2007) 'Social Neuroscience Approaches to Interpersonal Sensitivity', *Social Neuroscience* (2): 3–4, 151–7.

Decety, J. & Chaminade, T. (2003) 'When the Self Represents the Other: A New Cognitive Neuroscience View on Psychological Identification', *Consciousness and Cognition* 12: 577–96.

Decety, J., Chaminade, T., Grèzes, J., & Meltzoff, A.N. (2002) 'A PET Exploration of the Neural Mechanisms Involved in Reciprocal Imitation', *NeuroImage* 15: 265–72.

Decety, J. & Grèzes, J. (2006) 'The Power of Simulation: Imagining One's Own and Other's Behavior', *Brain Research* 1079: 4–14.

Decety, J. & Hodges, S.D. (2006) 'The Social Neuroscience of Empathy'. In: *Bridging Social Psychology: Benefits of Transdisciplinary Approaches*, P.A.M. Van Lange (ed.), pp. 103–9. Mahwah, NJ: Lawrence Erlbaum Associates.

Decety, J. & Ickes, W. (2009) (eds) *The Social Neuroscience of Empathy*. Cambridge, Mass.: MIT Press.

Decety, J. & Jackson, P.L. (2004) 'The Functional Architecture of Human Empathy', *Behavioral and Cognitive Neuroscience Reviews* 3: 71–100.

Decety, J. & Jackson, P.L. (2006) 'A Social Neuroscience Perspective on Empathy', *Current Directions in Psychological Science* 12: 406–11.

Decety, J. & Lamm, C. (2006) 'Human Empathy Through the Lens of Social Neuroscience', *The Scientific World Journal* 6: 1146–63.

Decety, J. & Lamm, C. (2007) 'The Role of the Right Temporoparietal Junction in Social Interaction: How Low-level Computational Processes Contribute to Meta-cognition', *The Neuroscientist* 13: 580–93.

Decety, J. & Lamm, C. (2009) 'Empathy Versus Personal Distress—Recent Evidence from Social Neuroscience'. In: *The Social Neuroscience of Empathy*, J. Decety & W. Ickes (eds.), pp. 199–213. Cambridge: MIT press.

Decety, J. & Meyer, M. (2008) 'From Emotion Resonance to Empathic Understanding: A Social Developmental Neuroscience Account', *Development and Psychopathology* 20(4): 1053–80.

Decety, J., Michalska, K.J., & Akitsuki, Y. (2008) 'Who Caused the Pain? An fMRI Investigation of Empathy and Intentionality in Children', *Neuropsychologia* 46: 2607–14.

Decety, J., Michalska, K.J., Akitsuki, Y., & Lahey, B. (2009) 'Atypical Empathic Responses in Adolescents with Aggressive Conduct Disorder: A Functional MRI Investigation', *Biological Psychology* 80: 203–11.

Decety, J. & Moriguchi, Y. (2007) 'The Empathic Brain and its Dysfunction in Psychiatric Populations: Implications for Intervention Across Different Clinical Conditions', *Biopsychosocial Medicine* 1: 22.

Decety, J. & Sommerville, J.A. (2003) 'Shared Representations Between Self and Others: A Social Cognitive Neuroscience View', *Trends in Cognitive Sciences* 7: 527–33.

Deigh, J. (2004) 'Primitive Emotions'. In: *Thinking about Feeling: Contemporary philosophers on emotions*, R.C. Solomon (ed.), pp. 9–27. Oxford: Oxford University Press.

Deleuze, G. (1964/2000) *Proust and Signs*, R. Howard (trans.). Minneapolis: University of Minnesota Press.

Dennett, D.C. (1991) *Consciousness Explained*. Boston: Little, Brown and Company.

Dilman, I. (1975) *Matter and Mind*. London: Macmillan.

Dinstein, I., Hasson, U., Rubin, N., & Heeger, D.J. (2007) 'Brain Areas Selective for Both Observed and Executed Movements', *Journal of Neurophysiology*, 98(3), 1415–27.

Dobbs, D. (2006) 'A Revealing Reflection', *Scientific American Mind* (April): 22–7.

Doerr, H. (1984) *Stones for Ibarra*. New York: Viking.

Dokic, J. (2003) 'The Sense of Ownership: An Analogy Between Sensation and Action'. In: *Agency and Self-Awareness*, J. Roessler & N. Eilan (eds), pp. 321–44. Oxford: Oxford University Press.

Doris, J. & Stich, S. (2009) 'Moral Psychology: Empirical Approaches', *Stanford Encyclopedia of Philosophy*. http://plato.stanford.edu/entries/moral-psych-emp/

Duan, C. & Hill, C.E. (1996) 'The Current State of Empathy Research', *Journal of Counseling Psychology* 43(3): 261–74.

Dunning, D., Griffin, D.W., Milojkovic, J.D., & Ross, L. (1990) 'The Overconfidence Effect in Social Prediction', *Journal of Personality and Social Psychology* 58(4): 568–81.

Duranti, A. (2008) 'Further Reflections on Reading Other Minds', *Anthropological Quarterly* 81: 483–94.

Durrell, G. (1956) *My Family and Other Animals*. Harmondsworth, UK: Penguin.

Eaton, Marcia (2001) *Merit, Aesthetic and Ethical*. Oxford: Oxford University Press.

Einolf, C.J. (2008) 'Empathic Concern and Prosocial Behaviors: A Test of Experimental Results Using Survey Data', *Social Science Research* 37(4): 1267–79.

Eisenberg, N. (1983) 'Children's Differentiations among Potential Recipients of Aid', *Child Development* 54(3): 594–602.

Eisenberg, N. (1986) *Altruistic Emotion, Cognition, and Behavior*. Hillsdale, NJ: Erlbaum.

Eisenberg, N. (2000) 'Empathy and Sympathy'. In: *Handbook of Emotions*, M. Lewis & J. Haviland-Jones (eds), pp. 677–91. New York: The Guilford Press.

Eisenberg, N. (2002) 'Emotion-related Regulation and its Relation to Quality of Social Functioning'. In: *Child Psychology in Retrospect and Prospect: In Celebration of the 75th Anniversary of the Institute of Child Development. The Minnesota Symposia on Child Psychology* vol. 32, W. Hartup & R.A. Weinberg (eds), pp. 133–71. Mahwah, NJ: Erlbaum.

Eisenberg, N. (2007) 'Empathy-related Responding and Prosocial behaviour'. In: *Empathy and Fairness* (Novartis Foundation), G. Brock, G. & J. Good (eds), pp. 71–80. Chichester, UK: John Wiley & Sons.

Eisenberg, N. (2009a) 'Empathy'. In: *The Child: An Encyclopedic Companion*, R. Shweder, T. Bidell, A.C. Dailey, S.D. Dixon P.J. Miller, & J. Modell (eds), pp. 316–18. Chicago: University of Chicago Press.

Eisenberg, N. (2009b) 'Moral Development'. In: *Oxford Companion to the Affective Sciences*, D. Sander & K. Scherer (eds), pp. 260–2. Oxford: Oxford University Press.

Eisenberg, N, Bridget, C.M., & Shepard, S. (1997) 'The Development of Empathic Accuracy'. In: *Empathic Accuracy*, W. Ickes (ed.), pp. 194–215. New York: The Guilford Press.

Eisenberg, N. & Eggum, N.D. (2009) 'Empathic Responding: Sympathy and Personal Distress'. In: *The Social Neuroscience of Empathy*, J. Decety & W. Ickes (eds), pp. 71–83. Cambridge, Mass.: The MIT Press.

Eisenberg, N. & Fabes, R.A. (1990) 'Empathy: Conceptualization, Measurement, and Relation to Prosocial behavior', *Motivation and Emotion* 14(2): 131–49.

Eisenberg, N., Fabes, R.A., Miller, P.A., Fultz, J., Shell, R., Mathy, R.M., & Reno, R. R. (1989) 'Relation of Sympathy and Personal Distress to Prosocial Behavior: A Multimethod Study', *Journal of personality and social psychology* 57: 55–66.

Eisenberg, N., Fabes, R.A., Murphy, B., Karbon, M, Maszk, P., Smith, M., O'Boyle, C., & Suh, K. (1994) 'The Relations of Emotionality and Regulation to Dispositional and Situational Empathy-Related Responding', *Journal of Personality and Social Psychology* 66: 776–97.

Eisenberg, N., Fabes, R.A., & Spinrad, T.L. (2006a) 'Prosocial Development'. In: *Handbook of Child Psychology: Social, Emotional, and Personality Development*, N. Eisenberg (ed.), pp. 646–718. New York: Wiley.

Eisenberg, N. & Lennon, R. (1983) 'Sex Differences in Empathy and Related Capacities', *Psychological Bulletin* 94: 100–31.

Eisenberg, N. & Miller, P. (1987) 'Relation of Empathy to Prosocial Behavior', *Psychological Bulletin* 101: 91–119.

Eisenberg, N., Murphy, B.C., & Shepard, S. (1997) 'The Development of Empathic Accuracy'. In: *Empathic Accuracy*, W. Ickes (ed.), pp. 73–116. New York: The Guilford Press.

Eisenberg, N., Schaller, M., Fabes, R.A., Bustamante, D., Mathy, R.M., Shell, R., & Rhodes, K. (1988) 'Differentiation of Personal Distress and Sympathy in Children and Adults', *Developmental Psychology* 24(6): 766–75.

Eisenberg, N., Shea, C.L., Carlo, G., & Knight, G.P. (1991) 'Empathy-related Responding and Cognition: A "Chicken and the Egg" Dilemma'. In: *Handbook of Moral Behavior and Development, vol. 2: Research*, W.M. Kurtines & J.L. Gewirtz (eds), pp. 63–88. Hillsdale, NJ: Erlbaum.

Eisenberg, N., Spinrad, T.L., & Sadovsky, A. (2006b) 'Empathy-related Responding in Children'. In: *Handbook of Moral Development*, M. Killen & J.G. Smetana (eds), pp. 517–48. Mahwah, NJ: Lawrence Erlbaum Associates.

Eisenberg, N. & Strayer, J. (1987) 'Critical Issues in the Study of Empathy'. In: *Empathy and its Development*, N. Eisenberg & J. Strayer (eds), pp. 3–13. Cambridge: Cambridge University Press.

Eisenberg, N., Valiente, C., & Champion, C. (2004) 'Empathy-Related Responding: Moral, Social, and Socialization Correlates'. In: *The Social Psychology of Good and Evil*, A.G. Miller (ed.), pp. 386–414. New York: The Guilford Press.

Eisenberg-Berg, N. (1979) 'The Development of Children's Prosocial Moral Judgment', *Developmental Psychology* 15: 128–37.

Ekman, P. (1972) 'Universals and Cultural Differences in Facial Expression of Emotion'. In: *Nebraska Symposium on Motivation* (xix), J. R. Cole (ed.), pp. 207–83. Lincoln, NE: University of Nebraska Press.

Ekman, P. (1980) 'Biological and Cultural Contributions to Body and Facial Movements in the Expression of the Emotions'. In: *Explaining Emotions*, A. O. Rorty (ed.), pp. 73–101. Los Angeles: University of California Press.

Ekman, P. (1992) 'An Argument for Basic Emotions', *Cognition and Emotion* 6: 169–200.

Ellis, H. & Young, A. (1990) 'Accounting for Delusional Misidentifications', *British Journal of Psychiatry* 157: 239–48.

Etlin, R. (1998) 'Aesthetics and the Spatial Sense of Self', *The Journal of Aesthetics and Art Criticism*, 56: 1–19.

Fadiga, L., Fogassi, L., Pavesi, G., & Rizzolatti, G. (1995) 'Motor Facilitation During Action Observation: A Magnetic Stimulation Study', *Journal of Neurophysiology* 73(6): 2608–11.

Farrer, C., Franck, N., Frith, C.D., Decety, J., Georgieff, N., d'Amato, T., & Jeannerod, M. (2004) 'Neural Correlates of Action Attribution in Schizophrenia', *Psychiatry Research: Neuroimaging* 131: 31–44.

Farrer, C., Franck, N., Georgieff, N., Frith, C.D., Decety, J., & Jeannerod, M. (2003) 'Modulating the Experience of Agency: A Positron Emission Tomography Study', *NeuroImage* 18: 324–33.

Farrer, C. & Frith, C. D. (2002) 'Experiencing Oneself vs. Another Person as Being the Cause of an Action: The Neural Correlates of the Experience of Agency', *NeuroImage* 15: 596–603.

Farrow, F.D. & Woodruff, W.R. (2007) (eds) *Empathy in Mental Illness*. New York: Cambridge University Press.

Feagin, S. (1988) 'Imagining Emotions and Appreciating Fiction', *Canadian Journal of Philosophy* 18: 485–500.

Feagin, S. (1996) *Reading with Feeling: The Aesthetics of Appreciation*. Ithaca, NY: Cornell University Press.

Fehr, E. & Gächter, S. (2002) 'Altruistic Punishment in Humans', *Nature* 415: 137–40.

Feigenson, N.R. (1997) 'Sympathy and Legal Judgment: A Psychological Analysis', *Tennessee Law Review* 65: 1–78.

Feinman, S., Roberts, D., Hsieh, K.-F., Sawyer, D., & Swanson, D. (1992) 'A Critical Review of Social Referencing in Infancy'. In: *Social Referencing and the Social Construction of Reality in Infancy*, S. Feinman (ed.), pp. 15–54. New York: Plenum.

Felman, S. & Laub, D. (1992) *Testimony: Crises of Witnessing in Literature, Psychoanalysis, and History*. New York: Routledge.

Fenichel, O. (1953) *The Collected Papers of Otto Fenichel*. Fenichel, H. & Rappaport, D. (eds). New York: W. W. Norton.

Ferrari, P.F. & Gallese, V. (2007) 'Mirror Neruons and Intersubjectivity'. In: *On Being Moved: From Mirror Neurons to Empathy*, S. Bråten (ed.), pp. 73–88. Amsterdam: John Benjamin's Publishing Company.

Ferrari, P.F., Gallese, V., Rizzolatti, G., & Fogassi, L. (2003) 'Mirror Neurons Responding to the Observation of Ingestive and Communicative Mouth Actions in the Monkey Ventral Premotor Cortex', *European Journal of Neuroscience* 17: 1703–14.

Feshbach, N.D. (1975) 'Empathy in Children: Some Theoretical and Empirical considerations', *The Counseling Psychologist* 5(2): 25–9.

Feshbach, N.D. & Roe, K. (1968) 'Empathy in six- and seven-year-olds', *Child development* 39(1): 133–45.

Field, T.M., Woodson, R., Greenberg, R., & Cohen, D. (1982) 'Discrimination and Imitation of Facial Expression by Neonates', *Science* 219: 179–81.

Figley, C. (1995) *Coping with Secondary Stress Disorder in Those who Treat the Traumatized*. New York: Brunner/Mazel.

Fisher, H. (2004) *Why We Love: The Nature and Chemistry of Romantic Love*. New York: Henry Holt.

Fisher, J.C. (2006) 'Does Simulation Theory Really Involve Simulation?', *Philosophical Psychology* 19(4): 417–32.

Fiske, S. (2004) *Social Beings: A Core Motives Approach to Social Psychology*. New York: Wiley.

Fliess, R. (1942) 'The Metapsychology of the Analyst', *Psychoanalytic Quarterly* 11: 211–27.

Flory, Dan (2008) *Philosophy, Black Film, Film Noir*. University Park: Pennsylvania State University Press.

Fodor, J. (1999) 'Let Your Brain Alone', *London Review of Books* (30 September).

Fogassi, L., Ferrari, P.F., Gesierich, B., Rozzi, S., Chersi, F., & Rizzolatti, G. (2005) 'Parietal Lobe: From Action Organization to Intention Understanding', *Science* 308: 662–7.

Fontaine, P. (1997) 'Identification and Economic Behavior: Sympathy and Empathy in Historical Perspective', *Economics and Philosophy* 13(2): 261–80.

Foot, P. (1997) 'Virtues and Vices'. In: *Virtue Ethics*, R. Crisp & M. Slote (eds), pp. 163–77. Oxford: Oxford University Press.

Frankfurt, H. (2004) *The Reasons of Love*. Princeton: Princeton University Press.

Freeborn, R. (1960) *Turgenev, the Novelist's Novelist: A Study*. Oxford: Oxford University Press.

Freedberg, D. & Gallese, V. (2007) 'Motion, Emotion and Empathy in Esthetic Experience', *Trends in Cognitive Science* 11: 197–203.

Freud, Sigmund (1915) 'Thoughts for the Times on War and Death'. In his *Collected Papers* (1949), Joan Riviere (ed.), vol IV, p. 307. London: Hogarth Press. Also Standard Edition, vol 14: 273–89.

Freud, Sigmund (1919/1948) 'Introduction to the War Neuroses'. In his *Collected Papers* (1948–1950), Joan Riviere, A. Strachey, & J. Strachey (eds), vol. V. London. The Hogarth Press. Also Standard Edition, vol 17: 207–10.

Freud, Sigmund (1922/1949) *Group Psychology and the Analysis of the Ego*. International Psychoanalytic Library, No. 6. Ernest Jones (ed.). James Strachey (trans.). London: Hogarth Press.

Freud, S. (1953) *The Standard Edition of the Complete Psychological Works of Sigmund Freud*. J. Strachey (ed.). London: Hogarth Press.

Freud, S. (1991) *Penguin Freud Library, vol. 12. Civilization, Society and Religion: Group Psychology, Civilization and its Discontents and Other Works*, J. Strachey (trans.). Harmondsworth: Penguin Books.

Fried, I., Wilson, C.L., Maidment, N.T., Engel, J., Behnke, E., Fields, T.A., MacDonald, K.A., Morrow, J.W., & Ackerson, L. (1999) 'Cerebral Microdialysis Combined with Single-neuron and Electroencephalographic Recording in Neurosurgical Patients. Technical Note', *Journal of Neurosurgery* 91: 697–705.

Friedberg, A. (2006) *The Virtual Window: From Alberti to Microsoft*. Cambridge: MIT Press.

Frith, U. (1989) *Autism: Explaining the Enigma*. Oxford: Blackwell.

Fromm-Reichmann, F. (1959) *Psychoanalysis and Psychotherapy, Selected Papers*. Chicago: University of Chicago Press.

Gabrielsson, A. (2002) 'Emotion Perceived and Emotion Felt: Same or Different?', *Musicae Scientiae* (special number 2001–2002): 123–47.

Gaita, R. (1991) *Good and Evil: An Absolute Conception*. Basingstoke, UK: Macmillan Press.

Gallagher, H.L. & Frith, C. (2003) 'Functional Imaging of "Theory of Mind"', *Trends in Cognitive Sciences* 7: 77–83.

Gallagher, S. (2001) 'The Practice of Mind: Theory, Simulation, or Interaction?', *Journal of Consciousness Studies* 8: 83–107.

Gallagher, S. & Meltzoff, A.N. (1996) 'The Earliest Sense of Self and Others: Merleau-Ponty and Recent Developmental Studies', *Philosophical Psychology* 9: 211–33.

Gallese, V. (2006) 'Intentional Attunement: A Neurophysiological Perspective on Social Cognition and its Disruption in Autism', *Brain Research* 1079(1): 15–24.

Gallese, V., Fadiga, L., Fogassi, L., & Rizzolatti, G. (1996) 'Action Recognition in the Premotor Cortex', *Brain* 119(2): 593–609.

Gallese, V. & Goldman, A. (1998) 'Mirror Neurons and the Simulation Theory of Mind-reading', *Trends in Cognitive Sciences* 2: 493–501.

Gallese, V., Keysers, C., & Rizzolatti, G. (2004) 'A Unifying View of the Basis of Social Cognition', *Trends in Cognitive Science* 8(9): 396–403.

Gardner, J. (1978) *On Moral Fiction*. New York: Basic Books.

Gaut, B. (1999) 'Identification and Emotion'. In: *Passionate Views: Film, Cognition, and Emotion*, C. Plantinga & G.M. Smith (eds), pp. 200–16. Baltimore: Johns Hopkins University Press.

Gazzola, V., Aziz-Zadeh, L., & Keysers, C. (2006) 'Empathy and the Somatotopic Auditory Mirror System in Humans', *Current Biology* 16: 1824–9.

Geist, R.A. (2009) 'Empathic Understanding: The Foundation of Self-Psychological Psychoanalysis', *Annals of the New York Academy of Sciences* 1159: 63–74.

Gendler, T.S. (2006) 'Imaginative Resistance Revisited'. In: *The Architecture of the Imagination*, S. Nichols (ed.), pp. 149–74. Oxford: Oxford University Press.

Gendler, T.S. (2008) 'Alief and Belief', *Journal of Philosophy*, 105(10): 634–63.

Giacomo, R., Fogassi, L., & Gallese V. (2006) 'Mirrors in the Mind', *Scientific American*, 57: 34–7.

Gibbs, J., Arnold, K., & Burkhart, J. (1984) 'Sex Differences in the Expression of Moral Judgment', *Child Development* 55: 1040–3.

Gilbert, D.T. (2006) *Stumbling on Happiness*. New York: Knopf.

Gill, K.L. & Calkins, S. (2003) 'Do Aggressive/Destructive Toddlers Lack Concern for Others? Behavioral and Physiological Indicators of Empathic Responding in 2-year-old Children', *Development and Psychopathology* 15: 55–71.

Gilligan, C. (1982) *In a Different Voice: Psychological Theory and Women's Development*. Cambridge: Harvard University Press.

Giovanelli, A. (2008) 'In and Out: The Dynamics of Imagination in the Engagement with Narratives', *The Journal of Aesthetics and Art Criticism* 66(1): 11–24.

Giovanelli, A. (2009) 'In Sympathy with Narrative Characters', *The Journal of Aesthetics and Art Criticism* 67: 83–95.

Gladstein, G.A. (1983) 'Understanding Empathy: Integrating Counseling, Developmental, and Social Psychology Perspectives', *Journal of Counseling Psychology* 30(4): 467–82.

Gladstein, G.A. (1984) 'The Historical Roots of Contemporary Empathy Research', *Journal of the History of the Behavioral Sciences* 20(1): 38–59.

Gladstein, G.A. & Brennan, J. (1987) *Empathy and Counseling: Explorations in Theory and Research*. New York: Springer-Verlag.

Goldie, P. (1999) 'How We Think of Others' Emotions', *Mind & Language* 14, 394–423.

Goldie, P. (2000) *The Emotions: A Philosophical Exploration*. Oxford: Clarendon.

Goldie, P. (2002a) 'Emotion, Personality and Simulation'. In: *Understanding Emotions: Mind and Morals*, P. Goldie (ed.), pp. 97–109. Aldershot, UK: Ashgate Publishing.

Goldie, P. (2002b) 'Emotions, Feelings and Intentionality', *Phenomenology and the Cognitive Sciences* 1: 235–54.

Goldie, P. (2003) 'Narration, Emotion, and Perspective'. In: *Imagination, Philosophy, and the Arts*, M. Kieran & D.M. Lopes (eds), pp. 54–68. London: Routledge.

Goldie, P. (2004a) *On Personality*. London: Routledge.

Goldie, P. (2004b) 'Emotion, Reason and Virtue'. In: *Emotion, Evolution and Rationality*, D. Evans & P. Cruse (eds), pp. 249–67. Oxford: Oxford University Press.

Goldie, P. (2007) 'Seeing What is the Kind Thing to Do: Perception and Emotion in Morality', *Dialectica* 61: 347–61.

Goldie, P. (2008a) 'Misleading Emotions'. In: *Epistemology and the Emotions*, D. Kuenzle, G. Brun, & Dogluogu, U. (eds), pp. 149–67. Aldershot, UK: Ashgate Publishing.

Goldie, P. (2008b) 'Thick Concepts and Emotion'. In: *Reading Bernard Williams*, D. Callcut (ed.). pp. 94–109. London: Routledge.

Goldman, A.I. (1992) *Liaisons: Philosophy Meets the Cognitive and Social Sciences*. Cambridge, MA: MIT Press.

Goldman, A.I. (1995a) 'Empathy, Mind, and Morals'. In *Mental Simulation: Evaluations and Applications*, M. Davies & T. Stone (eds), pp. 185–208. Oxford: Blackwell,.

Goldman, A.I. (1995b) 'Interpretation Psychologised'. In: *Folk Psychology: The Theory of Mind Debate*, M. Davies & T. Stone (eds), pp. 74–99. Oxford: Blackwell.

Goldman, A.I. (1995c) 'Simulation and Interpersonal Utility', *Ethics* 105: 709–26.

Goldman, A.I. (2006a) *Simulating Minds: The Philosophy, Psychology, and Neuroscience of Mindreading*. Oxford: Oxford University Press.

Goldman, A.I. (2006b) 'Imagination and Simulation in Audience Responses to Fiction'. In: *The Architecture of the Imagination*, S. Nichols (ed.), pp. 41–57. Oxford: Oxford University Press.

Goldman, A.I. (2008) 'Hurley on Simulation', *Philosophy and Phenomenological Research* 77(3): 775–88.

Goldman, A.I. (2009a) 'Mirroring, Simulating and Mindreading', *Mind & Language* 24(2): 235–52.

Goldman, A.I. (2009b) 'Replies to Perner and Brandl, Saxe, Vignemont, and Carruthers', *Philosophical Studies* 144: 477–91.

Goldman, A.I. & Sripada, C.S. (2005) 'Simulationist Models of Face-based Emotion Recognition', *Cognition* 94: 193–213.

Goldstein, T.R. (2009) 'Psychological Perspectives on Acting', *Psychology of Aesthetics, Creativity, and the Arts* 3(1): 6–9.

Goncourt, E.L. (1962) *Pages from the Goncourt journals*, R. Baldick (ed. and trans.). Oxford: Oxford University Press.

Gopnik, A. & Wellman, H.M. (1994) 'The theory theory'. In: *Mapping the Mind: Domain Specificity in Cognition and Culture*, L.A. Hirschfeld & S.A. Gelman (eds), pp. 257–93. New York: Cambridge University Press.

Gordon, R. (1986) 'Folk Psychology as Simulation', *Mind and Language* 1: 158–71.

Gordon, R. (1995) 'Simulation Without Introspection or Inference From Me to You'. In: *Mental Simulation: Evaluations and Applications*, M. Davies & T. Stone (eds), pp. 53–67. Oxford: Blackwell.

Gordon, R. (2005) 'Intentional Agents Like Me'. In: *Perspectives on Imitation: From Neuroscience to Social Science*, S. Hurley & N. Chater (eds), pp. 95–106. Cambridge: MIT Press,.

Gordon, R.M. (2009) 'Folk Psychology as Mental Simulation', *Stanford Encyclopedia of Philosophy*. http://plato.stanford.edu/entries/folkpsych-simulation/

Graham, T. & Ickes, W. (1997) 'When Women's Intuition Isn't Greater than Men's'. In: *Empathic Accuracy*, W. Ickes (ed.) pp. 117–43. New York: The Guilford Press.

Grammer, K., Keki, V., Striebel, B., Atzmüller, M., & Fink, B. (2003) 'Bodies in Motion: A Window to the Soul'. In: *Evolutionary Aesthetics*, E. Voland & K. Grammer (eds), pp. 295–323. Berlin: Springer Verlag.

Green, M. (2008) 'Empathy, Expression, and What Artworks Have to Teach'. In: *The Ethical Criticism of Art*, G. Hagberg (ed.), pp. 95–122. Oxford: Blackwell.

Greenberg, L.S., Watson, J.C., Elliot, R. & Bohart, A.C. (2001) 'Empathy', *Psychotherapy* 38(4): 380–4.

Greenfield, P.M. & Suzuki, L. (1998) 'Culture and Human Development: Implications for Parenting, Education, Pediatrics and Mental Health'. In: *Handbook of Child Psychology, Fifth edition, vol. 4: Child Psychology in Practice*, I.E. Sigel & K.A. Renninger (eds), pp. 1059–109. New York: Wiley.

Greenhouse, L. (2005) *Becoming Justice Blackmun*. New York: Times Books.

Greenspan, P. (1988) *Emotions and Reasons: An Inquiry into Emotional Justification*. New York: Routledge.

Griffiths, P.E. (1997) *What Emotions Really Are*. Chicago University of Chicago Press.

Griswold, C.L. (1999) *Adam Smith and the Virtues of Enlightenment*. New York: Cambridge University Press.

Griswold, C.L. (2006) 'Imagination: Morals, Science, and Arts'. In: *The Cambridge Companion to Adam Smith*, K. Haakonssen (ed.), pp. 22–56. New York: Cambridge University Press.

Grondin, J. (1994) *Introduction to Philosophical Hermeneutics*, J. Weinsheimer (trans.). New Haven, CT: Yale University Press.

Groos, K. (1892) *Einleitung in die Aesthetik*. Giessen, Germany: Ricker.

Gusnard, D.A., Akbudak, E., Shulman, G.L., & Raichle, M.E. (2001) 'Medial Prefrontal Cortex and Self-referential Mental Activity: Relation to a Default Mode of Brain Function', *Proceedings of the National Academy of Sciences USA* 98: 4259–64.

Guyer, P. (2005) *Values of Beauty*. Cambridge: Cambridge University Press.

Hall, G.B.C., Szechtman, H., & Nahmias, C. (2003) 'Enhanced Salience and Emotion Recognition in Autism: A PET Study', *American Journal of Psychiatry* 160: 1439–41.

Halpern, J. (2001) *From Detached Concern to Empathy: Humanizing Medical Practice*. New York: Oxford University Press.

Halpern, J. (2007) 'Empathy and patient-physician conflicts', *Journal of General Internal Medicine: Official Journal of the Society for Research and Education in Primary Care Internal Medicine* 22(5): 696–700.

Halpern, J. (2009) 'Groupthink and caregivers' projections: addressing barriers to empathy', *The Journal of Clinical Ethics* 20(1): 75–8.

Hamilton, A.F., & Grafton, S.T. (2008) 'Action Outcomes are Represented in Human Inferior Frontoparietal Cortex', *Cerebral Cortex* 18(5): 1160–8.

Hamilton, N.G. (1981) 'Empathic Understanding', *Psychoanalytic Inquiry* 1: 417–22.

Hampshire, S. (1972) 'Sincerity and Single-mindedness'. In his *Freedom of Mind and Other Essays*, pp. 232–56. Oxford: Oxford University Press.

Han, S., Fan, Y. & Mao, L. (2008) 'Gender Difference in Empathy for Pain: An Electrophysiological Investigation', *Brain Research* 1196: 85–93.

Hancock, M. & Ickes, W. (1996) 'Empathic Accuracy: When Does the Perceiver-Target Relationship Make a Difference?', *Journal of Social and Personal Relationships* 13(2): 179–99.

Hanne, M. (1994) *The Power of the Story*. Cambridge: Berghahn Books.

Hare, R.D. (1991) *The Hare Psychopathy Checklist—Revised*. Toronto: Multi-Health Systems.

Hareli, S., & Weiner, B. (2002) 'Dislike and envy as antecedents of pleasure at another's misfortune', *Motivation and Emotion* 26: 257–77.

Harold, J. (2000) 'Empathy with Fictions', *British Journal of Aesthetics* 40: 340–55.

Harris, P.L. (2000) *The Work of the Imagination*. Oxford: Blackwell.

Hartmann, H. (1964) *Essays on Ego Psychology*. New York: International Universities Press.

Hassabis, D., Kumaran, D., Vann, S.D., & Maguire, E.A. (2007) 'Patients with Hippocampal Amnesia Cannot Imagine New Experiences', *Proceedings of the National Academy of Sciences USA* 104: 1726–31.

Hatfield, E. (2009) 'Emotional Contagion and Empathy'. In: *The Social Neuroscience of Empathy*, J. Decety & W. Ickes (eds), pp. 19–30. Cambridge: MIT Press.

Hatfield, E., Cacioppo, J.T. & Rapson, R.L. (1992) 'Primitive Emotional Contagion'. In: *Review of Personality and Social Psychology: Emotion and Social Behavior*, M. Clark (ed.), pp. 151–77. Thousand Oaks, CA: Sage.

Hatfield, E., Cacioppo, J.T., & Rapson, R.L. (1993) 'Emotional Contagion', *Current Directions in Psychological Science* 2: 96–9.

Hatfield, E., Cacioppo, J.T., & Rapson, R.L. (1994) *Emotional Contagion*. Cambridge: Cambridge University Press.

Hatfield, E., Rapson, R, & Le, Y. L. (2009) 'Emotional Contagion and Empathy'. In: *The Social Neuroscience of Empathy*, J. Decety & W. Ickes (eds), pp. 19–30. Cambridge: MIT Press.

Hauk, O., Johnsrude, I., & Pulvermüller, F. (2004) 'Somatotopic Representation of Action Words in Human Motor and Premotor Cortex', *Neuron* 41: 301–7.

Heal, J. (1994) 'Simulation vs. Theory Theory: What is at Issue?'. In: *Objectivity, Simulation, and the Unity of Consciousness*, C. Peacocke (ed.), pp. 129–44. Oxford: Oxford University Press.

Heal, J. (1996/2003a) 'Simulation and Cognitive Penetrability', *Mind and Language* 11: 44–67. Reprinted in her *Mind, Reason and Imagination*, pp. 63–88. Cambridge, Cambridge University Press.

Heal, J. (1997/2003a) 'Indexical Predicates and their Uses', *Mind* 106(424): 619–40. Reprinted in her *Mind, Reason and Imagination*, pp. 153–73. Cambridge, Cambridge University Press.

Heal, J. (1998) 'Co-cognition and Off-line Simulation: Two Ways of Understanding the Simulation Approach', *Mind and Language* 13(4): 477–98.

Heal, J. (2003a) *Mind, Reason and Imagination: Selected Essays in Philosophy of Mind and Language*. Cambridge: Cambridge University Press.

Heal, J. (2003b) 'Simulation and Cognitive Penetrability'. In her *Mind, Reason and Imagination: Selected Essays in Philosophy of Mind and Language*, pp. 63–88. Cambridge: Cambridge University Press.

Heal, J. (2003c) 'Co-cognition and Off-line Simulation: Two Ways of Understanding the Simulation Approach'. In her *Mind, Reason and Imagination: Selected Essays in Philosophy of Mind and Language*, 91–114. Cambridge: Cambridge University Press.

Heal, J. (2003d) 'Indexical Predicates and their Uses'. In her *Mind, Reason and Imagination: Selected Essays in Philosophy of Mind and Language*, pp. 153–73. Cambridge: Cambridge University Press.

Heise, M. (2005) 'Brown v. Board of Education, Footnote 11, and Multidisciplinarity', *Cornell Law Review* 90/02: 279–320.

Held, V. (2001) 'Caring Relations and Principles of Justice'. In: *Controversies in Feminism*, J.P. Sterba (ed.), pp. 67–82. Lanham, MD: Rowman and Littlefield.

Held, V. (2006a) 'The Ethics of Care'. In: *The Oxford Handbook of Ethical Theory*, D. Copp (ed.), pp. 537–66. New York: Oxford University Press.

Held, V. (2006b) *The Ethics of Care: Personal, Political, and Global*. New York: Oxford University Press.

Henderson, L.N. (1985) 'Legality and Empathy', *Michigan Law Review* 85: 1574–653.

Herder, J.G. (1778) *Vom Erkennen und Empfinden der Menschlichen*. Seele, Riga: Hartknock.

Herder, J.G. (2002) *Sculpture*, J. Gaiger (ed. & trans.). Chicago: Cambridge University Press.

Herman, J. (1992/1997) *Trauma and Recovery: The Aftermath of Violence—From Domestic Abuse to Political Terror*. New York: Basic Books.

Hess, U. & Blairy, S. (2001) 'Facial Mimicry and Emotional Contagion to Dynamic Emotional Facial Expressions and their Influence on Decoding Accuracy', *International Journal of Psychophysiology* 40: 129–41.

Heyes, C. (2005) 'Imitation by association'. In: *Perspectives on Imitation, vol. 1, Mechanisms of Imitation and Imitation in Animals*, S. Hurley & N. Chater (eds), pp. 157–76. Cambridge, MA: MIT Press.

Hirsch, J (2004) 'Post-Traumatic Cinema and the Holocaust Documentary'. In: *Trauma and Cinema: Cross-cultural Explorations*, E.A. Kaplan & B. Wang (eds), pp. 95–123. Hong Kong: Hong Kong University Press.

Hobson, R.P. (2002) *The Cradle of Thought*. Oxford: Macmillan.

Hodges, S.D. & Wegner, D.M. (1997) 'Automatic and Controlled Empathy'. In: *Empathic Accuracy*, W. Ickes (ed.), pp. 311–39. New York: The Guilford Press.

Hoffman, M.L. (1970) 'Moral Development'. In: *Carmichael's Manual of Child Psychology*, P. Mussen (ed.), pp. 261–359. New York: Wiley.

Hoffman, M.L. (1977) 'Sex Differences in Empathy and Related Behaviors', *Psychological Bulletin* 84(4): 712–22.

Hoffman, M.L. (1978) 'Empathy, its Development and Prosocial Implications'. In: *Nebraska Symposium on Motivation*, C.B. Keasey (ed.). 25: 169–218.

Hoffman, M.L. (1979) 'Development of Moral Thought, Feeling, and Behavior', *American Psychologist* 34(10): 958–66.

Hoffman, M.L. (1981a) 'The Development of Empathy'. In: *Altruism and Helping Behavior: Social, Personality, and Developmental Perspectives*, J.P. Rushton & R.M. Sorrentino (eds), pp. 41–63. Mahwah, NJ: Lawrence Erlbaum.

Hoffman, M.L. (1981b) 'Is Altruism Part of Human Nature?', *Journal of Personality and Social Psychology* 40: 121–37.

Hoffman, M.L. (1982) 'Development of Prosocial Motivation: Empathy and Guilt'. In: *The Development of Prosocial Behavior*, N. Eisenberg (ed.), pp. 281–313. New York: Academic Press.

Hoffman, M.L. (1983) 'Affective and Cognitive Processes in Moral Internalization: An Information Processing Approach'. In: *Social Cognition and Social Development: A Socio-Cultural Perspective*, E.T. Higgins, D.N. Ruble & W.W.Hartup (eds), pp. 236–74. New York: Cambridge University Press.

Hoffman, M.L. (1984a) 'Empathy, its Limitation and its Role in a Comprehensive Moral Theory'. In: *Morality, Moral Development and Moral Behavior*, J. Gewirtz & W. Kurtines (eds), pp. 283–302. New York: John Wiley.

Hoffman, M.L. (1984b) 'Interaction of Affect and Cognition in Empathy'. In: *Emotions, Cognition, and Behavior*, C.E. Izard, J. Kagan & R.B. Zajonc (eds), pp. 103–31. Cambridge and New York: Cambridge University Press.

Hoffman, M.L. (1987) 'The Contribution of Empathy to Justice and Moral Judgment'. In: *Empathy and its Development*, N. Eisenberg & J. Strayer (eds), pp. 47–80. Cambridge: Cambridge University Press.

Hoffman, M.L. (1991) 'Is Empathy Altruistic?', *Psychological Inquiry* 2(2): 131–3.

Hoffman, M.L. (2000) *Empathy and Moral Development: Implications for Caring and Justice.* Cambridge: Cambridge University Press.

Hoffman, M.L. (2001a) 'Empathy is Fickle but Beneficial', *New York Newsday* (2 April).

Hoffman, M.L. (2001b) 'A Comprehensive Theory of Prosocial Moral Development'. In: *Constructive and Destructive Behavior*, A.C. Bohart & D.J Stipek (eds), pp. 61–86. Washington, D.C.: American Psychological Association.

Hoffman, M.L. (2004) 'Empathy and Vicarious Traumatization in Clinicians', unpublished manuscript, New York University.

Hoffman, M.L. (2007) 'What We Know about Empathy and Where to Go from Here', paper presented at the Conference on Understanding Other Minds and Moral Agency, at Holy Cross College.

Hoffman, M.L. (2008) 'Empathy and Prosocial Behavior'. In: *Handbook of Emotion,* (third edition), M. Lewis, J. Haviland-Jones, & L. Feldman Barrett (eds), pp. 449–52. New York: Guilford.

Hogan, P.C. (2003) *Cognitive Science, Literature, and the Arts.* Lond London: Routledge.

Hogan, R. (1969) 'Development of an Empathy Scale', *Journal of Consulting and Clinical Psychology* 33(3): 307–16.

Hojat, M. (2007) *Empathy in Patient Care: Antecedents, Development, Measurement, and Outcomes.* New York: Springer-Verlag.

Holton, R. (1999) 'Intention and Weakness of Will', *Journal of Philosophy* 96: 241–62.

Hommel, B., Müsseler, J., Aschersleben, G., & Prinz, W. (2001) 'The Theory of Event Coding: A Framework for Perception and Action', *Behavioral and Brain Sciences* 24: 849–78.

Honderich, T. (2005) (ed.) *Oxford Companion to Philosophy* (New Edition). Oxford: Oxford University Press.

Hopkins, R. (1998) *Picture, Image and Experience.* Cambridge: Cambridge University Press.

Hopkirk, P. (1990) *The Great Game.* Oxford: Oxford University Press.

Hornby, N. (1992) *Fever Pitch.* London: Victor Gollancz.

Hornby, N. (1996) *Fever Pitch.* London: Indigo.

Hornby, N. (2000) *Fever Pitch.* London: Penguin.

Horowitz, M.J. (1969) 'Psychic Trauma: Return of Images after a Stress Film', *Archives of General Psychiatry* 20: 552–9.

Hume, D. (1739/1978). *A Treatise of Human Nature.* P.H. Nidditch (ed.). Oxford: Oxford University Press.

Hume, D. (1751/1957) *An Inquiry Concerning the Principle of Morals.* New York: Liberal Arts Press.

Hume, D. (1757) *Of the Standard of Taste.* http://www.csulb.edu/~jvancamp/361r15.html

Hume, D. (2000). *A Treatise of Human Nature.* D.F. Norton & .M.J. Norton (eds). Oxford: Oxford University Press.

Hume, D. (2007) *An Enquiry Concerning Human Understanding and Other Writings*. S. Buckle (ed.). New York: Cambridge University Press.

Hurley, S. (2008) 'The Shared Circuits Model (SCM): How Control, Mirroring, and Simulation Can Enable Imitation, Deliberation, and Mindreading', *The Behavioral and Brain Sciences* 31(1): 1–22.

Hurley, S. & Chater, N. (2005) (eds) *Perspectives on Imitation: From Neuroscience to Social Science*. Cambridge: MIT Press.

Husserl, E. (1989) *Ideas Pertaining to a Pure Phenomenology and to a Phenomenological Philosophy: Second Book: Studies in the Phenomenology of Constitution*. R. Rojcewicz & A. Schuwer (trans.). Dordrecht: Kluwer Academic Publishers.

Hutchison, W.D., Davis, K.D., Lozano, A.M., Tasker, R.R., & Dostrovsky, J.O. (1999) 'Pain-Related Neurons in the Human Cingulate Cortex', *Nature Neuroscience* 2: 403–5.

Huttenlochers, P.R. & Dabholkar, A.S. (1997) 'Regional Differences in Synaptogenesis in Human Cerebral Cortex', *Journal of Comparative Neurology* 387: 167–78.

Hutto, D. (2002) 'The World is Not Enough: Shared Emotions and Other Minds'. In: *Understanding Emotions: Mind and Morals*, P. Goldie (ed.), pp. 37–54. Aldershot, UK: Ashgate Publishing.

Hutto, D. (2005) 'Starting without Theory'. In: *Other Minds: How Humans Bridge the Divide between Self and Others*, B. Malle & S.D. Hodges (eds.), pp. 56–72. New York: The Guilford Press.

Iacoboni, M. (2005) Neural Mechanisms of Imitation, *Current Opinion in Neurobiology*, 15(6): 632–7.

Iacoboni, M. (2007) 'Neurons For a Secular Morality', *Neuron* 56: 438–9.

Iacoboni, M. (2008) *Mirroring People: The New Science of How We Connect with Others*. New York: Farrar, Straus, & Giroux.

Iacoboni, M. (2009a). 'Imitation, Empathy and Mirror Neurons', *Annual Review of Psychology* 60: 653–70.

Iacoboni, M. (2009b) 'Neurobiology of Imitation', *Current Opinion in Neurobiology* 19(6): 661–5.

Iacoboni, M. & Dapretto, M. (2006) 'The Mirror Neuron System and the Consequences of its Dysfunction', *Nature Reviews—Neuroscience* 7(12): 942–51.

Iacoboni, M. & Mazziotta, J.C. (2007) 'Mirror Neuron System: Basic Findings and Clinical Applications', *Annals of Neurology* 62(3): 213–18.

Iacoboni, M., Molnar-Szakacs, I., Buccino, G., Mazziotta, J., & Rizzolatti, G. (2005) 'Grasping the Intentions of Others with One's Own Mirror Neuron System', *Public Library of Science Biology* 3: 529–35.

Iacoboni, M., Woods, R.P., Brass, M., Bekkering, H., Mazziotta, J.C., & Rizzolatti, G. (1999) 'Cortical Mechanisms of Human Imitation', *Science* 286: 2526–8.

Ickes, W. (1993) 'Empathic Accuracy', *Journal of Personality* 61(4): 587–610.

Ickes, W. (1997a) (ed.) *Empathic Accuracy*. New York: Guilford.

Ickes, W. (1997b) 'Introduction'. In: *Empathic Accuracy*, W. Ickes (ed.), pp. 1–16. New York: The Guilford Press.

Ickes, W. (2003) *Everyday Mind Reading*. Amherst, NY: Prometheus Books.

Ickes, W. Gesn, P.R., & Graham, T. (2000) 'Gender Differences in Empathic Accuracy: Differential Ability or Differential Motivation?' *Personal Relationships* 7: 95–109.

Ickes, W. & Simpson, J.A. (1997) 'Managing Empathic Accuracy in Close Relationships'. In: *Empathic Accuracy*, W. Ickes (ed.), pp. 218–50. New York: The Guilford Press.

Ickes, W., Stinson, L., Bissonnette, V., & Garcia, S. (1990) 'Naturalistic Social Cognition: Empathic Accuracy in Mixed-sex Dyads', *Journal of Personality and Social Psychology* 59: 730–42.

Irvin, S. (2008) 'Scratching an Itch', *Journal of Aesthetics and Art Criticism* 66: 25–35.

Irwin, T.H. (1980) 'Reason and Responsibility in Aristotle'. In: *Essays on Aristotle's Ethics*, A.O. Rorty (ed.), pp. 117–56. Berkeley: University of California Press.

Isen, A.M. & Levin, P.F. (1972) 'The Effect of Feeling Good on Helping: Cookies and Kindness', *Journal of Personality and Social Psychology* 21: 384–8.

Jabbi, M., Swart, M., & Keysers, C. (2007) 'Empathy for Positive and Negativ Emotions in the Gustatory Cortex', *NeuroImage* 34: 1744–53.

Jackson, F. (1982/1990) 'Ephiphenomenal Qualia'. Reprinted in: *Mind and Cognition: A Reader*, W. Lycan (ed.), pp. 469–77. Oxford: Basil Blackwell.

Jackson, P.L., Brunet, E., Meltzoff, A.N., & Decety, J. (2006) 'Empathy Examined through the Neural Mechanisms Involved in Imagining How I Feel Versus How You Feel Pain: An Event-related fMRI Study', *Neuropsychologia* 44: 752–61.

Jackson, P.L. & Decety, J. (2004) 'Motor Cognition: A New Paradigm to Study Self–Other Interactions', *Current Opinion in Neurobiology* 14: 259–63.

Jackson, P.L., Meltzoff, A. N., & Decety, J. (2004) 'How Do We Perceive the Pain of Others? A Window into the Neural Processes Involved in Empathy', *NeuroImage* 2: 771–9.

Jackson, P.L., Meltzoff, A.N., & Decety, J. (2006) 'Neural Circuits Involved in Imitation and Perspective-taking', *NeuroImage* 31: 429–39.

Jackson, P.L., Rainville, P., & Decety, J. (2006), 'To What Extent Do We Share the Pain of Others? Insight from the Neural Bases of Pain Empathy', *Pain* 125: 5–9.

Jacob, P. (2008) What do Mirror Neurons Contribute to Human Social Cognition? *Mind & Language* 23: 190–223.

Jaffee, S. & Hyde, J.S. (2000) 'Gender Differences in Moral Orientation: A Meta-analysis', *Psychological Bulletin* 126: 703–26.

Janata, P. & Grafton, S.T. (2003) 'Swinging in the Brain: Shared Neural Substrates for Behaviors Related to Sequencing and Music', *Nature Neuroscience* 6: 682–7.

Jaspers, K. (1968) *General Psychopathology*, 2 vols. J. Hoenig & M.W. Hamilton (trans.). Chicago: University of Chicago Press.

Jeannerod, M. (1999) 'To Act or Not to Act: Perspectives on the Representation of Actions', *Quarterly Journal of Experimental Psychology* 52A: 1–29.

Jellema, T., Baker, C.I., Perrett, M.W., & Perrett, D.I. (2002) 'Cell Populations in the Banks of the Superior Temporal Sulcus of the Macaque, and Imitation'. In: *The Imitative Mind*, A.N. Meltzoff & W. Prinz (eds), pp. 267–90. Cambridge: Cambridge University Press.

Juslin, P.N. & Laukka, P. (2003) 'Communication of Emotion in Vocal Expression and Music Performance: Different Channels, Same Code?', *Psychological Bulletin* 129(5): 770–814.

Juslin, P.N. & Västfjäll, D. (2008) 'Emotional Responses to Music: The need to Consider Underlying Mechanisms', *Behavioral and Brain Sciences* 31: 559–75.

Kagitcibasi, C. (1996) 'Individualism and collectivism'.In: *Handbook of Cross-Cultural Psychology*, J.W. Berry, M.H. Segall, & Kagitcibasi, C. (eds), vol 3: 1–49.

Kahn, E. & Rachman, A.W. (2000) 'Carl Rogers and Heinz Kohut: A Historical Perspective', *Psychoanalytic Psychology* 17(2): 294–312.

Kalven, H. & Zeisel, H. (1966) *The American Jury*. Chicago: University of Chicago Press.

Kamisar, Y. (2000) 'Can (Did) Congress Override Miranda?', *Cornell Law Review* 85: 883–955.

Kandel, S., Orliaguet, J.P., & Viviani, P. (2000) 'Perceptual Anticipation in Handwriting: The Role of Implicit Motor Competence', *Perception & Psychophysics* 62: 706–16.

Kaplan, E.A. (2005). *Trauma Culture: The Politics of Terror and Loss in Media and Literature*. New Brunswick, NJ: Rutgers University Press.

Kaplan, E.A. (2006) 'Empathy, Global Trauma, and Public Feeling: Viewing Images of Catastrophe', presented in part at the California State University Fullerton conference on empathy, June 2006.

Kaplan, E.A. & Wang, B. (2004) *Trauma and Cinema: Cross-Cultural Explorations*. Hong Kong: Hong Kong University Press.

Kaplan, J. T. & Iacoboni, M. (2006) 'Getting a Grip on Other Minds: Mirror Neurons, Intention Understanding and Cognitive Empathy', *Social Neuroscience* 1: 175–83.

Karniol, R., Gabay, R., Ochion, Y., & Harari, Y. (1998) 'Is Gender or Gender-role Orientation a Better Predictor of Empathy in Adolescence?', *Sex Roles* 39: 45–59.

Keefe, Rosanna & Smith, Peter (1996) (eds) *Vagueness: A Reader*. Cambridge, MA: MIT Press.

Kelly, M. (2008) (ed.), *Encyclopedia of Aesthetics*, 4 vols. Oxford: Oxford University Press.

Keniston, K. (1968) *Young Radicals*. New York: Harcourt.

Kennett, J. (2002) 'Autism, Empathy, and Moral Agency', *Philosophical Quarterly* 52: 340–57.

Kenny, A. (1963) *Action, Emotion, and Will*. London: Routledge and Kegan Paul.

Keysar, B., Lin, S. & Barr, D.J. (2003) 'Limits on theory of mind use in adults', *Cognition* 89(1): 25–41.

Keysers, C. (2009) 'Mirror Neurons', *Current Biology* 19(21): 971–3.

Keysers, C. & Fadiga, L. (2009) *The Mirror Neuron System*. London: Psychology Press.

Keysers, C. & Gazzola, V. (2006) 'Toward a Unifying Neural Theory of Social Cognition', *Progress in Brain Research* 156: 379–401.

Keysers, C. & Perrett, D. (2004) 'Demystifying Social Cognition: A Hebbian Perspective', *Trends in Cognitive Sciences* 8: 501-7.

Keysers, C., Wicker, B., Gazzola, V., Anton, J.-L., Fogassi, L., & Gallese, V. (2004) 'A Touching Sight: SII/PV Activation During the Observation of Touch', *Neuron* 42: 335–46.

Kielburger, C. (1998) *Free the Children: A Young Man's Personal Crusade Against Child Labor*. New York: Harper Collins.

Kim, J., Doop, M., Blake, R., & Park, S. (2005) 'Impaired Visual Recognition of Biological Motion in Schizophrenia', *Schizophrenia Research* 77: 299–307.

Kinder, M. (1991) *Playing with Power in Movies, Television and Video Games*. Berkeley: University of California Press.

King, J.A., Blair, R.J., Mitchell, D.G., Dolan, R.J., & Burgess, N. (2006) 'Doing the Right Thing: A Common Neural Circuit for Appropriate Violent or Compassionate Behavior', *Neuroimage* 30(3): 1069–76.

Kivy, P. (1987) 'How Music Moves'. In: *What Is Music? An Introduction to the Philosophy of Music*, P. Alperson (ed.), pp. 149–63. New York: Haven.

Kivy, P. (1989) *Sound Sentiment*. Philadelphia: Temple University Press.

Kivy, P. (1993) 'Auditor's Emotions: Contention, Concession and Compromise', *Journal of Aesthetics and Art Criticism* 51: 1–12.

Kivy, P. (1994) 'Armistice, But No Surrender: Davies on Kivy', *Journal of Aesthetics and Art Criticism* 52: 236–7.

Kivy, P. (2002) *Introduction to a Philosophy of Music*. Oxford: Clarendon.

Kivy, P. (2006) 'Critical Study: Deeper than Emotion', *British Journal of Aesthetics* 46: 287–311.

Klein, K.J.K. & Hodges, S.D. (2001) 'Gender Differences, Motivation and Empathic Accuracy: When it Pays to Understand', *Personality and Social Psychology Bulletin* 27: 720–30.

Klein, S.B. & Loftus, J. (2002) 'Memory and Temporal Experience: The Effects of Episodic Memory Loss on an Amnesic Patient's Ability to Remember the Past and Imagine the Future', *Social Cognition* 20: 353–79.

Kluger, R. (1975) *Simple Justice: The History of Brown v. Board of Education and Black. America's Struggle for Equality*. New York: Vintage Books.

Knights, L.C. (1964) *Explorations: Essays in Criticism Mainly on Literature of 17th Century*. Harmondsworth, UK: Penguin.

Knoblich, G., Seigerschmidt, E., Flach, R., & Prinz, W. (2002) 'Authorship Effects in the Prediction of Handwriting Strokes: Evidence for Action Simulation During Action Perception', *Quarterly Journal of Experimental Psychology A* 55(3): 1027–46.

Koelsch, S., Fritz, T., von Crammon, D. Y., Müller, K., & Frederici, A.D. (2006) 'Investigating Emotion with Music: An fMRI Study', *Human Brain Mapping* 27(3): 239–50.

Kögler, H. & Stueber, K. (2000) (eds) *Empathy and Agency: the Problem of Understanding in the Human Sciences*. Boulder, CO: Westview Press.

Kohlberg, L. (1976) 'Moral Stages and Moralization: The Cognitive-Developmental Approach'. In: *Moral Development and Behavior*, T. Lickona (ed.), pp. 31–53. New York: Holt, Rinehart & Winston.

Kohler, E., Keysers, C., Umiltà, M.A., Fogassi, L., Gallese, V., & Rizzolatti, G. (2002) 'Hearing Sounds, Understanding Actions: Action Representation in Mirror Neurons', *Science* 297: 846–8.

Kohut, H. (1971) *The Analysis of the Self*. New York: International Universities Press.

Kohut, H. (1975) 'The Psychoanalyst in the Community of Scholars', *Annual of Psychoanalysis* 3: 341–70.

Kohut, H. (1977) *The Restoration of the Self*. New York: International Universities Press.

Kohut, H. (1982) 'Introspection, Empathy, and the Semicircle of Mental Health', *International Journal of Psycho-Analysis* 63: 395–407.

Kohut, H. (1984) *How Does Analysis Cure?* Chicago: University of Chicago Press.

Kolnai, A. (1978) *Ethics, Value and Reality*. Indianapolis: Hackett.

Kondo, H., Saleem, K.S., & Price, J.L. (2005) 'Differential Connections of the Perirhinal and Parahippocampal Cortex with the Orbital and Medial Prefrontal Networks in Macaque Monkeys', *Journal of Comparative Neurology* 493: 479–509.

Kosslyn, S.M. (2007) 'On the Evolution of Human Motivation: The Role of Social Prosthetic Systems'. In: *Evolutionary Cognitive Neuroscience*, S. Platek, J.P. Keenan, & T. Shackelford (eds), pp. 541–54. Cambridge: MIT Press.

Kripke, S.A. (1980) *Naming and Necessity*. Cambridge: Harvard University Press.

Krumhansl, C.L. (1997) 'An Exploratory Study of Musical Emotions and Psychophysiology', *Canadian Journal of Experimental Psychology* 51: 336–52.

Kurtz, R.R. & Grummon, D.L. (1972) 'Different Approaches to the Measurement of Therapist Empathy and their Relationship to Therapy Outcomes', *Journal of Consulting and Clinical Psychology* 39(1): 106–15.

Lakoff, G. (2002) *Moral Politics: How Liberals and Conservatives Think* (second edition). Chicago: University of Chicago Press.

Lakoff, G. (2004) *Don't Think of an Elephant: Know Your Values and Frame the Debate*. White River Junction, VT: Chelsea Green Publications.

Lamarque, P. (1996) *Fictional Points of View*. Ithaca, NY: Cornell University Press.

Lamarque, P. (2001) 'Literature'. In: *The Routledge Companion to Aesthetics*, B. Gaut & D.M. Lopes (eds), pp. 449–61. London: Routledge.

Lamb, R.B. (1974) 'Adam Smith's System: Sympathy not Self-Interest', *Journal of the History of Ideas* 35(4): 671–82.

Lamb, R. (1987) 'Objectless Emotions', *Philosophy and Phenomenological Research* 48: 107–17.

Lamm, C., Batson, C.D., & Decety, J. (2007) 'The Neural Substrate of Human Empathy: Effects of Perspective-taking and Cognitive Appraisal', *Journal of Cognitive Neuroscience* 19(1): 42–58.

Lamm, C., Meltzoff, A.N., & Decety, J. (2010) 'How Do We Empathize with Someone Who is Not Like Us? A Functional Magnetic Resonance Imaging Study', *Journal of Cognitive Neuroscience* 22(2): 362–76.

Langfeld, H. (1920) *The Aesthetic Attitude*. New York: Harcourt, Brace and Company.

Laster, K. & O'Malley, P. (1996) 'Sensitive New-age Laws: The Re-assertion of Emotionality in Law', *International Journal of Sociology and Law* 21: 23–4.

Laub, D. (1995) 'Truth and Testimony: The Process and the Struggle'. In: *Trauma: Explorations in Memory*, C. Caruth (ed.), pp. 61–75. Baltimore: Johns Hopkins Press.

Lavenex, P., Suzuki, W.A., & Amaral, D.G. (2002) 'Perirhinal and Parahippocampal Cortices of the Macaque Monkey: Projections to the Neocortex', *Journal of Comparative Neurology* 447: 394–420.

Lazarus, R.S. (1991) *Emotion and Adaptation*. Oxford: Oxford University Press.

Lazarus, R.S., Speisman, J.C., Mordkoff, A.M., & Davison, L.A. (1962) 'A Laboratory Study of Psychological Stress Produced by a Motion Picture Film', *Psychological Monographs* 76(34): 1–35.

Le Doux, J. (1996) *The Emotional Brain*. New York: Simon and Schuster.

Lee, V. (1913) *The Beautiful: An Introduction to Psychological Aesthetics*. Cambridge: Cambridge University Press.

Lee, V. & Anstruther-Thomson, C. (1897) 'Beauty and Ugliness', *Contemporary Review* 72: 544–69 and 669–88.

Lemma, A. (2003) *Introduction to the Practice of Psychoanalytic Psychotherapy*. West Sussex, UK: John Wiley & Sons.

Lennon, R. & Eisenberg, N. (1987) 'Emotional Displays Associated with Preschoolers' Prosocial Behavior', *Child Development* 58(4): 992–1000.

Leonard, J. (2003) 'Not What Happened but Why', review of Susan Sontag, *Regarding the Pain of Others*, in *New York Review of Books* (23 March), 11–12.

Lerner, J., Goldberg, J., & Tetlock, P. (1998) 'Sober Second Thought: The Effects of Accountability, Anger, and Authoritarianism on Attributions of Responsibility', *Personality and Social Psychology Bulletin* 24: 563–74.

Lerner, J.S. & Tiedens, L. (2006) 'Portrait of The Angry Decision Maker: How Appraisal Tendencies Shape Anger's Influence on Cognition', *Journal of Behavioral Decision Making* 19: 115–37.

Lerner, M.J. Ross, M., & Miller, D.T. (2002) *The Justice Motive in Everyday Life*. New York: Cambridge University Press.

Leung, K. & Bond, M.H. (1984) 'The Impact of Cultural Collectivism on Reward Allocation', *Journal of Personality and Social Psychology* 47: 793–804.

Levenson, R.W. & Ruef, A.M. (1997) 'Physiological Aspects of Emotional Knowledge and Rapport'. In: *Empathic Accuracy*, W. Ickes (ed.), pp. 44–72. New York: The Guilford Press.

Levine, L. (1997) 'Reconstructing Memory for Emotions', *Journal of Experimental Psychology: General* 126(2): 165–77.

Levinson, J. (1996) 'Musical Expressiveness'. In his *The Pleasures of Aesthetics*, pp. 90–125. Ithaca, NY: Cornell University Press.

Levinson, J. (2006) 'Musical Expressiveness as Hearability-as-expression'. In: *Contemporary Debates in Aesthetics and the Philosophy of Art*, M. Kieran (ed.), pp. 192–204. Oxford: Blackwell.

Lewis, D. (1988) 'What Experience Teaches'. In: *Mind and Cognition: A Reader*, W. Lycan (ed.), pp. 499–519. Oxford: Basil Blackwell.

Lhermitte, F., Pillon, B., & Serdaru, M.D. (1986) 'Human Autonomy and the Frontal Lobes. Part I: Imitation and Utilization Behavior. A Neuropsychological Study of 75 Patients', *Annals of Neurology* 19(4): 326–34.

Lichtenberg, J.D. (1981) 'The Empathic Mode of Perception and Alternative Vantage Points for Psychoanalytic Work', *Psychoanalytic Inquiry* 1(3): 329–55.

Linden, T. (2008) 'Explaining Civil Society Core Activism in Post-Soviet Latvia', Ph.D. Dissertation, Stockholm University, Sweden.

Linder, D. O. (1996) 'Juror Empathy and Race', *Tennessee Law Review* 63: 887–916.

Lipps, T. (1903a) *Ästhetik*, Teil I. Leipzig, Germany: Leopold Voss Verlag.

Lipps, T. (1903b) 'Empathy, Inward Imitation, and Sense Feelings', In: *Philosophies of Beauty: From Socrates to Robert Bridges being the Sources of Aesthetic Theory*, E.F. Carritt (ed.), pp. 252–6. Oxford: Clarendon Press (1931).

Livingston, A. & Murray, M. (2009) 'Context of Obama's "empathy remark"' *Msnbc.com*. http://firstread.msnbc.msn.com/_news/2009/05/01/4430634-context-of-obamas-empathy-remark

Lopes, D.M. (1996) *Understanding Pictures*. Oxford: Oxford University Press.

Lopes, D.M. (2003) 'Pictures and the Representational Mind', *The Monist* 86(4): 35–52.

Lopes, D.M. (2005) *Sight and Sensibility: Evaluating Pictures*, Oxford: Oxford University Press.

Lotze, H. (1856) *Mikrokosmos*, i. Leipzig, Germany: Hirzel.

Lotze, H. (1868) *Geschichte der Aesthetik in Deutschland*. Munich: Cotta.

Lynch, M.P. (1998) *Truth in Context: An Essay on Pluralism and Objectivity*. Cambridge, Mass.: MIT Press.

Lyons, W. (1980) *Emotions*. Cambridge: Cambridge University Press.

McCall Smith, Alexander (2006) *The Right Attitude to Rain*. New York: Random House.

McFee, G. (2000) *Free Will*. Teddington, UK: Acumen.

McFee, G. (2005) 'The Artistic and the Aesthetic', *British Journal of Aesthetics* 45(4): 368–87.

Macfie, A.L. (1959) 'Adam Smith's Moral Sentiments as foundation for his Wealth of Nations', *Oxford Economic Papers* 11(3): 209–28.

McIntosh, D.N., Reichmann-Decker, A., Winkelman, P., & Wilbarger, J.L. (2006) 'When the Social Mirror Breaks: Deficits in Automatic, but not Voluntary, Mimicry of Emotional Facial Expressions in Autism', *Developmental Science* 9: 295–302.

Maddell, G. (2002) *Philosophy, Music and Emotion*. Edinburgh: Edinburgh University Press.

Makkreel, R.A. (1992) *Dilthey: Philosopher of the Human Studies*. Princeton, NJ: Princeton University Press.

Makkreel, R.A. (1996) 'How is Empathy Related to Understanding?'. In: *Issues in Husserl's Ideas II*, T. Nenon & L.Embree (eds), pp. 199–212. The Hague: Kluwer Academic Publishers.

Makkreel, R.A (2000) 'From Simulation to Structural Transposition: A Diltheyan Critique of Empathy and Defense of *Verstehen*'. In: *Empathy and Agency: The Problem of Understanding in the Human Sciences*, Kögler & Stueber (eds), pp. 181–93. Boulder, CO: Westview Press.

Malcolm, J. (2006) 'The Art of Testifying', *The New Yorker* (13 March), p. 70.

Malcolm, N. (1977) 'The Privacy of Experience'. In his *Thought and Knowledge*, pp. 104–32. Ithaca, NY: Cornell University Press.

Malle, B.F. (2004) *How the Mind Explains Behavior: Folk Explanations, Meaning, and Social Interaction*. Cambridge, MA: The MIT Press.

Malle, B.F. (2005). 'Three Puzzles of Mindreading'. In *Other Minds: How Humans Bridge the Divide between Self and Others*, B. Malle & S.D. Hodges (eds), pp. 26–43. New York: The Guilford Press.

Mallgrave, H.F. & Ikonomou, E. (1994) (eds) *Empathy, Form, and Space: Problems in German Aesthetics 1873–1893*. Santa Monica, CA: Getty Center for the History of Art and Humanities.

Maroney, T.A. (2006) 'Law and Emotion: A Proposed Taxonomy of an Emerging Field', *Law and Human Behavior* 30: 119–42.

Martin, A., Wiggs, C.L., Ungerleider, L.G., & Haxby, J.V. (1996) 'Neural Correlates of Category-Specific Knowledge', *Nature* 379: 649–52.

Martin, G.B. & Clark, R.D. (1987) 'Distress Crying in Neonates: Species and Peer Specificity', *Developmental Psychology* 18: 3–9.

Massumi, B. (1996) 'The Autonomy of Affect'. In: *Deleuze: A Critical Reader*, P. Patton (ed.), pp. 217–39. Oxford: Blackwell.

Maynard, P. (1997a) *The Engine of Visualization: Thinking through Photography*. Ithaca, NY: Cornell University Press.

Maynard, P. (1997b) 'Drawing Distinctions I: The First Projects', *Philosophical Topics* 25(1): 231–53.

Mehrabian, A. & Epstein, N. (1972) 'A Measure of Emotional Empathy', *Journal of Personality* 40 (4): 525–43.

Meltzoff, A.N. (1995) 'Understanding the Intentions of Others: Re-enactment of Intended Acts by 18-month-old Children', *Developmental Psychology* 31: 838–50.

Meltzoff, A.N. (2007a) ' "Like Me": A Foundation for Social Cognition', *Developmental Science* 10: 126–34.

Meltzoff, A.N. (2007b) 'The "Like Me" Framework for Recognizing and Becoming an Intentional Agent', *Acta Psychologica* 124: 26–43.

Meltzoff, A.N. & Brooks, R. (2008) 'Self-experience as a Mechanism for Learning About Others: A Training Study in Social Cognition', *Developmental Psychology* 44: 1257–65.

Meltzoff, A.N. & Decety, J. (2003) 'What Imitation Tells Us About Social Cognition: A Rapprochement Between Developmental Psychology and Cognitive Neuroscience', *The Philosophical Transactions of the Royal Society, London* 358: 491–500.

Meltzoff, A.N. & Gopnik, A. (1993) 'The Role of Imitation in Understanding Persons and Developing a Theory of Mind. In: *Understanding Other Minds: Perspectives from Autism*, S. Baron-Cohen, H. Tager-Flusberg, & D. Cohen (eds). pp. 335–66. New York: Oxford University Press.

Meltzoff, A.N., Kuhl, P.K., Movellan, J., & Sejnowski, T.J. (2009) 'Foundations for a New Science of Learning', *Science* 325: 284–8.

Meltzoff, A.N. & Moore, M.K. (1977) 'Imitation of Facial and Manual Gestures by Human Neonates', *Science* 198: 75–8.

Meltzoff, A.N. & Moore, M.K. (1983) 'Newborn Infants Imitate Adult Facial Gestures', *Child Development* 54: 702–9.

Meltzoff, A.N. & Moore, M.K. (1994) 'Imitation, Memory, and the Representation of Persons', *Infant Behavior & Development* 17: 83–99.

Meltzoff, A.N. & Moore, M.K. (1995) 'Infants' Understanding of People and Things: From Body Imitation to Folk Psychology'. In: *The Body and the Self*, J.L. Bermúdez, A.J. Marcel, & N. Eilan (eds), pp. 43–69. Cambridge: MIT Press.

Meltzoff, A.N. & Moore, M. K. (1997) 'Explaining facial imitation: A theoretical model', *Early Development and Parenting* 6: 179–92.

Meltzoff, A.N. & Moore, M.K. (1998) 'Infant Intersubjectivity: Broadening the Dialogue to Include Imitation, Identity and Intention'. In: *Intersubjective Communication and Emotion in Early Ontogeny*, S. Bråten (ed.), pp. 47–62. New York: Cambridge University Press.

Mercer, P. (1972) *Sympathy and Ethics: a Study of the Relationship between Sympathy and Morality with Special Reference to Hume's Treatise*. Oxford: Clarendon Press.

Meskin, A. & J.M. Weinberg (2006) 'Imagine That!'. In: *Contemporary Discussions in Aesthetics and the Philosophy of Art*, M. Kieran (ed.), pp. 222–35. Oxford: Blackwell.

Mikhail, J. (2002) 'Aspects of the Theory of Moral Cognition: Investigating Intuitive Knowledge of the Prohibition of Intentional Battery and the Principle of Double Effect', Georgetown University Law Center Public Law and Legal Theory Working Paper No. 762385.

Miles, J. (2003) Other Bodies and Other Minds in Edith Stein. In: *Husserl and Stein* W. Sweet & R. Feist (eds), pp. 119–26. Washington, D.C.: Council for Research in Values and Philosophy.

Milinski, M. (2003) 'Perfumes'. In: *Evolutionary Aesthetics*, E. Voland & K. Grammer (eds), pp. 325–39. Berlin: Springer Verlag.

Mill, John S. (1861/1979) *Utilitarianism*. In: *American State Papers*, R.M.Hutchins (ed.) 43: 445–76. Chicago: University of Chicago Press.

Millar, A. (2000) 'The Scope of Perceptual Knowledge', *Philosophy* 75: 73–88.

Milliman, R.E. (1982) 'Using Background Music to Affect the Behavior of Supermarket Shoppers', *Journal of Marketing* 46(3): 86–91.

Milliman, R.E. (1986) 'The Influence of Background Music on the Behavior of Restaurant Patrons', *Journal of Consumer Research* 13(2): 286–9.

Mitchell, J.P. (2008) 'Activity in the Right Temporo-Parietal Junction is not Selective for Theory of Mind', *Cerebral Cortex* (18): 262–71.

Mitchell, W. (1907) *Structure and Growth of the Mind*. London: Methuen.

Mohedano-Moriano, A., Pro-Sistiaga, P., Arroyo-Jimenez, M.M., Artacho-Pérula, E., Insausti, A.M., Marcos, P., Cebada-Sánchez, S., Martínez-Ruiz, J., Muñoz, M., Blaizot, X., Martinez-Marcos, A., Amaral, D.G., & Insausti, R. (2007) 'Topographical and Laminar Distribution of Cortical Input to the Monkey Entorhinal Cortex', *Journal of Anatomy* 211: 250–60.

Mondero, B. (2006) "Proprioception as an Aesthetic Sense', *The Journal of Aesthetics and Art Criticism* 64: 231–42.

Montag, C., Gallinat, J. & Heinz, A. (2008) 'Theodor Lipps and the Concept of Empathy: 1851–1914'. *The American journal of psychiatry* 165(10): 1261.

Montaigne, Michel de (1993) *Essays*. Harmondsworth, UK: Penguin.

Montmarquet, J. (1993) *Epistemic Virtue and Doxastic Responsibility*. Lanham, MD: Rowman and Littlefield.

Moore, A. (2006) 'Maxims and Thick Ethical Concepts', *Ratio* 19(2): 129–47.

Moore, B.S. (1990) 'The Origins and Development of Empathy', *Motivation and Emotion* 14(2): 75–80.

Moran, D. (2000) *Introduction to Phenomenology*. London and New York: Routledge.

Moran, D. (2004) 'The Problem of Empathy: Lipps, Scheler, Husserl and Stein'. In: *Amor Amicitiae: On the Love that is Friendship: Essays in Medieval Thought and Beyond in Honor of the Rev. Professor James McEvoy*, T.A.F. Kelly & P.W. Rosemann (eds), pp. 269–312. Leuven/Paris/Dudley, MA: Peeters.

Moran, R. (2001) *Authority and Estrangement: An Essay on Self-knowledge*. Princeton: Princeton University Press.

More, E.S. & Milligan, M.A. (1994) (eds) *The Empathic Practitioner: Empathy, Gender, and Medicine*. Piscataway, NJ: Rutgers University Press.

Morrison, I., Lloyd, D., di Pellegrino, G., & Roberts, N. (2004) 'Vicarious Responses to Pain in Anterior Cingulate Cortex: Is Empathy a Multisensory Issue?', *Cognitive, Affective, Behavioral Neuroscience* 4: 270–8.

Morrow, G.R. (1923) 'The Significance of the Doctrine of Sympathy in Hume and Adam Smith', *The Philosophical Review* 32(1): 60–78.

Morton, A. (1990) *Disasters and Dilemmas*. Oxford: Blackwell.

Morton, A. (2004) *On Evil*. London: Routledge.

Morton, A. (2006) 'Imagination and Misimagination'. In: *The Architecture of the Imagination*, S. Nichols (ed.), pp. 57–72. Oxford: Oxford University Press.

Moser, C. (1972) *Columbia Essays on Modern Writers*. New York: Columbia University Press, 4.

Mukamel, R., Ekstrom, A.D., Kaplan, J., Iacoboni, M., & Fried, I. (2007) 'Mirror Properties of Single Cells in Human Medial Frontal Cortex', presented on November 4, 2007 at the Society for Neuroscience in San Diego, California.

Muñoz, J.E. (2000) 'Feeling Brown: Ethnicity and Affect in Ricardo Bracho's *The Sweetest Hangover (and other STD's)*', *Theater Journal* 52: 67–79.

Murata, A., Fadiga, L., Fogassi, L., Gallese, V., Raos, V., & Rizzolatti, G. (1997) 'Object Representation in the Ventral Premotor Cortex (Area F5) of the Monkey', *Journal of Neurophysiology* 78: 2226–30.

Murdoch, I. (1998) *Existentialists and Mystics*. London: Chatto and Windus.

Nash, J.M. (2007) 'The Gift of Mimicry', *Time* (29 January): 108–10, 113.

Neill, A. (1993) 'Fiction and the Emotions', *American Philosophical Quarterly* 30: 1–13.

Neuberg, S.L., Cialdini, R.B., Brown, S.L., Luce, C., Sagarin, B.J., & Lewis, B.P. (1997) 'Does Empathy Lead to Anything More than Superficial Helping? Comment on Batson et al (1997)', *Journal of Personality and Social Psychology* 73: 510–16.

Neumann, R. & Strack, F. (2000) ' "Mood Contagion": The Automatic Transfer of Mood Between Persons', *Journal of Personality and Social Psychology* 79: 211–23.

Nichols, S. (2004) *Sentimental Rules*. Oxford: Oxford University Press.

Nichols, S. & Stich, S.P. (2003) *Mindreading: An Integrated Account of Pretence, Self-Awareness, and Understanding Other Minds*. Oxford: Clarendon.

Nichols, S., Stich, S.P., Leslie, A., & Klein, D. (1996) 'Varieties of Off-Line Simulation'. In: *Theories of Theories of Mind*, P. Carruthers & P.K. Smith (eds), pp. 39-74. Cambridge: Cambridge University Press.

Niedenthal, P.M., Brauer, M., Halberstadt, J., & Innes-Ker, A. (2001) 'When Did Her Smile Drop? Facial Mimicry and the Influences of Emotional State on the Detection of Change in Emotional Expression', *Cognition and Emotion* 15: 853–64.

Nisbett, R.E. & Ross, L. (1991) *The Person and the Situation*. New York: McGraw-Hill.

Noddings, N. (1984) *Caring: a Feminine Approach to Ethics and Moral Education*. Berkeley, CA: University of California Press.

North, A.C. & Hargreaves, D.J. (1997), 'Music and Consumer Behaviour'. In: *The Social Psychology of Music*, D.J. Hargreaves & A.C. North (eds), pp. 268–89. Oxford: Oxford University Press.

Novalis (Georg Philipp Friedrick von Hardenberg) (1802/1960) 'Die Lehrlinge zu Sais'. In: *Novalis Schriften*, volume 1 (second edition), Paul Kluckhohn & Richard Samuel (eds), pp. 79–110. Stuttgart, Kohlhammer.

Nozick, R. (1981) *Philosophical Explanations*. Cambridge: Harvard University Press.

Nussbaum, M. (2001) *Upheavals of Thought: The Intelligence of Emotions*. Cambridge: Cambridge University Press.

Oatley, K. & Jenkins, J.M. (1996) *Understanding Emotions*. Oxford: Blackwell.

Odling-Smee, F.J., Laland, K.N., & Feldman, M.W. (2003) *Niche Construction: The Neglected Process in Evolution*. Princeton: Princeton University Press.

Okuda, J., Fujii, T., Ohtake, H., Tsukiura, T., Tanji, K., Susuki, K., Kawashima, R., Fukuda, H., Itoh, M., & Yamadori, A. (2003) 'Thinking of the Future and the Past: The Roles of the Frontal Pole and the Medial Temporal Lobes', *NeuroImage* 19(4): 1369–80.

Okun, M.A., Shepard, S.A. & Eisenberg, N. (2000) 'The Relations of Emotionality and Regulation to Dispositional Empathy-Related Responding Among Volunteers-in-Training', *Personality and Individual Differences* 28(2): 367–82.

Oliner, S.P. & Oliner, P.M. (1988) *The Altruistic Personality*. New York: The Free Press.

Oliver, K. (2001) *Witnessing: Beyond Recognition*. Minneapolis: University of Minnesota Press.

Oliver, K. (2004) *The Colonization of Psychic Space: A Psychoanalytic Social Theory Of Oppression*. Minneapolis: The University of Minnesota Press.

Olson, G. (2008) 'Radical Empathy: From Mirror Neurons to Moral Neuropolitics', unpublished manuscript, Moravian College, Political Science Department, Bethlehem, PA.

Orange, D. (1995) *Emotional Understanding*. New York: Guilford Press.

Ornstein, P.H. & Ornstein, A. (1995) 'Some Distinguishing Features of Heinz Kohut's Self Psychology'. *Psychoanalytic Dialogues* 5(3): 385–91.

Palágyi, M. (1924) *Naturphilosophische Vorlesungen über die Grundprobleme des Bewusstseins und des Lebens* (second edition). Leipzig, Germany: Johann Ambrosius Barth.

Palágyi, M. (1925) *Wahrnehmungslehre*. Leipzig, Germany: Johann Ambrosius Barth.

Pearlman, L.A. & MacIan, P.S. (1995) 'Vicarious Traumatization among Trauma Therapists: Empirical Findings on Self-Care: Traumatic Stress Points', *News for the International Society for Traumatic Stress Studies* 7(3): 5.

Pearlman, L.A. & Saakvitne, K.W. (1995) *Trauma and the Therapist*. New York: W. W. Norton.

Pedersen, R. (2010). Empathy Development in Medical Education—A Critical Review, *Medical Teacher* 32(7): 593–600.

Pellegrino, G. di, Fadiga, L., Fogassi, L., Gallese, V., & Rizzolatti, G. (1992) 'Understanding Motor Events: A Neurophysiological Study', *Experimental Brain Research* 91: 176–80.

Pérez-Reverte, A. (2002) *The Queen of the South*, A. Hurley (trans). Harmondsworth, UK: Penguin.

Perner, J. & Kuhberger, A. (2005) 'Mental Simulation: Royal Road to Other Minds?' In: *Other Minds: How Humans Bridge the Divide between Self and Others*, B. Malle & S.D. Hodges (eds), pp. 174–89. New York: The Guilford Press.

Perner, J. & Ruffman, T. (1995) 'Episodic Memory and Autonoetic Consciousness: Developmental Evidence and a Theory of Childhood Amnesia', *Journal of Experimental Child Psychology* 59: 516–48.

Peterson, J.M. & Cary, J. (2002), 'Organizational Justice, Change Anxiety, and Acceptance of Downsizing', *Motivation and Emotion* 26: 83–103.

Pfeifer, J.H. & Dapretto, M. (2009) ' "Mirror, Mirror, in My Mind": Empathy, Interpersonal Competence, and the Mirror Neuron System'. In: *The Social Neuroscience of Empathy*, J. Decety & W. Ickes (eds), pp. 183–97. Cambridge, MA: The MIT Press.

Pfeifer, J.H., Iacoboni, M., Mazziotta, J.C., & Dapretto, M. (2008) 'Mirroring Others' Emotions Relates to Empathy and Interpersonal Competence in Children', *NeuroImage* 39: 2076–85.

Piaget, J. (1954) *The Construction of Reality in the Child*. M. Cook (trans.). New York: Basic Books.

Piaget, J. (1962) *Play, Dreams and Imitation in Childhood*. C. Attegno & F.M. Hodgson (trans.). New York: Norton.

Pigman, G.W. (1995) 'Freud and the History of Empathy', *The International Journal of Psycho-Analysis* 76 (Pt 2): 237–56.

Pillsbury, S. H. (1999), 'Harlan, Holmes, and the Passions of Justice'. In: *The Passions of Law*, S. Bandes (ed.), pp. 330–62. New York: New York University Press.

Pineda, J. (2009a) (ed.) *Mirror Neuron Systems*. New York: Humana Press.

Pineda, J. (2009b) 'Preface'. In: Pineda (2009a), pp v–viii. New York: Humana Press.

Pineda, J.A. & Hecht, E. (2009) 'Mirroring and Mu Rhythm Involvement in Social Cognition: Are There Dissociable Subcomponents of Theory of Mind?', *Biological Psychology* 80(3): 306–14.

Pinker, S. (1999) *How the Mind Works*. London: Penguin.

Plantinga, C. (1999) 'The Scene of Empathy and the Human Face on Film'. In: *Passionate Views: Film, Cognition, and Emotion*, C. Plantinga & G.M. Smith (eds), pp. 239–55. Baltimore: Johns Hopkins University Press.

Plutchik, R. (1980) 'A General Psychoevolutionary Theory of Emotions'. In: *Emotion: Theory, Research, and Experience. Vol 1. Theories of Emotion*, R. Plutchik & H. Hellerman (eds), pp. 3–33. New York: Academic Press.

Plutchik, R. (1987) 'Evolutionary Bases of Empathy'. In: *Empathy and its Development*, N. Eisenberg & J. Strayer (eds), pp. 38–46. Cambridge: Cambridge University Press.

Posner, M.I. & Rothbart, M.K. (2000) 'Developing Mechanisms of Self-regulation', *Development and Psychopathology* 12: 427–41.

Posner, R.A. (1999) 'Emotion vs. Emotionalism in Law'. In: *The Passions of Law*, S. Bandes (ed.), pp. 309–29. New York: New York University Press.

Preston, S.D. & de Waal, F.B.M. (2002) 'Empathy: Its Ultimate and Proximate Bases', *Behavioral and Brain Sciences* 25: 1–72.

Prinz, J.J. (2004) *Gut Reactions: A Perceptual Theory of Emotion*. Oxford: Oxford University Press.

Prinz, J.J. (2007) *The Emotional Construction of Morals*. Oxford: Oxford University Press.

Prinz, W. (1997) 'Perception and Action Planning', *European Journal of Cognitive Psychology* 9: 129–54.

Prinz, W. (2002) 'Experimental Approaches to Imitation'. In: *The Imitative Mind: Development, Evolution, and Brain Cases*, A.N. Meltzoff & W. Prinz (eds), pp. 143–62. Cambridge: Cambridge Uuniversity Press,

Prinz, W. (2005) 'An ideomotor approach to imitation'. In: *Perspectives on Imitation: From Neuroscience to Social Science*, vol. 1, S. Hurley & N. Chater (eds), pp. 141–56. Cambridge, MA: MIT Press.

Provine, R.R. (1996) 'Laughter', *American Scientist* 84 (January-February), 38–45.

Pulvermüller, F., Hauk, O., Nikulin, V., & Ilmoniemi, R. (2005) 'Functional Links Between Motor and Language Systems', *European Journal of Neuroscience* 21(3): 793–7.

Putnam, H. (1988) *Representation and Reality*. Cambridge: Bradford/MIT.

Rachman, A.W. (1988) 'The Rule of Empathy: Sandor Ferenczi's Pioneering Contributions to the Empathic Method in Psychoanalysis', *The Journal of the American Academy of Psychoanalysis* 16(1): 1–27.

Radford, C. (1975) 'How Can We be Moved by the Fate of Anna Karenina?', *Proceedings of the Aristotelian Society* 49 (Supplement): 67–80.

Radford, C. (1989) 'Emotions and Music: A Reply to the Cognitivists', *Journal of Aesthetics and Art Criticism* 47: 69–76.

Radford, C. (1991) 'Muddy Waters', *Journal of Aesthetics and Art Criticism* 49: 247–52.

Radke-Yarrow, M. & Zahn-Waxler, C. (1984) 'Roots, Motives, and Patterns in Children's Prosocial Behavior'. In: *The Development and Maintenance of Prosocial Behavior: International Perspectives on Positive Morality*, E. Staub, K.D. Bartal, J. Karylowski, & J. Raykowski (eds), pp. 81–99. New York: Plenum Press.

Raine, A. (1996) 'Autonomic Nervous System Factors Underlying Disinhibited, Antisocial, and Violent Behavior: Biosocial Perspectives and Treatment Implications', *Annals of the New York Academy of Sciences* 794: 46–59.

Raine, A., Venables, P., Mednick, S., & Sarnoff, A. (1997) 'Low Resting Heart Rate at Age 3 Years Predisposes to Aggression at Age 11 Years: Evidence from the Mauritius Child Health Project', *Journal of the American Academy of Child & Adolescent Psychiatry* 36: 1457–64.

Ramachandran, V.S. (2000) 'Mirror Neurons and Imitation Learning as the Driving Force Behind "the Great Leap Forward' in Human Evolution. *Edge Website article* http://www.edge.org/3rd_culture/ramachandran/ramachandran_p1.html.

Ramachandran, V.S. & Oberman, L.M. (2006) 'Broken Mirrors: a Theory of Autism', *Scientific American* (November): 62–9.

Raposo, A., Moss, H., Stamatakis, A. & Tyler. L. (2009) 'Modulation of Motor and Premotor Cortices by Actions, Action Words and Action Sentences' *Neuropsychologia* 47: 388–96

Ratcliffe, M. (2008) *Feelings of Being: Phenomenology, Psychiatry, and the Sense of Reality*. Oxford: Oxford University Press.

Ravenscroft, I. (1998) 'What Is It Like to Be Someone Else? Simulation and Empathy', *Ratio* 11 (2): 170–85.

Regan, D. (1979) 'Rewriting Roe v. Wade', *Michigan Law Review* 77: 1569–617.

Reichmann, F.F. (1950) *Principles of Intensive Psychotherapy*. Chicago: University of Chicago Press.

Reik, T. (1948). *Listening with the Third Ear*. New York: Farrar, Straus, & Giroux.

Renzi, E. de, Cavalleri, F., & Facchini, S. (1996) 'Imitation and Utilisation Behaviour', *Journal of Neurology, Neurosurgery, and Psychiatry* 61: 396–400.

Repacholi, B.M. & Meltzoff, A.N. (2007) 'Emotional Eavesdropping: Infants Selectively Respond to Indirect Emotional Signals', *Child Development* 78: 503–21.

Repacholi, B.M., Meltzoff, A.N., & Olsen, B. (2008) 'Infants' Understanding of the Link Between Visual Perception and Emotion: "If She Can't See Me Doing it, She Won't Get Angry"', *Developmental Psychology* 44: 561–74.

Rich, W.J. (2005) 'Betrayal of the Children with Dolls: The Broken Promise of Constitutional Protection for Victims of Race Discrimination', *Cornell Law Review* 90(2): 419–42.

Richardson, H. (1994) *Practical Reasoning about Final Ends*. Cambridge: Cambridge University Press.

Richell, R.A., Mitchell, D.G.V., Newman, C., Leonard, A., Baron-Cohen, S., & Blair, R.J.R. (2003) 'Theory of Mind and Psychopathy: Can Psychopathic Individuals Read the "Language of the Eyes"?', *Neuropsychologia* 41(5): 523–6.

Ripp, V. (1980) *Turgenev's Russia from "Notes of a Hunter" to "Fathers and Sons"*. Ithaca, NY: Cornell University Press.

Rizzolatti, G., Camarda, R., Fogassi, L., Gentilucci, M., Luppino, G., & Matelli, M. (1988) 'Functional Organization of Inferior Area 6 in the Macaque Monkey. II. Area F5 and the Control of Distal Movements' *Experimental Brain Research* 71: 491–507.

Rizzolatti, G., Fadiga, L., Gallese, V., & Fogassi, L. (1996) 'Premotor Cortex and the Recognition of Motor Actions', *Cognitive Brain Research* 3: 131–41.

Rizzolatti, G., Fadiga, L., Matelli, M., Bettinardi, V., Perani, E., Fasio, D., & Fasio, S. (1996) 'Localization of Grasp Representations by PET Observation Versus Execution', *Experiment Brain Opinion* 111: 246–52.

Rizzolatti, G., Fogassi, L., & Gallese, V. (2001) 'Neurophysiological Mechanisms Underlying the Understanding and the Imitation of Action', *Nature Review Neuroscience* 2: 661–70.

Rizzolatti, G. & Luppino, G. (2001), 'The Cortical Motor System', *Neuron* 31: 889–901.

Rizzolatti, G. & Sinigaglia, C. (2008) *Mirrors in the Brain: How Our Minds Share Actions, Emotions, and Experience*. New York: Oxford University Press.

Roberts, R.C. (1987) 'Will Power and the Virtues'.In: *The Virtues: Contemporary Essays on Moral Character*, R. Kruschwitz & R. Roberts (eds), pp. 121-36. Belmont, CA: Wadsworth Publishing Company.

Roberts, W. & Strayer, J. (1996) 'Empathy, Emotional Expressiveness, and Prosocial Behavior', *Child Development* 67(2): 449–70.

Robinson, J. (1994) 'The Expression and Arousal of Emotion in Music', *Journal of Aesthetics and Art Criticism* 52: 13–22.

Robinson, J. (2005) *Deeper than Reason: Emotion and its Role in Literature, Music and Art*. Oxford: Clarendon.

Rochat, P. & Striano, T. (2000) 'Perceived Self in Infancy', *Infant Behavior & Development* 23: 513–30.

Rogers, C.R. (1957) 'The Necessary and Sufficient Conditions of Therapeutic Personality Change', *Journal of Consulting and Clinical Psychology* 22: 95–103.

Rogers, C.R. (1959) 'A Theory of Therapy, Personality, and Interpersonal Relationships, As Developed in the Client-Centered Framework'. In: *Psychology: A Study of a Science*, Vol. 3: *Formulations of the Person and the Social Context*, S. Koch (ed.), pp. 184–256. New York: McGraw Hill.

Rogers, C.R. (1961) *On Becoming a Person*. London: Constable.

Rogers, C.R. (1975) 'Empathic: An Unappreciated Way of Being', *The Counseling Psychologist* 5 (2): 2–10.

Rogers, S.J. (1999) 'An Examination of the Imitation Deficit in Autism: The Roles of Imitation and Executive Function'. In: *Imitation in Infancy*, J. Nadel & G. Butterworth (eds), pp. 254–83. Cambridge: Cambridge University Press.

Rozin, P., Lowery, L., Imada, S., & Haidt, J. (1999) 'The CAD Triad Hypothesis: A Mapping Between Three Moral Emotions (Contempt, Anger, Disgust) and Three Moral Codes (Community, Autonomy, Divinity)', *Journal of Personality and Social Psychology* 76: 574–86.

Ruby, P. & Decety, J. (2001) 'Effect of Subjective Perspective Taking During Simulation of Action: A PET Investigation of Agency', *Nature Neuroscience* 4: 546–50.

Ruby, P. & Decety, J. (2004) 'How Would You Feel Versus How Do You Think She Would Feel? A Neuroimaging Study of Perspective-taking with Social Emotions', *Journal of Cognitive Neuroscience* 16: 988–99.

Ruddick, S. (1989) *Maternal Thinking: Toward a Politics of Peace*. Boston, MA: Beacon Press.

Ryle, G. (1949) *The Concept of Mind* (2002 Edition). Chicago: University of Chicago Press.

Safire, W. (2006) Magazine Section, *New York Times* (30 April), p. 30.

Sagi, A. & Hoffman, M.L. (1976) 'Empathic Distress in the Newborn', *Developmental Psychology* 12(2): 175–6.

Salgado, S. (2004) *Sahel: The End of the Road*. Berkeley: University of California Press.

Sandweiss, M.A. (2004) 'Death on the Front Page', *The New York Times* (4 April).

Sante, L. (2007) 'On the Road Again', review of Howard Cunnell (ed.), *On the Road: The Original Scroll*, in *New York Times Book Review* (29 August), 12–13.

Sawicki, M. (1997) 'Empathy Before and After Husserl', *Philosophy Today* 41: 123–7.

Sawyier, F.H. (1975) 'A Conceptual Analysis of Empathy', *Annual of Psychoanalysis* 3: 37–47.

Saxe, R. (2006) 'Uniquely Human Social Cognition', *Current Opinion in Neurobiology* 16: 235–9.

Saxe, R. (2009) 'The Neural Evidence for Simulation is Weaker Than I Think You Think It Is', *Philosophical Studies* 144(3): 447–56.

Saxe, R. & Kanwisher, N. (2003) 'People Thinking about Thinking People: The Role of the Temporo-Parietal Junction in Theory of Mind', *NeuroImage* 19: 1835–42.

Saxe, R. & Powell, L.J. (2006) 'It's the Thought that Counts: Specific Brain Regions for One Component of Theory of Mind', *Psychological Science* 17(8): 692–9.

Schacter, D.L. & Addis, D.R. (2007) 'The Cognitive Neuroscience of Constructive Memory: Remembering the Past and Imagining the Future', *Philosophical Transactions of the Royal Society of London, Series B: Biological Sciences* 362: 773–86.

Schacter, D.L. & Addis, D.R. (2009) 'On the Nature of Medial Temporal Lobe Contributions to the Constructive Simulation of Future Events', *Philosophical Transactions of the Royal Society*, B 364: 1245–53.

Schacter, D.L., Addis, D.R., & Buckner, R.L. (2007), 'Remembering the Past to Imagine the Future: The Prospective Brain', *Nature Reviews Neuroscience* 8: 657–61.

Schacter, D.L., Addis, D.R. & Buckner, R.L. (2008) 'Episodic Simulation of Future Events', *Annals of the New York Academy of Science* 1124: 39–60.

Schachter, S. & Singer, J.E. (1962) 'Cognitive, Social, and Physiological Determinants of Emotional States', *Psychological Review* 69: 379–99.

Schapiro, Leonard B. (1979) *Turgenev: His Life and Times*. Oxford: Oxford University Press.

Scheler, M. (1970/1979) *The Nature of Sympathy*. London: Routledge & Kegan Paul.

Scheper-Hughes, N. (2003) *Migrations: The Work of Sebastiao Salgado*. Berkeley: Townsend Center Publishing.

Schmid Mast, M.S. & Ickes, W. (2007) 'Empathic Accuracy: Measurement and Potential Clinical Applications'. In: *Empathy and Mental Illness*, T.F.D Farrow & W.R.Woodruff (eds), pp. 408–27. Cambridge: Cambridge University Press.

Schmitt, C. (1996) *The Concept of the Political*. G. Schwab (trans.). Chicago: University of Chicago Press.

Schuhmann, K. & Smith, B. (1987) 'Adolf Reinach: An Intellectual Biography'. In: *Speech Act and Sachverhalt: Reinach and the Foundations of Realist Phenomenology*, Mulligan, K. (ed.), pp. 3–27. Dordrecht/Boston/Lancaster: Martinus Nijhoff Publishers.

Schulte-Rüther, M., Markowitsch, H.J., Shah, N.J., Fink, G.R. & Piefke, M. (2008) 'Gender Differences in Brain Networks Supporting Empathy', *NeuroImage* 42(1): 393–403.

Schulz, Armin W. (2011) 'Simulation, Simplicity, and Selection: An Evolutionary Perspective on High-Level Mindreading,' *Philosophical Studies* 152(2): 271–85.

Schwaber, E. (1981) 'Empathy: A Mode of Analytic Listening', *Psychoanalytic Inquiry* 1(3): 357–92.

Scruton, R. (2000) *An Intelligent Person's Guide to Modern Culture*. South Bend, IN: St Augustine's Press.

Searle, J. (2002) 'Twenty-One Years in the Chinese Room'. In: *Views into the Chinese Room*, J. Preston & M. Bishop (eds), pp. 51–69. Oxford: Clarendon.

Sedgwick, E.K. (1995) *Shame and Its Sisters: A Silvan Tompkins Reader*. Durham, NC: Duke University Press.

Shanton, K. (2007) 'Episodic Memory and Mindreading Share a Common Simulational Strategy', unpublished manuscript, Rutgers University, Department of Philosophy.

Shanton, K. & Goldman, A.I. (2010) 'Simulation Theory'. In: *Wiley Interdisciplinary Reviews: Cognitive Science* 1(4): 527–38.

Shapiro, T. (1974) 'The Development and Distortions of Empathy', *The Psychoanalytic Quarterly* 43(1): 4–25.

Shapiro, T. (1984) 'On Neutrality', *Journal of the American Psychoanalytic Association*, 32(2): 269–82.

Shatin, L. (1970) 'Alteration of Mood via Music: A Study of the Vectoring Effect', *Journal of Psychology* 75: 81–6.

Sherman, N. (1998) 'Empathy and Imagination'. In: *Midwest Studies in Philosophy Vol. XXII: Philosophy of Emotions*, P.A. French & H.K. Wettstein (eds), pp. 82–119. Notre Dame: University of Notre Dame Press.

Shevrin, H. (1978) 'Semblance of Feeling in the Imagery of Affect in Empathy, Dreams and Unconscious Processes: A Revision of Freud's Several Affect Theories'. In: *The Human Mind Revisited*, S. Smith (ed.), pp. 263–94. New York: International Universities Press.

Shirtcliff, E.A.,Vitacco, M.J., Graf, A.R., Gostisha, A.J., Merz, J.L. & Zahn-Waxler, C. (2009) 'Neurobiology of Empathy and Callousness: Implications for the Development of Antisocial Behavior', *Behavioral Sciences & the Law* 27(2): 137–71.

Silver, M.A., Portnoy, S., & Peters, J.K. (2004) 'Stress, Burnout, Vicarious Trauma, and Other Emotional Realities in the Lawyer/Client Relationship: A Panel Discussion', *Touro Law Review* 19: 847–73.

Singer, T. (2006) 'The Neuronal Basis and Ontogeny of Empathy and Mind Reading: Review of Literature and Implications for Future Research', *Neuroscience and Biobehavioral Reviews* 30 (6): 855–63.

Singer, T. (2007) 'The Neuronal Basis of Empathy and Fairness'. In: *Empathy and Fairness* (Novartis Foundation), Frith, C. (ed.) pp. 20–30. Chichester, West Sussex UK: Wiley.

Singer, T., Critchley, H.D. & Preuschoff, K. (2009) 'A Common Role of Insula in Feelings, Empathy and Uncertainty', *Trends in Cognitive Sciences* 13(8): 334–40.

Singer, T. & Lamm, C. (2009) 'The Social Neuroscience of Empathy', *Annals of the New York Academy of Sciences* 1156: 81–96.

Singer, T., Seymour, B., O'Doherty, J., Kaube, H., Dolan, R., & Frith, C. (2004) 'Empathy for Pain Involves the Affective but not Sensory Components of Pain', *Science* 303(5661): 1157–62.

Singer, T., Seymour, B., O'Doherty, J., Sephan, K.E., Dolan, R.J., & Frith, C. (2006) 'Empathic Neural Responses are Modulated by the Perceived Fairness of Others', *Nature* 439: 466–9.

Slote, M.A. (2003) 'Sentimentalist Virtue and Moral Judgment: Outline of a Project', *Metaphilosophy* 34(1/2): 131–43.

Slote, M.A. (2004) Moral Sentimentalism', *Ethical Theory and Moral Practice* 7(1): 3–14.

Slote, M.A. (2005) 'Moral Sentimentalism and Moral Psychology'. In: *The Oxford Handbook of Ethical Theory*, D. Copp (ed.), pp. 219–40. Oxford: Oxford University Press.

Slote, M.A. (2007) *The Ethics of Care and Empathy*. London: Routledge.

Slote, M.A. (2010) *Moral Sentimentalism*. Oxford: Oxford University Press.

Smetana, J. & Braeges, J. (1990) 'The Development of Toddlers Moral and Conventional Judgments', *Merrill-Palmer Quarterly* 36: 329–46.

Smith, A. (1759/1976) *The Theory of Moral Sentiments*. D.D. Raphael & A.L. Macfie (eds). Oxford: Clarendon.

Smith, A. (1759/2002) *The Theory of Moral Sentiments*. K. Haakonssen (ed.). Cambridge: Cambridge University Press.

Smith, A.M. (2006) *The Right Attitude to Rain*. New York: Random House.

Smith, D.W. (2007) *Husserl*. London and New York: Routledge.

Smith, M. (1995) *Engaging Characters: Fiction, Emotion and the Cinema*. Oxford: Clarendon.

Smith, M. (1997) 'Imagining From the Inside'. In *Film Theory and Philosophy*, R. Allen & M. Smith (eds), pp. 412–30. Oxford: Clarendon.

Sober, E. & Wilson, D.S. (1998) *Unto Others: the Evolution and Psychology of Unselfish Behavior*. Cambridge, MA: Harvard University Press.

Solomon, R.C. (1976) *The Passions*. New York: Anchor.

Sommers-Flanagan, J. & Sommers-Flanagan, R. (2004) *Counseling and Psychotherapy Theories in Context*. UK: Wiley.

Sonnby-Borgstrom, M., Johnson, P., & Svenson, O. (2003) 'Emotional Empathy as Related to Mimicry Reactions at Different Levels of Information Processing', *Journal of Nonverbal Behavior* 27: 3–23.

Sontag, S. (1977) *On Photography*. New York: Farrar, Strauss, & Giroux.

Sontag, S. (2003) *Regarding the Pain of Others*. New York: Farrar, Strauss, & Giroux.

Sousa, R. de (1990) *The Rationality of Emotions*. Cambridge: MIT Press.

Spence, S.A., Brooks, D.J., Hirsch, S.R., Liddle, P.F., Meehan, J., & Grasby, P.M. (1997) 'A PET Study of Voluntary Movement in Schizophrenic Patients Experiencing Passivity Phenomena (Delusions of Alien Control)', *Brain* 120: 1997–2011.

Spiegelberg, H. & Schuhmann, K. (1994) *The Phenomenological Movement: A Historical Introduction* (third revised edition). Dordrecht: Kluwer Academic Publishers.

Stamenov, M. & Gallese, V. (2002) (eds) *Mirror Neurons and the Evolution of Brain and Language*. Amsterdam: John Benjamin's Publishing Company.

Staub, E. (1978) *Positive Social Behavior and Morality, vol. 1: Personal and Social Influences*. New York: Academic Press.

Staub, E. (1987) 'Commentary on Part I of Empathy and its Development'. In: *Empathy and its Development*, Eisenberg & Strayer (eds), pp. 103–15. New York: Cambridge University Press.

Staub, E., Tursky, B. & Schwartz, G.E. (1971) 'Self-Control and Predictability: Their effects on Reactions to Aversive Stimulation', *Journal of Personality and Social Psychology* 18(2): 157–62.

Stein, E. (1989) *On the Problem of Empathy (The Collected Works of Edith Stein, Volume 3)*, (third revised edition), W. Stein (trans.). Washington, D.C.: ICS Publications.

Stepien, K.A. & Baernstein, A. (2006) 'Educating for Empathy. A Review', *Journal of General Internal Medicine: Official Journal of the Society for Research and Education in Primary Care Internal Medicine* 21(5): 524–30.

Stern, D.N. (2004) *The Present Moment in Psychotherapy and Everyday Life*. New York: Norton.

Stocker, M. (1979) 'Desiring the Bad', *Journal of Philosophy* 76: 738–53.

Stocker, M. & Hegeman, E. (1996) *Valuing Emotions*. Cambridge: Cambridge University Press.

Stone, V.E., & Gerrans, P. (2006) 'What's Domain-Specific About Theory of Mind', *Social Neuroscience* 1(3–4): 309–19.

Stotland, E. (1969) 'Exploratory Investigations of Empathy'. In: *Advances in Experimental Social Psychology*, vol. 4, L. Berkowitz (ed.), pp. 271–314. New York: Academic Press.

Stotland, E., Mathews, K.E., Sherman, S.E., Hansson, R.O. & Richardson, B.Z. (1978) *Empathy, Fantasy, and Helping*. Beverly Hills, CA: Sage Publications.

Stowe, H. (1852/2009) 'Autobiographical Letter to Eliza Cabot Fallon'. In: *Stowe in Her Own Time*, S. Belasco (ed.), pp. 62–9. Iowa City: University of Iowa Press.

Strauss, C. (2004) 'Is Empathy Gendered and, If So, Why? An Approach from Feminist Psychological Anthropology', *Ethos* 32(4): 432–57.

Stueber, K. (2000) 'Understanding Other Minds and the Problem of Rationality'. In: *Empathy and Agency: The Problem of Understanding in the Human Sciences*, H. Kögler & K. Stueber (eds), pp. 144–62. Boulder, CO: Westview Press.

Stueber, K. (2006) *Rediscovering Empathy: Agency, Folk Psychology, and the Human Sciences.* Cambridge, Mass.: MIT Press.

Stueber, K. (2008) 'Empathy', *Stanford Encyclopedia of Philosophy*. http://plato.stanford.edu/entries/empathy/

Stürmer, S., Snyder, M., & Omoto, A. (2005) 'Prosocial Emotions and Helping: The Moderating Role of Group Membership', *Journal of Personality and Social Psychology* 88: 532–46.

Sullivan, H.S. (1953) *The Interpersonal Theory of Psychiatry*. Perry & Gawel (eds). New York: Norton.

Sullivan, H.S. & Perry, H.S. (1954) *The Psychiatric Interview*. New York: W.W. Norton.

Szporn, A. (2001) 'The Impact of Life-Condition Information on Empathy', Ph.D. Dissertation, New York University.

Szpunar, K.K., Watson, J.M., & McDermott, K.B. (2007) 'Neural Substrates of Envisioning the Future', *Proceedings of the National Academy of Sciences USA* 104: 642–7.

Taylor, C. (1985) *Human Agency and Language: Philosophical Papers I.* Cambridge: Cambridge University Press.

Thielman, S. (2007) 'David Cronenberg Speaks', interview (21 September), *Variety* http://www.variety.com/awardcentral_article/VR1117972489.html?nav=news

Thomas, E. (2000) *Robert Kennedy: His Life*. New York: Simon and Shuster.

Thompson, R. A. (1987) 'Empathy and Emotional Understanding: The Early Development of Empathy'. In: *Empathy and Its Development*, N. Eisenberg & J. Strayer (eds), pp. 119–45. Cambridge: Cambridge University Press.

Thornhill, R & Gangestad, S.W. (2003) 'Do Women have Evolved Adaptation for Extra-Pair Copulation?'. In: *Evolutionary Aesthetics*, E. Voland & K. Grammer (eds), pp. 342–60. Berlin: Springer Verlag,

Throop, C.J. (2008) 'On the Problem of Empathy: The Case of Yap, Federated States of Micronesia', *Ethos* 36(4): 402–26.

Tichener, E. (1909) *Lectures on the Experimental Psychology of the Thought Processes*. New York: Macmillan.

Tobin, J.J., Wu, D.Y.H., & Davidson, D.H. (1989) *Preschool in Three Cultures: Japan, China, and the United States*. New Haven, CT: Yale University Press.

Toi, M. & Batson, C.D. (1982) 'More Evidence That Empathy is a Source of Altruistic Motivation', *Journal of Personality and Social Psychology* 43(2): 281–92.

Tolias, A.S., Keliris, G.A., Smirnakis, S.M., & Logothetis, N.K. (2005) 'Neurons in Macaque Area V4 Acquire Directional Tuning After Adaptation to Motion Stimuli', *Nature Neuroscience*, 8(5): 591–3.

Trevarthen, C. (1979) 'Communication and Cooperation in Early Infancy'. In: *Before Speech: The Beginning of Interpersonal Communication*, M. Bullowa (ed.), pp. 321–47. Cambridge: Cambridge University Press.

Trevarthen, C. & Aitken, K.J. (2001) 'Infant Intersubjectivity: Research, Theory, and Clinical Applications', *Journal of Child Psychology and Psychiatry* 42: 3–48.

Triandis, H.C. (1995) *Individualism and Collectivism*. Boulder, CO: Westview.

Trivers, R.L. (1971) The Evolution of Reciprocal Altruism, *Quarterly Review of Biology* 46: 35–57.

Truax, C.B. & Carkhuff, R.R. (1964) 'Significant Developments in Psychotherapy Research'. In: *Progress in Clinical Psychology*, L.E. Abt & B.F. Riess (eds), pp. 136–50. New York: Grune & Stratton.

Truax, C.B. & Carkhuff, R.R. (1967) *Towards Effective Counseling and Psychotherapy: Theory and Practice*. Chicago: Aldine.

Tsoudis, O. (2002) 'The Influence of Empathy in Mock Jury Criminal Cases: Adding to the Affect Control Model', *Western Criminology Review* 4(1): 55–67.

Tulving, E. (1983) *Elements of Episodic Memory*, ii. Oxford: Oxford University Press.

Tulving, E. (1985) 'Memory and Consciousness', *Canadian Psychologist* 25: 1–12.

Tulving, E. (2001) 'Episodic Memory and Common Sense: How Far Apart'? In: *Episodic Memory: New Directions in Research*, A. Baddeley, M.A. Conway, & J.P. Aggleton (eds), pp. 269–88. New York: Oxford University Press.

Turgenev, I. S. (1852) *A Sportsman's Sketches*. London: William Heineman.

Uddin, L. Q., Iacoboni, M., Lange, C., & Keenan, J.P. (2007) 'The Self and Social Cognition: The Role of Cortical Midline Structures and Mirror Neurons', *Trends in Cognitive Sciences* 11: 153–7.

Umiltà, M.A., Kohler, E., Gallese, V., Fogassi, L., Fadiga, L., Keysers, C., & Rizzolatti, G. (2001) 'I Know What You Are Doing: A Neurophysiological Study', *Neuron* 31: 155–65.

Underwood, B. & Moore, B. (1982) 'Perspective-taking and Altruism', *Psychological Bulletin* 91: 43–73.

Ungerer, J.A., Dolby, R., Waters, B., Barnett, B., Kelk, N., & Lwein, V. (1990) 'The Early Development of Empathy: Self-regulation and Individual Differences in the First Year', *Motivation and Emotion* 14: 93–106.

Vaage, M. (2008) 'Seeing is Feeling', Ph.D. Dissertation, University of Oslo.

Valentino, B. (1994) *Final Solutions: Mass Killing and Genocide in the Twentieth Century*. Ithaca, NY: Cornell University Press.

Van Boven, L. & Loewenstein, G. (2003) 'Social Projection of Transient Drive States', *Personality and Social Psychology Bulletin* 29(9): 1159–68.

Van der Kolk, Bessel A. (1984) (ed.) *Post-Traumatic Stress Disorder: Psychological and Biological Sequelae*. Washington, D.C.: American Psychiatric Press.

Van Lange, P.A. (2008) 'Does Empathy Trigger Only Altruistic Motivation? How About Selflessness or Justice?', *Emotion* 8(6): 766–74.

Verducci, Susan (1998) 'Moral Empathy: the Necessity of Intersubjectivity and Dialogic Communication', *Philosophy of Education*, pp. 335–42.

Verducci, S. (2000a) 'A Moral Method? Thoughts on Cultivating Empathy through Method Acting', *Journal of Moral Education* 29(1): 87–99.

Verducci, S. (2000b) 'A Conceptual History of Empathy and a Question it Raises for Moral Education', *Educational Theory* 50(1): 63–80.

Vignemont, F. de (2008) 'Empathie Miroir et Empathie Reconstructive', *Revue Philosophique de la France and de l'Etranger*, 133(3): 337–45.

Vignemont, F. de (2010) 'Knowing Other People's Mental States as if they Were One's Own'. In *Handbook of Phenomenology and Cognitive Science*, S. Gallagher & D. Schmicking (eds), pp. 283–99. Berlin: Springer.

Vignemont, F. de & Singer, T. (2006) 'The Empathetic Brain: How, When, and Why?', *Trends in Cognitive Sciences* 10: 435–41.

Vischer, R. (1873) 'Über das Optische Formgefühl' ('On the Optical Sense of Form: A Contribution to Aesthetics'). In: *Empathy, Form and Space: Problems in German Aesthetics, 1873–1893*, H. Mallgrave & E. Ikonomou (eds and trans.), pp. 89–124. Santa Monica, CA: Getty Centre for the History of Art and the Humanities.

Vitz, R. (2004) 'Sympathy and Benevolence in Hume's Moral Psychology', *Journal of the History of Philosophy* 42(3): 261–75.

Viviani, P. (2002) 'Motor Competence in the Perception of Dynamic Events: A Tutorial'. In: *Common Mechanisms in Perception and Action: Attention and Performance*, vol. xix, W. Prinz & B. Hommel (eds), pp. 406–42. Oxford: Oxford University Press.

Viviani, P. & Stucchi, N. (1992) 'Biological Movements Look Constant: Evidence of Motor-Perceptual Interactions', *Journal of Experimental Psychology: Human Perception and Performance* 18: 603–23.

Waal, F.B. de (2008) 'Putting the Altruism Back into Altruism: The Evolution of Empathy', *Annual Review of Psychology* 59: 1146.

Waal, F.B. de (2009) *The Age of Empathy: Nature's Lessons for a Kinder Society*. New York: Crown Publishing Group.

Wahlstrom, D. (1990) 'On Liberating Dachau'. In: *Witnesses to the Holocaust: An Oral History*, R.G. Lewin (ed.). Boston: Twayne Publishers.

Walker, L.J. (1984) 'Sex Differences in the Development of Moral Reasoning. A Critical Review', *Child Development* 55: 677–91.

Walton, K.L. (1984) 'Transparent Pictures: On the Nature of Photographic Realism', *Critical Inquiry* 11: 246–77.

Walton, K.L. (1990) *Mimesis as Make-Believe: On the Foundations of the Representational Arts*. Cambridge: Harvard University Press.

Walton, K.L. (1997) 'Spelunking, Simulation, and Slime: On Being Moved by Fiction'. In: *Emotion and the Arts*, M. Hjort & S. Laver (eds), pp. 37–49. Oxford: Oxford University Press.

Walton, K.L. (1999) 'Projectivism, Empathy, and Musical Tension', *Philosophical Topics* 26: 407–40.

Walton, K.L. (2006) 'The (So-called) Problem of Imaginative Resistance'. In: *The Architecture of the Imagination*, S. Nichols (ed.), pp. 137–148. Oxford: Oxford University Press.

Ward, J.H. (1896) 'Instant Power of "Uncle Tom's Cabin"', *The Washington Post* (1 August).

Weiner, B. (1985) '"Spontaneous" Causal Thinking', *Psychological Bulletin* 7: 74–84.

Weston, M. (1975) 'How Can We be Moved by the Fate of Anna Karenina?', *Proceedings of the Aristotelian Society* 49 (Supplement): 81–93.

Weyant, J.M. (1978) 'Effects of Mood States, Costs, and Benefits on Helping', *Journal of Personality and Social Psychology* 36: 1169–76.

Wheeler, L. (1966) 'Toward a Theory of Behavioral Contagion', *Psychological Review* 73: 179–92.

Wheeler, T. (2004) *The Stratocaster Chronicles*. Milwaukee, WI: Hal Leonard Corporation.

Wicker, B., Fonlupt, P., Hubert, B., Tardif, C., Gepner, B. & Deruelle, C. (2008) 'Abnormal Cerebral Effective Connectivity During Explicit Emotional Processing in Adults with Autism Spectrum Disorders', *Social Cognitive and Affective neuroscience* 3(2): 135–43.

Wicker, B., Keysers, C., Plailly, J., Royet, J.-P., Gallese, V., & Rizzolatti, G. (2003) 'Both of Us Disgusted in My Insula: The Common Neural Basis of Seeing and Feeling Disgust', *Neuron* 40: 655–64.

Wiggins, D. (1980) 'Deliberation and Practical Reason'. In: *Essays on Aristotle's Ethics*, A.O. Rorty (ed.), pp. 221–40. Berkeley: University of California Press.

Wilke, M., Logothetis, N.K., & Leopold, D.A. (2006) 'Local field potential reflects perceptual suppression in monkey visual cortex', *Proceedings of the National Academy of Sciences U S A*', 103 (46): 17507–12

Willett, C. (1995) *Maternal Ethics and Other Slave Moralities*. New York: Routledge

Williams, B. (1978) *Descartes: The Project of Pure Enquiry*. Harmondsworth, UK: Penguin.

Williams, B. (1981) *Moral Luck*. Cambridge: Cambridge University Press.

Williams, B. (1985) *Ethics and the Limits of Philosophy*. Cambridge: Harvard University Press.

Williams, J. & Stickley, T. (2010) 'Empathy and Nurse Education', *Nurse Education Today* 30: 752–5.

Williams, L.A. & Desteno, D. (2008) 'Pride and Perseverance: The Motivational Role of Pride', *Journal of Personality and Social Psychology* 94: 1007–17.

Williamson, R.A., Meltzoff, A.N., & Markman, E.M. (2008) 'Prior Experiences and Perceived Efficacy Influence 3-year-olds' Imitation', *Developmental Psychology* 44: 275–85.

Williamson, Timothy (1994) *Vagueness*. London: Routledge.

Wilson, J.P.R. (1972) *Emotion and Object*. Cambridge: Cambridge University Press.

Wisdom, J. (1953) *Philosophy and Psycho-Analysis*. Oxford: Blackwell.

Wispé, L. (1986) 'The Distinction between Sympathy and Empathy: To Call Forth a Concept, A Word is Needed', *Journal of Personality and Social Psychology* 50(2): 314–21.

Wispé, L. (1987), 'History of the Concept of Empathy'. In: *Empathy and Its Development*, N. Eisenberg & J. Strayer (eds), pp. 17–37. Cambridge: Cambridge University Press.

Wispé, L. (1991) *The Psychology of Sympathy*. New York: Plenum Press.

Wittgenstein, L. (1953) *Philosophical Investigations*. G.E.M. Anscombe (trans). Oxford: Blackwell.

Wittgenstein, L. (1966) *Lectures & Conversations on Aesthetics, Psychology and Religious Belief*. Cyril Barrett (ed.). Oxford, Blackwell.

Wittgenstein, L. (1969) *On Certainty*. Oxford: Blackwell.

Wittgenstein, L. (1976) *Wittgenstein's Lectures on the Foundations of Mathematics, Cambridge 1939*. C. Diamond (ed.). Hassocks: Harvester Press.

Wittgenstein, L. (1993) *Philosophical Occasions*. J. Klagge & A. Nordmann (eds). Indianapolis: Hacket.

Wittgenstein, L. (2001) *Philosophical Investigations: 50th Anniversary Edition*. G.E.M. Anscombe (trans.). Oxford: Blackwell.

Wittgenstein, L. (2005) *The Big Typescript: TS 213*. Oxford: Blackwell.

Wittgenstein, L. & Waismann, F. (2003) *Voices of Wittgenstein*. G. Baker (ed.). London: Routledge.

Wollheim, R. (1984) *The Thread of Life*. Cambridge: Harvard University Press.

Wollheim, R. (1987) *Painting as an Art*. London: Thames and Hudson.

Wollheim, R. (1993) *The Mind and Its Depths*. Cambridge: Harvard University Press.

Wood, J. (2008) *How Fiction Works*. New York: Farrar, Straus, & Giroux.

Worth, S. E. (2000) 'Understanding the Objects of Music', *Journal of Aesthetic Education* 34(1): 102–7.

Zagzebski, L.T. (1996), *Virtues of the Mind*. Cambridge: Cambridge University Press.

Zahavi, D. (2001) Beyond Empathy: 'Phenomenological Approaches to Intersubjectivity', *Journal of Consciousness Studies* 85(7): 151–67.

Zahavi, D. (2008) 'Simulation, Projection and Empathy', *Consciousness and Cognition* 17: 514–22.

Zahn-Waxler, C., Cummings, E.M., & Iannotti, R. (1986) (eds) *Altruism and Aggression: Biological and Social Origins*. Cambridge and New York: Cambridge University Press.

Zahn-Waxler, C. & Radke-Yarrow, M. (1990) 'The Origins of Empathic Concern', *Motivation and Emotion* 14(2): 107–30.

Zahn-Waxler, C., Radke-Yarrow, M., Wagner, E., & Chapman, M. (1992) 'Development of Concern for Others', *Developmental Psychology* 28: 126–36.

Zahn-Waxler, C., Robinson, J.L., & Emde, N.E. (1992) 'The Development of Empathy in Twins', *Developmental Psychology* 28: 1038–47.

Zaki, J., Bolger, N. & Ochsner, K. (2008) 'It Takes Two: The Interpersonal Nature of Empathic Accuracy', *Psychological Science: A Journal of the American Psychological Society / APS* 19(4): 399–404.

Zaki, J., Bolger, N. & Ochsner, K. (2009) 'Unpacking the Informational Bases of Empathic Accuracy', *Emotion* 9(4): 478–87.

Zaki, J. & Ochsner, K. (2009) 'The Need for a Cognitive Neuroscience of Naturalistic Social Cognition. *Annals of the New York Academy of Sciences*', 1167: 16–30.

Zaki, J., Weber, J., Bolger, N. & Ochsner, K. (2009) 'The Neural Bases of Empathic Accuracy', *Proceedings of the National Academy of Sciences of the United States of America* 106(27): 11382–7.

Zipursky, B. (1990) '*Deshaney* and the Jurisprudence of Compassion', *New York University Law Review* 65: 1101–47.

Zunshine, L. (2006) *Why We Read Fiction: Theory of Mind and the Novel*. Columbus, OH: Ohio State University Press.

Index

Note: page numbers in *italic* indicate figures and illustrations.

Lightning Source UK Ltd.
Milton Keynes UK
UKOW04n1332100614

233167UK00001B/22/P